Income Property
Appraisal and Analysis

Income Property Appraisal and Analysis

Jack P. Friedman, Ph.D., C.P.A., S.R.P.A.
Laguarta Professor of Real Estate
Real Estate Center
Texas A & M University
College Station, Texas

Nicholas Ordway J.D., Ph.D.
Hawaii Chairholder of Real Estate
Director of Hawaii Real Estate
Research and Education Center
University of Hawaii
Honolulu

A RESTON BOOK
PRENTICE-HALL
Englewood Cliffs, New Jersey 07632

Library of Congress Cataloging in Publication Data

Friedman, Jack P.
Income property appraisal and analysis.

Bibliography: p.
Includes index.
1. Real property—Valuation. 2. Real estate investment. I. Ordway, Nicholas. II. Title.
HD1387.F694 333.33'2 81-1335
ISBN 0-8359-3057-2 AACR2

A Division of Simon & Schuster
Englewood Cliffs, New Jersey 07632

10 9 8 7 6 5 4 3 2

PRINTED IN THE UNITED STATES OF AMERICA.

to ANITA and KATHY

Contents

CODE OF ETHICS

OF

THE NATIONAL SOCIETY OF

REAL ESTATE APPRAISERS, INC.

The professional real esate appraiser occupies a necessary and important niche in the economic affairs of people.

In recognition of their solemn responsibility, the members of the National Society of Real Estate Appraisers mutually pledge to themselves, and the public as follows:

1. That they will render no evaluation for a fee contingent upon the value reported.
2. That they will keep confidential their conclusions and report only to their client.
3. That they will accept no appraisal assignments in which they have an undisclosed personal interest, present or prospective.
4. That they will ever strive to preserve and increase their competency as appraisers.
5. That they will conduct their business activities in such a manner as to reflectc credit upon themselves, fellow appraisers, and the real estate business in general and that they will refrain from criticizing the reputation of fellow members of this society.

Illustrations

Tables

Preface

The objective of this book is to give its user problem-solving abilities capable of dealing with any situation likely to be encountered when analyzing income-producing real estate. It differs from many other texts in that it stresses an understanding of processes, rather than a simple memorization of ideas or definitions.

In the future, the real estate market will continue to become more complex. New financing devices will appear, tax laws will change, and new ownership vehicles will emerge. As this evolution continues, the face amount that is paid for property will become less meaningful as an indication of value than before. Investors are recognizing that they are purchasing not only real estate but also a certain package of terms. Consequently, prices paid for property will require substantial adjustments to derive market value estimates.

Students who have learned how to approach and solve complex problems in real estate will be able to cope with current situations and forthcoming changes. They will have a sound basis for estimating the value of an income stream produced by real estate regardless of the financing pattern, leasing arrangement, income tax consequences, or ownership vehicle. The authors hope that this text instills in students, the problem-solving abilities that are needed to face a rapidly changing business environment.

The text has been structured with a benchmark example that is used as a common thread to link many chapters together. Variations on the benchmark example are used to illustrate certain points or techniques. The benchmark example is intended to provide continuity and avoid unnecessary repetition of background information in order to effectively focus on the points under consideration. It is hoped that this thread is helpful to students.

The authors are deeply grateful to scholars who have helped to shape appraisal education. These include Dr. Paul F. Wendt, Dr. Byrl N. Boyce, Dr. William N. Kinnard, Jr., Dr. Carl J. Tschappat, Dr. Alfred A. Ring, Dr. Frederick M. Babcock, Dr. William M. Shenkel, Dr. Halbert C. Smith, Dr. James Graaskamp, Dr. Kenneth

Lusht, Dr. Stephen D. Messner, Dr. Richard Ratcliff, and Dr. James R. Cooper. Practitioners who have contributed much to appraisal literature and applications who also deserve deep gratitude include Charles Akerson, McCloud Hodges, Jr., Dr. Stephen Roulac, Dr. John McMahan, L. W. Ellwood, Irwin Johnson, Gene Dilmore, Henry Harrison, and others.

The authors thank their former and present students, professors and employers for their encouragement in this effort. We acknowledge the support and many hours of hard work from several wonderful people including Mrs. M. T. Barnhill, Jr., Mrs. Garland Williams, Mrs. Gleneva Collette, Ms. Lynn Dunning, Ms. Susan Worthington, Mr. Roy Vajdak, and Mr. Nanda Rangan. Despite the assistance received, the authors remain solely responsible for any errors.

Jack P. Friedman
Nicholas Ordway

Chapter 1

Introduction and Purpose

This book was written to help appraisal students, appraisers, and other real estate analysts solve problems involving income-producing properties. Income-producing properties have many distinctive characteristics that provide a challenge to real estate professionals. These characteristics include:

1. *Uneven cash flows.* Real estate investments require expenditures in uneven sums of money. Normally, during the construction and development of a project cash flows are negative. During the lease-up of the project, cash flows shift from negative to positive. While the property is in operation there may be substantial expenditures for renovation or capital additions. In some years money might be withdrawn by refinancing. Finally, a large sum of money might be expected when the property is sold.

2. *Potential appreciation of land.* One important characteristic of land is its potential for appreciation. This may occur because of changes in the land use pattern, relative scarcity of sites with similar locations, inflation, and other factors.

3. *Depreciation of improvements.* Improvements tend to decline in relative value over time. This decline is due to wear and tear from use and from exposure to the elements, changes in technology, and other factors from outside the property.

4. *Flexible financing arrangements.* Income-producing properties may have several layers of equity and debt financing. This financing may be complicated by timing, methods of calculating interest, participation shares, and various partial interests.

5. *Divided legal interests.* Each property may be composed of different mixes of legal rights and interests. One property may be

subject to a lease, with separation of air, surface, and mineral rights, and encumbered by liens; whereas another property may be in "fee simple absolute" free and clear of any claims.

6. *Distinctive tax considerations.* Federal and state governments have spun an intricate web of tax laws and regulations that affect real estate investments. This web provides both opportunities and constraints. In many cases the tax consequences of an investment in income-producing properties are the prime reason for a transaction.

7. *Risk and uncertainty.* Because real estate is physically immobile, it is subject to a greater range of risks than most other types of investment. This requires inspection of both the asset itself and the surrounding physical environment before a value recommendation can normally be made.

8. *Stratified markets.* Real estate markets tend to be narrow, localized, segmented, and personalized. Data are difficult to collect and verify for competitive properties in a geographic area. Prices at which transactions take place are not normally set by the interaction of large numbers of buyers and sellers, but are made on the basis of individual negotiation.

NEED FOR VALUE ESTIMATES

The types of problems that appraisers are usually asked to solve require an estimate of value. The value estimate may be important in helping the buyer or the seller arrive at a fair transaction price. It may be important to a lender in the mortgage-underwriting decision. An insurance company may require an estimate for the purpose of indemnification. The government may be condemning the property, and the owner may require an estimate for the purpose of challenging the government's offer of "just compensation." The problem may involve value for tax assessment purposes. A lease may include an escalation clause setting rental levels as a percentage of market value. Allocation of purchase price to land and improvements may be important in justifying a depreciation schedule for income tax purposes. One corporation seeking to acquire another corporation may require a current value estimate of the other company's real estate holdings.

WHAT IS VALUE?

Value is the cash or cash equivalent that a buyer is willing to exchange for some object or thing. It is important to distinguish among the concepts of *value, cost,* and *price.* Value is conventionally analyzed from the viewpoint of the prospective purchaser (see Figure 1-1). *Value* is a measurement of how much a hypothetical purchaser would be willing to exchange for the property being appraised. *Cost* is a measurement of the expenditures necessary to produce a similar property to the one being appraised. This cost may not be the same as the prospective purchaser would be willing to pay. Depending on several factors including purchaser needs, availability of substitute properties, and activities of other purchasers, this cost could be higher or lower than the current value. *Price* is the historic fact of how much was spent on similar properties in past transactions. Price is also used to indicate the "asking price" of a seller. Neither past prices nor asking prices will necessarily represent a fair measurement of current value.

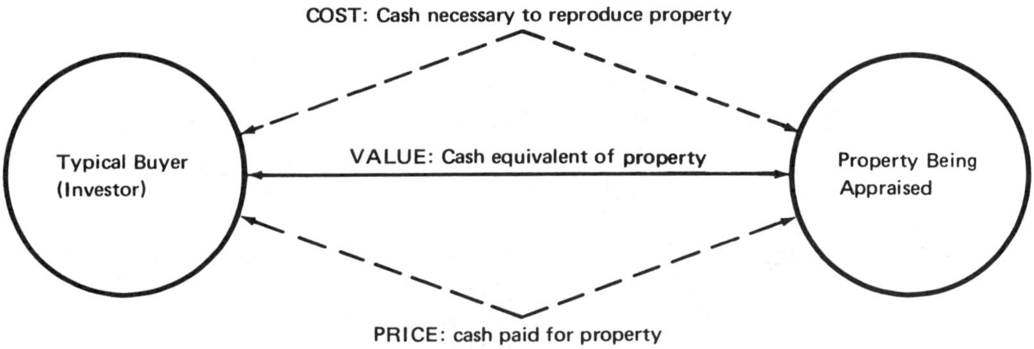

FIGURE 1-1. Value as Compared to Cost and Price.

There are many different kinds of value. These various kinds of values are necessary because of different needs and functions. Included are such values as loan value, insurable value, fair market value, book value, rental value, salvage value, investment value, and many others. In general, however, value may be divided into two broad categories: value in exchange and value in use.

Value in Exchange

Value in exchange is the price that would tend to prevail in a free, open, and competitive market on the basis of an equilibrium set by the forces of supply and demand. This is also sometimes referred to as *objective value* because it is based on observable economic forces. A common form of value in exchange that will be used frequently throughout this book is *market value.*

Market value has been defined as:

> The highest price in terms of money that a property will bring in a competitive and open market under all conditions requisite to a fair sale, the buyer and seller each acting prudently and knowledgeably, and assuming that the price is not affected by undue stimulus.[1]

This definition contains a number of important implicit assumptions:

1. The market is open and competitive, allowing sufficient numbers of buyers and sellers of competitive properties to interact freely.
2. The buyer and seller of the appraised property are typical in motivation, economically rational, under no undue pressure, reasonably prudent and knowledgeable, and acting to maximize their self-interests.
3. The property will be on the market for a reasonable time to give it sufficient exposure to potential buyers.
4. Payment to the seller is in cash or cash equivalent.
5. The buyer is able to purchase the property with financing and terms typical in the market.

Quite often some or all of these assumptions will be violated in an actual transaction. Market value is an ideal standard that is not always realizable. For this reason the transaction price is frequently not the same as the fair market value. It should be observed that market value is conventionally estimated from the perspective of the potential buyer typical in the market.

Because of the nature of market value assumptions, sometimes an appraiser will be asked to find "the most probable selling price." This concept is less rigid than the market value definition. It is an indication of the likely price for which a property can be exchanged, given existing market conditions and actual knowledge and behavior of buyers and sellers. This type of value estimate is a forecast of the probable transaction price in the near future. It often includes a range of prices within a probability distribution in contrast to market value, which is a single figure estimate.

---

[1] Adapted from Byrl Boyce, ed., *Real Estate Appraisal Terminology* (Cambridge, Mass.: Ballinger Publishing Co., 1975), p. 137.

Value in Use

Value in use is the worth of a property to a specific user or set of users. Another way to look at it is to consider the value of the property when put to a specific use as part of a going concern (e.g., real estate used for a factory). Because value in use is related to specific user needs, it is often referred to as *subjective value.*

One category of value in use that is frequently noted is *investment value.* Investment value is the value of the appraised property to a specific investor. Unlike market value, which assumes the existence of a "typical" purchaser or a "typical" investor, investment value is based on needs and characteristics of a specific individual. Investment value is concerned with the present worth of future income streams resulting from the operation of a property. Important to an investor are such factors as risk, quantity and cost of financing, future appreciation or depreciation, and income tax consequences.

This book provides a discussion of the various analytical techniques needed to solve a wide variety of appraisal problems. Whether or not the problems require the estimate of value in exchange or value in use, it will usually be necessary to collect market data to utilize these techniques.

The next chapter includes a discussion of the types of data that an appraiser would normally collect within the context of the appraisal process. However, it is important to understand that certain types of information collected may have bias or other limitations. To some extent, the bias and limitations may stem from the nature of real estate markets.

REAL ESTATE MARKETS

Data must be collected from the appropriate real estate market in order to develop a defensible estimate of value. Data-gathering difficulties can occur if an appraiser is unfamiliar with the nature and peculiarities of a local market.

A real estate market is a set of mechanisms by which property rights and interests are transferred, prices are established, and space is allocated among various competing land uses. As diagrammed in Figure 1–2, a real estate market is a complicated structure that has the purpose of bringing buyers and sellers together.

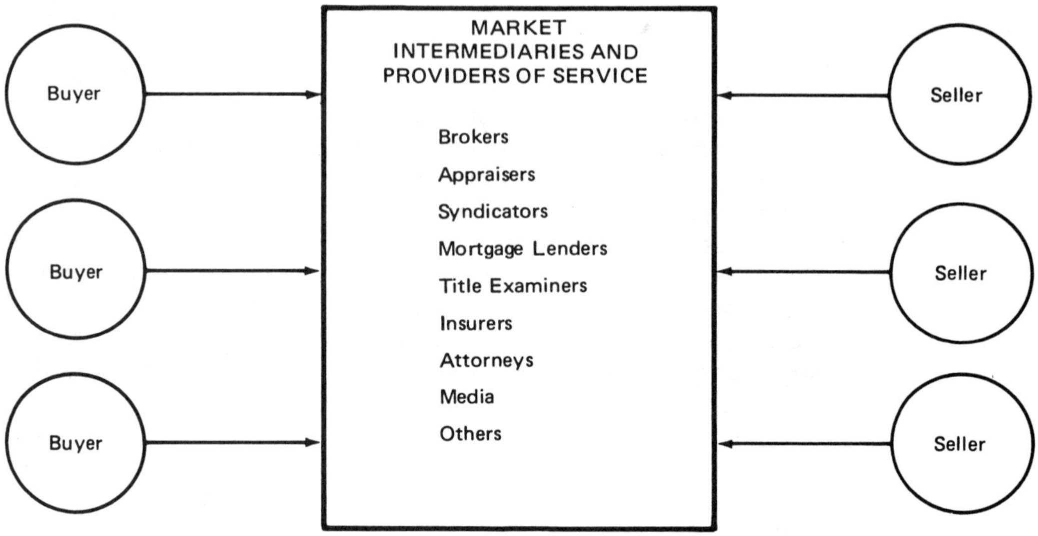

FIGURE 1–2. Simplified Model of Participants in a Real Estate Market.

A real estate market is localized and segmented. It is local because real estate is immobile, and it is subject to the physical environment. Each parcel of land is highly differentiated. This means that each parcel of land has unique attributes. A market in New York is different from a market in California. Different laws regulate transactions, different climates exist, and different economies operate. A real estate market is segmented because different users have different needs and different resources. It may be segmented in many ways:

- *By use*—Different markets exist for residential, commercial, industrial, and agricultural properties.
- *By geography*—Each neighborhood may be a different market. One segment of a city may be subject to different market conditions than another segment.
- *By price*—A different set of buyers may exist for houses in the $150,000 to $200,000 range than for houses in the $70,000 to $90,000 range.
- *By quality of product*—Office space in a Class A category may be in a separate market segment from office space in a Class D category, even when both properties are on the same street.

- *By investment motivation*—Some investors may be interested in property requiring little management, with no cash flow but with a great amount of appreciation potential. Others may want properties with a good tax shelter and a positive cash flow.
- *By types of property interest*—Different markets exist for various real estate interests. These interests may include unencumbered fees, easements, mineral rights, leaseholds, and time-share condominium interests.

Real estate transactions tend to be private in nature. Published information in the public records is often incomplete or misleading. This means that for some appraisal assignments, time must be planned for additional data collection and verification. It cannot be assumed that all data found in the public records are a correct description of a transaction.

Some events in a real estate market occur because of emotions or lack of information on the part of various participants. Either the buyer or the seller may base judgments on rumors or on unspecified psychological needs. This can result in a wide variance in selling prices, in terms offered, and in other aspects of a transaction. Therefore, care should be taken in the analysis of data.

Unlike other kinds of markets where many individuals interact to set prices through supply and demand, real estate market segments often have only a few buyers or sellers. This is particularly true of specialized or single-purpose properties. This situation requires special attention for identifying the characteristics of potential purchasers of such a property.

Real estate is fixed in location. Construction is time consuming. Improvements are relatively durable. All of these factors result in an inelastic supply of real estate products in the short run. This means that even if demand increases and prices are pushed up, it is very difficult to increase rapidly the quantity of useful real estate in a particular market. Likewise, in situations of overbuilding, prices may remain depressed for several years until the oversupply is absorbed.

Demand can be very changeable. For example, the opening of a new factory in a small town can cause a significant migration of new workers, requiring large amounts of new housing, retail, recreational, and institutional space. On the other hand, shortages of mortgage money and high interest rates can dampen the demand for real estate.

All of these factors suggest that an appraiser must be aware of changing market conditions and trends. Care should be taken to collect data that correctly reflect conditions in the particular market segment that pertains to the properties being appraised or analyzed.

ORGANIZATION OF CHAPTERS—THE BUILDING-BLOCK APPROACH

A key feature of this book is the structure of its organization. It uses a systematic building-block approach to develop an understanding of the subject matter. Analytical techniques begin with simple income configurations; more comprehensive examples are offered as the book progresses. Figure 1–3 illustrates the sequence of topics covered. It shows how each chapter is integrated into the organization of the book.

Chapter 2 introduces real estate valuation principles and describes how they relate to the appraisal process. This process is an orderly method of problem solving, applicable to most income-property situations.

Chapters 3 and 4 concern compound interest and discounting. They serve as a foundation for mathematical calculations that underlie sophisticated analytical techniques. The reader is offered a sound background in comprehending and manipulating the six functions of compound interest. Upon mastery of the six functions, the reader will have an understanding of the use of compound interest and discounting functions as they apply to real estate appraisal and investment situations. Financial calculator usage is described in Chapters 3 and 4, but use is suggested only after mastery of the basic mechanics of compound interest functions.

Chapter 5 introduces the reader to capitalization rates. In real estate appraisal terminology, a capitalization rate is composed of two elements: one is an interest or discount rate; the other is a recovery rate, which provides for a return of the capital invested in the asset. Chapter 5 explains how to derive an interest rate (a return on investment) and how to distinguish it from a capital recovery rate. The various ways to account for capital recovery or capital growth are explained.

The income from some investments can be separated in accordance with the various components that earn income. From a physical aspect, this separation divides a real estate asset into the improvements and the land. Financially, the components are the mortgage and equity investments. Chapter 6 considers the physical separation method. Three residual techniques are explained. The concept of a reversionary value to be received upon the resale of a real estate asset is introduced.

As a preliminary step toward valuing income-producing real estate, it is important to gather accurate financial information about operations of the property. An important source of this information is the accounting data. However, since accounting data do not always reflect economic realities, and because the data are not necessarily organized in the manner most convenient for appraisal applications, they must be reorganized and analyzed to be useful in the appraisal process. Chapter 7 describes how accounting information can be converted into meaningful data and ratios that are useful for real estate appraisal and analytical applications. An example of a hypothetical income-producing property is introduced in this chapter. This benchmark example continues throughout the book to serve as a common thread. In later chapters, modifications and increasingly sophisticated tools are applied to the basic example, thereby linking various concepts while maintaining continuity.

Results of the application of mechanical techniques are sterile without realistic assumptions and forecasts of the amounts and timing of expected future income. Chapter 8 describes the methods typically used to forecast cash flow from the operation of real estate and the proceeds from its resale.

The permanent financing instrument that has been most prevalent in real estate since the 1930s is the level-payment self-amortizing mortgage. Analysis of its payment plan serves as a building block for the understanding of more complex income configurations. Chapter 9 explores the important manipulations of payments, principal, rate, and amortization terms. In addition, it discusses the analysis of other widely used financing patterns.

The amount that an investor is willing to pay for a certain property is often influenced by the nature of the financing structure that is part of the transaction. A given financing arrangement, whether good or poor, is bound to influence the price. Chapter 10 explains the process that one would use to adjust actual prices that result from different financing terms.

Mortgage-equity analysis is a technique that separates income-producing property into two financial components. It is predicated on the concept that sophisticated real estate owners will pay a certain amount for property, given a specific or typically available financing pattern. The price is based on the forecast cash flow and reversionary value that investors expect to receive after subtracting all other costs and expenses of operation and financing. Chapters 11, 12, and 13 explain refined analytical techniques and how they can be applied to income derived from the three stages of ownership (acquisition, operation, disposition). These chapters tie together the band of investment, conventional, and Ellwood techniques.

Market value is viewed from the perspective of the most probable purchaser. However, each investor is in a unique circumstance. One of the most important considerations is the effect that ownership of a property will have on the individual's income tax situation. Chapter 14 describes highlights of income tax implications at the different stages of ownership. Techniques for measuring after-tax cash flows are discussed in Chapter 15. The methods explained consider amounts and timing of income.

The value of income-producing property is generally best measured by considering forecast income. In certain situations, the direct sales comparison and cost approaches can offer valuable information. Chapters 16, 17, and 18 describe how these approaches are related to the income approach within the appraisal process. These chapters offer information concerning strengths, limitations, and important applications of the cost and direct sales comparison approaches.

Chapter 19 provides a review of various analytical techniques as applied to income-producing real estate. Chapter 20 is an application of techniques discussed in this book to analyze partial interests in real estate such as leaseholds, air rights, easements, and others.

SUMMARY

Income-producing real estate has distinct characteristics that provide a challenge to real estate professionals. These characteristics concern income configurations; future value changes; complex financial, legal, and tax implications; and risk and market considerations.

Appraisers are frequently asked to estimate the value of property; since there are many different kinds of value, it is important to understand each of them and the type of value sought. The value of a property to a specific investor, the property user, or the most probable purchaser is likely to differ substantially.

The value of income-producing property is usually best measured by the amount and timing of all the forms of income that it is likely to generate. An appraiser or analyst must gather estimates of likely income from the appropriate segment of the real estate market. This is quite difficult to accomplish because of complex transactions and private agreements, and especially because of the long-lasting nature of real estate in a constantly changing market environment.

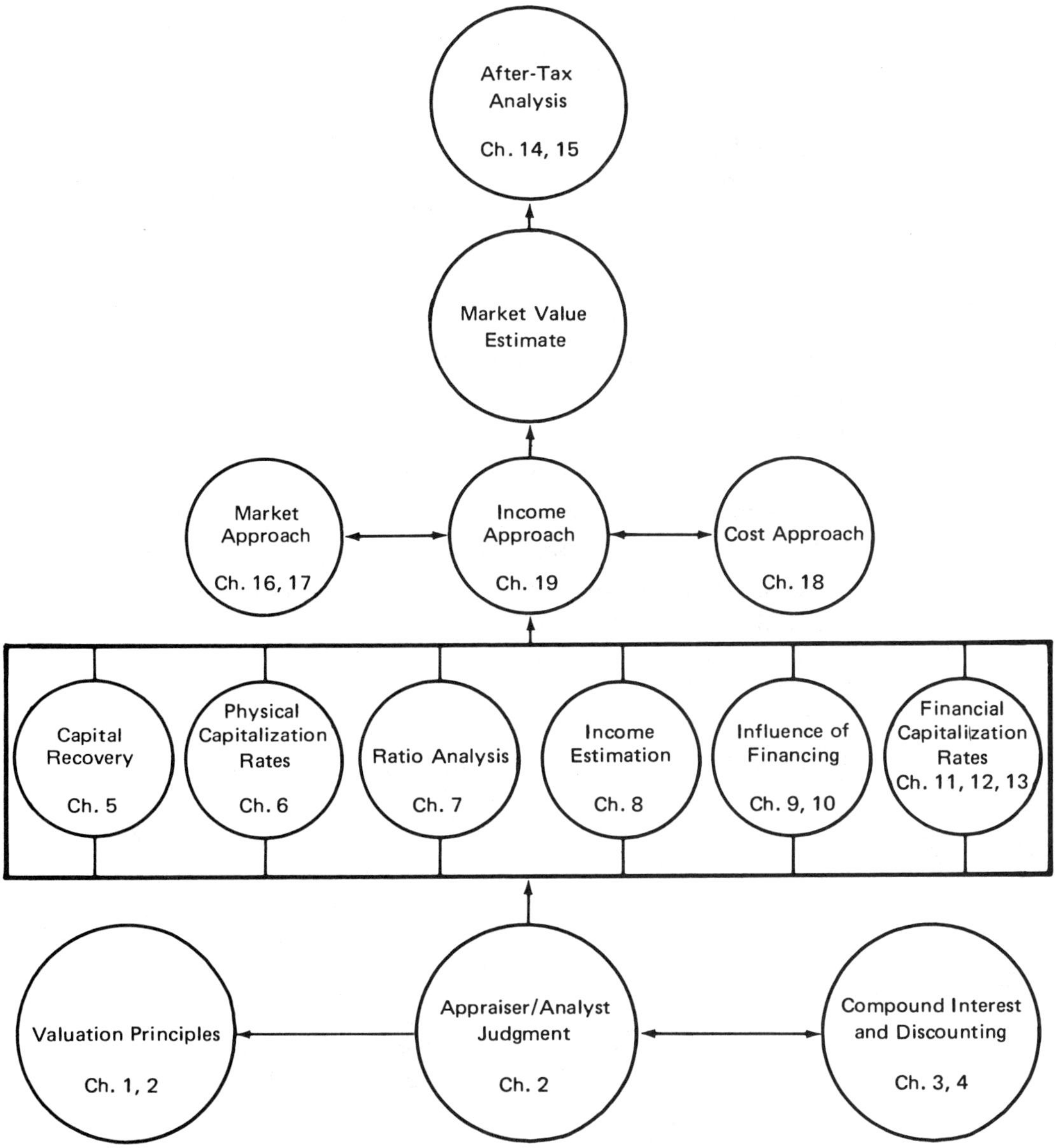

FIGURE 1–3. Building Blocks for Income Property Valuation.

The organization of this book is structured into systematic building blocks, using a benchmark example as a common thread. Reading the material and answering the questions and problems at the end of each chapter will offer the user an opportunity to understand and apply the basic financial, economic, and mathematical principles to situations that are frequently encountered in income-property appraisal and analysis situations.

Essay Questions

1. What are some of the characteristics of income-producing properties?
2. What are some of the purposes for which real estate appraisals are required?
3. What are some of the kinds of value?
4. Define *market value.* How does it differ from *cost* and *price?*
5. What are some of the functions of the real estate market?
6. In what ways is the real estate market different from the stock market or commodities markets?

Chapter 2

How the Income Approach Fits into the Appraisal Process

The value of an income-producing property is based on the quantity, quality, and duration of benefits that the property is expected to produce over time. These benefits are converted to a lump sum present value by an appraiser who carefully considers relevant market data.

How does the appraiser or analyst estimate this value? Why are two income streams of similar amount valued differently? What factors are likely to change the future benefits that are expected from the operation or resale of a real estate project?

The appraisal profession has developed a logical and systematic approach for estimating the values of various types of real estate. The process allows for the measurement of different types of value such as investment value, market value, most probable selling price, or whatever type of value estimate is required by the assignment. This appraisal process is a problem-solving approach. It is a series of steps allowing for the consideration of all important and relevant facts in the market that could influence the value of a property. This process is described in this chapter.

The theoretical foundation of the appraisal process is a unified set of valuation principles. These principles are based on the observed economic behavior of human beings as they have dealt with real estate in the past. As a prelude to discussing how the income approach fits into the appraisal process, these important principles are discussed and defined on the following page.

REAL ESTATE VALUATION PRINCIPLES

Real estate valuation principles may be grouped into four categories. These categories are:

1. Principles based on user perceptions.
2. Principles associated with land and improvements.
3. Principles associated with the market environment.
4. The principle of the highest and best use.

As diagrammed in Figure 2-1, these principles are related to each other. Several may be in operation at any one time with respect to a particular property being examined. It should be noted that these principles do not apply to every appraisal problem. Human beings often act without adequate rationale. One principle may override another principle depending on the particular situation or the individual involved. Real estate markets may operate imperfectly, or government intervention may prevent the full operation of a principle. For such reasons, these principles indicate merely the tendency of human economic behavior and not the certainty of behavior.

Principles Based on User Perceptions

Principles based on user perceptions include: utility, substitution, and anticipation.

Utility. Real estate has value when it is useful to some potential owner. It can be useful because it is needed to carry out some economic function such as the operation of a manufacturing plant or the growing of crops. It can be useful because someone is willing to pay rent for its temporary possession. Or it can be useful because it creates pride of ownership or satisfies some other psychological need. These are examples of benefits that owners of rights in real estate can realize.

Definition of utility: Utility is the ability of real estate to satisfy user needs at a particular location and within a given time period.

For income-producing properties, the satisfaction of user needs can ultimately be translated into a stream of income. For an owner-user this income stream would be treated as "imputed rent." In other words, how much would one have to pay someone else if the property

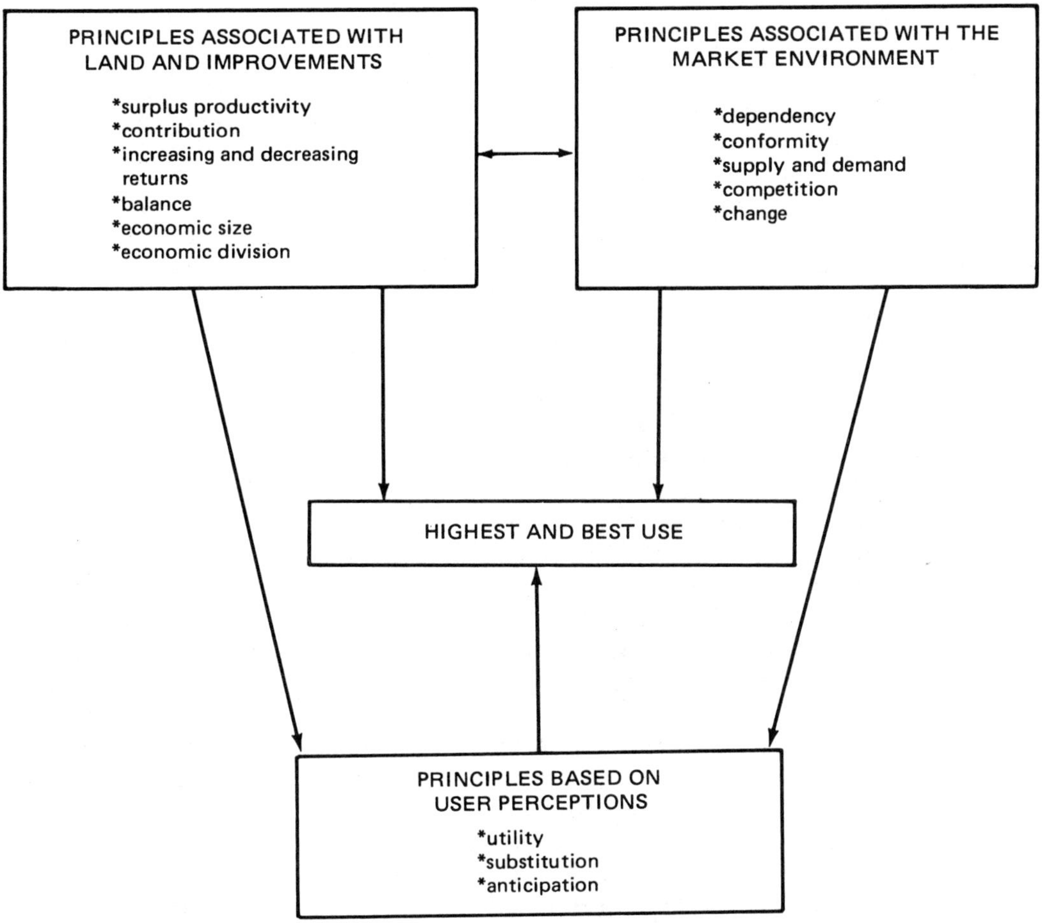

FIGURE 2-1. Real Estate Valuation Principles.

were being leased? This savings is imputed to the property even though no dollars actually change hands.

Substitution. A rational purchaser would pay no more for a property than the lowest price being charged for another property of equivalent utility. Likewise, it would not be prudent to pay more for an existing project if another one of equivalent utility could be reproduced, without unreasonable delay, for a lower cost. If an investor is analyzing an income stream, the maximum price would be set by examining the price of other income streams of similar risk and quality.

Definition of substitution: The principle of substitution holds that the maximum value of a property is set by the lowest price or cost at which another property of equivalent utility may be acquired.

This principle underlies each of the three traditional approaches to value used in the appraisal process. These are: (1) direct sales comparison, (2) income, and (3) cost approaches. These three approaches will be covered in this chapter.

Similar to the principle of substitution is the concept of *opportunity cost.* Opportunity cost is a measurement of what an investor would lose by giving up alternative uses of funds to invest in a particular venture.

Anticipation. In general, the utility of property is related to the value of forecast future benefits. For income-producing properties, value is based on how a prospective buyer perceives the net receipts from the operation of the asset plus any amounts to be received upon resale. Methods of net income calculations and forecasting are discussed in later chapters. What is important to the investor is the quantity, quality, and duration of the expected future income stream. However, expectations with respect to this income stream can change. For example, current events such as the announcement of a nearby new regional airport or the construction of a new highway can influence the way people think about a particular property.

Definition of anticipation: Anticipation is the determination of the present worth of income or other benefits one expects to receive in the future from the ownership of property.

Because money earns interest, one dollar to be received in the future has a smaller value than a dollar held at the present time. This is referred to as *the time value of money.* The process of adjusting future dollars to present values is called *discounting*. Both concepts are discussed in the next chapter. To properly analyze future dollars anticipated from the ownership of real estate, it is important to adjust forecast future receipts for time value.

Principles Associated with Land and Improvements

Principles associated with land and improvements include: surplus productivity, contribution, increasing and decreasing returns, balance, economic size, and economic division.

Surplus Productivity. The value of land is based on its surplus productivity. To understand this concept, one must recognize that economic activities normally require four factors in production (see Table 2-1). Each factor must be paid from the earnings created by the activity.

TABLE 2–1

Factors in Production and Their Compensation(s)

Factors	*Compensation(s)*
Labor	Wages, salaries, fees, commissions
Capital (money or what money buys)	Interest, dividends
Entrepreneurship (coordination)	Profit, management fees
Land	Rent

Because land is physically immobile, the factors of labor, capital, and entrepreneurship must be attracted to it. This means that these factors are compensated first. If any money is left over, this residual amount is paid as rent to the owner. In economic theory, land is said to have "residual value" and is worth something only if there is a surplus after paying the other factors in production.

Definition of surplus productivity: Surplus productivity is defined as the net income attributed to land after the costs of labor, capital, and entrepreneurship have been paid.

Surplus productivity may result because land allows a user to maximize revenues, minimize costs, satisfy amenity needs, or some combination of these. Examples follow:

- *Revenue maximization* — A convenience store operator will pay extra for a site with high visibility and easy access to a large volume of consumer traffic.

- *Cost minimization* — A manufacturer of automobiles will pay more for a site on a railroad spur than for one in the center of a downtown business district.
- *Amenity satisfaction* — A residential user will pay more for a site with a scenic view than for one without such a view.

Contribution (marginal productivity). A builder is considering whether to add a swimming pool to an apartment complex. The cost of this feature is $17,500. With the swimming pool, the complex is worth $1,165,000. Without this pool, it is worth $1,140,000. Thus the pool would add $25,000 to the overall value. Since the cost of adding this amenity is less than its contribution, a prudent builder would construct the pool.

Contribution is the value increment to an economic good by the addition of some new factor rather than the actual cost of the new factor itself. In real estate, some things add more than their cost of production, whereas other things may actually detract from value. For example, new paint on the exterior of a house may improve its appearance and make it more salable. However, if the color is outlandish by market standards, the impact on value may be negative.

Definition of contribution: Contribution is the amount by which the value or the net income of an economic good is increased or decreased by the presence or absence of some additional factor in production.

Increasing and decreasing returns. A common problem faced by the owners of land is how intensively their land should be developed. An example of this type of problem is the following.

The XYZ Development Company has one acre of land. If the company builds one house, it will make a profit of $10,000. As more houses are placed on the same parcel, the per unit land cost will decrease, but the market will pay less for each house because of the smaller lot size. The calculation of profits for each density is summarized in the schedule below:

Number of houses	*Profit per house*	*Total profit*
0	0	0
1	$10,000	$10,000
2	$15,000	$30,000
3	$12,000	$36,000
4	$10,000	$40,000
5	$ 8,000	$40,000
6	$ 6,000	$36,000
7	$ 4,000	$28,000

For up to two houses, profits increase at an increasing rate due to economies of scale. Then, although profits on each house decrease, a density of up to four or five houses actually increases overall profits to the development company. However, once the company builds its sixth house, it will begin losing overall profits.

Definition of increasing and decreasing returns: This principle holds that as resources are added to fixed agents in production, net returns will tend to increase at an increasing rate up to a point at which total returns will increase at a decreasing rate until the increment to value is less than the cost of resource unit input.

Balance (proportionality). If too few factors in production are combined with the land, it is underimproved. If too many factors in production are combined, the land is overimproved. In both cases the land is not being used efficiently, and according to the principle of surplus productivity, the value of land would suffer. All factors in production must be in the proper proportion to each other in order to maximize overall returns to land.

Definition of balance: For any type of land use there are optimal amounts of different factors in production that can be combined to create maximum land values.

In the example above, the XYZ Development Company found that maximum returns could be made by combining either four or five houses with the land. In both cases, the profits would be $40,000. However, if the construction of four houses would yield the same profits at a lower risk than the construction of five houses, the principle of balance would suggest that four was the correct number. Risk might be lower with four houses because fewer transactions would be necessary to achieve the same profits. The decision of the company would depend on its strategic marketing objectives.

The principle of balance also applies in a community or region. There are one or more mixes of land uses in a community that will yield the highest overall value to all land resources. To achieve this balance, there ordinarily must be intelligent cooperation between the private and public sectors. This balance can be encouraged by the exercise of sound planning and logical application of zoning regulations and police power devices.

Economic Size. Appropriate scale of land development is determined by competitive market conditions and the requirements of users. Land at a good location that is too small or too large for probable users can suffer a discount in the marketplace. For example, a corner lot may be an ideal location for a gasoline station. If the site is too small, access problems will be created and there may not be enough space for service and storage areas. If the site is too large, the excess land will add no additional revenues to the operation of the station. The principle of economic size is another way of considering the principle of balance.

An example of this principle is *plottage value*. Plottage value occurs when two or more parcels of land are assembled into one tract and the value of the new tract is greater than the sum of the separate parcels. For example, assume that a developer can buy Lot A for $15,000 and Lot B for $10,000. If these lots are put together, the new tract is worth $33,000. The plottage value would be $8,000, as noted in the following calculation:

Value of assembled tract	$33,000
Less: cost of Lot A	– 15,000
Less: cost of Lot B	– 10,000
Plottage value	$ 8,000

Definition of economic size: Economic size is the quantity of land proportionately necessary to develop the appropriate scale of land use justified by the market at a particular location.

Economic Division. The system of property law in the United States allows interests in land to be divided and sold separately. This is referred to as the *bundle of rights* theory of property. Each right may be thought of as a single stick in a bundle of sticks. Together all of the sticks represent all property rights recognized by law.

The principle of economic division suggests that property rights should be separated and packaged in such a manner as to increase the total value of property. Division can take place in many different ways. Examples follow:

- *Physical division* — separating air rights, surface rights, and mineral rights; or subdividing a tract of land.
- *Division of time of possession* — leases, life estates, future interests.
- *Division of right to use* — easements, licenses, deed restrictions.
- *Division by right of ownership* — joint tenancies, partnerships, trusts, corporations, options, conditional sales contracts.
- *Division by security interests* — first mortgages, junior mortgages, tax liens, judgment liens, equity interests.

One important area of economic division that will be explored in subsequent chapters is the division of equity and mortgage positions in an investment. Consideration will be given to the financial impact of the relationship of the two positions.

Definition of economic division: Economic division occurs if rights in real property can be subdivided into two or more property interests resulting in an overall increase in aggregate value.

Principles Associated with the Market Environment

Principles associated with the market environment include: dependency, conformity, supply and demand, competition, and change.

Dependency. Location is one of the most important factors creating value in real estate. Good location is dependent on the physical relationship of land to the surrounding land use pattern and on its proximity to the economic environment. Together these two characteristics form the *situs* or economic location of the land use.

The concept of situs is illustrated in Figure 2–2 as it pertains to a typical retail property use. Similar relationships could be diagrammed for other kinds of uses. Situs is dependent on the mutual interaction of the specific land use and the economic environment on at least four levels. These four levels are indicated by the concentric circles of off-site, immediate neighborhood, trade or subarea, and overall area or region (see Figure 2–2). For certain types of use such as large manufacturing operations, dependency levels may also exist on a national or international scale.

If either the surrounding land use pattern or the economic environment changes, the value of a real estate use would probably be affected. Some examples of land use pattern changes include: construction of a nearby shopping center, creation of a lake, development of a school, or the opening of a sewage treatment plant. These land use pattern changes could have a positive or a negative value impact. The magnitude of the impact is related to the extent of the new land use and to the linkages between the subject property and the new use.

A *linkage* is measured by cost. It is the cost of reaching a supporting facility for a specific purpose, from the subject property. Linkages can be measured as time cost, distance cost, or money cost, from the subject property. Some of these linkages are difficult to measure. For example, if one site has a scenic view, how is this to be

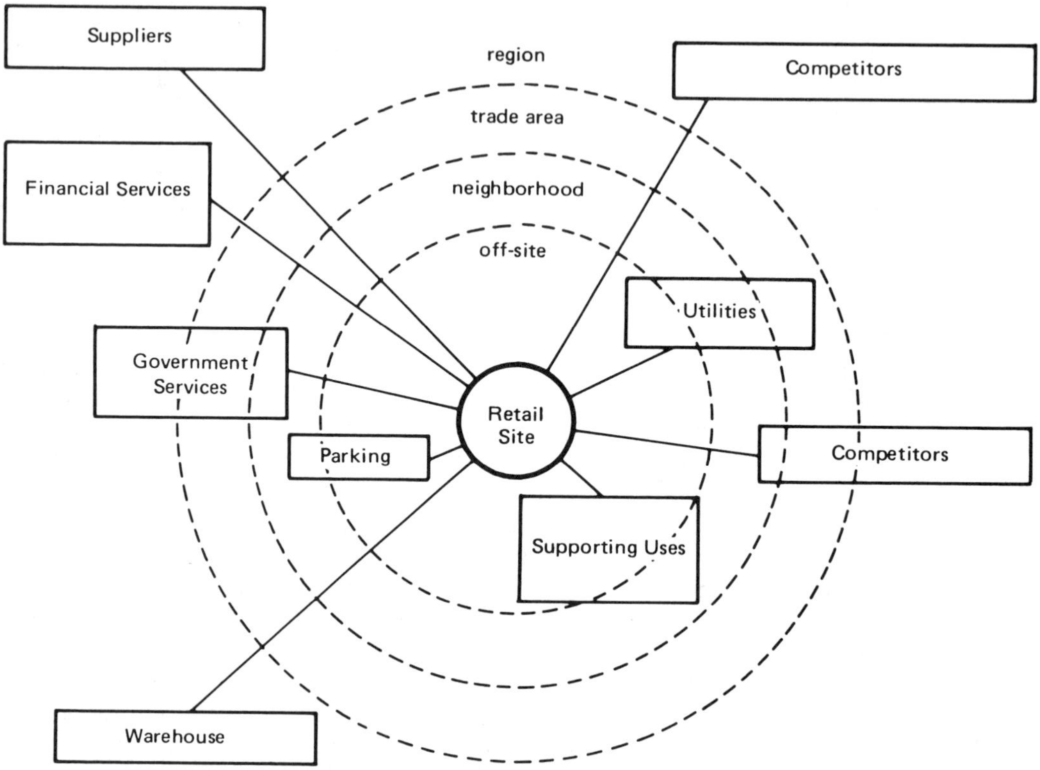

FIGURE 2–2. Situs of a Typical Retail Property Use.

measured? The value of the linkage would be the difference between a site with a view and one without the view.

Linkage costs can be imposed in several ways. For example, if an expressway were constructed, this could shorten the time and distance costs of linking the suburbs with a downtown job center. If a toll were imposed, this would increase the money linkage cost. By changing the speed limit from 70 mph to 55 mph, the time linkage costs would be increased.

Income flows are highly dependent on how a location relates to a user's market. For example, interference with linkages through highway construction, or by a retail competitor positioning itself to intercept traffic, could significantly reduce revenues to a retail location user.

Definition of dependency: The value of a particular real estate use is influenced by and also influences the nature and operation of land use values in the surrounding environment.

Conformity. A project that fails to conform to market standards is likely to suffer a financial penalty. Assume that the market standard in a community is for apartment units to have three bedrooms in order to achieve maximum rental per square foot. A project composed of two-bedroom units would face market resistance if the rental rates were the same as for the three-bedroom apartments. This would be the case even if both types of unit had the same square footage. Therefore, to market the less desirable units, it might be necessary to reduce the rental rate.

Real estate projects must conform to the land use pattern. This does not mean that all buildings must be of the same architectural style. However, the architectural styles and the land use must be compatible. Consider the consequences of constructing a brightly painted Victorian house in a neighborhood of ranch-style houses. Consider also what would happen if a municipal incinerator were constructed next to a nursing home. The nursing home might be closed because of the health hazard imposed by the smoke and other pollution.

Definition of conformity: Conformity is how well the architectural style and levels of amenities and services offered by a real estate development measure up to market needs and expectations.

Related to the principle of conformity are the principles of *regression* and *progression*. Regression occurs when a real estate use is an overimprovement for a market area. For example, if a $175,000 house is constructed in a neighborhood of houses in the $70,000 to $80,000 range, the market value of the more expensive house would not reflect its true cost. The sales price would probably be lower than the actual construction costs. Progression occurs when a real estate project experiences positive value changes because of the operation of the surrounding land uses. For example, if several stores in a shopping area are renovated, all stores in the area would probably experience positive value changes.

Supply and Demand. Real estate has value if it has utility to some user or group of users. Utility, however, is not the only consideration. Real estate must also be relatively scarce. Supply is the quantity of real estate that is available on the market at a given price schedule. Demand is based on the desire of potential purchasers to acquire real estate, provided that they also have sufficient sources of financing to act on their desires.

Because real estate markets are imperfect, supply and demand do not always dictate the price at which real estate will change ownership. Negotiating ability, number and sophistication of participants, emotion, cost of financing, and other factors are also important in establishing selling prices.

Over the long run, supply and demand are relatively effective forces in determining the direction of price changes. In the short term, the forces of supply and demand may not have an opportunity to operate effectively in the real estate market. Market distortions can come from monopoly control of land by private owners. Or markets may be influenced by government controls. For example, local governments may impose growth controls or rent controls or may distort markets in many other ways.

If there is an excessive supply or lack of demand, this will tend to depress prices and rent levels. Supply is relatively inelastic in the short run. This means that it takes a long planning horizon to increase the supply of real estate; even if prices are raised, supply cannot be increased very quickly. It is also difficult to decrease the supply of real estate. Once too much real estate of a particular type has been produced, vacancy rates may remain high for a long time. This creates an excellent opportunity for bargain hunters as prices remain low or fall.

A contrary pressure on prices occurs when there is either an inadequate supply or a high demand. Demand tends to be more volatile than supply. It is more responsive to price changes and trends. Changes in the money supply, interest rate changes, surges of emotional speculation, fear, and other factors can influence the nature of demand at any given time.

When supply and demand are in balance, the market price tends to reflect the cost of production. If market prices are higher than production costs, more real estate would be produced until the two came into balance. If market prices are lower, new production would slow down or stop until the demand caused market prices to rise.

Definition of supply and demand: Supply is the quantity of goods available at a given price schedule; demand is the quantity of goods desired at the price schedule. Together supply and demand interact to establish prices.

Competition. People try to maximize their own wealth. If they see others making excess or monopoly profits in real estate, they will try to enter the market themselves. Excess or monopoly profits are amounts beyond those reasonably necessary to compensate entrepreneurial activities. Higher than usual profits give incentive to the creation of new competition.

New competition will cause the supply of a given real estate use in an area to increase. Unless demand also increases, the average net income for all real estate of the type being produced will tend to fall. If competition is excessive, profits could fall below normal or in some situations disappear entirely.

Definition of competition: Where profits exist beyond the income necessary to pay for the factor in production, competition will tend to enter the market, causing average net incomes to fall.

This principle is important to an analyst attempting to estimate the value of an income stream that is above the market norm. Unless the excess profits are locked in with a long-term lease or for some other reason, the income stream should be considered carefully. Basically, the analyst could take one of two approaches. First, the excess profits can be isolated from the normal profits and treated as a separate income stream. Alternatively, the entire net income stream can be treated as more risky than normal and can be capitalized at a higher rate. Annuities and capitalization rates are discussed in subsequent chapters.

Change. Objects wear out. New businesses are started and others are stopped. The land use pattern is modified by private and public actions. Money supply and interest rates fluctuate. Economic conditions create opportunities. International events affect the cost of commodities. New technology and social patterns create new demands for real estate. Demographics create needs for different kinds of housing. People's desires and tastes undergo transitions. Neighborhoods go through cycles of growth, maturity, decline, and renewal. Any of these factors and many others can change the utility of real estate at a given location.

Definition of change: Real estate values tend not to remain constant but are likely to vary over time.

Analysts must monitor events that are likely to have an impact on real estate. Conditions that existed in the past are not certain to exist in the future. To properly assess the value of future income from a real estate venture, the underlying assumptions justifying revenue and cost forecasts must be carefully scrutinized. Because events and conditions are constantly changing, it is a professional standard in the appraisal profession to make appraisals *as of* a given date.

The Principle of Highest and Best Use

The principle of highest and best use is a synthesis of the principles in each of the three categories previously discussed. A definition that has become accepted in the appraisal profession is as follows:

Definition of highest and best use: The reasonable and probable use that will support the highest present value, as defined, as of the effective date of the appraisal. Alternatively, that use, from among reasonable, probable, and legal alternative uses, found to be physically possible, appropriately supported, and financially feasible, and which results in highest land value.[1]

A discussion of this principle is reserved for Chapter 16. Highest and best use offers a conceptual model for analyzing the various factors that influence the value of a site. It considers important factors in the physical, legal, social, and economic areas that influence real estate values. It also serves as a bridge spanning other value principles including: utility, substitution, anticipation, surplus productivity, contribution, increasing and decreasing returns, balance, economic size, economic division, dependency, conformity, supply and demand, competition, and change.

THE APPRAISAL PROCESS

Appraisal of income-producing properties is an orderly process based on the value principles discussed in this chapter. This process requires problem identification, data collection, and data analysis in order to arrive at a supportable estimate of value. The appraisal process is based on the scientific method and is applicable to the solution of a wide variety of valuation problems. Through this problem-solving process, market-based data are used to justify assumptions and facts that lead to a logical and defensible conclusion. The process may be divided into six steps (see Figure 2–3):

1. Definition of problem.
2. Plan of appraisal.
3. Collection and verification of data.
4. Application of relevant valuation approaches.
5. Reconciliation.
6. Report of the final value estimate.

Step One: Definition of Problem

What problem does the client need solved? Normally the purpose of the appraisal is to find some value estimate that is a necessary ingredient to a client's decision-making needs. The client may be

[1]Adapted from Byrl Boyce, ed., *Real Estate Appraisal Terminology* (Cambridge, Mass.: Ballinger Publishing Co., 1975), p. 107.

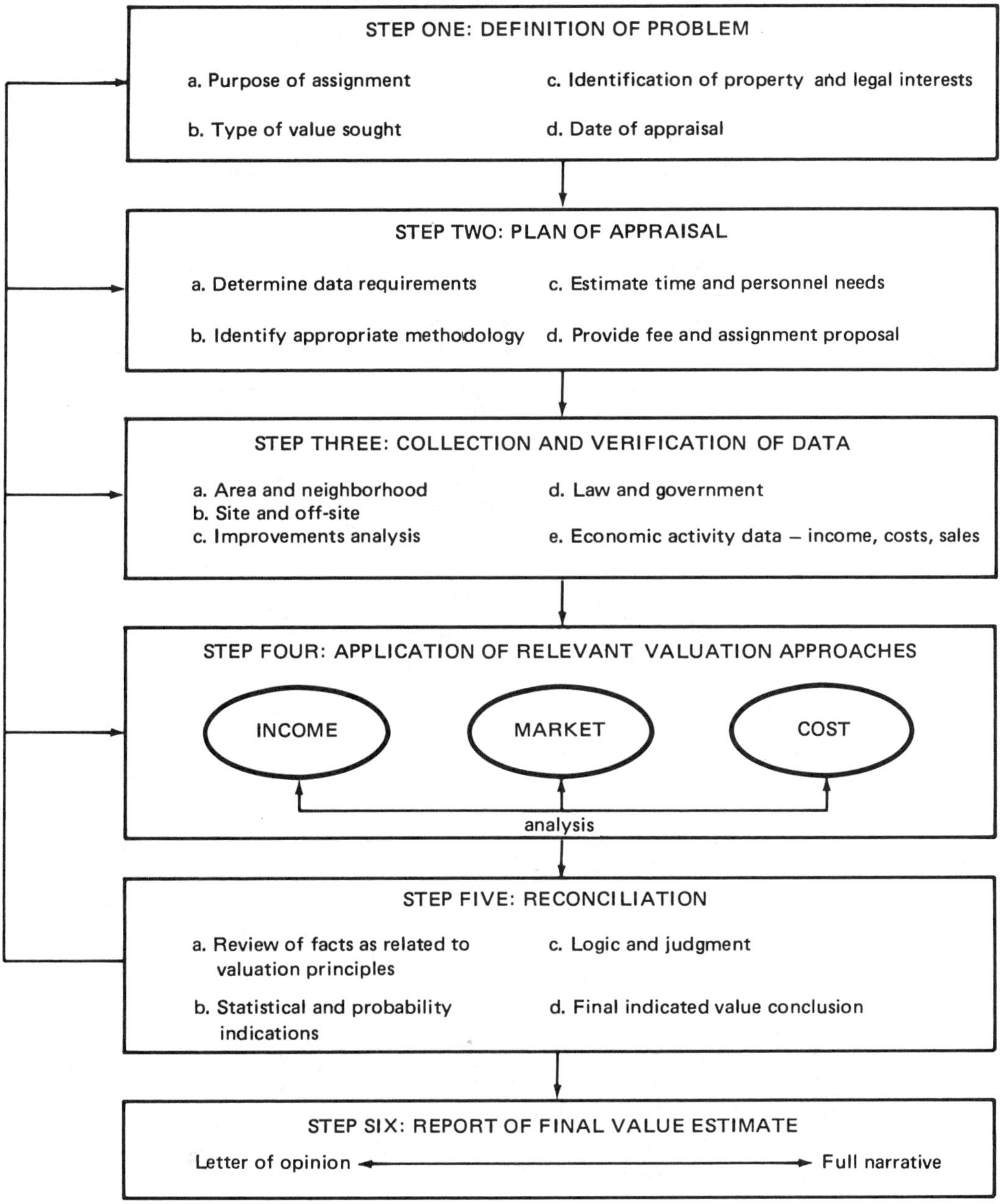

FIGURE 2-3. The Appraisal Process.

interested in purchasing an office building as an investment. How does this investment compare to alternative ways of using the money? The client may wish to sell a warehouse. What is the most probable selling price? The client may wish to lend money to an apartment building owner. The owner has agreed to pledge the property in order to secure the loan. How valuable is that security? The government wishes to take the client's shopping center. What is the fair market value of the center? Each of the problems mentioned requires the appraiser to find a different type of value because the client's needs are different. Utility, substitution, and anticipation are the underlying principles in helping the analyst understand the nature of the problem involved.

In the appraisal it is important to identify the physical property and the legal interest involved. The size and nature of the physical asset must be carefully measured and identified. The client may have only a leasehold or an easement. The fractional or partial interest involved may be a share in a joint tenancy or a partnership. The property may be encumbered with a deed of trust (mortgage) or some other kind of lien. Zoning restrictions may prohibit a planned use. Deed restrictions may limit the size of the use. The principles of balance, economic size, and economic division may apply and provide insights about what kind of information should be collected.

The principle of change makes it important for the appraiser to select an effective date for the valuation. Without a date, someone could inadvertently pick up an appraisal report years later and use it in decision making. Since conditions and assumptions are likely to change, the client must know the time framework within which the value estimate is appropriate.

Step Two: Plan of Appraisal

An appraisal problem is solved by carrying out and completing a research program. Once the problem has been understood and defined, the analyst will direct attention to a probable solution of the problem. Experience has shown that the most efficient way of achieving the solution is through the appraisal framework. This framework is designed to allow the appraiser to begin with general value forces on the national and regional level. From the general information the appraiser then begins to consider more specific value forces on the market and submarket level. Finally the appraiser focuses on very specific forces influencing the value of the particular site and improvements.

Normally, the appraiser will make a plan to determine what data will be necessary to solve the problem. This plan is made to avoid unnecessary duplication, to eliminate unproductive costs, and to save time. The appraiser will attempt to concentrate on those factors that will be relevant in the solution of the problem.

In the plan, the market and submarket will be identified. This step is important whether the value being sought is investment value, market value, or some other type. On the supply side, substitute properties likely to be competitive with the subject will be identified for further analysis. On the demand side, identification will be made of probable purchasers or users for the type of property being appraised. Such information as the terms of financing in the market, size and competitive attributes of comparable properties, and characteristics of probable users will be noted.

The next consideration is determining the applicability of the three traditional approaches to value. Although it is generally true that the income approach will be the most suitable procedure for analyzing income-producing properties, this will not always be the case. The income approach is only one indicator of value. The market and cost approaches can also provide useful information. In some situations, the cost or market approaches may be more accurate or more efficient. In many situations, each approach can be used as a check against the value estimate provided by the other approaches.

The market or direct sales comparison approach is particularly useful where there is an active market for comparable properties. The accuracy of this approach is dependent on the quality of data collected. Accurate information should be collected about recent sales of comparable properties. Among the data collected about the sales of comparable properties are the following: physical characteristics, time of sale, location, conditions of sale, and terms of financing. This approach tends to be weak if there have been few transactions, if the transactions are not recent, or if the market is abnormal. Because this approach depends on historical transactions, a value indication using old data may be misleading if the market is rapidly changing.

The cost approach is very useful for appraising special-purpose properties and new or proposed construction, for estimating the highest and best use of land, and for insurance purposes. Information collected should generally include such data as land prices, building specifications, wage rates, material costs, equipment expenses, and profits and overhead of builders in the local market. This approach is difficult to use for certain properties such as buildings with unique architectural or aesthetic features, building improvements suffering from excessive accrued depreciation, or buildings of historic merit.

From a theoretical standpoint, it can be argued that the cost and income approaches are part of the market approach. Each deals with different kinds of information derived from the market. For example, data for the cost approach are based on current market prices for materials, labor, and other inputs. And the income approach requires the use of capitalization rates that are derived from the market. As a practical matter, however, cost and income approaches are useful techniques, separate from the market approach, which is based on sales of comparable property.

The next stage involves outlining the appraisal and developing work schedule and budget. Estimates are made of the expected cost and time necessary to collect and verify the data. This will depend partly on the extensiveness of the appraiser's data files, the human resources available, the uniqueness or difficulty of the problem, and the experience of the appraiser. It may be necessary to include in the budget various fees for other professionals or experts. Depending on the complexity of the problems, these individuals may include engineers, art experts, cost estimators, attorneys, accountants, or other appraisers. The client's problem may require the collection of original primary data. These data may have to be collected through extensive marketing questionnaires and will require computer time to tabulate and classify. The research may require travel. If a narrative appraisal must be written, the appraiser may also need to budget costs for developing tables, charts, diagrams, maps, and other exhibits.

The final consideration is the preparation and submission of a written fee proposal. The fee should be based on the difficulty of the problem, the expenditures anticipated, a fair allocation of overhead expenses, the amount of legal risk exposure, and the range of services rendered. The fee may be a flat lump sum or an hourly rate. It is considered to be a conflict of interest if the fee is set as a percentage of the final value estimate.

The *assignment proposal* is a means of clarifying the responsibilities of both the appraiser and the client. It is also a way of making sure that the appraiser has understood the nature of the client's problem. Gaining the client's formal approval of the assignment proposal and fee will help avoid future misunderstandings.

Step Three: Collection and Verification of Data

The credibility of the appraiser's conclusions depends on the data used to reach those conclusions. If the data are inaccurate or of poor quality, it will be very difficult to develop a supportable conclusion.

An attempt should be made to collect the best data available. The appraiser should take all reasonable steps to verify the accuracy and credibility of data used in the report or in the analysis. At a minimum, the following questions should be answered in the appraiser's mind:

1. Are the data collected important and relevant to the solution of the appraisal problem? Extraneous information that is included as a filler rarely enhances the credibility of a report.

2. How useful are the data? Are the facts drawn from the same set of market conditions as influence the subject property? Are these facts sufficiently specific or are they vague? How timely is the information?

3. Have the data been verified? Has the appraiser personally inspected the property? Has the information on the sales comparables been confirmed by knowledgeable parties to the transactions? Are the financial figures used to construct a reasonable income stream comparable to the operation of similar properties in the market?

4. Is there any reason to believe that the data are inaccurate? What possible biases or distortions could exist?

5. On the basis of the appraiser's experience and knowledge, does the information collected seem reasonable?

Step Four: Application of Relevant Valuation Approaches

The data collected will be analyzed within the context of the applicable valuation approaches. No attempt will be made to provide a detailed discussion of the approaches in the following paragraphs. For coverage of market and cost approaches, the reader may wish to consult Chapters 16, 17, and 18.

In general, the market approach is based on the application of the principle of substitution. Competitive properties are selected for comparison. Usually there are differences between the comparables selected and the subject property, and adjustments are required. The underlying basis of these adjustments is the principle of contribution.

The cost approach is also based on the principle of substitution. Additional principles underlying this approach include highest and best use, contribution, balance, economic size, and economic division.

For the purpose of analysis, the appraiser considers the land separately from the improvements. The land is valued using the principle of highest and best use. Alternative hypothetical development schemes are considered to estimate the highest residual value of the land. With respect to income-producing properties this procedure may lead the appraiser to the conclusion that the existing use is inappropriate for the location or that it is underimproved.

In the valuation of the improvements, consideration is given to the cost of reproducing the improvements as if these were new. Techniques used by the appraiser range from the very detailed quantity survey method to more simplified methods based on cost per square foot.

The next step in the cost approach is to estimate any accrued depreciation that may exist. Accrued depreciation is a summary of the loss of utility suffered by the property. Loss of utility normally comes from physical deterioration, functional obsolescence, and economic (locational) obsolescence.

Physical deterioration may be a result of age and possible lack of proper maintenance. The amount of deterioration existing will have an impact on the remaining useful life of a property. This estimate of remaining useful life is also important in the income approach. It helps an appraiser estimate the length of an income stream.

Functional obsolescence may be a result of a developer's failure to consider the principles of balance, economic size, or economic division. For example, the building may be an overimprovement for the property. Or the principle of change may be in operation, e.g., increasing energy costs may make an office building with large glass panels functionally obsolete.

Economic (locational) obsolescence can be explained by an application of the principles of change and dependency. Such obsolescence occurs when the land use pattern, linkages, or customer markets change. Because real estate is fixed at a particular location, it cannot be moved and may suffer a loss of utility.

The income approach is a process of estimating the present value of future benefits one expects to derive from the operation and possible future disposition of the property. The operational value principle involved is that of anticipation.

Each of the three approaches provides the appraiser with a different perspective. Although these approaches depend on data collected from the same market, each deals with a different aspect of the market. In a perfect market, all three approaches would tend to converge on the same value. However, real estate markets are not perfect. Often supply and demand are not in equilibrium. Potential users may be misinformed. Producers may be inefficient. For these reasons, among others, each of the approaches may provide a different value indication.

Step Five: Reconciliation

Reconciliation is a process of using judgment and logic to develop a final estimate of value. As a prelude to the judgment process, the appraiser reviews all facts and checks the accuracy of the computations. All assumptions are tested for reasonableness and credibility.

Reconciliation has been described as "an examination of conscience." In this process, the appraiser reviews the applicability of value principles as these pertain to the various stages of problem identification, data collection, and analysis — using each valuation approach. The indications of value are reconsidered. How valid are they? Are they justified on the basis of the data? Do they make sense? The original problem is reexamined. The appraiser may use statistical calculations to develop probability distributions. He may then consider a value range within which the value sought is expected to fall. Normally, the appraiser is expected to provide the client with a single value estimate. On the basis of this process, the appraiser must now make that decision.

Observe that reconciliation is not a process of mechanical averaging of results derived using the three approaches. It is a process of human logic, judgment, and decision.

Step Six: Report of Final Value Estimate

As a last step, the appraiser writes a report of the findings and conclusions, which is then transmitted to the client. Depending on the original agreement with the client, this report may be a simple letter, a completed standardized form, or a comprehensive narrative report.

SUMMARY

The income approach to property appraisal must be considered within the context of a systematic, problem-solving process. This process is based on a unified theory of value principles. The principles discussed in this chapter were divided into four groups. The first group contained principles based on user characteristics. These were the principles of utility, substitution, and anticipation. The second group contained principles associated with land and improvements. These were the principles of surplus productivity, contribution, increasing and decreasing returns, balance, economic size, and economic division. The third group contained principles associated with the market environment. These were the principles of dependency, conformity, supply and demand, competition, and change. The last principle to be described was a bridge joining the other principles. This was the principle of highest and best use.

Described also in this chapter was the appraisal process. It was discussed in six steps:

Step One — Definition of problem.
Step Two — Plan of appraisal.
Step Three — Collection and verification of data.
Step Four — Application of relevant valuation approaches.
Step Five — Reconciliation.
Step Six — Report of the final value estimate.

Questions

1. A developer has paid $200,000 for ten acres of land to be used for the development of a residential subdivision. At a density of one house per acre, each house will cost $60,000 to construct and will be marketed for $80,000 after paying all selling expenses. For each additional house that is put on an acre of land the construction cost will drop by $2,000, but the market price after selling expenses will fall by $4,000.
   a. How many houses should be built?
   b. What are the total profits?
   c. What value principle is involved?
2. XYZ Fast Foods is examining a site for possible lease. The site is expected to attract 2,000 customers per month. On the average, each customer will consume $2.00 worth of hamburgers and soft drinks. The company must make a profit margin of 10¢ on each dollar of sales. The cost of labor and materials for each dollar of sales is 80¢.
   a. How much is the maximum rent that the company can afford to pay each month and still meet its profit margin requirements?
   b. What principle or principles are involved in creating value in the land?

3. An appraiser is using the market approach to estimate the indicated value of a subject property. She has found a recent sale that is nearly identical to the subject property. That property has a swimming pool but the subject property does not. The appraiser has learned that such a pool will cost $20,000 to construct. The first comparable property sold for $120,000. In checking her files, the appraiser finds two other comparable sales in that neighborhood. One was for $97,000 without a swimming pool; the other sale was for $112,000 with a swimming pool. All other differences are minor.
   a. Estimate a value range for the subject property.
   b. What are the pitfalls of making adjustments using the information provided?
   c. What value principle applies?

Essay Questions

1. In an open and free market, what potential problems are associated with an income stream based partly on excess profits? What economic principle is likely to come into operation?
2. What is the concept of *situs?* At what stages in the appraisal process is the concept important?
3. Why does the appraisal process rely on three different approaches to value? How different are these approaches?
4. Why is the real estate market relatively slow in adjusting supply to demand?
5. Define each of the following:
   a. Reconciliation.
   b. Highest and best use.
   c. Market value.
   d. Substitution.
   e. Contribution.

Chapter 3

Compound Interest, Discounting, and Annuities

The value of income-producing properties is based on the present value of dollars expected to be received at various time intervals in the future. A dollar received one year from now or ten years from now is worth less than a dollar received today. Therefore, an adjustment must be made to future receipts to estimate their present value.

Consider two alternative investments. Investment A costs $100,000 and will pay back an income of $10,000 each year for thirty years. Investment B costs $50,000 and will be worth $100,000 twelve years from now. Given that risks are perceived to be equal, which is the better investment? To determine the answer, the analyst must be familiar with the concepts of *compounding* and *discounting.* These concepts will allow for a proper consideration of an investment.

JUDGMENTS REQUIRED

Compound interest and discounting are mechanical techniques that can be applied to income that is forecast from an investment. Before applying the techniques, it is crucial to carefully judge (1) the *amounts* of money that are expected to be involved; (2) the *timing* of when amounts are to be paid or received; (3) the *risks* perceived to be inherent in the investment; and (4) an appropriate *rate of return* (interest or discount rate) based on market conditions and perceived risk.

These four elements can be succinctly stated as: (1) amounts, (2) timing, (3) risk, and (4) rate of return. Only after amounts, timing, risk, and rate of return have been properly melded together can an analyst offer a sophisticated judgment concerning the value of an investment.

Amounts

Cash dollars or their cash equivalents are the common denominator of amounts. It is important to forecast the total amount of dollars expected to be paid for and received from an investment proposal, with the highest possible degree of accuracy. The amounts of dollars expected to be invested and recovered can answer the crucial question of whether the investment offers a positive rate of return. When cash inflows are expected to exceed outflows, a positive rate of return on investment is expected. But the amounts, even if known with certainty, do not offer information concerning the rate of return nor the risk involved. For example, suppose $100 is to be invested and $200 is to be returned at a later date. Is it a good investment? That question cannot be answered properly without an estimate of the likelihood of the $200 being returned (or a greater or lesser amount) and an estimate of when it will be returned.

Timing

One of the investor's most precious and irreplaceable resources is time. Once lost, time can never be regained. Benjamin Franklin constantly reminded his readers that "time is money." He pointed out that time nonproductively used was money lost. One way to use time productively is to put capital to work. Money is used to earn interest. The timing of the interest is important because the interest that is earned may be used to earn still more interest. The timing of investment returns is measured in intervals, or periods. An interval or period may be a day, week, month, quarter, half-year, or year. The timing of amounts to be paid or received is crucial to any investment analysis.

For example, if $100 is paid for an investment, and $200 is expected to be received, whether the $200 will be received the next day, next year, or 5 years or 50 years later makes a great deal of difference. As a general rule, the sooner amounts are received, the better the investment. Returns from the investment can then be reinvested to realize greater earnings over a given time span.

Risk

Risk is the variability or uncertainty associated with an investment. That is, risk is the probability that returns from the investment will be greater or less than was originally forecast.

For example, a $100 bet on a 50 to 1 long shot in a horse race has a great deal of risk. It can result in the loss of $100 or a gain of $5,000. On the other hand, $100 invested in a U.S. government bond has less risk. After a given period of time, it will be worth $150 with an extremely high degree of certainty. The analyst should keep in mind that there are different types of risk, and that no investment is entirely free of risk.

Rate of Return

Rate of *return on investment* is a percentage relationship between earnings and invested capital. A properly derived rate of return considers the amounts and timing of expected earnings, and it can be used as a common denominator to rank investment proposals. The rate of return on investment is also called the *yield to maturity.* For consumer loans, it is the "Annual Percentage Rate" (APR).

Unless investment criteria include nonfinancial reasons, the investment offering the highest rate of return on investment is chosen first. But when all elements are not equal, forecast rates of return are balanced against risk. The greater the risk, the higher the rate of return must be to compensate an investor for assuming the risk.

COMPOUND INTEREST FUNCTIONS

Since compound interest is a mechanical process and because of the variety of income configurations that can result from different investments, tables have been prepared and included in *Appendix B* at various interest rates. Each page of the tables considers at least 30 years of income and has six columns for convenient application to a variety of income streams. Column functions and headings are listed below. See Appendix B for examples.

- Compound amount of one (Column 1)
- Accumulation of one per period (Column 2)
- Sinking fund factor (Column 3)
- Present worth of one (Column 4)
- Present worth of an annuity (Column 5)
- Installment to amortize one (Column 6)

This chapter describes the composition and use of three of the functions: compound amount of one, present worth of one, and present worth of an annuity. The other three functions are described in the following chapter.

COMPOUND AMOUNT OF ONE

In devising the "rate of return on investment" as a financial yardstick, it is essential to consider the compound interest effect. Compound interest means that interest that has been earned—if it is left on deposit with the initial investment—becomes part of the principal. Therefore, that interest along with the initial deposit will earn interest the next period. In contrast, simple interest does not provide for interest to be earned on interest.

For example, suppose that \$100 is deposited in an account that pays a 10% rate of interest, compounded annually. The \$100 will earn \$10 interest the first year (10% of \$100.00 = \$10.00). After one year, the balance will be \$110.00 (\$100.00 + \$10.00 = \$110.00). Provided that the full \$110.00 remains on deposit for the second year, \$11.00 of interest will be earned in the second year (10% of \$110.00 = \$11.00). After five years, the balance will be \$161.05, provided all interest was left on deposit. This is shown in Table 3–1. In comparison, simple interest would provide \$10.00 per year interest; so after five years, \$150.00 (\$100.00 + 5 × \$10.00 = \$150.00) would be the full principal. This, too, is shown in Table 3–1.

TABLE 3-1.
\$100.00 Deposit—Compound versus Simple Interest (Rate = 10%)

Year		*Compound Interest*	*Simple Interest*
0	Deposit	\$100.00	\$100.00
1	Interest earned	10.00	10.00
1	Balance, end of year	110.00	110.00
2	Interest earned	11.00	10.00
2	Balance, end of year	121.00	120.00
3	Interest earned	12.10	10.00
3	Balance, end of year	133.10	130.00
4	Interest earned	13.31	10.00
4	Balance, end of year	146.41	140.00
5	Interest earned	14.64	10.00
5	Balance, end of year	\$161.05	\$150.00

The power of compound interest becomes evident when one considers that if the Canarsie Indians, who sold Manhattan Island to Peter Minuit in 1626, for \$24.00 worth of merchandise, had invested \$24.00 at 6% compounded annually, the principal amount in 1983 would be worth nearly 26 billion dollars. If the Indians had invested at 7% compounded annually, the principal sum would be worth an astounding 741 billion dollars. On the other hand, \$24.00 at 6% simple interest for the same time period is only \$538.08, and at 7% simple interest it is only \$623.76.

The logic of compound interest is obvious. All money that has been left on deposit should earn interest. Further, only the money that has been on deposit should earn interest. This investment logic should be firmly ingrained in the minds of all analysts and appraisers.

Figure 3–1 graphically portrays the growth of today's principal to a calculated future value with compound interest.

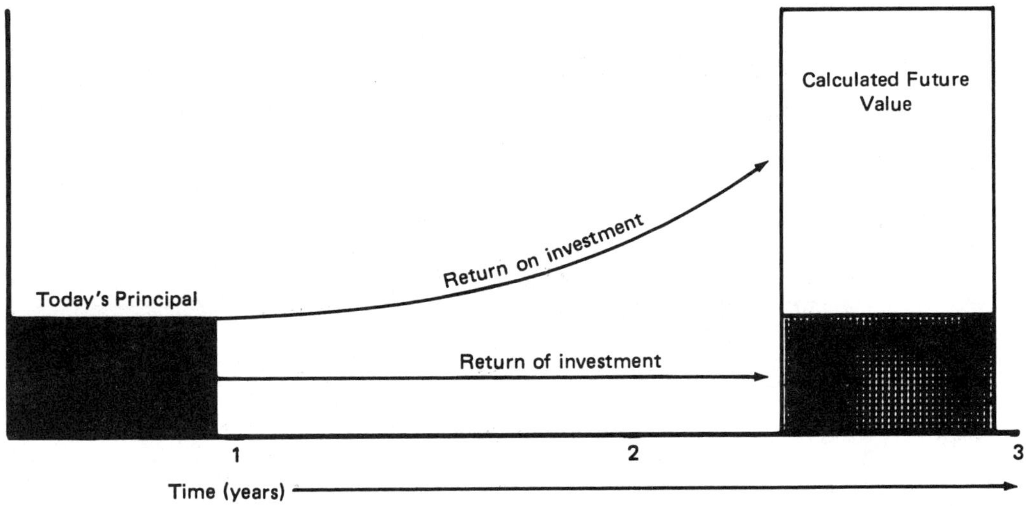

FIGURE 3–1. Growth of Principal at Compound Interest.

Precomputed Tables for Compound Interest

Because compound interest is used so regularly and extensively, investors have found it convenient and advisable to become acquainted with standardized tables that have precalculated compound interest factors. A *factor* is one of two or more numbers that when multiplied together produce a given product. If an investor knows how much the number one is worth at the end of 23 years, when compounded annually at 10%, he will also know how much \$43.22 will be worth merely by multiplying it by the value of one at the end of 23 years. All compound interest tables use the formula

$$S^n = (1 + i)^n$$

where

S^n = the sum after n periods
i = the periodic rate of interest
n = the number of periods

Most "six-function" precomputed tables show the growth of \$1.00 per period at compound interest in column 1. Table 3-2 is a sample of compound interest tables at 10% interest with annual compounding. When the beginning balance is greater (or less) than \$1.00, simply multiply the beginning amount by the factor in the table to find the resulting lump sum amount. For example, when \$10,000 earns 10% annual compound interest for five years, the balance will become \$16,105.10 (\$10,000 × 1.61051 = \$16,105.10).

TABLE 3-2

Compound Amount of \$1.00 at 10%

Year	*Compound Amount*
1	\$ 1.10
2	1.21
3	1.331
4	1.4641
5	1.61051
6	1.771561
7	1.948717
8	2.143589
9	2.357948
10	2.593742
20	6.727500
30	17.449402
50	117.390853

This occurs because each and every dollar invested earns at the same rate of interest. Each dollar alone would grow from \$1.00 to approximately \$1.61 in five years at 10% annual compound interest, so \$10,000 would grow to \$10,000 × 1.61.

Rule of 72's

The "rule of 72's," which is based on logarithms, uses the number 72 as a short-cut approximation for the number of years it will take money to double when interest is left on deposit. The rule states that a sum will approximately double in the number of years as determined by dividing 72 by the interest rate expressed as a whole number. This rule works reasonably well in the 3 to 18% range.

For example, at 3% compound interest, it will take approximately 24 years ($72 \div 3 = 24$) for money to double (at simple interest, it will take $33^1/_3$ years). At 4% interest, it will take approximately eighteen years to double; at 6% interest, about twelve years; at 12% interest, about six years. The rule works in reverse just as well. If a \$10,000 investment doubles to \$20,000 in six years, the compounded annual rate of interest is approximately 12% (72 divided by six years is 12%). If money doubles in ten years, the compounded rate is about 7.2%. This is shown graphically in Figure 3-2.

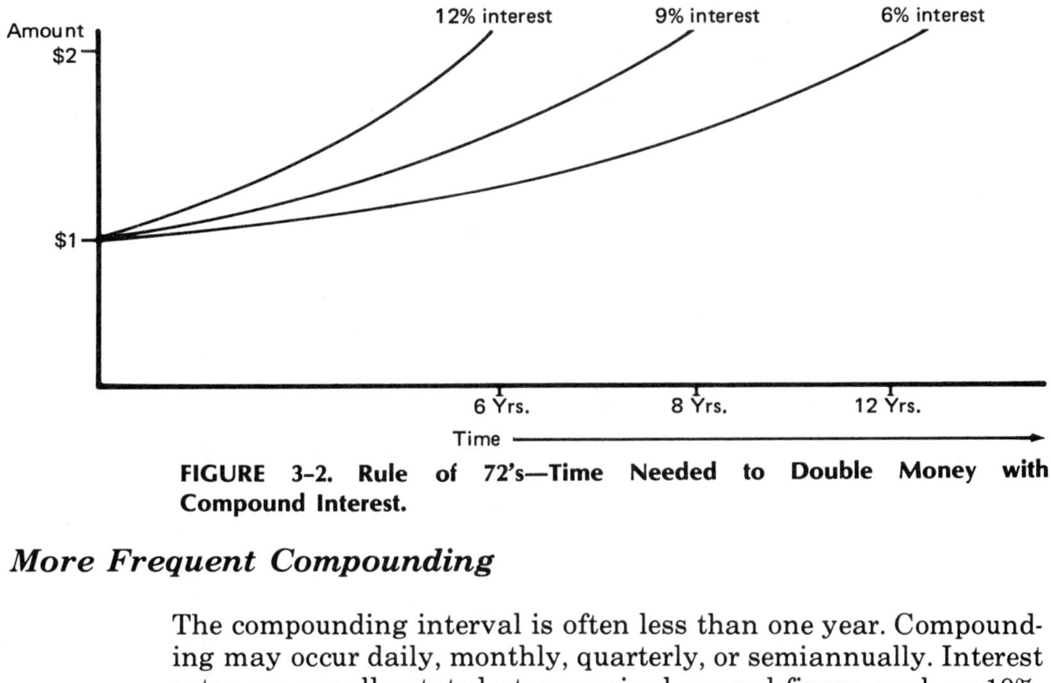

FIGURE 3-2. Rule of 72's—Time Needed to Double Money with Compound Interest.

More Frequent Compounding

The compounding interval is often less than one year. Compounding may occur daily, monthly, quarterly, or semiannually. Interest rates are usually stated at a nominal annual figure, such as 10%, but more frequent compounding serves to increase the effective rate. The general formula is the same:

$$S^n = (1 + i)^n,$$

but it must be modified to reflect the smaller compounding interval.

The modification necessary is to multiply the number of years by the compounding frequency per year, and divide the nominal annual rate by the compounding frequency. The result will indicate an effective interest rate per compounding period.

For example, 10% interest with quarterly compounding actually means that the interest will be paid at the rate of $2^1/_2$% per quarter of each year. If the compounding is monthly, the interest would be paid at .00833 per month (.10 ÷12 = .00833). There are precomputed tables that consider more frequent compounding. Table 3-3 shows the growth of $1.00 at 10% interest with quarterly compounding. The more frequent the compounding interval, the more rapidly money grows (see Table 3-4). This means the effective annual rate would be higher (for more frequent compounding) than the nominal annual rate.

TABLE 3-3
Growth of $1.00 with Quarterly Compounding (Nominal Annual Rate = 10%)

Year	*Quarter*	*Compound Amount*
1	1	$1.025
	2	1.050625
	3	1.076891
	4	1.103813
2	5	1.131408
	6	1.159693
	7	1.188686
	8	1.2184029

TABLE 3-4
Growth of $1000.00 for Various Compounding Intervals (Nominal Rate = 10%)

Compounding Interval	*Amount at End of One Year*	*Effective Annual Rate*
Annual	$1,100.00	10.00%
Semiannual	1,102.50	10.25%
Quarterly	1,103.81	10.38%
Monthly	1,104.71	10.47%
Weekly	1,105.06	10.50%
Daily	1,105.15	10.50%

Discrete versus Continuous Compounding

The term *discrete* means that the compounding interval is fixed, such as a year, quarter, or month. Continuous compounding implies that interest is earning interest with the shortest possible time period. Although the shortest possible time period is infinitely short, daily compounding gives a very close approximation of continuous compounding. At a 10% rate, daily compounding for a "360-day year" would be determined by the following formula where S^n is the sum after *n* periods.

$$S^n = (1 + i)^n$$

$$S^n = \left(1 + \frac{.10}{360}\right)^{360}$$

$$S^n = 1.105156$$

Use of Calculators for Compound Interest

The keyboard of most financial calculators has a row with five buttons for financial computations, as shown in Figure 3-3. The [N]

FIGURE 3-3. Financial Calculator Keyboard Row.

key is for the number of periods. The [%i] key is for the periodic interest rate; [PMT] for periodic payment; [PV] for the present value of an amount; and [FV] for the future value of an amount. In addition, there is a [CPT] button or [COMPUTE] designation for a row.

When dealing with compound interest for a lump sum amount at a specified rate of interest for a specified time interval, three items are known. The calculator will solve for the fourth. Some calculators require that the CI mode (Compound Interest) be selected in advance.

For example, to find the future value of $10,000 at 10% interest with annual compounding for five years, touch the keys shown in Figure 3-4.

The same problem, but with quarterly compounding, can be solved by multiplying the number of years by 4 to reflect the number of quarters, and dividing the rate of interest by 4 to reflect the periodic interest rate. Figure 3-5 shows the keystrokes using quarterly compounding.

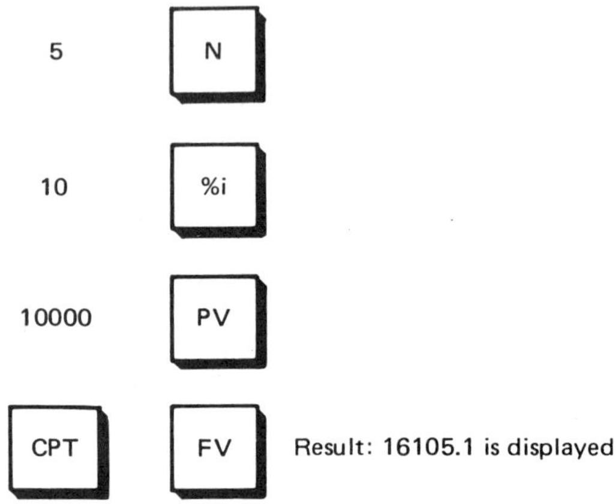

FIGURE 3-4. Calculator Keystrokes for Compound Interest—at 10% Interest, Annual Compounding for 5 Years, and $10,000 Beginning Principal.

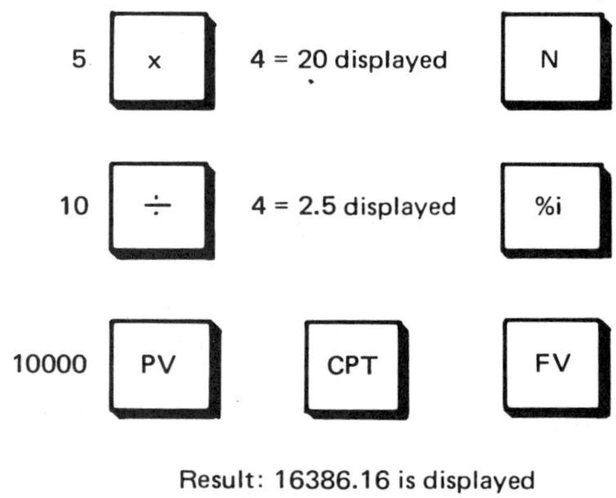

FIGURE 3-5. Calculator Keystrokes for Quarterly Compounding at 10% Interest for 5 Years (20 Quarters) and $10,000 Beginning Principal.

PRESENT VALUE OF A REVERSION

The present value of a reversion is the reciprocal of the compound amount of one. It is the value now of one dollar expected to be received in the future. Since the purpose of investing is to receive returns in the future, applying the present value of a reversion factor to anticipated future income is a crucial step in valuing an investment.

The present value of a reversion (V^n) is graphically illustrated in Figure 3-6. Its usefulness is to estimate the present worth of a known (or forecast) future lump sum receipt of money, at a specified interest rate. When applying a present worth factor, the term *discounting* or *discount rate* is used, as contrasted with *compounding* or *interest rate,* which is used in compound amounts of one.

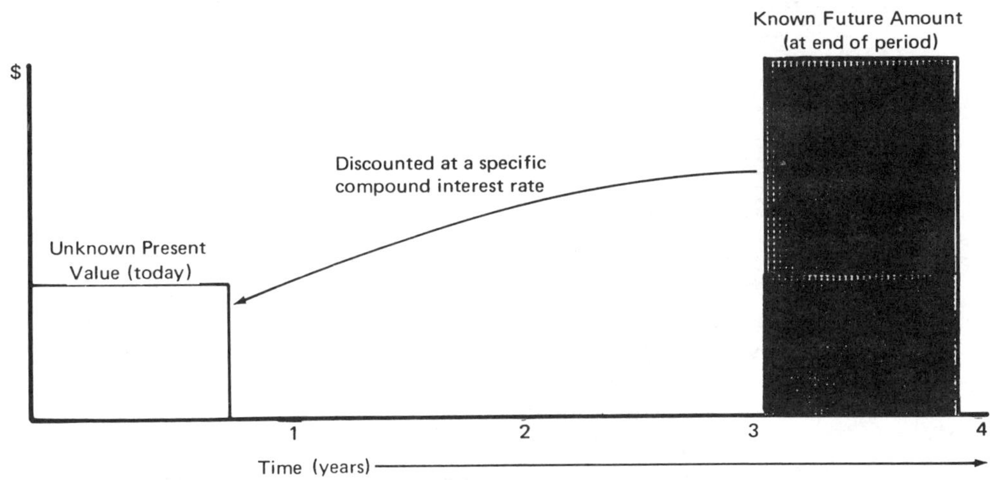

FIGURE 3-6. Present Value of Reversion—Graphic Illustration.

Since money has a time value, one dollar to be received in the future is worth less than one dollar now. How much less (the amount of discount) depends on (a) the time span between the cash outflow and inflow, and (b) the necessary rate of interest or discount.

For example, at a 10% rate of interest (discount rate), \$100.00 that is expected to be received one year from now has a present value of \$90.91. As a check on the arithmetic, if an investor has \$90.91 now and can earn 10% during the next year, the interest will amount to \$9.09; so with the interest added, the principal in one year will be \$100.00 (\$90.91 + \$9.09 = \$100.00).

An investor who expects to receive $100.00 in two years and pays $82.64 now will receive a 10% annual rate of interest. As a check, after one year, $82.64 will grow to $90.91 with 10% interest, then to $100.00 in two years.

An application of this in real estate would be the problem of estimating the amount to pay today for land that is expected to be resold in the future at a gain. For example, an investor expecting to resell certain property in two years for $10,000 is faced with the problem of how much to offer for the land today. If the investor requires a 10% annual rate of return on capital invested, the maximum offer would be $8,264. A price lower than that will result in a higher rate of return on investment. Conversely, a higher price would prevent achievement of the 10% annual required rate of return.

Formula for Present Worth of Reversion

The formula for the present value reversion of one is:

$$V^n = \frac{1}{(1 + i)^n} \quad \text{also} \quad \frac{1}{S^n}$$

The reader will observe that this factor is the reciprocal of the amount of one at compound interest. Therefore, any problem that can be answered using the compound amount of one factor can also be solved using the reversion factor, but by division instead of multiplication, or vice versa.

For example, as described earlier, $100.00 at 10% compound interest will grow to $161.05 in five years. Since $100.00 will become $161.05 in five years, then $62.09 is the amount that will grow to $100.00 in five years. The ratio analysis is shown below for the example:

Now		*5 Years*
$100.00	is to	$161.05
as x	is to	$100.00

$$\text{Since } \$161.05x = 10{,}000$$

$$x = \frac{10{,}000}{161.05}$$

$$x = \$62.09$$

Construction of Tables

As in the compound amount of one, regular and extensive use of the present worth of one factor created a need for standardized precalculated tables. The present worth of one is found in column 4 of many compound interest tables. It is derived using the formula described earlier:

$$V^n = \frac{1}{(1+i)^n} \quad \text{also} \quad \frac{1}{S^n}$$

Since it is the reciprocal of the compound amount of one, tables can be constructed simply by considering it as a reciprocal, as shown in Table 3-5.

TABLE 3-5
Construction of Present Value of Reversion Table (Annual Rate = 10%)

Year	*Compound Amount*	*Reciprocal*		*Present Value of One*
1	1.1	1/1.1	=	.909091
2	1.21	1/1.21	=	.826446
3	1.331	1/1.331	=	.751315
4	1.4641	1/1.4641	=	.683013
5	1.6105	1/1.6105	=	.620921

Certain tables are constructed with the present value of one at various rates of discount (interest) on the same page. Such tables may be convenient, for example, to highlight the purchasing power of $1.00 in the future at various rates of inflation. Table 3-6 shows this at 3, 6, 10, and 15% rates. Present worth of one line at various discount rates are graphed in Figure 3-7.

TABLE 3-6
Future Purchasing Power of $1.00 at Various Rates of Inflation

	Rate of Inflation			
Year	*3%*	*6%*	*10%*	*15%*
1	.9709	.9434	.9091	.8696
2	.9426	.8900	.8264	.7561
3	.9151	.8396	.7513	.6575
4	.8885	.7921	.6830	.5718
5	.8626	.7473	.6209	.4972

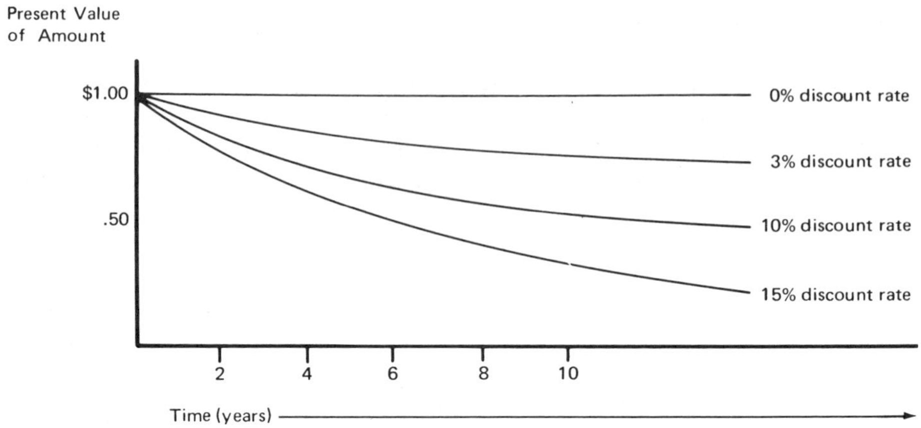

FIGURE 3-7. Present Value Time Lines At Selected Discount Rates.

More Frequent Discounting

Just as with compound interest, the interval between discounting periods may be shorter (more frequent) than one year. This is accomplished in the same manner as for compound interest. The nominal discount rate is divided by the interval frequency (if quarterly, then divide by 4, for example), and the number of periods per year is multiplied by the number of years.

Financial Calculator Applications

To discover the present value of a known future amount using a financial calculator, input the number of time intervals as [N], periodic interest rate as [%i], and known future value as [FV]. Then press [COMPUTE] [PV]. The present value is displayed. (Some calculators require a CI mode to be selected first. Figure 3-8 shows the calculator keystrokes necessary to find the present value of $10,000, which is to be received in five years at a 10% annual discount rate.

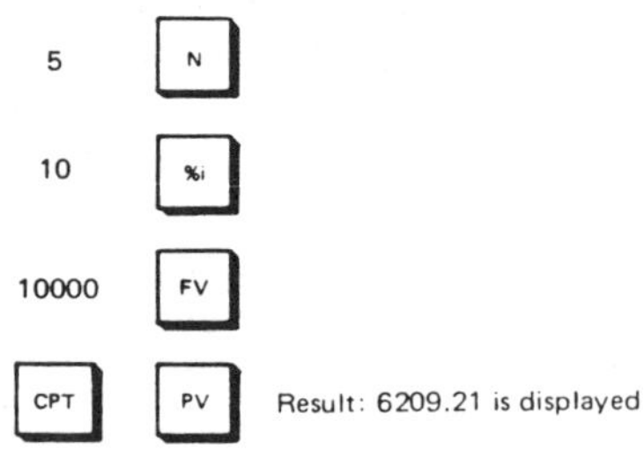

FIGURE 3-8. Calculator Keystrokes for Present Value of Reversion at 10% Discount Rate, Annual Discounting for 5 Years, and $10,000 Future Value.

PRESENT WORTH OF AN ANNUITY

An ordinary annuity is defined as a series of equal payments, the first payment to be made one period from the present. It is also defined as a series of receipts. As an example, the right to receive $100 at the end of each year for the next four years creates an ordinary annuity. Similarly, the obligation to pay $100 per month for the next 300 months is an ordinary annuity. The present value of an annuity is graphically shown in Figure 3-9.

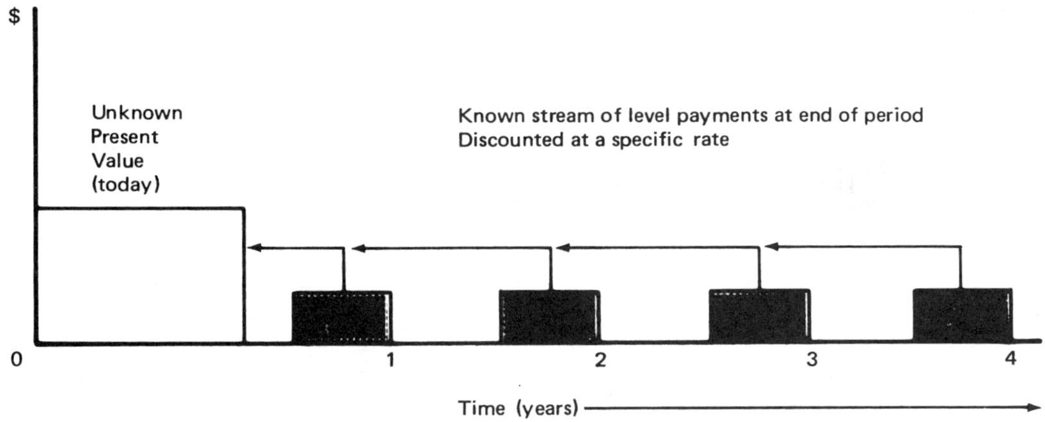

FIGURE 3-9. Present Value of Ordinary Annuity.

The present value of an annuity at a given rate of discount can be derived by treating each individual payment (or receipt) separately. Each payment is multiplied by the appropriate present value of one factor.

For example, the right to receive $100 net rental income at the end of each year for the next four years can be valued by considering each of the four receipts as individual reversions. At a 10% discount rate, the first year's receipt is worth $90.91 ($100.00 × .90909 = $90.91); the second year's receipt is worth $82.64; the third year's $75.13; the fourth, $68.30. The present value of the entire four-year annuity is \$316.98, which is the sum of \$90.91 + \$82.64 + \$75.13 + 68.30. Therefore, at a 10% interest rate, a \$316.98 investment today (present value) is a fair exchange for the receipt of \$100.00 per year for the next four years.

Precomputed Tables. Extensive and widespread use of the present value of an annuity has led to the compilation of precomputed tables. These tables show factors assuming each payment to be \$1.00 per period. The factors are called *annuity factors* or *Inwood factors,* named after William Inwood (1771–1843). The factor is shown in column 5 of many compound interest tables.

The formula for the Inwood factor is:

$$a_n = \frac{1 - \frac{1}{(1 + i)^n}}{i} \quad \text{or} \quad \frac{1 - V^n}{i}$$

It is also the summation of present values of \$1.00 for the specified time period, which is:

$$a_n = \sum_{t=1}^{t=n} \frac{1}{(1 + i)^t}$$

To compile an annuity chart, simply add the present-value-of-one factors for the appropriate number of years. This is shown in Table 3-7.

TABLE 3–7
Relation of Present Value of One to Present Value of Annuity (Rate = 10%)

Year	Present Value of One	Present Value of Annuity
1	.9091	.9091
2	.8264	1.7355
3	.7513	2.4868
4	.6830	3.1698

"Bankbook" Proof Method

As a method to check or prove that the present value of an annuity is correct, consider the "bankbook" method. In this approach, whatever amounts are on deposit should earn interest. Amounts withdrawn stop earning interest. The present value of an annuity shows the amount of deposit today that, with interest on the remaining balance, will allow the withdrawal of a certain amount per year for the term of the annuity.

For example, consider a deposit of $316.98 today. If it were deposited in a noninterest-bearing checking account, and equal amounts withdrawn each year for four years, then only $79.24 could be withdrawn each year without causing an overdraft. But, if interest were paid on the remaining balance each year, annual withdrawals could be greater than $79.24. The higher the interest rate, the greater the possible annual withdrawal. At a 10% interest rate, the withdrawal could be $100.00 each year. As a check, see Table 3–8. Notice that interest is added at the end of each year based on the amount on balance throughout the year. Simultaneously with crediting interest, $100 is withdrawn at the end of each year.

TABLE 3–8
Bankbook Method ($316.98 Deposit at 10% Interest with $100 Annual Withdrawal)

Year	Balance at Beginning of Year	Add Interest at 10% of Balance	Subtract End of Year Withdrawal	Balance at End of Year
1	$316.98	+$31.70	−$100.00	=$248.68
2	248.68	+ 24.87	− 100.00	= 173.55
3	173.55	+ 17.36	− 100.00	= 90.91
4	90.91	+ 9.09	− 100.00	= -0-

Calculator Applications

To use a financial calculator when valuing an annuity, input the number of periods [n], interest rate [%i], and known periodic payment [PMT]. Then press [COMPUTE] [PV]. The present value of an annuity is displayed. An example is shown in Figure 3–10.

Shorter Intervals

Receipts from an ordinary annuity frequently occur monthly, quarterly, and semiannually, as well as annually. To accommodate them, the nominal interest rate is divided by the number of periods per year. The total number of periods is the number of years multiplied by the number of periods per year.

4 [N]

10 [%i]

100 [PMT]

[CPT] [PV] Result: $316.98 is displayed

FIGURE 3–10. Calculator Keystrokes for Present Value of Annuity at 10% Discount Rate, Annual Discounting for 4 years, with Payment of $100.00 per Year.

Annuity in Advance (Annuity Due)

Some annuities are structured so that the first receipt (or payment) of the income stream occurs immediately. Subsequent payments occur at the regular interval. These are called *annuities in advance* or *annuities due.*

To value such annuities, consider the first payment at its full amount. It occurs immediately, so there is no need to discount that first receipt. Other receipts are discounted. Since the second receipt is one time interval from the present, it can be treated using the present value of a reversion factor for the first interval (from standard tables). To modify an ordinary annuity factor into an annuity due factor, find the ordinary annuity factor for an income stream that is one period shorter than the income stream considered, and add one to the factor. Adding one reflects the first receipt. One period shorter takes into account the present value of the remaining payments.

For example, net rental income is $100 per year, payable at the beginning of each year for four years. The present value of the income stream, discounted at a 10% rate, is $348.68. The first payment has a present value of $100.00; the second, $90.91; the third, $82.64; the fourth, $75.13 ($100.00 + $90.91 + $82.64 + $75.13 = $348.68).

Some calculators have a [DUE] key to accommodate an annuity due. Keystrokes are shown on the next page.

4 [N]

10 [%i]

100 [PMT]

[2nd] [DUE] [PV] Result: $348.68 is displayed

Use of Two Factors

Income that is expected to be generated from real estate is often composed of two distinct forms: (a) a stream of income and (b) a lump sum amount from the resale of the asset. It is convenient to value such income using two compound interest factors.

For example, suppose that income-producing real estate is expected to generate $65,000 of annual income at the end of each year for 25 years, after which it is expected to be resold for $500,000. The appropriate discount rate is 12%. The present worth of an annuity (column 5) can be used to value the anticipated $65,000 of annual income ($65,000 × 7.8431 = $509,804) and the present worth of one factor (column 4) to value the lump sum resale amount ($500,000 × .05882 = $29,411). The total value of the property is an estimated $539,000 ($509,804 + $29,411 = $539,215, which rounds to $539,000). Here, two compound interest factors have been used to analyze the two different income configurations that are expected.

Use of Split Rates

Investment offerings may be forecast to produce income configurations with a difference in the degree of risk that is perceived for some of the forecast income. Different discount rates can be applied to some of the forecast income in order to adjust for risk.

As an example, suppose that a building is leased to the U.S. government for 25 years at a net rental of $65,000 per year, at the end of which term the building is expected to be resold for $500,000. The income stream is absolutely certain. But the resale price is not at all certain; the building may resell for a much greater (or smaller) amount than $500,000. To adjust for the uncertainty of the resale price, a higher discount rate may be applied to the forecast resale price. Selection of the rates is a matter for one's judgment, considering current market rates.

As an application, the $65,000 annual income stream that is certain may be discounted using a 12% rate, and the $500,000 forecast resale proceeds may be discounted at a 15% rate. The estimated property value is $524,000 as follows:

$ 65,000 × 7.8431	=	$509,802
$500,000 × .0304	=	15,200
Total		525,002
Rounded to		$525,000

Step-Up or Step-Down Income Streams

Leases or mortgages may require the payments to increase or decrease periodically. When an increase is required, it is a "step-up" lease, frequently used by lessors as a hedge against inflation. Step-down leases are sometimes used to acknowledge the depreciation of property as it ages. The mechanics of compound interest for step-up or step-down income streams can be handled in several ways.

For example, suppose that the net rental income will be payable at the end of each year as shown below:

Years	*Net Rent Payable*
1–5	$60,000
6–25	70,000

A 12% discount rate is appropriate. The reversion (resale) is to be considered separately. Three mechanical methods are:

1. Value an income stream of $70,000 per year for 25 years; then subtract the present value of $10,000 per year for the first 5 years as follows:

$70,000 × 7.843	=	$549,020
Less $10,000 × 3.605	=	−36,050
Present value of income		$512,970

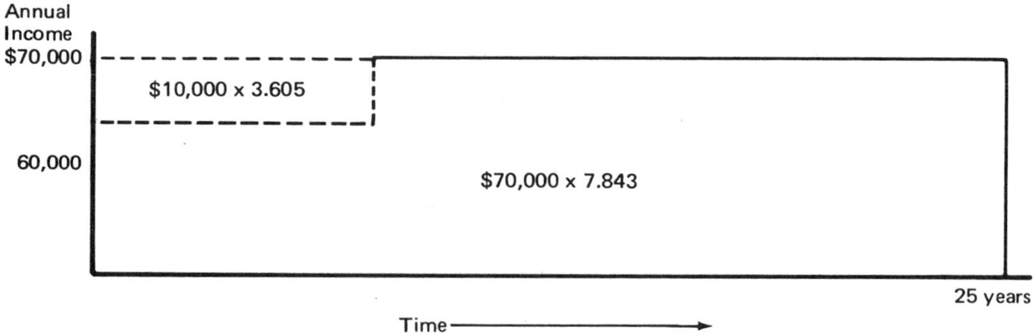

2. Value an income stream of \$60,000 per year for 25 years; then add the present value of \$10,000 per year for 20 years, deferred by 5 years as follows:

\$60,000 × 7.843	=	\$470,580
Add \$10,000 × 7.469 × .5674	=	42,381
Present value of income		\$512,961

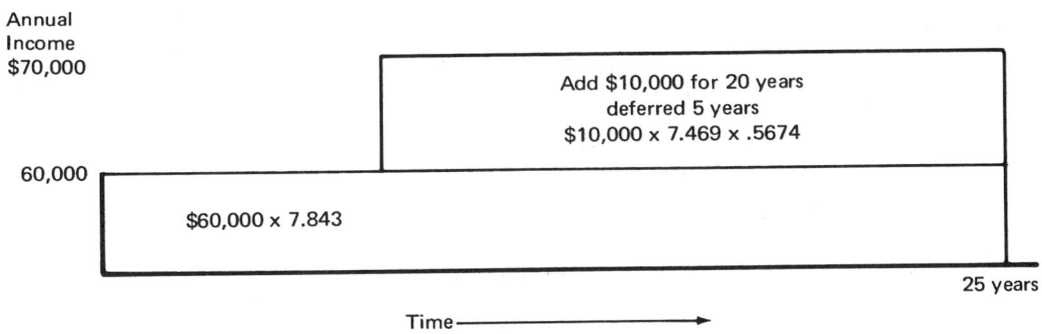

3. Value an income stream of \$60,000 per year for 25 years, and add the present value of \$10,000 per year to be received between the fifth and twenty-fifth years as follows:

\$60,000 × 7.843	=	\$470,580
Add 10,000 × (7.843 − 3.605)	=	42,380
Present value of income		\$512,960

(Differences between the three results are caused by rounding.)

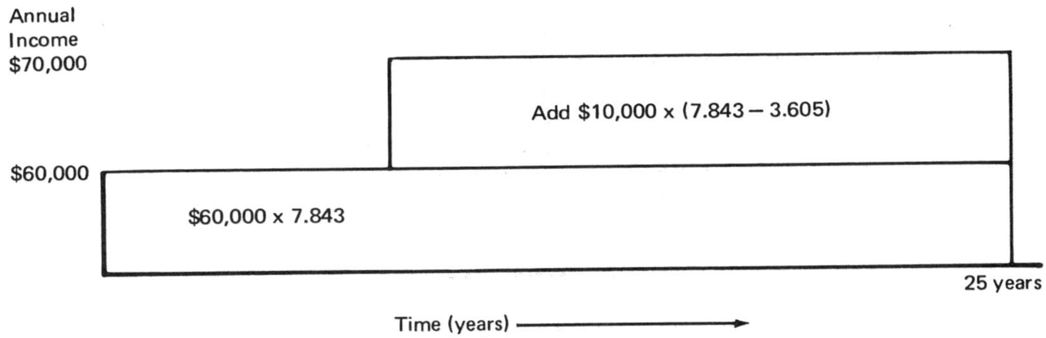

SUMMARY

Compound interest serves as the cornerstone of sophisticated investment analysis. It considers that all money on deposit will earn interest, both beginning principal and accrued but unpaid interest. The present value of a reversion is the reciprocal of compound interest. It offers the current value of an amount that is expected to be received in the future. The present value of an annuity is the value of a series of payments or receipts that is due in the future.

After the amounts and timing of cash inflows of an investment are estimated, their present value can be estimated, based on an appropriate discount rate. The risk or uncertainty associated with various investments and the rate of return offered can be compared, to estimate whether forecast returns adequately justify the expenditure required for the investment.

Questions

1. Land, purchased for $20,000 cash, appreciates at the rate of 15%, compounded annually. How much is it worth after five years? Disregard taxes, insurance, and selling expenses.
2. A land speculator expects that a certain 100-acre tract can be sold to a subdivider four years from now, for $10,000 per acre. Disregarding holding and selling costs, what cash price today would allow the speculator to realize a 15% compounded annual rate of return?
3. What is the present value of a mortgage loan that calls for a $1,000 annual payment, payable at the end of each year for 25 years, discounted at a 10% annual rate?
4. How much must be deposited today, in a bank that pays a 10% annual rate with annual compounding, in order to realize $10,000 in four years?
5. Ms. Brown has just paid $100 for a purchase option on some land. The option gives her the right to buy the property for $10,000 at the end of two years. The $100 paid for the option will not be applied toward the purchase price. How much must Ms. Brown put aside today, in a bank that pays a 10% rate of interest with monthly compounding, so that the balance will be $10,000 in two years?
6. Mr. Green just bought a parking lot for $18,000 cash. He assumes that he can rent it to an operator for $2,000 net annual rent, payable at the end of each year for ten years. He assumes that he can resell the property at the end of the tenth year for $40,000. At a 15% discount rate:

a. How much is the value of the annual rent?

b. How much is the value of the resale proceeds?

c. What price for the property would generate a 15% yield?

d. Will Mr. Green receive a 15% yield rate, based on his assumptions? Explain.

7. A lease calls for $10,000 annual rent for the first five years, and $20,000 per year for the next ten years. Rent is payable at the end of each year. At a 10% nominal annual rate, how much is the value of the lease payments?

8. At a 13% annual interest rate, construct a table of compound interest, present worth of one, and ordinary annuity factors, for three years.

9. Mary owns a lease entitling her to receive payments of $10,000 at the end of each year for five years; at the end of that time, the lease payments will step up to $12,500, payable at the end of each year for another ten years. At the end of the fifteenth year the property is expected to be resold at a price of $100,000. How much would Mary sell these property rights for today if she expected 10% interest compounded annually?

Essay Questions

1. Distinguish between *compound interest* and *simple interest.*
2. Explain the concept of the time value of money.
3. What major factors determine the value of expected future income?
4. How is the compound amount of one related to the present worth of one?
5. How is the present worth of an annuity factor related to the present worth of one factor?
6. Define:

   a. Ordinary annuity.

   b. Annuity due (in advance).

   c. Rule of 72's.

   d. Compound interest.

Chapter 4

Installment to Amortize One, Accumulations, Sinking Funds, and Important Relationships of Functions

Three functions of compound interest discussed in this chapter are: (1) installment to amortize one, (2) the accumulation of one per period, and (3) the sinking fund factor. The installment to amortize one is the regular periodic payment necessary to retire an interest-bearing loan. It is the reciprocal of the present worth of an annuity. The accumulation of one per period shows the balance of a savings account in which one dollar is deposited at the end of each period. The sinking fund factor is the periodic deposit necessary to reach one dollar at the end of a specified period, with compound interest. The sinking fund factor is the reciprocal of the accumulation of one per period.

INSTALLMENT TO AMORTIZE ONE

Loans are frequently structured to require equal payments large enough to exceed interest and fully amortize the loan over a set period of time. *Amortization* is defined as the process of liquidating a debt over time. The mathematical relationship of one payment divided by the original principal is the installment to amortize a loan. The installment to amortize one indicates the required periodic payment on a loan, including interest and principal repayment, that will retire the loan over a specified period.

In the previous chapter, it was shown that $1.00 to be received at the end of each year for four years has a present value of $3.1698 at a 10% annual rate of interest. The first $1.00 is worth $.90909 today; the second $1.00 is worth $.8264; the third $.7513; the fourth $.6830. The sum of the four present value amounts is $3.1698 ($.90909 + $.8264 + $.7513 + $.6830 = $3.1698).

The installment to amortize $1.00 seeks the reciprocal of that result. For example, given a loan of $3.1698 at 10% interest, it answers the question, "What annual payment is required to amortize (retire) that loan in four years?" The answer is $1.00.

The mathematical relationship of one payment to the original principal is $1.00/$3.1698 = .315477. That factor, .315477, shows the periodic payment necessary to retire a loan. For each dollar that is borrowed, $.315477 must be repaid at the end of each year for four years to fully retire the debt with interest applied to the outstanding balance at a 10% rate. A loan that is 100 times larger will require payments 100 times the $1.00 amount. So, if the loan were $316.98, the required payment would be $100.00 per year for four years. As a check, use the bankbook method as shown in Table 4-1.

TABLE 4-1.
Bankbook Method (Amount Borrowed = $316.98; Interest Rate = 10%; Annual Payment = $100)

Year	*Loan Balance at Beginning of Year*	*Add Interest at 10%*	*Less Interest and Principal Payment*	*Balance, End of Year*
1	$316.98	+$31.70	−$100.00	= $248.68
2	248.68	+ 24.87	− 100.00	= 173.55
3	173.55	+ 17.36	− 100.00	= 90.91
4	90.91	+ 9.09	− 100.00	= 0

Effect of Term and Rate on Payment

As interest rates increase and/or as the amortization term shortens, the required periodic payment is increased. Conversely, lower interest rates and longer repayment periods reduce the required periodic payment. Each level payment in the installment to amortize one factor is a blend of interest (return on investment) and a reduction of the original principal amount (return of investment). This blend changes with each payment as is illustrated in Figure 4-1.

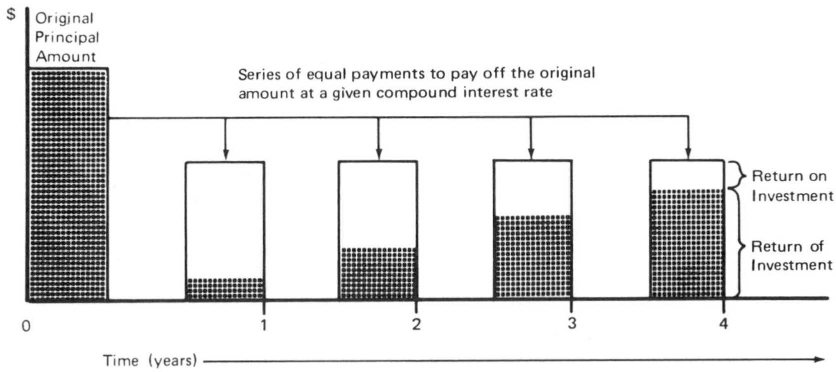

FIGURE 4-1. Installment to Amortize One.

Precomputed Tables

Extensive and widespread use of the installment to amortize one dollar led to the compilation of precomputed tables. Some tables show the factor per $1.00 borrowed, generally in column 6 of compound interest tables. Other tables have been prepared at selected loan principal amounts, generally in $100 or $1,000 increments.

Tables use a formula that is the reciprocal of the present worth of an annuity. It is:

$$\frac{1}{a_n} = \frac{i}{1 - V^n} \qquad \text{or} \qquad \frac{i}{1 - \dfrac{1}{(1 + i)^n}}$$

where i = interest rate
n = number of periods
V^n = present value of one
a_n = present value of annuity

To compile a set of tables, divide the present worth of an annuity into the number one. Derivation of the present worth of an annuity was described in the previous chapter.

Calculator Applications

To use a financial calculator to find the required periodic payment for a loan, input the number of periods [N], interest rate [%i], and original principal [PV]. Then, press [COMPUTE] [PMT]. The periodic payment that is required to amortize the loan will appear in the display. An example is shown in Figure 4–2.

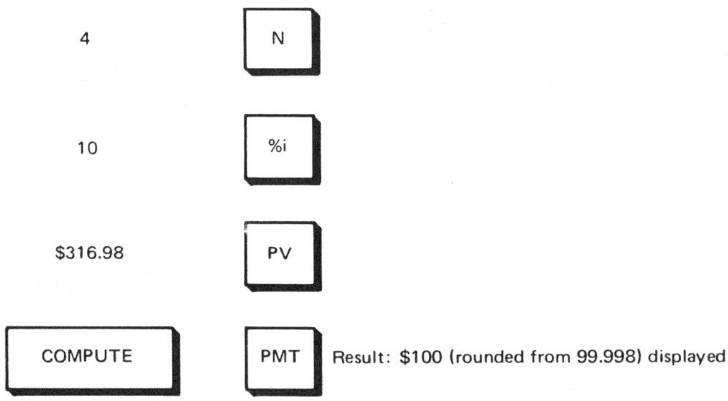

FIGURE 4–2. Calculator Keystrokes for Payment to Amortize a Loan, at a 10% Interest Rate, $316.98 Principal, with 4 Years of Equal Payments.

Shorter Intervals

Many loans are structured to require monthly, quarterly, or semiannual payments. To accommodate them, divide the nominal annual interest rate by the compounding frequency (i.e., if monthly, divide the rate by 12), and multiply the number of periods per year by the number of years (i.e., if monthly, multiply the number of years by 12 to derive the number of periods for the loan).

ACCUMULATION (GROWTH) OF ONE PER PERIOD

The factor of accumulation of one per period helps answer the question of how much a series of equal amounts deposited at the end of periodic intervals will be worth at the *end* of the total term. The reader may be able to conceptualize what this factor does by considering what happens when an individual deposits one dollar at the end of each of four years at a 10% rate of interest compounded annually. The dollar deposited at the end of the first year will draw interest for three years; the dollar deposited at the end of the second year will draw interest for two years; the dollar deposited at the end of the third year will draw interest for one year; and finally the dollar deposited at the end of the fourth year will draw no interest.

As an example, a college student is able to save $1,000 at the end of each summer, which he deposits in an account that bears a 10% rate of interest. At the end of the fourth summer, he will have $4,641 to apply as a down payment on a condominium unit. A graphic presentation is shown in Figure 4–3. Table 4–2 presents the composition of an accumulation.

TABLE 4–2
Accumulation of One Per Period (Periods = 4; Interest Rate = 10%; Periodic Deposit = $1.00)

End of period 1, initial deposit	$1.00
Interest, period 1	–0–
Balance, end of period 1	1.00
Interest, end of period 2	.10
Deposit, end of period 2	1.00
Balance, end of period 2	2.10
Interest, end of period 3	.21
Deposit, end of period 3	1.00
Balance, end of period 3	3.31
Interest, end of period 4	.331
Deposit, end of period 4	1.00
Balance, end of period 4	4.641

Precomputed Tables

Widespread use of the accumulation of one per period has led to the compilation of precomputed tables showing factors per dollar of periodic deposit. In most six-function tables, this factor is shown in column 2. Factors are based on amounts contributed at the end of each period.

The formula for the accumulation of one per period is:

$$S_n = \frac{S^n - 1}{i} \quad \text{or} \quad \frac{(1 + i)^n - 1}{i}$$

where

i = periodic interest rate
n = number of periods considered
S_n = accumulation of one per period

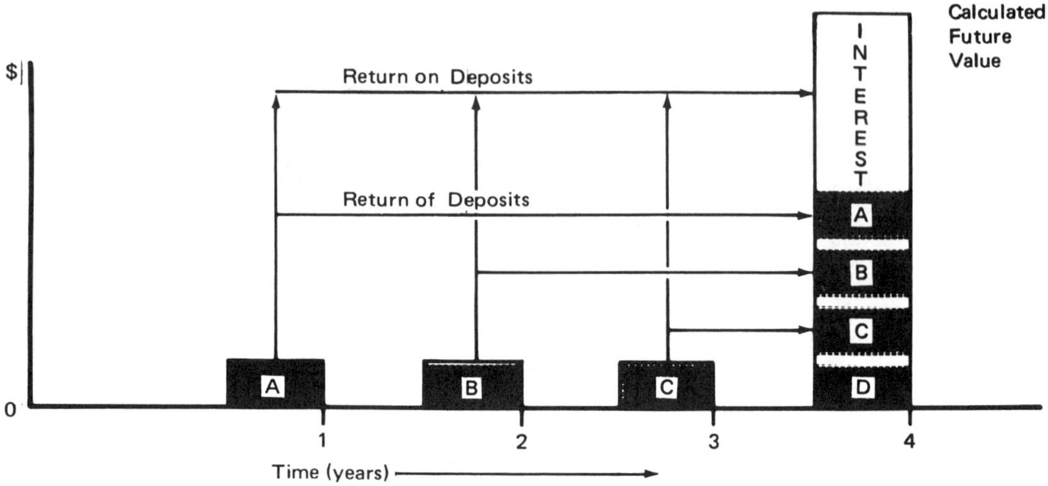

FIGURE 4-3. Accumulation of One Per Period. A, B, C, and D each represent one dollar deposited at the end of a year. Each deposit earns compound interest from the date deposited until the date that a terminal amount is sought. Thus, all deposits and interest are allowed to accumulate. The terminal value is the sum of all deposits plus compound interest.

To compile a set of tables, one can use the formula set forth on page 65 or modify and sum column 1 (compound interest factor) for the periods considered. The modification can be effected by totaling column 1 for one period shorter (i.e., sum three years of column 1 when a four-year accumulation is desired); then add 1.

Accumulations that are based on deposits at the *beginning* of each year may be derived by adding the column 1 amounts for the length of the time span considered.

Calculator Applications

To find the future value of an accumulation of one per period using a financial calculator, input the term for the accumulation [N], the interest rate that deposits will earn [%i], and the amount of one deposit [PMT]. Then, press [COMPUTE] [FV]. The result will be displayed. A sample is shown in Figure 4-4. (The [DUE] button of a calculator should be used when amounts are deposited at the beginning of each period.)

Shorter Intervals

Periodic deposits that accumulate interest may be more frequent than one a year, and the interest rate paid may be compounded more frequently than once a year. To find the accumulation factor

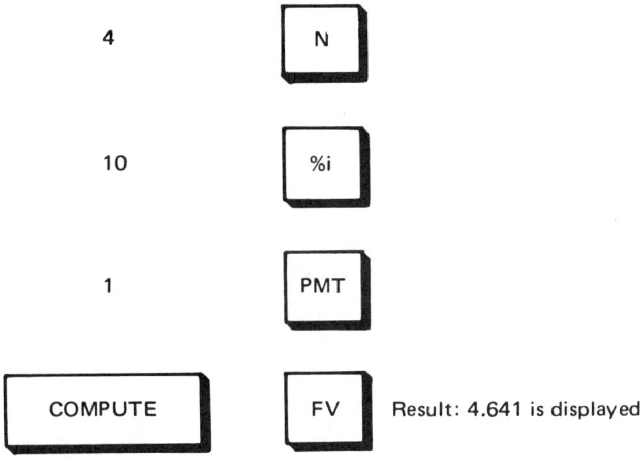

FIGURE 4-4. Calculator Solution for Accumulation of One Period for 4 Periods at a Rate of 10% with each Deposit=$1.00.

per dollar contributed for each period, divide the interest rate by the number of periods per year, and multiply the number of years by the frequency. For example, if one dollar is to be deposited at the end of each quarter for four years, and it will earn interest at 10% compounded quarterly, the periodic interest rate is $2^1/_2$% (10 ÷ 4) and the number of periods is 16 (4 × 4 = 16).

SINKING FUND FACTOR

The sinking fund factor shows the deposit that is required at the end of each period (periodic deposit) to reach $1.00 after a certain number of periods. The factor considers interest that will be earned on the deposits.

For example, at a 0 rate of interest, 25¢ must be deposited at the end of each year for four years in order for it to accumulate to $1.00 at the end of four years. If, instead, the deposits earn compound interest at 10%, only $.215471 need be deposited at the end of each of the four years. The difference between $1.00 and the four deposits (4 × .215471 = $.861884) is interest that will be earned on the fund.

As an example, a coed wishes to accumulate $4,641 at the end of four years by depositing an equal amount at the end of each year. Amounts on deposit earn a 10% annual rate of interest. The required annual deposit is $1,000 (.215471 × $4,641 = $1,000).

Sinking funds are frequently established to retire the principal balance of loans, when interest-only is paid to the creditor until maturity. Each period the debtor places into a separate interest-earning fund an amount that, with interest, is calculated to retire the principal when the loan matures. At maturity, the fund is withdrawn and its balance applied against the loan.

Relationship to Other Factors

The sinking fund factor (column 3 in Appendix B) indicates the payment that must be deposited each period in order to reach $1.00 at the end of the specified number of periods. It is the reciprocal of the accumulation of one per period (column 2).

The sinking fund factor is a component of the installment to amortize $1.00. That function consists of two rates. One rate is interest, or a return *on* investment. The other is the sinking fund factor, a recovery or return *of* investment. The sinking fund factor, selected at the same rate of interest as the loan bears, is the rate of principal retirement for the loan. For example, the factor for the installment to amortize a $1.00 loan at 10% interest over four years is .315471. Of that factor, .10 represents interest at 10% (.10), and .215471 is the sinking fund factor at 10% interest.

If interest on the loan is to be paid annually, and the .215471 per period sinking fund factor is set aside in a separate fund earning a 10% interest rate, the fund would become exactly enough to pay off the $1.00 loan at its maturity in four years. Computations are shown in Table 4–3. A graph of the sinking fund factor is shown in Figure 4–5.

TABLE 4–3
Sinking Fund Factor (Interest Rate = 10%; Number of Periods = 4; Periodic Deposit = .215471)

Deposit, end of period 1	.215471
Interest, for period 1	–0–
Balance, end of period 1	.215471
Interest, for period 2	.021547
Deposit, end of period 2	.215471
Balance, end of period 2	.452489
Interest, for period 3	.045249
Deposit, end of period 3	.215471
Balance, end of period 3	.713209
Interest, for period 4	.071321
Deposit, end of period 4	.215471
Balance, end of period 4	1.000000

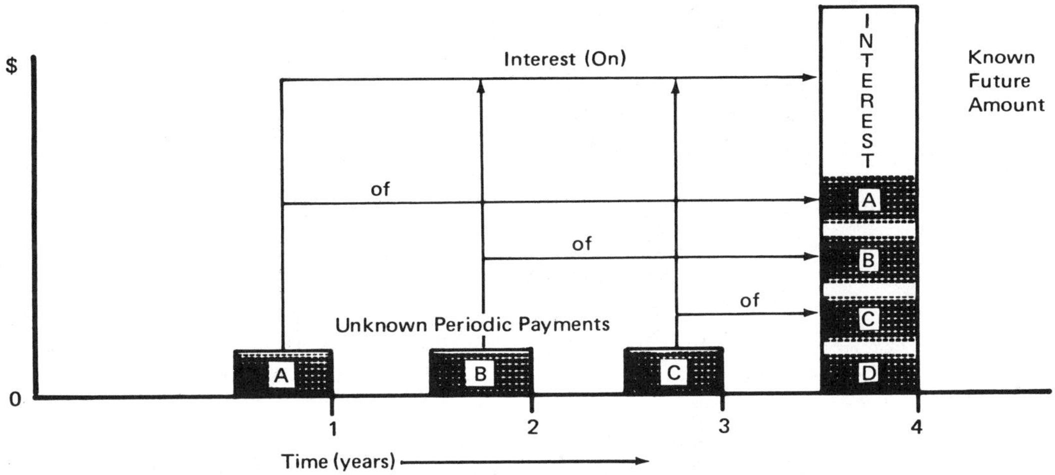

FIGURE 4-5. Sinking Fund Factor—Graphic Presentation. A, B, C, and D are equal amounts deposited at the end of each year. Each deposit earns compound interest for the period of time it remains on deposit. At the end of the time period considered, the depositor can withdraw the terminal value. The sinking fund factor is computed such that the terminal value will always equal one (dollar).

Precomputed Tables

Precomputed tables have been prepared for sinking fund factors. The figure that is at the intersection of the number of periods and the appropriate column (column 3 of tables in Appendix B) indicates the level periodic payment necessary to amass \$1.00 after that number of periods, at the rate of interest selected.

Tables use the formula:

$$\frac{1}{S_n} = \frac{i}{S^n - 1} \quad \text{or} \quad \frac{i}{(1 + i)^n - 1}$$

where n = number of periods

i = periodic interest rate

$\frac{1}{S_n}$ = sinking fund factor

Shorter Intervals

Contributions to a sinking fund may be deposited more frequently than once each year, and interest can be compounded more frequently, such as monthly, quarterly, or semi-annually. Tables have been prepared that presume more frequent contributions in conjunction with more frequent compounding. They indicate the periodic payment needed to amass \$1.00 at the periodic interest rate.

RELATIONSHIPS OF FUNCTIONS

The six functions of compound interest represent manipulations of the basic formula $(1 + i)^n$ for the compound amount of one. All factors are derived from that basic expression. All consider that interest is earned on funds that are on deposit, while they are on deposit. All consider the effect of compound interest, which is that interest, once earned, is converted to principal.

Although standard tables offer six functions for convenience, only three are needed because the other three are reciprocals. Manipulations that require multiplication can be effected by division using a reciprocal, and vice versa (see Table 4–4).

TABLE 4–4
Basic Functions of Compound Interest and Their Reciprocals

Function	*Reciprocal*
Compound amount of one (column 1)	Present value of one (column 4)
Accumulation of one per period (column 2)	Sinking fund factor (column 3)
Present value of an annuity (column 5)	Installment to amortize $1 (column 6)

Other Relationships

The sinking factor (column 3), when added to the periodic interest rate, will equal the installment to amortize one dollar (column 6). This relationship points out that the installment to amortize one dollar is the sum of two elements. One element is interest, a return *on* investment; the other is capital recovery, a recovery *of* investment. By calculating loan payments based on the installment to amortize one dollar, borrowers repay the principal over the term of the loan, with interest. Had loan payments been nonamortizing, with interest-only required, the borrower could put aside each period, in a separate account, the amount indicated by the sinking fund factor. Provided that the sinking fund earns interest at the same rate as the loan bears, the sinking fund balance could be applied to exactly offset the loan balance at its maturity.

The installment to amortize one dollar (column 6) is related to the interest rate in that the installment must always exceed the periodic interest rate, no matter how long the term of the loan. Unless each loan payment exceeds the periodic interest requirement, the loan will not be retired through periodic payments.

TABLE 4-5

A Six-Function Compound Interest Table

10 % = ANNUAL RATE   COMPOUND INTEREST TABLES   ANNUAL RATE = 10 %

NOMINAL ANNUAL INTEREST RATE = 10 %   COMPOUNDING FREQUENCY (PER YEAR) = 1

YEAR	AMOUNT OF 1 AT COMPOUND INTEREST (COL 1)	ACCUM OF 1 PER PERIOD (COL 2)	SINKING FUND FACTOR (COL 3)	PRESENT VALUE REVERSN OF 1 (COL 4)	PRESENT VALUE ORD ANN 1 PER PERIOD (COL 5)	INSTALL TO AMORT 1 (COL 6)	PERIOD
1	1.1000	1.0000	1.000000	0.9091	0.9091	1.1000000	1
2	1.2100	2.1000	0.476190	0.8264	1.7355	0.5761905	2
3	1.3310	3.3100	0.302115	0.7513	2.4869	0.4021148	3
4	1.4641	4.6410	0.215471	0.6830	3.1699	0.3154708	4
5	1.6105	6.1051	0.163797	0.6209	3.7908	0.2637975	5
6	1.7716	7.7156	0.129607	0.5645	4.3553	0.2296074	6
7	1.9487	9.4872	0.105405	0.5132	4.8684	0.2054055	7
8	2.1436	11.4359	0.087444	0.4665	5.3349	0.1874440	8
9	2.3579	13.5795	0.073641	0.4241	5.7590	0.1736405	9
10	2.5937	15.9374	0.062745	0.3855	6.1446	0.1627454	10
11	2.8531	18.5312	0.053963	0.3505	6.4951	0.1539631	11
12	3.1384	21.3843	0.046763	0.3186	6.8137	0.1467633	12
13	3.4523	24.5227	0.040779	0.2897	7.1034	0.1407785	13
14	3.7975	27.9750	0.035746	0.2633	7.3667	0.1357462	14
15	4.1772	31.7725	0.031474	0.2394	7.6061	0.1314738	15
16	4.5950	35.9497	0.027817	0.2176	7.8237	0.1278166	16
17	5.0545	40.5447	0.024664	0.1978	8.0216	0.1246641	17
18	5.5599	45.5992	0.021930	0.1799	8.2014	0.1219302	18
19	6.1159	51.1591	0.019547	0.1635	8.3649	0.1195469	19
20	6.7275	57.2750	0.017460	0.1486	8.5136	0.1174596	20
21	7.4003	64.0025	0.015624	0.1351	8.6487	0.1156244	21
22	8.1403	71.4028	0.014005	0.1228	8.7715	0.1140051	22
23	8.9543	79.5430	0.012572	0.1117	8.8832	0.1125718	23
24	9.8497	88.4973	0.011300	0.1015	8.9847	0.1112998	24
25	10.8347	98.3471	0.010168	0.0923	9.0770	0.1101681	25
26	11.9182	109.1818	0.009159	0.0839	9.1609	0.1091590	26
27	13.1100	121.0999	0.008258	0.0763	9.2372	0.1082576	27
28	14.4210	134.2099	0.007451	0.0693	9.3066	0.1074510	28
29	15.8631	148.6309	0.006728	0.0630	9.3696	0.1067281	29
30	17.4494	164.4940	0.006079	0.0573	9.4269	0.1060792	30
31	19.1943	181.9434	0.005496	0.0521	9.4790	0.1054962	31
32	21.1138	201.1378	0.004972	0.0474	9.5264	0.1049717	32
33	23.2252	222.2516	0.004499	0.0431	9.5694	0.1044994	33
34	25.5477	245.4767	0.004074	0.0391	9.6086	0.1040737	34
35	28.1024	271.0244	0.003690	0.0356	9.6442	0.1036897	35
36	30.9127	299.1268	0.003343	0.0323	9.6765	0.1033431	36
37	34.0040	330.0395	0.003030	0.0294	9.7059	0.1030299	37
38	37.4043	364.0434	0.002747	0.0267	9.7327	0.1027469	38
39	41.1448	401.4478	0.002491	0.0243	9.7570	0.1024910	39
40	45.2593	442.5926	0.002259	0.0221	9.7791	0.1022594	40
41	49.7852	487.8518	0.002050	0.0201	9.7991	0.1020498	41
42	54.7637	537.6370	0.001860	0.0183	9.8174	0.1018600	42
43	60.2401	592.4007	0.001688	0.0166	9.8340	0.1016880	43
44	66.2641	652.6408	0.001532	0.0151	9.8491	0.1015322	44
45	72.8905	718.9049	0.001391	0.0137	9.8628	0.1013910	45
46	80.1795	791.7954	0.001263	0.0125	9.8753	0.1012630	46
47	88.1975	871.9749	0.001147	0.0113	9.8866	0.1011468	47
48	97.0172	960.1724	0.001041	0.0103	9.8969	0.1010415	48
49	106.7190	1057.1896	0.000946	0.0094	9.9063	0.1009459	49
50	117.3909	1163.9086	0.000859	0.0085	9.9148	0.1008592	50

Similarly, the present worth of an ordinary annuity (column 5) can never increase beyond the factor that results from the operation of dividing $1.00 by the periodic interest rate. For example, if the annual interest rate is 10% (.10), the maximum column 5 factor is 10 ($1 ÷ .10 = 10). The maximum column 5 figure at any interest rate indicates an amount sufficient to generate $1.00 per period in perpetuity. A $10 balance at 10% interest will generate $1.00 per year of interest. The interest can be disposed at one's discretion without affecting the principal, thereby generating a perpetual income stream. Table factors for the present value of an annuity, since they are shown for a finite period of time, will approach but not exceed $1.00 divided by the periodic rate of interest. A sample six-function compound interest table is shown in Table 4–5.

Using the Tables. In using the tables, the analyst should consider the following:

1. Are you certain that you understand the problem? Is it a problem that involves compounding or discounting? Is it a composite problem that requires more than one function?

2. If the compounding frequency is more than annual, are you using the correct effective rate of interest?

3. Are the inflows or outflows of cash at the beginning or end of each compounding period? Is this consistent with the way the appropriate factor is calculated in the table? It may be necessary to make an adjustment.

4. Have you checked the accuracy of the arithmetic? Does the solution make sense?

Expansion of Tables

Column 1 of the tables can be expanded to any number of years or periods by multiplying factors to derive the factor for the period desired. This is effected by adding the periods to the one desired, then multiplying factors for those periods. For example, the factor for 80 years at 10% interest can be found by adding the periods and then multiplying the 40-year factor by itself (40 years + 40 years = 80 years, and 45.2593 × 45.2593 = 2048.4); or by adding the periods and multiplying the 50-year factor by the 30-year factor (50 years + 30 years = 80 years and 117.3909 × 17.4494 = 2048.4); or by adding the periods and multiplying the 30-year factor by the 22-year factor and the result by the 28-year factor (30 + 22 + 28 = 80 years and 17.4494 × 8.1403 × 14.42104 = 2048.4).

Column 4 of the tables can be expanded in a similar manner. The factor for 80 years at 10% interest can be derived by adding the periods and multiplying the factor for 40 years by itself ($40 + 40 = 80$ and $.0221 \times .0221 = .0004884$); or by adding the periods and multiplying the 50-year factor by the 30-year factor (50 years + 30 years = 80 years and $.0573 \times .0085 = .000487$). Differences are caused by rounding.

The accumulation of one period can be expanded by adding factors for compound amounts of one dollar, lagged by one year. For example, to find the accumulation of one for eleven years, add the ten-year compound amount of the one to the tenth-year accumulation of one per period. The sinking fund factor can be expanded by using the reciprocal of the accumulation of one per period.

Expansion of the present value of an annuity (column 5) can be effected by adding the column 4 amount for the future years. For example, the present value of an annuity for eleven years is the sum of the tenth-year present value of annuity and the eleventh-year present value of a reversion.

Since the installment to amortize one dollar (column 6) is the reciprocal of the present value of an annuity, expansion can be effected by the use of a reciprocal.

CAPITALIZATION RATE

A capitalization rate is a rate that is used to convert an income stream into one lump sum value. The formula used is:

$$V = \frac{I}{R}$$

where V = present value
I = periodic income
R = capitalization rate

In real estate appraisal and investment terminology, a capitalization rate is defined as being composed of a return on and a recovery of investment; whereas in finance and economic terminology, a capitalization rate is defined as simply a rate of return on investment.

When income from a real estate investment is forecast to be level in perpetuity, or when level income is forecast and no change is expected in the capital value of the income-producing asset, capital recovery is not necessary. Then, the capitalization rate is the same as the interest or discount rate.

When the forecast income is level, but the capital of an investment declines over time, as for self-amortizing mortgages, then the capitalization rate in real estate terminology is the factor for the installment to amortize one dollar. The factor includes interest on the remaining capital and recovery of the capital at the sinking fund rate. Capitalization rates are more fully discussed in the next chapter.

SUMMARY

The six functions of compound interest, explained in Chapters 3 and 4, can be helpful in estimating the value of real estate. The compound amount of one answers the question, "What will my property resell for, based on its current market value and an expected compound growth rate?" The accumulation of one per period shows how regular deposits will grow with compound interest. The sinking fund factor indicates the deposit needed each period to accumulate to one dollar with compound interest after a number of periods. It indicates the necessary annual rate needed to recover the investment in an asset.

The present worth of one indicates the value now of a lump sum to be received in the future, such as land that is expected to be sold. The annuity factor shows the value of a stream of income, such as would be received from rented property or payments on a mortgage loan. The installment to amortize one factor indicates the periodic payment necessary to amortize a loan, including interest and principal repayment.

All of the six functions are based on compound interest, which holds that all principal on deposit should earn interest, including interest that remains on deposit from previous periods. Further, that interest is due only on amounts of principal, not on amounts of withdrawn interest or principal.

The six functions of compound interest can be helpful in solving nearly all arithmetic problems that involve income-producing real estate.

Questions

1. What is the annual payment required on a $100,000 mortgage at 12% interest, with annual payments required and 25 years for amortization?

2. How much is the monthly payment required for a $100,000, 25-year self-amortizing loan at a nominal annual interest rate of 12%?
3. Mr. & Mrs. Young Married are saving for a down payment on a home. If they deposit $100 per month into an account that earns 10%, with monthly compounding, how much will they have after five years?
4. Mr. & Mrs. Young Married want to accumulate $10,000 in five years by depositing an equal amount each month. Amounts on deposit will earn at a 10% rate compounded monthly. What is their required monthly deposit?
5. A $100,000 mortgage loan requires that only interest be paid. However, the full principal balloons (is due) in ten years. Ms. Smith, the borrower, wants to put aside a certain amount each year in an interest-earning fund that in ten years will be adequate to offset the loan. The fund will earn 10% interest compounded annually. How much is Ms. Smith's annual deposit?
6. What annual payment is needed to retire a $1,000 loan at 10% interest over four years? Prepare an amortization schedule.
7. Dick lends $10,000, payable in equal annual installments at the end of each year for 30 years, at a 10% rate of interest. How much is each annual payment?
8. An investment will pay $100,000 at the end of twelve years. A debt of $50,000 must be paid off by the owner of the investment asset at the end of the third year. If an investor expects to make 10% compounded annually on his invested equity, how much should he pay for the offered investment asset?
9. Mildred is saving up to retire 40 years from today. She has just deposited $500 at a compound interest rate of 10% per annum. She intends to deposit the same amount at the beginning of each year until she retires at the end of the fortieth year. How much will she have accumulated at the time of retirement?
10. A condominium is planning to replace the roofing on all their buildings in ten years. They anticipate the cost will be $150,000 at the tenth year. How must should they deposit at the end of each year in an account that compounds at the rate of 10% per annum?

Essay Questions

1. How is the installment to amortize one related to the annuity factor?
2. How is the accumulation of one per period related to the sinking fund factor?

3. Define and explain each:
   a. Capitalization rate.
   b. Return on investment.
   c. Return of investment.
   d. Amortization.
   e. Sinking fund.

Chapter 5

Introduction to Capitalization Rates and Capital Recovery

The mechanics of the income approach to property valuation are based on the principles of compound interest discussed in the previous two chapters. In its purest form, value through the income approach is calculated by the following formula:

$$V = \frac{I}{R}$$

where: V = value
I = net operating income
R = capitalization rate

On this simple skeleton is constructed a very elaborate theory of income property valuation. This chapter and the next explain basic principles used to develop capitalization rates for simple income streams. Once the reader understands how to handle a simple income stream, more complicated income streams will be discussed.

WHAT IS INCOME CAPITALIZATION?

Income capitalization is a process of translating a stream of future income receipts into a single present value sum. It takes into account:

1. Amount of future income.
2. When the income is to be received.
3. Duration of the income.

The term *capitalization rate* as used in real estate terminology must include a return *on* and a return *of* investment. Return *on* investment is the compensation necessary to pay an investor for the time value of money, risk, and other factors associated with a particular investment. In other words, it is the interest paid for the use of money. This is also referred to as *yield.* Return *of* investment deals with repayment of the original principal. This is referred to as *capital recovery.*

A *yield* is a percentage relationship describing how much one earns on an investment. Two general types of yield must be contrasted: (1) current yield and (2) yield to maturity.

Current yield is a measurement of the present productivity of the current cash returns from an investment compared to the investment outlay. This may be calculated by the following formula:

$$\text{Current yield} = \frac{\text{Annual income}}{\text{Investment price}}$$

A more sensitive measurement is *yield to maturity.* This is a measurement of the effective annual earnings as a percentage of the price of an investment, from the present until it is sold or redeemed. It considers the amounts and timing of forecast income. Yield to maturity includes an adjustment from the current yield to reflect anticipated capital gains or losses during the investment holding period. The yield to maturity is an effective rate of return on investment that considers current income and expected capital gain or loss prorated in a manner that reflects the timing of the eventual capital gain or loss realization. The rate itself considers but does not incorporate capital recovery. Because yield to maturity considers anticipated capital gain or loss, it is much more meaningful than current yield. However, determination of the yield to maturity requires a trial-and-error process and is much more difficult to calculate than current yield. There are some general rules for estimating whether the yield to maturity exceeds the current yield. The rules are that the yield to maturity will be:

1. Greater than the current yield when capital appreciation is anticipated.
2. Less than the current yield when a capital loss is anticipated.
3. Exactly equal to the current yield when neither gain nor loss is anticipated.
4. Negative when the total of all current income plus capital resale value is less than the purchase price.

Yield to Maturity Versus Capitalization Rate

A yield-to-maturity rate incorporates only a return *on* investment; whereas a capitalization rate, as used in real estate appraisal terminology, includes a capital recovery provision as well as a rate of return on investment.

In theory, a capitalization rate for current income should either explicitly or implicitly account for the following factors:

1. Compensation for a risk-free, liquid investment.
2. Compensation for risk.
3. Compensation for illiquidity.
4. Compensation for investment management.
5. Provision for forecast appreciation or depreciation of an asset.

To illustrate how some of these factors can be accounted for in a capitalization rate, the build-up method is discussed in the next paragraphs. Provisions for forecast appreciation or depreciation are discussed in this chapter as part of the treatment of capital recovery.

Build-Up Method

The Build-Up Method is a process of constructing an interest rate using a risk-free rate as a foundation and adding to this base the necessary compensations for risk, illiquidity, and burden of investment management. This method permits an analyst to make specific provisions for differences between real estate income streams and other income streams.

The analyst begins with a liquid, risk-free rate. This may be the rate on passbook accounts offered by financial institutions whose depositors' accounts are insured by a U.S. government agency. The rate is the minimum that must be paid as compensation for the time value of money.

Added to this risk-free rate is a provision for risk associated with the specific type of real estate being appraised. For example, risk is low where there is a strong tenant with captive customers such as a U.S. post office; but risk is high for property leased to weak tenants who have fickle customers such as an undercapitalized discotheque.

Provisions must be made for illiquidity. Liquidity is a measurement of how quickly an asset can be converted into cash. Real estate is illiquid compared to stock and bonds. This is particularly true in real estate markets when there is a tight mortgage money situation.

Some investments require very little management, whereas others require a great deal. The investment management burden requires additional compensation. For example, a demand deposit in a savings bank requires very little investment management. Investment management entails filing tax returns, choosing among financing alternatives and decisions of holding or selling assets; it is not to be confused with property management, which requires day-to-day supervision and is a property operating expense.

To illustrate how an interest rate could be developed for different types of investments, see Table 5-1.

TABLE 5-1
Interest Rate Through Build-Up Method

	Blue Chip Stock	*Income from Triple Net Lease to Major Corporate Tenant*	*Income From Small Apartment Project*
Risk-free rate	6.0%	6.0%	6.0%
Allowance for risk	6.0%	4.0%	7.0%
Allowance for illiquidity	0.0%	3.0%	5.0%
Allowance for investment management	0.5%	1.0%	2.0%
Rate derived by build-up	12.5%	14.0%	20.0%

Where does the analyst find the proper adjustments for risk, loss of liquidity, and burden of management? As noted in Table 5-1, these costs are not the same for all investments. Many of these adjustments are subjective characteristics derived from the goals, objectives, and income tax situation of the client-investor. In later chapters we will discuss procedures for deriving an overall capitalization rate from the market, band of investment methods, and mortgage-equity provisions.

CAPITALIZATION RATES ADJUSTED FOR CAPITAL RECOVERY

A capitalization rate is a rate which, when divided into the current income generated by an investment, offers a value estimate for an investment. Income streams that are forecast to be level in perpetuity are appropriately capitalized at the interest (or discount) rate. Capitalization at the interest (or discount) rate is also appropriate when there is no forecast change in the capital value of an investment. In that case, the investment expenditure is recovered upon resale. All of the income stream is yield (return on investment).

However, when the asset is wasting (that is, a capital loss is forecast) a portion of the current income must be considered a recovery of the investment. The balance of current income is a return on investment. In such a situation, the capitalization rate must be increased so that it mathematically computes a lump sum asset value whereby some of the current income is a return on the investment and some is a recovery of the investment. On the other hand, when asset appreciation is forecast, all of the current income and some of the resale proceeds are producing a return on investment. Resale proceeds offer all of the capital recovery. Given forecast appreciation, a capital growth rate can be subtracted from the discount rate to derive a capitalization rate.

To dramatize the need for capital recovery, consider this investment offering:

> Invest $10,000 now, and get $2,500 per year! That's a 25% return! Act now!

The promoter promises to pay $2,500 per year as a return, for each of the next four years. (After that, the investment will be worthless! The promoter was silent on that aspect!) Would the investor get a 25% return? Certainly not. After four years the investor will merely recover his capital of $10,000, without a penny of earnings. Or it can be considered that the investor received a 25% return *on* investment but lost the entire principal! From either approach, it is clear that this investment offering a 25% return is misleading.

INCOME STREAM

Consider an income stream. A *stream* is a series of receipts expected periodically, as contrasted with one lump sum receipt.

Examples of income streams are:

1. Receipt of $60 *semiannually* for interest from a $1,000 face value bond that pays a 12% interest rate and matures at face value in 15 years.
2. Receipt, through a mortgage loan, of $4,212.90 *per month* for the next 25 years.

3. Receipt of $14,445 *per year* for the next 10 years in the form of cash flow from an apartment building equity ownership interest.

Notice that the three income stream examples are for finite periods: none of the income streams lasts forever.

To properly capitalize an income stream, divide one payment of the income stream by a capitalization rate. In real estate finance, a capitalization rate is the sum of two rates: one is a percentage interest rate for the return *on* investment; added to that is a percentage rate for principal recovery (return *of* investment).

Here we will consider capitalizing an income stream under three forecasts of capital (principal) change:

1. No change in capital (principal) value.
2. Forecast depreciation in capital value.
3. Forecast appreciation in capital value.

Partial capital recovery situations and comments on capital recovery are also discussed.

No Change in Capital Value

When there is no forecast change in the principal value of an investment, all of the capital recovery is found in the asset value at resale. The current income is earnings that can be capitalized at the interest rate (rate of return *on* investment). For example, suppose that a corporate bond is issued for $1,000 and matures fifteen years later. It has a 12% coupon rate of interest, so the interest would be $120 per year. (Most bonds pay interest twice a year, so each bond would pay $60 every six months.) Thus the income stream can be capitalized at a 12% rate by dividing the annual income by 12%, or:

$$\frac{\$120}{.12} = \$1{,}000 \text{ (principal value)}$$

There is no need to provide capital recovery because the same amount of purchase capital as invested will be returned upon bond maturity or redemption. This technique holds for all bonds (or other income streams) that are purchased and redeemed at exactly the same price. However, when a bond is bought at face value and is resold at a discount, there is a capital loss. That situation will require considering a capital recovery rate. A bond purchased at a discount and redeemed at face value offers capital gain. Capitalizing current income by division of an interest rate fails to consider forecast changes in capital value. The bond example is used here because of the fixed amounts of income and principal.

In real estate investments, a capitalization rate need not include a capital recovery provision when resale will bring the same amount as was paid for an investment, and level income is forecast. This would be the situation where land, a warehouse, or an industrial plant or some other facility is under a net lease for a specified level annual rent in perpetuity. Or when the proceeds of a resale from the property (perhaps through a purchase option) will bring exactly the same amount as the initial cost of the property.

Inflation expectations often justify the absence of capital recovery. For example, in apartments, increases in rental income are often expected to more than offset increases in operating expenses; and inflation-caused appreciation is often expected to offset the losses caused by physical deterioration and obsolescence.

The example of a corporate bond illustrates a situation without a need for capital recovery. Suppose a bond is issued at par, $1,000, and matures fifteen years later at the same $1,000. There is no capital recovery since the principal remains intact. All of the interest is income and yield; all of the capital is recovered upon redemption. If interest income is $60 every six months, this is a 6% rate semiannually, which is the same as a 12% interest rate with semiannual discounting.

Forecast Depreciation in Capital Value

When the capital (principal) of an investment is expected to decline in value, some or all of the capital recovery is received through current income. Therefore, the capitalization rate for current income must include both a return *on* investment, and a recovery of the expected loss.

For example, consider a self-amortizing mortgage loan that generates $4,212.90 in monthly income. It carries a face interest rate of 12% per year—more precisely, 1% per month. In order to derive the value of that income, we must consider (a) how long the income stream will last and (b) the amount of principal that the investment can command upon a resale. In this case, the monthly income stream will be $4,212.90 for 25 years (300 months), followed by no principal value since the loan will have been fully retired. Capitalization of income at just the interest rate would imply that the principal remains unchanged, and therefore would overstate the value of the mortgage loan. A capital recovery rate provision must be added to the interest rate to derive a proper capitalization rate.

There are three methods of capital recovery to select from:

1. Straight-line capital recovery.
2. Sinking fund capital recovery at investment earnings rate.
3. Sinking fund capital recovery at safe interest rate.

Straight-Line Capital Recovery. The straight-line method, also called the *Ring Method,* assumes that an equal amount of principal is recovered each year. For example, assume a $1,000 loan payable over four years, at a 12% interest rate (see Table 5-2). The straight-line annual capital recovery rate would be 25%, based on a 100% asset write-off over four years (100%/4 years = 25% per year). The capitalization rate then would be 25% + 12% = 37%. Each year, 25% of the $1,000 principal would be recovered, along with 12% interest. The 12% interest rate applied to the $1,000 principal requires a first year interest payment of $120. Payment for the first year would include $250 of principal; so the total payment would be $370 for the first year. This is shown in Figure 5-1 as are years 2-4.

TABLE 5-2
Straight-Line Capital Recovery ($1,000 Loan at 12% for 4 Years)

Year	*Principal Recovery*	*Principal Remaining at End of Year*
1	$250.00	$750.00
2	250.00	500.00
3	250.00	250.00
4	250.00	0

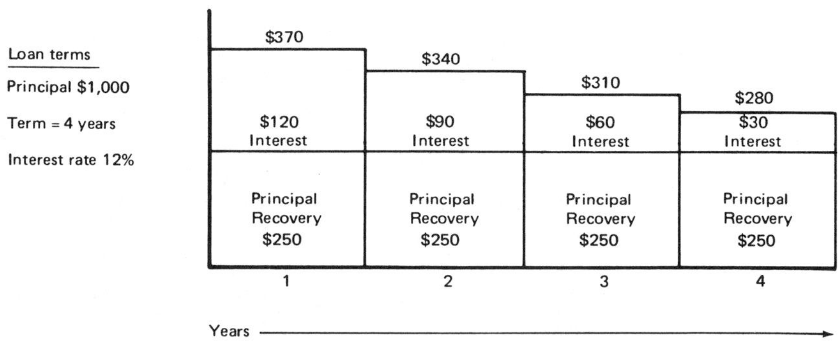

FIGURE 5-1. Level Capital Recovery.

In the second year, interest should be 12% of the remaining principal. Since $250 of the $1,000 initial principal was recovered in the first year's payment, $750 is the remaining principal; and at a 12% interest rate, $90 is the interest payment required for the second year. After two years, only $500 of principal is left; interest for the third year is 12% of $500 or $60; for the fourth year, $250 of principal is left; interest at 12% is $30. Note that Table 5-2 and Figure 5-1 relate to the same income stream.

Notice that the annual loan payment declines under the straight-line capital recovery assumption. This consideration is important: it points out that straight-line capitalization is appropriate for declining income but is *not* to be used for level income streams. Capitalization of level income using straight-line capital recovery underestimates the value of the income stream.

Applying a straight-line capitalization rate to the $1,000 four-year loan at 12% interest, the "cap" rate would be 37% as described earlier. Given the first year's income of $370, a $1,000 capital value can be derived by division: $370 divided by .37 = $1,000 of principal.

Sinking Fund Capital Recovery at Investment Earnings Rate. Capital recovery at the investment earnings (interest or yield) rate is called the *Inwood Method.* It is also called *level annuity capital recovery.*

The capital recovery rate component of the capitalization rate is the sinking fund factor at the same interest rate as the investment offers. A portion of the income stream represents earnings, a return *on* investment. The balance of the income stream represents capital recovery, a return *of* investment. In the case of 100% capital depreciation, the capital recovery portion of income, if it is reinvested at the return on investment (interest) rate, will grow to exactly the same amount as the initial principal, thus recovering the entire original capital.

For example, a four-year loan of $1,000 at 12% interest requires *equal* annual payments of $329.23 for full amortization, based on the installment to amortize one (column 6). Interest for the first year is $120, and principal recovery is $209.23. The annual interest could be spent by the lender, but if the $209.23 principal receipts are retained each year, the annual principal recovery would grow to $836.92 after four years (4 × $209.23 = $836.92) without any interest being paid on reinvested principal receipts. If the $209.23 principal amount received annually is reinvested at a 12% interest rate, it will grow to $1,000, the same amount as the initial loan principal, as follows:

Principal receipt, end of year 1*	$ 209.23
Interest earned, year 2 @ 12%	25.11
Principal receipt, end of year 2	209.23
Balance at end of year 2	443.57
Interest earned, year 3 @ 12%	53.23
Principal receipt, end of year 3	209.23
Balance at end of year 3	706.03
Interest earned, year 4	84.72
Principal receipt, year 4	209.23
Balance at end of year 4	999.98
Rounding error	.02
Total	$1,000.00

*Year 1—No interest was earned during the first year because the payment was received at the end of the year.

When a level income stream is considered, the capitalization rate is normally the sum of the earnings rate (interest or discount) plus the sinking fund factor at the same rate. In the previously mentioned example, the .209234 four-year sinking fund factor at 12% (column 3) is added to the 12% interest rate, the result being a cap rate of .329234.

Thus, if the income is known to be level at $329.23 per year, and the payments are to be received regularly at the end of each year for four years, the capital value is computed as follows: $329.23 divided by .32923 equals $1,000.00. Keep in mind, however, that this type of capital recovery involves two implicit assumptions. They are:

1. The annual interest at a 12% rate may be spent by the owner without affecting the principal.
2. The annual capital recovery must be reinvested at a 12% annual rate for the principal amount to remain intact.

Level annuity capital recovery may be graphed as shown in Figure 5-2.

Note that direct capitalization of the $329.23 annual income at the discount or interest rate of 12% would yield the following erroneous results: $329.23 divided by .12 = $2,743.58, an erroneous value for the loan. The four-year loan described requires total payments, interest, and principal, amounting to 4 × $329.23 = $1,316.92, much less than the $2,743.58 erroneous value. This point emphasizes the need to add a provision for capital recovery to the discount or interest rate. The amount of capital recovery depends on the length (term) of the income stream and the discount or interest rate. The longer the term of the income stream, the less the annual capital recovery required. If the income stream is forecast as one of a perpetual duration, or if no capital loss in principal is forecast, income may be capitalized at (divided by) the interest (discount) rate.

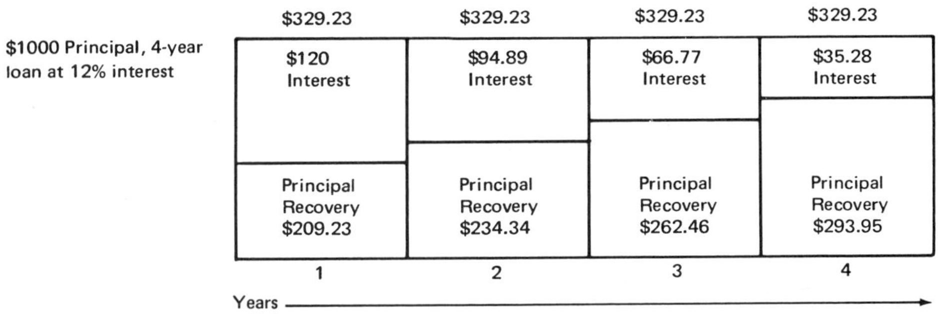

Year	Principal Recovery	Principal at End of Year
1	$209.23	$790.77
2	234.34	556.43
3	262.46	293.97
4	293.95	.02
Total	999.98	
Rounded	$1,000.00	

FIGURE 5–2. Interest and Principal Distribution.

Sinking Fund Capital Recovery at Safe Interest Rate. Sometimes, specific investments are so lucrative that reinvestment at the same rate that they are yielding is considered unlikely. What is likely for reinvested funds is that they can earn income at a lower "safe" rate. This "safe" approach to capital recovery is called the *Hoskold Method.*

Suppose that an investor discovers a gold mine or oil well. Will he be so lucky the next time? When the minerals are depleted, will he get his principal back? Probably not. The Hoskold Method presumes a safe rate of earnings as its assumption for capital recovery.

Suppose, for example, that an investment proposal offers a 12% interest rate and has a four-year life. Capital recovery amounts can be safely reinvested at only a 5% rate. Since the four-year sinking fund factor at 5% interest is .232, the capitalization rate is .12 + .232 = .352.

To find the value of this four-year income stream, divide the first year's income by .352. If the first year's expected income is $352, the value of the stream is $1,000; $352 divided by .352 equals $1,000.

Looking at the example in greater detail, from the first year's income of $352, subtract $120 for interest, leaving $232 of principal. If that amount is reinvested at a 5% rate, and a similar amount is added to it at the end of each year and reinvested until the end of the fourth year, it will become $1,000 in principal.

Although the Hoskold Method is seldom used in real estate appraisals, a modification of it, the Financial Management Rate of Return (see Chapter 15), is being used increasingly in investment analysis.

Partial Capital Recovery

An investment may be partially wasting, but *less* than a 100% decline in value is expected. When this is forecast, the capital recovery rate should be a fraction of the 100% rate. This allows a fraction of the capital to be recovered from resale, instead of from current income.

For example, using straight-line capital recovery, an asset that is expected to be resold after four years for 50% of its current value would have 50% of 25% (four-year life = 25% per year) or 12.5% of its annual income as a capital recovery rate. The 12.5% for capital recovery plus a 12% earnings rate totals 24.5% as an income capitalization rate.

Annuity capital recovery with a 50% forecast decline in value at a 12% interest (or discount) rate would give a capitalization rate as follows:

Yield or discount or interest rate	=	.12
Add Capital recovery:		
50% loss × .209 sinking fund	=	.1045
Capitalization rate		.2245

Component Separation. Another approach to partial capital recovery is available through the separation of the components that represent different investments.

For example, suppose that an investor pays $2,000 for a building and land, combined. A 12% interest or discount rate is expected. The appraisal report indicates that the market value of the land alone is $1,000; the building alone is worth $1,000, with a four-year life, after which time it will be worthless. Income attributable to the building will gradually decline, whereas the land value and income to the land will remain level in perpetuity. Therefore, the total capital recovery component for the building is 50% of the total investment. Considering a 25% recovery (four-year straight-line) rate, this amounts to a 12.5% rate of capital recovery for the total investment. The capitalization rate for the property therefore is 12% + 12.5% = 24.5%.

The composition of this rate with separate rates for buildings and land is described below:

		Decimal Weighted
Building:		
Return on investment: 50% of total investment at 12% interest rate	=	.06
Return of investment: 50% of total investment (over 4 years)	=	.125
Land:		
Return on investment: 50% of total investment at 12% interest rate	=	.06
Return of investment: Not applicable	=	0
Capitalization rate	=	.245 = 24.5%

Capital Recovery Situations

Whenever an investment is expected to lose some or all of its capital (principal) value, capital recovery must be provided in the income stream because it won't be in the resale proceeds. An example is the improvements of an older hotel. As its reputation declines, so do its room rates and the nature of its clientele. Its revenue will decline, but expenses may increase because of necessary repairs. After a while, it will be ripe for demolition. A recent purchaser who has allocated any of its purchase price to improvements must look to the income stream for capital recovery. Considering its declining income, it is appropriate to use straight-line capital recovery. The same would be true for older housing, offices, and shopping facilities.

For example, a capital recovery situation is faced by a real estate owner who holds a long-term lease at a fixed net rental but has given the tenant a purchase option at a nominal amount, exercisable when the lease terminates. All of the capital must be recovered in the income steam. Similarly, owners of self-amortizing mortgages face a loss in capital value through systematic amortization. Their receipts remain level until full amortization; then the principal is zero. Therefore capital recovery by the sinking fund method would be appropriate.

For example, consider a $400,000 loan at 12% interest, payable over 25 years. Monthly payments are $4,212.90. Its holder (the lender) might be tempted to consider that the monthly interest rate is above 1% ($4,212.90/$400,000 equals 1.05%). But he must remember that the asset will be worthless after 25 years; therefore the actual monthly earnings rate is exactly 1%. The monthly receipts that are in excess of 1% serve to recover the $400,000 capital investment. The monthly capital recovery rate for the situation is the sinking fund factor at 12% interest for 25 years, using monthly payments. The exact monthly factor is .000532; that added to the monthly 1% (.01) interest rates gives a capitalization rate of .010532 to be applied to the monthly income. By division, the capital value of the loan at origination is $400,000, as follows: $4,212.90 divided by .010532 equals $400,000.

Forecast Appreciation in Capital Value

Some investments are expected to appreciate in value. The purchaser anticipates future growth in value and so does the seller. Through negotiations with the seller, the price paid may reflect a premium over the property's value in its present use; the premium reflects further value gains that are anticipated. Current income may be quite low; so the price will be high relative to current income.

Given that expectation, it is theoretically defensible to subtract a provision for future capital gain from the interest or discount rate, to derive a rate to capitalize current income.

For example, let's say that a 12% interest (or discount) rate is desired. Current income is level at $100 per year. The investment is expected to increase in value by 30% over the next four years. The capitalization rate is computed as follows:

Yield rate desired	=	.12
Less: Deferred return (appreciation): .3 × .209*	=	.0627
Capitalization rate	=	.0573

Therefore, the current value of the asset is $100 divided by .0573, or

Value: $100 ÷ .0573 = $1,745

The income stream is graphically pictured in Figure 5–3.

*Sinking fund factor at a 12% interest rate for four years.

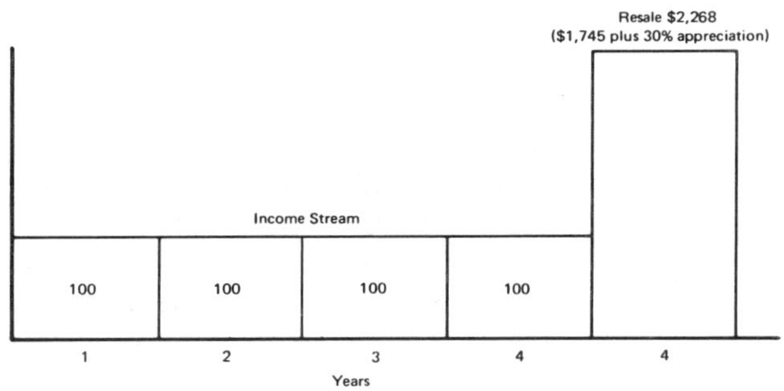

FIGURE 5-3. Income Stream and Reversion for Appreciating Asset.

A "growth chart" for this investment, using the "bankbook" technique that shows transactions if recorded in a passbook savings account, is shown in Table 5-3.

TABLE 5-3
Growth Chart for Sample Investment Using Bankbook Techniques

	Deposit	*Interest at 12%*	*Less Withdrawal of Current Income*	*Balance End of Year*
1	$1,745	$209	$100	$1,854
2		224	100	1,978
3		238	100	2,116
4		254	100	2,268

In this situation of appreciation in capital value, all of the capital recovery, plus some of the income required to receive a 12% yield to maturity, is found in the proceeds from resale. Notice that the balance at the end of four years ($2,268) exceeds by 30%, the initial deposit ($1,745).

Calculations Providing for Capital Appreciation. The price of land and improvements may be expected to rise: (1) as inflation causes more dollars to be paid for the property, and (2) as demand for certain property increases due to population growth and local area desirability. In many instances, investors buy at prices that offer a rather low current income stream in anticipation of a deferred return. That is, they will buy at a price that anticipates appreciation.

Suppose inflation is expected to cause higher property prices, more than compensating for depreciation and obsolescence; or when local demand is expected to cause a rise in value. Then the reversion received upon resale offers 100% capital recovery plus additional income. It is unnecessary to deplete current income to obtain a capital recovery provision since the opposite—capital growth—will occur. Then, the capitalization rate is to be reduced for the expected capital gain.

This provision may be appropriate for land or modern improvements in an inflationary period provided that market prices reflect low current yields in exchange for capital gains. For example, suppose an investor wants a 15% equity yield rate (rate of return on investment) with a $100,000 equity investment. Annual forecast cash returns are $14,445. If the resale proceeds will be exactly $100,000, then the return will be 14.445%, slightly below the 15% desired.

Suppose the investor is willing to defer receipt of $555 per year ($15,000 minus $14,445 = $555) in exchange for appreciation to be received later. To account for capital growth in the capitalization rate, the procedure shown in Table 5-4 can be used:

TABLE 5-4
Appreciation Needed to Achieve Desired Yield to Maturity

Current Yield	=	*Desired Yield to Maturity*	−	*Sinking Fund Factor*	×	*Fraction of Forecast Equity Value Change over Holding Period*
.14445	=	.15	−	.049252	×	x (unknown)
	Subtract .15 from both sides of the equation					
−.00555	=			−.049252	×	x
	Multiply both sides of the equation by −1					
.00555	=			.049252	×	x
	Divide both sides of the equation by .049252					
$\frac{.00555}{.049252}$	=					x
.112686	=					x

Appreciation (x) = 11.2686 %

Therefore, the value of equity must increase by 11.27% (rounded) for the investment to offer a 15% yield to maturity.

When forecast appreciation and current income are given, a capital growth rate can be computed. For example, suppose it is forecast that the equity in subject property would appreciate by 20% over a ten-year projection period. Annual cash flow is level at

$14,445; the investor wants a 15% yield to maturity. The investor can pay $103,061 for the equity as shown below:

Current Equity Dividend Rate		*Desired Yield to Maturity*		*Sinking Fund Factor*		*Forecast equity Appreciation*
D	=	.15	−	.049252	×	.20

Solve for *D* (equity dividend):

$$D = .14015$$

Thus the investor can capitalize a current income of $14,445 by the .14015 rate to get a maximum investment that would yield a 15% earnings rate, given a 20% increase in the value of the invested equity: $14,445 divided by .14015 = $103,061. With that investment, the receipt of $14,445 per year for ten years, followed by a proceeds of resale 20% above the $103,061, generates a yield rate of 15%.

When adjusting a current yield rate to a yield to maturity rate, the analyst must be careful to use appropriately matched levels of income and value. The preceding examples considered the equity dividend rate and equity yield rate. Consequently, the appreciation (depreciation) percentage is applied to the amount of equity. A parallel application is the treatment of net operating income and property value (overall rate of return). In that consideration, forecast appreciation or value decline is applied to the entire property cost, not just to the cost of equity.

SUMMARY

In any investment situation, the periodic income and proceeds from resale can be divided into two components: a return *on* investment and a return *of* investment. The return *on* investment is an interest, discount, or yield to maturity. The return *of* investment is a capital recovery rate. As a rule, the capital recovery rate depends on the term of the investment, the current yield rate, the expected stability of periodic income, and the amount of principal (capital) gain or loss expected over the holding period. In general:

1. When the expected reversion is exactly equal to the initial investment, all of the capital recovery is in the reversion, so there is no need to provide for capital recovery in the capitalization rate. (Periodic earnings represent the return on investment.)

2. When the expected reversion is less than the initial investment, some or all of the capital recovery is in the current income; therefore a capital recovery provision must be included in the income capitalization rate.

3. When the expected reversion exceeds the initial investment, all of the capital recovery is in the reversion, and some of the reversion, plus all of the periodic income, produces the yield to maturity.

4. When the expected reversion plus all of the expected periodic income total is less than the "initial investment," there is a capital loss with no return on investment.

The three methods for providing capital recovery are annuity, sinking fund, and straight-line. The annuity method presumes level income and reinvestment at the asset earnings rate. The sinking fund method assumes reinvestment at a specified safe (low) rate. Straight-line capital recovery presumes a declining income stream.

Estimating the amount or rate of capital is quite difficult for real estate investments because it is based on future events. Only through a careful physical and financial analysis of the property, its environment, economic condition and trends does one gather enough information to estimate a capital recovery rate.

Questions

1. What is the monthly capital recovery rate for a $200,000 level-payment mortgage, self-amortizing over 30 years at 10% interest per year, with monthly payments?
2. A systematically declining income stream that will end in five years generates $1,000 income this current year. What is its present value, using straight-line capital recovery at a 10% discount rate?
3. For the income stream described in Question 2, prepare a table that distributes total income as to interest and principal.
4. A $1,000 loan calls for four equal annual payments at 15% interest, each $350.27, for full amortization. What is the annual capital recovery rate?
5. For Question 4, construct a table showing payments and their annual distribution of interest and principal.

6. A $1,000 annual return is forecast from a $7,500 investment. The investment is expected to be sold after five years for $10,000.
   a. What is the current yield?
   b. What is the yield to maturity?

Essay Questions

1. Distinguish between a return *on* and a return *of* investment.
2. Why is it necessary to include a capital recovery provision for the income capitalization rate of a wasting asset? Explain.
3. What are three methods of providing for capital recovery? What are the conditions for each?
4. State the general rules for determining whether capital recovery comes from the periodic income or the reversion (resale).
5. Distinguish between *current yield, yield to maturity,* and *capitalization rate.*

Chapter 6

Physical Residual Techniques of Income Capitalization

In income capitalization, residual techniques are used to value improved real estate when the value and income claim of the building or the land is known. Whatever income is left over after satisfying known income requirements for building or land is attributable to the other component. Thus, the residual income is the amount left over after satisfying known income requirements, and can be capitalized to estimate the value of the residual component asset.

LAND ECONOMICS—RESIDUAL THEORY

Classical land economic theory, originally developed for agricultural land, holds that all income to land should be treated as a residual. The land value is based on this residual income. For example, suppose that one acre of farm land can produce a crop valued at \$100.00. To produce that crop, there is a certain optimal mix of land, labor, capital, and entrepreneurship. Assume that the following expenditures per acre are the optimal mix for a certain farm:

Labor (to till, seed, weed, harvest)	\$50.00
Capital (equipment usage)	25.00
Entrepreneurship (farmer's risk and talent)	10.00
Total	\$85.00

Since the crop promises a price of $100, and nonland known costs are $85, the $15 residual income is attributable to land. If that income is expected to be received each year in perpetuity, and the appropriate capitalization rate is 10%, the acre of land is estimated to be worth $150 ($15 divided by .10 = $150).

In agriculture, land is thought to hold residual value as contrasted with other factors in production that have a first claim against income because land doesn't do anything. Something is done to it. In contrast, other factors of production have an earlier claim. For example, if laborers are paid less than $50 per acre for their efforts, they will choose to work in a factory or on another farm; if farm equipment manufacturers don't receive enough from the sale of tractors, they will make different products; and farmers, unless they are paid adequately for their talent and risk, will work for a salary or enter another business venture instead of farming.

Since the above example assumed that the combination of inputs was of an optimal efficiency mix, considering the principle of increasing and decreasing returns, there is no further cost savings to be gained by changing the mix, given current prices and technology. Labor, capital, and entrepreneurship must be paid the amounts indicated. In a competitive environment, they need not be paid more. But they must be paid before the land can earn rent. After those payments, land receives the residual income, and the residual is called *land rent.* It is also called *economic rent* in this example because the land did nothing to earn the income. "Economic rent" in economics terminology is an "unearned" form of income. (In appraisal terminology, economic rent is the market rental rate.)

Fertile land will command a higher residual and hence will have a higher value than poorer land. If the price of the crop should increase, residual incomes to land and values of land will increase. Land once thought to be virtually worthless will then be brought into cultivation. Classical economists have always felt that land has no inherent price or value; it commands a residual only.

APPLICATION OF RESIDUAL TECHNIQUES TO INCOME-PRODUCING REAL ESTATE

Residual techniques can be applied to income-producing property. The three most commonly used types are: land, building, and property residual techniques. In the land residual technique, the value of the improvements are given, and the land receives the residual of income after satisfying the income requirements of the improvement's value. The building residual technique is used when the value of the land is estimated and given. The property residual technique is used when an estimated income stream and resale value for all of the property are given.

Land Residual Technique

The land residual technique has its roots in classical land economics. It is useful when improvements are relatively new or have not yet been built. Their value (or proposed cost) can be closely approximated, as can their estimated useful lives. For example, suppose recently constructed real estate improvements cost $450,000. These improvements have a 50-year economic useful life. The appropriate rate of return on investment is 12% because that rate is competitive with other investment opportunities perceived to have equal risk. Straight-line capital recovery is considered appropriate for the improvements. The annual recovery rate is 2% (100%/50 years = 2% per year). So the total required rate of return for the improvements is 14% (12% + 2% = 14%). Annual net operating income for the first year is estimated to be $65,000. (See table 7–4). The improvements require a 14% return on $450,000 of cost, which equals $63,000 of income. Subtracting this amount from the $65,000 net operating income leaves a $2,000 residual for the land. That amount, capitalized in perpetuity at 12%, offers a land value of $16,666.67. Capitalization of land income in perpetuity is appropriate because land is thought to not wear out. This is summarized in Table 6–1.

TABLE 6–1.
Land Residual Technique—Straight-Line Capital Recovery for Buildings

Net operating income (first year)	$65,000.00
Less: Income attributable to improvements:	
12% (on) + 2% (of) = 14%; .14 × $450,000 =	63,000.00
Residual income to land	$ 2,000.00
Capitalized at 12% return on investment in perpetuity	$16,666.67

The total property value is then estimated at $467,000.00 ($450,000 for improvements plus $16,666.67 for land = $466,666.67; rounded to $467,000.00).

The land residual technique is analogous to the agricultural example. The improvements to real estate, which require labor, capital, and entrepreneurship, hold the first claim on income, as they do in the agricultural model. Remaining income is attributable to land and may be capitalized to derive a land value estimate.

The straight-line capital recovery approach in Table 6–1 inherently assumes that income attributable to the building systematically declines with time. Had the income to the building been projected to be level for 50 years, an annuity capital recovery rate would have been appropriate. In that event the land residual approach would indicate a land value of $90,102, based on $10,812 annual income to land, as shown in Table 6–2.

TABLE 6–2
Land Residual Technique—Annuity Capital Recovery for Building Income

Net operating income		$65,000
Less: Income to improvements:		
$450,000 × .120417 *	=	54,188
(column 6, 50 years @ 12%		
Income to land		$10,812
Land value: $10,812 divided by .12	=	$90,102

The property value would then be $540,102 based on $90,102 for land plus $450,000 for improvements.

*Given a $450,000 construction cost for improvements with a 50-year useful life and level income, the annual income requirement is based on the installment to amortize one factor at the appropriate rate of interest.

The capitalization method used must match the income that is forecast to be received. Unless the income stream assumptions and capitalization rates are properly matched, the resulting present values will be invalid.

Diagrams of income to buildings and to land under two different capital recovery assumptions are shown as Figures 6–1 and 6–2. Notice that the capital recovery assumption has a great influence on the residual income and value.

The land residual technique can be successfully used when the value of improvements can be accurately estimated. However, once the improvements are built, the land and improvements become one unit, and it is seldom possible to separate them afterwards.

Another use of the land residual technique is in estimating the highest and best use of land. Costs of different proposed im-

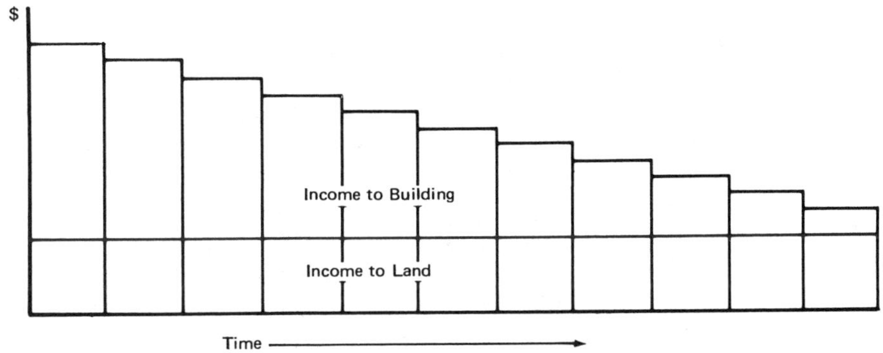

FIGURE 6–1. Land Residual with Straight-Line Building Capital Recovery.

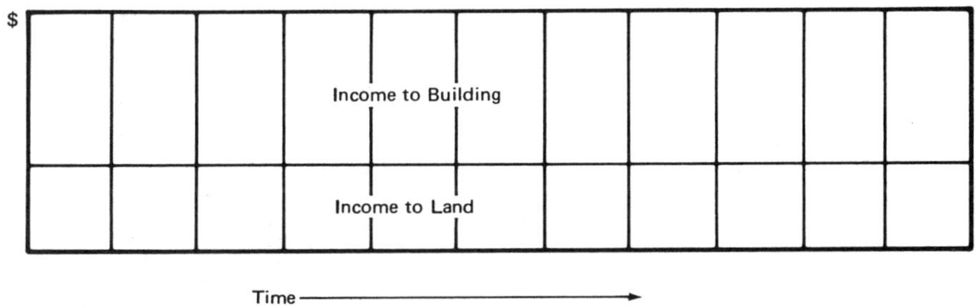

FIGURE 6–2. Land Residual with Annuity Building Capital Recovery.

provements can be estimated, as can the net operating income for each type of improvement. A capitalization rate is multiplied by the estimated improvement cost and the result subtracted from forecast net operating income. The result is forecast land income. Whichever type or level of improvement offers the highest residual income to land is the highest and best use of the land, subject to legal and physical constraints. The subject of highest and best use is discussed further, with examples, in Chapter 16.

Building Residual Technique

The building residual technique works in reverse of the land residual technique. When the land value can be estimated with a high degree of confidence (as when there are many recent sales of comparables), income attributable to the land can be subtracted from net operating income. The residual of income is attributable to the improvements and can be capitalized to estimate their value. Then the capitalized value of improvements can be added to the land value to result in a total property value estimate.

The building residual technique is unfounded in classical economic theory. In economics, it is the land that receives the residual income, not the improvements. In practice, however, land values may be readily ascertainable in the market. For example, in the central business district of a city or in the suburbs there may be recent sales of comparable land. Attempting to value a building, particularly an older one that is outmoded in many respects, is especially difficult. Given these circumstances, the building residual technique adds a useful tool to a real estate market value estimate, despite the absence of an adequate theoretical basis.

As an example of the building residual technique, suppose that the land value is estimated at $50,000 through a careful analysis of several recent sales of comparable vacant tracts of land. A 12% discount rate is considered appropriate. From the estimated $65,000 of annual net operating income, $6,000 (12% of $50,000 land value = $6,000) is attributable to the land. Capital recovery for land income is unnecessary since the land will last forever. The $59,000 balance of the net operating income is attributable to the improvements. Improvements would be worth $421,429 using a straight-line capital recovery rate and 50-year life; or $489,964 using a level income assumption, as shown in Table 6-3. The total property value is the building value plus $50,000 for land. Based on straight-line capital recovery, the total property value is $471,429; or it is $539,965 based on level annuity capital recovery.

TABLE 6-3
Building Residual Technique

Net operating income		$65,000
Less: Income to land: 12% of $50,000	=	6,000
Income to improvements		$59,000
Improvement value at straight-line capital recovery: (over 50 years) $59,000/.14	=	$421,429
Improvement value at level annuity capital recovery: (over 50 years) $59,000/.120417	=	$489,965

Negative Residuals

It is possible that application of the building or land residual technique will result in negative values. In that situation it may be possible to detect important information about the property.

For example, suppose that the land residual technique indicates a negative amount (residual) of income to the land. Before arriving at a conclusion, the analyst should recheck the capitalization rate assumptions, as to both the return on and the return of investment. If the assumptions are valid, it is likely that the building is an overimprovement for that site. That is, the income claimed by the building fails to offer an adequate return on and of the investment in the building. Alternatively, a different management approach may be needed to make the property more attractive to tenants by adjusting the rental rate schedule or the tenant mix or by changing the level of services offered to tenants.

Should the building residual technique offer a negative value to the building, then, after reviewing capitalization rate assumptions, the analyst may offer property management suggestions. Or, if a negative residual remains, a suggestion might be the demolition of the building and a replacement that will conform to the property's highest and best use.

Property Residual Technique

The use of the word *residual* in *"property residual technique"* is misleading. A more descriptive term would be *reversion. Reversion* indicates a remaining value to be received when the income stream has ended. The reversion may be realized upon termination of the economic useful life of the property or upon a resale that will occur at an earlier date.

When the net operating income can be forecast with reasonable certainty over a building's economic useful life, the property residual technique can provide a good estimate of its value. Then there is no need to attempt to separate building-generated income from that commanded by the land. This avoids the difficult building-land separation step, which is awkward from a theoretical viewpoint because of the unitary feature of one property generating an income stream. The estimated resale price at the end of the improvement's useful life, even if it is misjudged by a wide margin, will have only a slight effect on the property's present value because the resale may be many years away. However, the estimated useful life of improved real estate is seldom the typical investment holding period.

Reversion at End of Economic Useful Life of Property. Consider improved real estate that is expected to generate $65,000 of level annual net operating income for the next 50 years, after which the improvements will be worthless as income-producing assets. For simplicity, assume that the land value will remain unchanged at $50,000. A 12% rate of return on investment is considered appropriate. Valuation of the $65,000 per year income stream should be computed using a level annuity factor (multiply by the annuity factor), and the $50,000 reversion using a present worth of one factor. Notice that the results (see Table 6–4) are exactly equal to those shown previously for the land residual technique with annuity capital recovery.

TABLE 6–4

Property Residual Technique

	Amount		Factor		Present Value
Income stream	$65,000	×	8.3045	=	$539,792
Reversion	$50,000	×	.00346	=	+173
Total present value					$539,965
Rounded to					$540,000

A straight-line capital recovery rate should be applied to the building income when it is assumed that the income to the building will decline systematically. It is necessary, however, to separate the income attributable to the land from the income to the building in order to treat just the building income as declining, since the land value (and its income claim) is considered to be level and nonwasting. This is shown in Table 6–5.

Resale of Property with Reversion Prior to End of Economic Life. The property residual technique can be employed considering a resale prior to the end of the property's economic useful life. An assumed resale price could be a purchase option price if one is offered to the tenant in the lease, or the value of the remaining income stream that the property is expected to generate after resale. For example, suppose the property considered earlier with an estimated 50-year useful life is to be resold 10 years into its estimated useful life. The reversion at resale is based on 40 years of *remaining* annual level net operating income of $65,000, plus a $50,000 reversion for the land. The assumed resale price after 10 years is $536,382 as in Table 6–6.

The property residual will thus be estimated at $536,382 to be received in 10 years. The present value of that amount, plus the present value of the 10 years of net operating income received during the holding period, is computed as shown in Table 6–7.

TABLE 6–5
Property Residual with Straight-Line Capital Recovery for Improvements

Net operating income			$65,000
Less: Income to land: 12% of $50,000 value			6,000
Income to building			$59,000
Capitalization of income:			
	Capitalization Factors		
Income to land:	$ 6,000 × 8.3045[a]	=	$ 49,827
Income to improvements:	$59,000 × 7.1428[b]	=	421,429
Reversion: Land value	$50,000 × .00346[c]	=	173
Total value of property			$471,429

[a] 50-year annuity (column 5) at 12% interest.
[b] 1/(.12 + .02) = 7.1428 (50-year straight-line factor at 12% interest).
[c] 50-year reversion factor (column 4) at 12% interest.

TABLE 6–6
Resale Price Prior to End of Economic Life

	40-Year Factor		*Value at Resale*
Annual income stream	$65,000 × 8.2438[a]	=	$535,845
Reversion	$50,000 × .010746[b]	=	+537
Resale price in 10 years			$536,382

[a] Annuity factor at 12% interest for 40 years.
[b] Present worth of one factor at 12% interest for 40 years.

TABLE 6–7
Property Residual Technique with Resale Prior to End of Economic Useful Life

	Income		*Factor*		*Present Worth*
Annual income stream	$ 65,000	×	5.6502[a]	=	$367,265
Reversion in 10 years	$536,382	×	.32197[b]	=	+172,700
Total present value in 10 years					$539,965

[a] 10-year annuity factor (column 5) at 12%.
[b] 10-year reversion factor (column 4) at 12%.

Purchase Option. Suppose that the subject property is under an absolute net lease for $65,000 per year rental, payable at the end of each year for 25 years. The tenant has the option to buy the property at the end of 25 years for $500,000. The present value, at a 12% interest or discount rate, using the property residual technique and assuming exercise of the option, is shown in Table 6–8. Note that even if the tenant vacates after 25 years and fails to exercise the purchase option, there is little difference in the present value of the property. When discounted 25 years, today's value of the reversion is worth under 6% (.05882) of the resale price, at a 12% interest (discount) rate.

TABLE 6–8
Income Stream and Resale Price at Purchase Option Amount

Source of Income	*Amount*		*Factor*		
Net annual rent	$ 65,000	×	7.8431[a]	=	$509,804
Resale	$500,000	×	.0588[b]	=	+29,411
Total present value					$539,215

[a] 25-year annuity factor at 12% interest.
[b] 25-year reversion factor at 12% interest.

The property residual technique is diagrammed in Figure 6–3.

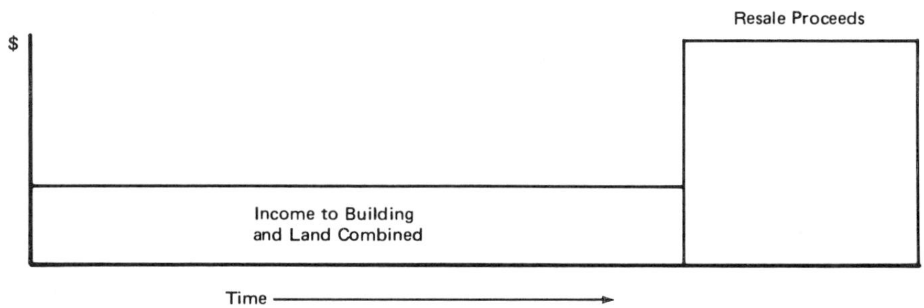

FIGURE 6–3. Property Residual Technique—Level Income Assumption.

Summary of Residual Techniques and Reconciliation of Differences

Employing different residual techniques mechanically to the same income assumptions can result in slightly different answers due to different inherent assumptions or estimates concerning the current

TABLE 6–9
Property Value Estimates under Different Techniques

Residual Technique	*Total Property Value Considering Building Income Assumptions*	
	Level Income	*Declining Income*
Land residual	$540,102	$466,666
Building residual	$539,965	$471,429
Property residual	$539,965	$471,429

value of the buildings or land. There should be no cause for concern over the mathematics used or the mechanical process unless the variations are substantial.

For each of the three types of residual techniques demonstrated, two different capital recovery assumptions were shown. One capital recovery assumption assumed level income; the other assumed that the income to improvements declines. A summary of (unrounded) results is shown in Table 6–9.

Results for the building and property residual techniques are consistent with each other. In both of these, it was assumed that the land value was $50,000. The mechanical technique employed made no difference. However, results from the land residual technique were inconsistent with the two other techniques. This was caused by a different assumption from the outset. In the land residual technique, it was assumed that the improvements were known to be worth $450,000. In contrast to the other techniques, the land value was not known. As a result, the land residual technique ascribed a different assumption concerning the amount of reversion (resale of land at the end of the income stream) and the amount of declining building income (for the case of straight-line capital recovery). Despite the discrepancy, there is no significant difference in the estimate of values using any of the three residual techniques. A significant difference is caused by the income assumption. A great deal of difference in value is indicated, depending on whether income is expected to remain level over time or decline.

PHYSICAL OVERALL CAPITALIZATION RATE TECHNIQUES

On the basis of the estimated proportions of the value of land and improvements, respectively, a capitalization rate can be derived. That rate is a physical overall rate that can be used to capitalize all of the net operating income.

Application of this technique requires an initial estimate of the improvement ratio. Suppose that improvements are estimated to represent 90% of the property's total value. The land is estimated to be worth 10% of the property value. Building and land capitalization rates can then be weighted according to their fraction of capital value, and their income requirements.

Consider these assumptions:

Improvement ratio: 90%
Improvement economic life: 50 years
Discount (interest) rate: 12%

The physical overall capitalization rate is as shown in Table 6–10.

TABLE 6–10
Straight-Line Presumption (Declining Income) and Level Annuity Presumption (Level Income)

Straight-Line Presumption (Declining Income)

Asset	*Ratio*		*Capitalization Rate*		*Weighted Rate*
Improvements	.90	×	.14	=	.126
Land	.10	×	.12	=	+.012
Weighted capitalization rate					.138
Value estimate: $65,000 divided by .138				=	$471,015
Rounded to					$471,000

Level Annuity Presumption (Level Income)

Asset	*Ratio*		*Capitalization Rate*		*Weighted Rate*
Improvements	.90	×	.120417	=	.108375
Land	.10	×	.12	=	+.012
Weighted capitalization rate					.120375
Value estimate: $65,000 divided by .120375				=	$539,979
Rounded to					$540,000

In the case of deriving physical capitalization rates, the presumptions reflect improvements at 90% of the value estimate; land at 10%. This offers a slightly different variation in presumptions from the residual techniques discussed earlier. In the residual techniques, either the improvement or land was estimated at a certain dollar value as contrasted with a ratio here. For example, improvements were assumed to be worth $450,000 in the land residual techniques (Table 6–2); and land was $50,000 in the building and property residual techniques (Tables 6–3 and 6–6). However, in this ratio approach, note (in Table 6–10) that the dollar figures were close but not identical to figures that would be derived by applying the improvement or land ratio to the value estimate. That is, 10% of $471,015 or of $539,979 is not exactly equal to $50,000 of land. This explains why value estimates using ratios were close but not identical to the results using dollar amounts. However, unless there is a substantial discrepancy between the value estimates and ratios used, there is no need to reconcile differences.

Inflation Adjustment and Use of Sinking Fund Factor

During economic times when inflation is anticipated, investors will bid up prices for real estate, sacrificing current returns for appreciation they expect to realize later. A preferred approach to this type of analysis is the mortgage-equity technique. The mathematics of an inflation-adjusted capitalization rate can also be applied to physical residual techniques. For example, suppose that land is 10% of a property's current value, and it is expected to grow in value by a 5% per year compounded inflation rate for the next 10 years. Improvements represent 90% of value, and they are expected to grow by 3% per year compounded (5% inflation less 2% depreciation in real terms equals 3% net growth). Total appreciation, then, will be 37.24% as shown in Table 6–11.

TABLE 6–11

Resale Price Growth with Inflation

Asset	*Ratio*		*Growth Factor*		*Weighted Growth Factor*
Improvements	.9	×	1.3439[a]	=	1.20951
Land	.1	×	1.6289[b]	=	+.16289
Total resale/present value					1.3724
Subtract 1, leaving .3724 or 37.24% appreciation					

[a] Column 1 for 10 years at 3%.

[b] Column 1 for 10 years at 5%.

The rate to capitalize current income can be modified to reflect expected future appreciation in value. Since the investor will be sacrificing current cash returns for future value growth, and since the benefit of future appreciation will be received in a lump sum at a later date, the annual rate of appreciation must be converted into an effective annual capitalization rate. This is accomplished using the sinking fund factor. Multiply the sinking fund factor for the holding period by the expected appreciation percentage for the same period. The result is subtracted from the desired yield to maturity. This is shown in Table 6–12.

TABLE 6–12
Adjusting Capitalization Rate for Expected Value Appreciation

Step 1. Adjust target capitalization rate (C.R.) by subtracting the product of forecast appreciation and the sinking fund factor:

C.R. = .12 − .3724 × .057
C.R. = .12 − .02123
C.R. = .09877

Step 2. Divide forecast income by capitalization rate to derive present value (P.V.):

P.V. = $65,000 ÷ .09877
P.V. = $658,094
Rounded = $658,000

Step 3. Estimate resale price:

$658,094 + 37.24% appreciation = $903,168

Step 4. Consider reasonableness of resale amount.

The present value estimate and resale price can be checked by adding together the present value of the two sources of income at the desired yield-to-maturity rate. This is shown in Table 6–13.

The sinking fund factor at the desired yield to maturity is used to adjust desired yields into capitalization rates. Capitalization rates can then be applied to current income, given expectations of appreciation or decline in value. The sinking fund factor is used because it inherently shows the annual rate of growth necessary to reach a desired lump sum future payment. The capitalization rate is derived by subtracting the estimated appreciation multiplied by the sinking fund factor, from the desired yield to maturity rate. See Table 6–12.

TABLE 6–13
Present Value Estimate with Expected Appreciation

Source of Revenue	Amount		10-Year Factor		Present Value
Net operating income	$ 65,000	×	5.65[a]	=	$367,250
Resale principal	903,085	×	.322[b]	=	290,793
Present value					$658,043

Notice that the $903,085 resale amount exceeds the $658,043 present value estimate by 37.24%

[a] Annuity factor at 12% for 10 years.
[b] Present worth of one factor at 12% for 10 years.

SENSITIVITY ANALYSIS: PRESENT VALUE GIVEN ASSUMED RESALE PRICES

By using the sinking fund factor in a capitalization rate, an analyst can estimate the maximum current value based on alternative expectations of resale price. This is known as *sensitivity analysis.*

For example, suppose an investor desires a 12% yield to maturity on the total purchase price of unmortgaged real estate that generates a level annual net operating income of $65,000. The investor is uncertain of the resale value in ten years but wants to know the present prices that will be justified by different value change assumptions. The assumptions are that resale prices may be 10 or 25% higher or lower than present prices. Capitalization rates and value estimates are computed in Table 6–14.

When a decline in value is anticipated, some of the capital must be recovered through the income stream. Adding to the capitalization rate produces a lower value estimate. It allows more of the income stream to be considered as capital recovery, and less of the reversion as capital recovery. Subtracting from the capitalization rate assumes that some of the rate of return on investment and all of the capital recovery will be received upon resale of the property.

From that analysis, the investor can justify the maximum amount to bid for property. Results show the highest price to pay that with the forecast value change will result in the desired 12% yield-to-maturity. The investor may be willing to bid up the price to $615,000 if expectations are that a 25% or greater appreciation gain

TABLE 6–14
Capitalization Rates and Value Estimates at Selected Resale Price Assumptions

Resale Price Assumption	Overall Capitalization Rate	=	Desired Yield to Maturity (decimal)	+	(Sinking Fund Factor	×	Forecast Depreciation (−) Appreciation)	=	Overall Capitalization Rate	Property Value Estimate
10% decline	CR_1	=	.12	+	.057	×	(.10)	=	.1257	$571,104
25% decline	CR_2	=	.12	+	.057	×	(.25)	=	.13425	$484,171
10% decline	CR_3	=	.12	+	.057	×	(−.10)	=	.1143	$568,678
25% decline	CR_4	=	.12	+	.057	×	(−.25)	=	.10575	$614,657

Note: Property value estimates are based on dividing $65,000 of annual net operating income by the capitalization rate.

Forecast depreciation raises the capitalization rate thereby reducing property value estimates; forecast appreciation does the reverse.

CR = Capitalization rates at selected resale assumptions.

is to be realized over the ten-year period. It should be noted that an investor who buys at the higher price must sacrifice current annual returns in order to realize the forecast appreciation benefits.

Estimate Yield Given Assumed Resale Prices

An alternative use of sensitivity analysis is to estimate yields, given present prices and forecast value changes. For example, suppose that property is offered for sale at \$500,000 free and clear of any liens. Net operating income (NOI) is expected to be level at \$65,000. The investor wants to know yield rates, given a resale in ten years at three alternative prices: \$400,000, \$500,000, and \$600,000. The analysis can be done using the same steps as in Table 6–12 except that the unknowns are different and a trial-and-error process must be used.

The overall capitalization rate (OAR) is 13%, based on \$65,000 NOI and \$500,000 of value. Different yield to maturity rates and sinking fund factors at those rates are tested in a formula until an equality is found between overall rates and yields to maturity with value changes. For example, assuming a \$400,000 resale price, which implies that depreciation will be 20%, the equation to seek an equality solution becomes:

$$\text{OAR} = \text{Y} + (\text{dep.})\ (\text{SFF at Y})$$
$$.13 = \text{Y} + (.2)\ (\text{SFF at Y})$$

Try Y = 12%:

$$.13 = .12 + (.2)\ (.057)$$
$$.13 = .1314$$

Try Y = 11%:

$$.13 = 11 + (.2)\ (.0598)$$
$$.13 = .12196$$

where: OAR = Overall rate of return
Y = Yield to maturity
dep. = Forecast property value depreciation over holding period
SFF at Y = Sinking fund factor at yield to maturity (Y).

The results at 11% and 12% yield to maturity rates indicate overall rates of 12.196% and 13.14%, respectively. Since they bracket the targeted 13% overall rate, the yield to maturity is between 11% and 12%. A 12% yield to maturity brought results quite close to the 13% overall rate; therefore the yield to maturity is slightly below 12%, assuming a $400,000 resale price.

At a $500,000 resale price, the yield to maturity will be exactly equal to 13%. The resale price equals the original price, so all of the income is yield. Income of $65,000 per year offers a 13% return on the $500,000 investment, with capital recovery at resale.

The $600,000 resale price will offer a yield above 13%. It will be approximately 14%, based on the trial-and-error process:

$$.13 = .14 - (.20)(.0517)$$
$$.13 = .14 - .01034$$
$$.13 = .12966$$

Results can be graphed, as shown in Figure 6–4.

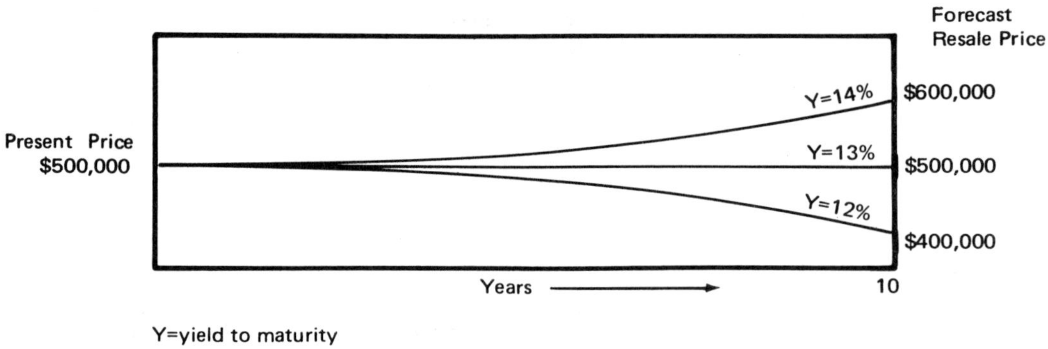

FIGURE 6–4. Forecast Yield Rates at Selected Resale Prices.

SUMMARY

Residual techniques of income capitalization have their roots in classical land economics. After income requirements for given factors of production are subtracted from total income, the residual income applies to land. The land residual technique in appraisal is to be used when the value of improvements and the capitalization rate are easily estimated. The building residual technique can be used when the estimated land value is a readily available amount. Capitalization of residual income can be applied using straight-line or annuity capital recovery rates, depending on whether the forecast income stream is declining or level.

The property residual technique assumes that a single income stream is generated by all of the property. The present value of the income stream, added to the present value of the estimated resale price, offers an estimate of the present value of the property. The resale may be forecast to occur at the end of the economic life of the property or at an earlier date. The technique is quite appropriate when there is a predetermined income stream and a fixed resale price as through a purchase option.

Building, land, and property residual techniques, when they are applied consistently, will yield identical results. Often, regardless of whether dollar amounts or percentages of improvement ratios are specified, residual techniques of capitalization can result in different value estimates. This may be due to slightly different inputs as assumptions. However, unless there is a significant difference between estimates, there is no need to refine the assumptions for consistency.

Input assumptions that require sound judgment and will influence value estimates, include values of asset with the first claim against income, their estimated useful lives, interest (or discount) rates, and the capital recovery assumption. Capital recovery assumptions, such as for straight-line capital recovery, annuity capital recovery, or appreciation expectations, can significantly affect the value estimate and therefore must be matched with the anticipated income stream and reversion.

Questions

1. A certain older office building in the heart of a downtown metropolitan area currently generates $40,000 net operating income. Income is expected to decline systematically over the estimated ten remaining years of the building's useful life. Therefore, straight-line capital recovery (declining income to the building) is considered appropriate. The land is currently valued at $250,000 by numerous recent sales of comparable properties. For the type of property, investors want a 10% interest (yield to maturity) rate.
   a. How much of the first year's $40,000 NOI is attributable to the land?
   b. How much of the NOI is attributable to the building?
   c. What is the building capitalization rate, assuming straight-line capital recovery?
   d. What is the value of the building, using the building residual technique?
   e. What is the combined value of the building and land?

2. A free-standing retail store is under an absolute net lease for the next 25 years with $10,000 per year rent payable at the end of each year. The tenant has a purchase option to buy the property at the end of the lease term for $75,000. The property is free and clear of debt. For this situation, investors seek a 12% rate of return on investment.
   a. What is the present value of the rental income?
   b. Assuming that the tenant will exercise the purchase option, what is the present value of the reversion?
   c. What is the present value of the property?
   d. What is the name of the technique applied?

Essay Questions

1. What is the justification (in land economics) for the land residual technique?
2. What is the significance of negative residual income?
3. Why is the property residual technique really a reversion technique?

Chapter 7

Pro Forma Financial Statements and Ratio Analysis

Whenever income-producing real estate is purchased as an investment, its owner is looking forward to benefits that are expected to be received in the future. During property ownership, real estate owners can receive several financial benefits, which are generally classified as: (1) cash flow, (2) income tax savings, (3) appreciation in value, and (4) mortgage reduction. Generally accepted accounting principles recognize accounting-defined net income and capital gains upon resale, but not precisely the same four categories of benefits that real estate owners measure. Consequently, there is a gap between real estate analysts and their accountants. The accounting profession has made efforts in recent years to reflect accrued but unrealized asset appreciation on balance sheets for certain companies, and to prepare a cash flow statement ("Sources and Applications of Funds") together with other financial statements. Still, a gap exists.

This chapter will not attempt to bridge or cure that gap. Instead, it will point out how accounting information is used by real estate owners, appraisers, and analysts. The chapter should aid in the understanding of financial statements for real estate projects. It describes how and why those in real estate revise financial statements to suit their purposes, and the ratio analysis techniques that they use. It stresses ratio analysis as a tool for property analysis.

BALANCE SHEET

For recently acquired real estate, an accounting-prepared balance sheet may appear as shown in Table 7-1. Real estate owners and analysts will recast this balance sheet, painting with a broad brush, and thus omitting the items of smaller value. They mentally recognize that most of the cash is set aside as tenant rental deposits. In the example provided, the $500 inventory of supplies probably consists of minor items such as unused furnace filters, janitorial supplies, and paint. Insurance for the year has already been paid. The $500 rental income receivable is not enough to raise a concern over delinquencies. Deferred mortgage and leasing fees were already paid to brokers. Accountants will amortize these deferred fees over the life of mortgage and lease terms, respectively, but, for the real estate analyst these fees have no further value. The substantial amounts are for buildings and land. Buildings will be depreciated over their useful lives; land will remain at cost. So real estate analysts and appraisers are concerned with the real property, not the small amounts of cash, receivables, and prepaid items.

As for the liability side, accounts payable consist of a recent utility bill and bills for some supplies. These will soon be paid. Tenant rental deposits will be refunded as tenants vacate. Accrued real estate taxes are not yet due. The portion of long-term debt that comes due this year will be satisfied with monthly payments. Only the total mortgage amount and owner's equity are of serious interest to analysts.

Thus, in this process, real estate analysts will disregard the small amounts and consider only the most important items, and they will condense and simplify the balance sheet for analysis purposes as shown in Table 7-2.

INCOME STATEMENT

The same type of condensation and simplification can be effected by appraisers for the income statement. However, for real estate analysis purposes, cash flow is considered more meaningful than accounting-defined "net income." Further, to be consistent with traditional real estate appraisal and investment analysis techniques, the cash flow statement takes on a particular structure. Shown in Table 7-3 is an accounting-derived income statement; following that are revised statements that are helpful to facilitate real estate analysis.

For real estate analysis purposes, it is convenient and traditional to categorize certain levels of income and expenses. The first step is to include potential rental income to show that amount as

TABLE 7–1
An Accounting Prepared Balance Sheet

ASSETS		
Current		
Cash		$ 2,500
Rental income receivable		500
Inventory of supplies		500
Prepaid insurance		1,500
Total current assets		$ 5,000
Noncurrent		
Deferred leasing expense		$ 1,000
Deferred mortgage commitment fee		4,000
Buildings at cost	$445,000	
Less: Accumulated depreciation	0	$445,000
Land		50,000
Total noncurrent assets		$500,000
Total assets (current plus noncurrent)		$505,000
LIABILITIES AND OWNER'S EQUITY		
Current liabilities:		
Accounts payable		$ 2,000
Tenant rental deposits		2,000
Accrued real estate taxes		1,000
Current portion of long-term debt		2,000
Total current liabilities		$ 7,000
Long-Term liabilities		
Mortgages payable (less current portion)		$398,000
Deferred federal income tax liability		
Total long-term liabilities		$398,000
Total liabilities		$405,000
OWNER'S EQUITY		
Capital contributed		$100,000
Retained earnings		0
Total equity		$100,000
Total liabilities and owner's equity		$505,000

TABLE 7–2
Simplified Balance Sheet

ASSETS	
Building (and other improvements)	$450,000
Land	50,000
Total	$500,000
LIABILITIES AND EQUITY	
Mortgage (12% interest rate, 25-year term)	$400,000
Equity	100,000
Total	$500,000

TABLE 7–3
Accounting Income Statement for the Year Ended December 31, 19__

Income	
Rental income	$95,000
Miscellaneous income	3,000
Total income	$98,000
Expenses:	
Utilities	$ 3,500
Repairs	2,500
Swimming pool maintenance	1,000
Management fee	6,000
Payroll	4,000
Payroll taxes	500
Supplies	1,500
Advertising	500
Interest	47,854
Legal and accounting	2,000
Property taxes	8,000
Depreciation	20,000
Miscellaneous	1,500
Total expenses	$98,854
Pretax net income (loss)	($ 854)

well as the vacancy rate. Consequently, a real estate appraiser or analyst will restructure the accountant's statement as shown in Table 7–4.

Notice in Table 7–4 that the real estate analyst, besides providing for a vacancy and collection allowance, has lumped together as "current operating expenses" all of the expenses from the Accounting Income Statement (Table 7–3) except interest and depreciation. Interest is treated together with principal repayment as a later step in the real estate pro-forma cash flow statement on Table 7–4. Depreciation accounting, since it is a noncash item, does not appear on the cash flow statement. The cash flow statement does include a reserve for replacements to "stabilize" expenses. Since the appliances, carpets, water heaters, air-conditioning compressors, and other short-lived items will be replaced in future years, a replacement reserve is established on the cash flow statement. Interest and principal repayment are considered together as debt service. They are financing costs, not operating expenses. Any mortgage principal reduction benefits will be realized upon a resale, not as current cash flow.

TABLE 7–4
Traditional Real Estate Cash Flow Statement (Pro Forma)

Potential gross income:		
Units *Description* *Rate*		
4 1-Bedroom @ $355 =	$1,420	
12 2-Bedroom @ $425 =	5,100	
4 3-Bedroom @ $453 =	1,812	
Monthly potential gross	$8,332	
Multiply by 12 months for annual amount (rounded)		$100,000
Less: Vacancy and collection allowance		5,000
Add: Miscellaneous income		3,000
Effective gross income		$ 98,000
Less: Current operating expenses*, and	$31,000	
Replacement reserve	2,000	33,000
Net operating income		$ 65,000
Less: Debt service (interest and principal)		50,555
Before-tax cash flow (cash throw-off)		$ 14,445

*Operating expenses include:

Utilities	$ 3,500
Repairs	2,500
Swimming pool maintenance	1,000
Management fee	6,000
Payroll	4,000
Payroll taxes	500
Supplies	1,500
Advertising	500
Legal and accounting	2,000
Property taxes	8,000
Miscellaneous	1,500
Total	$31,000

The real estate cash flow statement has four tiers of income as shown in Table 7–4. The highest tier is that of *potential gross income,* which assumes that all units are rented for the entire year. The second tier, *effective gross income,* is after vacancies have been subtracted and miscellaneous income included. The third tier, *net operating income,* shows the amount of income available without regard to financing costs. It is useful in analyzing property that is free and clear of debt. The fourth tier, *before-tax cash flow* or *cash throw-off,* is the amount of cash available to the owner annually after subtracting all cash outflows. By rearranging financial statements for income-producing property consistently in these four tiers, the analyst is able to compare properties with each other and to compute certain financial ratios for the subject property. The ratios so derived can be of important use in the acquisition, operations, and resale aspects of ownership.

FINANCIAL RATIO ANALYSIS

Upon the acquisition of any business enterprise, it is important to compute certain financial ratios and to monitor them periodically. The analysis of ratios and their change from one period to the next can often detect facets of the enterprise that are within norms as well as those that become unhealthy. An alert businessman can use ratio analysis to compare potential acquisitions and select the one offering the greatest potential. By monitoring constantly changing ratios, it is possible to detect areas of weakness for both management and capital employment in order to bring ratios back to the desired balanced level of safety and risk.

For real estate investments, the 50 to 100% debt structures commonly used have an extreme influence on the prices paid and on ratios for both operating (cash flow) and capital accounts. For this reason, both operating ratios and capital account ratios will be described, as well as ratios of the two statements taken together. To be consistent, balance sheets and cash flow statements for the same property will be used in the description of ratio analysis that follows.

The pro forma cash flow statement in Table 7-4 and the simplified balance sheet in Table 7-5 provide an example of a real estate investment from which ratios can be computed. These ratios are defined in the next section and their significance is explained for each statement and for the two statements taken together.

Ratios that Apply to Balance Sheets

Improvement Ratio. The improvement ratio is the ratio of buildings and site improvements to the total price of the property, which is 90% ($450,000/$500,000 = 90%) in the example in Table 7-5. The improvement ratio generally indicates the fraction of the total cost that can be depreciated for income tax purposes. The higher the fraction that is depreciable, the greater the noncash tax deductions for depreciation. The complement of this ratio (10%) also indicates the fraction of price that is nondepreciable, nondestructible, and nonwasting, namely, land.

TABLE 7–5
Simplified Balance Sheet

ASSETS	
Building (and other improvements)	$450,000
Land	50,000
Total	$500,000
LIABILITIES AND EQUITY	
Mortgage (12% interest rate, 25-year term)	$400,000
Equity	100,000
Total	$500,000

The improvement ratio for real estate generally ranges from 60 to 95%. Shopping center sites typically need expensive land because of the need for access and driving convenience. Moreover, considerable land is needed for parking, and improvements are seldom higher than two stories for the convenience of shoppers. Consequently, shopping centers tend to have a relatively low improvement ratio. Downtown high-rise office buildings will have a higher ratio because of the ability to spread the land cost over more improvements. For example, if $100 per square foot is paid for land on which a 50-story building is erected, completely covering the land, the land cost accounts for only $2 per square foot of floor space for the improved property. The improvement ratio range for homesites may be wide. The same improvement may be built on a $10,000 homesite as on one costing upwards of $25,000.

Loan-to-Value Ratio

The loan-to-value ratio is the ratio of the mortgage debt to the property value, 80% ($400,000/$500,000 = 80%) in the example in Table 7-5. For developed property, although the ratio is actually of the loan to price, it is still referred to as the *loan-to-value ratio.* From a borrower's viewpoint, the ratio indicates the degree of leverage—higher ratios mean more leverage; lower ratios mean more equity.

From a lender's standpoint, higher ratios imply a greater risk of default and foreclosure. Institutional lenders have certain limits for loan-to-value ratios. Federal savings and loan associations, for example, cannot lend over 80% of the price of a home financed by a conventional loan unless there is mortgage insurance. (Mortgage insurance protects lenders in the event of default.) Life insurance companies in many states cannot lend over 75% of the value of property that they finance.

When a real estate developer arranges permanent financing for a planned project, lenders will commit to a certain loan amount based on the estimated property value when it is a finished product. The developer's construction cost is considered unimportant compared to the value of forecast income. Consequently, if development costs are low, the loan may exceed 100% of the project cost and still be within 75% of value.

Ratios That Affect the Cash Flow Statement

Suppose that the cash flow statement (pro forma) in Table 7-6 is generated by the same property as the balance sheet. The *vacancy and collection allowance ratio* is computed by dividing the allowance by the potential gross income. It is 5% ($5,000/$100,000 = 5%) as shown in Table 7-6, and its complement is the occupancy ratio, 95%.

TABLE 7-6
Real Estate Analyst Pro Forma Cash Flow Statement

Potential gross income	$100,000
Less: Vacancy and collection allowance	5,000
Plus: Miscellaneous income	3,000
Effective gross income	$ 98,000
Less: Operating expenses including replacement reserve	33,000
Net operating income	$ 65,000
Less: Debt service	50,555
Before-tax cash flow (cash throw-off)	$ 14,445

It is important to maintain a low vacancy ratio for real estate investments because most of the cash outflows are fixed regardless of the occupancy rate. Cash payments for real estate taxes, insurance, and debt service show little variation for most properties whether they are 25, 50, or 100% occupied. The marginal cost of renting to a tenant is small, so it is important that all or nearly all of the space be rented to tenants. For owners, it is preferable to have a 90 to 100% occupied building at slightly below market rate rentals, rather than to have an 80% or lower occupancy rate at above market rental rates.

Vacancy rates range widely with the type of property. Freestanding retail stores are either 100% occupied or they are vacant. Occupancy is imperative to provide rental income for the real estate owner. Hotels and resorts expect a lower effective occupancy rate than do stores or apartment buildings. For resorts, this is due to the seasonal nature of their business. Hotel occupancy may vary for this reason or because of weekend traffic and conventions. The national average hotel occupancy rate is 60 to 70%. Managers of apartments and office buildings generally try to maintain an occupancy rate of 93 to 97%. When leased property is fully occupied, with a waiting list, there is an obvious opportunity for a sharp rental rate increase that will provide greater rental income, despite an accompanying vacancy rate increase. Should the occupancy rate fall below the 80 to 85% mark, management may offer rental concessions to gain more tenants.

Market value appraisals should be based on rental rates and occupancy levels typical for that type of property in the local market. Superior or inferior management talents, although they do affect financial performance, do not affect the market value of property. Rental rates and vacancy assumptions for pro forma statements should be based on typically competent management in the local market.

The *break-even ratio,* also called the *default point,* is the minimum occupancy ratio needed to cover all of the cash expenses. It is computed by adding together operating expenses and debt service, then dividing by the potential gross income. Miscellaneous income is usually omitted. For the given figures, the break-even ratio is about 84%, as follows:

$$\frac{33{,}000 \text{ operating expense} + \$50{,}555 \text{ debt service}}{\$100{,}000 \text{ potential gross income}} = 83.55\%$$

Computation of the break-even ratio allows lenders and equity investors to determine the minimum occupancy rate at which there will be some cash throw-off. The term *default point* implies that the owner will default on the mortgage payment when the occupancy rate falls below that point. That suggestion is misleading. Nearly all investors will remain as owners at that point; most will continue when the ratio drops below the default point in the hope of income increases and/or capital gain upon resale.

The *operating expense ratio* is the ratio of operating expenses to potential gross income—33% ($33,000/$100,000 = 33%) in the example. Sometimes effective gross income is used as the denominator.

Operating expenses are necessary to maintain and run the property even if the property was paid for all in cash. Operating expenses include utilities, repairs, replacement reserves, real estate taxes, management, insurance, payroll, payroll taxes, advertising, postage, and other items. Excluded are debt service, depreciation, and income taxes.

The operating expense ratio will vary with each property. When property is subject to an absolutely net lease, the tenant pays all operating expenses, and the real estate owner incurs none. The ratio then is 0. The ratio may be below 15% on semi-net leased property where the owner is responsible for just certain items such as insurance or real estate taxes. For most apartments, the typical ratio is 33 to 45%, unless the rental rate includes all utilities; then it may go above 50%. Office buildings that include cleaning services and have other costly services to maintain, as on elevators, lobbies, and restrooms, will have a high (45 to 60%) operating expense ratio. Owners should continually monitor the ratio to detect and follow up on any changes. Such an analysis might pinpoint areas that need additional attention or opportunities for cost reductions.

An appraiser must attempt to estimate operating expenses under typically competent management. Any efficiencies (or extravagances) that differ from the norm are usually attributable to management talents, not to the property.

The *debt service coverage ratio* is found by dividing the annual debt service into the net operating income. In the example shown, the debt service coverage ratio is approximately 1.29 ($65,000/$50,555 = 1.2857). Like the break-even ratio, it offers information concerning the cushion of income (net operating income) over the fixed debt service payments.

The debt service coverage ratio offers important information that is of concern to both lenders and investors. Many lenders impose minimum coverage ratios, in addition to a minimum loan-to-value ratio. The minimum coverage ratio will vary according to each property, economic conditions, and the geographic area. For example, a 1.05 ratio may be an acceptable ratio for a free-standing store that is net-leased over a long term (nearly as long as the mortgage term) to an AAA credit-rated tenant. For a shopping center with 50% "credit" tenants, a 1.2–1.25 ratio would be appropriate. A property without strong tenants on long-term leases, such as apartments and some office buildings, will require a 1.25–1.50 ratio. The variability of hotel and resort income creates the need for a higher ratio. Recreational facilities such as racquette ball, tennis, and skating arenas typically deserve ratios of 1.5 to 2.5.

Ratios from Balance Sheet and Cash Flow Statements

Certain ratios are computed combining figures from both the balance sheet and cash flow statements. These ratios include the gross rent multiplier, overall rate of return, mortgage constant, equity dividend, and band of investment rates.

The *gross rent multiplier* (GRM) is the relationship of the purchase price to gross rental income. As it is defined, either potential gross income (before vacancies have been subtracted) or effective gross income (net of a vacancy allowance) may be used. Analysts should ascertain which rental income figures are used and be consistent. From Tables 7-5 and 7-6, the GRM is 5 computed as follows:

$$\frac{\text{Purchase price}}{\text{Rental income}} = \frac{\$500{,}000}{\$100{,}000} = 5$$

This method is one of the most widely used techniques for real estate purchase analysis. It is easy to compute and involves readily available figures. However, its widespread use stems from the ease of computation and comparison to other projects, not from its reliability as a measuring device.

The GRM fails to account for operating expense variations among projects, financing, resale prices, and income taxes. It disregards the amounts and timing of spendable income. The technique can be expected to be used for many years to come, but the reality is that it provides an unsophisticated, unrefined measure, one that should be used only to compare unmortgaged properties that are physically similar and in the same geographical area.

The *overall rate of return* (OAR) is computed by dividing the net operating income by the sales price. In the pro forma statement tables, Tables 7-5 and 7-6, the OAR is 13% ($65,000/$500,000 = 13%). This result is the rate of return on the entire purchase capital, without regard to the contributor (i.e., equity investor or mortgage lender), and without regard to the length or term over which income is forecast. From the OAR must come a return *on* the entire investment plus a return *of* the wasting portion of the investment.

This improves on the GRM in that operating expenses are taken into acount. The OAR is an acceptable ranking device for comparable, unmortgaged properties since it evaluates properties free and clear of any financing. However, when property is subject to an existing mortgage, a market-derived OAR fails to acknowledge the particulars of existing debt. With Ellwood's modifications, the OAR can include provisions for specific before-tax equity dividend rates, mortgage loans, loan-to-value ratios, and forecast property appreciation.

The *mortgage constant* is a ratio or percentage of the annual debt service to the amount borrowed. In the given example the ratio is about 12.64% ($50,555/$400,000 = .1263875). The mortgage constant is a function of the interest rate, full mortgage amortization term, and compounding frequency.

The constant percentage must exceed the mortgage face interest rate to assure loan amortization. The excess of the constant over the face interest rate of the mortgage reduces the loan principal balance. In the event that the constant exactly equals the mortgage interest rate, there will be a balloon payment of the full original principal. Should the constant be less than the interest rate, the loan payments do not cover the interest requirement. Consequently, unpaid interest will be added to the principal, and the balance will grow. Increasing principal balance loans are indeed rare. Nearly all loans require some amortization.

The *equity dividend rate* is the annual cash throw-off divided by the cash down payment. It is also called the *cash-on-cash return, percentage cash flow,* or *current yield.* For the given example, the rate is 14.44% ($14,445/$100,000 = .14445).

The equity dividend rate is widely used by investors who are considering property as an investment. This technique, although it disregards current income tax consequences, future appreciation (or value decline), mortgage reduction, and forecast net operating income changes, provides a measure of current performance to the equity investment. Some investors will determine the minimum required rate of cash return, then estimate the price to pay.

For example, if the minimum acceptable equity dividend rate is 20%, a cash throw-off of $14,445 would be divided by 20% (.2) to derive the maximum equity, $72,225 ($14,445/.20 = $72,225). To that, the $400,000 mortgage is added, which results in a price of $472,225. A required equity dividend rate of 12% results in an equity value of $120,375, and a property price of $520,375 including the $400,000 mortgage debt.

Some investors use the equity dividend rate as a device for ranking comparable investments. Others use it as a screening device with a minimum specified rate. More sophisticated investors will judge the trade-off between current equity dividend rates of return and forecast appreciation (or value decline) to estimate the appropriate price to pay.

The *band of investment* (BOI) technique is a method of deriving an overall rate of return from the annual mortgage constant and equity dividend rate. Given market information about those ratios, one can derive a market-based overall rate of return. The process involves weighting proportions for mortgage and equity positions and their respective currently required cash rates of return.

In the given example, the $400,000 mortgage represents 80% of the purchase capital. Its constant is 12.64%. Thus, the mortgage requires $.8 \times .1264 = .10112$ of the property's purchase price as an annual requirement. Equity paid is 20% of the purchase capital with a 14.44% requirement. Weighted, this becomes .02888 of the purchase price. Together, the band of investment overall rate is 13% (.10112 + .02888 = .13). This is summarized in Table 7-7.

TABLE 7-7
Band of Investment Technique

	Purchase Capital Contributed		Current Requirement		Weighted Rate
Mortgage	80%	×	.1264	=	.10112
Equity	20%	×	.1444	=	.02888
Total purchase capital weighted rate					.13 or 13%

The BOI approach is useful in estimating a value for property in the absence of adequate information on the sales prices of comparable properties and reliable net operating income information. However, in the absence of comparable sales, it is often difficult to judge required equity dividend rates, loan-to-value ratios, and other data that are required as inputs to derive a band of investment ratio. A summary of commonly used ratios is given in Table 7-8 on page 130.

SUMMARY

Traditional income property analysis for real estate requires financial statements that differ from statements prepared in accordance with generally accepted accounting principles. The nature of income from real estate does not easily lend itself to accounting-defined net income and asset appreciation received upon resale. Real estate analysts will therefore reconstruct financial statements to the effect of (1) considering only the most important balance sheet items at market value, not depreciated historical cost, (2) considering a cash flow statement with four tiers of income. If financial statements are consistently prepared, reconstructed statements can be used to derive meaningful relationships for the subject property and as a comparison device to apply against other properties. Examination of the relationship is called *ratio analysis*.

Ratio analysis is an important analytical tool for income-producing property. Upon the acquisition of an investment, bal-

TABLE 7–8

Commonly Used Ratios

Balance Sheet Ratios	
Improvement ratio:	Improvement cost / Total cost or value
Loan-to-value ratio:	Mortgage principal / Property value
Equity ratio:	Equity value / Property value
Cash Flow Statement Ratios	
Vacancy ratio:	Vacancy and collection allowance / Potential gross income
Break-even ratio:	Operating expenses and debt service / Potential gross income
Operating expense ratio:	Operating expenses / Potential or effective gross income
Debt coverage ratio:	Net operating income / Annual Debt Service
Balance Sheet and Cash Flow Statement Together	
Gross rent multiplier:	Purchase price / Gross rental income (potential or effective)
Overall rate of return:	Net operating income / Purchase Price
Mortgage constant:	Annual debt service / Mortgage principal
Equity dividend rate:	Cash throw-off / Equity investment

ance sheet ratios are useful in determining appropriate proportions of improvements to land, as well as the degree of leverage. Cash flow statements can provide such measures as the occupancy break-even point, appropriate vacancy rate, and operating expense ratio. The balance sheet and income statement, taken together, can provide meaningful results such as gross rent multipliers, overall rates of return, mortgage constants, and equity dividend rates.

Questions

1. Given a building with 10,000 leasable sq ft, 400 of which are vacant, the balance of space rented at $12 per sq ft, with an operating expense ratio of 45% of potential gross income, how much is:
   a. Potential gross income? $120,000
   b. Effective gross income? $115,200
   c. Net operating income? $66,000
2. An 8000-sq ft warehouse is net-leased at $3 per sq ft for the next 10 years. It is subject to a $100,000 mortgage, self-amortizing over 20 years at an 11% rate of interest with monthly payments. How much is:
   a. Net operating income? $24,000
   b. Annual debt service? 12,386.26
   c. Before-tax cash flow? 11,613.74
3. A $2,000,000 shopping center is purchased with a 75% loan-to-value ratio mortgage, payable over 25 years at 12% interest with monthly payments. It generates $205,000 annual net operating income. Land is considered to be worth $600,000; the balance of costs are land improvements.
   a. What is the improvement ratio? 70%
   b. What is the overall rate of return? .1025
   c. What is the annual mortgage constant? .126386897
   d. What is the equity dividend rate? .308393088
   e. What is the debt service coverage ratio? 1.081335723
4. Investors for apartments are seeking a 10% cash-on-cash return in the current market. Current interest rates on 30-year mortgages for this type of property are 12% with monthly payments. Lenders will fund up to a 75% loan-to-value ratio. What is the overall rate of return using the band of investment technique?

Essay Questions

1. Why do real estate analysts and appraisers reconstruct financial statements that have been prepared in conformity with generally accepted accounting principles?
2. What purposes can ratio analysis serve?
3. What is the significance of the debt service coverage ratio? Why does it vary with different improvements to real estate?

4. What is the gross rent multiplier? What are some of its shortcomings?
5. What is the overall rate of return? Discuss its importance.
6. Discuss the influence of exceptionally efficient management on the market value of real estate.

Chapter 8

Income Estimation and Forecasting

Expected financial benefits from an income-producing property must be estimated and verified by the analyst. The value of the property is based on its productivity over time. To estimate its productivity, the following questions must be considered:

1. How much is the net operating income?
2. When will the income be received?
3. For how long is this income expected?
4. How certain is the future income stream?
5. What are the net proceeds expected from the sale of the property at the end of its holding period?

Answers to these questions depend on the ability of the analyst to make accurate forecasts. These forecasts are based on many factors, including: market behavior and trends, quality and location of the site and improvements, announced changes to the land-use pattern and linkage connections, capability of property management, and national economic indicators. A forecast is based on the logical evaluation of how these underlying factors are likely to influence the quantity, quality, and duration of the income produced by the property.

Forecasts are not simple mechanical projections of numbers reflecting past economic behavior. Nor are these predictions specifying exactly what will happen in the future. Unfortunately, analysts do not have crystal balls that produce a perfect picture of future events. Forecasts are the best human judgments that can be made in the context of information available and trends suggested by economic theory and market behavior.

HOW MUCH IS THE NET OPERATING INCOME?

The following discussion is restricted to properties that are currently in existence and fully leased, and are subject to a normal market vacancy rate. Special problems associated with improvements not yet in existence, properties under construction, and properties in the leasing phase will be discussed in other chapters.

Appraisers use several sources to collect information necessary to construct the "stabilized income" of the property being investigated. These sources include income statements and other information provided by the owner, data about other comparable properties in the same market, and published reports by government agencies, universities, trade associations, and national or local service organizations. Stabilized income is not as important in investment analysis since actual revenues and expenditures are discounted in the actual year that these are expected to be received or paid.

Stabilized income is the income that is normally expected from the operation of the subject property during a typical year of the projection period, adjusted to a present value. Some expenditures, such as the recarpeting of the hallways in an apartment building, take place in large lump sums and can distort the income in a particular year. Likewise, some expenditures can be deferred and thus create an overstatement of the true income. Stabilized income is a smooth stream. Unusual lump sum revenues and expenditures, actual or deferred, are allocated over the appropriate useful lives of improvements or activities creating the cash flows.

To examine how an appraiser would deal with information provided by an owner, the following paragraphs will refer to a proforma income statement reproduced in Table 8-1. This income statement summarizes the cash flow of an apartment building during a prior year, which was considered by the owner to represent the normal operation of the project.

It is the analyst's job to determine the validity of the figures in the income statement. These figures may be distorted either intentionally or negligently. Distortions may also occur because the preparer of the income statement was unaware of conventional practices of reporting these figures in the real estate industry.

Ordinarily, the analyst will collect information from three basic sources at this stage of the investigation. These sources are: (1) information provided by the owner, (2) information collected by personal inspection and interviews, and (3) information collected from the market.

TABLE 8–1
Apartment Pro Forma Statement Provided by Owner

Potential Gross Income:

Units	*Description*	*Rate*			
4	1-Bedroom	@ $387	=	$1,548	
12	2-Bedroom	@ $464	=	$5,568	
4	3-Bedroom	@ $495	=	$1,980	
Monthly potential gross				$9,096	
Multiply by 12 months for annual amount					$109,152
Less: Vacancy allowance (3.5%)					3,820
Add: Miscellaneous income					5,000
Effective gross income					$110,332
Less: Current operating expenses					25,000
Net operating income					$85,332
Less: Debt service (interest and principal)					50,555
Before-tax cash flow (cash throw-off)					$34,777

The owner might be asked to provide the following types of data: utility bills, property tax assessments, insurance policies, receipts and reports from property management companies, title insurance policies, W-2 forms and other wage information for employees, copies of the actual leases in force, and income tax forms pertaining to the operation of the project. Any books or ledgers prepared by accountants should also be checked.

The analyst should personally inspect the physical asset. This inspection should also include the off-site and neighborhood environment. A checklist might be used to record features and the condition of the improvements. Any possible deferred maintenance problems should be noted as well as any needed capital improvements. Tenants might be interviewed to verify information in the leases. Questions may also disclose strengths or weaknesses of the property management function. In addition, public title records, planning documents, and other information provided by public agencies may be examined.

Market data on competitive properties will provide benchmarks against which to judge the subject property. This information might include market rental rates, vacancy rates, and typical expense ratios. Recent sales may be analyzed to determine capitalization rates suggested by the market.

Potential Gross Income

In estimating the potential gross income, the analyst must be able to distinguish between *economic rent* (market rent) and *contract rent.* Economic rent is the rent prevailing in the market for similar properties. It is the basis for establishing the market value of a property through the income approach. Contract rent is the sum agreed to between the landlord and each tenant. If the leases are for a long term, the contract rent serves as an important ingredient in calculating the investment value of the project. In the case of short-term agreements, the analyst will determine whether it is reasonable to assume that the contract rent will equal the economic rent at the time the leases are renegotiated. With a mix of several leases encumbering a property, the analyst should prepare a schedule with the expiration date of each lease. This will assist in estimating the quality and duration of the income stream.

In the hypothetical project shown in Table 8–1, The analyst will seek verification of the potential gross income reported. Information on comparable properties in the market indicates a normal monthly rental range of 43¢ to 48¢ per square foot of leasable space. The following calculations are performed to determine the rental per square foot for each of the categories of units in the subject property:

Units (size)	*Calculation*		*Rent per Square Foot (monthly)*
1-bedroom (800 sq ft)	\$387/800	=	.484
2-bedroom (900 sq ft)	\$464/900	=	.516
3-bedroom (1000 sq ft)	\$495/1000	=	.495

The analyst observes that the rental rates are slightly higher than the indicated market range. A physical inspection of the property does not reveal a more attractive project, nor is this project in an advantageous location that might justify the higher rates. In questioning the tenants it is discovered that a separate agreement exists giving each tenant one month's free rent at the end of each full year of occupancy. After adjusting for the rent concession, it is determined that the rate is more in line with the market. Rental concessions are common in some real estate markets. For this reason it is important not to assume that figures collected for a single month, or a single year, necessarily represent the true monthly rent over the entire term. The calculation used by the analyst to adjust the potential gross income is summarized in Table 8–2.

TABLE 8–2
Calculation to Adjust Potential Gross Income for a Project that Offers a Rent Concession

One-Bedroom:		
a. \$387 × 11/12 = \$355	b. \$355 × 12 × 4 =	\$ 17,040
Two-Bedroom:		
a. \$464 × 11/12 = \$425	b. \$425 × 12 × 12 =	\$ 61,200
Three-Bedroom:		
a. \$495 × 11/12 = \$453	b. \$453 × 12 × 4 =	\$ 21,744
Total potential gross income (rounded from \$99,984)		\$100,000

Note: Formulas used for adjustments:

a. $\dfrac{\text{Monthly rate} \times \text{number of months that rent was collected}}{\text{Total months in term}} = \text{Effective monthly rate}$

b. Effective monthly rate × 12 × number of units = Potential gross income

Less: Vacancy and Collection Allowance

The potential gross income is the total rent that would be received if every unit were fully occupied 100% of the time. From this figure must be subtracted the loss from the expected average vacancy rate and an allowance for bad debts.

Special problems can occur in analyzing projects occupied by a single tenant. The analyst would evaluate the credit worthiness of the tenant and the length of the lease term. The analyst would attempt to make a judgment on whether there was a high or low probability of a vacancy in the future and when this vacancy would be likely to occur.

Although the hypothetical project referred to in this chapter is fully occupied, this happy state of affairs is not likely to continue. The records of the project indicate that approximately 28% of the units have turned over during each year. This turnover is the same for each of the three categories of apartment size. The average period over which a unit remains vacant is 1.5 months. On the basis of this information the analyst confirms the owner's estimate of a 3.5% vacancy rate. A sample calculation is found in Table 8–3. The vacancy rate is consistent with the rate in the local market for similar properties.

TABLE 8–3
Vacancy Rate Calculation for the Two-Bedroom Units

Formula used:

$$\frac{\text{Percent of units turning over during year} \times \text{Average time period unit vacant}}{\text{Number of rental periods in year}} = \text{Average vacancy rate}$$

$$\frac{.28 \times 1.5 \text{ months}}{12 \text{ months/year}} = .035\text{/year or } 3.5\% \text{ vacancy rate}$$

Although the analyst is able to confirm the vacancy rate, several unpaid bills are found in a shoe box. Upon inquiry, the owner states that some tenants have left without paying their bills. It is hoped that someday they will settle their bills. This is not convincing to the analyst who finds it necessary to deduct 1.5% from the potential gross income to reflect this bad debt experience. This adjustment is also consistent with the market.

Add: Miscellaneous Income

Miscellaneous income includes such sources as the following: revenues from laundry rooms, concession income, parking space or storage bin rentals, and income from associated services integral to the operation of the project. This income is any money reasonably related to the ordinary operation of the project. It does not include money that is the result of individual entrepreneurial activities of the owner or property manager.

In the hypothetical income statement, $5,000.00 is noted in the miscellaneous income account. Of this money, $3,000.00 comes from the operation of a laundry room and soft drink machines at the swimming pool. The remaining $2,000.00 is earned from Tupperware parties held by the owner and from occasional baby-sitting services provided by the owner's spouse. This latter sum is not considered to be part of the project's earnings and is subtracted from the account.

Effective Gross Income

Effective gross income is the amount remaining after the vacancy rate and bad debt adjustments are subtracted from the potential gross income and after any justifiable miscellaneous income is added to it. In the revised hypothetical income statement, the effective gross income is $98,000.00 and not the $110,332.00 indicated in the owner's statement in Table 8-1.

Less: Current Operating Expenses

Current operating expenses may be divided into two categories—fixed and variable. *Fixed expenses* are those that do not change as the rate of occupancy changes. One example of this category of expenses is property taxes. It may be noted that property taxes change from year to year. However, this change is not normally related to the level of occupancy of a building. *Variable expenses* are directly related to the occupancy rate. As more people occupy and use a building, the variable expenses increase. Examples of variable expenses are heating bills, trash removal, and water usage.

Fixed expenses differ from project to project. These include property taxes, license and permit fees, and property insurance. There may also be a fixed component in expenses normally classified as variable. For example, there may be a fixed management cost whether a building is full or empty.

Variable expenses include cost of utilities, management fees, payroll and payroll taxes, security costs, annual landscaping costs, advertising fees, and the cost of supplies and fees for various services provided by local government or private contractors.

The analyst should compare the expenses reported to the experience of comparable properties. This information may be obtained from published reports of trade organizations such as the Building Owners and Managers Association or the National Apartment Association. Information may also be collected from interviews of property managers, appraisers, and other professionals.

Another way that income may be distorted is when the cost of minor repairs is capitalized instead of being expensed. In accounting, capitalization is a process of spreading costs over more than one year. If the cost is for some improvement that will benefit the earning potential of the property over several years, capitalization of the expenditure is justified. If, however, the expenditure is one for ordinary maintenance, capitalization will understate the expenses in the reported year. The contrary may also occur. A cost may be reported as an expense when it should be capitalized. In both situations the expense account will be distorted.

In stabilizing the expense account the analyst must determine whether any expense items are likely to change substantially in the future. Some items such as property taxes and energy costs can change substantially in a short time. The analyst should consider the nature of the external environment and underlying economic conditions in forecasting possible trends affecting these expenditures. When an examination is made of historical figures reporting the costs of operation, care should be taken to assure that reporting practices have been consistent throughout the period. For instance, during one year the owner might have paid all of the utilities; whereas during the next year a separate metering system might have been installed with the tenants being required to pay for some of the utilities.

In the hypothetical project, the analyst discovers that no provision has been made for a management fee. The owner has been managing the property personally, and no actual expenses have been incurred. It is a conventional practice in estimating market value to assume that a project is being operated by management typical in the market for similar projects. A typical management fee might range between 5 and 8% of rents collected for a project of similar size. The analyst decides to charge the account with a $6,000.00 management fee to fairly reflect the economic cost of this function.

Less: Replacement Reserve

Provisions must be included for the replacement of short-lived items. Such items as carpeting and some mechanical equipment need to be replaced periodically as these wear out. Since these expenditures are likely to occur in large lump sums, it is appropriate to set aside a portion of the expected cost every year to stabilize the expenses. The reason such an account exists is that as objects wear out the owner is suffering a hidden loss of income. If this economic fact is not reported, the net operating income will be overstated. In the owner's statement, no such replacement reserve was established. The analyst determines that $2,000.00 would be a proper allocation to this account, based on short-lived asset costs, useful lives, and the interest rate earned on funds in the reserve account.

Net Operating Income

Net operating income is estimated by subtracting from the effective gross income the operating expenses and the replacement reserve. Table 8–4 shows the reconstructed income statement for the hypothetical project. In the reconstructed statement the net operating income is $65,000 instead of the $85,332 reported by the owner. If the owner's figures had been used without verification, the value estimate would be 31% higher than would have been justified by the market. Each dollar by which the revenues are overstated or expenses understated causes a magnification in the final value estimate. For this reason great care must be taken to verify the accuracy of reported figures.

TABLE 8–4
Reconstructed Owner's Income Statement

Account	Reason for Adjustment	Owner's Statement	Adjusted Statement
Potential gross income		$109,152	$100,000
	Note: Owner's statement fails to adjust for concession of one month's free rent every year for each apartment.		
Less: Vacancy and collection allowance		3,820	5,000
	Note: Owner's statement did not include an allowance of 1.5% for bad debt collection.		
Add: Miscellaneous income		5,000	3,000
	Note: Owner's figures include $2,000 in income from Tupperware parties and other sources not connected with operation of project.		
Effective gross income		$110,332	$ 98,000
Less: Current operating expenses		25,000	31,000
	Note: Since owner personally managed the property, a $6,000 management cost was not included.		
Less: Replacement reserve		None	2,000
	Note: Owner had no replacement reserve account.		
Net operating income		$ 85,332	$ 65,000
Less: Debt service (interest and principal)		50,555	50,555*
Before-tax cash flow (cash throw-off)		$ 34,777	$ 14,445

* New investor will probably have a new financing structure. This table is included to show how the before-tax cash flow was prepared.

WHEN WILL THE INCOME BE RECEIVED?

The discussion of stabilized income streams was based on the assumption that a project was completed and fully in operation. Special problems occur when the appraiser is asked to determine the value of a project that is in the planning and design stage, the construction stage, or the leasing stage. Figure 8–1 illustrates projected cash flows for a typical project with multiple tenants over its investment life cycle. Each phase of the life cycle creates a unique set of forecasting problems for the analyst.

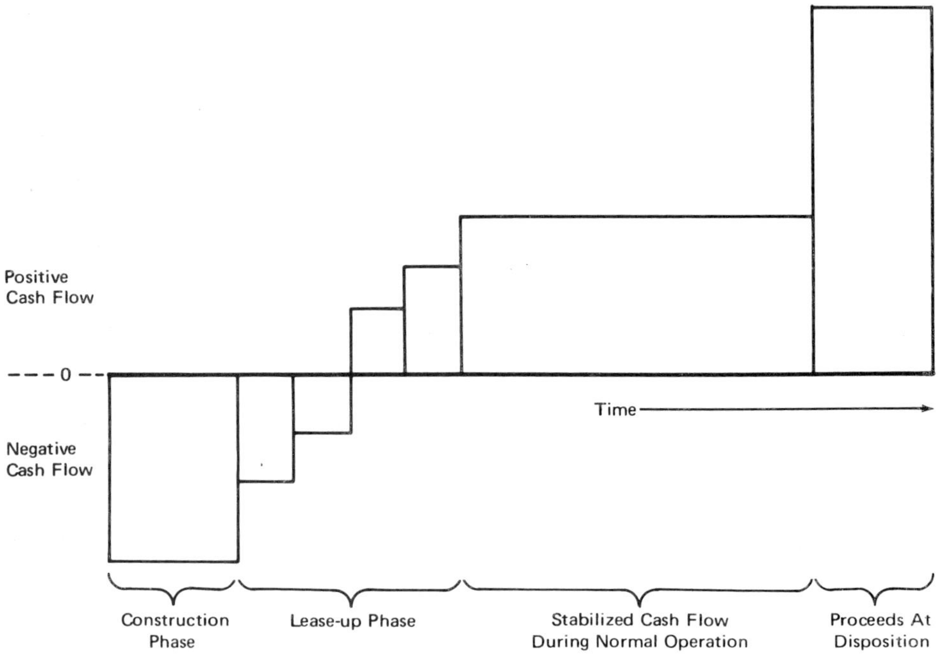

FIGURE 8–1. Expected Cash Flows During Investment Life Cycle of Project.

During the *construction stage,* cash flows are negative. The expected duration of the construction should be estimated. This can be done by examining schedules and expected times of completion. During this period, interest is to be paid to the construction lender, or added to the loan balance. Quite often this interest is based on a floating rate that is tied to the performance of the short-term prime interest rate. A forecast must be made assessing the expected range of the interest costs during this period. Use of the computer to perform a sensitivity analysis of the projected cash flows can provide early warning of possible problems if the interest rate is raised too high.

During the *leasing stage,* cash flows ordinarily will be negative at the beginning and will rise as the project is leased to various tenants. Some projects avoid this problem by preleasing the units before construction is completed. To forecast the expected leasing schedule the analyst will need to calculate the absorption rate in the market for the land use in question. Then an estimate must be made of the subject property's capture rate.

The *absorption rate* is a measurement of how many units of a particular land use will be purchased or leased during a particular time interval in a geographic area. For leased properties the following general formula is used:

$$\text{Absorption rate} = \frac{\text{Units leased per period}}{\text{Number of units available for lease in market}}$$

The higher the absorption rate, the more likely it is that the subject property will have a short leasing period. A low absorption rate is a danger sign that there may have been overbuilding of similar land uses in the market. If the absorption rate is estimated during the planning and design stage, adjustments can be made to the scale and phasing of the proposed subject property. There is less flexibility after construction contracts have been awarded and construction has commenced.

The *capture rate* is a measurement of the expected leasing experience of the subject property. The capture rate can also be calculated for projects that can be sold in increments such as residential condominiums or individual offices in a large office park. The capture rate is a function of the leasing skills of the property manager and the competitive position of the project in the context of the market. The general formula for the capture rate of leased properties is:

$$\text{Capture rate} = \frac{\text{Units in project leased per period}}{\text{Number of competitive units leased per period in market}}$$

It should be evident that the earlier a project is able to generate positive cash flow, the more value can be attributed to the income stream. Because of the nature of compound interest on amounts received in the future, the early stages of a project have a heavy weight in the determination of the investment value. Care should be taken to forecast cash flows during these early stages.

FOR HOW LONG IS THIS INCOME EXPECTED?

The analyst must be able to forecast the length of time over which the subject property is expected to produce income. For investment value this period is determined by various considerations, including the intended use of the property, the investor's tax situation, and the investor's business strategy. Normally, for market value appraisals, the analyst should attempt to evaluate the expected holding period of the typical investor. This is important in order to estimate the period for capital recovery where appropriate.

In evaluating the forecast income during the holding period, a judgment must be made about the trend of the income stream. Is it likely to remain stable? Is it expected to go up? Is it expected to go down? Because of the nature of compound interest, special care should be taken to forecast any short-term changes affecting the subject property. A miscalculation of the holding period is more serious if the annuity is a short-term annuity than if it is a long-term annuity. Consider Table 8–5.

TABLE 8–5
Value of Annuities of One Dollar Discounted at 10% for Different Periods

Time (years)	5	10	15	20	25	30	35	40
Value	3.79	6.14	7.61	8.51	9.07	9.43	9.64	9.78
Percentage difference between periods		62%	24%	12%	7%	4%	2%	1%

Making a mistake of 5 years between the 5 and 10-year annuity periods would result in a 62% error. The same mistake between the 35- and 40-year annuities would be a mistake of approximately 1%. Misjudgments in forecasting resale proceeds are also reduced as the projection period lengthens. It can thus be shown that forecasting mistakes in the near future are more serious than similar mistakes in the distant future. This explains the necessity for careful inspection of the subject property and evaluation of current market trends and conditions before forecasts are undertaken. It should be noted that forecasts for the near future are less likely to be in error by a significant margin than long-term forecasts.

HOW CERTAIN IS THE FUTURE INCOME STREAM?

Even the best available data forecasts contain elements of uncertainty. This uncertainty is commonly referred to as *risk*. Risk is the probability that forecast income and other benefits will not achieve expectations. Most people tend to think of risk as the possibility of loss. It is actually a more comprehensive concept. Risk also includes the idea that one might receive more than expected.

In normal real estate markets, people tend to be risk-adverse. As their perception of risk increases, a higher rate of return is required as compensation. The behavior of investors usually follows the pattern diagrammed in Figure 8–2. People require compensation for the use of their money even if no risk is perceived. This interest is measured by the "risk-free rate." A proxy for the risk-free rate might be U.S. government-backed securities. Built on top of this rate are the additional yields necessary as compensation for increased risks undertaken in an investment. There also seems to be a curvilinear relationship between risk and the required yield. As risks become too high, a disproportionately higher rate of return may be required.

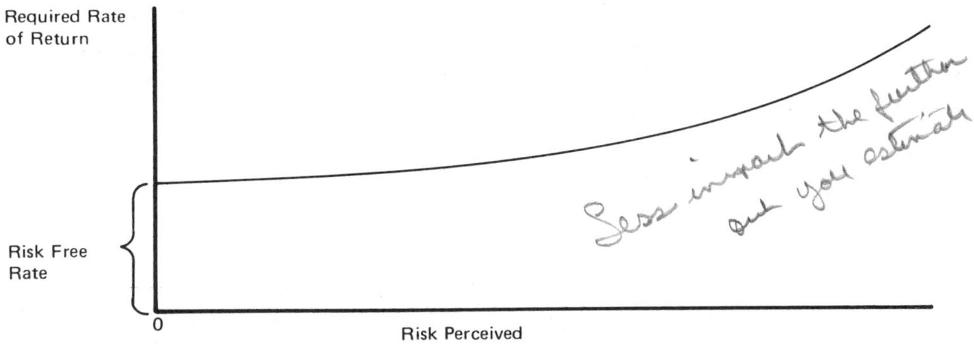

FIGURE 8–2. Relationship of Risk Perceived and Required Rate of Return. Investments that are relatively risk free, such as federally insured savings accounts, do not require as high a rate of return as other investments which have greater risk. As perceived risk increases, a higher rate of return must be expected to compensate for the increased risk.

The reason for this discussion is that if an annuity stream is perceived as being more risky than another, it would have a lower value in the marketplace. Thus investors are concerned not only about the quantity and duration of income streams but also about the quality of the expected cash flows.

Systematic risk prevails on the overall market level. The value of a particular income-producing property may be related to the functioning of economic and institutional conditions on the market level. Examples of this category of risk include possibilities of the following kinds: overbuilding of competitive properties, the closing of a manufacturing plant representing a large portion of the area employment base, passage of environmental restrictions, and/or imposition of rent controls. *Unsystematic risk* is that which is specifically related to the subject property and is independent of risks affecting similar properties. Examples of this type of risk are possibilities of the following kinds: cracks in the foundation, condemnation of the land for public acquisition, bankruptcy of the major tenant, destruction of the structure by fire, and/or development of a nearby incompatible land use.

Static risk is the possibility of loss from physical or human events that can be actuarially anticipated. In other words, these are possible events for which an insurance company would be willing to assume the risk in exchange for the payment of premiums. *Dynamic risks* have been defined as "profit or loss of entrepreneurial opportunity and economic competition."[1] Dynamic risks occur because of changes in the land use pattern and linkage connections. The actions or inactions of competitors in the market can also create opportunities for losses as well as increased profits.

These risks can affect various aspects of a subject property that are important to investors. These risks include:

1. Principal.
2. Income.
   a. Market rentals.
   b. Occupancy rates.
   c. Costs of operation.
3. Interest rates.
4. Availability of mortgage financing.
5. Appreciation.
6. Taxation of income and capital gains.
7. Purchasing power of money.

The ability to forecast potential risks affecting the future income stream and other expected investment benefits becomes more difficult as the time frame of the forecast increases. Figure 8–3 illustrates that the range of uncertainty, both on the upside and the

[1] James A. Graaskamp, *A Guide to Feasibility Analysis* (Chicago, Ill.: Society of Real Estate Appraisers, 1970), p. 32.

downside, increases over time at a compounding rate. The analyst may feel more confident with short-range projections than with long-range projections. Forecasts attempting to specify prices or market conditions 20 or 30 years in the future should be viewed with skepticism.

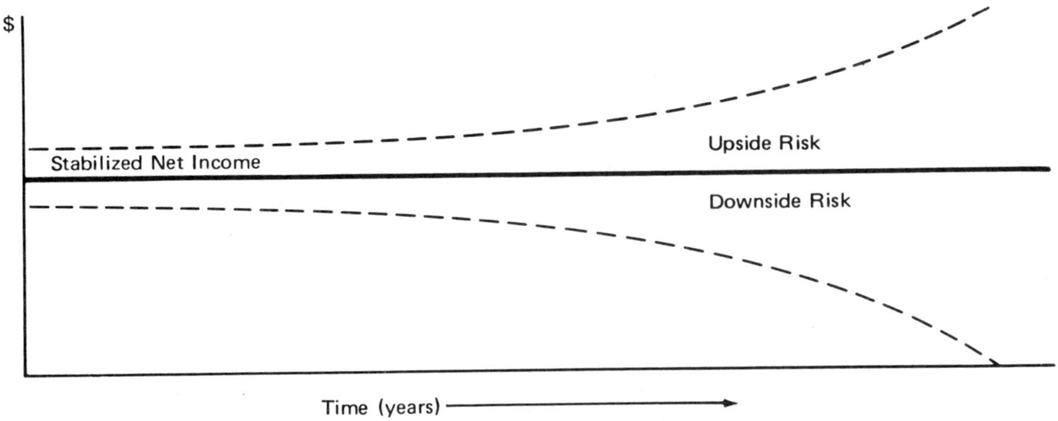

FIGURE 8–3. Range of Uncertainty Increases Over Time.

Risk Categories

There are two sets of risk categories. The first set consists of "systematic" and "unsystematic" risks. The second set consists of "static" and "dynamic" risks.

The terms "systematic risk" and "unsystematic risk" are adapted from similar concepts in finance literature on portfolio management.

WHAT ARE THE NET PROCEEDS EXPECTED FROM THE SALE OF PROPERTY AT THE END OF ITS HOLDING PERIOD?

One of the most difficult tasks for the forecaster is to estimate accurately the net proceeds expected from the resale of the subject property at the end of its holding period. The following factors should be considered.

Possible Appreciation of the Land

Depending on what happens to the surrounding land use pattern, the land could increase or decrease in value. For example, if the local government plans to build a rapid transit station in proximity to the subject site, the highest and best use for the land will probably change, and its value will change accordingly. Conditions of future scarcity of buildable sites with similar locational attributes might also be viewed as a possible upward value indication. On the other hand, if the land use succession is toward blight, the land may actually decline in value.

Depreciation of the Improvements

In real economic terms, the value of improvements is expected to decline over time. The rate of this depreciation can be determined by examining the depreciation experience of similar properties.

Amortization

The analyst should determine how much of the principal will be repaid at the end of the holding period for any mortgages encumbering the property. This will affect the total amount that the owner will receive from the proceeds of the expected sales price.

Transaction Costs

At the time of the future disposition, various transaction costs will typically be paid by the owner. These include real estate brokerage commissions, transfer taxes, discount points, and other closing charges not normally passed on to the buyer.

Capital Gains and Recapture

Because income tax laws are subject to the political process, over the long run there is no certainty as to how much tax will need to be paid at the time of disposition. Over the short run, the tax rules are specified and taxes can be determined with reasonable accuracy. Income taxation is more fully discussed in Chapter 14.

Inflation Rate

Consideration must be given to expected inflationary pressures on real estate values. In times of high inflation, failure to consider the implications of inflation is like making measurements with a rubber ruler.

SUMMARY

Estimation of future income or forecasting is not a simple mechanical process. Forecasting depends on logic and analysis of data collected about the subject property and the conditions of the market. Determination is made on the basis of perceived trends in the market and plans that have been announced for the future.

In this chapter, five questions involving income-producing properties were explored. To answer these questions is the goal of real estate property forecasts:

1. How much is the net operating income?
2. When will this income be received?
3. For how long is this income expected?
4. How certain is the future income stream?
5. What are the net proceeds expected from the sale of the property at the end of its holding period?

Questions

1. An analyst has been provided with the following information. An apartment project has fifty 2-bedroom units. The rental rate for each unit is $400.00 per month. All leases are for one-year terms. When a new tenant signs a lease, a black and white television set is given to the tenant as a welcoming gift. The cost of the television is $100.00. On the average, 40% of the units turn over during the year. The average time necessary to fill an empty unit is two months. In addition, there is a bad debt collection rate of one-half of 1% of all rents due. The apartment manager receives $5,000.00 a year plus a free unit in the complex to live in. He makes an additional $4,000.00 each year filling out income tax forms for the tenants. Fixed expenses are $50,000.00 and variable expenses are $200.00 per occupied unit per year. An additional 3% of the effective gross income is set aside as a replacement reserve. Fill out the following income statement:

   a. Potential gross income.
   b. Less: Vacancy and bad debt allowance.
   c. Add: Miscellaneous income.
   d. Effective gross income.

e. Less: Current operating expenses.

f. Less: Replacement reserve.

g. Net operating income.

2. A building has new carpeting installed with an expected life of seven years and costing $10,000.00. How should this expenditure be handled in estimating stabilized cash flow?
3. If there are 5,000 empty apartment units in a market that is expected to absorb 100 units each month, what is the absorption rate?
4. If the subject property can gain five new tenants each month, what is its capture rate?

Essay Questions

1. What factors might cause the remaining economic life of a project to change?
2. Why is the chronological age of a project not always a good indication of its effective age?
3. Why do real estate forecasts greatly depend on human judgment?

Chapter 9

Analysis of Financing Instruments

The valuation and analysis of financing instruments provide an excellent foundation for the analysis of income real estate. There are two reasons for this. First, the income generated by most mortgages is more certain in amounts and timing than that provided by most equity interests in real estate. Second, application of the mechanics of compound interest to mortgages is cut and dried. Prices for mortgages are clearly displayed in financial markets. In contrast, the sale of most real estate equities and the calculation of the prices paid will be determined by local practices combined with substantial negotiation, variations in prior management practice that can produce inconsistent historical rental income and expense, and differing opinions in the forecast of future income, expense, and resale values. This chapter concentrates on the valuation of *permanent mortgages,* as a background for the analysis of an income stream.

PERMANENT MORTGAGES

Most *permanent* mortgages used in the United States since the 1930s are of the level-payment, self-amortizing type. A lender decides the maximum loan principal amount based on a fraction (often 75 or 80%) of the property's value, fixes the maximum term (which will be shorter than the property's estimated useful life), and offers an interest rate based on prevailing market conditions. The periodic (usually monthly) mortgage payment is then computed using those three factors, which are:

1. Principal.
2. Term (remaining).
3. Interest.

Considering the periodic payment as a fourth factor, there are four factors in any loan. When any three of the four are known, the fourth factor can be determined.

Solve for Payment

The first factor to be solved for is the payment. Suppose the three known factors are as follows:

Principal	= $400,000
Term	= 25 years (300 months)
Interest rate	= 12% (1% monthly)

From these factors it is apparent that the monthly payment must be greater than $4,000. This is because the interest rate is 1% per month, and the principal $400,000. Interest alone will be $4,000 for the first month (1% of $400,000 equals $4,000), so the payment must exceed $4,000 in order to amortize the principal. It is calculated that a total monthly principal and interest payment of $4,212.90 will be sufficient. Of the $4,212.90 payment in the first month, the extra $212.90 will reduce the principal. The loan's outstanding principal balance will then be $399,787.10 ($400,000 minus $212.90). For the second month, the interest will be $3,997.87 (1% of the $399,787.10 principal), and the $215.03 difference between the payment and interest will go toward reducing the principal balance. As the loan progresses, more of each $4,212.90 payment will be applied toward principal, and less toward interest. At the end of 300 months, the loan will be fully paid off.

The monthly $4.212.90 payment for this loan was calculated by considering two elements: (1) the interest, which is a return *on* the lender's invested principal, and (2) the capital recovery, which is a return or recovery *of* the lender's invested principal. The 12% annual interest rate is really 1% monthly or .01 in decimal form. Added to this 1% is the sinking fund factor that will recover the principal (capital) over 25 years (300 months) by reinvestment at the same 12% rate of earnings (1% per month) that the mortgage bears. The monthly sinking fund factor is .0005322 (column 3 of 12% tables with monthly compounding). Thus the total monthly payment required for a return *on* and *of* the self-amortizing 25-year loan at 12% is .01 + .0005322 = .0105322 (see column 6). Multiplied by $400,000 of principal, this results in a monthly payment of $4,212.90, which, for the first month, includes $4,000 interest and $212.90 (sinking fund) principal repayment. As a check, by reinvesting $212.90 per month, at a 1% per month interest rate, in 300 months a total of $400,000 will be amassed. This can be shown by multiplying the $212.90 by 1878.8466 (column 2, accumulation of one per period), which almost exactly equals $400,000.

Financial calculators are handy in calculating mortgage payments. Given the above facts:

Input principal	$400,000		PV
Input rate	12 ÷ 12	=	%i
Input term	25 × 12	=	n
Compute	PMT	Result: $4,212.90	

Loan Constants

A *mortgage loan constant* is the relationship between the required annual payments of a loan and the original principal of a loan. For example, monthly payments of $4,212.90 total $50,555 in one year. The annual payment of $50,555 divided by $400,000 of principal gives a rate of .126387, or 12.6387%. That rate is called *an annual loan constant* because it must be paid every year. Constants include interest and principal retirement; therefore constants must exceed the loan's face interest rate.

The loan constant can be found in column 6 of compound interest tables. Longer amortization terms and/or lower interest rates reduce the constant. Shorter terms and higher interest rates raise the constant. Table users must be careful to multiply monthly constants by 12 to derive an annual constant.

The constant is a convenient tool to quickly determine the trade-offs of amortization terms and interest rates, and to compute the debt service. At a given interest rate and amortization term, the constant is the required payment per dollar borrowed. The constant can be multiplied by the principal to determine the actual loan payment.

Many borrowers seek the lowest possible constant to minimize current cash outflows, even though it means paying more interest and reducing equity build-up through mortgage liquidation payments. A chart of loan constants is presented in Table 9-1.

Solve for Principal

Whenever the interest rate, remaining term, and monthly payment are known, it is possible to solve for the unpaid principal balance.

TABLE 9-1

Loan Constant Chart

AMORT. TERM	INTEREST RATES 7%	8%	9%	10%	11%	12%	13%	14%	15%
1	103.83	104.39	104.94	105.50	106.06	106.62	107.18	107.75	108.31
2	53.73	54.27	54.82	55.38	55.93	56.49	57.05	57.62	58.18
3	37.05	37.60	38.16	38.72	39.29	39.86	40.43	41.01	41.60
4	28.74	29.30	29.86	30.44	31.01	31.60	32.19	32.79	33.40
5	23.76	24.33	24.91	25.50	26.09	26.69	27.30	27.92	28.55
6	20.46	21.04	21.63	22.23	22.84	23.46	24.09	24.73	25.37
7	18.11	18.70	19.31	19.92	20.55	21.18	21.83	22.49	23.16
8	16.36	16.96	17.58	18.21	18.85	19.50	20.17	20.85	21.53
9	15.01	15.62	16.25	16.89	17.55	18.22	18.90	19.60	20.31
10	13.93	14.56	15.20	15.86	16.53	17.22	17.92	18.63	19.36
11	13.06	13.70	14.35	15.02	15.71	16.41	17.13	17.86	18.61
12	12.34	12.99	13.66	14.34	15.04	15.76	16.50	17.25	18.01
13	11.74	12.40	13.08	13.77	14.49	15.22	15.97	16.74	17.52
14	11.22	11.90	12.59	13.30	14.03	14.78	15.54	16.33	17.12
15	10.79	11.47	12.17	12.90	13.64	14.40	15.18	15.98	16.80
16	10.41	11.10	11.81	12.55	13.31	14.08	14.88	15.69	16.52
17	10.08	10.78	11.51	12.25	13.02	13.81	14.62	15.45	16.29
18	9.79	10.50	11.24	12.00	12.78	13.58	14.41	15.24	16.10
19	9.53	10.25	11.00	11.78	12.57	13.38	14.22	15.07	15.94
20	9.30	10.04	10.80	11.58	12.39	13.21	14.06	14.92	15.80
21	9.10	9.85	10.62	11.41	12.23	13.06	13.92	14.80	15.69
22	8.92	9.67	10.45	11.26	12.09	12.94	13.80	14.69	15.59
23	8.76	9.52	10.31	11.13	11.96	12.82	13.70	14.59	15.50
24	8.61	9.38	10.18	11.01	11.86	12.72	13.61	14.51	15.43
25	8.48	9.26	10.07	10.90	11.76	12.64	13.53	14.45	15.37
26	8.36	9.15	9.97	10.81	11.68	12.56	13.47	14.39	15.32
27	8.25	9.05	9.88	10.73	11.60	12.50	13.41	14.33	15.27
28	8.16	8.96	9.80	10.66	11.54	12.44	13.36	14.29	15.23
29	8.07	8.88	9.72	10.59	11.48	12.39	13.31	14.25	15.20
30	7.98	8.81	9.66	10.53	11.43	12.34	13.27	14.22	15.17
31	7.91	8.74	9.60	10.48	11.38	12.30	13.24	14.19	15.15
32	7.84	8.68	9.54	10.43	11.34	12.27	13.21	14.16	15.13
33	7.78	8.62	9.49	10.39	11.30	12.24	13.18	14.14	15.11
34	7.72	8.57	9.45	10.35	11.27	12.21	13.16	14.12	15.09
35	7.67	8.52	9.41	10.32	11.24	12.19	13.14	14.11	15.08
36	7.62	8.48	9.37	10.29	11.22	12.17	13.12	14.09	15.07
37	7.57	8.44	9.34	10.26	11.19	12.15	13.11	14.08	15.06
38	7.53	8.41	9.31	10.23	11.17	12.13	13.10	14.07	15.05
39	7.49	8.37	9.28	10.21	11.16	12.12	13.08	14.06	15.04
40	7.46	8.34	9.26	10.19	11.14	12.10	13.07	14.05	15.04

* This chart shows the annual total of 12 monthly payments required to amortize a $100.00 loan over the amortization term. To use, find the intersection of the amortization term with the interest rate. The result is one year of payments (12 payments) per $100.00 borrowed.

For example, suppose that the three known factors have the values below:

Term (remaining)	= 25 years (300 months)
Interest rate	= 12% (1% per month)
Monthly payment	= $4,212.90

To determine the principal balance, simply multiply one monthly payment by the annuity factor (column 5) for the remaining term of the loan. With the given factors, the annuity factor is 94.946551 for monthly payment loans. The computation (94.946551 × $4,212.90) gives a principal balance of almost exactly $400,000. This computation provides the present value of the loan's payments.

A new loan that is issued at its face principal and at a specified interest rate requires a certain monthly payment. That payment is an annuity. The present value of that annuity, at that interest rate, is the loan principal balance.

The present principal balance of an aged loan can be found similarly. Consider the face interest rate, monthly payment, and *remaining* term. For example, when the mortgage considered above is 5 years old, it will have 20 remaining years. Find its present balance by multiplying the annuity factor at 20 years by its monthly payment. In this example the balance is $382,613.11 ($4,212.90 × 90.819416). Selected balances for this loan (originally a 25-year loan) at various ages are shown in Table 9–2.

TABLE 9–2
Selected Balances for a $400,000 Loan at 12% Interest

Age (End of Year)	*Remaining Term*	*Annuity Factor*		*Monthly Payment*		*Principal Balance*
1	24	94.305647	×	$4,212.90	=	$397,300.26
2	23	93.583461	×	$4,212.90	=	394,257.76
3	22	92.769683	×	$4.212.90	=	390,829.39
4	21	91.852697	×	$4,212.90	=	386,966.22
5	20	90.819416	×	$4,212.90	=	382,613.11
10	15	83.321664	×	$4,212.90	=	351,025.83
15	10	69.700522	×	$4,212.90	=	293,641.32
20	5	44.955038	×	$4,212,90	=	189,391.07
25	0	0	×	$4,212.90	=	0

To find the remaining principal balance on a loan using a financial calculator, perform the following:

Input periodic payment	$4,212.90	[PMT]
Input periodic interest rate	12 ÷ 12 =	[%i]
Input remaining term (periods)	12 × 25 =	[n]
[Compute] [PV]	Result: $400,000	

Solve for Term

The principal payments, when reinvested in a fund that earns interest at the same rate of interest as the mortgage bears, will ultimately equal the remaining principal of the loan. That time period is the remaining term of the loan.

It is possible to solve for the term of a loan when the three other factors are given. Even in the absence of a financial calculator, there are several methods. One involves the use of a set of tables. A second involves preparing an amortization schedule month by month. Logarithms may also be used.

Suppose the following information about a mortgage loan is given:

Principal balance	= $400,000
Interest rate	= 12% (1% per month)
Monthly payment	= $4,212.90
Remaining term	= ?

To solve using tables, divide the monthly payments by the loan principal balance. Consider the result, and search in column 6 of the tables for the figure closest to it. Applied to these facts, divide: $4,212.90/$400,000.00 = .0105322. Search column 6 of the monthly compound interest tables at a 12% interest rate until the number closest to that result is located. It is at 25 years, so that is the term of the loan. Often the figure derived by dividing the monthly payment by the principal will not be precisely the same as the one printed in the tables. In that case, find the numbers on the table that bracket the subject figures; the remaining term of the loan is between the years represented by the bracketing amounts. Further interpolation will not provide the exact term because figures for different years in the tables do not have a linear relationship with each other. Interpolation will generally point out the nearest year, but not the exact remaining life.

The remaining term of an aged (existing) loan can be found in a similar fashion. Divide the monthly P&I (principal and interest) payment by the present outstanding balance. Using the table page at the mortgage's face rate of interest, find the figure derived, in column 6 of the tables.

For example, suppose that the P&I payment is $4,212.90, and the present principal balance is $351,025.83. By division, the result is .01200168 ($4,212.90/$351,025.83 = .01200168), which is found in column 6 at 15 years on the 12% rate table with monthly payments. That mortgage, therefore, has 15 years left for full amortization.

Financial calculators can be used to find the term as follows:

Input principal	$400,000		PV
Input rate	12 ÷ 12	=	%i
Input monthly payment	$4,212.90		PMT
Compute n	Result: 300		

The result is the remaining term in months.

Solve for Rate

Solving for any interest rate is a trial-and-error process. Self-amortizing level-payment loans ease the process because all monthly payments will be equal. The interest rate is the rate at which the discounted present value of outflows (payments) equals the present value of inflows (principal balance), or vice versa.

To find the rate, divide the monthly payment by the principal; then find the resulting factor (quotient) in column 6 of the tables at the remaining term. For example, given this data:

Principal	= $400,000
Term	= 25 years (300 months)
Monthly payment	= $4,212.90
Rate	= ?

To find the rate, first divide $4,212.90/$400,000 = .0105322. Then, search the pages of the tables until column 6 of a monthly payment table at 300 months shows or brackets the figure. It is on the 12% interest rate page in this situation.

Calculator use requires the following steps:

Input principal	$400,000		PV
Input term (months)	25 × 12	= 300	n
Input monthly payment	$4,212.90		PMT
Compute %i	Result: .01		

Wait for the result, which is a monthly rate. Result × 12 = annual rate.

Loan Schedules

Amortization is the process of liquidating a debt. An *amortization schedule* shows, month by month or year by year, the principal balance of a loan. It further indicates that amount of each payment that applies to interest (return *on* investment) and to principal. A schedule may be computed in several ways. The easiest to understand is the long method, which is shown in Table 9-3.

TABLE 9-3
Long Method for Amortization Schedule (Principal = $400,000; Rate = 12% or (1% per month); Term = 25 years; Payment = $4,212.90)

Month	Monthly Payment	Interest at 1% per Month	Principal Retirement	End of Month Balance
0				$400,000.00
1	$4,212.90	$4,000.00	$ 212.90	$399,787.10
2	$4,212.90	3,997.87	215.03	399,572.07
3	$4,212.90	3,995.72	217.18	399,354.89
↓	↓	↓	↓	↓
298	$4,212.90	123.90	4,089.00	8,301.07
299	$4,212.90	83.02	4,129.88	4,171.19
300	$4,212.90	41.71	4,171.19	0
Total			$400,000.00	

Interest is computed each month based on the principal balance outstanding at the end of the previous month. The portion of the monthly payment that exceeds interest reduces the principal balance from its balance of the preceding month. As the loan ages, more of the periodic payment applies toward principal. Eventually, the loan will be retired.

A short-cut procedure for finding the principal balance at any time was described earlier. It involves valuing the mortgage payments at the mortgage's face rate of interest for the remaining term. A portion of Table 9-2 is shown below:

Age (End of Year)	Remaining Term	Annuity Factor		Monthly Payment		Principal Balance
1	24	94.305647	×	$4,212.90	=	$397,300.26
2	23	93.583461	×	4,212.90	=	394,257.76

Using principal balances of different times, it is possible to determine how much of the payment was applied toward principal during a certain time period, by subtracting one balance from another, and therefore how much interest was paid. During year 2, \$3,042.50 (\$397,300.26 minus \$394,257.76 equals \$3,042.50) was paid toward principal. Total payments during the year were 12 × \$4,212.90, which comes to \$50,554.80. Subtracting \$3,042.50 from \$50,554.80 gives the interest paid in year 2, which is \$47,512.30. A graphic presentation of mortgage payment application is shown in Figure 9-1.

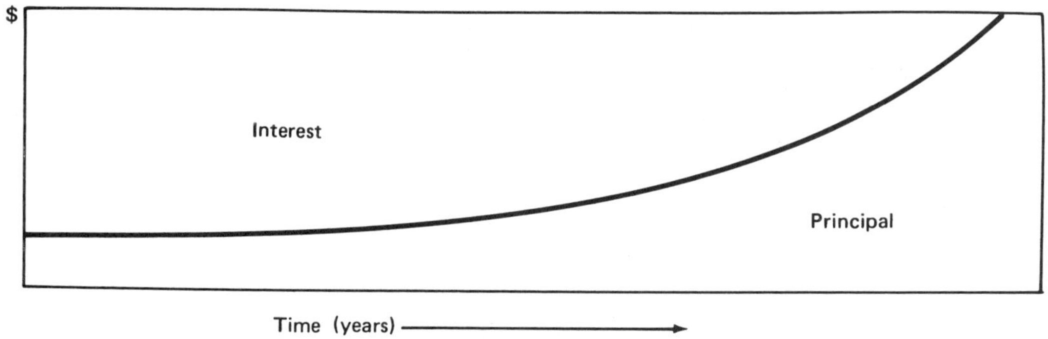

FIGURE 9-1. Mortgage Payment Application.

Loan Discounts and Loan Yields

Real estate mortgage loans are often offered at a discount to borrowers, and mortgage loans are frequently sold at a discount to mortgage investors. In both cases, the loan's face interest rate is not its true rate of return (yield to maturity) on a discounted principal.

Discounts on loans are stated as *points*. Each point is 1% of the principal balance. For example, a \$400,000 loan that carries 3 discount points means that the lender advances 97% of the \$400,000 face principal when the loan is issued (97% of \$400,000 = \$388,000), but requires the full \$400,000 to be repaid, together with interest on the full \$400,000. Thus, the lender increases the return on investment (yield to maturity) by discounting the loan.

To calculate the yield to maturity on the actual cash advanced (which is also the true effective interest rate to the borrower), consider three *actual* factors, which are:

Actual loan (cash advanced)	= \$388,000
Term	= 25 years (300 months)
Monthly payment	= \$4,212.90

Divide the monthly payment by the cash advanced; then search column 6 of table pages to find the resulting factor. For this example, the factor is .0108579 ($4,212.90/$388,000 = .0108579). The true interest rate is about 12.44% by interpolation from tables.

As a rule of thumb, each discount point is equivalent to adding about 1/8% to the face interest rate of a 25- or 30-year mortgage. So, 3 points charged on a 12% face interest rate mortgage is roughly equivalent to a 12 3/8% face interest rate mortgage without points.

A financial calculator can offer a more precise answer, computed as follows:

Input actual loan	$388,000		[PV]
Input term	25 × 12	=	[n]
Input payment	$4,212.90		[PMT]
[Compute] [%i]	Result: 1.0365766	=	monthly rate
	× 12	=	12.44% annual rate

Compute Loan Discounts, Given Yield

Maximum face rates of mortgage loans may be held to a ceiling, but higher yields are required. The rate ceiling may be imposed by law (FHA, VA, usury) or for property marketing purposes. When this is the situation, loans must be discounted so that they offer appropriate yields. The question is, "How many points are required to get the desired yield?"

For example, suppose $400,000 is the maximum face principal offered for a loan based on a percentage of the property's appraised value. The amortization term will be 25 years, and the ceiling interest rate is 12%. The monthly payment is then $4,212.90. The yield rate required to attract lenders is 12½%. A loan discount is required to raise the 12% face rate up to a 12½% yield.

To compute the actual principal (cash advance) to be loaned, multiply the monthly payment by the annuity factor at the desired yield (interest) rate. The maximum actual principal to be advanced is then $4,212.90 × 91.713322 = $386,379.05. The loan discount is the difference between the $400,000 face principal and the $386,379.05 actual loan, which is a $13,620.95 discount. The $13,620.95 is about 3.4% of $400,000. Therefore, a discount of nearly 3½ points is required to bring the yield up from the 12% rate to 12½%.

To use a financial calculator:

Input rate desired	12.5 ÷ 12	=	%i
Input monthly payment	$4,212.90		PMT
Input term	25 × 12	=	n
Compute PV	Result: $386,379.05		

Loan Discounts and Prepayments

More than half of all permanent loans are paid off prior to full amortization. A discounted loan that is paid off early will result in a higher yield because the discount charged will be amortized over a shorter time. For example, a 12% face rate loan with 3 points that is paid off after one year will effectively yield about 15%, which is 12% interest plus 3 points spread over only one year.

It is likely that a 25-year loan will be paid off within 10 years because of a sale or refinancing, so the points are spread over that period of time. As an example of solving for the rate on a presumed prepayment, consider a $400,000 loan with a 12% face rate, 25-year term, and 3 discount points. Ten years later, the balance on the loan will be $351,025.83. To compute the true yield (interest rate), which is a trial-and-error process, consider these facts:

Actual loan (cash advanced)	= $388,000 ($400,000 less 3%)
Monthly payments for 10 years	= $4,212.90
Prepaid balance in 10 years	= $351,025.83
Face rate	= 12%
Yield to full amortization	= 12.44%

It is known that the actual yield will be above 12.44% because that rate, derived earlier, considered the points to be spread over 25 years, whereas the presumed early repayment will cause only a 10-year spread of the discount; so the trial-and-error process should begin above 12.44% (see Table 9–4). At a 12.5% interest rate, the present value of receipts is $389,036.18. At 12.75%, the present value is $383,713.27. Since these two results bracket the $388,000 cash advanced, the yield to maturity assuming repayment in 10 years is between 12.5 and 12.75%; it is closer to 12.5%. Further interpolation through trial-and-error would result in a rate of 12.55%. This is the rate at which the present value of outflows and inflows is equal.

By financial calculator:

Input rate, 12.55%	12.55 ÷ 12	[%i]
Input monthly payment	$4,212.90	[PMT]
Input term	10 × 12	[n]
[Compute] [PV] for payments	$287,239.96	
Save PV of payments		[STO] [1]
Clear payment		[0] [PMT]
Enter remaining balance	$351,025.83	[FV]
Compute PV of balance	[Compute] [PV]	$100,723.29
ADD: PV of payments		
+ [RCL] [1]	Result:	$387,963.25
Rounded to		$388,000

TABLE 9-4
Trial-and-Error Process for Computing the Yield to Maturity Rate

	Try 12.5% (monthly tables)	*Try 12.75% (monthly tables)*
Step 1: Value of $4,212.90 monthly for 10 years	$287,813.25	$284,963.84
Step 2: ADD: Value of $351,025.83 in 10 years	101,222.93	98,749.43
Totals	$389,036.18	$383,713.27

This shows that an effective yield of 12.55% will result from the loan. It had 3 discount points and a 25-year amortization term and is presumed to be retired upon its tenth anniversary.

VARIABLE PAYMENT MORTGAGES

Not all mortgages are of the fixed-payment, self-amortizing type. Others include:

1. Balloon payment loans.
2. Fixed principal payment loans.
3. Participation.
4. Graduated payments.
5. Reverse annuity.
6. Variable rate.
7. Canadian rollover.
8. Wraparound.

9. Add-on interest.
10. Shared appreciation mortgage.

The basic approach to analysis of these mortgages as income-producing investments has much in common with level-payment, self-amortizing mortgages. Lenders in all situations must look to a return *on* and a recovery *of* the money that they lend.

Balloon Payment Loans

Balloon payment loans require a large final payment on the debt, which is known as the "balloon" payment. During the first several months or years of the loan, little or no principal is amortized. Then the entire balance becomes due. Real estate owners usually try to arrange replacement financing in advance so that when the balloon comes due, they will not lose the property through default on the balloon principal payment.

Balloon mortgages can be structured in basically three ways:

1. Dormant interest until maturity.
2. Interest-only payments, then balloon.
3. Some amortization prior to balloon.

Dormant Interest until Maturity. The dormant type requires absolutely no payments until maturity. Then, the original principal plus accrued compounded interest is due. For example if a dormant $400,000 mortgage at 12% annual interest is due in two years, the balloon would be $501,760, as shown below:

Amount of loan	$400,000
Interest, year 1 @ 12%	48,000
Balance end of year	$448,000
Interest, year 2 @ 12%	53,760
Balance end of year 2	$501,760

Use a calculator to compute the future balance of a dormant mortgage as follows:

Input original loan	$400,000	[PV]
Input interest rate	12	[%i]
Input term	2	[n]
[Compute] [FV]	Result: $501,760	

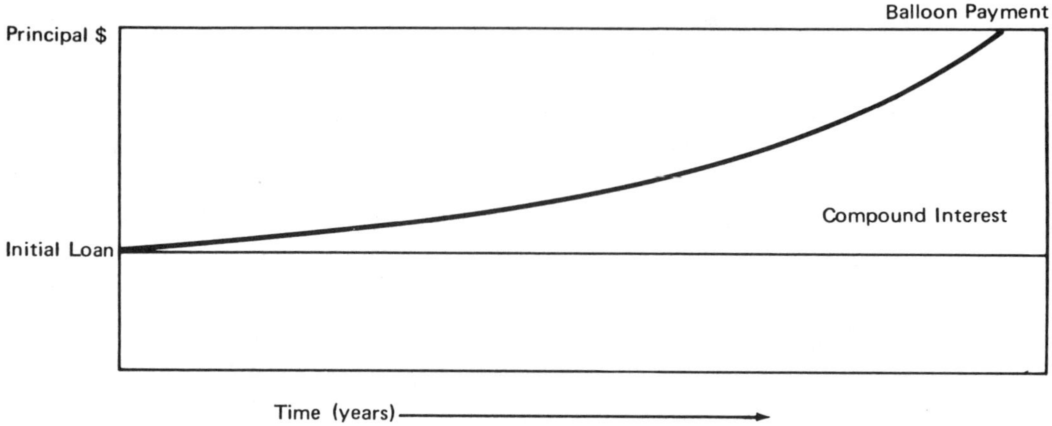

FIGURE 9–2. Dormant Mortgage Principal Balance.

There are very few dormant mortgages. Most of these are held by sellers of raw land; often, the land offers the possibility of being developed before the balloon payment. The borrower, who is often a land speculator, wants a loan with low payments to minimize holding costs.

A seller-lender who wants cash prior to loan maturity can try to sell the loan but will probably sell it at a rather high yield (deep discount) because of the risk of default and its illiquidity. At a yield rate of 25%, a balloon of $501,760 is worth 64 cents (from column 4, 2 years, 25% rate) per dollar, or $321,126.40. So the $400,000 dormant loan might be discounted by nearly 20 discount points to effect its sale.

Use a calculator as follows:

Input final balance	$501,760	[FV]
Input desired rate	25	[%i]
Input term	2	[n]
[Compute] [PV]	Result: $321,126.40	

Interest-Only Payments. Interest-only loans, with a balloon payment, require interest to be paid periodically. A $400,000 mortgage at 12% would call for $48,000 annual interest, payable at the end of each year; or $4,000 of interest at the end of each month if monthly payments are required. At the end of the loan term, the full $400,000 principal becomes due. Since there were no earlier principal payments, nor was there deferred interest, at maturity the original principal amount borrowed is due as a balloon payment.

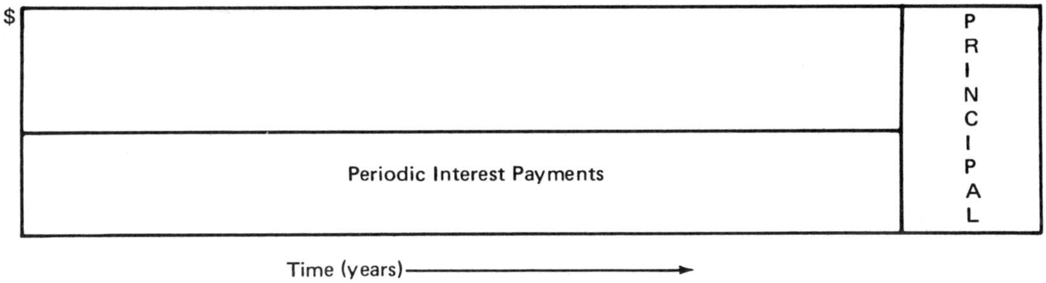

FIGURE 9–3. Interest-Only With Balloon Payment.

To value such a loan at any yield rate is a three-step computation:

Step 1. Treat the interest as an annuity, and find the present value of interest payments.
Step 2. Treat the balloon payment as a reversion, and find its present value.
Step 3. Step 1 + 2 = present value.

For example, a $400,000, 12% face interest rate mortgage, with interest-only payments will balloon in 2 years. Its value, to yield a 25% rate, is computed as follows:

Step 1. $48,000 × 1.44	=	$ 69,120.00
Step 2. $400,000 × .64	=	256,000.00
Step 3. Present value to yield 25%	=	$325,120.00

Use a financial calculator as follows:

Input interest payment	$48,000	[PMT]
Input rate	25	[%i]
Input term	2	[n]
[Compute] [PV]	Result: $69,120	[STO] [1]
Clear payment	0	[PMT]
Input balloon principal	$400,000	[FV]
[Compute] [PV]	Result: $256,000	

Add: Present value of payments
\+ [RCL] [1] = Result: $325,120.00

Some Amortization Prior to Balloon. A balloon payment loan can require some amortization prior to maturity. Projecting the balloon and valuing such mortgages is the same procedure as a self-amortizing mortgage that is paid off prior to full amortization. This was discussed earlier.

Fixed Principal Payment Loans

Some mortgage loans require equal payments toward principal, with interest on the unpaid balance. These are called *Springfield loans;* their P&I payment is variable.

Land speculators sometimes use this type; often, years of interest-only payments precede any principal payments. The payment stream is shown in Figure 9–4 with five years of interest-only payments followed by four equal annual principal payments, with interest in addition.

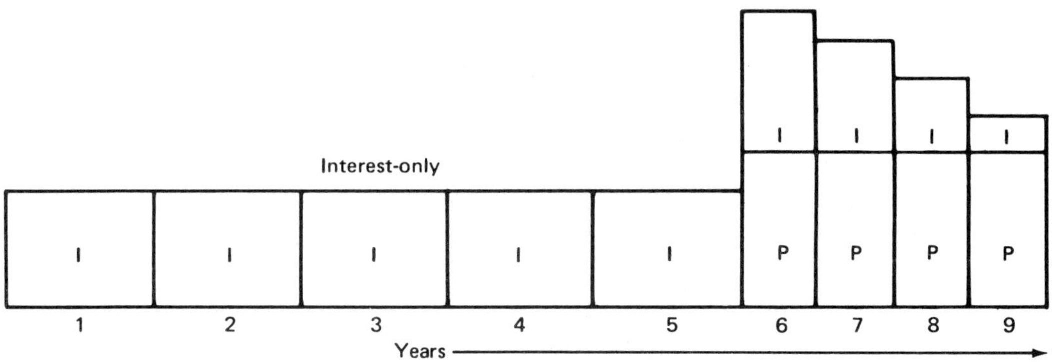

FIGURE 9–4. "Springfield" Loans With Interest-Only. I = Interest payment required. P = Principal payment required. Graphic presentation of loan that requires five years of interest-only payments followed by four equal payments of principal with interest on the unpaid balance.

Pricing this type of loan to offer a certain yield is best computed considering each payment. For example, assume a loan has $400,000 of principal, a 12% interest rate, and a five-year interest-only period followed by a four-year principal payout. To price that loan at a 25% yield rate, you should discount the payments by each year's reversion factor (column 4 of the tables). Computations are shown in Table 9–5.

TABLE 9-5
"Springfield" Mortgage Schedule (with Interest Only)

	Payment Distribution		Total		Reversion		Present
Year	Interest	Principal	Payment		Factor at 25%		Value
1	$48,000	$ -0-	$ 48,000	×	.8	=	$ 38,400
2	48,000	-0-	48,000	×	.64	=	30,720
3	48,000	-0-	48,000	×	.512	=	24,576
4	48,000	-0-	48,000	×	.4096	=	19,661
5	48,000	-0-	48,000	×	.32768	=	15,729
6	48,000	100,000	148,000	×	.262144	=	38,797
7	36,000	100,000	136,000	×	.209715	=	28,521
8	24,000	100,000	124,000	×	.167772	=	20,804
9	12,000	100,000	112,000	×	.134218	=	15,032
	Total for 25% return						$232,240

Participation

Participation loans are common on income-producing property. They usually require self-amortizing principal and interest payments as debt service, plus a "kicker." The "kicker" is that the lender shares in the equity investor's good fortune.

Kickers take various forms, including:

1. A portion of rent in excess of a base amount, or
2. A portion of net operating income above a base amount, or
3. A fraction of before-tax cash flow.

These participation mortgage loans are the same as self-amortizing mortgages except for the "kicker." Any income generated by the kicker provision can be analyzed separately. Whether the amount of kicker is expected to increase, decrease, or remain the same, this income, because of its uncertainty, should be valued at a higher discount rate than the minimum interest and principal portion of the payments.

For example, a 12% interest rate, $400,000 principal, 25-year term loan requires $4,212.90 in monthly payments. As additional interest, the lender is to receive 15% of the annual rental income (effective gross) in excess of $100,000. If the rental income is $120,000 for the first year, of the $20,000 excess, 15% ($3,000) is additional interest, i.e., the "kicker." It is suggested that the $3,000 and any forecast changes in that figure be capitalized at a higher rate than the 12% mortgage face interest rate to compensate for the uncertainty of that income.

Graduated Payments

Graduated payment mortgages (GPM) require variable payments. To value such loans, payments may be grouped according to the timing of receipts, then discounted to a present value at the desired yield rate.

GPMs are for homeowners who expect rising income levels. Mortgage payments are kept low during the early years, but then rise during the first five to ten years to the level that will fully amortize the loan. Figure 9-5 compares GPM payments to standard plan mortgages.

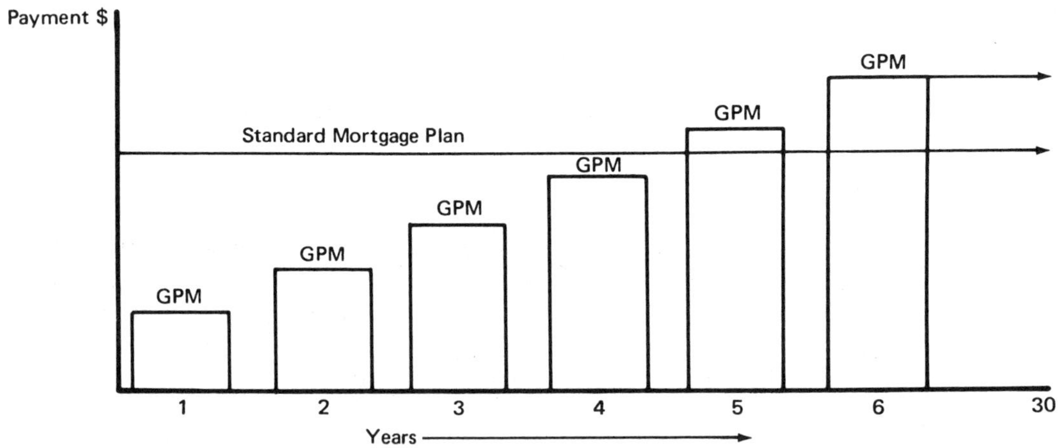

FIGURE 9-5. Graduated Payment Mortgage versus Standard Mortgage Payments.

The early years of GPMs provide negative amortization; principal balances actually increase. Payments are calculated to rise above the level of standard mortgages later so that full amortization will occur.

Reverse Annuity

Reverse annuity mortgages (RAMs) were established for retired homeowners. At the present time, there are very few mortgages of this type outstanding. RAMs require few or no payments at all until the property is sold, or until its owners are deceased, or until the loan-to-value ratio exceeds a specified limit. With an assumed time span for maturity, these mortgages can be valued by the same method as described for dormant mortgages. The assumed time span may be the remaining life expectancy of the owner-occupant or the contractually specified limit. RAMS can be structured for the homeowner to receive monthly payments until maturity.

Variable Rate

Variable interest rate mortgages (VRMs) have an interest rate that fluctuates with an index tied to money market conditions. This type of mortgage was introduced to allow a choice for borrowers and lenders who desire not to commit themselves to a fixed interest rate for a long term.

The maximum interest rate charged each year may be limited; there may be a ceiling and a floor on the highest and lowest rates. Interest rate increases and decreases will result in changed amortization terms and/or monthly payments. Higher interest rates require longer terms and/or higher payment; lower rates have the opposite effect.

Variable interest rate mortgages do not lend themselves easily to mechanical applications of yields due to the absence of an accurate forecast of future interest rates. Present values can be determined on the basis of minimum and maximum interest rates. However, the best approach is to consider that the yield will be tied to a prearranged index, but not over the ceiling rate, nor less than the floor.

Canadian Rollover

Canadian rollover mortgages are generally issued for 25- or 30-year terms. At prearranged time intervals, such as every five years, the interest rate is adjusted, upward or downward, to the prevailing interest rate at that time. *Renegotiated rate mortgages* (RRMs) are a modification of the Canadian rollover mortgage plan. The main difference is that the interest rate for RRMs is bounded by a floor and ceiling. Typically, all renegotiated rates must be within 5% of the initial interest rate. Interest rate changes are not to exceed ½% per year.

Wraparound

Wraparound mortgages (WAMs) may be structured in a variety of ways. When pricing or valuing one, it is very important to have a complete understanding of the terms of the WAM, and of those of the underlying mortgage(s).

Wraparound mortgages are a form of second (subordinate or junior) financing. A lender can offer a straight second mortgage on property that has an existing first mortgage or, instead, offer a wraparound. The wraparound overstates the second portion of the lien by including, in its balance, a surviving first mortgage.

For example, suppose property is encumbered by a first mortgage at 10% interest, $300,000 remaining balance, and 25 years left to run. Monthly P&I payments are $2,726.10. The property owner wants to borrow $100,000 as a second mortgage, and approaches a lender. The lender, instead of offering a $100,000 second mortgage, will advance $100,000 in cash to the property owner and receives a wraparound for $400,000. The $300,000 principal balance of the underlying first mortgage remains intact.

The WAM mortgage lender states that the interest rate on the $400,000 WAM will be 12%. Monthly payments for the 25-year term are to be $4,212.90 on the WAM, which the property owner will pay monthly to the WAM lender or his agent. The WAM lender will then forward $2,726.10 to the first mortgage holder, keeping the difference, $1,486.80 ($4,212.90 minus $2,726.10 = $1,486.80) as the monthly receipt. The WAM lender has thus leveraged around the 10% interest rate underlying first mortgage.

In this situation the effective yield on the WAM will be in excess of 17.6%. The rate is based on a $100,000 investment that provides monthly receipts of $1,486.80 for 25 years. To solve using a calculator:

Input principal	$100,000	[PV]
Input monthly payment	$1,486.80	[PMT]
Input term	25 × 12 = 300	[n]
[Compute] [%i]	Result: 01.46803	

Multiply by 12 for annual rate = .17616 or 17.6%

Since wraparounds may be structured in a variety of ways—interest-only, dormant, balloon—and since the underlying first mortgage may have a variety of forms, an understanding of the entire financing is necessary. After that is accomplished, consider the actual amount advanced by the WAM lender, expected net receipts, and their timing. Then, solve for a rate by trial and error.

Add-on Interest

Some loans, notably second mortgages, require add-on interest. Interest is added on to the principal, and the result is divided by the number of months to determine the monthly payment. The interest rate is stated quite low, but the effective yield may be high. Prepayment penalties are usually computed using the "rule of 78's." That rule is a sum-of-the-digits technique, not a discounted present value approach.

For example, consider a \$100,000 second mortgage at an 8% add-on rate, 25-year term. Over 25 years, total interest will be 25 × 8% = 200% of the principal. The principal is thus \$100,000 actual loan, plus \$200,000 for interest. A total of \$300,000 will be repaid, over 25 years (300 months). Dividing \$300,000 by 300 months gives \$1,000 as the monthly payment. This computes to an effective rate of 11.27% (see column 6 at 25 years at 11.25% interest).

A financial calculator output is below:

Input principal	\$100,000	[PV]
Input payment	1,000	[PMT]
Input term	25 × 12 = 300	[n]
[Compute] [%i]	Result: .939517	

Multiply by 12 = .112742 = 11.27%

The "rule of 78's" is frequently used to compute interest rebates on prepaid installment loans. The number *78* is the sum of the digits found by adding the numbers from 1 to 12. For a one-year installment loan with monthly payments, prepaid after one month, 12/78 of the interest will be charged; the remaining 66/78 of interest will be refunded. If it is prepaid after two months, 23/78 (11 + 12 = 23) will be charged as interest.

The formula for the sum of the digits in *N* years, which will be the denominator, is:

$$\text{Sum} = \frac{N(N+1)}{2}$$

As an example, consider a mortgage as before, \$100,000 principal at 8% add-on interest for a 25-year term, with annual payments. Since there is \$300,000 of total payments (\$100,000 principal plus \$200,000 interest) spread over 25 years, the annual payment is \$12,000. That loan, if prepaid after only three years, will deserve an interest charge of \$44,307.69 as computed below:

$$\begin{aligned}\text{Interest charge} &= \frac{25 + 24 + 23}{\frac{25(26)}{2}} \times \$200{,}000 \\ &= .22153846 \times \$200{,}000 \\ &= \$44{,}307.69\end{aligned}$$

From total interest of \$200,000, \$155,692.31 will be "refunded" (\$200,000 minus \$44,307.69 = \$155,692.31) if the loan is prepaid after three years.

The borrower will have received \$100,000 cash upon loan origination, paid \$12,000 per year for three years, then have to pay another \$108,307.69 to retire the loan, as shown below:

Total payment required:	\$300,000.00
Less: Three years of payments at \$12,000 per year	−36,000.00
Less: Interest rebate	−155,692.31
Amount due on prepayment after three years	\$108,307.69

A financial calculator can be used to determine the effective rate, as follows:

Input principal	\$100,000	STO 0
Input repayment year 1	12,000	STO 1
Input repayment year 2	12,000	STO 2
Input repayment year 3	\$ 12,000 +	
\$108,307.69 = \$120,307.69		STO 3

Compute 2nd IRR Result: 14.406%

Add-on interest rate loans and the prepayment penalties are quite common for personal property loans such as those on autos, mobile homes, and boats. This type of financing is sometimes used on real estate. Their general popularity of use in conjunction with personal property financing has resulted in preprinted tables with effective yield computations and prepayment amounts. After mastery of the calculations, you can use preprinted tables as a convenience.

Shared Appreciation Mortgage

The shared appreciation mortgage (SAM) is a type of participating loan. The contract allows the lender to participate in capital gains or resale proceeds realized from a sale of the property. In exchange, the lender typically reduces the interest rate on the loan. For example, the lender may reduce the interest rate by one third in exchange for one third of the appreciation. In the event that the property is not sold within a specified time, the lender's share of appreciation may be determined by an appraisal. Each party selects an appraiser. A third appraiser is called when the two do not agree. Other provisions can include call and prepayment privileges, minimum effective interest rates, deferred interest payment, maximum interest reduction, and maximum participatory shares.

SUMMARY

The arithmetic involved with the yields and prices for mortgage loans provides a foundation for valuing any stream of income. In nearly all mortgage loans, amounts of periodic payments and principal balances are fixed. This provides a certain stream of income, in the absence of a default. From that stream, one can estimate the value of the forecast income, which depends on the timing of payments, the length of the loan, the amount of amortization, and most importantly, the rate of interest or yield to maturity sought.

Since there are many different types of mortgage, some requiring level payments, and others requiring variable payments, and since mortgages have different amounts of collateral, one must be careful to determine the amounts and timing of payments, and to judge the risk involved and required yield to maturity. Once this is done, valuation of the loan to determine the discount, or valuation of a discounted loan to determine the yield rate, is a mechanical process. Mastery of that process is a vital step toward analysis of the more complex income configurations as provided by equity interests in real estate.

Questions

1. A 12% face interest rate loan for a 30-year term requires monthly payments for full amortization. Its initial principal is $100,000.
   a. What is the monthly payment?
   b. What is the debt service constant?
   c. What will the mortgage principal balance be in eight years?
2. An 11% face interest rate loan has a $250,000 principal, and requires payment of $2,580.47 per month.

a. How long will it take for full amortization?

b. How much discount will be required on that loan to allow a 12% yield to maturity?

c. How many "points" does the discount represent?

3. A mortgage loan has eighteen years left to run for full amortization; payments are $10,000 monthly; its face rate of interest is 8%.

   a. What is its principal balance?

   b. How much principal will be paid in the next year?

4. A $100,000 mortgage loan at a 10% annual interest rate requires five years of interest-only payments, then a balloon at the end of year 5.

   a. What is the amount of the balloon?

   b. If the loan is sold to yield 20% to maturity, what is the sales price?

5. A wraparound mortgage is written at an 11% rate of interest on its entire $100,000 balance, for twenty years. The underlying first mortgage is for $60,000 at 9% interest. Both require monthly payments.

   a. What is the total monthly payment for the entire wraparound?

   b. What is the total monthly payment on the underlying first mortgage?

   c. What is the effective yield rate of the additional funds provided by the wraparound?

6. A loan has a $10,000 principal, 10% annual interest rate, and four-year amortization term. It requires annual payments.

   a. What is the annual payment?

   b. What is the loan constant?

   c. Show an amortization schedule.

7. Define:

   a. Balloon payment loan

   b. Graduated payment loan

   c. Add-on interest.

   d. Rule of 78's.

   e. Participation loan.

   f. Springfield mortgages.

   g. Discount points.

   h. Shared appreciation mortgage.

Chapter 10

Influence of Financing on Price

Nearly all real estate purchases are completed with the assistance of a mortgage loan. Whenever borrowed money is used to complete an investment transaction, the borrower is said to be using *financial leverage.*

Often, property is refinanced by its new owner, which means that the purchaser arranges a new loan with a principal amount greater than the remaining principal on the old loan. This will retire the old loan and reduce the necessary cash down payment. A new loan may provide upwards of 75% of the purchase price. In other transactions, existing loans remain with the sold property and are assumed by buyers who pay for the owner's equity with a cash down payment. Some sellers will accept second mortgages and wraparounds; some institutional lenders also offer junior financing.

Most buyers of income-producing real estate want loans on it for several reasons. First, few have enough cash to pay the entire price in cash. Second, even those with enough to pay all in cash want to diversify their investments, thus spreading the risk. "Don't put all your eggs in one basket!" the expression goes. A third consideration is taxation: interest on borrowed money is nearly always tax deductible. Depreciation deductions are generally allowed for the full price, not just the equity. Fourth, borrowing money allows an investor to control more property.

From the borrower's viewpoint, there are two main drawbacks to loans. One is that interest must be paid. The second is that the principal must be repaid. Default on either could cause a foreclosure, loss of any equity, and a deficiency judgment.

EFFECT OF FINANCING ON VALUE

The financing of real estate will *not affect* the property's *value.* However, the financing, whether favorable or poor, can have a highly significant influence on the *price.* To the novice in real estate, this will seem strange. Why are price and value not the same? How can something affect price but not value? These questions are commonly asked. Consider exploring for oil. Costs are the same, whether a gusher or a dry hole is found. Value and price are not the same.

As for real estate sold as an investment, buyers and sellers do not always agree on value. They do agree on a price. The price, but not the value, is influenced by financing. Financing, whether good or bad, does not physically change the property. It does not increase market rental rates. However, financing does affect an owner's cash down payment and subsequent monthly payments. For example, if a seller willingly finances property with a 1% interest rate loan with a 40-year amortization term, a buyer can afford a much higher price for the property, while still enjoying below-market loan payments. The higher price includes the value of the property plus the value of favorable financing. Financing affects the rate of return on equity and the risk of the investment.

When estimating the market value of property, assume that typical financing available in the market for that type of property will be utilized. "Typical" financing is the amount of money that will be advanced by a third-party lender and the interest rate charged. Often, real estate prices are raised to include several seller-paid discount points charged on third-party financing. This changes the price but not the value of the real estate. Actually, the price reflects both the real estate and the financing.

Sellers may provide financing for buyers in instances where third-party lenders are unwilling to lend. The better the financing, the higher the price they will seek. Since the value has not been affected by financing, the value is much lower than the price. When adjusting price to equate with the value of real estate, find the market value (not face amount) of the mortgage(s) given in the transaction, and add that to the cash down payment. The value of the mortgage is likely to be much less than its face amount; so the value of the property is less than the price.

TYPES OF FINANCIAL INSTITUTIONS

The six most significant types of financial institutions in real estate are:

1. Life insurance companies (LICs).
2. Savings and loan associations (S&Ls).
3. Mutual savings banks (MSBs).
4. Commercial banks (CBs).
5. Real estate investment trusts (REITs).
6. Pension funds (PFs).

Their main involvement in income-producing real estate follows.

Life Insurance Companies

Generally, large life insurance companies are interested only in loans that exceed $1 million. They do not have the facilities to service tens of thousands of smaller loans; so they prefer a smaller number of larger loans. With billions of dollars in assets, some life insurance companies can achieve adequate diversification even though $10 million or more is placed in a single project. Life insurance companies rarely offer construction loans; they want the yield and safety provided by permanent mortgages on finished products.

Savings and Loan Associations and Mutual Savings Banks

Savings and loan associations (S&Ls) and mutual savings banks (MSBs) primarily offer residential first mortgages on local property. These include one-to-four-family homes. Only the largest S&Ls offer loans of more than $1 million on a single project, although many are willing lenders on multifamily properties in the $100,000–$1,000,000 range. Generally, these lenders require private mortgage insurance for single-family home loans in excess of 80% of value; they require a minimum of 20–25% down on multifamily property. Many S&Ls and MSBs offer construction loans to builders. For a "commitment fee", some offer the privilege of permanent financing at a predetermined interest rate.

Commercial Banks

Commercial banks (CBs) are active in issuing construction loans on all types of property. These are offered only with a "take-out" commitment from a permanent lender; upon project completion, the permanent loan will take them out of the construction loan.

Real Estate Investment Trusts

Real estate investment trusts (REITs) invest in construction loans, permanent mortgage loans, equities, and leasing arrangements. Each REIT may specialize in just one or two of these types of investments.

Pension Funds

Pension funds (PFs) often acquire permanent mortgages on income-producing properties. In recent years many have acquired ownership of equities in large income-producing properties, or have acquired properties without the aid of mortgage financing.

EFFECT OF FINANCIAL LEVERAGE

Financial leverage is using borrowed money to complete an investment transaction. If the assets bought with borrowed money offer annual financial benefits at a rate in excess of the loan's interest rate, leverage is positive or favorable. The investor makes money by borrowing.

On the other hand, if assets bought with borrowed money fail to increase in value, or if they fail to provide benefits in excess of the interest rate on the borrowed money, then leverage is "negative." Leverage is "neutral" when the property earns at the same rate as the interest rate on borrowed money.

To demonstrate the effect of financing, first consider property free and clear with a price of $500,000. The balance sheet is shown in Table 10–1. Suppose that property produces net operating income as shown in Table 10–2.

TABLE 10–1
Balance Sheet for Property Free and Clear of Debt

ASSETS	
Buildings (and other improvements)	$450,000
Land	50,000
Total	$500,000
LIABILITIES AND EQUITY	
Liabilities	$ 0
Equity	$500,000
Total	$500,000

TABLE 10–2
Net Operating Income, Property Free and Clear of Debt

Potential gross income	$100,000
Less: Vacancy and collection allowance	5,000
Add: Miscellaneous income	3,000
Effective gross income	$ 98,000
Less: Operating expenses (excludes financing expenses and depreciation)	33,000
Net operating income (NOI)	$ 65,000

An all-cash buyer at $500,000 will receive $65,000 of current income, which gives an overall rate of return (OAR) of 13% ($65,000/$500,000 = 13%). The yield to maturity will be higher if the net operating income (NOI) increases and/or the property appreciates and resells for more than the initial cost. On the other hand, a loss at resale or reduced NOI will cause the yield to maturity to be less than the 13% OAR. For the most part, loans on income-producing real estate are supplied by third parties; so the seller gets paid all in cash.

Using the previous example, suppose that instead of an all-cash purchase for $500,000, the purchaser arranges a $400,000 first mortgage loan, self-amortizing over 25 years, with monthly payments at 12% interest. The balance sheet and cash flow statement are shown in Tables 10–3 and 10–4.

TABLE 10–3
Balance Sheet with First Mortgage on Property

ASSETS	
Buildings (and other improvements)	$450,000
Land	50,000
Total	$500,000
LIABILITIES AND EQUITY	
Mortgage loan	$400,000
Equity (cash down payment)	100,000
Total	$500,000

By arranging $400,000 of first mortgage financing, the cash down payment is reduced to 20% of the price (instead of 100%), but the owner controls the entire property. Should the property appreciate in value, or the net operating income increase, the equity owner reaps these additional rewards, not the mortgage holder.

However, should the property decline in value by 20% and/or its effective gross income diminish by a similar rate, the value of the equity will become negligible; a deficiency occurs when the mortgage debt exceeds the property value.

TABLE 10–4
Cash Flow Statement for Mortgaged Property

Potential gross income	$100,000
Less: Vacancy and collection allowance	5,000
Add: Miscellaneous income	3,000
Effective gross income	$ 98,000
Less: Operating expenses	33,000
Net operating income	$ 65,000
Less: Debt service: 12 × $4,212.90	50,555
Before-tax cash flow (cash throw-off)	$ 14,445

Presuming that the given level of cash flow in the example will remain stable, the equity owner enhances the current rate of return from 13% when free and clear ($65,000 ÷ $500,000 = 13%) to 14.44% ($14,445 ÷ $100,000 = 14.44%) with the indebtedness. This indicates favorable leverage. In the absence of financing, a 13% current return (overall rate) was available. Since the financing has a mortgage loan constant of less than 13% ($50,555 ÷ $400,000 = .126387), current cash returns to the equity owner are enhanced by the leverage. Further benefits for the equity holder may be found in three areas other than the current cash return, as follows:

1. *Income taxes.* The entire $450,000 of improvements (but not land) can be depreciated in most circumstances for income tax purposes, regardless of the extent of equity invested. Interest on the mortgage is tax deductible.

2. *Appreciation.* The equity owner will enjoy all the gain in value of the entire asset, not just the equity contribution. This form of return is deferred, usually to be realized upon resale. It is often called a *capital gain.*

3. *Mortgage reduction.* Some of the mortgage payment reduces the loan principal. This type of return is also deferred until a sale.

Many investors seek to employ leverage to the greatest possible extent. However, unless the property provides returns in excess of the cost of borrowed money, leverage will be negative. Extreme leverage is demonstrated by the following example.

Suppose the equity owner is able to arrange a $100,000 second mortgage in addition to the $400,000 first mortgage on the property described earlier. The second mortgage requires interest-only payments at a 14% rate, and has a balloon payment in three years. Since the investor borrowed the entire cost, there is no down payment. This situation, where a real estate owner has borrowed the entire cost (or more), is defined as *mortgaging out.*

The balance sheet and cash flow statement appear in Tables 10–5 and 10–6. Since the owner has no cash investment in the property, the $445 cash throw-off provides an infinite rate of return on "equity." In addition, the owner may realize some income tax savings due to interest and depreciation accounting deductions, plus benefits from property appreciation. Further, the owner gains from gradual reduction of the first mortgage as it amortizes.

TABLE 10–5
Balance Sheet, First and Second Mortgage Financing on Property

ASSETS	
Buildings	$450,000
Land	50,000
Total	$500,000
LIABILITIES AND EQUITY	
Mortgage (first)	$400,000
Mortgage (second)	100,000
Equity	0
Total	$500,000

TABLE 10–6
Cash Flow Statement, First and Second Mortgages on Property

Potential gross income	$100,000
Less: Vacancy and collection allowance	5,000
Add: Miscellaneous income	3,000
Effective gross income	$ 98,000
Less: Operating expenses	33,000
Net operating income	$ 65,000
Less: First mortgage debt service, and	50,555
Second mortgage interest	14,000
Before-tax cash flow (cash throw-off)	$ 445

However, there are very sobering aspects. One is that if rental income should decline and/or operating expenses increase, cash throw-off will be negative. The owner then must find the cash to fund the deficit or face losing the property. A second problem will arise in three years when the second mortgage balloon is due. When that time comes, the equity owner stands to lose the property unless somehow arrangements are made to accommodate the $100,000 second mortgage balloon principal. Possible arrangements include (1) renegotiating with the second mortgage lender for an extension, (2) securing another second mortgage to retire the existing one, (3) refinancing the entire debt through a new first mortgage or wraparound, or (4) raising $100,000 cash from sources external to the property to retire the second mortgage. If these efforts should fail, the equity owner will lose the property through foreclosure, and unless the first and/or second mortgage carried nonrecourse provisions, the owner will be personally liable for a deficiency judgment. The deficiency judgment is the difference between the value of property upon foreclosure and the debts against it.

Exculpation

Any opportunity to insert nonrecourse (exculpatory) provisions in mortgage loans occurs when the loan is first issued. *Nonrecourse* means that the lender must look only to the property to satisfy the debt, not to the borrower. With such a provision included in mortgage loans, highly levered property becomes more desirable. The borrower can lose whatever little equity was paid, but is not personally liable for the debt.

Leverage and Price

Many real estate investors will pay more for property if they can arrange a high degree of leverage on a nonrecourse basis. In the previous example, it is not unusual for optimistic or risk-taking investors to pay 10 to 20% more for the property than its market value, provided that they can borrow nearly 100% of the price. They stand to lose little or none of their own money, and they have the opportunity to gain much if the property income increases or the value increases. Favorable financing, as measured by high leverage, can add to the price. However, it does not affect the property value.

Other investors are much more conservative. They are willing to make a substantial down payment to assume a low-interest loan. The low-interest loan will enhance the amount of cash flow to equity and provide a cushion in the event of reduced rental income and/or increased vacancies and operating expenses. The increased equity will reduce the possibility of an unwanted foreclosure and will provide more cash upon a resale.

For example, suppose that property is offered for sale for \$500,000 with an assumable 8% \$300,000 mortgage that has 20 years left for full amortization. The monthly payment is \$2,509.32; the annual debt service, therefore, is \$30,112.

Upon acquisition, the balance sheet and cash flow statement will be as shown in Tables 10-7 and 10-8. Notice that the cash throw-off of \$34,888 produces a 17.44% dividend rate on the \$200,000 of equity. Although the mortgage provides less leverage than an 80% loan, the favorable interest rate allows a substantial current cash return. In addition, equity build-up through mortgage retirement will occur more quickly for this loan with 20 remaining years than would a new loan with a 25- or 30-year term.

TABLE 10-7
Balance Sheet for Assumable Low-Interest-Rate Loan on Property

ASSETS	
Buildings (and other improvements)	\$450,000
Land	50,000
Total	\$500,000
LIABILITIES AND EQUITY	
Mortgage loan	\$300,000
Equity (cash down payment)	200,000
Total	\$500,000

TABLE 10-8
Cash Flow Statement with Assumable Low-Interest-Rate Loan on Property

Potential gross income	\$100,000
Less: Vacancy and collection allowance	−5,000
Add: Miscellaneous income	+3,000
Effective gross income	\$ 98,000
Less: Operating expenses	−33,000
Net operating income	\$ 65,000
Less: Debt service: 12 × \$2,509.32 =	−30,112
Before-tax cash flow (cash throw-off)	\$ 34,888

Because of these potential benefits, astute buyers may pay slightly over the market value for property with assumable low-interest-rate financing. It is possible to measure the ceiling amount of increase in payment for the property arising from the low-interest-rate loan (admittedly, transactions will not occur at the ceiling increase). To do so, first, find the difference in payments for the existing loan compared to a loan of the same principal and term at the market interest rate. Second, measure that difference by multiplying by the annuity factor for the term of the loan at the prevailing interest rate. The difference is the present value of the savings in loan payments. Given a current interest rate of 12%, the steps are:

1. \$3,303.26 − \$2,509.32 = \$793.94
2. \$793.94 × 90.8194 =\$72,105.15

This computation, yielding \$72,105.15 in this situation, attempts to value the present amount of savings from a low-interest-rate loan. It indicates that an investor who arranges a loan at the current prevailing (12%) interest rate can borrow only \$227,894.83 (\$300,000 minus \$72,105.17 = \$227,894.83) over 20 years and keep the monthly payment the same as the existing (8% interest rate) financing. However, a property encumbered by low-interest-rate financing seldom commands the full premium of the payment savings because it generally offers less leverage and less income tax savings.

Assumability. Many real estate mortgage loans cannot automatically be assumed by property buyers. The majority of conventional mortgages (non FHA or VA) on homes and other properties in most states have *due on sale* clauses. Such clauses provide for acceleration of the principal of a debt upon the sale of the mortgaged property unless the lender approves of the transaction. When current interest rates are above the face rate of a mortgage, many lenders will approve the proposed sale transaction only if they escalate the mortgage interest rate to current interest rates. Thus, an analyst should not presume automatic assumability of existing mortgage loans.

Effect of Loan Discount Points

Loan discount points may be paid in order to arrange a below-market interest rate loan. Each discount point represents a one-time charge by lenders equal to 1% of the loan principal. Often sellers pay these points to comply with government regulations.

Knowledgeable sellers, when they must pay discount points on buyers' new loans, devise legal ways to pass the points back where they belong: to the buyer since it is the buyer who is seeking the financing. In some situations, it is illegal for sellers to increase the price when they are to incur discount points; so they accomplish the price increase by using a more subtle approach. For example, they may have a high asking price, and they stick to that price if they are to pay points; yet they are willing to reduce the price when the financing does not require seller-paid discount points.

When an analyst or appraiser encounters a sale that involves two or more discount points, there is a likelihood that the property price was higher than it would have been with no seller-paid points. To arrive at a market value estimate, the amount of the seller-paid points should be subtracted from the actual price paid.

If an analyst is asked to consider the trade-off between interest rates and discount points, he should first attempt to find, for the market interest loan, the required monthly payment. Then he must find, for the lower-interest-rate loan, the principal balance that would carry that same monthly payment. The difference in principal balances represents the dollar value of points that may be added to the price to compensate for the low interest rate of the actual financing.

For example, suppose that the market rate of interest is 12% for a 25-year monthly-payment loan. A $400,000 principal balance loan is desired. The local state's usury ceiling is 11%, so the seller must pay several points. The monthly mortgage payment on a $400,000 loan at 12% interest will be $4,212.90. It is found that an 11% loan of $429,838 carries a $4,212.90 monthly payment. Therefore, the seller is apt to raise the price of the property sold by about $30,000 ($429,838 minus $400,000 = $29,838) to cover the points that must be paid.

As a shortcut, one may estimate using a rule of thumb. This rule holds that each discount point on a 25- or 30-year mortgage increases the effective yield to maturity of the mortgage by about ⅛ of 1%. Therefore, if there is a ½% interest rate spread between market interest rates and face mortgage rates, approximately 4 discount points are required (4 × ⅛% = ½%). A 1% rate differential justifies about 8 discount points.

Since sellers try to raise property prices when they pay points to secure a buyer's below-market interest rate for financing, the actual price must be adjusted to remove the influence of the points. Only by doing so can one estimate the property value free of the influence of points paid to arrange below-market interest rate financing.

SELLER FINANCING

For some properties, real estate is often financed by sellers at low interest rates. This occurs frequently for speculative acreage transactions since institutions seldom lend on this type of property. Lending institutions prefer to lend on property that generates an income stream, not on land that is lying fallow. They feel that an income stream will provide the cash needed to pay the debt service; they don't care to lend on raw land, since some day, through foreclosure, they could become the unwilling owners of a nonincome-producing asset. Therefore, many sellers must finance the speculative property they sell. In this case, sellers may offer the property at two different prices: a low amount when they are to receive all cash, or a much higher price if they provide long-term financing at a low interest rate. The price increases with longer terms, lower interest rates, and smaller cash down payments. In order to equate prices and terms with cash values, the process of "cash equivalent analysis" is necessary. The purpose of the process is to compare different prices and terms in order to achieve the same cash value.

For example, suppose a 100-acre tract of vacant land is worth $5,000 per acre in cash, as estimated by several recent sales of comparable property. Its cash value is $5,000 × 100 acres = $500,000. A seller offers the property for $600,000. The price is composed of a $100,000 cash down payment and a $500,000 purchase-money mortgage payable over 25 years at 8% interest with monthly installments of $3,859.08. Is the buyer justified in paying the $600,000 price? It is $100,000 above a cash price. Is the price reasonable for the seller to ask?

Consider this. If the buyer were able to arrange a $400,000 third-party mortgage at the prevailing interest rate of 12% with $100,000 cash for the down payment, the buyer would effectively be arranging to pay the seller $500,000 in cash for the property. The monthly payment on the $400,000 loan would be $4,212.90.

Instead of borrowing from a third party, the buyer could pay the seller $600,000 ($100,000 cash plus a $500,000 mortgage at 8%) and enjoy a monthly payment that is $353.82 less! In this situation the buyer can pay $100,000 more for property financed by the seller at a low-interest rate because of the low-interest mortgage that the seller will offer.

CASH EQUIVALENCE

To find the cash equivalent market value of property sold under favorable terms, you must add the *market value of the mortgage* accepted by the seller to the cash down payment that the seller receives. The market value of the mortgage will be less than the face value.

It is often difficult to estimate the market value of mortgages taken by sellers because they are infrequently traded. At the prevailing interest rate of 12% you should value the payments of the seller's mortgage using the annuity factor: $3,859.08 × 94.94655 = $366,406.34. The cash equivalent property value, considering the seller's 8% mortgage, is $466,406.34 ($100,000 cash down plus $366,406.34 mortgage). When negotiating, principals to the transaction should consider the trade-offs of higher prices with favorable financing, or lower prices with higher interest rates, less leverage, and shorter terms. Converting financing terms to a cash equivalent is a better program than the "gut feel" approach that many parties still use. This cash equivalence approach is well recognized in appraisal literature.

SUMMARY

The financing of real estate, whether favorable or not, can have a serious influence on the price paid for property. However, it does not affect the property value since any premium paid to obtain favorable financing is not attributable to the property itself.

Buyers may pay a higher price to get a high degree of leverage, low interest rate, or long amortization terms. Those seeking high leverage increase the uncertainty of income amounts but may reduce the amount they stand to lose by using nonrecourse financing. Conservative purchasers may pay a premium to assume low-interest-rate loans. The present value of the highest reasonable premium to be paid can be measured, although few transactions will occur at the full premium because of reduced leverage. Sellers may pay discount points or provide favorable financing, increasing the price of the property to compensate. In these situations, it is necessary to extract the premium paid for good financing from the transaction price, using cash equivalent analysis. In this manner, the market value of the property can be estimated, apart from the inherent value of low-interest-rate financing.

Questions

1. A 30-year self-amortizing $100,000 mortgage loan is issued. At an 11% rate of interest:

   a. What is the monthly payment?

b. How many discount points must be paid to increase the mortgage yield to 12%?

c. If the seller must pay the discount, what is the dollar amount of the discount?

2. A land seller receives a $10,000 cash down payment, plus a $90,000 principal, 20-year self-amortizing annual-payment mortgage at 8% interest. The mortgage can be readily sold to yield 15% to maturity.

   a. How much can the mortgage be sold for?

   b. Including the cash down payment, how much total cash can the seller realize by selling the land and then the mortgage?

3. A certain fourplex has an assumable $75,000 principal, 6% interest rate, monthly-payment mortgage with 15 years left to run. Current interest rates are 10%. How much is the maximum premium for the existing financing?

4. The estimated market value of a certain tract of land is $250,000. The seller is willing to finance all but $50,000 (the down payment) at 6% interest over 30 years with monthly payments. The market rate of interest is 12%. How much of a price increase should the seller obtain in exchange for the financing offered?

Essay Questions

1. Define or explain:

   a. Financial leverage.

   b. Refinancing.

   c. Nonrecourse loans.

   d. Cash equivalence.

   e. Diversification.

2. Distinguish between *price* and *value*.

3. Why does financing influence the price of property, but not the value?

4. Explain how financial leverage can become favorable and unfavorable.

Chapter 11

Introduction to Mortgage-Equity Analysis

Nearly all real estate investment transactions are completed with the aid of a mortgage loan. Benefits of mortgage financing to equity investors and mortgage lenders were described in Chapter 10.

As a brief summary, equity investors receive financial leverage that can provide higher current yields, greater appreciation benefits, more extensive diversification of assets, and increased depreciation and interest deductions for income tax purposes. Mortgage lenders receive a reasonably certain amount of income, with a secured principal. They have the first claim against income from operation and against assets in the event of default.

Mortgage-equity analysis is a residual technique. Equity investors pay the residual of the initial cost. They receive the residual of net operating income and the resale price, after full payment to mortgage lenders, both during operations and upon resale.

Mortgage financing for income-producing real estate affects all three of the phases of property ownership. The three phases are:

I. Acquisition (purchase)
II. Operations (holding).
III. Disposition (resale).

The effect of a mortgage loan on the equity investment in real estate for each of these phases and the value of the residual benefits are discussed in this chapter. An example will be given to illustrate all three phases.

PHASE I—ACQUISITION (PURCHASE) AND FINANCING TERMS

Most real estate investors, when buying property, seek the best financing terms. Opinions differ as to the definition of the *best* terms. The most important financial factors are: (1) interest rate, (2) degree of leverage, and (3) amortization terms.

To all, the interest rate is of prime concern. Interest is a charge for the rental of money. The lower the interest rate, the more attractive the loan. The degree of leverage is also important. Many investors will pay a significantly higher interest rate in order to enjoy a lower cash down payment and therefore be able to exercise more leverage. Some equity investors will pay higher prices for property if this is needed in order to achieve more leverage. Sellers sometimes accommodate by financing themselves or by paying discount points on a buyer's loan; but they will try to raise their price to compensate. Consequently, prices are generally increased by favorable financing.

The amortization term of a mortgage loan is of some importance. The longer the term, the lower the annual debt service, and therefore the annual cash throw-off is greater. However, there are diminishing returns to the trade-off of longer amortization terms because the debt service payment change does not have a linear relationship to the amortization term. Once loan terms are stretched beyond 30 years, the annual mortgage payment requirement declines, but the change is quite small. The annual payment for self-amortizing loans can never become less than the interest rate applied to the principal.

Other major considerations in arranging mortgage loans include:

1. Prepayment privileges.
2. Exculpation.
3. Assumability and escalation.
4. Call or acceleration.
5. Subordination.

Prepayment privileges allow the borrower the right to pay off the remaining debt. In some loans there are penalties for prepayment, although usually the penalty declines with time. For example, the penalty may be 3% if the loan is prepaid during the first five years, 2% the next five years, then declining by ½ of 1% for each of the following years until there is no penalty. Some mortgage loans are locked in for the first five to ten years; prepayment without the lender's consent is prohibited.

Exculpation (nonrecourse) means that the property is the sole collateral for the loan (as discussed in the previous chapter). Should the property be foreclosed, the lender can look only to the property for full satisfaction of the debt, not to other property owned by the equity investors. In the absence of exculpation, borrowers are generally personally liable for their debts.

Assumability is the borrower's right to transfer the property and obligation to another party. Since the transferee is not necessarily as good a credit risk as the original owner, many lenders often reserve the right to approve ownership changes. In recent years, some lenders have been willing to approve changes routinely, provided that they can *escalate* (increase) the interest rate on the debt. Such provisions in mortgage loans make assumption privileges less attractive. Despite lender approval of changes in ownership, original borrowers remain liable for the mortgage debt. Sellers have recourse to those who assumed their debt, but they (the sellers) are solely liable if the new owner acquired the property "subject to" the debt.

Call or acceleration provisions are effectively *balloon* payment provisions. Although the loan has a 25- or 30-year term, lenders, at their option, can accelerate payment of the principal after ten or fifteen years, regardless of whether the loan is in default. This obviously puts the lender in a strong position. Upon reaching the "call" date, the lender can force repayment or escalate the interest rate. "Canadian rollover" mortgages are those in which the loan is not called, but its interest rate is adjusted to the market rate at fixed time intervals such as every five years.

Subordination means moving a mortgage loan to a lower priority. Property that is financed by a seller with a first mortgage and is now ready to be developed is not acceptable collateral for a construction lender. Construction lenders want a first lien. If the holder of an existing mortgage is willing to subordinate, the existing mortgage will be reduced to a second lien position to allow a first lien for another mortgage. If a subordination clause will be needed, the borrower should attempt to insert it initially; lenders are highly reluctant to reduce collateral later. Subordinated loans are more favorable to borrowers because they increase the flexibility of first-mortgage financing.

Lender Constraints

From a lender's standpoint, all of the above factors are important. Many institutional lenders have constraints and guidelines either set as company policy or imposed by regulatory authorities. Such constraints include loan-to-value ratios, debt service coverage ratios, diversification, interest rates, amortization terms, property location, and many others depending on company policy and state law. Since these constraints can vary with every lender and every state and change with legislation and with economic conditions, it is not feasible to catalog them here.

At some point in time, real estate lenders, as a group, will be flush with funds. They seem to offer liberal value estimates and high loan-to-value ratio loans. However, when economic conditions change, many may face an acute shortage of loanable funds, and they raise interest rates and impose more rigorous standards on borrowers and property. In sum, mortgage money availability changes with economic conditions.

Example

The example here of a $500,000 purchase of income-producing property (see Figure 11–1) assumes an 80% loan-to-value ratio, 12% interest rate, 25-year, self-amortizing loan. The loan, therefore, has a principal of $400,000. Monthly payments are $4,212.90. Of the $500,000 price, subtract the $400,000 mortgage; the residual, $100,000, was therefore paid as a cash down payment.

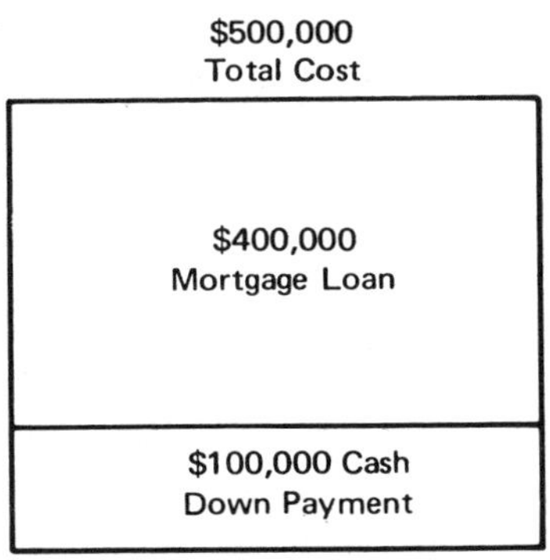

FIGURE 11–1. Sources of Acquisition Funds.

It is acknowledged that interest rates and loan-to-value ratios on new loans vary from time to time with individual lenders and their regulatory boards. Thus, use of the 80% ratio, 12% interest rate loan for 25 years is provided here only as an example; there is no inference that these terms will be available for all properties at all times or from any or all lenders. It is important to understand the method of analysis, not the specific ratio. The property under consideration in reality is likely to be of greater or lesser value than

$500,000; the loan-to-value ratio is apt to be other than 80%; and the interest rate is unlikely to be 12%. The framework for analysis presented here can be utilized no matter what the ratios, rates, terms, and amounts are. The $400,000 loan example will be used throughout much of the text, with variations to highlight important points.

Restated, the example is, upon acquisition:

Mortgage (25-year term, 12% interest)	$400,000
Equity (cash down payment)	100,000
Total	$500,000

PHASE II—OPERATIONS (HOLDING)

Suppose that the property under consideration generates net operating income (NOI) of $65,000, expected to be level and received annually at the end of each year. That net operating income will be divided between the mortgage lender and the equity investor. The mortgage lender has a first claim on income. Monthly debt service is $4,212.90 ($50,555 per year). Any net operating income in excess of that requirement is available for the equity investor to spend or to reinvest. As presented, the equity owner will receive $14,445 annually (before-income tax cash flow). Should the net operating income fall below the debt service requirement, the equity investor must make up the difference from sources outside the property, or face foreclosure and loss of all equity. Net operating income increases will pass through to the equity holder because of the fixed debt service (see Figure 11-2).

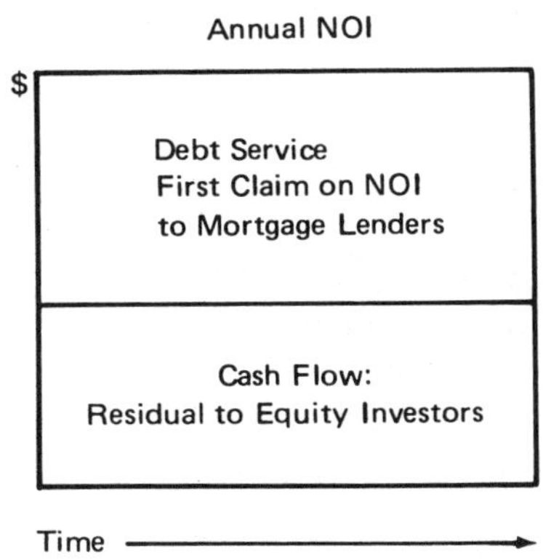

FIGURE 11-2. Distribution of Annual Net Operating Income. Net operating income (NOI) generated by mortgaged income-producing property is shared between mortgage lenders and equity investors. Lenders have the first (prior) claim for debt service; equity investors receive the residual which is cash flow.

Band of Investment

Rates of desired earnings from real estate, which are divided between mortgage lenders and equity investors, can be weighted by the portion of purchase capital contributed, to result in a discount rate applicable to the entire property. This method is called the *band of investment.* The discount rate is then used to capitalize all of the net operating income into one lump sum property value. This value would assume that a capital recovery provision is unnecessary because only interest rates are considered, not amortization or recovery of equity invested.

For example, suppose that lenders typically contribute 80% of the required purchase capital and seek a 12% rate of return on investment. Equity investors want a 15% rate of return on investment. The discount rate for the entire property would be 12.6% as shown below:

Source of Funds	*Purchase Capital Portion*		*Rate of Return on Investment*		*Weighted Rate*
Mortgage	.80	×	.12	=	.096
Equity	.20	×	.15	=	.03
Discount rate for entire property					.126

The result of application, using direct capitalization, would be $515,873 (rounded to $516,000), based on dividing the $65,000 net operating income by a 12.6% capitalization rate. This rate, since it consists purely of current interest, assumes no principal retirement of the loan and no capital appreciation or depreciation of the equity investment. Further, all of the NOI is paid each year to each investor: mortgage and equity. Repayment of all purchase capital will be made upon a resale at an indefinite time in the future.

Band of Investment with Amortization

The band of investment technique can be modified to include mortgage principal amortization. The modification consists of using the mortgage constant instead of the mortgage interest rate as the mortgage's required rate of return. This is shown in Table 11–1. Increasing the overall rate allows capital recovery for the mortgage portion of purchase capital to be reflected in the overall rate and therefore in the value estimate. The higher capitalization rate reduces the value estimate, which is appropriate when it is assumed that real property value depreciation, equalling the mortgage portion of the purchase price will occur. Therefore, capital recovery is needed for the mortgage portion of the property. The equity portion is considered to remain intact in value.

TABLE 11-1
Band of Investment with Mortgage Constant

Source of Funds	Purchase Capital Contributed		Rate Required		Weighted Rate
Mortgage	.80	×	.126387	=	.1011096
Equity	.20	×	.15	=	.03
Overall rate					.1311096
Value estimate: $65,000/.1311096				=	$495,768
Rounded to					$496,000

Residual of Earnings Technique

If it is known that the property generates an overall rate of a certain percentage, say 13% ($65,000/$500,000 = 13%), subtract the lender's interest claim on property earnings. At a mortgage interest rate of 12% and without regard to mortgage amortization, capital appreciation, or depreciation, the equity dividend rate is 17% as shown in Table 11-2.

TABLE 11-2
Band of Investment with Equity Residual

	Purchase Capital Contributed		Rate of Return on Investment		Weighted Rate
Total property	100%	×	.13	=	.13
Less: Mortgage	80%	×	.12	=	−.096
Equity	20%				.034
Rate of return on 20% down payment .034/.20 = 17%					

Consideration of mortgage amortization can be included in the residual of earnings technique. Then, the mortgage constant is subtracted from total property income, instead of subtracting just the mortgage interest rate. The result is the equity dividend rate or current yield. Assuming neither equity growth nor decline, the current yield will be equal to the yield to maturity. This is shown in Table 11-3.

TABLE 11-3
Equity Residual in Band of Investment with Mortgage Constant

Source	*Purchase Capital Contributed*		*Rate of Return*		*Weighted Rate*
Total property	100%	×	.13	=	.13
Less: mortgage	80%	×	.126387	=	.10111
Equity	20%				.02889
Equity percentage rate of return: .02889/.20 = .14445 or 14.44%					

The rate of return on equity will be 14.44%, assuming constant level cash flow for the equity investor and a proceeds from the sale exactly equal to the equity invested. The inference, then, is that the property will decline in value by the same amount as the mortgage is amortized.

Percentages versus Dollar Amounts

The use of loan-to-value ratio percentages in lieu of dollar amounts can result in inconsistencies when estimating an overall rate of return. The inconsistency is due to different assumptions. In the preceding examples, value estimates of $516,000 and $496,000 were reached, respectively. Based on these results, 80% loans would carry principal balances of $412,800 and $396,000, respectively. Neither amount is exactly equal to a loan with a $400,000 principal balance. Should dollars be known instead of typical percentage estimates, the dollars can be used to derive the necessary net operating income as shown in Table 11-4.

TABLE 11-4
Net Operating Income to Satisfy Purchase Capital Requirements

Source of Funds	*Purchase Capital Contributed*		*Current Rate Requirement*		*Required Current Income*
Mortgage	$400,000	×	.126387	=	$50,555
Equity	100,000	×	.14445	=	14,445
Net operating income required					$65,000

Discounted Cash Flow

Level annual cash flow may be discounted to a present value using an annuity factor. To do so, the annuity factor (column 5) for the holding period is multiplied by the level annual cash flow. Results at various yield-to-maturity rates, considering a ten-year income projection period, are shown in Table 11-5.

TABLE 11–5
Discounting Annuity Income at Selected Discount Rates

Interest or Discount Rate	Annuity Factor for 10 years		Annual Cash Flow		Present Value of Cash Flow
8%	6.71	×	$14,445	=	$96,926
12%	5.65	×	14,445	=	81,614
15%	5.019	×	14,445	=	72,499
20%	4.192	×	14,445	=	60,553

Variable Cash Flow

In the event that cash flow is expected to vary during the holding period, the cash flow can be discounted as a series of reversions to estimate present value. This is shown in Table 11–6 at a 15% discount rate.

TABLE 11–6
Discounting Variable Cash Flows at 15%

Year	Cash Flow		Present Value Factor at 15%		Amount at Present Value
1	11,000	×	.8696	=	$ 9,566
2	13,000	×	.7561	=	9,829
3	15,000	×	.6575	=	9,863
4	17,000	×	.5718	=	9,721
5	19,000	×	.4972	=	9,447
6	20,000	×	.4323	=	8,646
7	21,000	×	.3759	=	7,894
8	22,000	×	.3269	=	7,192
9	23,000	×	.2843	=	6,539
10	24,000	×	.2472	=	5,932
Total present value					$84,629

When no reversion (resale proceeds) is forecast, the present value of the cash flow provides an estimate of the value of equity. This is because the cash flow will be the only (nontax) item of benefit to the equity investor; there will be no appreciation in value and no mortgage reduction. This may be the situation where the investor anticipates abandoning the property when a certain event occurs, such as a balloon payment on a nonrecourse mortgage, or the expiration of a land lease where the investor owned only the improvements.

Cash-on-Cash Method (Percentage Cash Flow or Equity Dividend Rate)

For many investors, the only relevant criterion is current cash flow. They estimate the price that they are willing to pay without carefully considering the consequences upon resale. Some feel that the resale will occur so far into the future that the effect of resale on the current price is insignificant. A second reason is the problem of uncertainty. The resale price is unknown. Reinforcing this is the likelihood that comparable properties being considered as alternative investment opportunities, when they are resold, will show similar appreciation (or decline in value) percentage changes. Since this variable—the value change—is considered similar for both properties, there is no need to consider it when choosing among the alternative investment opportunities, and the purchaser therefore considers only the cash return on cash invested.

For example, suppose property is expected to generate $14,445 annual cash flow after subtracting debt service on a $400,000 principal balance mortgage. If the investor requires a 12% cash-on-cash rate (equity dividend rate), the price offered will be $520,000 computed as follows:

Annual cash flow $14,445/.12 =	$120,375	equity
Add: Mortgage loan	400,000	principal
Total price	$520,375	
Rounded to	$520,000	

An investor who insists on a 14% cash-on-cash rate will offer $503,000 as follows:

Annual cash flow $14,445/.14 =	$103,179
Add: Mortgage principal	400,000
Total price	$503,179
Rounded to	$503,000

At a 20% cash-on-cash return, the price drops to $472.000.

For a cash-on-cash return to be equal to a yield-to-maturity rate, the proceeds from resale must equal the initial investment, or the cash flow must be received annually in perpetuity. A more sophisticated approach to property analysis is to reflect the effect of a resale of the property. This requires an estimate of the holding period and the resale price. A discussion of the disposition (resale) of real estate follows.

PHASE III—DISPOSITION (RESALE)

Upon the resale of property, mortgage lenders have the first claim on the proceeds from the transaction. Paying off the remaining balance of a debt cannot be escaped; a routine title examination will discover the existing debt. Purchasers will not take on more debt than the purchase contract calls for.

Financing of Resale

There are basically four ways to finance the resale of real estate, with many variations on each. The four are:

1. All-new financing from a third party to repay the existing debt.
2. All-cash to assumption (by the new owner) of existing debt.
3. Junior lien or wraparound from a third-party lender.
4. Junior lien or wraparound for part or all of the equity, from the seller.

All-New Financing. When a buyer arranges all-new financing, some or all of the new loan taken out, added to the cash down payment, is used to repay the existing debt on the property. After subtracting for the seller's transaction costs, such as brokerage commissions, discount points, title fees, and so on, the remaining proceeds from the sale go to the seller, who may also have a Section 1231 or capital gain tax liability or capital loss. Effectively, the seller receives payments from the sale in cash at closing; however, he must also pay transaction costs and retire the remaining principal balance of the initial debt. The buyer's costs and the distribution of those funds in the sale are graphically shown in Figure 11–3 for a resale at $650,000.

All-Cash to Assumption. A buyer can purchase the property, paying all in cash to the seller for the equity. The buyer assumes the mortgage or takes the property subject to the existing debt. Property sale via loan assumption is generally favored by sellers since it usually minimizes transaction costs and the seller receives payment for the equity all in cash at closing. Although sellers may remain liable on the existing debt, a receipt of substantial cash for the equity provides a comfortable cushion against the possibility of a foreclosure and deficiency judgment at a future date. Because the transaction costs are minimized, some sellers, through negotiations, are willing to pass this savings through in the form of a lower price. The composition of a buyer's payment and the distribution of the proceeds to a seller are shown in Figure 11–4 at a price of $640,000.

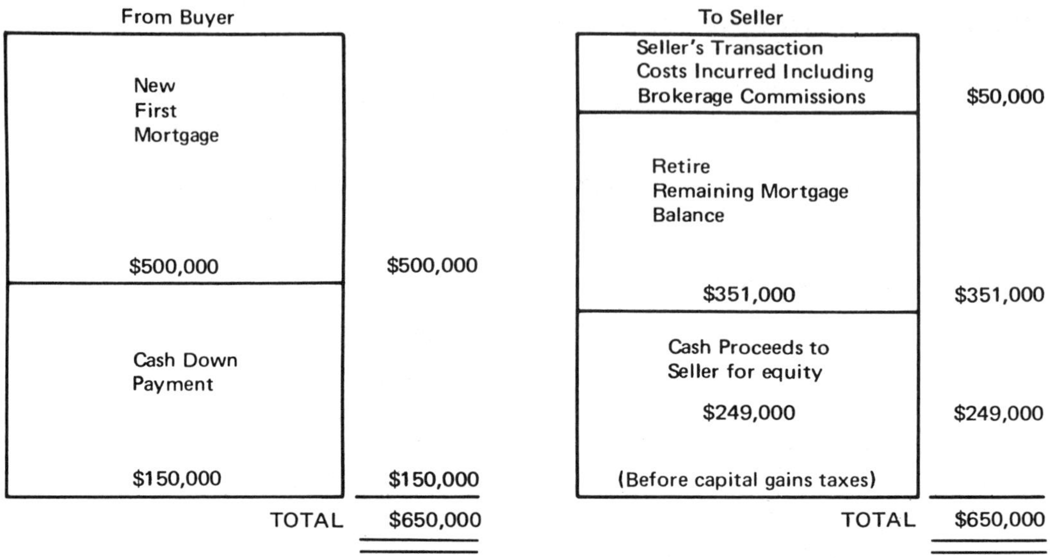

FIGURE 11-3. Resale of Property with New Loan, Showing Sources of Buyer's Money and Distribution.

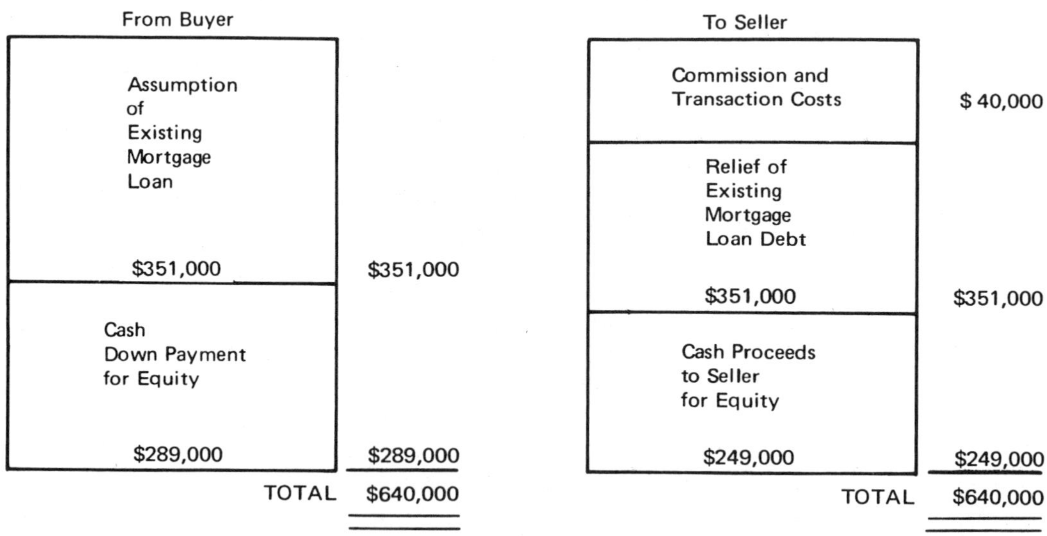

FIGURE 11-4. Resale of Property, Showing Cash to Assumption and Sources of Buyer's Money and Distribution.

Junior Lien from Third Party. A junior lien is a mortgage of lower priority than a first mortgage. Buyers can sometimes arrange a junior lien from a third party to raise part of the cash needed for a down payment. To sellers, this makes little difference when compared to a loan assumption since the seller will receive full payment from the sale in cash. Figure 11-5 shows the sources of the buyer's money and their distribution.

From Buyer	
Assumption of Existing First Mortgage $351,000	$ 351,000
Second Lien $189,000	$ 189,000
Cash for Equity $100,000	$100,000
TOTAL	$ 640,000

To Seller	
Commissions and Transaction Costs	$ 40,000
Relief of Existing Mortgage Debt $351,000	$351,000
Cash Proceeds to Seller for Equity $249,000	$249,000
TOTAL	$640,000

FIGURE 11-5. Resale of Property with First Mortgage Assumption and Third-Party Junior Lien, Showing Source of Buyer's Money and Distribution.

Junior Lien from Seller. An income-property seller may be willing to accept a junior lien in the form of a second mortgage or wraparound mortgage on property sold. This is often the case when new financing with high leverage is not available to buyers, and/or to preserve a low-interest-rate existing first mortgage. In addition, sellers may want to reduce the amount of capital gains taxes currently payable from the sale, and so may finance the sale using installment sale reporting for income taxes. Most sellers, however, after considering all factors, still want payment all in cash from the sale. They may have reinvestment opportunities that are superior to the interest that would be received on a second lien on property sold. They realize that someday they may have to foreclose and become reluctant owners of real estate, forced to keep up first mortgage payments and operating expenses instead of receiving collections on the second mortgage. Knowledgeable sellers will therefore raise the price of property when they supply the financing to compensate for whatever risk is not adequately reflected in the interest rate.

For example, suppose that a seller is asked to provide second financing at 8% interest for fifteen years, in lieu of $189,000 of the cash down payment. Considering the risk involved and the alternative investment opportunities, the seller feels that a 15% interest rate would be more appropriate. Since a mortgage for $189,000 at 15% over fifteen years carries a $2,645.22 monthly payment, that payment is acceptable to the seller. If the seller, through negotiations, becomes obligated to carry an 8% interest rate junior lien, the seller may attempt to raise the principal balance of the lien so that it bears a $2,645.22 payment. The principal balance at 8% interest that bears a monthly payment of $2,645.22 per month for fifteen years is approximately $277,000. Therefore, the seller will attempt to raise the principal balance on the second mortgage by $88,000 ($277,000 minus $189,000 = $88,000) and raise the price by $88,000 accordingly. The price would then become $728,000 ($640,000 + $88,000 = $728,000). Figure 11-6 displays the sources of a buyer's money and credit and the distribution.

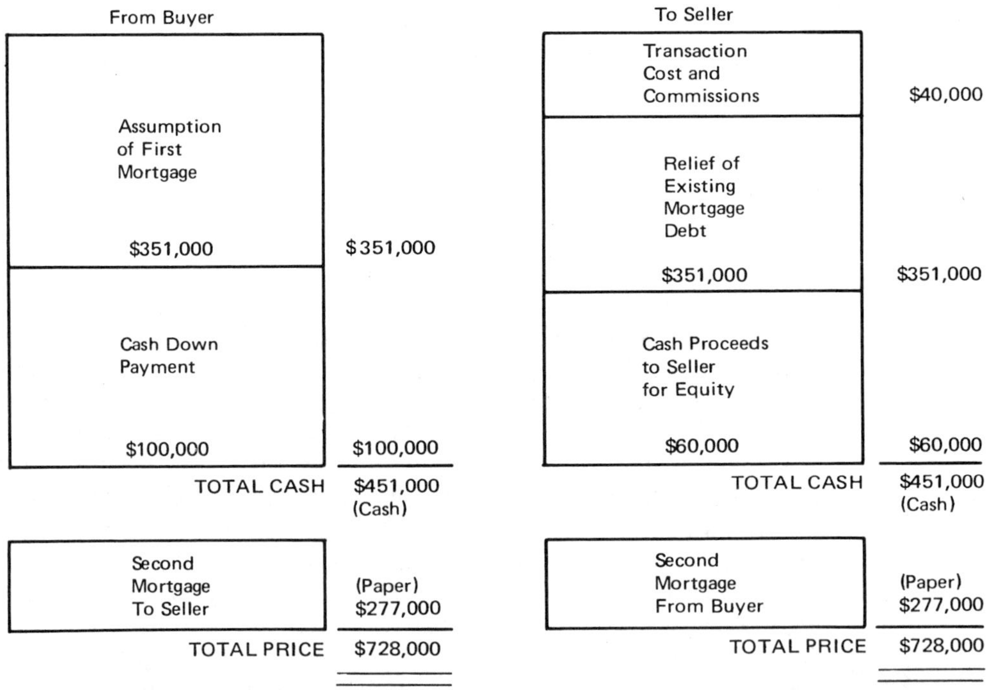

FIGURE 11-6. Resale of Property with First Mortgage Assumption and Seller Junior Financing, showing Sources of Buyer's Money, Credit, and Distributions.

There are many variations on the four themes of financing for property that is sold. New mortgages may be of various types: variable-rate, participating, callable, assumable, etc. Loan assumptions may or may not require rate escalation, personal debt liability, escrows, etc. Third-party second financing may have a balloon payment, variable payments, permanent subordination, and so on. Seller financing can be accomplished with whatever legal provisions the parties agree to, including amounts, rates, timing of payments, collateral substitutions, and so on. Four basic types were considered here, with the effect of each on the seller.

Present Value of Reversion

Most real estate purchasers can rightfully expect to receive something of value when they resell their property. What equity owners receive is called the *reversion* (to equity). Despite the fact that the reversion is not expected to be received for many years, it is possible to forecast a reasonable amount and estimate a present value of that amount using a lump sum reversion factor (column 4).

For example, suppose that the proceeds from resale are expected to be $249,000, and they are expected in ten years. The present value of the reversion at various rates of interest (discount) are shown in Table 11–7:

TABLE 11–7
Present Worth of Reversion at Selected Discount Rates for 10-Year Projection Period

Interest (Discount Rate)	*Present Worth Factor (Column 4)*		*Amount of Reversion*		*Present Worth of Reversion*
8%	.4632	×	$249,000	=	$115,337
12%	.3220	×	249,000	=	80,178
15%	.2472	×	249,000	=	61,553
20%	.1615	×	249,000	=	40,215

Mortgage-equity analysis is completed when the present worth of the reversion is added to the present worth of cash flow and to the present mortgage balance. These items together represent the present worth of cash benefits in real estate investment. For example, suppose that the present value of expected cash flow for ten years is $72,000. At that time, the property is expected to be resold. The estimated present value of the reversion, after subtracting the then existing mortgage from the resale price and applying a reversion factor, is $62,000. Then the present value of equity is the sum of $62,000 plus $72,000, which adds to $134,000. The $134,000 represents the present value of equity after considering mortgage debt service and the remaining unpaid balance of a loan at resale. Equity investors can therefore pay $134,000 plus the mortgage debt for the property. If the present mortgage debt is $400,000, a property price that is justified is $534,000.

SUMMARY

The mortgage-equity technique is a residual method of property analysis. Ownership of real estate can be divided into three phases: acquisition, operations, and disposition. During all of these three phases, the equity owners share in the residual. Equity owners pay the required down payment, which is the residual of price after subtracting the amount of mortgage loan that is taken on as a debt. Equity owners receive the residual of property earnings from operations, after subtracting required debt service. Upon resale of the property, the equity owner receives cash from the resale price.

The value of income-producing property can be financially estimated by adding together the initial mortgage debt and the estimated value of equity. The basis for the value of equity is the present value of future benefits expected: residual cash flows during the operation phase and the residual of the resale price. The sum of the mortgage debt plus the estimated equity value offers an estimate of the price for the property. The technique of adding together the mortgage balance and equity value to estimate a price (or a value) for property is further described in the next chapter.

Questions

1. A strip shopping center can be financed at 75% of its estimated value over 30 years at a 10% interest rate, monthly payment mortgage. Equity investors seek a 13% equity dividend rate.
   a. What fraction of the total purchase price is the cash down payment?
   b. What is the overall rate of return via the band of investment approach, reflecting mortgage amortization?
2. Purchase capital for a small office building is supplied via a $1,000,000 first mortgage at 12% interest over 30 years with monthly payments, plus $300,000 of equity, which seeks a 14% annual cash-on-cash return.

a. What is the debt service constant?

b. How much annual net operating income is required to satisfy the combined needs of lenders and equity investors?

c. What is the maximum equity paid to obtain a 17% cash-on-cash return on equity?

3. An apartment complex was purchased for $1,500,000, using a $500,000 cash down payment and a new 25-year monthly payment first mortgage loan of $1,000,000 at a 12% interest rate. Ten years later, the property is resold, leaving $2.5 million cash after subtracting transaction costs. NOI was $170,000 per year for the first 5 years; and $230,000 for the next 5 years of ownership.

   a. What is the annual cash flow during the first and last 5 years?

   b. What is the cash-on-cash return during the first 5 years? Last 5 years?

   c. What is the mortgage balance at the end of 10 years?

   d. What is the proceeds from resale to the equity owner, after subtracting the unpaid debt?

   e. If the annual cash flow and proceeds from resale were valued to yield a 15% return, would their total be greater or less than the $500,000 beginning equity?

Essay Questions

1. Define each term:

   a. Loan-to-value ratio.

   b. Subordination.

   c. Residual technique.

   d. Junior lien.

   e. Mortgage-equity analysis.

2. Explain each of the three phases of real estate ownership.
3. Explain five financing considerations aside from those that determine the periodic debt service payment.
4. Why may sellers expect to receive a higher price when they provide financing for the property that they are selling?

Chapter 12

Mortgage-Equity Analysis: Conventional Technique

The conventional mortgage-equity technique is a method of estimating the value of property based on the total amount of purchase capital contributed by mortgage lenders and equity investors. It considers the present values of cash flow and resale proceeds that the equity investor anticipates, and adds these amounts to the mortgage principal to derive a property value estimate. In this manner, all of the forecast property net operating income as well as the resale amount is valued.

The conventional technique requires estimates of the forecast cash flow that the equity owner is to receive and the proceeds of resale. Those two elements combined offer the estimated present value of the equity position. The initial loan balance (whether it is a new loan or one that is assumed) is then added to the estimated value of the equity position to derive an estimated price. In the case of a new loan with current market terms, and the use of current market equity yield-to-maturity requirements, the result will be the estimated market value of the real estate. Note that the technique does not include income tax considerations.

PRINCIPLE OF THE CONVENTIONAL TECHNIQUE

The underlying principle of the conventional technique is that both equity investors and mortgage lenders receive income that can be valued. The combined present values of the incomes for mortgage and equity make up the maximum purchase capital that can be raised; therefore this is the appropriate price to be paid for the property. This technique improves on the cash-on-cash method by considering resale proceeds. Resale proceeds include property value appreciation (or decline) and mortgage amortization recovered by the equity owner upon resale.

Income received by both mortgage and equity investors should consider a return both *on* and *of* investment. For the mortgage portion, the current income is debt service. Self-amortizing mortgages require interest (return *on* mortgage principal investment) and amortization (return *of* mortgage principal) payments combined over a certain term. The remaining principal balance of a mortgage at any time is equal to the present value of all the payments remaining until full amortization, discounted at the face mortgage interest rate.

Mortgages are often retired prior to their full amortization term. In this case, the balance of the mortgage is paid off in a lump-sum cash payment, thus retiring the loan. The face value of the loan is equal to the sum of the present value of the periodic cash payments plus the present value of the lump-sum cash payment received on retirement, discounted at the mortgage face rate of interest.

Similarly, the present value of the equity investment is equal to the sum of the income stream plus the proceeds from termination (resale), discounted at an appropriate equity yield rate. Instead of considering that they pay a given price for *property,* sophisticated equity investors recognize that they pay a certain price for *equity*. This equity price, with certain mortgage terms, is justified by the cash flow that the investors expect to receive and the proceeds from the resale. The present value of the equity is therefore the sum of the present value of the cash flow plus the present value of the resale proceeds, discounted at a yield-to-maturity rate that is appropriate for the risks involved. Thus, the amount and timing of benefits to equity are considered.

To illustrate, assume that an equity investor expects to receive $20,000 over ten years in various combinations of annual income and net resale proceeds. Table 12-1 summarizes how much *above* the mortgage amount could be paid (for equity) under each of three cash-flow alternatives. Although each investment provides $20,000 cash flow (after the payment of debt service), the net present value of each income stream discounted at 10% shows how the timing of the cash flow influences the price that can be paid for the income attributable to the equity.

TABLE 12-1
Purchase Price for Property Derived from the Sum of the Present Value of Cash Flow, the Net Resale Proceeds, and the Mortgage Principal Balance

Year	*Investment A*	*Investment B*	*Investment C*
1 (cash flow)	$ 1,000	$ 500	$ 0
2 (cash flow)	1,000	500	0
3 (cash flow)	1,000	500	0
4 (cash flow)	1,000	500	0
5 (cash flow)	1,000	500	0
6 (cash flow)	1,000	500	0
7 (cash flow)	1,000	500	0
8 (cash flow)	1,000	500	0
9 (cash flow)	1,000	500	0
10 (cash flow)	1,000	500	0
10 (net resale proceeds)	10,000	15,000	20,000
Total amount received	$20,000	$20,000	$20,000
Amount at net present value, 10% rate	$10,000[a]	$ 8,860[b]	$ 7,720[c]
Add mortgage principal	50,000	50,000	50,000
Purchase price	$60,000	$58,860	$57,720

[a] Annuity factor of 6.14 × $1,000 annual income plus reversion factor .386 × $10,000 = $10,000.
[b] Annuity factor of 6.14 × $500 annual income plus reversion factor of .386 × $15,000 = $8,860.
[c] Reversion factor of .386 × $20,000 = $7,720.

After establishing an estimated value of equity, investors will add the mortgage principal to this amount to derive a price for the property. At this price, equity investors expect to receive an adequate rate of return on their investment. The equation is simple:

$$\text{Price} = \text{Equity purchase capital} + \text{Mortgage purchase capital}$$

For example, if the equity value is $134,000 above a $400,000 mortgage debt, the price would be $534,000.

Equity Value Formula

The value of equity capital is the sum of two components: cash flow and resale proceeds. Both components are discounted at the appropriate yield rate, and their present values are derived using present value factors. When the forecast cash flow is expected to be level, the annuity factor is multiplied by the forecast annual cash flow. The reversion—or proceeds from resale—is valued by a present worth reversion factor since it is received in one lump sum.

The formula for equity value (equity purchase capital) is:

$$\text{Equity value} = \text{PWAF (CF)} + \text{PWF (PS)}$$

where:

PWAF = Present worth of an annuity factor at equity yield rate
CF = Cash flow
PWF = Present worth of reversion factor at equity yield rate
PS = Proceeds from resale

For example, suppose that annual before-tax cash flow is forecast to be $14,445 and the appropriate annuity factor is 5.01877. The forecast resale proceeds are $249,000 and the present worth factor is .2472. Therefore, the present value of the equity is $134,049 as shown below:

$$\text{Equity value} = 5.01877\ (\$14{,}445) + .2472\ (\$249{,}000)$$
$$\text{Equity value} = \$134{,}049\ (\text{rounded to } \$134{,}000)$$

The present mortgage principal balance is added to the equity value to estimate the property value. In this manner, all of the income is valued. Present values for cash flow, property value increases (or declines), and equity build-up through amortization payments are estimated in the equity value. The mortgage principal is equal to the present value of required debt service payments, discounted at the mortgage face interest rate. Thus the property value estimate—the sum of the equity value and the mortgage principal—considers all of the net operating income and the resale price of the property.

APPLICATION OF THE CONVENTIONAL TECHNIQUE

Application of the conventional technique requires a three-stage computation for a certain income projection period (see Table 12-2). The projection period is the term for which the owner anticipates holding the property.

TABLE 12–2
Three Stages in the Conventional Technique

Stage I. Estimate present value of annual cash flow
- A. Estimate: Annual net operating income (NOI)
  1. From: Potential gross income
  2. Subtract: Vacancy and collection allowance
  3. Add: Miscellaneous income
  4. Subtract: Operating expenses
  5. Result: Net operating income
- B. Estimate expected mortgage payments
  1. Initial principal
  2. Full amortization term
  3. Interest rate
  4. Monthly payment
  5. Annual debt service
- C. Annual cash flow is NOI minus annual debt service (I-A-5 less B-5)
- D. Value anticipated annual cash flow (present value of I-C for holding period)

Stage II. Estimate present value of resale proceeds at end of projection period
- A. Resale price
- B. Less: Transaction costs
- C. Less: Unpaid mortgage debt at resale
- D. Result: Resale proceeds
- E. Value anticipated proceeds from resale (present value of II-D)

Stage III. Estimate present value of equity and property
- A. Add: I-D plus II-E for estimated value of equity
- B. Add: III-A (equity value) plus I-B-1 (initial principal for estimated value of property

In the *first stage,* the analyst must estimate the net operating income (NOI) by subtracting operating expenses, and vacancy and collection allowances from the potential gross income. From the NOI, the amount necessary to pay the debt service must be subtracted to estimate the annual cash flow that is available for the equity investor. Then the present value of the forecast annual cash flow must be calculated.

In the *second stage,* the present value of the resale proceeds must be computed. To estimate the resale proceeds the analyst must forecast a resale price or change in property value, and then subtract all transaction costs that are to be paid by the seller upon resale, such as commissions, title expenses, and the unpaid mortgage balance at resale. The present value of the resale proceeds is then calculated.

In the *third stage,* the present value of the resale proceeds is added to the present value of the cash flow to derive an estimated value of equity. The property is estimated to be worth the equity value plus the present mortgage debt. In mortgage-equity analysis, the value of property is the combined values of mortgage and equity purchase capital contributions. This is diagrammed in Figure 12–1.

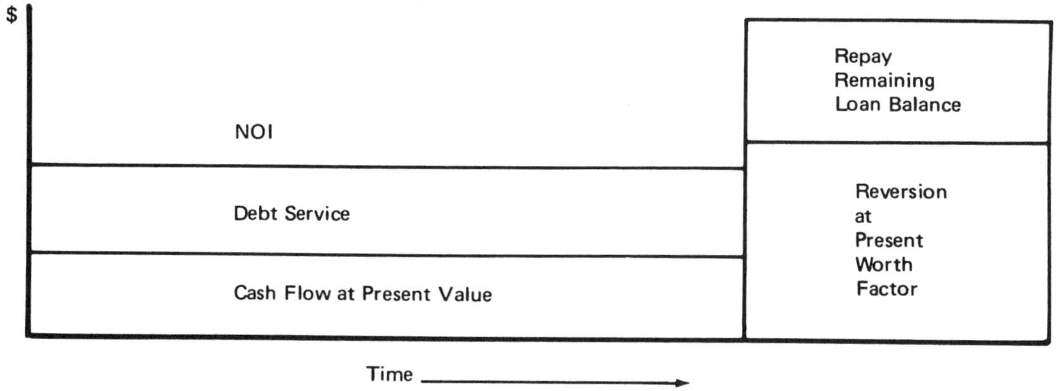

Property Value (V) = PWAF (NOI − DS) + PWF (RP − OS loan) + Present Mortgage Balance

Where:
PWAF=Present Worth of an Annuity Factor at Equity Yield Ratio
NOI=Net Operating Income
DS=Debt Service (annual requirement)
PWF=Present Worth Reversion Factor at Equity Yield Rate
RP=Resale Price for Property
OS=Outstanding Mortgage Balance at Resale

FIGURE 12–1. Mortgage-Equity Analysis.

Use of Algebra

Algebra is often required in the conventional technique. Employing algebra is aided by abbreviating symbols. Instead of *x*'s, *y*'s, and *z*'s, more descriptive abbreviations are used as symbols, as listed below for each stage.

Stage I *Estimate present value of cash flow.*

NOI = net operating income
DS = debt service (annual)
f = mortgage constant percentage (annual)
CF = cash flow (annual)

n = projection period
PWAF = present worth annuity factor
PWCF = present worth of cash flow (CF × PWAF)

Stage II *Estimate present worth of resale proceeds.*
RP = resale price of property
OS = outstanding mortgage balance at resale
b = fraction of loan principal remaining at resale
PS = proceeds (to the equity investor) from resale
PWF = present worth factor for reversion
PWR = present worth of reversion (PS × PWF)

Stage III *Estimate present worth of equity and property.*
MP = present mortgage principal
V = property value (initial)
LTV = loan-to-value ratio (initial)

The general formula:

Property value = Equity purchase capital + Mortgage purchase capital

can be expanded, to become

Property value = Present worth of cash flow + Present worth of proceeds from resale + Mortgage principal

or, with abbreviations:

$$V = \text{PWCF} + \text{PWR} + \text{MP}$$

The elements PWCF and PWR can be expanded as follows:

$$\text{PWCF} = \text{PWAF}\ (\text{NOI} - \text{DS})$$
$$\text{PWR} = \text{PWF}\ (\text{RP} - \text{OS})$$

Therefore:

$$V = \text{PWAF}\ (\text{NOI} - \text{DS}) + \text{PWF}\ (\text{RP} - \text{OS}) + \text{MP}$$

Depending on the known and unknown variables, amounts or rates can be substituted into the equation when they can be related to other factors.

Free and Clear Example of Conventional Technique

As a simplified example, consider property that is purchased with 100% equity capital. It is free and clear of any lien. The loan-to-value ratio is thus 0. The property generates $65,000 level annual net operating income and is expected to be resold in ten years for $600,000 after paying transaction costs. Equity investors desire a 15% yield-to-maturity (equity yield) rate. Since there is no mortgage to require debt service, net operating income and cash flow are the same amount: $65,000 annually. Similarly, the proceeds from resale (reversion) and the net sales price will be the same—$600,000—because there is no unpaid debt at resale. Valuation of the income and reversion at a 15% rate is $475,000, as shown in Table 12–3.

TABLE 12–3
Conventional Technique Applied to Property Free of Debt

Source of Income	*Amount*		*15% Rate Factor*		*Present Value of Income*
Annual cash flow	$ 65,000	×	5.01877	=	$326,220
Proceeds from resale	$600,000	×	.2472	=	148,320
Total present value					$474,540
Rounded to					$475,000

Therefore, where the property is free and clear of debt, investors are justified in paying only $475,000 for the property in order to receive a 15% yield rate to maturity. Annual cash flow of $65,000 provides a 13.7% cash-on-cash return to the $475,000 price. The yield to maturity is increased from 13.7% to 15% because the forecast reversion ($600,000 resale proceeds) exceeds the initial $475,000 investment. Therefore, all of the capital recovery and some of the income are found in the resale proceeds.

Conventional Technique with Mortgage Debt

Suppose that, in the preceding example, $400,000 of mortgage debt would typically be available to purchase the property. The debt would have a 25-year term and require $4,212.90 as the monthly payment at 12% interest. Equity investors want a 15% yield-to-maturity (equity yield) rate. The property will be held for ten years and is then expected to be sold for $600,000. The outstanding mortgage balance in ten years will be $351,000. The conventional technique is shown below, separated into the three stages.

Stage I.	
Net operating income	\$65,000
Less: Annual debt service:	
12 × \$4,212.90	−50,555
Annual cash flow (to equity)	\$14,445
Multiply by: Annuity factor	× 5.01877
Present value of cash flow	\$72,496

Stage II.	
Resale price (after transaction costs)	\$600,000
Less: Outstanding debt in 10 years	−351,000
Proceeds (to equity)	\$249,000
Multiply by: Reversion factor	× .2472
Present value of resale proceeds	\$ 61,553

Stage III.	
Stage I: Present value of cash flow	\$ 72,496
Add: Stage II: Present value of resale proceeds	+ 61,553
Present value of equity	\$134,049
Add: Initial mortgage balance	+400,000
Present value of property	\$534,049
Rounded to	\$534,000

The justified present price for the property is \$534,000. Although equity receives only a 10.8% cash-on-cash return, (\$14,445 ÷ 134,000 = 10.8%), the \$134,000 equity investment captures all of the property appreciation, which increases the equity yield to 15%. The \$534,000 price is higher than the free-and-clear price of \$475,000 since the leverage factor is favorable: the mortgage constant is less than the overall rate, and property appreciation is forecast. The favorable leverage adds to the value. With favorable leverage, forecast yields to equity investors will improve despite a higher price for the property.

Effect of Leverage. In most situations, equity investors demand a higher yield-to-maturity rate for highly levered property because of the increased risk. However, when debt is nonrecourse, leverage reduces the amount the investor stands to lose and allows greater equity diversification into other projects. The mortgage reduces the equity investment required, thereby increasing the number of potential investors who could consider the project as an investment. Thus, mortgages can add to property price. Terms of a typical third-party mortgage are considered for real estate appraisals that have the purpose of estimating the market value of the subject real estate.

Effect of Equity Yield Rates on Value. The property value is sensitive to equity yield rates. The higher the rate required, the lower the property value. Shown in Table 12–4 are value estimates at selected equity yield rates.

TABLE 12–4
Property Value Estimates at Selected Equity Yield Rates

Equity Yield Rate	*Present Worth of Cash Flow*		*Present Worth of Reversion*		*Initial Mortgage Balance*		*Value Estimate*
8%	\$96,926	+	\$115,337	+	\$400,000	=	\$612,263
12%	81,614	+	80,178	+	400,000	=	561,792
15%	72,499	+	61,553	+	400,000	=	534,052
20%	60,556	+	40,215	+	400,000	=	500,771

Conventional Technique Given More Than One Unknown

Use of algebra is necessary in the conventional technique when there is more than one unknown. Frequently, the forecast resale price is based on the present value of the property. The potential mortgage principal is sometimes based on the present property value. Application of the conventional technique is demonstrated for the following situations:

1. The resale price but not the fractional change in property value is offered, or vice versa.
2. The mortgage principal, but not the loan-to-value ratio, is known, or vice versa.

Given Resale Price or Fractional Change in Value. If the dollar amount of a resale price is estimated, the resale amount is substituted for RP in the equation:

$$V = \text{PWAF (NOI} - \text{DS)} + \text{PWF (RP} - \text{OS)} + \text{MP}$$

However, if an estimated fraction change in value over the projection period is offered instead of a resale price estimate in dollars, the estimated resale can be related as a fraction of V, to reduce the number of unknowns. For example, if it is forecast that the property will decline in value by 30% over the projection period, then RP = .7*V*. That is, the estimated resale price will be 70% (.7) of the present value.

When appreciation is forecast, the resale price will be greater than the present value, and also can be stated in terms of *V*. Appreciation of 30% would be shown as 1.3*V*. Putting unknown values in terms of *V* minimizes mathematical manipulation.

Given Mortgage Principal or Loan-to-Value Ratio. When the mortgage principal is known, as are other loan factors, it is possible to solve for debt service and annual cash flow, as well as for the mortgage balance at the end of the projection period. However, when a loan-to-value ratio is given, more intricate computations are required.

It is best to express as many unknowns as possible in terms of *V*. When an 80% loan-to-value ratio is quoted, it is appropriate to substitute .8*V* for the mortgage principal. Since the mortgage principal has an effect on annual debt service, it also affects the cash flow.

When the loan-to-value ratio is given (but not the mortgage principal) along with other terms, it is necessary to compute a debt service constant. The annual debt service can then be expressed in terms of *V*. For example, given an 80% loan, with a 12.6387% constant (.126387), the annual debt service requirement will be $.126387 \times .8V$, or .10111*V*. In the equation, annual cash flow will be: NOI minus .10111*V*.

The mortgage balance at the end of the projection period can be expressed in terms of *V*, as well. A 12% 25-year monthly-payment self-amortizing mortgage will have an outstanding balance in 10 years equal to .8775 of its original balance. This relationship holds regardless of the amount of principal. Therefore, such a loan that is currently 80% (.8) of value will have a balance in 10 years that is $.8 \times .8775 = .702V$. This indicates the mortgage's future balance in relation to the property's present value. It does not indicate the future property value.

ADAPTATIONS OF CONVENTIONAL TECHNIQUE

Employing algebraic relationships, it is possible to derive estimates of value under the following conditions:

1. Solve for value, given mortgage principal and a dollar estimate of resale price.

2. Solve for value, given mortgage principal. The resale price is expressed in terms of the present value.
3. Solve for value, given the loan-to-value ratio and a dollar estimate of the resale price.
4. Solve for value, given the loan-to-value ratio and the resale price expressed in terms of the present value.
5. Solve for equity yield rate, given present price.

For each of those situations, equations are presented below. Solutions are presented in Appendix A in the back of the book.

Given:

\$400,000 (MP)*	=	mortgage principal (12% interest, 25-year term, debt service of \$50,555 per year)
\$65,000 (NOI)	=	annual NOI
\$50,555 (DS)*	=	annual debt service
\$14,445 (CF)*	=	annual cash flow
10(N)		projection period in years
\$351,000 (OS)*	=	mortgage balance at end of projection period
5.01877 (PWAF)	=	factor for the present worth of a 10-year annuity at 15% rate
.2472 (PWF)	=	factor for the present worth of a 10-year reversion
\$500,000 (RP)*	=	resale price in 10 years

*Except where a ratio is indicated; then amounts are unknown.

Practice Problem 1

Solve for value, given mortgage principal and a dollar estimate of the resale price. The estimated resale price is \$500,000.

$$V = \text{PWAF (NOI} - \text{DS)} + \text{PWF (RP} - \text{OS)} + \text{MP}$$

Substituting:

$V = 5.01877\ (\$65{,}000 - \$50{,}555) + .2472\ (\$500{,}000 - \$351{,}000) + \$400{,}000$

$V = \$509{,}328$ (see Appendix A for details)

Practice Problem 2

Solve for value, given mortgage principal and percentage of property value change over projection period. Percentage value change is 10% appreciation.

$$V = \text{PWAF (NOI} - \text{DS)} + \text{PWR (RP} - \text{OS)} + \text{MP}$$

Substituting given components:

V = 5.01877 (\$65,000 − \$50,555) + .2472 (1.1V − \$351,000) + \$400,000
V = \$529,775 (see Appendix A for details)

Notice that 1.1V was substituted for RP. This was done because it was given that the resale price would be 10% greater than the present value. This substitution makes V the only unknown value in the equation.

Practice Problem 3

Solve for value given a loan-to-value ratio estimate, interest rate, and term. (Loan-to-value ratio is estimated at 80%; mortgage principal is unknown.)

$$V = \text{PWAF (NOI} - \text{DS)} + \text{PWF (RP} - \text{OS)} + \text{MP}$$

Substituting amounts:

V = 5.01877 [\$65,000 − .8V (.126387)] + .2472 [V − .8V (.8775)] + .8V
V = \$514,719 (see Appendix A for details)

Notes on substitutions:

(a) MP = .8V since the loan-to-value ratio is given at 80%.
(b) OS = .8V (.8775).

The outstanding mortgage balance in 10 years will be .8775 of the present balance. The present balance is .8V. Therefore, the *OS* balance in 10 years is .8V (.8775).

(c) DS = .8V(.126387). The loan is .8V and the debt service constant is .126387. Therefore DS = .8V (.126387).
(d) RP = V assumes no value change over the projection period.

Practice Problem 4

Solve for value, given percentage loan-to-value ratio (80%) and fraction value change = 30% appreciation. Mortgage principal and resale price are unknown. Loan-to-value ratio is 80%.

$$V = \text{PWAF (NOI} - \text{DS)} + \text{PWF (RP} - \text{OS)} + \text{MP}$$

Substitutions:

$$V = 5.01877\ [\$65{,}000 - .8V\,(.126387)] + .2472\ [1.3V - .8V\,(.8775)] + .8V$$

V = \$582,931 (see Appendix A for details)

Practice Problem 5

Solve for equity yield rate, given other variables including the present price. Present price is \$500,000.

$$V = \text{PWAF (NOI} - \text{DS)} + \text{PWF (RP} - \text{OS)} + \text{MP}$$

$$\$500{,}000 = \text{PWAF}\ (\$65{,}000 - \$50{,}555) + \text{PWF}\ (\$500{,}000 - \$351{,}000) + \$400{,}000$$

Substitute PWAF and PWF at different yield rates until the solution provides an equality. See Appendix A for details. Solution: Equity yield rate is between 16% and 17%.

Effect of Existing Mortgage

The conventional mortgage-equity technique can be used to estimate a price when there is an existing mortgage on the property. In this situation, the present mortgage principal balance, rather than the initial balance, is MP. The outstanding balance at the end of the projection period, or this balance as a fraction of the current principal balance, can be used in the equation.

For example, let us suppose that the subject property is encumbered by a mortgage that was originally \$400,000. It was taken out 5 years ago at a 12% rate, over a 25-year amortization term. The present balance is \$382,613. Ten years from now, the balance will be \$293,641, which is 76.75% of the current principal balance (\$293,641/\$382,613 = .767463). In the equation, let MP = \$382,613, OS = \$293,641, and b = .767463. Then:

$$V = \text{PWAF (NOI} - \text{DS)} + \text{PWF (RP} - \text{OS)} + \text{MP}$$

Let RP = V, and equity yield = 15%. Thus:

V = 5.01877 ($65,000 − $50,555) + .2472 ($V$ − $293,641) + $382,613
V = $508,131
Rounded to $508,000

Effect of Two Mortgages

Two or more mortgages on the property add little difficulty to the basic conventional mortgage-equity technique. However, all three stages must be modified to accommodate the mortgages. It is convenient to assign numbers to the symbols used for each mortgage, as shown below:

Stage I.	DS_1 and DS_2 represent debt service on the two mortgages.
Stage II.	OS_1 and OS_2 represent outstanding balances on the mortgages at the end of the projection term.
Stage III.	MP_1 and MP_2 represent present mortgage principal balances of the mortgages.

Then:

$$V = \text{PWAF}(\text{NOI} - DS_1 - DS_2) + \text{PWF}(\text{RP} - OS_1 - OS_2) + MP_1 + MP_2$$

Effect of Projection Period

The holding or projection period, which is the estimated time span from acquisition to resale, has an influence on the value estimate. The analyst should carefully select the most likely projection period. Many income-producing properties are sold within ten years or refinanced during that time; so ten years is a projection period that is often used. Although ten years is reasonable and is often used in practice because of diminishing income tax deductions for depreciation and interest expense, the optimal holding period should consider investment opportunities outside the subject property—that is, whether the investor can, with no perceived change in risk, equal or exceed the rate of return that is forecast to be received from the subject property by investing the proceeds from resale into alternative investments. It is a question that cannot be answered by the subject property alone. Alternative investment opportunities must be considered.

Nonetheless, the projection period does have an influence on the value estimate using the conventional technique. The influence is a function of an ever-changing leverage situation. The longer the holding period, the lower the present value estimate (assuming no refinancing and favorable leverage). As time passes, the loan-to-value declines; so the effect of favorable leverage is diminished. This is illustrated in Figure 12-2.

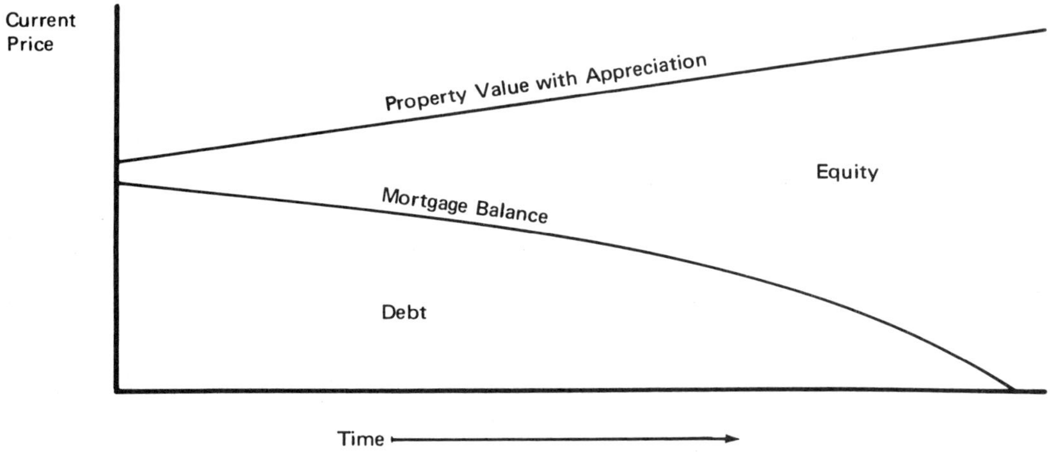

FIGURE 12-2. Changing Debt-Equity Structure.

As an example, situations A and B considered the same mortgage, equity yield rate, and net operating income (see Table 12-5). Both assumed neither appreciation nor depreciation in the property value over the projection term. The $7,000 difference in current value estimates for A versus B is attributable to the reduced leverage over time of the longer holding period of situation B. Consequently, the income projection period must be chosen carefully, considering the expected time span from acquisition until disposition or refinancing.

TABLE 12-5
Effect of Projection Term on Value Estimates

	Situation	
Description	*A*	*B*
Mortgage (25 years, 12%)	$400,000	$400,000
Value change during projection	0	0
Equity yield to maturity	15%	15%
Annual cash flow	$ 14,445	$ 14,445
Projection term	10 years	20 years
Value estimate	$517,000	$510,000

In situation A, the value estimate is about $517,000; whereas in B, it is $510,000.

Situation A:
$V = 5.01877\ (\$14{,}445) + .2472\ (V - \$351{,}000) + \$400{,}000$
$V = \$72{,}496 + .2472V - \$86{,}767 + \$400{,}000$
$V = \$517{,}078$

Situation B:
$V = 6.25933\ (14{,}445) + .0611\ (V - \$189{,}391) + \$400{,}000$
$V = \$90{,}416 + .0611V - \$11{,}572 + \$400{,}000$
$V = \$510{,}005$

Variable Cash Flow

When it is expected that net operating income will fluctuate from one year to the next, or in cases where the annual debt service is variable, cash flow will vary from year to year. Given those conditions, Stage I of the conventional technique would then be altered to treat the annual cash flow as a series of individual reversions, instead of an annuity. No change is required for Stages II and III.

SUMMARY

The conventional technique of mortgage-equity analysis is a method of valuation within the income approach. It considers that the value of the property is the sum of the mortgage debt and the equity value. The value of equity is the sum of the present value of the annual cash flow for a given projection period plus the present value of the proceeds from resale at the end of the projection period. Adding the mortgage debt to the equity value offers an estimate of the price that is expected to yield certain benefits to the equity investor and mortgage lender.

In mortgage-equity analysis, either the mortgage loan principal or the loan-to-value ratio must be given with the mortgage facts. An estimate of the resale price or fractional change in value over the projection period must be included. Finally, the net operating income and the desired equity yield rate are to be included.

The technique can be employed if there is an existing loan to be assumed or if a new loan is arranged. It can be modified to accommodate more than one mortgage and variable cash flows. In instances where the price is known, the technique can be used to estimate the equity yield rate. In conclusion, the conventional mortgage-equity technique is a flexible one that can accommodate almost all situations. Resulting value estimates, however, are no better than the assumptions that are input.

Questions

1. A small industrial warehouse is net-leased for $10,000 per year rental for the next 25 years, with rent payable at the end of each year. It is estimated that the property will be worth $60,000 when the lease expires. Investors want a 13% yield rate to maturity.
   a. What is the present value of the income stream?
   b. What is the present value of the reversion?
   c. What is the estimated present value of the property?
2. The warehouse in Question 1 is subject to a $75,000 first mortgage at an 11% interest rate, payable in annual installments over 25 years.
   a. What is the annual cash flow?
   b. What is the present value of the cash flow at a 15% equity yield rate?
   c. What is the forecast resale price?
   d. What is the forecast resale proceeds?
   e. What is the present value of the estimated resale proceeds at a 15% equity yield rate?
   f. What is the estimated present value of the property?
3. A free-standing retail store is net-leased for $15,000 per year for the first 5 years, and $12,000 per year for the following 5 years. It is subject to a $100,000, 25-year monthly-payment mortgage at a 10% interest rate. Equity investors want a 14% yield rate.
   a. What is the present value of the cash flow?
   b. What will the outstanding mortgage balance be in 10 years?
   c. If the property is expected to resell for $200,000 at the end of the tenth year, what is the expected proceeds from resale?
4. Net operating income for an apartment complex is expected to be level at $30,000 per year for 5 years. The apartment complex is subject to a $200,000 principal, 12% interest rate, monthly-payment mortgage, self-amortizing over 30 years. Equity investors seek a 12% equity yield rate.
   a. What is the annual cash flow?
   b. What is the estimated value of the property, assuming no change in its value over a 5-year projection period?

Essay Questions

1. How does the conventional mortgage-equity technique differ from the cash-on-cash method?
2. How does the conventional technique account for value change (appreciation or decline) and equity's recovery of mortgage reduction benefits. Discuss the timing of the realization of those benefits.
3. What are the assumptions about the property that must be given if the conventional mortgage-equity technique is to be used?
4. How does the projection term affect the value estimate in the conventional mortgage-equity technique?

Chapter 13

Ellwood's Mortgage-Equity Technique

L.W. Ellwood's contribution to mortgage-equity analysis was in devising a certain shortcut formula offering results that are identical to the conventional mortgage-equity technique. Although Ellwood is frequently credited with the development of the six-function compound interest tables, these tables were actually compiled several centuries before his birth.

This chapter describes the application of Ellwood's formula under a variety of circumstances, its relationship to the conventional technique, its derivation from the band of investment technique, and its uses for sensitivity analysis. Since the Ellwood technique parallels the conventional mortgage-equity technique, many portions of this chapter will parallel the preceding one.

ADVANTAGES OF ELLWOOD'S TECHNIQUE VERSUS CONVENTIONAL MORTGAGE-EQUITY TECHNIQUE

The main attraction of the Ellwood technique is that it offers a shortcut mortgage-equity formula when given the loan-to-value ratio and the estimated fraction change in property value over the projection period. The conventional technique is more easily applied when dollar amounts for the mortgage principal and resale price are given; Ellwood's is easier to use when ratios are given. However, either technique can be applied in either situation, and the results will be mathematically identical; so the choice of one over the other is a matter that depends on the analyst's personal preference and on the assumptions that are given.

Ellwood was employed by a life insurance company. In most states, a life insurance company's mortgage investments are restricted to a certain loan-to-value ratio. He discovered that precomputed tables allowed for more efficient processing of mortgage applications. His technique allows an analyst to compute quickly capitalization rates at any given loan-to-value ratio. The analyst can solve for value, then lend a fraction (75% or whatever other percentage is appropriate) of that amount.

THE ELLWOOD FORMULATION

The Ellwood formulation is:

$$r = Y - mC; \qquad \text{also} \qquad R = Y - mC + \text{dep (SFF@Y)}$$

where:

r	= the overall rate of return to capitalize net operating income into value without considering property appreciation or value decline.
R	= the overall rate of return to capitalize net operating income into value, given a forecast change in value over the projection period.
Y	= equity yield rate (yield to maturity on equity).
m	= the loan-to-value ratio.
C	= a mortgage coefficient that Ellwood derived.
dep	= the fraction decline (depreciation) in property value over the projection period.
app	= the fraction increase (appreciation) in property value over the projection period. Can be inserted into equation as − dep.
SFF@Y	= the sinking fund factor at the equity yield rate for the projection period.

Using the Ellwood "C Table"

Table 13-1 is a page of Ellwood's "C Factors." To use the "C Table," first find the mortgage amortization term and interest rate range that includes the subject mortgage, across the top of the page. Then find the specific column across the top of the page at the mortgage interest rate. Next, find the desired equity yield rate and projection term within the two columns on the left side of the page. The intersection of the mortgage interest rate column with the equity yield rate and projection period row offers the C factor.

TABLE 13-1
Sample of Ellwood "C" Table 25 Year Mortgage Amortization: 10.75% to 12%

	Interest Rate	10.75%	11%	11.25%	11.50%	11.75%	12.00%	Sinking Fund Factor at Equity Yield
	Equity Yield	MORTGAGE	COEFFICIENTS				"C"	
	6%	-0.0462	-0.0487	-0.0512	-0.0537	-0.0562	-0.0587	.1774
	7%	-0.0363	-0.0388	-0.0413	-0.0438	-0.0463	-0.0488	.1739
	8%	-0.0265	-0.0290	-0.0315	-0.0340	-0.0365	-0.0390	.1705
	9%	-0.0167	-0.0192	-0.0217	-0.0241	-0.0266	-0.0291	.1671
	10%	-0.0069	-0.0093	-0.0118	-0.0143	-0.0168	-0.0193	.1638
	11%	0.0030	0.0005	-0.0020	-0.0045	-0.0069	-0.0094	.1606
	12%	0.0128	0.0103	0.0079	0.0054	0.0029	0.0005	.1574
	13%	0.0226	0.0202	0.0177	0.0153	0.0128	0.0103	.1543
Pro-jection	14%	0.0325	0.0300	0.0276	0.0251	0.0227	0.0202	.1513
	15%	0.0423	0.0399	0.0374	0.0350	0.0325	0.0301	.1483
	16%	0.0522	0.0497	0.0473	0.0448	0.0424	0.0399	.1454
Period	17%	0.0620	0.0596	0.0571	0.0547	0.0523	0.0498	.1426
	18%	0.0719	0.0694	0.0670	0.0646	0.0621	0.0597	.1398
5 Years	19%	0.0817	0.0793	0.0769	0.0744	0.0720	0.0696	.1371
	20%	0.0916	0.0892	0.0867	0.0843	0.0819	0.0795	.1344
n = 5	21%	0.1014	0.0990	0.0966	0.0942	0.0918	0.0893	.1318
	22%	0.1113	0.1089	0.1065	0.1041	0.1017	0.0992	.1292
	23%	0.1212	0.1188	0.1164	0.1140	0.1115	0.1091	.1267
	24%	0.1311	0.1287	0.1263	0.1238	0.1214	0.1190	.1242
	25%	0.1409	0.1385	0.1361	0.1337	0.1313	0.1289	.1218
	26%	0.1508	0.1484	0.1460	0.1436	0.1412	0.1388	.1195
	27%	0.1607	0.1583	0.1559	0.1535	0.1511	0.1487	.1172
	28%	0.1706	0.1682	0.1658	0.1634	0.1610	0.1586	.1149
	29%	0.1804	0.1781	0.1757	0.1733	0.1709	0.1685	.1127
	30%	0.1903	0.1880	0.1856	0.1832	0.1808	0.1784	.1106
	6%	-0.0447	-0.0472	-0.0496	-0.0521	-0.0546	-0.0571	.0759
	7%	-0.0352	-0.0376	-0.0401	-0.0426	-0.0450	-0.0475	.0724
	8%	-0.0257	-0.0281	-0.0306	-0.0330	-0.0355	-0.0379	.0690
	9%	-0.0161	-0.0186	-0.0210	-0.0234	-0.0259	-0.0283	.0658
	10%	-0.0066	-0.0090	-0.0114	-0.0138	-0.0163	-0.0187	.0627
Pro-jection	11%	0.0030	0.0006	-0.0018	-0.0042	-0.0066	-0.0091	.0598
	12%	0.0126	0.0102	0.0078	0.0054	0.0030	0.0006	.0570
	13%	0.0222	0.0199	0.0175	0.0151	0.0127	0.0103	.0543
Period	14%	0.0319	0.0295	0.0271	0.0247	0.0223	0.0199	.0517
	15%	0.0415	0.0392	0.0368	0.0344	0.0320	0.0296	.0493
10 Years	16%	0.0512	0.0488	0.0465	0.0441	0.0417	0.0394	.0469
	17%	0.0609	0.0585	0.0562	0.0538	0.0515	0.0491	.0447
n = 10	18%	0.0706	0.0682	0.0659	0.0635	0.0612	0.0588	.0425
	19%	0.0803	0.0780	0.0756	0.0733	0.0709	0.0686	.0405
	20%	0.0900	0.0877	0.0854	0.0830	0.0807	0.0783	.0385
	21%	0.0997	0.0974	0.0951	0.0928	0.0904	0.0881	.0367
	22%	0.1095	0.1072	0.1049	0.1026	0.1002	0.0979	.0349
	23%	0.1193	0.1170	0.1147	0.1123	0.1100	0.1077	.0332
	24%	0.1290	0.1267	0.1244	0.1221	0.1198	0.1175	.0316
	25%	0.1388	0.1365	0.1342	0.1319	0.1296	0.1273	.0301
	26%	0.1486	0.1463	0.1440	0.1417	0.1394	0.1371	.0286
	27%	0.1584	0.1561	0.1539	0.1516	0.1493	0.1469	.0272
	28%	0.1682	0.1660	0.1637	0.1614	0.1591	0.1568	.0259
	29%	0.1780	0.1758	0.1735	0.1712	0.1689	0.1666	.0247
	30%	0.1879	0.1856	0.1833	0.1811	0.1788	0.1765	.0235

For example, the heading on Table 13-1 is "25 Years Amortization: 10.75% to 12%." The next-to-last column is headed "12%" which is the interest rate of the mortgage considered. In the first column is "Projection." The bottom half of Table 13-1 is for ten-year projection terms at various equity yield rates. The intersection of the 15% equity yield rate row with the 12% interest rate offers a C factor of .0296. The column on the extreme right is the sinking fund factor for the projection term at the equity yield rate.

C factors at which the mortgage interest rate exceeds the equity yield rate, will generally have a negative sign. Either the negative coefficient can be used including the minus sign, or the absolute value may be inserted, changing a sign to give:

$$r = Y + mC$$

Free and Clear Example

As an example, suppose property is forecast to generate level NOI of \$65,000 per year for a ten-year projection period. Appreciation of 27% is anticipated over the holding period. There is no mortgage debt, therefore $mC = 0$. Equity owners want a 15% yield rate. The formula would be as follows:

$$R = Y - mC + \text{depreciation (SFF@Y)}$$

Substitute knowns:

$$
\begin{aligned}
\text{Y} &= .15 \text{ (given)} \\
m &= 0 \text{ (given free and clear)} \\
C &= .02964 \text{ (from "C Table")} \\
\text{dep/app} &= .27 \text{ (given 27\% appreciation)} \\
\text{SFF@Y} &= .04925 \\
R &= .15 - 0 \times C + .27\ (.04925) \\
R &= .15 - .0133 \\
R &= .1367
\end{aligned}
$$

Since:

$$\text{R} = \frac{\text{NOI}}{V}$$

then:

$$V = \frac{\text{NOI}}{R} \text{ (by direct capitalization)}$$

$$V = \frac{\$65{,}000}{.1367}$$

$$V = \$475{,}494$$

As a check, use the conventional technique:

Stage I.	PWAF (NOI − DS):		
	5.01877 ($65,000 − 0)	=	$326,220
Stage II.	PWF (RP − OS);		
	RP = 1.27*V*:		
	.2472 [1.27 ($475,494) − 0]	=	$149,278
Stage III.	Free and clear		-0-
Total			$475,498

Note: A slight difference in the result compared to the conventional technique occurs because of rounding.

Ellwood Technique with Mortgage Debt

Suppose that property which generates $65,000 of level annual net operating income is offered for sale at whatever price it takes to offer a 15% rate of return to equity (equity yield). An 80% loan-to-value ratio mortgage is assumed to be available, at a 12% interest rate, payable over a 25-year self-amortizing term. There is no forecast change in value over the 10-year holding period. The value estimate, unrounded, using the Ellwood technique, is $514,688 as shown below:

$$r = Y - mC$$
$$r = .15 - .80\,(.02964)$$
$$r = .15 - .02371$$
$$r = .12629$$
$$V = \text{NOI}/r$$
$$V = \$65{,}000/.12629$$
$$V = \$514{,}688$$

Checking Ellwood: Use Conventional Technique. The value estimate (via Ellwood) in the example above was $514,688. Since the loan-to-value ratio was 80%, the beginning loan principal is estimated at $411,750 (80% of $514,688 = $411,750). The mortgage constant on such a debt is 12.6387%; so the annual debt service requirement is (.126387 × $411,750 = $52,040). The loan balance in 10 years will be $361,310. The three-stage conventional technique can be used to check results, as follows:

Stage I.	PWAF (NOI − DS):*	
	5.01877 ($65,000 − $52,040) =	$65,043
Stage II.	PWF (RP − OS):*	
	.2472 ($514,688 − $361,310) =	37,915
Stage III.	Mortgage principal	411,750
	Total	$514,708

The checking procedure shows that the price derived by the Ellwood technique does indeed offer a 15% yield rate to maturity for the equity investor, with the given assumptions. The assumptions include a mortgage loan at 80% of the value estimate; a mortgage at exactly 80% of the value estimate (via Ellwood) was substituted as the loan principal in the conventional technique check. This result, using the conventional technique check, and a mortgage principal amount, gave an identical value estimate as obtained by the conventional approach, except for a $20 difference due to rounding.

Whenever the Ellwood technique is used, it is a good policy to check results via the conventional technique. The results should confirm each other except where there is a technical difference in assumptions or an arithmetic error.

Substitute Dollar Amounts for Symbols

In the Ellwood formula, dollar amounts can be inserted in lieu of fractions or ratios for some of the terms. The actual mortgage principal of a loan and the resale price estimate are often substituted for ratios.

Loan-to-Value Ratio. Instead of a loan-to-value ratio inserted for *m,* the actual mortgage principal divided by *V* can be used as a substitute. That is, the loan-to-value ratio is expressed by the fraction:

Mortgage principal/Value, or MP/*V**

*The abbreviations used here were explained in Chapter 12.

So, if it were given that the mortgage principal were $400,000, for example, the formula would become:

$$r = Y - \left[\left(\frac{\$400{,}000}{V}\right)(C)\right]$$

Resale Price or Fraction Change in Value. In the Ellwood formulation, *R* is the overall capitalization rate for net operating income, reflecting forecast appreciation or value decline over the projection period. The forecast value change fraction, multiplied by the sinking fund factor at the equity yield rate, is used to adjust the capitalization rate for resale assumptions. In the case of forecast appreciation, the result will be subtracted; for depreciation, it is added to the capitalization rate to result in this formula:

$$R = \mathrm{Y} - mC \begin{matrix} + \\ - \end{matrix} \left[\begin{matrix}\text{dep}\\ \text{app}\end{matrix} \quad (\text{SFF@Y})\right]$$

or

$$R = r \begin{matrix} + \\ - \end{matrix} \left[\begin{matrix}\text{dep}\\ \text{app}\end{matrix} \quad (\text{SFF@Y})\right]$$

If a resale price estimate is offered instead of a fractional change in value, the resale price can be converted into a fraction as follows:

$$\frac{V - \text{RP}}{V}$$

The Ellwood formula then becomes:

$$R = Y - mC + \left[\left(\frac{V - \text{RP}}{V}\right)(\text{SFF@Y})\right]$$

Although it is not known whether the resale price will exceed the present property value, it doesn't matter in the formula. If *V* exceeds RP, depreciation is indicated. If RP exceeds *V*, other signs will change to reflect the forecast appreciation.

Substitutions for R

Ellwood's formulation seeks the solution for R, which is then divided into the estimated annual net operating income to estimate the property value. Since $V = \text{NOI}/R$, then $R = \text{NOI}/V$. It is often convenient to substitute NOI/V in place of R in the formulation, so that it reads,

$$\frac{\text{NOI}}{V} = Y - mC + \text{dep (SFF@Y)}$$

Since m and "dep" may be altered to be expressed in terms of V, the NOI/V substitution serves the purpose of having all of the unknowns expressed in terms of V.

ADAPTATIONS OF ELLWOOD TECHNIQUE

Like the conventional mortgage-equity technique, the Ellwood technique can be adapted to fit a variety of conditions. Sample equations are provided below, for different circumstances paralleling the five examples from the previous chapter.

Practice Problem 1

Solve for value, given the mortgage principal and dollar estimate of the resale price.

$$R = Y - mC + \text{dep (SFF@Y)}$$

Substitutions:

$$\frac{\text{NOI}}{V} = Y - \left[\frac{\text{MP}}{V}(C)\right] + \left[\left(\frac{V - \text{RP}}{V}\right)(\text{SFF@Y})\right]$$

$$\frac{\$65{,}000}{V} = .15 - \left[\left(\frac{\$400{,}000}{V}\right)(.02964)\right] + \left[\left(\frac{\text{V} - \$500{,}000}{V}\right)(.04925)\right]$$

Solve for V (see Appendix A).

Practice Problem 2

Solve for value, given mortgage principal and percentage of property value change over projection period.

$$R = Y - mC + \text{dep(SFF@Y)}$$

$$\frac{\$65{,}000}{V} = .15 - \left[\left(\frac{\$400{,}000}{V}\right)(.02964)\right] - .1(.04925)$$

Solve for V (see Appendix A).

Practice Problem 3

Solve for value, given a loan-to-value ratio and dollar estimate of the resale price.

$$R = Y - mC + \text{dep(SFF@Y)}$$

$$\frac{\$65{,}000}{V} = .15 - .8(.02964) + \left[\left(\frac{V - \text{RP}}{V}\right)(.04925)\right]$$

Practice Problem 4

Solve for value, given a loan-to-value ratio and fraction value change. LTV = 80% and dep = −.30 (appreciation of 30%).

$$R = Y - mC + \text{dep(SFF@Y)}$$

$$\frac{\$65{,}000}{V} = .15 - .8(.02964) - .30(.04925)$$

Solve for V (see Appendix A).

Practice Problem 5

Solve for equity yield rate, given other variables including the present price. Present price is \$500,000; no value change is forecast.

$$R = Y - mC + \text{dep(SFF@Y)}$$

$$\frac{\$65{,}000}{\$500{,}000} = Y - \left[\left(\frac{\$400{,}000}{\text{V}}\right) C\right]$$

$$.13 = Y - \left[\left(\frac{\$400{,}000}{\text{V}}\right) C\right]$$

Substitute values for Y and C at different equity yield rates until an equality is found (see Appendix A).

Computing the C Factor and the Effect of Existing Mortgages

The Ellwood "C Tables" show mortgage terms in 5-year increments. Amortization terms of 20, 25, and 30 years are common for new mortgages. For existing mortgages, seek out the remaining (not original) term on the tables.

However, an existing mortgage is unlikely to have a remaining term that is an exact multiple of 5 years. In that case, find the remaining term, and compute the C factor using this formula:

$$C = Y + P\ (\text{SFF@Y}) - f$$

where:

C = Ellwood mortgage coefficient.
Y = the equity yield rate.
P = the fraction of the present loan balance that will be paid off over the projection period.
SFF@Y = the sinking fund factor at the equity yield rate over the projection period.
f = the annual mortgage constant, based on the annual payment and present (not original) balance.

For example, suppose a 12% mortgage has 20 remaining years. (Although the C factor is shown in the tables, it can be computed in the manner below.) The projection term is 10 years; equity yield is 15%. In 10 years, 23.25% of the present mortgage balance will be retired. The mortgage constant is 13.213%, based on the present balance and annual payment.

$$C = Y + P\ (\text{SFF@Y}) - f$$
$$C = .15 + .2325\ (.04925) - .13213$$
$$C = .15 + .011451 - .13213$$
$$C = .029321$$

Effect of Two Mortgages. If there are two mortgages on the property, the loan-to-value ratio or principal for each should be multiplied by the C factor for each mortgage. The formula is shown below:

$$R = Y - mC_1 - mC_2 + \text{dep}\ (\text{SFF@Y})$$

When mortgage balances are given, the mortgage principal divided by V can be substituted for m.

Effect of Projection Period

The Ellwood technique, like the conventional technique, indicates different present values, given different projection terms. When leverage is favorable, longer projections offer lower value estimates due to the declining leverage ratio as time passes. Therefore, an analyst must give ample thought to the projection period selected. Of paramount consideration is the length of time the typical investor will own the property.

Expansion of Ellwood's Tables

Ellwood provided capitalization rate tables at loan-to-value ratios of 66⅔% and 75%. In these tables $r = Y - mC$ has been precomputed. Adjustment is required for appreciation and depreciation. Irvin Johnson further expanded Ellwood's tables to indicate precomputed overall capitalization rates at various loan-to-value ratios and appreciation or depreciation assumptions. These tables are in *The Instant Mortgage-Equity Technique.*[1] See Tables 13-2 and 13-3 which are likenesses of Ellwood "r" and Johnson tables, respectively.

For example, consider a 12% interest rate mortgage loan with a 25-year amortization term, 15% equity yield rate, and 10-year projection period on property that is not expected to change in value. The overall "r" capitalization rate using the "C" factor is computed as follows:

$$r = Y - mC$$
$$r = .15 - .75\ (.02964)$$
$$r = .12777$$

That overall rate, .12777, is on both Ellwood and Johnson tables, Tables 13-2 and 13-3. Johnson's table factors are overall rates that incorporate selected appreciation or depreciation changes.

ELLWOOD DERIVATION FROM BAND OF INVESTMENT

Ellwood's overall capitalization rate, *r*, can be derived from the band of investment (BOI) approach. The pure band of investment considers the portions of purchase capital provided by mortgage

[1]Irvin E. Johnson, *The Instant Mortgage—Equity Technique* (Lexington, Mass.: D.C. Heath & Company, 1972).

TABLE 13-2
Sample of Ellwood Capitalization Rate Tables Assuming 75% of Purchase Price Financed by Mortgage 25 Years Amortization: 10. 75% to 12%

	Interest Rate	10.75%	11%	11.25%	11.50%	11.75%	12.00%	Sinking Fund Factor at Equity Yield
	Equity Yield	Basic Overall Capitalization Rate "r"						
	6%	0.0946	0.0965	0.0984	0.1002	0.1021	0.1040	.1774
	7%	0.0973	0.0991	0.1010	0.1029	0.1047	0.1066	.1739
	8%	0.0999	0.1018	0.1036	0.1055	0.1074	0.1092	.1705
	9%	0.1025	0.1044	0.1062	0.1081	0.1100	0.1118	.1671
	10%	0.1052	0.1070	0.1089	0.1107	0.1126	0.1145	.1638
	11%	0.1078	0.1096	0.1115	0.1133	0.1152	0.1171	.1606
	12%	0.1104	0.1123	0.1141	0.1160	0.1178	0.1197	.1574
	13%	0.1130	0.1149	0.1167	0.1186	0.1204	0.1223	.1543
Pro-	14%	0.1156	0.1175	0.1193	0.1212	0.1230	0.1249	.1513
jection	15%	0.1183	0.1201	0.1219	0.1238	0.1256	0.1275	.1483
	16%	0.1209	0.1227	0.1245	0.1264	0.1282	0.1300	.1454
Period	17%	0.1235	0.1253	0.1271	0.1290	0.1308	0.1326	.1426
	18%	0.1261	0.1279	0.1297	0.1316	0.1334	0.1352	.1398
5 Years	19%	0.1287	0.1305	0.1323	0.1342	0.1360	0.1378	.1371
	20%	0.1313	0.1331	0.1349	0.1368	0.1386	0.1404	.1344
n = 5	21%	0.1339	0.1357	0.1375	0.1394	0.1412	0.1430	.1318
	22%	0.1365	0.1383	0.1401	0.1419	0.1438	0.1456	.1292
	23%	0.1391	0.1409	0.1427	0.1445	0.1463	0.1482	.1267
	24%	0.1417	0.1435	0.1453	0.1471	0.1489	0.1507	.1242
	25%	0.1443	0.1461	0.1479	0.1497	0.1515	0.1533	.1218
	26%	0.1469	0.1487	0.1505	0.1523	0.1541	0.1559	.1195
	27%	0.1495	0.1513	0.1531	0.1549	0.1567	0.1585	.1172
	28%	0.1521	0.1539	0.1557	0.1574	0.1592	0.1610	.1149
	29%	0.1547	0.1564	0.1582	0.1600	0.1618	0.1636	.1127
	30%	0.1572	0.1590	0.1608	0.1626	0.1644	0.1662	.1106
	6%	0.0935	0.0954	0.0972	0.0991	0.1010	0.1028	.0759
	7%	0.0964	0.0982	0.1001	0.1019	0.1038	0.1056	.0724
	8%	0.0993	0.1011	0.1029	0.1048	0.1066	0.1085	.0690
	9%	0.1021	0.1039	0.1057	0.1076	0.1094	0.1112	.0658
	10%	0.1049	0.1067	0.1085	0.1104	0.1122	0.1140	.0627
	11%	0.1077	0.1095	0.1113	0.1132	0.1150	0.1168	.0598
	12%	0.1105	0.1123	0.1141	0.1159	0.1177	0.1196	.0570
	13%	0.1133	0.1151	0.1169	0.1187	0.1205	0.1223	.0543
Pro-	14%	0.1161	0.1179	0.1197	0.1214	0.1232	0.1250	.0517
jection	15%	0.1189	0.1206	0.1224	0.1242	0.1260	0.1278	.0493
	16%	0.1216	0.1234	0.1251	0.1269	0.1287	0.1305	.0469
Period	17%	0.1243	0.1261	0.1279	0.1296	0.1314	0.1332	.0447
	18%	0.1271	0.1288	0.1306	0.1323	0.1341	0.1359	.0425
10 Years	19%	0.1298	0.1315	0.1333	0.1350	0.1368	0.1386	.0405
	20%	0.1325	0.1342	0.1360	0.1377	0.1395	0.1413	.0385
n = 10	21%	0.1352	0.1369	0.1387	0.1404	0.1422	0.1439	.0367
	22%	0.1379	0.1396	0.1413	0.1431	0.1448	0.1466	.0349
	23%	0.1406	0.1423	0.1440	0.1457	0.1475	0.1492	.0332
	24%	0.1432	0.1449	0.1467	0.1484	0.1501	0.1519	.0316
	25%	0.1459	0.1476	0.1493	0.1511	0.1528	0.1545	.0301
	26%	0.1485	0.1503	0.1520	0.1537	0.1554	0.1572	.0286
	27%	0.1512	0.1529	0.1546	0.1563	0.1581	0.1598	.0272
	28%	0.1538	0.1555	0.1572	0.1590	0.1607	0.1624	.0259
	29%	0.1565	0.1582	0.1599	0.1616	0.1633	0.1650	.0247
	30%	0.1591	0.1608	0.1625	0.1642	0.1659	0.1676	.0235

TABLE 13-3
Irvin Johnson's Expansion of Ellwood's "R" Table—Table of Overall Capitalization Rates

10 YEAR HOLDING PERIOD
15% EQUITY YIELD RATE
75% LOAN-TO-VALUE RATIO

YEARS LOAN TERM	PCT APPRE -DEP	MORTGAGE INTEREST RATES 7.0	8.0	9.0	10.0	11.0	12.0	13.0	14.0	15.0
10	40%	.08534	.09004	.09486	.09979	.10483	.10998	.11524	.12060	.12607
10	30%	.09026	.09496	.09978	.10471	.10975	.11491	.12017	.12553	.13100
10	20%	.09519	.09989	.10471	.10964	.11468	.11983	.12509	.13046	.13592
10	10%	.10011	.10481	.10963	.11456	.11960	.12476	.13002	.13538	.14085
10	0%	.10504	.10974	.11456	.11949	.12453	.12968	.13494	.14031	.14577
10	-10%	.10996	.11466	.11948	.12441	.12945	.13461	.13987	.14523	.15070
10	-20%	.11489	.11959	.12441	.12934	.13438	.13953	.14479	.15016	.15562
10	-30%	.11981	.12451	.12933	.13426	.13930	.14446	.14972	.15508	.16055
10	-40%	.12474	.12944	.13426	.13919	.14423	.14938	.15464	.16001	.16547
15	40%	.07851	.08427	.09019	.09625	.10246	.10880	.11527	.12186	.12856
15	30%	.08344	.08920	.09511	.10118	.10739	.11373	.12020	.12679	.13348
15	20%	.08836	.09412	.10004	.10610	.11231	.11865	.12512	.13171	.13841
15	10%	.09329	.09905	.10496	.11103	.11724	.12358	.13005	.13664	.14333
15	0%	.09821	.10397	.10989	.11595	.12216	.12850	.13497	.14156	.14826
15	-10%	.10314	.10890	.11481	.12088	.12709	.13343	.13990	.14649	.15318
15	-20%	.10807	.11382	.11974	.12580	.13201	.13836	.14482	.15141	.15811
15	-30%	.11299	.11875	.12466	.13073	.13694	.14328	.14975	.15634	.16303
15	-40%	.11792	.12367	.12959	.13566	.14186	.14821	.15467	.16126	.16796
20	40%	.07530	.08160	.08807	.09468	.10143	.10831	.11529	.12236	.12952
20	30%	.08022	.08653	.09299	.09961	.10636	.11323	.12021	.12729	.13445
20	20%	.08515	.09145	.09792	.10454	.11129	.11816	.12514	.13221	.13937
20	10%	.09007	.09638	.10284	.10946	.11621	.12308	.13006	.13714	.14430
20	0%	.09500	.10130	.10777	.11439	.12114	.12801	.13499	.14206	.14922
20	-10%	.09992	.10623	.11270	.11931	.12606	.13293	.13991	.14699	.15415
20	-20%	.10485	.11115	.11762	.12424	.13099	.13786	.14484	.15191	.15907
20	-30%	.10977	.11608	.12255	.12916	.13591	.14278	.14976	.15684	.16400
20	-40%	.11470	.12100	.12747	.13409	.14084	.14771	.15469	.16176	.16892
25	40%	.07351	.08015	.08695	.09388	.10092	.10807	.11529	.12259	.12994
25	30%	.07844	.08508	.09187	.09880	.10585	.11299	.12022	.12751	.13487
25	20%	.08336	.09001	.09680	.10373	.11077	.11792	.12514	.13244	.13979
25	10%	.08829	.09493	.10173	.10865	.11570	.12284	.13007	.13736	.14472
25	0%	.09321	.09986	.10665	.11358	.12062	.12777	.13499	.14229	.14964
25	-10%	.09814	.10478	.11158	.11850	.12555	.13269	.13992	.14721	.15457
25	-20%	.10307	.10971	.11650	.12343	.13047	.13762	.14484	.15214	.15949
25	-30%	.10799	.11463	.12143	.12835	.13540	.14254	.14977	.15706	.16442
25	-40%	.11292	.11956	.12635	.13328	.14032	.14747	.15469	.16199	.16934

and equity contributors. It weights purchase capital shares by the interest rate and equity yield-to-maturity rate desired, respectively.

For example, suppose the mortgage lender provides 80% of the purchase capital at a 12% interest rate, and equity contributes 20% of the purchase capital at a 15% yield rate. The pure band of investment rate is as shown in Table 13–4.

TABLE 13–4

Pure Band of Investment

Purchase Capital Contributor	*Share of Purchase Capital*		*Yield Rate Capital*		*Weighted Desired Rate*
Mortgage	80%	×	12%	=	9.6%
Equity	20%	×	15%	=	3.0%
Weighted rate: Pure band of investment					12.6%

The pure BOI rate requires two adjustments to become equivalent to an Ellwood *r* overall capitalization rate (before property appreciation or depreciation). Both adjustments relate to mortgage amortization.

Adjustment #1 is to acknowledge that mortgage amortization payments are required from annual net operating income. This reduces the current income available to the equity investor. Since it is a current requirement that the equity investor must pay, it is added to the pure BOI rate. The amortization payment on a mortgage is the excess of the mortgage loan constant over the interest rate. The proper amount is derived by weighting the excess (constant versus interest rate) by the loan-to-value ratio. Given a loan constant of .126387 and an interest rate of .12, the .006387 difference, multiplied by the 80% loan-to-value ratio, offers an adjustment of .0051096 (.8 × .006387 = .0051096). The result, after adding that amount to the pure BOI rate, is the same as the BOI rate modified to include mortgage amortization.

Adjustment #2 is required to consider the future date when the equity investor will receive the benefit of mortgage amortization. Upon resale of the property, equity investors recover the resale price less the sum of transaction costs and the unpaid mortgage balance. The mortgage reduction is then recovered by the equity position at resale. Since this is a benefit that the equity investor will receive at a later date, the effective annual benefit is computed using the sinking fund factor; then it is subtracted from the BOI rate. The effective benefit to equity investors depends on the loan-to-value ratio and the amount of the mortgage that is paid off over the projection period. Conversion to an effective annual rate of equity benefit is effected via the sinking fund factor at the equity yield rate.

For example, on a 25-year mortgage loan at a 12% interest rate, 12.25% of the loan will be paid off over a ten-year projection period. If the loan is 80% of value, and equity investors want a 15% yield rate, adjustment #2 will be:

$$.80 \times .1225 \times .04925 = .0048265$$

Based on the given variables, the Ellwood *r* factor is composed as shown in Table 13-5.

TABLE 13–5

Ellwood Adjustments to Band of Investment

Source of Purchase Capital	*Share of Purchase Capital*		*Yield Desired*		*Weighted Rate (Desired)*
Mortgage	80%	×	12%	=	.096
Equity	20%	×	15%	=	.030
Pure BOI rate					.126
Ellwood Modifications:					
Add: Adjustment #1:	80%	×	.006387	=	.0051096
Subtract: Adjustment #2:	80%	×	(.1225 × .04925)	=	−.0048265
Ellwood *r*					.1262827
Value estimate: $65,000 NOI/.1262827				=	$514,718

Forecast appreciation or depreciation is added to the basic Ellwood *r* by multiplying the forecast fraction property value change by the sinking fund factor at the equity rate. The result is subtracted from the overall rate when given an appreciation forecast, or added for a forecast decline in value.

COMPOSITION OF THE C FACTOR

The Ellwood *C* factor, which is called a *mortgage coefficient,* is the pivotal function in the Ellwood technique. The *C* factor represents a synthesis of various mortgage and equity relationships.

The formula for *C* is:

$$C = Y + P\ (\text{SFF@Y}) - f$$

where:

Y = the equity yield rate.
P = the fraction of the loan paid off over the projection period.
$SFF@Y$ = the sinking fund factor at the equity yield rate over the projection term.
f = the annual mortgage constant.

By consolidating these variables and multiplying them by the loan-to-value ratio, the equity yield rate is adjusted to result in an overall capitalization rate. The overall rate then reflects financial leverage, mortgage amortization, and the equity build-up via mortgage amortization that will be recovered by the equity owner upon resale of the property. The *C* factor thus consolidates the BOI with adjustments #1 and #2. The *C* result is properly weighted by *m* in the expression:

$$r = Y - mC$$

By using the precomputed *C* factors, the overall capitalization rate and the resulting property value estimate can be derived without going through the three-stage conventional technique or the modified band of investment approach. In cases where *C* factors do not exist on preprinted tables, they can be computed.

SUMMARY

The Ellwood technique is an approach to mortgage-equity analysis that derives the same result as the conventional mortgage-equity technique, given the same assumptions. The Ellwood technique provides a shortcut when the loan-to-value ratio and/or fraction change in value is given, but can also be used when given a mortgage principal and resale price estimate. The technique can be used if there is new financing to be arranged or if an existing loan is to be assumed.

The Ellwood technique requires the same assumptions as the conventional mortgage-equity technique and is affected by those assumptions in an identical manner. Assumptions include certain financing terms, resale price or value change estimates, and a projection period. Users must be aware of the importance that the assumptions have for the value estimate. In the Ellwood technique, the *C* factor is a pivotal one. *C* results from a synthesis of other variables.

The Ellwood technique provides a powerful shortcut to mortgage-equity analysis. Users should be careful to review input assumptions because the value estimate is no better than the assumptions that are input.

Questions

1. Consider a free-standing retail store that is under a ten-year lease at an annual net rental of $12,000 per year. Typical financing is a mortgage at 75% of value for twenty years at a 10% interest rate. Equity investors want a 14% yield rate. The property is expected to be worth the same amount in ten years as it is now.
   a. What is the overall capitalization rate, r, using $r = Y - mC$? *Note:* $C = .03813$.
   b. What is the estimated property value, V, using $V = \text{NOI}/r$?
   c. At that value estimate, what is the principal of a 75% LTV mortgage?
2. Given the value estimate and mortgage derived in Question 1, how much is the:
   a. Annual cash flow?
   b. Proceeds from resale?
   c. Present value of (a) and (b) at the equity yield rate?
   d. Property value estimate using the conventional technique?
3. Given a loan principal balance of $75,000, how can the figure be substituted for the loan-to-value ratio, m?
4. Given a forecast resale price of $120,000, how can this amount be substituted for the fraction change in value, "app" or "dep," in the Ellwood formula?

Essay Questions

1. What are the advantages of the Ellwood formulation over the conventional technique?
2. What variables are considered by the Ellwood C factors?
3. What are the two adjustments from the pure BOI technique to derive Ellwood's r? Why are they needed?
4. What are the steps needed to locate the C factor in the Ellwood tables? What must be done to derive the C factor when it is not shown on the tables?

Chapter 14

After-Tax Cash Flow and After-Tax Resale Proceeds

The conventional mortgage-equity (and Ellwood) techniques consider three of the four financial rewards flowing from income property ownership to equity investors. The three rewards are: cash flow, appreciation, and mortgage reduction. However, these techniques do *not* consider the income tax implications of real estate ownership.

Income tax implications affect property owners during the acquisition and ownership phases and upon resale of the property. Since ordinary income tax rates for individuals are graduated up to 33% of taxable income under the Tax Reform Act of 1986, taxes can have a significant effect on the owner's after-tax return.

Some real estate investments offer cash flow that is fully taxable; others offer partially taxable cash flow; others offer tax-free cash flow and some even generate tax losses that can shelter taxable income from outside the property. However, the Tax Reform Act of 1986 limits one's ability to apply losses from real estate against other forms of income.

Real estate investments have three phases:

1. Purchase (acquisition).
2. Ownership period (operations).
3. Disposition (resale).

There are income tax implications at each of the three phases. Effective planning can serve to minimize or postpone income taxation at each phase.

DIFFERENT ENTITIES EXPERIENCE DIFFERENTIAL TAX TREATMENT

The income tax situation for each tax-paying unit or entity is different. Entities include single individuals, married couples who file either joint or separate tax returns, heads of households, partnerships, limited partnerships, corporations, Subchapter S corporations, nonprofit organizations, trusts, Real Estate Investment Trusts, and others. Each entity faces different tax laws and rates.

Income Tax Implications to Underlying Owner

The income tax implications to the underlying owner depend not only on the income generated by a particular investment but also on the income and deductions provided by sources outside the subject investment. Therefore, it is difficult to generalize about the consequences of a given investment proposal for the overall tax situation of any investor. It is possible, however, to generalize about the forecast taxable income (or loss) and capital gain (or loss) that is expected to be generated by a subject investment. The amount of tax payment (or saving) from ownership of the investment is dependent on the type of ownership vehicle (entity) and its other income, as well as on the underlying owner's entity and outside income.

For example, suppose a corporation is one of the partners in a partnership that owns a manufacturing facility and an apartment complex. The corporation itself may own municipal bonds, a retail store, and other investments, in addition to being a partner in the manufacturing-apartment partnership. Stockholders of the corporation may have income from wages, interest, royalties, and capital gains. The tax effect of the apartments on the corporate stockholders cannot be determined without unraveling all of the other sources and amounts of income and tax to the different entities, with and without the apartments. Furthermore, whether the partnership is general or limited, whether the corporation's partnership interest is general or limited, and whether the corporation is Subchapter C, Subchapter S, or a personal holding company, as well as the filing status and past income or loss of all of the entities; all of these factors can make a huge difference in the tax implications of the apartments to the underlying owner.

What can be done toward investment analysis is to consider the apartment alone, and to estimate the income tax implications to one level of ownership, based on assumptions concerning the income tax rate of that owner.

Value of Income Tax Deductions to Different Entities

A real estate investment opportunity that is a tax haven to one party can hold unwanted tax or financial consequences for another and vice versa. For example, an individual who is in a high ordinary tax bracket might benefit from an investment that offers a tax loss but no cash flow. The benefit arises from a reduction of taxes that would otherwise be paid on nonproject income. However, the ability to use losses generated by rental real estate has been limited by the Tax Reform Act of 1986.

On the other hand, a nonprofit organization such as a qualified pension fund normally does not pay an income tax. If this organization did own a noncash-producing, tax-shelter-generating investment, it is of no real use to it. The tax shelter feature is of no value because the organization pays no income taxes. An investment that provides only tax losses provides no financial income.

Tax-paying investors should be cautioned that there must be a genuine economic purpose to a transaction, not just the reduction of taxes. There are two reasons. The first is that transactions that are motivated solely to avoid income taxes will be disallowed by the Internal Revenue Service. Second, the tax-shelter aspects taken alone seldom provide adequate financial justification for an investment. The highest income tax rate is 33%, so the maximum tax benefit from a total loss of investment dollars is 33 cents per dollar invested. In most cases, the tax recovery from a loss will be much less. Unless an investment provides some nontax rewards, it is highly unlikely to be a worthwhile investment. The U.S. government will share in an investor's genuine losses, but it does not effectively underwrite the entire loss. A taxpayer is better off receiving taxable income in cash, and paying taxes on the income, than paying cash for losses and claiming a tax deduction. Sometimes, through real estate investments, a tax deduction can be generated without a cash outlay, as by depreciation accounting that provides a tax deduction without related cash outflows. This is welcomed by nearly all tax-paying entities.

Investment Value versus Market Value

The purpose of most real estate appraisals is to estimate the market value of property. There are numerous definitions of market value; many assume a prudent, typically motivated, knowledgeable purchaser. However, when an analyst considers the value of a certain proposed real estate investment for a specific individual or other entity, taking into account the income tax and other financial implications of ownership that are unique to that particular investor, it is the "investment value" that is sought. *Investment value* is the estimated value of an investment to a particular investor. Investment value is seldom the same as market value. Market value represents an impersonal synthesis of sellers and buyers, whereas investment value is the estimated value for one individual.

PHASE I—PURCHASE (ACQUISITION)

There is some opportunity to realize tax deductions during the acquisition phase. Before 1969, many investments were arranged with five years of prepaid interest. Purchasers paid tax-deductible cash as interest in lieu of all or part of the equity. Other deductions included interest and taxes paid during construction, advance payments for services to general partners by limited partners, retroactive allocations of losses that accrued during the year to investors who purchased later in the year, and, in some cases, disproportionate allocations of deductions whereby a minority interest in a partnership was allocated all of the partnership's depreciation deductions. Especially since 1969, Congress has plugged those loopholes and others.

Investment property buyers are no longer allowed to claim deductions for discount points they pay to arrange financing, nor for most other expenses that they may incur at closing. Interest and taxes that are paid during construction must be added to the tax basis of the property and depreciated. The pre-1969 era of substantial deductions during the acquisition phase of real estate was gradually ended by a number of changes in tax law between 1969 and 1986.

Tax Basis

Borrowing is not normally a taxable event; so money provided by a mortgage loan is not taxable income, regardless of whether the money was provided by a third party or by the seller of real estate. The cash down payment together with the debt incurred constitutes the purchase price of property and its tax basis. *Tax basis* is a term used to describe one's investment in property. Capital expenditures, which are nondeductible improvements, are added to this basis. Also depreciation claimed for tax purposes is computed from this basis. Depreciation deductions are subtracted to result in an *ad-*

justed tax basis, which is the amount from which gain or loss from resale is computed.

Each succeeding owner begins with a tax basis based on the purchase price paid, no matter what the seller's adjusted tax basis was. This allows property to be depreciated several times, but only once by each owner.

PHASE II—OWNERSHIP PERIOD (OPERATIONS)

During operations, rental income is included in the income tax return, as are miscellaneous income and interest income. Business deductions are allowed for expenses that are ordinary and necessary in carrying out the business. These include maintenance and repairs, advertising, management fees, utilities, payroll and payroll taxes, deferred charge amortization, interest, and depreciation.

Operating Expenses

Normally, all of the "operating expenses" as classified by a real estate analyst are tax-deductible, except a replacement reserve. Deductions are not permitted on money that is simply put into a replacement reserve account to be used for a future need in the business. Later, when the replacement component—carpet, appliance, roof—is purchased, it can be depreciated over its estimated useful life.

Debt Service

Interest on property that is used in a trade or business is generally deductible in full. However, tax reform acts 1969 and 1976 placed limits on the amount of "investment interest expense." These limits applied to interest on loans for net-leased real estate. The 1986 tax act removed interest paid for rental real estate from investment interest rules. Regardless, most apartments, shopping centers, hotels, warehouses, and other properties are operated as a trade or business, as opposed to an "investment." Interest paid on such debts is deductible; however, there are limits on the application of losses against nonpassive income. Mortgage principal payments are not tax-deductible. There are no taxes due upon borrowing the principal, so it is consistent not to allow deductions for principal repayment.

On self-amortizing mortgage loans that require level payments, most of the cash debt service payments during the early years will be for interest. In later years, as the principal is reduced, most of the cash debt service payment will apply toward nontax-deductible principal repayment. From the same cash payment for a loan's annual debt service requirement, the tax-deductible (interest) portion will vary with principal balance, and the principal balance will vary with the age of the loan. As time passes, more taxable income will be generated by leveraged real estate, even if the cash flow remains unchanged.

Depreciation Accounting

Depreciation accounting is a method of allocating the cost of a wasting asset over its estimated economic useful life. For income tax purposes, depreciation is a provision for the estimated wear and tear of an asset. Depreciation deductions can be claimed as a tax deduction on real estate improvement (not land) regardless of whether the market indicates an increase or decrease in the value of the property. To claim depreciation on an income tax return, a bookkeeping entry is required, not a cash payment.

Advantages of Depreciation Deductions. In many real estate investment situations, depreciation deductions are of significant value. The deductions reduce income taxes without a cash payment. However, there will be a day of reckoning. Ultimately, the tax implications catch up with the real economic situation. Depreciation deductions serve to reduce the adjusted tax basis of property; so, upon a resale, there will be a greater capital gain on which a tax is due. Most investors prefer to enjoy substantial amounts of current depreciation deductions in the face of a future tax because of (1) the time value of money, and (2) the possibility of lower tax rates upon resale. Lower tax rates may be due to more favorable capital gains rates, or planning the sale to occur in a tax year when there are offsetting losses. The time value of money implies that taxpayers would rather pay taxes later than now. It is like getting an interest-free loan from the U.S. government.

Amount of Depreciation Deductions. The amount of depreciation deductions depends on three variables:

1. The amount to be depreciated.
2. The depreciable life.
3. The depreciation method.

Amount to Be Depreciated. The amount to be depreciated is usually the cost of improvements (not land), less their estimated salvage value (if any). For inherited property, gifts, property acquired in an exchange, and other special situations, another basis will be considered. For most purchased properties, the cost will be the basis for depreciation. Most real estate investment purchases involve the acquisition of two or more assets at one amount. The asset values must be separated to claim the appropriate amount of depreciation on each. The most common need is to separate a building from land when one property is purchased for a single amount. Personal property included in a sale, fences, and sitework may be separated. Purchasers will want to allocate as much of the cost to buildings and other improvements because they are eligible for depreciation deductions, and little to land because land isn't depreciable.

Salvage or scrap value is the estimated remaining value at the end of the economic useful life of property. Some real estate improvements require costly demolition when they are no longer useful. Some scrap may be quite valuable after many years. The scrap or salvage value of a property is difficult to estimate before demolition.

Depreciable Life. Under the Tax Reform Act of 1986, the depreciable life of real estate purchased after 1986 is 27.5 years for residential, and 31.5 years for nonresidential. An alternate life of 40 years is also provided. The depreciable life of real estate for tax purposes is mandated by whatever law Congress adopts and the President signs. For many years the lives allowed have been arbitrary, with no relation to the estimated actual life of the property nor historical lives of similar properties. See Table 14-1 for depreciable lives at different times. The Tax Reform Act of 1981 provided 15 year lives in an effort to stimulate the economy. Indeed it succeeded; from 1981 through 1986 there was a huge boom in office buildings, apartments and shopping center construction and sales. The 1984 tax act lengthened the period to 18 years; the next year it became 19 years. The purpose of those changes were to provide the government with more tax revenues. The 1986 tax act's purpose was to remove the effects of taxation on business decisions.

Depreciation Method. The straight-line method of depreciation is required by the 1986 tax act for all real estate. This provides for an equal amount of depreciation in every year except the year of acquisition and disposition. The Internal Revenue Service

TABLE 14–1
Real Estate Depreciation Lives Under Different Tax Laws

Year	*System*	*Real Estate Life (Years)*
1962	IRS Guideline Lives	40-60, or useful life Component (if new) Accelerated or S/L varied
1981	Accelerated Cost Recovery	15 Accelerated or S/L
1984	Accelerated Cost Recovery	18 Accelerated or S/L
1985	Accelerated Cost Recovery	19 Accelerated or S/L
1987	Tax Reform Act of 1986	
	Residential	27½ Straight line
	Nonresidential	31½ Straight line
	Alternate	40 Straight line

TABLE 14–2
Depreciation Percentages Under the Tax Reform Act of 1986

Unofficial Straight-Line Depreciation Percentages For Real Estate

27.5 Year Residential Real Property

Recovery Year(s)	*The applicable percentage is: (Use the column for the Month in the First Year the Property is Placed in Service)* 1	2	3	4	5	6	7	8	9	10	11	12	*Recovery Years*
1	.035	.032	.029	.026	.023	.020	.017	.014	.011	.008	.005	.002	1
2-27	.036	.036	.036	.036	.036	.036	.036	.036	.036	.036	.036	.036	2-27
28	.029	.032	.035	.036	.036	.036	.036	.036	.036	.036	.036	.036	28
29	0	0	0	.002	.005	.008	.011	.014	.017	.020	.023	.026	29
Total	1.000	1.000	1.000	1.000	1.000	1.000	1.000	1.000	1.000	1.000	1.000	1.000	Total

31.5 Year Nonresidential Real Property

Recovery Year(s)	*The applicable percentage is: (Use the column for the Month in the First Year the Property is Placed in Service)* 1	2	3	4	5	6	7	8	9	10	11	12	*Recovery Years*
1	.030	.028	.025	.022	.020	.017	.015	.012	.009	.007	.004	.001	1
2-31	.032	.032	.032	.032	.032	.032	.032	.032	.032	.032	.032	.032	2-31
32	.010	.012	.015	.018	.020	.023	.025	.028	.031	.032	.032	.032	32
33	0	0	0	0	0	0	0	0	0	.001	.004	.007	33
Total	1.000	1.000	1.000	1.000	1.000	1.000	1.000	1.000	1.000	1.000	1.000	1.000	Total

provides tables to indicate the amount of depreciation allowed in each year (see Table 14-2). A mid-month convention is built into the tables so the same amount of depreciation is allowable no matter which day of the month the property was bought. As shown by the tables, a January purchase provides more depreciation in the first year than would a February purchase. However, depreciation would be the same for a January 1 purchase as compared to a January 31 closing. Closing on February 1 instead of January 31 results in losing a month's depreciation.

Accelerated methods of depreciation had been allowed on real estate for purchases prior to 1987. Accelerated depreciation provides for high tax deductions in the early years of ownership, and less depreciation later. If accelerated depreciation were claimed, the amount in excess of straight line was generally subject to *recapture* or taxation at high tax rates upon a sale.

New versus Used. Since the tax act of 1981 the amount of depreciation on real estate is not affected by the age of the property or the number of times it sold.

Residential versus Nonresidential. The test of whether property is residential depends on the portion of gross income that is derived from dwelling units. Each year, at least 80% of the gross income must be from dwelling units for the property to be classified as residential. For example, suppose a high-rise apartment building has rent-paying stores on the ground floor that pay *over* 20% of the rent for the year. The entire building would then be considered non-residential. On the other hand, if the stores contributed *under* 20% of the total rent for the building, it would be residential. Transient-type establishments such as hotels are nonresidential.

One's personal residence is residential but cannot be depreciated for income tax purposes unless it is used in a trade or business, i.e., rented to tenants. *Residential property* as it is defined by tax law includes duplexes, triplexes, high-rise apartments, garden apartments, and others.

At-Risk. The 1986 tax act extended at-risk provisions to real estate. This prevents a real estate owner from taking a tax deduction beyond money that can be financially lost. Amounts at-risk include cash contributed to buy real estate, the basis of property contributed by the investor, and debt for which the investor is personally liable. Tax losses and tax-free cash distributions cannot exceed that total. One exception is allowed for third party nonrecourse loans: they can be added to amount at risk. However, this exception does not apply to seller financing. Lenders who foreclosed on property and provide a loan for its resale are not third parties, so such loans cannot be considered at risk by equity investors.

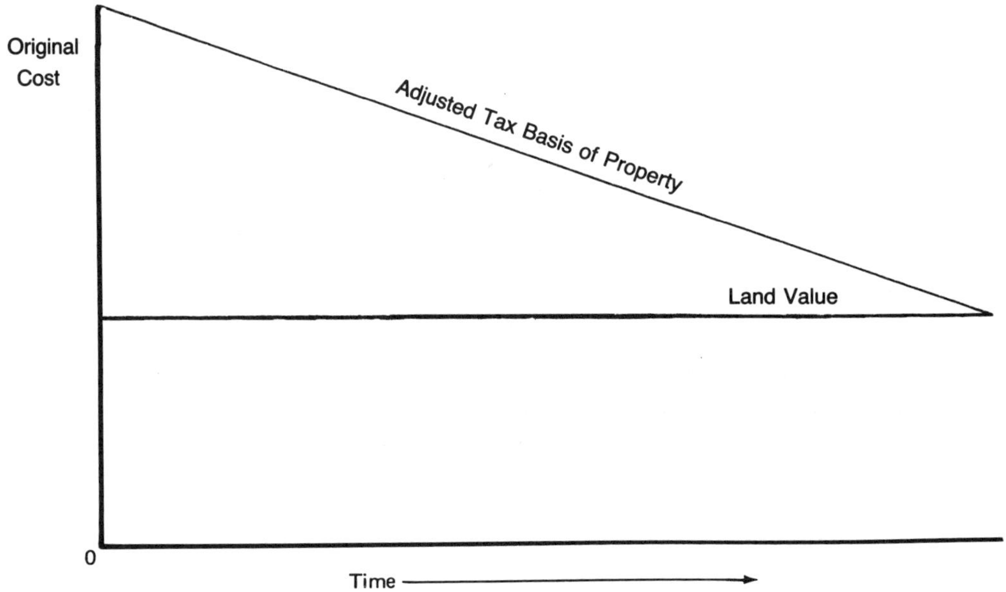

FIGURE 14-1. Adjusted Tax Basis of Depreciable Real Estate

Depreciation Example. As an example, suppose that apartments are purchased for \$500,000. The land value is \$125,000. Land cannot be depreciated. Appliances, carpets, certain fixtures, and other personal property included in the sale are worth \$100,000. They have a 10-year remaining life and no salvage value and are referred to as *short-lived assets*. The *long-lived assets* are the building shell and components that make up the remaining \$275,000 of cost. They have a 27½-year useful life for depreciation purposes and no salvage value. A summary is shown in Table 14-3.

TABLE 14–3

Costs, Lives, and First-Year Depreciation Using Selected Depreciation Methods

Asset	Cost	Life
Land	$125,000	Perpetual
Appliances, carpets (short-lived)	100,000	10 years
Building and components (long-lived)	275,000	35 years
Total	$500,000	

Taxable Income or Loss

The taxable income or loss from income-producing real estate is derived by subtracting from the effective gross income the sum of tax-deductible operating expenses, interest, and depreciation. Taxable income or loss for the first two years and the eleventh year, assuming no change in rentals or operating expenses, is shown on line 5 of Table 14-4.

In the first few years, tax losses are generated by the property. Had an accelerated depreciation method been used, tax losses in those early years would have been greater. In later years, as the interest payment declines, and as there is less depreciation to claim as deductions, taxable income is generated. The tax loss or taxable income situation arises even though cash flow was assumed to remain unchanged.

Reconciliation of Taxable Income with Cash Throw-off

Cash throw-off and taxable income are not the same amount because of tax-deductible noncash items (depreciation) and required nondeductible cash payments (principal amortization and replacement reserves). To reconcile the two, begin with taxable income; then subtract the cash requirements that are not deductible (principal amortization and replacement reserves), and add back the non-

TABLE 14–4

Taxable Income or Loss

Line	Year 1	Year 2	Year 11
1. Effective gross income	$98,000	$98,000	$98,000
2. Operating expenses ($2,000 replacement reserve is not tax-deductible)	$31,000	$31,000	$31,000
3. Interest (at 12%, 25-year, $400,000 mortgage)	47,854	47,512	41,644
Depreciation at straight-line:			
Short-lived assets	10,000	10,000	10,000
Long-lived assets	10,000	10,000	-0-
4. Total tax deductions	$98,854	$98,512	$82,644
5. Taxable income (or loss)	$ (854)	$ (512)	$15,356
6. Less: Principal amortization payments	(2,701)	(3,043)	(8,911)
7. Less: Replacement reserve	(2,000)	(2,000)	(2,000)
8. Add: Depreciation (noncash)	20,000	20,000	10,000
9. Cash throw-off	$14,445	$14,445	$14,445

cash tax deductions (depreciation). The result will be cash throw-off. Table 14–4, lines 6–9, shows this reconciliation. If, instead, one started with cash throw-off, the reverse procedures would be used: subtract depreciation from cash throw-off, and add back mortgage principal amortization and replacement reserves, to result in taxable income or loss.

Interaction of Depreciation and Mortgage Principal Payments

Depreciation claimed for income purposes allows a tax deduction without a cash payment. Mortgage payments that apply toward principal reduction require a cash payment but are not deductible for income tax purposes. So they have an opposite effect. When all the other operating expenses are tax-deductible (as when there is not a replacement reserve), the difference between the depreciation claimed for tax purposes and the mortgage principal payments is clearly reflected in taxable income. Any excess of depreciation over mortgage principal payments in a taxable year will cause some of the before-tax cash flow (cash throw-off) to be tax-free. When the principal amortization payment equals depreciation, all of the cash throw-off will be taxable. Should the principal amortization payments exceed depreciation, taxable income will exceed cash throw-off. Replacement reserves require cash payments and are not tax-deductible; so they are to be added to mortgage amortization payments when estimating the relationship of taxable income to cash throw-off.

Taxable Income versus Tax Payments

The taxable income (or loss) offered by a real estate investment is the amount generated by the subject investment that is to be added to the owning entity's other taxable income for the year (or subtracted in the event of a loss). To find the effective tax payment on the income (or tax savings on losses), one must determine the amount of taxes due on the entity's total income, with and without the real estate investment. The difference in tax is the tax payment or saving caused by the investment. When the tax is expressed as a percentage of the property's taxable income (or loss), it is called the *marginal tax rate* for the investor. *Marginal rate* is defined as the rate of tax saving or payment on the additional income (or loss) to the investor.

Taxable income is not the amount of tax. Federal income tax rates for individuals range from 0 to 33% of taxable income. The rate of tax is therefore some percentage of taxable income, but not over 33%. When deriving after-tax cash flow, be sure to subtract the estimated tax from (or add back the estimated tax savings to) cash throw-off. The estimated tax (or savings) is a percentage of the estimated taxable income (or loss).

For example, (using Table 14-4), if a forecast tax loss is $854 (year 1), an investor in the 40% tax bracket including state income taxes, will save $342. Cash throw-off of $14,445 plus $342 of tax savings results in an after-tax cash flow of $14,787 ($14,445 + $342 = $14,787). On the other hand, if there is $15,356 of taxable income (year 11) to be taxed at a 40% rate, $6,142 of taxes must be paid, so the cash throw-off of $14,445 is reduced by $6,142 to result in an after-tax cash flow of $8,303.

Passive Activity Income. The 1986 tax act made three categories of income: active, portfolio, and passive. Real estate rental activity is passive. A loss from a passive activity cannot offset nonpassive income; such loss would be suspended until passive activities generate income. One exception allows an active lessor to deduct up to $25,000 of passive losses. This is phased out as adjusted gross income exceeds $100,000. Table 14-5 assumes that the small losses in early years can offset other income.

TABLE 14–5
After-Tax Cash Flow for a Proposed Investment

Year	Before-Tax Cash Flow	Tax Saving (Payment)	After-Tax Cash Flow
1	$14,445	342	$14,787
2	14,445	205	14,650
3	14,445	51	14,496
4	14,445	(123)	14,322
5	14,445	(319)	14,126
6	14,445	(540)	13,905
7	14,445	(788)	13,657
8	14,445	(1068)	13,377
9	14,445	(1384)	13,061
10	14,445	(1740)	12,705

PHASE III—DISPOSITION (RESALE)

Upon resale of the property, a taxable gain or loss will occur. When the resale price is greater than the adjusted tax basis of the property, there will be a gain. Should the resale price be less than the adjusted tax basis, a tax loss results. To determine the after-tax proceeds from resale, the tax on the gain must be subtracted from the before-tax proceeds.

After-Tax Proceeds from Resale

The after-tax proceeds from resale is the before-tax proceeds minus taxes. Derivation of the before-tax proceeds was described in the chapters on the conventional and Ellwood techniques. As a review, to derive the before-tax proceeds, subtract from the resale price:

1. Transaction costs such as commissions.
2. Remaining mortgage balance at the sale.

Deriving the after-tax proceeds requires subtracting taxes from the resale.

To compute the gain or loss from resale, subtract from the resale price:

1. Transaction costs.
2. The adjusted tax basis of the property at sale.

The adjusted tax basis is generally the original cost, plus capital improvements (such as for remodeling, a new roof, an added wing, and other capital expenditures that are not tax-deductible when paid or incurred), minus accumulated depreciation that was claimed for income tax purposes. This is diagrammed in Figure 14-2.

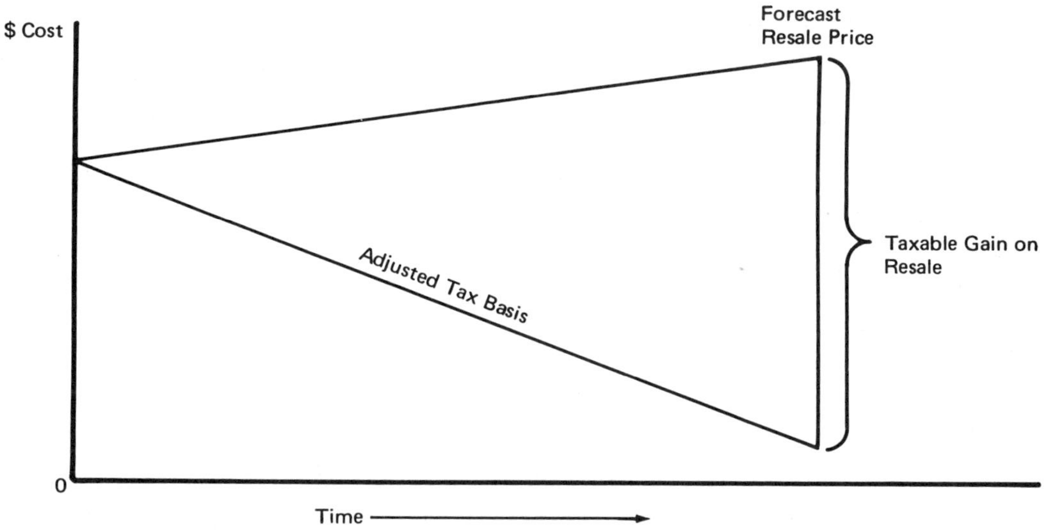

FIGURE 14-2. Diagram of Taxable Gain on Resale.

For example, suppose that property was purchased for \$500,000 and resold ten years later for \$640,000. Transaction costs were \$39,000; subtracting them leaves an "amount realized" of \$601,000. There were no capital improvements. Depreciation claimed during the holding period amounted to a total of \$200,000. The adjusted tax basis of the property at resale is therefore \$300,000 (\$500,000 cost minus \$200,000 depreciation). The taxable gain is \$301,000 (\$601,000 realized minus \$300,000 adjusted tax basis = \$301,000 gain).

Types of Income

The *Internal Revenue Code* specifies different types of income; some types are taxed at more favorable rates. Some of these types of income for real estate are:

1. *Ordinary income*—Taxed at regular rates ranging up to 70% for individuals.

2. *Long-term capital gains*—Gains from the sale of capital assets, which are taxed at ordinary tax rates after 1987.

3. *Section 1231 gains*—Gains from the sale of property used from the sale of capital assets that have been held over six months.

4. *Section 1250 gains*—Gains on the sale of Section 1231 assets due to the excess of accelerated depreciation. Such gains on real estate are generally taxed at ordinary tax rates.

Ordinary Income. Generally, taxable income (or loss) generated during the holding period of income-producing real estate is considered ordinary income. Ordinary tax rates also apply to salaries, dividends, interest, the sale of inventory or stock in trade, and certain other assets.

Long-Term Capital Gains. Long-term capital gains arise from the sale of capital assets that have been held over one year. The definition of a capital asset, according to the *Internal Revenue Code,* is as follows:

[Sec. 1221]

SEC. 1221. CAPITAL ASSET DEFINED.

For purposes of this subtitle, the term "capital asset" means property held by the taxpayer (whether or not connected with his trade or business), but does not include—

(1) stock in trade of the taxpayer or other property of a kind which would properly be included in the inventory of the taxpayer if on hand at the close of the taxable year, or property held by the taxpayer primarily for sale to customers in the ordinary course of his trade or business;

(2) property, used in his trade or business, of a character which is subject to the allowance for depreciation provided in section 167, or real property used in his trade or business;

(3) a copyright, a literary, musical, or artistic composition, a letter or memorandum, or similar property, held by—

(A) a taxpayer whose personal efforts created such property,

(B) in the case of a letter, memorandum, or similar property, a taxpayer for whom such property was prepared or produced, or

(C) a taxpayer in whose hands the basis of such property is determined, for purposes of determining gain from a sale or exchange, in whole or part by reference to the basis of such property in the hands of a taxpayer described in subparagraph (A) or (B);

(4) accounts or notes receivable acquired in the ordinary course of trade or business for services rendered or from the sale of property described in paragraph (1); or

(5) an obligation of the United States or any of its possessions, or of a State or Territory, or any political subdivision thereof, or of the District of Columbia, issued on or after March 1, 1941, on a discount basis and payable without interest at a fixed maturity date not exceeding one year from the date of issue.

Notice that the definition is negative: it describes what is *not* a capital asset. Anything else is a capital asset. One item specifically described as not qualifying as a capital asset is real property used in a trade or business. Such real property generally includes apartments, shopping centers, office buildings, industrial property, hotels, and others. These assets—property used in a trade or business—are known as "Section 1231 Assets" under Section 1231 of the *Internal Revenue Code.*

Section 1231 Gains. Section 1231 generally includes all depreciable property that is "used in a trade or business." If such property is sold at a gain, the gain is generally taxed as a capital gain, except in the case of depreciation. As it relates to real estate, the excess accelerated depreciation that was claimed during the holding period (beyond what straight-line depreciation would have been) is subject to tax as ordinary income under Section 1250. A net loss on Section 1231 property is deductible as an ordinary loss. A loss on such property implies that the depreciation claimed for tax purposes was inadequate compared to the true economic decline in value.

Section 1250 Gains. Section 1250 of the *Internal Revenue Code* applies to the excess accelerated depreciation claimed on real estate used in a trade or business. The provisions of Section 1250 have been altered several times during the 1960s and 1970s. With each change, the section was tightened up, and, at the present time, all of the post-1976 excess accelerated depreciation on all real estate except for certain low-income apartments is *recaptured* as ordinary income.

Taxable Gain versus Before-Tax Proceeds from Resale

Calculation of the gain on resale is not the same as for the before-tax proceeds from resale. Whereas the remaining balance of a mortgage at resale has a major effect on the before-tax proceeds from resale, it has no effect on the taxable gain. For example, suppose that income-producing real estate was purchased for $500,000, depreciated to an adjusted tax basis of $300,000, and sold in ten years for

\$601,000 net of transaction costs. The gain is \$301,000 (\$601,000 minus \$300,000) regardless of the debt against the property. Whether the property was mortgaged for \$600,000 or \$400,000 or was always free and clear of any mortgage makes no difference to the income tax collector. It can, however, make a great deal of difference to the seller. Highly leveraged property on which accelerated depreciation was claimed can create an awkward situation at resale. The before-tax proceeds from resale can be negligible because the remaining balance of the mortgage is nearly as much as the resale price. The gain and accompanying tax on the gain can be substantial because accelerated depreciation reduced the adjusted tax basis rapidly, and the excess accelerated depreciation is recaptured at ordinary tax rates. Upon resale, the seller may be in the uncomfortable position of having a substantial tax liability, with less cash from the sale than the tax that is due.

An extreme example occurs at a foreclosure. The foreclosure price is deemed to be at the mortgage balance. Should the mortgage balance at foreclosure exceed the adjusted tax basis, there is a taxable gain, but the former owner has no cash with which to pay the tax.

Taxable Gain and True Economics Ultimately Coincide. During the holding period, an owner of income-producing property can claim depreciation, accelerated depreciation for some property. Generally, the depreciation reduces taxable income during operations. But depreciation also increases the potential gain upon resale because it reduces the adjusted tax basis of the property. Eventually, the true economics of the situation and the tax implications will coincide. Unless the property's value declines by the same amount as the depreciation claimed for income tax purposes, there will be a taxable gain to be recognized. Despite that "day of reckoning" when the tax situation catches up with the true economics, most investors prefer to claim as much depreciation as possible for at least three reasons. First, it postpones taxes and the savings from a postponement alone is worthwhile. Second the gain on resale could be a capital gain with rates that might be lower than ordinary income rates. Third, through careful estate and gift tax planning, the tax on the potential gain may be avoided or minimized.

As an example of the after-tax proceeds from resale, suppose that property was purchased for \$500,000, and depreciated down to \$300,000 over ten years using the straight-line method. It was originally financed with a \$400,000 mortgage at 12% interest for a 25-year term. After 10 years, the mortgage balance is \$351,000. The property is resold for $640,000, of which $39,000 is paid as a brokerage commission and other transaction costs. The gain on the sale is $301,000 ($601,000 adjusted price less $300,000 adjusted tax basis). The additional tax to the owner is computed to be $72,000. The proceeds from resale after taxes are described in Table 14-6.

TABLE 14-6
After-Tax Proceeds from Resale

Resale price	$640,000
Less: Transaction costs	−39,000
Unpaid mortgage	−351,000
Taxes on sale	−72,000
After-tax proceeds from resale	$178,000

After estimating the after-tax proceeds from resale, all after-tax cash flow can be discounted to a present value, and an after-tax yield to maturity on equity can be estimated. Such calculations consider the amount of down payment, after-tax cash flow for each year, and the proceeds from resale. This technique is similar to the Ellwood and conventional methods except that it reflects income taxes. All of the net after-tax income that the equity owner expects to receive is included, as is the timing of the receipts. Methods of discounting after-tax cash flows, including the after-tax proceeds from resale, are described in Chapter 15.

Tax-Deferred Exchange

It is possible to defer taxation of the gain through a trade of the property under Section 1031 of the *Internal Revenue Code.* This section provides that none of the gain realized from the exchange of like property under certain conditions is taxable. The gain is deferred through a transfer of the tax basis from the old to the new property.

To qualify:

1. There must be an exchange.
2. Properties exchanged must be of like kind.
3. The properties given up and received must be held for use in trade or business or held as an investment.

Generally, an exchange will be tax-free (tax-deferred is more descriptive) except to the extent of receipt of "unlike" property, which is called *boot.* The receipt of boot (cash, net mortgage debt relief, personal property) triggers taxation of gain to the extent of boot or realized gain, whichever is less.

Installment Sale Reporting

When a seller finances part of a sale by accepting a purchase-money mortgage for part of the down payment, the seller may pay a tax on the gain as the principal payments on the note are collected. This method has the advantage of spreading the tax on the gain over the period during which the proceeds from the sale are collected. This can result in lower tax payments by not concentrating all the gain from a sale in one year.

Payments in the year of sale consist of cash and marketable obligations, plus the excess of the relief of indebtedness over the adjusted basis of the property.

For example, assume that property was originally purchased for $500,000, then depreciated to $300,000. After ten years, it is resold for $728,000. This is shown in Table 14–7.

TABLE 14–7
Taxable Gain on Resale

Cash down payment	$100,000
Assumption of first mortgage	+351,000
Second mortgage to seller	+277,000
Total price	$728,000
Less: Transaction costs	− 40,000
Seller's adjusted tax basis	−300,000
Gain on the sale	$388,000

Since the first mortgage, assumed by the buyer, exceeds the seller's adjusted tax basis by $51,000 ($351,000 minus $300,000 = $51,000), this amount and the $100,000 cash down payment are the "payments in the year of sale."

The *gross profit ratio* is the profit to the seller ($388,000) divided by the *contract price.* To determine the contract price, subtract the existing mortgage assumed by the buyer from the adjusted sales price, then add the excess of the mortgage assumed by the buyer over the tax basis, as shown in Table 14–8. In this situation, the gross profit ratio is 100% ($388,000 gross profit/$388,000 contract price). Therefore, 100% of each principal payment from the buyer is taxable as gain to the seller. Had the gross profit ratio been 90%, then 90% of each principal payment would be taxable gain to the seller. Interest income collected by the seller on the second mortgage is taxed as ordinary income.

TABLE 14–8
Contract Price of Installment Sale

Sales price	$728,000
Less: Transaction costs	−40,000
Less: Mortgage assumed by buyer	−351,000
Add: Mortgage assumed over basis	+51,000
Contract price	$388,000

SUMMARY

Cash throw-off from income-producing property may be subject to tax or be tax-free, or the property may generate tax losses. The principal reasons for the difference between cash throw-off and taxable income computations are noncash depreciation deductions and nontax-deductible mortgage principal payments. The depreciation claimed reduces taxable income during the holding period, but it also reduces the adjusted tax basis of the property. Upon resale, the true economics of the investment situation will be recognized for income tax purposes.

Upon resale, gain is measured by the difference between the selling price (after transaction costs) and the adjusted tax basis of the property. The extent of leverage employed is not a factor in determining the tax at resale, although it is important in determining the before-tax proceeds from resale. Subtracting the tax on the gain, which is likely to be at favorable capital gains rates unless accelerated depreciation has been claimed, from the before-tax proceeds determines the after-tax proceeds from resale.

Although the income tax situation of each investor varies, one can forecast the expected after-tax cash flow and its timing, then use the present value of that income as a yardstick to compare one investment proposal to another. In that manner, an investor can select the property that may be expected to yield the greatest benefits, taking into account cash throw-off, income tax implications, appreciation, and mortgage reduction.

Questions

1. A strip shopping center is offered for sale for $2,000,000, of which $1,500,000 represents improvements that can be depreciated over 30 years. How much depreciation can be claimed for each of the first *three* years using:
   a. Straight-line depreciation?
   b. 150% declining balance?
2. The shopping center in Question 1 is financed with a $1.4 million loan at 10% interest with annual payments at the end of each year, self-amortizing over 25 years.
   a. What is the interest deduction for each of the first three years?
   b. What is the annual debt service requirement?
3. The shopping center described in Questions 1 and 2 generates $290,000 effective gross income each year and offers $100,000 in tax-deductible operating expenses, exclusive of depreciation and interest deductions.
   a. What is the annual before-tax cash flow?
   b. What is the taxable income or loss for each of the first three years, using straight-line depreciation?
   c. Assuming that the owner is in the 30% marginal income tax bracket, how much is the after-tax cash flow for the first three years?
4. The shopping center described in Questions 1, 2, and 3 is resold at the beginning of the fourth year for $2.3 million. Brokerage fees and other transaction costs amount to $100,000. Straight-line depreciation was claimed. The large gain causes the investor to be in the 50% marginal tax bracket.
   a. What is the taxable gain on the transaction?
   b. Assuming that the gain is taxed as a capital gain, and therefore only 40% of the gain is included in the owner's ordinary taxable income, how much is the tax on the gain?
   c. What is the outstanding mortgage balance at the end of the third year (or beginning of the fourth year)?
   d. What is the after-tax proceeds from resale?

Essay Questions

1. What is the difference between *market value* and *investment value?*
2. Why do income tax effects alone rarely, if ever, justify an investment?
3. How does depreciation claimed for income tax purposes benefit a real estate investor?
4. What three factors affect the amount of depreciation deductions?
5. Distinguish between depreciation claimed for income tax purposes and a true economic loss in value.
6. Explain how the same property can be depreciated more than once.
7. Define *adjusted tax basis* and explain how it is affected by depreciation deductions.
8. Explain which deductions are allowed for tax purposes on property used in a trade or business, and which cash payments are not tax-deductible.
9. How is gain or loss on the resale of income-producing real estate computed?
10. What is *excess accelerated depreciation?* How does it affect the tax on resale?
11. Why do many investors prefer to claim accelerated depreciation even though the income tax implications generally will ultimately reflect the true economic changes in value?

Chapter 15

After-Tax Measuring Devices

This textbook has stressed the importance of using a discounted present value approach for estimating the value of income that is forecast to be received. Discounting is analogous to compounding. Interest or yield to maturity is based on the amounts invested, the forecast benefits, and timing of all receipts and payments. Stress has been placed on a yield-to-maturity approach as opposed to a simple one-year analysis, or methods that average annual income instead of allowing for the effect of the timing of cash inflows and outflows. This chapter describes both discounting and nondiscounting methods.

FOUR POPULAR DISCOUNTING METHODS

As analyses become more sophisticated, variations on discounted techniques have been developed and applied to the after-tax cash flows forecast to be received from income-producing property. The four most popular discounting methods are:

1. Net present value (NPV).
2. Internal rate of return (IRR).
3. Modified internal rate of return (MIR).
4. Financial management rate of return (FMRR).

The forecast after-tax cash flows and after-tax proceeds from resale from the example in the previous chapter are used as the starting point and are repeated in Table 15–1. The income configuration presented has only one cash outflow followed by a series of cash inflows; so it does not show variations of income patterns that certain of the four measuring devices accommodate better than others. These differences will be acknowledged.

TABLE 15–1
Forecast After-Tax Cash Inflows

End of Year	*After-Tax Cash Inflows (Outflows)*
0	($100,000)
1	14,787
2	14,650
3	14,496
4	14,322
5	14,126
6	13,905
7	13,657
8	13,377
9	13,061
10	12,705
10 (resale proceeds)	$178,000

Net Present Value Technique

In the net present value (NPV) technique, the analyst discounts all of the forecast cash inflows and outflows to a present value at a specified rate of return on investment. If the net result is negative, then the specified rate of return is not forecast to be achieved; so the proposed investment is not considered. If positive, the investment can be considered. Table 15–2 shows positive results, based on a 15% specified rate of return on investment. The present values of expected after-tax cash inflows are $115,050, and the present value of the investment is $100,000. The difference, $15,050, is positive, so the forecast rate of return is above 15%.

Selection of the rate for discounting forecast inflows and outflows is crucial to the analysis. In the example, 15% was arbitrarily selected. Had a higher rate been selected, the net present value would have been negative. Therefore the rate must be chosen carefully. It must exceed the marginal cost of capital to the investor who may have to raise the investment capital from other sources and therefore wants to be in a favorable leverage situation. It should also exceed rates offered on alternative investment situations that are perceived to bear equal risk, and allow for the risk involved in the subject investment considered.

Internal Rate of Return Technique

In the internal rate of return (IRR) technique, the rate of return expected to be received on the subject property is sought. It is the rate at which the cash inflows and outflows are exactly equal. The IRR

TABLE 15-2
Use of Net Present Value Method (Discount Rate = 15%)

End of Year	*After-Tax Cash Inflow (Outflow)*		*Present Value Factor at 15%*		*Amount at Present Value**
0	$(100,000)	×	1.000000	=	$(100,000)
1	14,787	×	.869565	=	12,858
2	14,650	×	.756143	=	11,078
3	14,496	×	.657516	=	9,531
4	14,322	×	.571753	=	8,189
5	14,126	×	.497177	=	7,023
6	13,905	×	.432328	=	6,012
7	13,657	×	.375937	=	5,134
8	13,377	×	.326902	=	4,373
9	13,061	×	.284262	=	3,713
10	12,705	×	.247185	=	3,140
10	178,000	×	.247185	=	43,999
Total NPV at 15% =					$ 15,050

*Total present value of inflows is $115,050; subtracting $100,000 investment cost paid at inception results in $15,050 net present value of investment.

is thus used as a measuring device to compare various investment proposals.

Solving for the IRR is a trial-and-error process. In the NPV example above, the 15% rate that was specified resulted in a present value of inflows that exceeded outflows. The greater the rate used, the lower the present value of inflows. (The present value of outflows in the example is unaffected by the rate selected because all outflows occurred at the inception of the investment and therefore were not discounted.) The internal rate of return for the subject property therefore exceeds 15%, and can be determined through trial and error.

Table 15-3 shows a trial at 20%, which results in a negative NPV of $11,620. Therefore, the rate is between 15% and 20%. Table 15-4 shows a trial at 17.5%, at which the present value of inflows is almost exactly equal to outflows. Therefore, the IRR approximates 17.5%. Through further interpolation, a more exact rate can be derived.

IRR versus NPV: A Comparison. The NPV technique seeks the difference between the present value of cash inflows and outflows at a specified rate, whereas the IRR technique derives the rate at which inflows and outflows are equal. See Figure 15-1.

From a theoretical standpoint, the NPV is preferable because it includes an inherent assumption that the earnings on reinvested funds occur at the selected rate, whereas the IRR implicitly as-

TABLE 15–3
Internal Rate of Return (Trial at 20%)

End of Year	After-Tax Cash Outflow (Inflow)		Present Value Factor at 20%		Amount at Present Value
0	$(100,000)	×	1.000000	=	$(100,000)
1	14,787	×	.833333	=	12,323
2	14,650	×	.694444	=	10,174
3	14,496	×	.578704	=	8,389
4	14,322	×	.482253	=	6,907
5	14,126	×	.401878	=	5,677
6	13,905	×	.334898	=	4,657
7	13,657	×	.279082	=	3,811
8	13,377	×	.232568	=	3,111
9	13,061	×	.193807	=	2,531
10	12,705	×	.161505	=	2,052
10	178,000	×	.161505	=	28,748
Total NPV at 20% = (negative)					$ (11,620)

TABLE 15–4
Internal Rate of Return (Trial at 17.5%)

End of Year	After-Tax Cash Inflow (Outflow)		Present Value Factor at 17.5%		Amount at Present Value
0	$(100,000)	×	1.000000	=	$(100,000)
1	14,787	×	.851064	=	12,585
2	14,650	×	.724310	=	10,611
3	14,496	×	.616434	=	8,936
4	14,322	×	.524624	=	7,514
5	14,126	×	.446489	=	6,307
6	13,905	×	.379991	=	5,284
7	13,657	×	.323396	=	4,417
8	13,377	×	.375231	=	3,682
9	13,061	×	.234239	=	3,059
10	12,705	×	.199352	=	2,533
10	178,000	×	.199352	=	35,485
Total NPV at 17.5% =					$ 413

sumes reinvestment at its rate. Since an analyst cannot determine that the IRR's reinvestment rate will be achieved, this bias is considered a drawback of the IRR. Further, the IRR technique will produce more than one mathematically correct rate for each year in which inflows are followed by outflows, and vice versa. In the NPV technique, the analyst introduces bias by specifying a rate, whereas the IRR technique has its own inherent biases. Despite its drawbacks, the IRR is widely used as a measuring device to rank alternative investments.

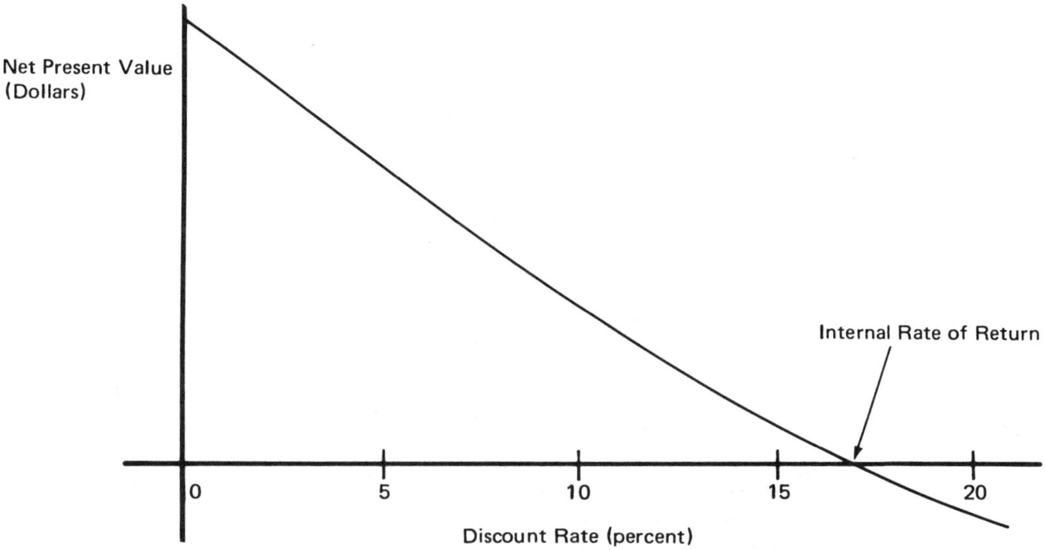

FIGURE 15–1. IRR Versus NPV. By definition, the internal rate of return (IRR) is the discount rate at which the net present value (NPV) of an investment is zero. The NPV is positive at discount rates that are less than the IRR. The NPV is negative at discount rates that are above the IRR.

Modified Internal Rate (MIR)

A modified internal rate of return (MIR) is sometimes used to avoid one of the drawbacks of the IRR, namely, the inherent presumption of reinvestment at the IRR. The MIR technique is most frequently used when the investment outflow is to occur over multiple periods.

For example, suppose that $100,000 of equity must be contributed in two installments: $50,000 immediately, with the second $50,000 due one year later. Use of the IRR technique assumes that the second $50,000, while waiting to be invested, can earn interest at the same rate as the IRR. This presumption is difficult to achieve in reality since the investor must keep the $50,000 adequately liquid in a relatively risk-free investment medium during the first year. Use of the MIR would allow the proposed real estate investment to be considered, with the assumption that the $50,000 installment-two contribution will earn at a lower rate while waiting to be invested. If the appropriate rate of earnings is 5% after taxes, then the outflows would be considered as shown in Table 15–5.

Internal rate of return computations are then applied, treating the outflow at the end of year 0 as $97,619, instead of $50,000 followed by $50,000 one year later. Presuming that the subject property promises to generate an internal rate of return above 5%, the modified internal rate (MIR) will be less than the unmodified internal rate of return.

TABLE 15-5
Discounting Equity Investment Installments at Safe Rate

	End of Year	Amount	Present Value Discounted at 5%
Installment 1	0	$50,000	$50,000
Installment 2	1	50,000	47,619
Total investment needed at year 0			$97,619

Financial Management Rate of Return (FMRR)

The financial management rate of return* is an attempt to further improve on the IRR. Applying the FMRR requires the analyst to specify two rates:

1. A safe, liquid after-tax rate (i_L).
2. A "run of the mill" after-tax rate (i_R).

The safe, liquid rate is one that can be earned on short-term investments, such as on tax-free (municipal) obligations that mature within one year. Basically, it is applied to investment outflows that are forecast to be incurred after the initial investment. Those outflows are generally discounted to a lump sum at the start of year 1 (or end of year 0). In this respect it is similar to the MIR. Under some conditions, cash outflows that are expected to occur during the holding period (operations) stage may be discounted using the safe, liquid rate (i_L).

Generally, cash inflows are compounded forward at a "run of the mill rate" (i_R) to a terminal value at the forecast resale point. The "run of the mill rate" is an after-tax rate of return on investment that is expected to be achieved by other investments that will be available during the operations phase.

The effective lump sum investment at the start of year 1 is then compared to the lump sum terminal value to derive a rate of return, using the internal rate of return method for two lump sums (from column 1 of compound interest tables). This is diagrammed in Figure 15-2. The result is the FMRR.

*M. Chapman Findlay, III, and Stephen D. Messner, "Real Estate Investment Analysis: IRR versus FMRR," *The Real Estate Appraiser,* V. 41 July/August 1975, pp 5-20.

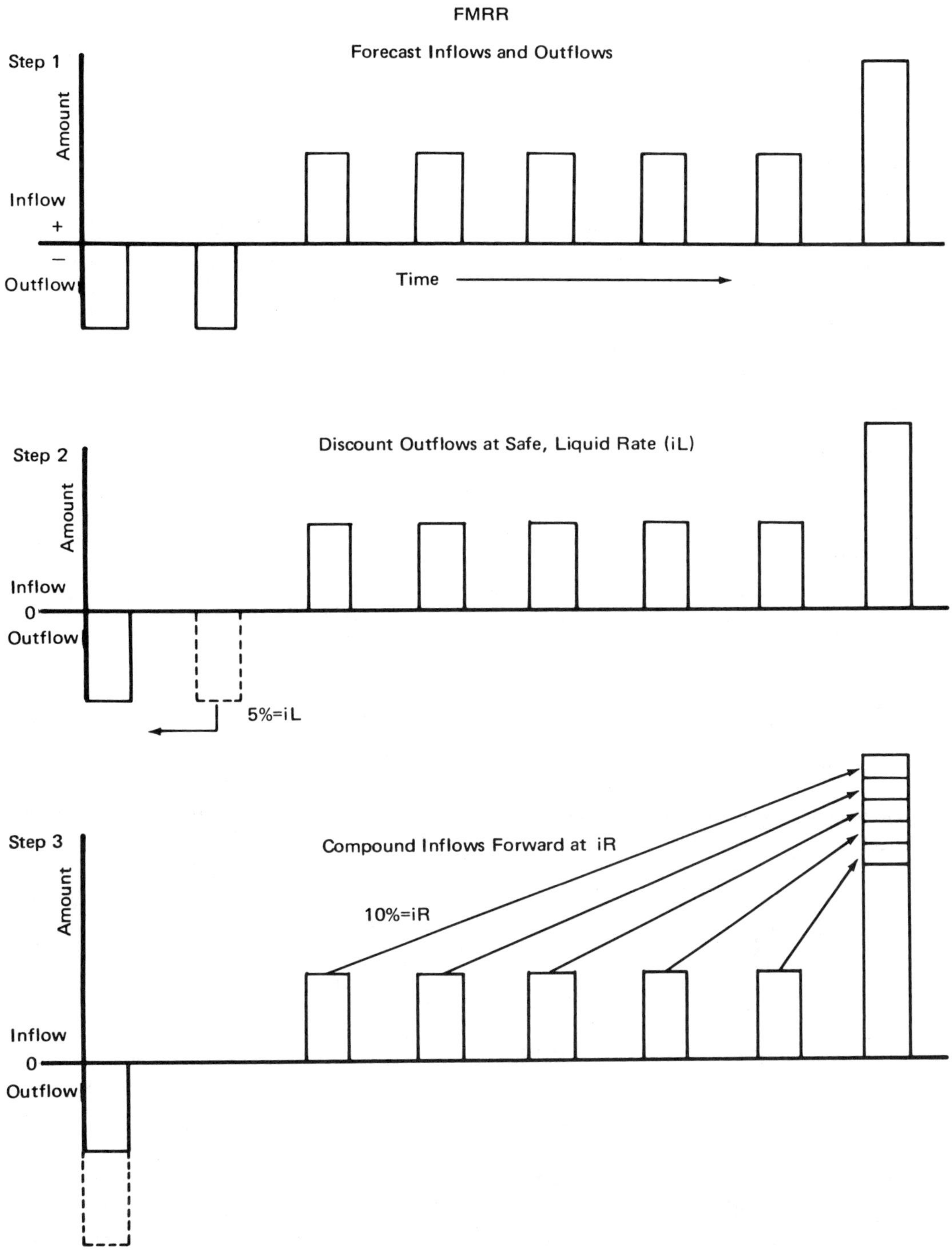

FIGURE 15–2. Financial Management Rate of Return (FMRR).

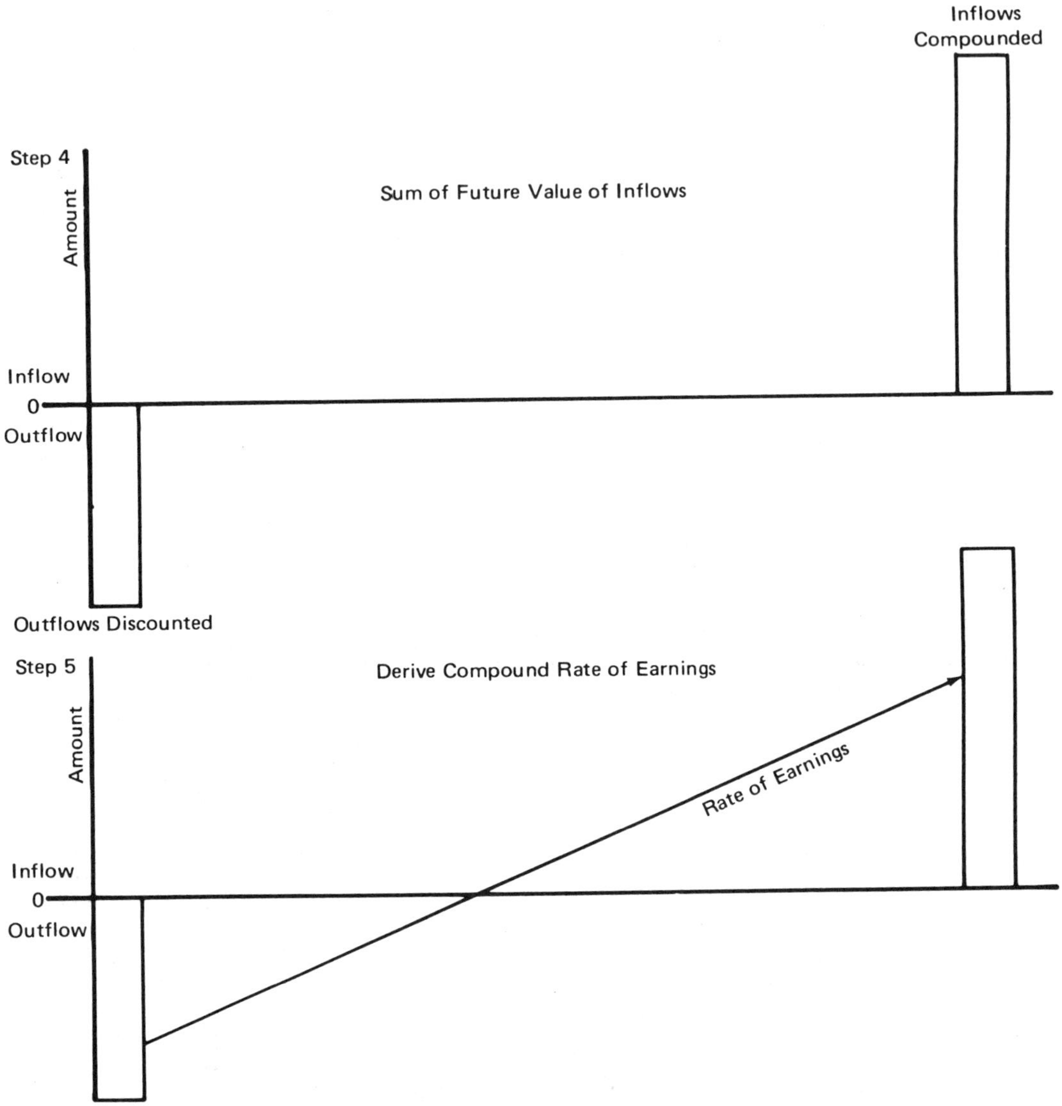

FIGURE 15-2. (Continued)

FMRR versus IRR and NPV. The FMRR has the distinct advantage over the IRR and NPV of applying different rates of return (discount rates) to cash inflows and outflows. Further, FMRR applications avoid the possibility of more than one mathematically correct rate of return, which is an IRR pitfall; and they also avoid the IRR's inherent presumption of reinvestment at the IRR. However, the FMRR requires two rates of return to be specified: a safe liquid rate and a run of the mill rate. Results of the FMRR rest heavily on the validity of these specified rates.

NONDISCOUNTED APPROACHES

Two of the most frequently used nondiscounted approaches to an after-tax rate of return are:

1. Net spendable income technique.
2. Average annual after-tax return.

Net Spendable Income

The net spendable income (NSI) technique offers a rate of return by dividing each year's after-tax cash flow by either the equity invested or the current equity. For example, the year 1 after-tax cash flow of $14,787, when divided by the $100,000 equity, offers a 14.787% after-tax return for the first year. The rate of return changes from year to year, with varying after-tax cash flows and equity investment. Therefore, this technique fails to accurately present a yield to maturity, which should be based on timing of cash inflows and outflows. Further, the technique disregards the potential tax liability on a resale.

Average Annual After-Tax Return

The average annual after-tax return method requires the summation of all of the after-tax cash flows, including the proceeds from resale. From that total, the investment outlay is subtracted, and the result is divided by the projected holding span of the investment, to result in the average annual after-tax income. This figure, in turn, is divided by the initial equity investment. The result offers an average annual rate of return on investment. However, such a rate is frequently misleading because it fails to indicate the timing of inflows. It is much preferred to receive inflows in the early years of an investment so they can be reinvested. This method fails to articulate the timing of receipts. The method is especially misleading when most of the income is forecast to be received upon a resale in the distant future.

AFTER-TAX RATE OF RETURN CONSIDERATIONS

There are three major factors that an analyst should consider when evaluating forecast after-tax rates of return (see Figure 15–3). These are:

1. Assumptions input or used as a basis for the projections.
2. Risks inherent with real estate investments.
3. Mathematics of the after-tax rates of return.

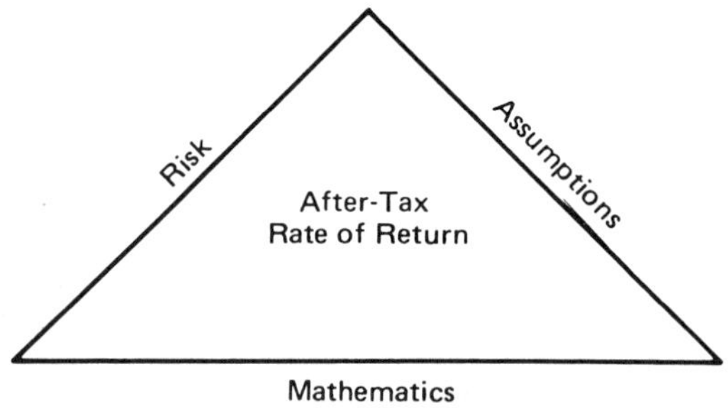

FIGURE 15–3. Three Factors Affecting After-Tax Rate of Return: Risk, Assumptions, and Mathematics.

Assumptions Input

Assumptions used in preparing after-tax forecasts concern four major variables, which are:

A. Net operating income.
B. Financing terms.
C. Income tax implications.
D. Forecast resale price.

All four assumptions are crucial to realization of the forecast after-tax rate of return.

Net Operating Income. Forecasts of unit rental rates, occupancy rates, and operating expenses are required to derive net operating income. Whether properties are new or have been in operation for many years, an appraiser who is faced with the assignment of estimating market value must estimate, on the basis of market data, the present dollar amounts or percentages of various inputs such as rents, occupancy rates, and operating expenses. (One exception is a situation when a property is encumbered by a long-term lease to a credit-worthy tenant.) Rates of return are highly sensitive to changes in the forecasts of these inputs.

Financing Terms. Market value appraisals consider the typical financing terms that are available in the market. Terms include principal, interest rate, amortization, participation, escalation provisions, personal liability, and others. These terms affect the amount of equity required, cash flows, resale proceeds, income tax implications, and risk. Any variance from the terms considered in the projection to those actually employed will affect the rate of return.

Income Tax Implications. Forecasts of after-tax cash flows and after-tax resale proceeds, by definition, consider income taxes. Deductions include operating expenses, depreciable lives and methods, and interest payments. The investment tax credit and energy credit may be claimed on certain property. The regular income and capital gains rates for investors may change due to income and deduction changes, changes in marital status, death, changes in the tax rate schedule, new laws, new regulations, court cases clarifying tax doctrines, and other possible events. All of these factors will affect the after-tax return.

Forecast Resale Price. The forecast resale price is often derived on the basis of an assumed value growth rate. It is impossible to predict with certainty the amount a property will bring in the future. Yet, a reversionary value is expected to be shown in forecast results. Often, the forecast resale price has a significant impact on the after-tax rate of return.

Risks Inherent with Real Estate Investments

Real estate investments are inherently subject to risks caused by factors external to the property. Assumptions underlying forecasts, although they may generally be "proven out," are subject to variability caused by a variety of influences, many of which cannot be controlled by the owner. The same four major variables that were described in the "Assumption Input" section are subject to risk. Added to these four is the additional variability of government influence.

Net Operating Income. General economic and local market fluctuations affect the stability of rental rates, occupancy rates, and operating expenses. Inflation, competition, personal taste changes, and other factors can affect net operating income and therefore the rate of return. Even when rental rates are fixed through a long-term lease to a credit-worthy tenant, risk is not totally avoided. Tenants can bankrupt as did W.T. Grant and the Penn Central. Risk in the investment capital is introduced due to the fixed income stream (unless an escalation provision has been included). In the future, a fixed income stream may offer an inadequate return based on building replacement cost, and thereby cause a loss of part of the invested capital.

Some factors are influenced by national or local business cycles. Consequently, there may be significant year-to-year fluctuations from the forecast trend line (see Figure 15–4).

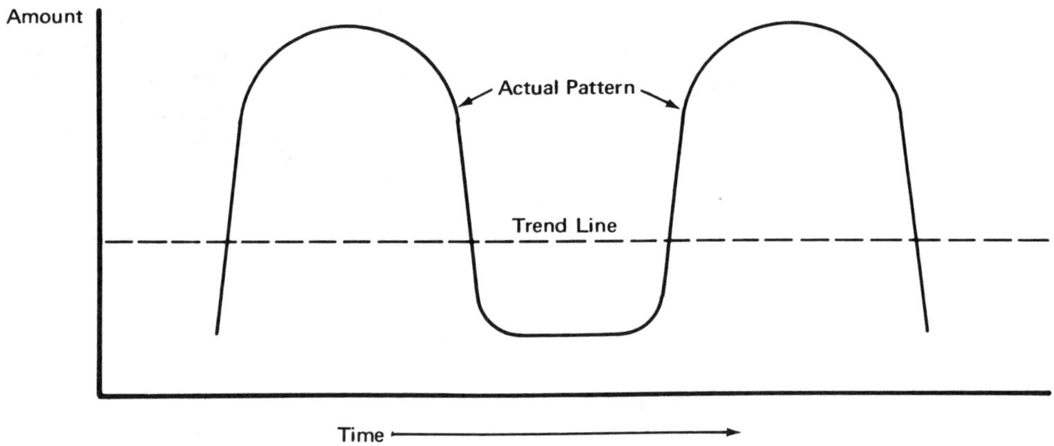

FIGURE 15–4. Trend Line Versus Actual Pattern of Net Operating Income.

Financing Terms. The degree of leverage affects the break-even point, which is the occupancy level that results in zero before-tax cash flow. Leverage may allow equity investors to diversify their assets into several projects, thus minimizing the amount they stand to lose in any one project. As leverage causes periodic debt service requirements to increase, the cash flow as a percentage of equity invested tends to become more volatile. Small changes in the net operating income become significant changes in percentages of after-tax cash flow. Some investors prefer stable cash flows, whereas others can accept fluctuations. Mortgages that include participation requirements, periodically renegotiated rates, and personal liability of the investor can affect the stability of forecast cash flows and after-tax rates of return.

Income Tax Implications. Fundamental changes in income tax laws are possible. These could significantly affect the forecast after-tax rate of return for a proposed real estate investment. There could be substantial tax rate differences; or changes in the computation of taxable income or loss, in deductions for operating expenses, in interest rates and depreciation, in capital and Section 1231 gains computations, in loss carrryover provisions, in estate and gift tax laws, and the like. The uncertainty of tax changes adds a degree of risk to any real estate investment.

Forecast Resale Price. Economic conditions, particularly inflation, can cause a drastic change from a forecast resale price. Functional obsolescence could cause a significant value change. An extreme example might be changes in the field of energy. If a technological breakthrough were discovered to efficiently harness solar energy, functional obsolescence of conventionally powered properties would be significant. Environmental obsolescence is the risk that forces outside a property will cause a change in the subject property's value.

Government Influence. Potential rent controls, condemnation, political turmoil, war, new legislation, and new judicial interpretations introduce risk to property owners. Unfortunately, projected after-tax rates of return do not explicitly articulate these possibilities.

Mathematics

The arithmetic of each after-tax measuring device provides a rate of return on investment. The question to be resolved by analysts and investors is whether the forecast rate of return is adequate compensation for the perceived risks in the light of alternative investment opportunities.

Some considerations posed by forecast after-tax rates of return on equity are:

1. Risk that is not explicitly considered.
2. Size of investment not indicated.
3. Explicit or inherent reinvestment assumptions.

Risk is not explicitly considered by rates because rates are simply numbers. Without reference points, such as rates offered by alternative investment opportunities, the meaning of a rate is limited. In addition, a rate that is based on equity invested does not explicitly consider exposure to loss beyond the amount invested. Furthermore, such rates do not consider the variability of returns caused by the use of leverage.

The size of an equity investment can have a profound impact on the rate of return. If leverage is favorable, the more that is employed, the higher the rate of return on equity (see Table 15-6). Yet, is it worth the time and effort to carefully scrutinize an investment that promises to repay 10 cents even if this is a high rate of return on an investment of one penny? Also, the rate of return on equity invested in one project fails to offer information concerning diversification and management requirements of an investor's entire portfolio.

TABLE 15-6
Effect of Favorable Leverage on Various Equity Deposits (Given a Project Cost of $100,000, Net Operating Income of $15,000, and a Mortgage Rate of 10% Interest-Only).

Equity Deposit	*Rate of Return*
100%	15%
50%	20%
25%	30%
10%	60%
1%	510%
0	Infinite

An explicit reinvestment rate is offered by the net present value technique, the modified internal rate, and the financial management rate of return. An explicit reinvestment rate is particularly important to an investor when (a) returns are to be reinvested rather than spent, (b) both cash inflows and outflows are expected during the operations stage, (c) rates offered by alternative investments are known, and (d) the investor's cost of capital is known. In contrast, the internal rate of return, which has inherent biases, is a technique that is mathematically free of an analyst's personal subjectivity. This is because the internal rate of return provides an internally generated rate.

SENSITIVITY ANALYSIS

The effects of the assumptions and risks that were previously described can be analyzed by additional forecasts. In each forecast, one variable is changed, and a rate of return computed considering that change. For example, a forecast can be prepared at a lower occupancy rate, another at a lower resale price, another at less favorable financing terms, and still another at unfavorable income tax assumptions. The effect of each variable on the rate of return can then be studied. The purpose is to estimate how sensitive the rate of return is to those variables. If desired, additional forecasts can be prepared indicating the interaction of changes in the variables. Instead of attempting to analyze all of the combinations of variables, it may be appropriate to consider just three forecasts: most probable, optimistic, and pessimistic. Should a project seem viable under even the pessimistic assumptions, it would surely be acceptable under all other conditions.

Another type of sensitivity analysis technique is called *Monte Carlo simulation.* A Monte Carlo simulation is a process of using a computer to run many different projections of a cash flow statement. Each separate projection is based on assumptions that are changed on the basis of estimated statistical probability distributions. This technique permits an analyst to judge how responsive the rate is to changed assumptions and other inputs. Figure 15–5 shows diagrams of Monte Carlo simulations to derive after-tax cash flow.

SUMMARY

There are various measuring devices that can be used to rank real estate investment offerings on the basis of after-tax cash flow. The internal rate of return (IRR) and net present value (NPV) techniques are the two traditional ones that consider amounts and timing of cash inflows and outflows. The IRR has inherent biases, whereas the analyst employing the NPV technique injects bias.

A modified internal rate of return (MIR) and the financial management rate of return (FMRR) both attempt to avoid some of the pitfalls of the IRR or NPV technique. They are preferable under many circumstances, though, like the traditional approaches, they are not entirely free of bias.

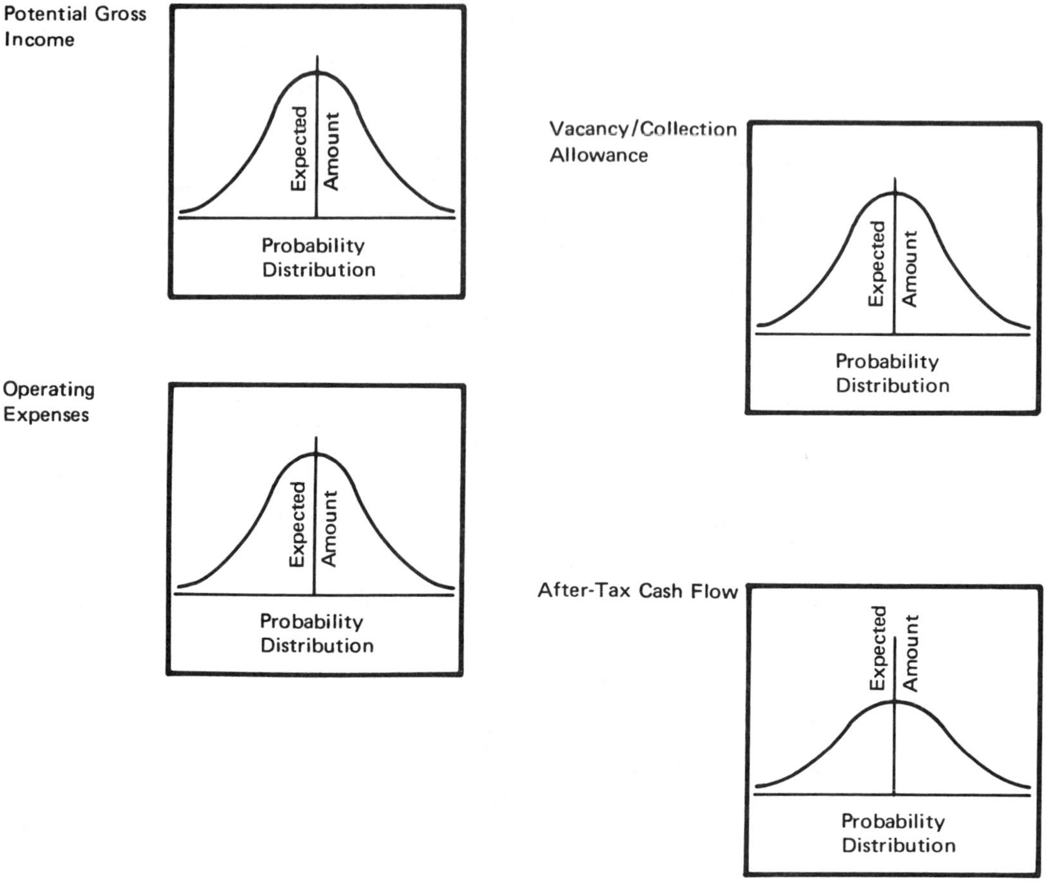

FIGURE 15–5. Monte-Carlo Probability Charts.

There are nondiscounted approaches to considering after-tax returns, as on an annual basis or on a yearly average basis. Their greatest shortcoming is their inability to consider the timing of cash inflows and outflows and to produce an effective yield to maturity.

Regardless of which analytical method is selected, it is of extreme importance to recognize that the mathematics employed offer results based only on the assumptions that are input. Therefore extreme care is needed in forecasting rental and vacancy rates, operating expenses, and the resale price. Unless these assumptions are carefully considered, results are of no value regardless of the mathematical validity of the technique used.

Questions

1. Find the net present value for all of the three investment offerings (A, B, and C) below. Each requires a $10,000 investment at the start of year 1 (end of year 0). Use a 15% rate.

	Cash Inflows		
End of Year	*A*	*B*	*C*
1	$ 0	$5,000	$6,000
2	0	5,000	5,000
3	15,000	5,000	4,000

2. Compute the internal rate of return for each of the three income streams of Question #1.
3. Assuming that the cash inflows provided by investments B and C of Question #1 could be reinvested at a 12% rate of return from receipt until the end of the third year, how much total cash would be available at the end of the third year?
4. Compute the FMRR for investment proposals B and C in Question #1, based on the information in Question #3.

Essay Questions

1. Compare the internal rate of return technique to the net present value technique.
2. At what rate will the IRR technique yield results that are identical to the NPV technique?
3. In what respect does the FMRR technique improve on the IRR? What biases are contained in the IRR and the FMRR?
4. What are two nondiscounted after-tax analytical techniques, and what are their weaknesses?
5. Why is it necessary to carefully analyze and forecast property performance in terms of net operating income and resale price?
6. Discuss three major factors that an analyst should consider when evaluating after-tax rates of return.
7. Why can't an analyst depend entirely on the mathematical answer provided by various after-tax measuring devices?

8. How might sensitivity analysis add a dimension to traditional real estate investment analysis?
9. Why does increased financial leverage also increase investment risks?

Chapter 16

Site Analysis and Application of the Principle of Highest and Best Use

What is the maximum price that should be paid for a specific parcel of land? This question underlies four general types of investment situations normally faced by a real estate analyst. These situations are:

1. Land requiring a user.
2. A user in search of specific types of land.
3. An investor looking for a satisfactory combination of land and user.
4. A speculator in search of land with good appreciation potential.

To provide the answers to these questions, an analyst has several alternative ways of making a determination. One such way is to perform a highest-and-best-use study. A highest-and-best-use study is a means of considering alternative development strategies to calculate which strategy will result in the highest residual value of the land. This approach can help solve the general problems of land requiring a user and a speculator in search of land with good appreciation potential. The market approach is useful in solving the other two types of problems. Both highest-and-best-use studies and the market approach to value are discussed in this chapter.

THE PRINCIPLE OF HIGHEST AND BEST USE

The theoretical foundation of the studies is the principle of "highest and best use." This has been defined as: "that use, from among reasonably probable and legal alternative uses, found to be physically possible, appropriately supported, financially feasible, and which results in highest land value."[1] There are several factors that interact to determine the highest and best use of a particular site. These factors are illustrated in Figure 16–1.

Before a decision is made to purchase and develop land or to purchase an existing building for immediate occupancy or redevelopment, the property's value potential must be investigated. The developer is interested in the answer to two major questions. The first question is whether the market will support a planned use, or alternatively, what planned uses will the market support. This involves the identification of market opportunities and an analysis of the competition. The second question concerns the cost and feasibility of developing the land or redeveloping the property. This requires an identification of the land's holding capacity and the constraints that are imposed on the development of the site. The factors that are considered in answering these questions are: location potential, market demand, legal right to develop use, resource quality of the site, technological feasibility, and financial feasibility.

Location Potential

The location of land is very important and is considered the prime determinant of value. Often the appraiser or analyst is evaluating a "site" rather than raw land. A site is land ready for development, with appropriate utilities and other facilities reasonably available. An important consideration is how a particular site relates to the surrounding land use pattern. A second consideration is the accessibility of the site. If a site is difficult to get to, it becomes less useful.

Consider a person who is interested in developing a breakfast cafe for motorists. This person has a choice of two sites—one across the street from the other. The site that is selected is the one that is most accessible to morning commuter traffic. If a developer is interested in constructing a warehouse facility, a location within easy

[1]Bryl Boyce, ed., *Real Estate Appraisal Terminology* (Cambridge, Mass.: Ballinger Publishing Co., 1975), p. 107.

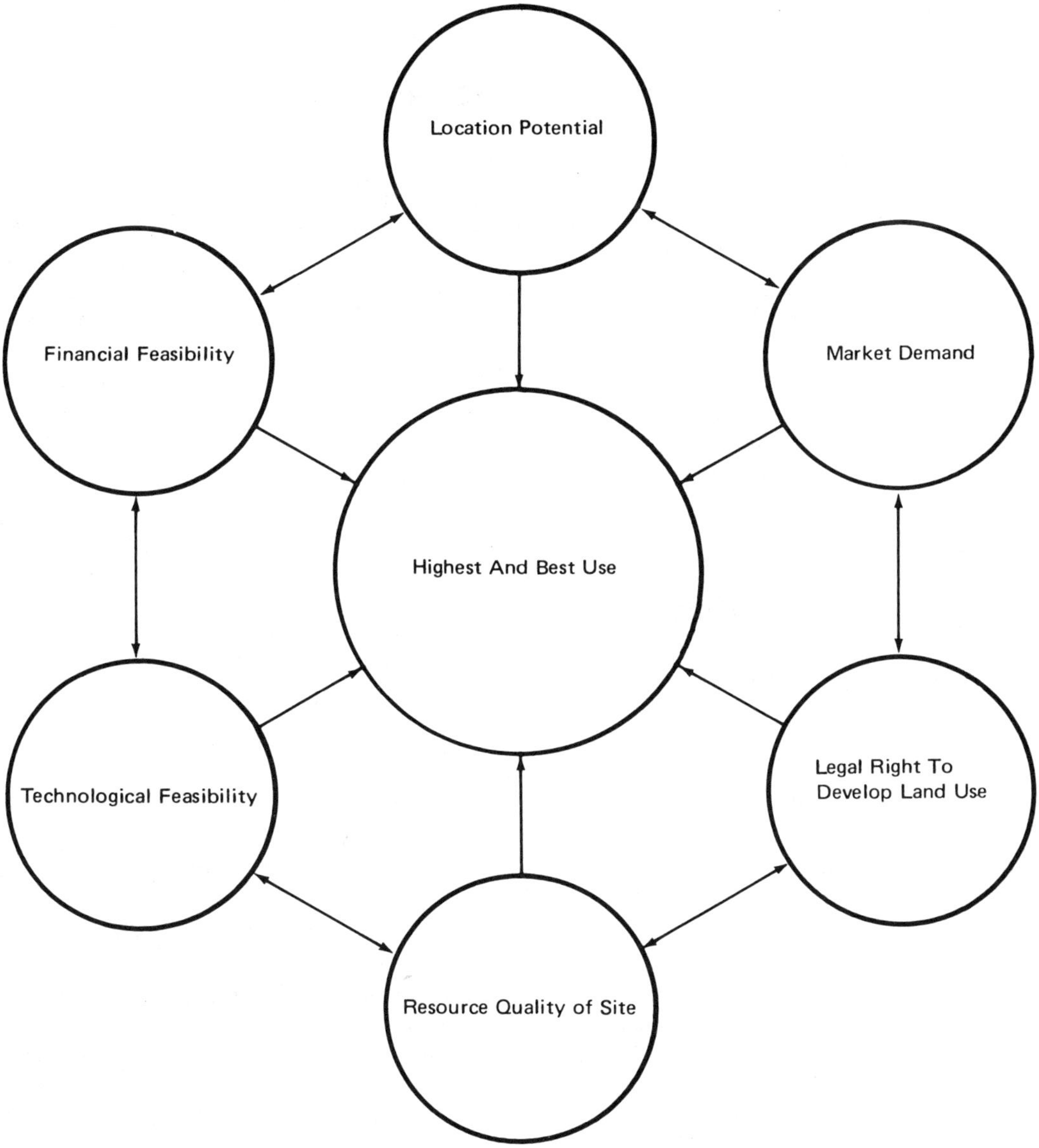

FIGURE 16–1. Several Factors Interact to Determine Highest and Best Use.

reach of an interstate highway system and/or a railroad spur would probably be selected. For certain types of real estate uses, such as convenience stores or fast food restaurants or motels, visibility from either side of the road for oncoming traffic is very important. This visibility may not be as important for a furniture store or an automobile dealership since their customers can ordinarily be attracted to the site through effective advertising.

Care should be taken to identify incompatible uses, nuisances, and hazards. This locational information should be plotted on a map. The map could contain information about driving times to job centers, traffic counts, and identification of important land uses. Some information can be acquired from the examination of aerial photographs; maps; published planning studies; tables containing demographic information; locational studies prepared by newspapers, radio, and television stations for their advertisers; data from the Chamber of Commerce; and other such sources.

Market Demand

Analysis of market demand is used to determine whether a planned use is "reasonably probable" given the nature of supply and demand interaction in the market. This analysis is used to determine the type of use or mix of uses that should feasibly be developed. It is also useful in estimating the proper timing or phasing of the development and the scale of the project.

Market analysis may be divided into four functional tasks: field analysis, quantitative analysis, qualitative analysis, and synthesis (see Figure 16–2). Within each of these four tasks certain objectives are sought.

The first objective is to identify pertinent supply and demand factors influencing the value of a particular land use. For example, the "target market" must be identified. The target market involves those users who are likely to purchase or rent the particular real estate properties. For example, the target market for two-bedroom apartments might be young professionals and married couples without children. Once the target markets have been identified, then amenities likely to produce a competitive differential between the subject property and all others are analyzed. A competitive differential is something that will give a project a comparative advantage. For example, an analyst may discover that competitive projects do not have enough tennis courts. Tenants must wait in long lines to play. Therefore building more than the standard number of courts may be a cost-efficient way to make the proposed project attractive to the target market. Amenities can include fireplaces in each unit, swimming pools, jogging trails, and miniwarehouses.

1. *Field Analysis:*

The basis for market analysis involves going out into the prospective market areas and physically researching needed data. This includes an extensive examination of both client's and competitor's facilities with regard to physical plant (sales area and volume), ingress-egress, merchandising efforts, pricing, personnel, and reputation within the community. This analysis also includes driving times around the prospective retail food outlet and customer surveys. Finally, an extensive geographic analysis of the area is made. This includes road patterns, traffic flow along the road patterns, neighborhood conditions, population characteristics, and income characteristics.

2. *Quantitative Analysis:*

This is the quantification of the field data into understandable symbols and terms. This involves the graphic and mathematical determination of the prospective food retail site(s), competitors, trade area, driving times, mileage rings (quad analysis), population, available food dollars, market share and drawing power of the prospective project and competitors.

3. *Qualitative Analysis:*

This is the data that is not mathematically or graphically determined but rather determined by experience and knowledge. This includes consumer demographic behavior patterns.

4. *Synthesis:*

The synthesis of all information in order to determine the practicality, feasibility, and profitability of retail outlets, whether they be new, enlarged, or remodeled.

FIGURE 16-2. Market Analysis Used by Major U.S. Food Retailer.

Developers are concerned with the rate and direction of growth in a community. Where are people moving? What kind of people are they? Analysis is made of demographic information. Demographics is a summary of population characteristics. These characteristics may include age distribution, household size, and income levels. This type of information is useful in predicting future housing demand.

An inventory is made of competing uses, with a description of their relevant amenities and other attributes. Competing uses are that part of the supply in a community that is likely to draw away some of the demand that might otherwise be captured by the subject property. In addition, it is important to forecast the number of competing uses that are likely to be constructed in the future. Public records containing new building permits and zoning applications provide lead indicators for such forecasts. Also informative are newspaper and public relations announcements, advertisements for construction bids, and information collected at professional meetings or through interpersonal contact.

Once the demand is estimated and an inventory is made of competing and expected future competing uses, then the absorption rate and capture rate are calculated. A discussion of these two measurements is provided in Chapter 8 of this book. These rates are used to determine the scale and timing of a project.

Legal Right to Develop Use

A careful examination is made of all public and private legal restrictions on the proposed project. Public restrictions include: zoning ordinances, environmental laws, planning requirements, permit requirements, building codes, housing codes, and subdivision regulations. In addition, analysis should be made of various tax policies in the community and whether local taxes are likely to change in the near future. Other public limitations may include energy rules, solar access restrictions, mandatory dedication of land for public use in exchange for the right to record a plat, and other requirements. Some jurisdictions require local citizen evaluation of major projects or of any projects requiring zoning changes. Other jurisdictions may require a developer to set aside 10% or more of the apartment units in a project or housing units in a subdivision at below-market rentals or prices for low-income people. Many of these restrictions and regulations can alter significantly the highest and best use of a site.

Private legal restrictions include deed restrictions, easements, and contractual agreements. Title defects may encumber a property. An adjoining landowner may have a building encroaching on the subject property. The land may have existing graveyards or historic buildings that cannot be moved.

If there is a question whether legal restrictions exist, the analyst should request an opinion from a qualified attorney. Care should be taken not to practice law without a license.

Resource Quality of the Site

The resource quality of a site is functionally related to its capacity and its efficiency in combining with other factors of production. Capacity is a measurement of how many factors can be added to the site. An example of this might be whether to build a five-story building or a ten-story building. Efficiency considers how profitably factors can be combined for different real estate products. For example, because of a scenic view or the prestige associated with a location, it may be more efficient to build an office park rather than a warehouse.

Resource quality is studied by determining whether the site is physically usable and what physical constraints operate to limit the uses of the land. This requires a personal examination of the land and of off-site relationships and dependencies.

In general, an examination should be made of the size and shape of the site, with a notation of any natural features like creeks, flood plains, large rocks, and vegetation. The topography of the site is measured, and any unbuildable slopes or major grading requirements are noted. The soil and subsoil are tested by taking boring samples from different spots on the land. The developer will be interested in the bearing quality of the soil and percolation or permeability. The bearing quality determines what kinds of structures can be placed on the land and what kind of foundation will be necessary to support each structure. A determination is made as to whether any rock formations exist that would require expensive blasting to remove. Percolation and permeability measure the ability of the soil to absorb water. This is very critical if septic tank systems are planned. Any drainage problems are investigated. The utilities and level of public services available are checked. Any off-site nuisances or detrimental uses should be investigated. This includes such factors as the zoning of the adjoining property. For example, if the developer is planning to construct a retirement home and an adjoining site is zoned for heavy industrial use, the retirement home may have marketing problems in the future if the adjoining land is developed for its zoned use.

Technological Feasibility

Technological feasibility is based on whether a project can be completed within a specified range of time and on cost and quality trade-offs. If the project takes too long to complete, if it costs too much, or if it falls below a minimum quality standard, it is not considered to be technologically feasible. There are seven basic constraints that define whether the project will be feasible. These are: physical, legal, safety, materials and supplies, financial, crew, and management. These various constraints may be established by law (Occupational Health and Safety Administration work safety rules); by suppliers (shortages or delivery delays); by lending agreements (restrictions on construction loan draws); or by other factors (union strikes or boycotts).

Financial Feasibility

Financial feasibility is based on whether the proposed project will attain a cash flow of sufficient quantity, quality, and duration to allow investors to recover the capital invested and achieve the necessary and expected rate of return. Factors to be considered are the timing of inflows and outflows of cash, revenues, costs, debt service, and the proceeds of a sale or refinancing.

The next section is a discussion of highest-and-best-use studies. Each of the above factors underlying the principle of highest and best use must be evaluated for the alternative development strategies being tested.

HIGHEST-AND-BEST-USE STUDIES

Highest-and-best-use studies involve the testing of various development strategies on a parcel of land. For each combination of improvements and land, the land residual value is calculated. The combination resulting in the highest residual value is the highest and best use of the land.

The first step is to select those uses that are reasonably probable within the context of market opportunities and constraints. Consideration is given to the location potential, market demand, and the legal right to develop the use. This procedure allows for the consideration of only those land uses that are likely to be feasible and reduces the need for unnecessary collection of data. If the zoning restricts the use of land to residential purposes, for example, it will be unnecessary to consider commercial or industrial uses. However, if the analyst believes that a zoning change is likely, a zoning restriction does not necessarily preclude consideration of other uses.

The second step is to determine the cost of developing each alternative development strategy. Consideration is given to the resource quality of the site and the technological feasibility of development. For example, assume that an analyst has identified three probable development strategies for a parcel of land. These development strategies are indicated below:

Development Strategy	*Cost of Building Structures*
Apartment project	$450,000.00
Shopping center	$721,500.00
Office building	$577,000.00

The third step is to determine the financial feasibility of each development strategy. As outlined in Chapter 8, an income statement is prepared for each hypothetical development possibility. To simplify comparison, Table 16-1 summarizes the stabilized income of each of the above three alternative development strategies. More properly, the analyst should include a projection of the negative cash flows during the construction and lease-up phases of each alternative. This more refined type of analysis will be illustrated in the next section.

TABLE 16-1
Comparison of Alternative Development Strategies Using Land Residual Technique

	Apartment Project	*Shopping Center*	*Office Building*
Gross annual income	\$100,000.00	\$250,000.00	\$150,000.00
Less: Vacancy and collection allowance	−5,000.00	−25,000.00	−20,000.00
Add: Miscellaneous income	+3,000.00	+10,000.00	+5,000.00
Effective gross income	\$ 98,000.00	\$235,000.00	\$135,000.00
Less: Operating expenses	−30,000.00	−120,000.00	−50,000.00
Less: Replacement reserve	−3,000.00	−10,000.00	−5,000.00
Net operating income	\$ 65,000.00	\$105,000.00	\$ 80,000.00
Less: Income Attributable to improvements	−59,000.00[a]	−101,000.00[b]	−75,000.00[c]
Net income remaining to land	\$ 6,000.00	\$ 4,000.00	\$ 5,000.00
Value of land indicated at 12% capitalization rate	\$ 50,000.00[d]	\$ 33,300.00[e]	\$ 41,700.00[f]

[a] \$450,000 (cost of improvement) × .1311 (capitalization rate) = \$58,995, say \$59,000.
[b] \$721,500 (cost of improvement) × .1400 (capitalization rate) = \$101,010, say \$101,000.
[c] \$577,000 (cost of improvement) × .1300 (capitalization rate) = \$75,010, say \$75,000.
[d] \$ 6,000 / .12 = \$50,000.
[e] \$ 4,000 / .12 = \$33,333, say \$33,300.
[f] \$ 5,000 / .12 = \$41,667, say \$41,700.

The net operating income is calculated for each development strategy on the basis of assumptions and judgment of what the market will justify. The next step is to allocate the income between the improvements and the land. The analyst may use capitalization rates derived from the market or based on investor expectation. There can be a different rate for each development strategy. This rate is functionally related to the risk, the time period of capital recovery, the financing structure, and the expected appreciation or depreciation. The calculation of the capitalization rate has been discussed in previous chapters.

In the hypothetical project alternatives, the capitalization rate was higher for the shopping center than for the other two development strategies (see footnotes to Table 16–1). The analyst perceived an overbuilding of shopping centers in the community. This was reflected in the loan-to-value ratios permitted by the lending institutions. On the basis of these calculations, the net income remaining to the land was found. This amount was capitalized to determine the residual land values. On the basis of the assumptions used, the apartment project was found to be the highest and best use. It might be noted that if the capitalization rate for the shopping center had been similar to the other two rates, the shopping center would have been the highest and best use.

SUBDIVISION AND DEVELOPMENT

In the previous section, projects were analyzed on the basis of stabilized incomes. As has been noted in Chapter 8, it is important to evaluate the impact of negative cash flows during the early stages of development. To illustrate the procedure that would be used, this section will consider how a tract of land that is to be subdivided into building sites is analyzed in order to determine the maximum price that can be paid for the land.

Raw land must be developed before it can be subdivided and sold as a number of individual parcels. Various expenditures are incurred in addition to the cost of the land itself. Some of these expenditures are a result of the resource quality of the land; others are a result of local subdivision regulations or state environmental laws. Costs incurred before beginning physical development are called "front-end" costs.

As a preliminary step to subdividing land, an examination should be made of local subdivision regulations. These regulations will specify the improvements that need to be made, what permits are required, and any additional costs that must be incurred. Usually land planners or landscape architects are hired to design a land use plan that will yield the maximum number of buildable lots from the tract being considered. It may be necessary to consult engineers for various services as well. Payment of all fees for permits must be included in the budget. Any liability insurance, bonds, and financing fees should be considered. Portions of the tract are cleared, future sites and roads are surveyed, and various topographic and planning studies are performed. These activities require the developer to make expenditures before even a single lot is sold.

In addition to the front end costs, the developer must also expend money for each site before it is sold. Many of these expenses are incurred during the year when the lot is transferred to a new owner. Some of these costs include additional streets, water drainage, sewerage, utilities, grading, and selling expenses. In addition, the developer must include a proper allocation of overhead, indirect expenses, and necessary profit.

A cash flow projection for a hypothetical subdivision is found in Table 16–2. This table is constructed on the basis of several assumptions in order to simplify the presentation. With the availability of computers, the information should be tabulated for each month and not annually as indicated in the table. In order to highlight the procedure, all planning, design, and preliminary expenditures are assumed to occur in the present; and all sales revenues and variable expenses are assumed to take place at the end of each year.

The tract of land being studied is 30 acres. "Front-end" costs are assumed to be $50,000. Design studies indicate a yield of three lots per acre. Each lot can be sold for $10,000. The variable cost for developing each lot, the selling expenses, and overhead are estimated to come to $4,667. It is estimated that 30 lots can be sold each year. Because of the cost of capital and risk expectations, the discount rate is 10%. On the basis of these assumptions specifying the cost of development, the developer can afford to pay a maximum price of $347,996 for the tract, or approximately $11,600 per acre.

In an analysis of similar types of problems, the analyst must test all assumptions against conditions and trends existing in the market. A number of factors should be evaluated. For example, are costs and revenues going to increase because of inflation? Will discounts be given to builders who purchase a large number of lots at any one time? Will the financing costs remain stable, or are they likely to fluctuate?

Determining the Scale of a Project

In many cases, a developer is able to select the size of a planned project. Flexibility may exist in the size of a tract that can be purchased for a subdivision, in the number of residential units that can

TABLE 16–2
Value of Land Based on Cost of Development

Cash Flow (Excluding Land Acquisition Cost)

Present expenditure for planning, design, and preliminary improvements			−$ 50,000
Year 1:	Site sales (30 @ $10,000)	$300,000	
	Less: Selling, development, and profit (30 @ $4,667)	−140.000	
			+$160,000
Year 2:	Site sales (30 @ $10,000)	$300,000	
	Less: Selling, development, and profit (30 @ $4,667)	−140,000	
			+$160,000
Year 3:	Site sales (30 @ $10,000)	$300,000	
	Less: Selling, development and profit (30 @ $4,667)	−140,000	
			+$160,000

Net Present Value at 10% Discount Rate

Year	*Amount*		*Discount Factor*		*Present Value*
0	−$ 50,000	×	1.000000	=	−$ 50,000
1	+$160,000	×	.909091	=	+$145,555
2	+$160,000	×	.826446	=	+$132,231
3	+$160,000	×	.751315	=	+$120,210
			Net present value		$347,996

Maximum Feasible Cost of Land

$347,996/30 acres = $11,600 per acre

be built, or in the number of square feet of commercial space that can be constructed.

In the previous hypothetical example, assume that a developer may choose to purchase a tract of land in increments of 10 acres. In other words, the developer may purchase 10 acres, 20 acres, 30 acres, or any other multiple of 10. The market price of the property is $11,000 per acre. If all of the other assumptions remain the same, how many acres should be purchased?

The procedure used by the analyst is to examine the net present value of a range of alternative development strategies. As was previously illustrated in Table 16–2, a separate cash flow projection is forecast for each alternative. Since the price of land is already stated, the analyst includes this figure as a front-end cost. If the land is financed by a mortgage with payments spread over the holding period, only the down payment should be put as a present cost. With computer software packages, it is feasible to perform such a cash flow projection on a monthly basis. Annual projections for alternatives are found in Table 16–3.

TABLE 16–3

Procedure for Estimating Optimal Subdivision Size

Size of Tract:	*10 Acres*	*20 Acres*	*30 Acres*	*40 Acres*	*50 Acres*	*Present Value Factor*
Year 0:						
Land	−$110,000	−$220,000	−$330,000	−$440,000	−$550,000	
Fixed costs	− 50,000	− 50,000	− 50,000	− 50,000	−50,000	
Present value	−$160,000	−$270,000	−$380,000	−$490,000	−$600,000	(1.000000)
Year 1:						
Revenues	+$300,000	+$300,000	+$300,000	+$300,000	+$300,000	
Variable costs	− 140,000	− 140,000	− 140,000	− 140,000	− 140,000	
	+$160,000	+$160,000	+$160,000	+$160,000	+$160,000	
Present value	+$145,455	+$145,455	+$145,455	+$145,455	+$145,455	(.909091)
Year 2:						
Revenues		+$300,000	+$300,000	+$300,000	+$300,000	
Variable costs		− 140,000	− 140,000	− 140,000	− 140,000	
		+$160,000	+$160,000	+$160,000	+$160,000	
Present value		+$132,231	+$132,231	+$132,231	+$132,231	(.826446)
Year 3:						
Revenues			+$300,000	+$300,000	+$300,000	
Variable costs			− 140,000	− 140,000	− 140,000	
			+$160,000	+$160,000	+$160,000	
Present value			+$120,210	+$120,210	+$120,210	(.751315)
Year 4:						
Revenues				+$300,000	+$300,000	
Variable costs				− 140,000	− 140,000	
				+$160,000	+$160,000	
Present value				+$109,282	+$109,282	(.683013)
Year 5:						
Revenues					+$300,000	
Variable costs					− 140,000	
					+$160,000	
Present value					+$ 99,347	(.620921)
Net Present Value (NPV)	−$ 14,545	+$ 7,686	+$ 17,890	+$ 17,178	+$ 6,525	

An examination of the data indicates that the highest net present value is the 30-acre subdivision tract. A 10-acre tract results in a negative net present value. This means that the developer would not achieve the necessary rate of return and could not afford the heavy front-end costs for a tract that small. The reader may observe that the difference in cost between 30 acres and 40 acres is $110,000. The additional present value increment in the fourth year at a 10% discount rate is only $109,282. This means that the fourth increment actually has a negative value of $718 (i.e., $110,000 minus $109,282 equals −$718).

A similar analysis can be performed by testing the internal rates of return of each alternative development strategy. The 30-acre development plan has the highest internal rate of return of 12.7%. This meets the 10% target rate. Spending an extra $110,000 now to buy an additional 10 acres will result in additional revenues of $160,000 in the fourth year. This incremental investment only has an internal rate of return of 9.8%. This is below the target rate.

Interim Uses. Sometimes land is not ready for development. The market may not justify a planned use until several years in the future. Many investors or speculators may select an *interim use* for the land. Interim uses are those that are expected to produce an income for a short time interval until the market is ripe for a more productive use. Interim uses might include parking lots, tree farms, mobile home parks, or other uses that have revenues justifying the temporary investment. Care should be taken to include the cost of demolition at the end of the holding period when analyzing the net present value or internal rate of return of the projected cash flows.

Using the Market Approach to Estimate Site Value

An investor would prefer not to pay any more for a site than the price of other sites of similar utility that are being exchanged in the market. To estimate the market value of a site, the appraiser should check recent sales of competitive properties to find the indicated value of the subject property.

To illustrate the procedure that would be used, assume that an appraiser has accepted an assignment to estimate the market value of a four-acre site in a developing neighborhood. In the same general location, subject to similar market forces, the appraiser has found five sales comparables. Evaluation of the attributes deemed relevant in the local market has caused the appraiser to make the notations as shown in Table 16–4.

TABLE 16–4
Appraisal Notations of Five Sales Comparables

Sales Comparable	*Price*	*Time*	*Size*	*Soil*	*Topography*
1	$11,500	4 months ago	4 acres	Same	Same
2	$11,800	2 months ago	3.5 acres	5% better	5% better
3	$14,600	1 month ago	5 acres	Same	Same
4	$19,300	1 year ago	7 acres	Same	10% better
5	$12,200	6 months ago	4.5 acres	2% worse	5% worse

Among the elements of comparison that were checked are the conditions of sales and terms of financing. These are found to be normal for all five market comparables. Except for the notations, the comparables are physically similar to the subject property. No locational advantages or disadvantages are discernible. From tracking trends in the market the appraiser notes that prices have been increasing at a 12% annual rate. The next step the appraiser takes is to adjust the comparables so that these are as identical as possible to the subject property. This means that if a comparable has a feature making it $500 more attractive than the subject property, it is assumed that the purchaser paid $500 more than otherwise would have been paid. The value of this feature is subtracted from the actual sales price for that site. Or if the subject property has a feature worth $700 in the market that the comparable does not, $700 should be added to the comparable. The adjustments are summarized in Table 16–5.

When an individual is appraising property using the market approach and the comparables are in a variety of sizes, it simplifies matters if everything is translated into some kind of standard unit of comparison. The standard of comparison may be rooms, rental units, square feet, cubic yards, or acres. In this problem, the appraiser translates prices for each comparable site into a price per acre. All adjustments are then performed on a per-acre basis.

It may be observed that the process of estimating the indicated market value of the subject property does not involve taking a simple average of the five adjusted value indications. It is a process of applying human logic and judgment.

TABLE 16-5
Adjustment Grid for Market Approach in Valuation of Subject Site

	Subject Property	*Comparable Number 1*	*Comparable Number 2*	*Comparable Number 3*	*Comparable Number 4*	*Comparable Number 5*
Price	?	$11,500	$11,800	$14,600	$19,300	$12,200
Size	4 acres	4 acres	3.5 acres	5 acres	7 acres	4.5 acres
Price per acre	?	$ 2,875	$ 3,371	$ 2,920	$ 2,757	$ 2,711
Soil	—	—	−169	—	—	+54
Topography	—	—	−169	—	−276	+136
Time	Today	+115	+67	+29	+331	+163
Indicated value		$ 2,990	$ 3,100	$ 2,949	$ 2,812	$ 3,064

(Therefore, the indicated value is $3,000 per acre or $12,000 for the subject property.)

To simulate the appraiser's thought process in the above example (see Table 16–5), a first observation is that Comparable Number 4, the largest property, is selling for the least money per acre after all of the adjustments have been made. The principle of balance may be in operation here. The market may be discounting the per-acre price because the site is larger than the economic size needed. The appraiser therefore puts the most reliability on Comparable Number 1 because it is the same size as the subject property and requires only one adjustment. Numbers 2 and 5 need the most adjustments. Two of the adjustments, for soil differences and topography, were very subjective in nature. Comparable Number 3 required very few adjustments. Although the site is larger than the subject property, the lower per-acre price reinforces the idea that the market may be discounting the large-sized tracts. The appraiser checks the zoning ordinance in the city or county zoning office and discovers that there is a minimum lot size of three acres for residential tracts. The five-acre tract is too small to be further subdivided. However, most sites are in the four- to five-acre range, so Number 3 is not penalized too severely because of its general conformity to market standards. On the basis of this analysis, the appraiser concludes that the indicated market value is $3,000 per acre. This results in a $12,000 market value for the subject property.

Lot prices in residential subdivisions are not proportionately associated with size. Very large lots that exceed the market norm may be heavily discounted. Several rules of thumb for depth adjustment have been reported in the literature. Among the more common are the 4-3-2-1 rule, the Davies rule, the Hoffman rule, the Hoffman-

Neill rule, the parabolic formula, and the Milwaukee rule.[2] Little reliance can be placed on these rules without first testing market behavior. In some markets very little price differentiation exists between different-sized lots within acceptable ranges. In other markets prices may be affected by size. A much preferable approach is the use of linear or multiple regression. This is a statistical technique used to calculate the mathematical relationships between variables. It requires the use of large numbers of data points to provide reliability. Using one of many calculators currently available, the appraiser can use regression to determine the existence of a relationship between lot depth and sales price.[3]

The market approach is commonly used in appraising properties consisting of improvements and land. The major difference is the increased complexity of making adjustments as a result of the improvements. Adjustments might include architectural style, construction quality, physical condition, number of rooms, number of stories, floor area, accessory buildings, functional adequacy, amenity features, and other such factors. The procedure is the same as described for dealing with site valuation. There are several excellent references that contain an adequate coverage of this approach to valuation.[4]

Abstraction or Allocation Technique for Site Value Estimate. The abstraction or allocation technique can be used in markets where there has been little or no market activity of site sales. It is a modification of the market approach and requires data on recent sales of improved properties. The abstraction or allocation method is based on the value principle of balance. It assumes that for competitive properties in a given market, a similar ratio would exist between land and improvements.

To illustrate the procedure, assume that an appraiser is trying to estimate the value of a site in a residential neighborhood. The neighborhood is 95% built up, and there have been no site sales in the last three years. As indicated in Table 16-6, recent sales of houses in the neighborhood have been found. As part of the data collection and analysis process, an estimate of the depreciated

[2] Alfred A. Ring, *The Valuation of Real Estate,* 2nd ed. (Englewood Cliffs, N.J.: Prentice-Hall, Inc., 1970), p. 104.; Ronald E. Gettel, *Real Estate Guidelines & Rules of Thumb* (New York: McGraw-Hill Book Company, 1976), pp. 55–62.

[3] William M. Shenkel, *Modern Real Estate Appraisal* (New York: McGraw-Hill Book Company, 1978), p. 358.

[4] See *The Appraisal of Real Estate,* 7th ed. (Chicago: American Institute of Real Estate Appraisers, 1978), Chapters 15 and 16.

value of the improvements is made using the cost approach. This approach is discussed in the next chapter.

TABLE 16–6
Recent Sales Used as Data in the Abstraction Approach

Sales Comparable	*Price*		*Depreciated Worth of Improvements*		*Indicated Value of Site*	*Site Value as Percentage of Sales Price*
1	$85,000	−	$68,425	=	$16,575	19.5%
2	$78,000	−	$61,620	=	$16,380	21.0%
3	$93,000	−	$75,795	=	$17,205	18.5%
4	$91,000	−	$73,710	=	$17,290	19.0%
5	$87,000	−	$66,600	=	$17,400	20.0%

As buildings grow older, the site value is likely to represent a higher proportion of the total sales price. For very old buildings, the abstraction method may be very inaccurate because of problems that may exist in estimating the accrued depreciation. Other factors may also influence the ratio between site and improvements, such as the over- or underimprovement of comparable sales or problems associated with odd shapes or sizes of sites. Because of these limitations the approach should be used only if the techniques discussed previously cannot be used. As in the hypothetical example, the technique is most useful when many developed properties of a similar type have sold recently. If the appraiser has concluded that the proper and appropriate development plan for the subject site is similar to the development represented by the sales comparables, this procedure is workable.

After evaluating the data in Table 16–6, the appraiser concludes that the indicated value of the subject site is $17,000. This will represent approximately 20% of the total cost of the property after it is improved.

SUMMARY

This chapter included a discussion of various approaches used to solve site valuation problems commonly faced by appraisers and analysts. These problems include land requiring a user, a user in search of specific types of land, an investor looking for a satisfactory combination of land and user, and a speculator in search of land with good appreciation potential.

The principle of highest and best use was analyzed. Factors considered included location potential, market demand, legal right to develop use, resource quality of the site, technological feasibility, and financial feasibility.

Several approaches used to determine the value of land were described. These approaches included highest-and-best-use studies, subdivision and development methods, the market approach, and the abstraction or allocation techniques. In addition, there was discussion of the method of determining the appropriate scale of a project.

Questions

1. Consider the following alternative development strategies:

   Alternative A (Shopping Center): Expected sales are $2,000,000; a percentage lease sets the rental at 6% of the gross sales; operating and advertising expenses equal 40% of received rentals; replacement reserve is $10,000; the improvements cost $350,000 and require a 15% capitalization rate.

   Alternative B (Office Park): Gross annual income is $200,000; vacancy and bad debt allowance are 5%; operating expenses are $75,000; replacement reserve is $3,000; the improvements cost $600,000 and require a 17% capitalization rate.

   The capitalization rate for the land is 10%.

   a. What is the value of the land as a shopping center site?

   b. What is the value of the land for office park use?

2. A developer is considering the purchase of a 30-acre tract. The front-end costs are $100,000. Each acre will yield four sites that will sell for $10,000 each. Selling expenses and variable development costs are $6,000 per lot payable when the lot is sold. The developer's discount rate is 15%.

   a. What is the value of the tract if the developer expects to sell 20 lots each year?

   b. What is the value of the tract if the developer expects to sell 40 lots each year?

3. Complete the following grid, making all appropriate adjustments. There is an appreciation rate of 1.5% simple interest each month.

	Subject Property	*Comparable Number 1*	*Comparable Number 2*	*Comparable Number 3*
Price	?	$12,700	$17,400	$20,500
Size	4 acres	3 acres	4 acres	5 acres
Shape	Normal	Same	$1,000 better	$2,000 worse
Soil	Good	Same	$500 worse	$500 worse
Topography	Good	Same	$1,000 worse	Same
Time	Today	1 year ago	6 months ago	3 months ago
Indicated value	____	____	____	____

Essay Questions

1. Explain how the principle of highest and best use provides the underlying theory for solving the four general types of investment problems normally faced by a real estate analyst.
2. In performing a highest-and-best-use study, why is it likely that the analyst will use a different capitalization rate for each alternative development strategy?
3. Criticize the abstraction method as an effective method for finding the value of a site suitable for a shopping center or an office park.

Chapter 17

Direct Sales Comparison Approach

The direct sales comparison approach is a technique for estimating the market value of a property from recent sales activity. Actual market transactions are analyzed by the appraiser and are compared to the subject property. This approach is based on the principle of substitution. It is assumed that a rational investor or purchaser will pay no more for a particular property than the cost of acquiring another similar property with the same utility. Therefore, prices that are paid for similar or comparable properties should indicate the market value of the subject property that is being appraised.

In the direct sales comparison approach, the appraiser considers the comparable properties that have sold in a relevant market; then makes adjustments for differences that may exist between the subject property and the comparables. The result is an estimate of each selling price of a comparable property as if it sold with the same salient features as the subject property. The adjusted price allows the appraiser to draw logical inferences of what the subject property is likely to be worth in the market. The direct sales comparison approach is also called the *comparative sales approach,* the *market approach,* and the *market data approach.*

The direct sales comparison approach is one of three approaches to appraising real estate. The other two approaches, *income* and *cost,* also require market data. In the income approach, capitalization rates are derived from market data. The cost approach requires estimates of replacement or reproduction costs that are based on market prices for material, labor, overhead, and normal profit.

HOW TO USE THE DIRECT SALES COMPARISON APPROACH

Normally an appraiser takes the following steps to apply the direct sales comparison approach:

Step 1. Identify recent sales of comparable properties in the relevant market. Data on the sale of comparable properties may be found in the appraiser's own files; courthouse records; records of lending institutions such as savings and loan associations or insurance companies; computer-based data banks such as multiple-listing services; and records of real estate brokers, title companies, attorneys, etc. In some markets it may be relatively easy to discover data on sales of comparable properties; in other markets, there may be few or no sales of comparable properties. When ample data is available, the appraiser must ascertain that the properties that sold are indeed comparable to the subject property being appraised. Considerations include whether the comparables or "comps" are in the same market area as the subject, are of the same age and size, offer the same amenities, and were sold at a time that would reflect similar economic conditions, including financing.

Step 2. Verify the the data of the sales transaction. Information collected on sales of comparable properties should be verified with one of the principals to the transaction (buyer or seller) or an authorized agent (broker, lender, title company). Care should be taken to assure that the comparables are competitive from the viewpoint of a typically informed purchaser in the market. The sales price should be based on a bona fide "arm's length" transaction. This means that there was no undue pressure on either party, that both parties were typically informed and economically rational, and that the payment or financing was similar to that normally found in the market. The appraiser should be suspicious of unduly hasty sales or sales that occurred between two closely related parties (e.g., parent/child, husband/wife, corporation/wholly-owned subsidiary). Sales that depend on the tax treatment to one or more of the parties, estate sales, and sales to avoid mortgage foreclosure should be discarded as a general rule.

Step 3. Adjust for any differences between each sales comparable and the subject property. To the extent that a comparable property is dissimilar to the subject, adjustments are required in order to derive what the probable estimated sales price of the comparable property would have been if it had the same features as the subject property.

When adjusting actual sales prices of comparable properties, adjustments are made *from* the comparable *to* the subject property. The adjustment process attempts to answer the question, "What would the comparable have sold for if it had the same features as the subject?" For example, if a comparable apartment complex has superior landscaping compared to the subject, and the superiority is valued in the market at $10,000, then the actual sales price of the comparable should be reduced by $10,000. When the comparable is inferior to the subject, the actual sales price of the comparable should be raised to the price at which it would have sold had it possessed the superior feature of the subject property.

Adjustments are also made from the perspective of how a difference would be valued by a typical purchaser in the market. A feature is therefore not necessarily worth the expenditure of including or excluding it, but rather it is worth the amount that it contributes to the property's overall value. For example, the cost of painting a building may be $2,000, but it will likely cause a prospective purchaser to pay $3,500 more. Thus, the proper adjustment would be $3,500, not $2,000.

Paired Sales

One way to determine what a proper adjustment should be is to find several sets of paired sales. *Paired sales* are properties that are nearly identical except for a feature that the appraiser is attempting to estimate in order to make the proper adjustment. For example, assume that an appraiser is trying to estimate the adjustment for a swimming pool. Table 17–1 summarizes the relevant information on five sets of paired sales that an appraiser found in a residential subdivision. Although the appraiser calculated the mean, median, and mode to help describe the distribution of the differences between each of the pairs, this was not a substitute for human judgment. Ultimately the appraiser had to make a decision as to the effect of the swimming pool on the total property value.

Adjustment Process

In general, the adjustment process can take one of three basic forms: (1) dollar adjustments, (2) percentage adjustments, or (3) overall bracketing.

Dollar adjustments are plus or minus amounts that are applied to each comparable.

TABLE 17–1
Paired Sales Used to Determine Adjustment for Swimming Pool Feature

	Sales Price				
	Pair #1	*Pair #2*	*Pair #3*	*Pair #4*	*Pair #5*
House with Pool	$85,000	$94,000	$88,000	$91,000	$91,000
House without Pool	$69,000	$78,500	$72,750	$75,000	$74,500
Difference	$16,000	$15,500	$15,250	$16,000	$16,500

Mean = $15,850 Median = $16,000 Mode = $16,000

Indicated Adjustment: $16,000

Percentage adjustments are used when it is difficult to find precise dollar amounts, but the market evidence indicates that a percentage differential exists. One important consideration in making adjustments on a percentage basis is whether these adjustments should be made on an independent plus-or-minus basis or on a cumulative basis. One would use an independent plus-or-minus basis only if it is determined that the adjusted features are considered by buyers in the market as independent of other features. An illustration of this may be found in Table 17-2. Once the percentage adjustments are determined, they are added together. The sales price of the comparable is then multiplied by the resulting percentage (−9% in Table 17-2), which indicates an adjustment of −$9,000 on the sales price. This amount is then added to or subtracted from the original sales price to find the adjusted value of the comparable, which is $91,000 [$100,000 −$9,000 = $91,000].

TABLE 17–2
Sales Comparison Adjustments: Independent versus Cumulative

	Sales Comparable	*Adjustments on Independent Plus or Minus Basis (Add or Subtract)*	*Adjustments on a Cumulative Basis (Multiply)*
Price	$100,000	—	—
Date	4 months ago	+ 4%	1.04
Landscaping	5% better than subject	− 5%	.95
Amenities	10% better than subject	−10%	.90
Condition	2% worse than subject	+ 2%	1.02
Total adjustments		− 9%	.906984
Adjusted value of comparable		$91,000	$90,689
Rounded to			$90,700

Percentage adjustments are made on a cumulative basis if the appraiser determines that each adjustment influences the other adjustments. However, this is rare. If adjustments must be made on a cumulative base, each percentage adjustment is added or subtracted from 100% to calculate a separate factor. Factors are multiplied by each other. For example, if the comparable is 4% worse than the subject, the percentage derived would be 1.04 (remember to adjust the comparable price as if the comparable had the same features as the subject). A separate percentage will then be calculated for each adjustment. Then, all of the percentage adjustments are multiplied together. The calculation to derive the cumulative adjustment in Table 17-2 is: 1.04 × .95 × .90 × 1.02 = .906984. This result is slightly different than would be achieved using an independent "plus-and-minus" method.

If adjustments must use actual dollar adjustments *and* percentage adjustments, all percentage adjustments must first be converted into dollar amounts. The usual sequence for making adjustments is: (1) time, (2) location, (3) terms and conditions of sale, and (4) other differences (physical, amenities, etc.).

Overall Bracketing

Overall bracketing can be used in an active market where sufficient sales can be found that would allow an appraiser to arrive at a market range that is very narrow. This method depends on the availability of relatively homogeneous properties. In such a case, an appraiser may decide not to make specific individual adjustments but rather compare the subject property on an overall basis to determine whether it is superior or inferior to each comparable. An aggregate adjustment is then made within the bracketed range. This makes it unnecessary to separately consider each feature that is different between the subject property and a sales comparable.

For example, assume that an appraiser found three apartment projects. Each was the same size as the subject with essentially the same number of units and same amenity features. The appraiser found the following information:

Comparable	*Sales Price*	*Quality Compared to Subject*
Project #1	$618,000	Better
Project #2	$610,000	Inferior
Project #3	$612,000	Slightly Inferior

These comparables have a range of only $6,000, which is less than 1% between the highest and lowest. On the basis of this finding, the appraiser may feel confident in estimating that the subject property is valued at $615,000.

Adjustments That Will Affect the Purchase Price

Adjustments should be made for all major features and amenities that would be considered to have value by a prospective purchaser. These include adjustments for:

1. Time
2. Location
   a. Situs
   b. Access
   c. Linkages
3. Terms and conditions of sale
   a. Conventional versus FHA or VA mortgages
   b. Buyer and seller motivations and knowledge
4. Financing terms
   a. Loan-to-value ratio
   b. Interest rate
   c. Term of loan
   d. Amortization and balloon payments
   e. Financing charges
   f. Participation agreements
5. Physical characteristics
   a. Physical features
   b. Quality of construction and maintenance
   c. Amenities
   d. Functional adequacy

UNITS OF COMPARISON

Because income-producing properties are often dissimilar in size and number of units, it may be very difficult to compare a market sales comparable with the subject property, and it is sometimes necessary to reduce the data to a common denominator. Consider the following attributes of the subject property and a recent sales comparable.

Subject Property—Apartment project with 20 units: four are 1-bedroom units; twelve are 2-bedroom units; four are 3-bedroom units.

Sales Comparable—Apartment project with 30 units: ten are 2-bedroom units; ten are 3-bedroom units; ten are 4-bedroom units.

To compare these properties we need to find a common denominator. This common denominator is either a physical unit of comparison (price per square foot) or an economic unit of comparison (price per dwelling unit).

Units of comparison are used by appraisers and other professionals in the real estate industry as a means of communicating information in an efficient and understandable manner. Different units of comparison are used by different real estate market segments. In comparing rural land sales, a price per acre would prove meaningful. On the other hand, in comparing sales of theater buildings, a price per theater seat would offer more useful information. Units of comparison are shorthand ways of communicating standardized information to investors or prospective purchasers in a particular market. The next several paragraphs will discuss various units of comparison that are commonly used in the real estate industry.

Land Sales

Units of comparison used in the analysis of land sales include the following:

- Price per acre
- Price per square foot
- Price per front foot
- Price per lot
- Price per unit of density

Price per Acre. Price per acre is a unit of comparison that is used to report sales of large tracts of land. This can include land ready for development and/or subdivision, farm land, purchases of industrial land, or land divided into residential lots.

Price per Square Foot. Land that is suitable for an office building, for a commercial development, or for a warehouse or other industrial use is often quoted at a price per square foot. To be considered comparable, sites should offer similar features, amenities, and attributes. For office buildings this could include access to transportation and parking facilities, other office buildings, banks, restaurants, and retail outlets. For industrial property, access to rail, water, transportation, fire protection, and labor markets is important. Access to transportation is especially important for warehousing. Facilities can include highway and rail access. For some warehousing activity, proximity to ports or rivers is also important. The price for land in downtown centers is frequently quoted on a per-square-foot basis. For a large office building site, the land must be of sufficient scale to permit construction. Small unassembled parcels of land do not sell for the same price per square foot as large tracts covering a city block. An exception may be a holdout parcel that prevents the final assemblage. The price for such parcels is not reflective of typical market prices for parcels of similar size.

Price per Front Foot. The price of land that is available for commercial property use is often cited at an amount per front foot. Value is considered proportionate to the length that fronts on a certain street or highway. For example, the price may be based on $1,000 per front foot. Thus, a site with 50 lineal feet would be worth an estimated $50,000.

A uniform depth is associated with front foot values. Sites that are deeper than the uniform depth are worth only slightly more, whereas those not as deep are worth almost as much. This is because the bulk of value is associated with the street or road frontage; little of the value can be allocated proportionately toward the rear of the site. Normally, homogeneous pricing per front foot is restricted to a small geographic area. It often occurs because of an agglomeration of specialized retail space that gives a unique value to land in the proximity.

Price per Lot. Prices of land in a residential subdivision may be priced on the basis of a buildable lot. Within standard sizes and shapes very little fluctuation will exist in prices. However, adjustments may be required for positive or negative amenity features, sharp slopes, drainage problems, and flood plains.

Price per Unit of Density. Zoning laws normally allow development up to a certain density on tracts located within various zoning districts. In some markets this is translated into land price quotations that are based on the density permitted by the zoning ordinance. For example, the price for land may be quoted on the basis of apartment dwelling units permitted. If the density permitted is twenty units per acre, and the price is quoted as $1,000 per unit, this makes $20,000 for an acre. On the other hand, if the density is restricted to twelve units per acre, then a price of $1,000 per unit means that the price per acre is $12,000. When the land is quoted at a price per unit of density, often no recognition is afforded any benefits to the dwellers derived from lower densities.

An example of a measurement of a unit of density is the floor-area-ratio (FAR). Many municipal zoning ordinances restrict building sizes in terms of the multiple of ground area that a building would cover. For example, if the FAR is 3, the total floor area in the building must not exceed three times the total site area. Broadly interpreted, this allows a 3-story building to cover the entire site, or a 6-story building on half the site, or a 12-story building on one-fourth of the site. The unbuilt portion of the site may be used for open space, parks, or perhaps parking. The price of the site may be quoted in terms of its maximum buildable size. For example, if the lot size is 10,000 square feet with a FAR of 3, the price may be quoted as $1.25 per floor square foot. This would make the price $37,500 (10,000 × 3 × $1.25 = $37,500). Usually this method of quoting prices occurs in markets where land is at a premium. For example, sites next to rapid transit rail stations might be quoted on this basis. A price on the basis of an amount per square foot of land is likely to be more widely used than is an amount per square foot of potential improvements.

Developed Properties

Units of comparison used in the analysis of developed properties include the following:

- Price per square foot of gross area.
- Price per square foot of net leasable area.
- Price of improvements per square foot.
- Price per cubic foot (or other capacity measurement).
- Price per room.
- Price per unit.
- Price per income production unit.

Price per Square Foot of Gross Area. In some markets, prices are quoted on a per-square-foot-of-gross-area basis. For most properties, prices per square foot on existing properties should be avoided because these prices might be misleading. Seldom are properties so comparable in services and amenities as to offer comparability on a per-square-foot basis.

Price per Square Foot of Net Leasable Area. The price per square foot of net leasable area has an advantage over the price per square foot of gross area in that nonproductive space such as that used for halls and elevators tends to be factored out. This permits an appraiser to account for some of the functional obsolescence of a building that has a less efficient design.

Price of Improvements per Square Foot. The price of improvements per square foot is computed by subtracting the land value from the sales price and dividing the remainder by the area of the building. This procedure has the advantage of separately accounting for land that may have a special value because of a locational advantage, which affects the overall sales price.

Price per Cubic Foot (or Other Capacity Measurement). For certain types of real estate products, the most reliable measurement is one that indicates the capacity. Examples are grain elevators and oil tanks. A capacity measurement might be the number of bushels the elevator will hold or the number of barrels the tank will hold.

Price per Room. The price per room unit of measurement is used in relatively few markets. When considered, it is important to determine what is counted as a room and what is not. For example, rooms include the kitchen, bedrooms, living room, dining room, and den. Bathrooms and hallways are normally excluded, although large foyers or enclosed patio are sometimes counted as "half" rooms. An example of pricing on the basis of price per room is shown below:

Comparable	*Sales Price*	*Number of Rooms*	*Resulting Price per Room*
Complex #1	$600,000	60	$10,000
Complex #2	$750,000	80	$ 9,375
Complex #3	$450,000	44	$10,227

The "Resulting Price per Room" amounts indicate a value range of $9,375 to $10,227. The median figure is $10,000 (an equal number is below and above the median) with an average of $9,867. Because apartment complexes may have different levels of amenities and services, or the location advantage may be significant, information on a per room basis is suspect.

Price per Unit. The price per unit is often used in some real estate markets. Usually this is restricted to residential rental projects, although it can also be used for such real estate products as miniwarehouses or standardized office units. To illustrate, suppose that prices and apartment dwelling units for three comparable complexes are as shown below:

Comparable	*Sales Price*	*Number of Apartment Units*	*Price per Unit*
Complex #1	$600,000	25	$24,000
Complex #2	$750,000	30	$25,000
Complex #3	$450,000	18	$25,000

From this information, one might conclude that the market price is about $25,000 per apartment unit. If the subject property has twenty units, it is worth about $500,000 (20 × $25,000 = $500,000). However, for a price per unit to be used as a comparison device, the units and services offered by the comparables must be truly similar to the subject property. In addition, the apartment units, as measures of comparison, must be used regularly by participants in the marketplace.

Whenever physical units of comparison such as unit or rooms are used, care must be exercised because of errors that can occur due to different mixes of rooms in a complex and the unequal costs associated with different rooms. For example, kitchens and bathrooms are generally more expensive to build because of plumbing and electrical needs, appliances, cabinets, and fixtures. Two different apartment complexes may have the same number of rooms, but one complex may offer a mix of apartment units that have more rooms, larger rooms, twice as many bathrooms, and more kitchen appliances and amenities. In such a situation, a per-room or a per-apartment-unit value comparison would be very misleading.

Price per Income Production Unit. Some types of real estate can best be compared by price per income production unit. A sports arena or a parking garage might be compared on such a basis. The sports arena might be valued on a per-seat amount, and the income production unit for the garage would be the amount per parking space.

Evaluating Projects on the Basis of the Relationship of Income to Sales Price

Units of comparison used to evaluate projects on the basis of the relationship of income to sales prices include the

- Gross rent multiplier (GRM), also known as *gross income multiplier* (GIM).
- Overall capitalization rate, also known as the *overall rate* (OAR).

Gross Rent Multiplier. The GRM is a ratio between a sales price and either the potential gross income or the effective gross income. Whether the potential gross income or the effective gross income is used depends on local custom or the appraiser's own preferences. In either case, it is important to use one or the other on a consistent basis in order to make meaningful comparisons. It is also common in some markets to use a gross *monthly* rent multiplier, which considers income on a monthly basis rather than on an annual basis.

To apply the GRM, an appraiser would ordinarily perform three steps:

1. Estimate the market rent for the subject property.
2. Determine the ratio of gross income to sales price from recent market transactions.
3. Multiply the market rent of the subject property by the multiplier ratio derived in step two.

The GRM is considered a market approach for income-producing properties because it uses sales prices and gross rents that are calculated from actual market transactions. It does not consider the operating expense ratio or the net operating income of either the subject property or the sales comparables.

To illustrate how to use the GRM approach, consider a case example. Suppose that data is collected on three comparable apartment complexes that recently sold. The following prices and potential gross rents are indicated:

Comparable	*Sales Price*	*Potential Gross Rent*	*Resulting GRM*
Apartment Complex #1	$600,000	$100,000	6.00
Apartment Complex #2	$750,000	$128,000	5.86
Apartment Complex #3	$450,000	$ 74,000	6.08

The indicated gross rent multiplier would be about 6: complex #1 sold at a 6 multiplier, #2 was slightly lower, #3 was slightly above 6. If the subject property's potential gross income is $100,000, its estimated sales price would be 6 times $100,000, which is $600,000.

Gross rent multipliers should not be adjusted for amenities or other differences between the comparables and the subject property. The GRM is based on the actual rents and sales prices prevailing in the market. If amenities or levels of services offered differ between a comparable and the subject, this difference is presumably reflected in both the sales price and the rent. That is, a comparable would have sold for less and rented for less if it had inferior features. The mathematical relationship would be unaffected. The mathematical relationship, however, does not obviate the need for a judicious selection of comparables.

There are many limitations in applying the GRM approach. First, the subject property must be in a market in which competitive properties are regularly bought and sold on the basis of their gross incomes. Second, the GRM technique is not considered very sensitive to differences in risk or rates of capital recovery between the comparables and the subject property. Third, the technique assumes a narrow range of vacancy and expenses ratios among all of the properties. This means the technique is not sensitive to differences that may exist in net operating incomes.

Overall Capitalization Rate. The overall rate of return (OAR) is part of the income approach of appraisal. Deriving an overall rate of return from market data overcomes some of the major objections than can be levied against the GRM approach. In order to derive an overall capitalization rate from market data, the appraiser must select similar properties that have sold recently and are characterized by income streams of similar risk and duration as is the income stream of the subject property. If sufficient comparables are available, it is possible to derive an OAR directly from the market. This permits the appraiser to use *direct capitalization* to convert forecast net operating income (NOI) into a market value estimate. Direct capitalization is defined as

> the conversion of anticipated net operating income into a lump sum present value by dividing the income by an appropriate rate which reflects the prevailing relationship of net operating income to selling price for comparable properties being sold in the market.

To illustrate the procedure, assume that an appraiser has found the following data:

Comparable	*NOI*	*Sales Price*	*Indicated OAR*
Apartment Complex #1	$72,000	$600,000	.120
Apartment Complex #2	$82,500	$750,000	.110
Apartment Complex #3	$47,250	$450,000	.105

After reviewing the quality of the comparables, the appraiser decides that the most appropriate overall rate estimate is 11.5%. The net operating income of the subject property is $65,000. The following calculation is performed:

$$V = \frac{\$65{,}000}{.115}$$

$$V = \$565{,}217$$

Rounded to $565,000

The advantage of this procedure for deriving the OAR is that it is based on market behavior and is mechanically easy to apply. Like the GRM approach, its validity is dependent on the quality of market data that can be collected and verified.

CASE EXAMPLE

As an example, suppose that the subject property is a 20-unit apartment complex. Three recent sales of comparable properties have been discovered, and the data has been verified with sellers and buyers. The three are as follows:

Comparable	Sales Price	Units	Potential Gross Income
#1	$600,000	25	$100,000
#2	$750,000	30	$128,000
#3	$450,000	18	$ 74,000

Comparable #1 offers amenities and location nearest to the subject property but has superior landscaping estimated to be worth $5,000 more than the subject. Its swimming pool is comparable to the subject's, judged to be valued at $16,000. It sold three months ago.

Comparable #2 also has a swimming pool; it sold six months ago with favorable seller financing judged to add $15,000 to the price that would have been paid had typical financing been employed.

Comparable #3 is two blocks from a bus stop, whereas the subject is eight blocks from the stop. Each block from the bus stop is judged to detract $3,000 from value. It sold two days ago. It does not have a pool.

Prices have been rising by ½% per month for the type of property in the local market.

Table 17–3 illustrates the required adjustments in grid form. The adjusted per unit values range from $24,160 to $25,250. Since #1 is close to the subject property in size, proximity, and time of sale, and requires few adjustments, it is given the most weight; and a value estimate of $24,500 per unit is estimated for the subject property.

TABLE 17-3

Grid with Appraisal Adjustments

Feature	Subject	Comparable #1	Comparable #2	Comparable #3
Sales price	—	$600,000	$750,000	$450,000
Time	Now	1½% + $9,000	3% + $22,500	0
Pool	Yes	Yes	Yes	No, +$16,000
Landscaping	Adequate	Superior, −$5,000	Adequate	Adequate
Financing	Market	Market	Favorable, −$15,000	Market
Location	—	Similar	Similar	Superior, −$18,000
Adjusted sales price		$604,000	$757,500	$448,000
Units	20	25	30	18
Amount per unit, adjusted		$ 24,160	$ 25,250	$ 24,888

SUMMARY

The direct sales comparison approach is a market-based procedure. It uses information gathered from recent sales activity of competitive properties as a means to develop logical conclusions of value of the subject property. Steps used to apply the direct sales comparison approach are:

1. Identify recent sales of comparable properties in the relevant market.
2. Verify the data on the sales transactions.
3. Adjust for any differences between each sales comparable and the subject property.

After the mechanical steps are completed, the appraiser must carefully consider the significance of each value indication. A logical analysis of the adjusted sales comparables will lead to a judgment regarding the value estimate of the subject property.

Because income properties are often very dissimilar in size and number of productive units, it is often necessary to use a common denominator to make meaningful comparisons. The common denominators used are called *units of comparison.* Appraisers use both physical units of comparison (e.g., price per square foot) and economic units of comparison (e.g., price per theater seat). In addition, information is often summarized in order to allow an evaluation of projects on the basis of the relationship of income and sales price. Two such measurements are the gross rent multiplier (GRM) and the overall capitalization rate (OAR).

Questions

1. You have been asked to estimate the value of a 500-seat theater. In the same market, three comparable theaters have recently sold. The following information is provided:

Comparable	*Total Price*	*Seats*
A	$230,000	450
B	$275,000	550
C	$195,000	375

Estimate the market value on the basis of the above information.

2. You have assembled the following data:

Feature	*Subject*	*Comparable #1*	*Comparable #2*	*Comparable #3*
Price	?	$800,000	$860,000	$660,000
Rooms	135	165	170	125
Units	44	50	49	40
Pool	Yes	No	Yes	No
Gross income	$150,000	$160,000	$168,000	$136,000

The pool is worth $16,000.

Estimate the value on a per-room, per-unit, and GRM basis. Derive a value estimate and briefly defend that estimate.

3. You have received the following financial information about three comparable office buildings. This information has been personally verified.

	Comparable A	*Comparable B*	*Comparable C*
Sales price	$1,000,000	$1,200,000	$900,000
Potential gross income	$200,000	$300,000	$185,000
Vacancy and bad debt	−10,000	−30,000	−9,000
Effective gross income	$190,000	$270,000	$176,000
Operating expenses	−90,000	−153,000	−85,000
NOI	$100,000	$117,000	$ 91,000

The indicated market rental for your subject property is $8.00 per square foot. It has 20,000 square feet of net leasable area. The estimated vacancy and bad debt allowance is 5%. The operating expense ratio is 45% of potential gross income. What is its indicated value using: (1) GRM and (2) OAR? Which value estimate gives you the most confidence? Why?

Essay Questions

1. What are the advantages and disadvantages of using the direct sales comparison approach in estimating the value of an income-producing property?
2. What are the limitations of the technique?
3. Why must sales data on each comparable be verified by the appraiser? What types of data must be collected and verified?
4. Why is it logical to make the time adjustment first in many appraisal problems?
5. For an income-producing property, which unit of comparison is likely to result in a more meaningful estimate: a physical unit of comparison or an economic unit of comparison?
6. Compare and contrast the GRM and OAR.

Chapter 18

Improvement Analysis and Application of the Cost Approach*

The cost approach to appraisal can be used as a valuation approach for income-producing property. Appraisers estimate the reproduction or replacement cost new of the subject property; then subtract the estimated depreciation sustained by the improvements. To the amount thus derived, the market value of the land as if vacant is added. The resulting total is one estimate of the property value.

The value of most income-producing property is best measured by the amount of income that it is expected to generate; asset costs do not indicate the value of forecast income. Consequently, one should not rely heavily on the cost approach as an indicator of the value for income-producing property. However, the cost approach can be employed in a variety of applications for income-producing properties. These applications and the limitations of the cost approach are described in this chapter.

*Portions of this chapter were adapted from *Appraising Income Property*, copyright 1979 by the Society of Real Estate Appraisers, Chicago, and prepared by Jack P. Friedman for Cassette Communications, Teton Village, Wyoming.

COST VERSUS VALUE

Appraisers should be cautioned that cost and value are not the same. A clear illustration of the difference between cost and value may be found in the petroleum industry. It may cost just as much to drill a dry hole as it does a producing oil well, but the difference in value is obvious. Similarly, there are obvious situations in real estate where land is not put to its highest and best use. One example would be constructing a sprawling home in the central business district of a large, thriving city. Suppose the land is worth $500,000, and the house cost $200,000 to build. The house adds nothing to the value of the property because an appropriate use of the land would be a different improvement—perhaps a high-rise office building or hotel. Someone wanting to buy the property with the intention of changing its use would pay only $500,000, which is the land value. The house adds nothing since it will be demolished. In fact, an appraiser might consider subtracting demolition costs from the value of the land.

REPRODUCTION COST NEW VERSUS REPLACEMENT COST NEW

It is important to distinguish between two terms by definition. First, *replacement cost new* is the cost of construction, at current prices, of a building having utility equivalent to the building being appraised but built with modern materials and according to current standards, design, and layout. *Reproduction cost new* is the cost of construction at current prices of an exact duplicate or replica, using the same materials, construction standards, design, layout, and quality of workmanship (which embodies all the deficiencies, "superadequacies," and obsolescence) of the subject building. In other words, one method is to *replace* the building with a suitable substitute, whereas the other method *reproduces* an exact replica.

For most appraisal purposes, reproduction cost new is preferred because replacement cost new would generate a building that is different from the subject being appraised. In addition, it is difficult to measure the difference in usefulness of an existing building compared to a proposed new one having a modern design. The measurements must come from an analysis of market behavior.

From a theoretical approach, replacement cost is preferred since it is unlikely that one would want to reproduce a building that is more than three years old with all of its functional inadequacies built in. If one were to start the building again, a building with the same or greater utility—built to modern standards, tastes, and design—would undoubtedly be preferred. However, reproduction cost is typically used in appraisals.

The choice of replacement cost or reproduction cost and the many subjective and difficult decisions in measuring depreciation make it difficult to apply the cost approach in a variety of valuation situations. Therefore, the first decision of the appraiser is to be knowledgeable as to conditions that are appropriate for the use of the cost approach.

WHEN TO USE THE COST APPROACH

There are several good reasons for using the cost aproach in an appraisal. It may be necessary when property tax assessment or condemnation dictates a separation of the value of improvements from land, or for income tax and accounting purposes when the improvements are subject to deduction as an allowance for depreciation expense. Aside from these mandated instances, the cost aproach is useful in other situations.

In many cases, replacement cost new tends to set the upper limit on the value of real estate. An informed purchaser would normally not pay as much for an existing structure as for a brand-new one having the same utility and built to modern standards. This is analogous to paying less for last year's model of an automobile than for this year's model. It employs the principle of substitution. One exception to the "normal" rule occurs when the buyer is in a hurry to buy or use the structure and cannot wait for a new one to be built. Also, if one wished to avoid the risks associated with development, one might pay more for an existing product than for a new one, using the "what you see is what you get" attitude.

Situations for which the cost approach is useful include:

1. Feasibility analysis for new construction.
2. Highest and best use of land.
3. Renovation.
4. Final value reconciliation.
5. Institutional and special-purpose buildings.
6. Inactive market appraisals.
7. Insurance purposes.
8. Income tax purposes.

New Construction

Consider new construction. Suppose that the minimum acceptable overall capitalization rate is 13%, and the proposed construction would cost $500,000 for an office building expected to generate only $30,000 of net operating income (NOI) annually. Is the project feasible? $500,000 at a 13% rate should generate $65,000 of earnings; so $30,000 NOI would not justify the expenditure. On the other hand, if the same $500,000 were expected to produce $100,000 of annual net operating income, the project is quite viable.

Highest and Best Use of Land

Suppose that land costs $50,000, and the market requires a 12% per-year return; in other words, the land would have a claim on $6,000 of annual net operating income. A duplex on that land would generate $5,000 of net operating income, which would be inadequate to pay for the land's claim alone, and the building would fail to justify its own construction cost. On the other hand, a 10-story apartment building could generate, say, twenty times the net operating income, or $100,000, which would be more than adequate to pay its own cost of, for example, $450,000 over its economic life and would also provide the $6,000 annual income commanded by the land. In contrast, a 100-story building, because of its high construction cost, anticipated vacancies, and maintenance expenses, might not provide a net operating income adequate to justify itself. So, in these extreme examples, the highest and best use of the $50,000 site has been narrowed to a building of between 1 and 100 stories. Ten stories is feasible, but 7, 9, 11, or 20 stories, or some other height might be *the* highest and best use. This illustrates the principle of increasing and decreasing returns.

Renovation

Should you renovate, or change the use of a property? This decision again rests on costs as compared to required returns. Should one pay $500,000 to renovate an old office building? Suppose the annual income increase expected is $25,000. Since this would provide only 5% annual return on the $500,000 investment, it would not be feasible in a market that expects 13%. But if the expected increase in net operating income were $150,000, to be realized each year over a long period of time, then the 13% requirement would be satisfied, and the expenditure seems justified.

Final Value Reconciliation

In reconciliation analysis, suppose that an existing property is considered, and income and market approaches have indicated a value of $500,000. The cost approach result is $750,000. Should the cost approach be disregarded? Perhaps not. It probably means that there won't be new competition for quite a while. The predicted absence of future competition could be an important piece of information even if it doesn't change the estimate of market value. Conversely, if the market and income approach values are well above that of the cost approach, the owner could be advised that new competition is likely and market prices could drop rapidly.

Institutional and Special-Purpose Buildings

It is not easy to appraise institutional and special-purpose properties using the market or income approach. What is the value of a now-vacant building that was once a school, a post office, a church, or a railroad station? An appraiser is not likely to find recent sales of comparable property in the same geographical area, and the property was not owned for its income-producing ability. So the cost approach, which considers reproduction or replacement cost new and the property's estimated remaining useful life, might provide some guide to the value of such properties.

"No-Market" Appraisals

In very small communities or in inactive markets, there may be no comparable sales data, and not enough information to apply a gross rent multiplier. Here, the cost approach may be the only alternative left to the appraiser.

Insurance Purposes

In estimating value for hazard insurance purposes, the cost is often preferred since reimbursement, from insurance, is usually based on costs.

Income Tax Purposes

Finally, since improvements to real estate but not land can be depreciated for income tax purposes, the cost approach in an appraisal may be used. It can be helpful in establishing the amount paid for improvements, as distinguished from land when one price has been paid for all of the property.

HOW TO USE THE COST APPROACH

The cost approach begins with an estimation of replacement or reproduction cost new. As noted earlier, these two terms are not interchangeable. *Reproduction* is the building of an exact duplicate of the subject property. *Replacement* is the building of property having the same functional utility but built to modern standards, tastes, and designs. Fifty years ago, for example, movie theaters were built with glorious chandeliers, richly upholstered seats, marble staircases, high ceilings, luxurious lobbies, and the like. Modern movie theaters have lower ceilings and minimal lobbies, which saves on construction costs and energy consumption. Modern lighting expenditures are minimal; and seats, staircases, and floor coverings are chosen for function and ease of maintenance, not for luxury. However, the modern theater may have better acoustics and fire safety mechanisms. It may be built with partitions to allow two or more movies to be shown simultaneously. To *reproduce* the 50-year-old theater is to build one exactly like it; to *replace* is to build a modern one.

The classic cost approach normally begins with reproduction cost new, but in many cases replacement cost new is preferable. For example, an appraiser could estimate the reproduction cost new of the 50-year-old theater and then subtract for all its functional inadequacies. But this is unrealistic in the present world. As a shortcut, an appraiser could instead estimate replacement cost. Then the appraiser would *not* subtract for the functional inadequacies since it is inappropriate to subtract anything that is not in the replacement cost estimate. When functional deficiencies are so acute and difficult to measure, and reproduction is highly unlikely, the use of a replacement cost estimate would be appropriate.

Methods of Estimating Cost New

The four most popular methods of estimating cost new are:

1. Quantity survey
2. Unit-in-place
3. Variations of the unit-in-place
4. Comparative unit

Quantity Survey Method. The quantity survey method involves detailing each and every part of the structure and multiplying the cost of each part by the number of such parts. If carried to its extreme, every nail of the same size would be counted, as would every drop of glue. This method is too cumbersome to be used for most appraisal purposes.

Unit-in-Place Method. The unit-in-place method involves finding the reproduction cost new, including installation, of various components on a per-unit basis. For example, suppose that the cost of one square foot of an exterior wall is \$2.00, comprised of \$1.00 for bricks, \$0.25 for mortar, \$0.25 for plaster, and \$0.50 for labor; then \$2.00 multiplied by the area would give the cost of the wall. The same method can be used for the floor, roof, plumbing, etc. Often, lump-sum additions are needed for heating and plumbing equipment and for fixtures. Further adjustment may be warranted for architects' fees, interest during construction, insurance, and other builder's overhead items. See Table 18–1.

Variations of the Unit-in-Place Method. Variations of the unit-in-place method are: (a) the subcontract method, (b) a trade breakdown, or (c) segregated costs. The subcontract method acknowledges that a builder typically employs subcontractors to do at least some of the work. It attempts to derive the reproduction cost by totaling the costs that each subcontractor would charge. The subcontractor may be hired for excavation work, foundations, brickwork, plumbing, and so on. The trade breakdown approach is similar. It requires a breakdown of costs by the trade that would perform the work. The trade may be carpentry, masonry, plumbing, etc. In the segregated costs method, component parts of a building are priced at their cost per square or cubic foot, then extended. Component parts may include foundations, floors, roof costs, etc. Any of these variations from the unit-in-place method requires lump-sum adjustments for fixtures and indirect costs.

Comparative Unit Method. The comparative unit method involves starting with a benchmark cost per square foot or cubic foot for an entire "typical" structure. From there, adjustments are effected to compensate for differences between the benchmark and the subject building. Be sure to recognize an adjustment for the *efficiency ratio,* that is, the ratio of leasable size to total size. For example, a high-rise office building that has 200,000 square feet might be only 80% efficient because 20% of the building area is used for elevators, hallways, etc. Adjustments may also be needed for equipment, overhead, and other elements of cost. See Table 18–2.

TABLE 18–1
Unit-in-Place Method for 1-Story Apartment Building

Base Costs	*Unit Cost*		*Number of Square Feet*		*Amount Extended*
1. Exterior walls with wood siding	$2.75	×	5,500	=	$ 15,125
2. Foundation wall	1.45	×	5,500	=	7,975
3. Parapet wall	.65	×	5,500	=	3,575
Horizontal Components					
4. Site preparation	.12	×	22,000	=	2,640
5. Interior foundations (included in base costs above)	0	×	22,000	=	0
6. Slab on ground	1.40	×	22,000	=	30,800
7. Framing (load-supporting walls)	2.50	×	22,000	=	55,000
8. Structural floor (included in base costs above)	0	×	22,000	=	0
9. Roof (shingles, plywood, joists, and rafters)	3.90	×	22,000	=	85,800
10. Floor finish (tile, carpeting)	1.80	×	22,000	=	39,600
11. Ceiling finish (drywall, taped, textured)	1.20	×	22,000	=	26,400
12. Partitions (studs, drywall, doors)	3.75	×	22,000	=	82,500
13. Plumbing (200 sq ft per $1,200 fixture)	2.50	×	22,000	=	55,000
14. Heating	2.80	×	22,000	=	61,600
15. Air conditioning/appliances	.95	×	22,000	=	20,900
16. Electrical	2.30	×	22,000	=	50,600
17. Fire protection	.15	×	22,000	=	3,300
18. Elevator (none)	0	×	22,000	=	0
19. Miscellaneous (kitchen and bath cabinets)	1.00	×	22,000	=	22,000
Total					$562,815
Location multiplier					× .97
Reproduction cost new					$545,930

TABLE 18–2
Comparative Unit Cost

Base unit cost per square foot	$24.55
Square feet required	× 22,000
Cost for benchmark unit	$540,100
Add: Additional appliances	20,000
Additional landscaping	4,000
Total	$564,100
Location multiplier	× .97
Estimate reproduction cost new	$547,177

Direct versus Indirect Costs

Direct costs are those that are directly associated with the structure. They include bricks, mortar, lumber, and all of the labor that goes into construction. *Indirect costs* are incurred or absorbed during construction but cannot be readily identified in the structure itself. These include developer's overhead and profit; insurance and interest during construction; architectural, legal, and engineering fees; feasibility studies; and many others.

Some items of costs are difficult to classify, such as permit and inspection fees, on- and off-site security, survey fees, etc. Because of inconsistent classifications, it is important for an appraiser to recognize just what is included in a given cost estimate.

Cost Services

Three commonly used cost services are:

1. *Boeckh Building Cost Manual,* 525 E. Michigan, Milwaukee, Wisconsin.
2. *Dodge Services,* F. W. Dodge Company, 1221 Avenue of the Americas, New York, N.Y.
3. *Marshall Valuation Service,* 1617 Beverly Blvd., Los Angeles, California.

These services usually provide (a) local adjustment factors in recognition of cost variations within the United States, and (b) time-adjustment factors in recognition of periodic cost changes. Local and time adjustment factors are multiplied by the basic figures shown in cost service manuals.

It is important to understand the material provided before using any of these services. For example, builder's overhead or other indirect costs may or may not be included in the costs shown. The benchmark unit in the comparative unit method may be based on a building that is much larger or smaller or of a shape quite different from the one being considered. Therefore the cost services must be used carefully. There are a variety of ways to use these services. For example, the services may include computer terminal input and response, costs from mailed-in plans and specifications, or manuals that can be used in the appraiser's office.

Appraisers should recognize that various cost estimation methods are likely to provide different results no matter how careful and well-documented the analyses. The quality and quantity of labor and materials used, labor strikes, material shortages, weather conditions, and the time it takes to complete a construction project all have a bearing on the cost. Not all of the foreseeable or unforeseeable factors are necessarily considered by cost estimates. When contractors are asked to submit secret bids on a completely specified project, it is not unusual to have variations of 20% or more among the bids. So, when estimating reproduction cost, an appraiser should recognize the potential variation. If the appraiser attempts more than one cost estimation method, and the variation among results is over 5 or 10%, it would be wise to check and recheck all figures. But a discrepancy of that magnitude does not necessarily mean an error. When considering a complicated structure, the appraiser would be well-advised to seek professional cost-estimating assistance or service.

ESTIMATING DEPRECIATION

After reproduction cost new is computed, depreciation must be deducted. The term *depreciation,* as used in appraisal, must be distinguished from *accounting depreciation.* In accounting, depreciation is a process of allocating the historical cost of an asset over its useful life, without attempting to value the asset. In appraisal, it is estimated as a factor in the current valuation, without regard to historical cost. Depreciation is defined as "a loss in utility, and hence value, from any cause."

In addition to the distinction between accounting depreciation and appraisal depreciation, a further distinction should be made between depreciation in the cost approach and depreciation in the Ellwood approach to mortgage-equity capitalization.

In the cost approach, depreciation is measured in terms of *current* dollars against *current* reproduction cost; whereas in the Ellwood technique, depreciation is simply an estimate that the resale price will be less than the historical purchase price. No attempt is made to allocate the decline in value among the various components of a building or the building structure in Ellwood's technique. The Ellwood technique for depreciation simply considers the forecast change in the value of an asset.

In the cost approach, the depreciation factor attempts to make adjustments between the attributes of the selected building, as if it were new, and the subject property's physical condition and economic setting. It is a way of adjusting the hypothetical new structure on which the cost estimate was based and distinguishing it from the subject property.

An appraiser may estimate depreciation through observation and/or by applying a formula based on the effective age and remaining life of each component of the property. An indirect method of estimating depreciation is to subtract values for the property, estimated from the market or income approach (or both), from the reproduction cost new of the subject property, plus land. The difference obtained is the total depreciation sustained. For example, if reproduction cost new plus the land at market value is $750,000, and both market and income approaches yield a value of $500,000, then the $250,000 difference is accrued depreciation. However, such a method fails to independently estimate depreciation in the cost approach.

A direct method is to estimate each type of depreciation for each component of the property that is being appraised. See Table 18–3. Three types of depreciation to be recognized are:

1. Physical deterioration (wear and tear).
2. Functional obsolescence (becoming outmoded).
3. Economic obsolescence (due to changes outside the subject property).

Physical Deterioration

Physical deterioration consists of all wear and tear, from faded paint to structural decay. Each item of depreciation may be considered either curable or incurable. It is *incurable* when the cost to correct the defect exceeds the value that would be added. *Curable* implies that the cost of correction is *less* than the value added. Any deficiency can be corrected, but if the expense exceeds the benefit to be derived, it is considered incurable.

TABLE 18–3

Estimate of Accrued Depreciation

1. Physical Deterioration
   A. Curable: Deferred maintenance

1. Painting and decorating	$2,500
2. Replace carpets in 5 units	1,750
3. Repair plumbing fixtures	2,200
Total physical curable	$6,450

   B. Incurable Short-Life Components

Component	*Reproduction Cost New*	*Actual or Effective Age*	*Normal Life Expectancy*	*Depreciation Incurred (%)*	*Depreciation Amount*
Window screens	$ 800	5	20	25	$ 200
Carpet (15 units)	5,250	5	10	50	2,625
Cabinets	22,000	5	25	20	4,400
Heating	61,600	5	30	16.7	10,288
Appliances	11,000	5	15	33.3	3,663
Air conditioning	11,000	5	15	33.3	3,663
Plumbing	55,000	5	40	12.5	6,875
Total incurable short-life	$166,650				$31,714

   C. Incurable Long-Life

Reproduction cost new	$545,930
Less: Physical curable	− 6,450
Reproduction cost new: Short-life	−166,650
Reproduction cost new: long-life	$372,830
Effective age: 5 years; est. total life 60 years	
5/60 = 8⅓%	
8⅓% × $372,830 =	$31,068

2. Functional Obsolescence
   A. Curable

Modernize appliances	$12,000
Less: Value of existing appliances	− 7,370
Total functional curable	$ 4,630

   B. Incurable

Rent loss caused by poor floor plan $10.00 × 12 months × 20 units × 5 GRM	$12,000

3. Locational Obsolescence:

Rent loss caused by nearby industrial plant $15.00 × 12 months × 20 units × 5 GPM	$ 18,000

Summary of Cost Approach

Estimated reproduction cost new		$545,930
Less: Accrued depreciation		
Physical: Curable	$ 6,450	
Incurable short-life	31,714	
Incurable long-life	31,068	
Functional: Curable	4,630	
Incurable	12,000	
Locational	18,000	
Total depreciation		−$103,862
Indicated depreciated value of improvements		$442,068
Estimated present worth of site		+ 50,000
Value estimate by cost approach		$492,068

Deferred maintenance is a type of curable depreciation that anticipates immediate expenditure by a prudent purchaser to bring property up to normal standards. This would include repainting where it is now necessary, repairing a leaking roof or dripping faucet, and the like. The existence of deferred maintenance items does not necessarily imply past neglect or abuse—only that it is appropriate to repair certain components immediately.

The measurement of remaining asset values considers effective age and remaining life. For example, a structure that has a chronological age of 10 years and suffers from normal depreciation, plus 50% for additional abuse, has an *effective age* of 15 years: 10 actual years, plus 5 years added for abuse. If its estimated physical life is 100 years, it shows 15% depreciation. If reproduction cost new is $100,000, then the charge for depreciation is $15,000. Some items, such as carpets and appliances, have short lives, whereas the main structure has a long useful life. After considering depreciation on short-lived assets, subtract the entire short-lived asset from the total reproduction cost to get the long-lived portion. Then apply depreciation against the long-lived portion. Failure to first subtract the cost of short-lived assets and deferred maintenance would result in depreciating those items twice.

Functional Obsolescence

Functional obsolescence means that something is outmoded. The cause may be a deficiency or an excess. The item in question may still work perfectly well, but it is not up to current standards. The item may be curable or incurable, depending on the cost of correction as compared to the benefits expected.

If obsolescence is curable but is caused by an absent element, such as the lack of air-conditioning in Texas, the depreciation is measured by the difference between the cost of adding air conditioning to the property and the cost of installing air conditioning in a new structure. In this way, the reproduction cost, which did not include air conditioning, is not penalized; but the extra cost of curing the deficiency is considered. For example, if it costs $30,000 to install air conditioning in apartments that are being built but $40,000 in existing ones because of additional labor efforts, the charge for functional obsolescence is the $10,000 difference. When the curable deficiency is caused by an out-of-date element, such as old-fashioned bathroom fixtures, the accrued depreciation is measured by the cost of replacing them.

When functional obsolescence is caused by an excess (also called a *superadequacy),* such as carpet that costs $25 per yard in an apartment where $10 per yard carpet would have been quite adequate, the reproduction cost new of the superadequacy (the $15 per yard excess) would be considered functional obsolescence. This excess is subtracted from the reproduction cost new to derive a value for the apartment. Be careful not to double-count depreciation. Since physical depreciation may already have been charged against the $25 per yard cost, the adjustment for the functional excess would be the undepreciated portion of the $15 per yard excess.

Incurable functional obsolescence caused by a deficiency is usually measured by the rent loss sustained. If a poor floor plan results in $10 per month less in rent, and the local monthly gross rent multiplier is 100, the deficiency is estimated at $1,000. (The gross rent multiplier is found in the market by dividing sales prices by monthly rent.) Incurable functional obsolescence may be caused by an excess. Suppose that a building was built strong enough to support ten more floors, but the height has not been and will never be increased. The undepreciated amount of the extra cost is subtracted from reproduction cost new as functional obsolescence, as is the capitalized value of additional operating expenses, if any, caused by the defect.

Two other sources of functional obsolescence stem from the floor-area ratio and the siting of improvements. The *floor-area ratio* measures the intensity of land use. For example, a 5-story building with 10,000 square feet on each floor, built on a 25,000 square foot site, has a floor-area ratio of 2 (5 floors × 10,000 sq ft per floor ÷ 25,000 sq ft land area). It covers 40% of the site (10,000 sq ft divided by 25,000 sq ft), but the height creates a floor-area ratio greater than 1. Unless this intensity is the highest and best use of the site, there may be functional obsolescence.

Siting is the positioning of improvements on a site. Improvements that are not properly positioned, for example, if they do not easily allow ingress and egress or fail to give highway exposure when this is desirable, are a cause of functional obsolescence.

Functional obsolescence, if it is acute, can have a dramatic influence on the value of improvements. A structure that is outmoded in many respects may not be able to command as much rental income as the operating expenses that will arise. In this event, the most feasible solution requires that the building be demolished. The fact that manually operated elevators of an office building still run, as do the window air conditioners and incandescent lighting, does not justify the continued existence of the building.

Economic Obsolescence

Economic obsolescence is due to factors outside the property. Such factors may include busy streets or an industrial plant near a residential area. Economic obsolescence is always considered incurable since the expense makes it impractical to buy surrounding properties and remove the offending elements just to increase the value of one property that is affected.

Economic obsolescence (also called *environmental* or *locational obsolescence*) is measured by the capitalized rent loss, estimated by using a gross rent multiplier. The portion of the capitalized loss that is attributable to the land is presumably reflected in the land value and should not be deducted from the reproduction cost of the improvements.

In relation to economic obsolescence, it is important to stress the difficulty in distinguishing between locational factors, which have perhaps diminished the utility of the improvements, and the locational factors, which have diminished the value of the site. For example, the "right" building may be at the "wrong" location or vice versa.

LIMITATIONS OF THE COST APPROACH

It is very difficult to measure the depreciation sustained by a building, particularly one that is more than ten years old. By definition, it is impossible to reproduce new an older building. In such cases, the cost approach may provide a poor indication of value, not only because of the impossibility of reproduction but also because improvements may not be the highest and best use of the site. Finally, the cost approach for existing buildings does not in itself consider the highest and best use of a site. Consequently, the cost approach must be employed carefully, and be judiciously considered in the reconciliation of value.

SUMMARY

The cost approach can offer an estimate of value for income-producing property, but it has many weaknesses. It is best used to determine the feasibility of new construction, the highest and best use of land, renovation analysis, hazard insurance evaluation, and other purposes.

In the cost approach, reproduction cost is first estimated (sometimes the replacement cost is estimated), and estimated depreciation is then subtracted. Depreciation may be physical, functional, or environmental. The value of the land is then added to the depreciated cost of improvements.

The primary weaknesses of the cost approach when applied to existing structures are: (1) the impossibility of erecting a new depreciated structure, (2) the unlikelihood of reproducing an obsolete structure, and (3) the inability to separate improvements from land. However, the cost approach can be useful in a variety of situations, as suggested above.

Questions

1. A 100 foot × 200 foot warehouse has exterior walls 25 feet high and includes 5% office space. Interior ceilings are 22 feet high with a clear span. The roof is flat.
   a. How many square feet are available for warehousing?
   b. How many square feet are available for office space?
   c. If the exterior walls cost 80¢ per square foot for labor, 80¢ per square foot for materials, and 40¢ per square foot for overhead, what is their total cost?
   d. A benchmark cost for the interior of a warehouse without offices is 60¢ per cubic foot. What would be the benchmark cost of the interior of the subject property if there were no office space?
   e. Refer to part (d) above. If the subject property is in a local area with a local adjustment factor of .96, what is the benchmark cost per cubic foot?
   f. Refer to parts (d) and (e) above. If the benchmark figure of 60¢ was prepared last year, and the time adjustment factor is 1.06 per year, what is the current benchmark cost for this geographic area?
   g. If office space costs an additional $5 per square foot for construction, plus $2,000 for air conditioning and heating equipment, what is the estimated cost of the additional office space?
2. Using the same subject property as in Question #1, consider that unit costs shown in a published manual are as follows: foundations, $1.50 per square foot; exterior wall, $2.00 per square foot; roof, $5.00 per square foot; plumbing, $20,000; electrical system, $15,000; mechanical equipment, $10,000; loading docks, $22,000; office space, $7.00 per square foot. Builder's and subcontractor's overhead and profit allowance are 19% of direct costs. What is the reproduction cost new of the property?

3. The warehouse in Questions #1 and #2 has a chronological and effective age of 12 years, and its estimated remaining useful life is 48 years. The office space requires $1,000 for immediate carpet and fixture replacements. The loading docks, because of abuse, show 25% more wear than normal; their typical total useful life is 30 years. They are in need of a $2,500 repair. The roof, electrical system, and mechanical equipment have an estimated remaining useful life of 18 years. Certain wiring needs replacement at a $3,000 cost to bring it up to code standards. How much is the incurable physical depreciation?

4. Last year, a new highway was completed that diverted most traffic four miles from the older road that the subject property is near. As a consequence, the subject property rents for 20¢ per square foot per year less than it would if it were closer to the new highway. The typical annual gross rent multiplier for this type of property in the area is 8. What is the amount of environmental obsolescence caused by the change?

5. The subject property needs additional security equipment. Such equipment is now essential for the type of materials normally stored in the warehouse, and it can be purchased and installed for $4,000. Moreover, the lighting in the warehouse is incandescent, whereas fluorescent lighting is currently needed. The cost of such a changeover would be $12,000. The annual rent loss is 5¢ per square foot of the entire warehouse.

   a. What is the amount of curable functional obsolescence?

   b. What is the amount of incurable functional obsolescence?

6. Referring to Questions #2, #3, #4, and #5, summarize reproduction cost and accrued depreciation.

7. A four-acre tract of land on an interstate highway is currently zoned for office space. The land is worth $50,000 per acre, judging from several recent sales of comparable tracts in the same geographic area. The owner is considering three alternative proposed buildings:

   A. A one-story building with 70,000 square feet of space having an efficiency ratio of 88%. Estimated rental rates will be $9 per square foot, occupancy 95%, and operating expenses 40% of potential gross income.

   B. A two-story walk-up with 100,000 square feet of space, 85% efficient, with 95% occupancy expected at $9 per square foot, and operating expenses of 40% of potential gross income.

   C. A ten-story elevator building with 500,000 square feet. The efficiency ratio would be 80% and occupancy 90% at $10 per square foot. Operating expenses would be 53% of potential gross income.

a. For each of the above, how much is the forecast net operating income?

b. Total construction costs, including necessary parking, architect's fees, overhead, etc., excluding land, are expected to be $35 per gross square foot of building for proposal A, $33 for proposal B, and $50 for proposal C. If investors want a 12% capitalization rate applied to the improvement cost, which of the three proposals represents the best use of the land?

Essay Questions

1. Distinguish between the following terms:
   a. Reproduction versus replacement cost new.
   b. Curable versus incurable depreciation.
   c. Accounting depreciation versus appraisal depreciation.
   d. Direct versus indirect costs.
2. Explain four methods of estimating reproduction cost new.
3. Describe three causes of depreciation.
4. Does replacement cost new set the upper limit for an improvement's value? Explain.

Chapter 19

Summary of Real Estate Valuation Tools and Capitalization Review

There are many commonly used decision tools for income-producing property. Some tools involve simple arithmetic; others are more complex. This chapter offers a summary of the various tools as they are applied to the benchmark example that has been used throughout the book. Specific comments are offered on the advantages, drawbacks, and pitfalls of each method. Following this is a review of capitalization techniques, including their mechanics and applicability.

REAL ESTATE VALUATION TOOLS AND BENCHMARK EXAMPLE

Inputs and assumptions to the benchmark example are summarized in Tables 19-1, 19-2, and 19-3 for the three stages of ownership: acquisition, operations, and resale. The inputs and assumptions are shown in Table 19-1. Table 19-2 is a summary of pro forma operations over a 10-year projection period; Table 19-3 shows pro forma results from resale.

TABLE 19–1
Benchmark Example Data Summary

Stage I. Acquisition	
Purchase price	$500,000
Physical composition	
Improvements	
Short-lived (10 years)	100,000
Long-lived (35 years)	350,000
Land	50,000
Total	$500,000
Financial composition	
Mortgage (25-year term, monthly payments at 12% interest)	$400,000
Equity	100,000
Total	$500,000
Stage II. Operations (level annual amounts)	
Potential gross income	$100,000
Less: Vacancy allowance (5%)	−5,000
Add: Miscellaneous income	+3,000
Effective gross income	$ 98,000
Less: Operating expenses (including $2,000 replacement reserve)	−33,000
Net operating income	$ 65,000
Less: Debt service	−50,555
Before-tax cash flow	$ 14,445
Tax rate on income from operations	40%
Stage III: Disposition	
Resale price (2.5% annual compound appreciation)	$640,000
Less: Expenses of resale	−39,000
Resale price after expenses of sale	$601,000
Less: Mortgage balance at resale (approx.)	−351,000
Less: Income taxes at resale	−72,000*
After-tax proceeds from resale (est.)	$178,000

*Tax rate on resale (capital or Section 1231 gain) 24%

TABLE 19–2
Pro Forma Summary of Operations over Ten Years for Benchmark Example

Year	Potential Gross Income	Vacancy Allowance	Misc. Income	Operating Expenses	Replacement Reserve
1	100,000	5,000	3,000	31,000	2,000
2	100,000	5,000	3,000	31,000	2,000
3	100,000	5,000	3,000	31,000	2,000
4	100,000	5,000	3,000	31,000	2,000
5	100,000	5,000	3,000	31,000	2,000
6	100,000	5,000	3,000	31,000	2,000
7	100,000	5,000	3,000	31,000	2,000
8	100,000	5,000	3,000	31,000	2,000
9	100,000	5,000	3,000	31,000	2,000
10	100,000	5,000	3,000	31,000	2,000

Year	Net Operating Income	Interest Expense	Principal Amortization	Before-Tax Cash Flow
1	65,000	47,855	2,700	14,445
2	65,000	47,512	3,043	14,445
3	65,000	47,126	3,428	14,445
4	65,000	46,692	3,863	14,445
5	65,000	46,202	4,353	14,445
6	65,000	45,650	4,905	14,445
7	65,000	45,027	5,527	14,445
8	65,000	44,326	6,228	14,445
9	65,000	43,537	7,018	14,445
10	65,000	42,646	7,908	14,445

Year	Depreciation Expense	Taxable Income	Tax Savings (−Payment)	After-Tax Cash Flow
1	20,000	−855	342	14,787
2	20,000	−512	205	14,650
3	20,000	−126	51	14.496
4	20,000	308	−123	14,322
5	20,000	798	−319	14,126
6	20,000	1,350	−540	13,905
7	20,000	1,973	−789	13,656
8	20,000	2,674	−1,069	13,376
9	20,000	3,463	−1,385	13,060
10	20,000	4,354	−1,741	12,704

TABLE 19-3
Pro Forma Proceeds from Resale for Benchmark Example

Year	Resale Price After Commission	Mortgage Balance	Adjusted Tax Basis	Straight-Line Basis
1	481,237	397,300	480,000	480,000
2	493,268	394,257	460,000	460,000
3	505,600	390,829	440,000	440,000
4	518,240	386,966	420,000	420,000
5	531,196	382,612	400,000	400,000
6	544,475	377,707	380,000	380,000
7	558,087	372,180	360,000	360,000
8	572,039	365,951	340,000	340,000
9	586,340	358,933	320,000	320,000
10	600,998	351,025	300,000	300,000

Year	Total Gain	Recapture Depreciation	Tax on Sale	After-Tax Proceeds	After-Tax Internal Rate of Return on Equity
1	1,237	0	296	83,642	−1.6%
2	33,268	0	7,958	91,053	10.5%
3	65,600	0	15,691	99,080	14.4%
4	98,240	0	23,499	107,775	16.1%
5	131,196	0	31,382	117,201	17.0%
6	164,475	0	39,343	127,426	17.4%
7	198,087	0	47,382	138,525	17.6%
8	232,039	0	55,504	150,584	17.7%
9	266,340	0	63,709	163,698	17.6%
10	300,998	0	71,999	177,975	17.5%

The decision tools considered are:

1. Payback period (payback)
2. Gross rent multiplier (GRM)
3. Overall rate of return (OAR)
4. Equity dividend rate (EDR)
5. Net spendable income (NSI)
6. Total annual equity returns
7. Average annual method
8. Net present value (NPV)
9. Ellwood technique
10. Internal rate of return (IRR)
11. Modified internal rate (MIR)
12. Financial management rate of return (FMRR)

Payback Period

The payback technique measures the amount of time required to recapture the cost of the investment through investment inflows. The result is a time period, not a rate of return. The payback technique fails to account for the investment inflows expected in periods beyond the payback period, and for the timing of inflows within the payback period.

The reciprocal of the payback period approximates the internal rate of return only in situations where investment inflows are level and in perpetuity, or in the case of a nonwasting asset (one in which the reversion is the same as the initial investment), or when the payback period is relatively short (four years or less) and level investment inflows continue for at least three times the payback period.

Payback can be computed on either a before- or an after-tax basis. It can be based on the entire property, or just on equity. For the benchmark property, the payback period is 7.7 years for the entire property: \$500,000 price/\$65,000 NOI = 7.7 years. It is approximately 7 years based on equity and cash flow before taxes: \$100,000 equity/\$14,445 = 7 years; and approximately 7 years based on after-tax cash flow (see Table 19–2).

Gross Rent Multiplier

The gross rent multiplier (GRM) is the relationship of the purchase or sales price to the gross rental income. As it is defined, either potential gross income (before vacancies have been subtracted) or effective gross income (net of a vacancy allowance) may be used. Analysts should ascertain which rental income figures are used and be consistent. In the given example, the GRM is 5, computed as follows:

$$\frac{\text{Sales price}}{\text{Rental income}} = \frac{\$500{,}000}{\$100{,}000} = 5$$

This method is one of the most widely used techniques. It is easy to compute and involves readily available figures. However, its widespread use stems from the ease of computation and comparison to other projects and not from its reliability as a measuring device. A more complete description of the GRM technique is in Chapter 17.

Although the GRM may be used as a rough indicator of over- or underpricing, it fails to account for operating expense variations among projects, financing, resale prices, and income taxes. It disregards the amounts and timing of after-tax cash flows to the equity investor. We can expect the technique to be used for many years to come, but the reality is that it provides an unsophisticated, unrefined measure.

Overall Rate of Return (OAR)

The overall rate of return is computed by dividing the net operating income by the sales price. The result is the rate of return on and of the entire purchase capital without regard to the contributor (i.e., equity investor or mortgage lender). For the benchmark property, the OAR is 13% as shown below:

$$\frac{\text{Net operating income}}{\text{Purchase price}} = \frac{\$65{,}000}{\$500{,}000} = 13\%$$

This method improves on the GRM in that operating expenses are taken into account. The OAR is a good ranking device for comparable, unmortgaged properties since it evaluates properties free and clear of any financing. It is also relatively easy to derive from the market. (The procedure for deriving the OAR from the market was described in Chapter 17.) However, when property is subject to an existing mortgage, a market-derived OAR fails to acknowledge the particulars of existing debt.

The OAR also fails to reflect individual income tax situations. However, with modifications as indicated in the Ellwood approach, it can include provisions for specific before-tax equity rates, mortgage loans, loan-to-value ratios, and forecast property value changes.

Equity Dividend Rate

The equity dividend rate (EDR) is also termed the *cash-on-cash-return* method, the *cash return on cash invested* method, and the *percentage cash flow technique.* Computation involves dividing the before-tax cash flow by the initial equity investment and converting the decimal result to a percentage.

The equity dividend rate fails to reflect income tax implications, property value changes, and reductions of mortgage principal. It also fails to describe a yield to maturity. This technique, however, is commonly used by real estate investors.

As it applies to the benchmark property, the EDR is as follows:

$$\frac{\text{Before-tax cash flow}}{\text{Equity invested}} = \frac{\$14{,}445}{\$100{,}000} = 14.45\%$$

Net Spendable Income

When the NSI technique is used, the rate is computed by dividing the sum of before-tax cash flow and the tax savings or payment (after-tax cash flow) by the initial equity investment. However, with this technique the resulting rate is misleading for the same reasons as those advanced for the equity dividend rate. Also, because accelerated depreciation and high interest payments during early years of income property ownership often cause large artificial accounting losses for those years (but not for later years), the percentage rates of the NSI can be deceiving, and they do not reflect taxes upon sale of a property.

As applied to the subject property, the net spendable income rates are as follows:

$$\text{Year 1:} \quad \frac{\$14{,}787}{\$100{,}000} = 14.79\%$$

$$\text{Year 2:} \quad \frac{\$14{,}650}{\$100{,}000} = 14.65\%$$

$$\text{Year 3:} \quad \frac{\$14{,}496}{\$100{,}000} = 14.50\%$$

Total Annual Equity Returns

With the total annual equity returns technique, the sum of forecast cash flow, tax savings (or payment), property appreciation (or depreciation), and mortgage reduction are compared with either the initial equity investment or the market value of equity to obtain a rate of return figure for each year.

In addition to the pitfalls described under the equity dividend and net spendable income techniques, this technique has an added shortcoming. Property appreciation and mortgage reduction cannot be realized until a sale, or, in some cases, until a refinancing, takes place. For the purpose of measuring the rate of return, it is better for the investor to include property appreciation and mortgage reduction figures in the year or years in which these are expected to be realized in cash.

As applied to the subject property, the total annual equity returns rates would be computed as follows:

$$\text{Year 1: } \frac{\underset{\text{(BTCF)}}{\$14{,}445} + \underset{\text{(TS)}}{\$342} + \underset{\text{(MR)}}{\$2{,}700} + \underset{\text{(APPREC)}}{\$12{,}500}}{\underset{\text{(Value)}}{\$500{,}000} - \underset{\text{(Mortgage)}}{\$400{,}000} = \underset{\text{(Equity)}}{\$100{,}000}} = \frac{\$29{,}987}{\$100{,}000} = 30.0\%$$

$$\text{Year 2: } \frac{\$14{,}445 + \$205 + \$3{,}043 + \$12{,}812}{\$512{,}500 - \$397{,}300 = \$115{,}200} = \frac{\$30{,}505}{\$115{,}200} = 26.5\%$$

$$\text{Year 3: } \frac{\$14{,}445 + \$51 + \$3{,}428 + \$13{,}133}{\$525{,}313 - \$394{,}257 = \$131{,}056} = \frac{\$31{,}057}{\$131{,}056} = 23.7\%$$

Where: BTCF = Before-tax cash flow
TS = Tax savings
MR = Mortgage reduction
APPREC = Property value appreciation

Average Annual Method

The average annual method involves averaging all investment inflows to an annual amount, and then dividing by the initial equity. Although this technique is commonly used by real estate investors to measure the rate of return, it disregards the timing of investment inflows. It would make no difference whether investment inflows were zero for the first five years of operations, and then $20,000 for the next five years, or the reverse. The method fails to distinguish the value of dollars that will be received immediately from those expected to be received in the distant future.

However, this method does have two strong points. One is the ease of computation, which is probably the reason why many property owners choose to use it. (Total investment outflows are subtracted from inflows, and the result is divided by the total holding period in years, and that quotient is divided by the initial equity to derive a rate.) The other strong point is that the average annual method will approximate the internal rate of return, provided that the following two conditions are met:

1. Annual investment inflows from operations are level in amount over the investment holding period.
2. The after-tax proceeds from the sale equal the initial equity investment.

Application of the average annual method to the benchmark property would depend on the selected holding period and whether a before- or an after-tax analysis was sought. As an example, assume a ten-year holding period and an after-tax basis as shown in Table 19–4.

TABLE 19–4
Example of Average Annual Method

Year	*After-tax Investment Inflows*
1	$ 14,787
2	14,650
3	14,496
4	14,322
5	14,126
6	13,905
7	13,656
8	13,376
9	13,060
10	12,704
Resale	$178,000
Total returns	$317,082
Less: Investment	−$100,000
Excess	$217,082
Divided by years (10)	
Average	$21,708
Divided by investment	($100,000)
Rate of return	21.7%

Net Present Value

The NPV technique involves discounting and summarizing investment inflows to a present value at a prespecified discount rate. The resulting present value is then compared to the present value of investment outflow(s). If the present value of investment outflow(s) exceeds the present value of inflow(s), the proposed investment is rejected because the investment fails to return the minimum acceptable rate of return. Otherwise, the proposed investment is considered.

In theory, the predetermined discount rate used for net present value computations is the entity's cost of capital. In practice, however, it is difficult to select an appropriate rate.

The net present value technique uses a discounting approach and thereby considers the time value of money. Unfortunately, this technique requires a predetermined hurdle (cutoff) discount rate and so fails to disclose the rate that the proposed investment is expected to earn (or that an actual investment has earned).

In the benchmark example, if an 18% or greater rate were used as the hurdle rate, the subject property would not be acquired. Acceptance would be permitted, however, if 17% or less were the cutoff point and a projection period in excess of five years was considered. The cutoff point is shown by the after-tax internal rate of return on equity (see Table 19–3). Inflows discounted above 18% would produce a present value that would be less than the equity investment; a rate below 17% produces contrary results.

Ellwood Technique

The Ellwood technique is a before-tax mortgage-equity method. It provides an overall rate, which is a blend of mortgage and equity rate requirements. It considers the before-tax cash flow and proceeds from a sale, discounted to a present value (value of equity), and adds the present mortgage balance to derive a property value estimate.

As applied to the subject property:

$$\frac{\text{NOI}}{V} = \text{Y} - mC + dep(SFF)$$

Where:

NOI = net operating income
V = property value estimate
Y = equity yield rate
m = loan-to-value ratio
P = the fraction of the loan paid off over the projection period
f = annual mortgage constant
SFF = sinking fund factor for the projection period at the equity yield rate
dep = fraction of decline in value over the projection period (negative for forecast appreciation)
C = $Y + P(SFF) - f$

For example, the overall rate for the subject property is:

$$\frac{\$\ 65{,}000}{\$500{,}000} = 13\%$$

In the Ellwood technique, given a level net operating income assumption and a 20% equity yield rate, the approximate Ellwood overall rate (OAR) is found as follows:

$$\begin{aligned} \text{OAR} &= Y - mC - dep(SFF) \\ \text{OAR} &= .20 - .8(.0783) - .202(.03852) \\ \text{OAR} &= .20 - .06264 - .00778 \\ \text{OAR} &= .12958 \end{aligned}$$

Internal Rate of Return

The internal rate of return (IRR) is usually defined as the rate at which the present values of investment outflows and investment inflows are equal. This rate is computed by solving for i (the internal rate of return) in the equation shown below.

$$\sum_{t=1}^{n} \frac{\text{Dollars of investment outflow in period } t}{(1+i)^t} = \sum_{t=1}^{n} \frac{\text{Dollars of investment inflow in period } t}{(1+i)^t}$$

This rate can be applied to the total property or to the equity, either before or after income taxes. The IRR shows the rate of return on capital generated by an investment. It is the rate of compound earnings per investment dollar per time period. In many cases the IRR is a useful device for ranking alternative investments. However, it has serious drawbacks; the three major ones are:

1. It requires a trial-and-error process for solution.
2. There exists the possibility of multiple outcomes.
3. Reinvestment is assumed.

Trial-and-Error Process. One drawback to the IRR technique is that a trial-and-error process is required to solve for the internal rate of return. With reasonably priced financial calculators on the market, this obstacle is not as formidable as it was several years ago.

Multiple Outcomes for Staggered Investment Outflows. In investment situations where there is more than one investment outflow, more than one internal rate of return can be computed. Since it is a common business practice in real estate to require just one investment outflow (subsequent outflows may occur because of the variability of NOI but are not predictable), this is seldom a drawback in the analysis of most real estate investments.

Reinvestment Assumption. The IRR is generated within an investment. Therefore, some analysts prefer to consider that the reinvestment of income is presumed to occur at the same rate as the IRR. As it relates to the benchmark property, the IRR is computed by solving for i in the following formula:

$$E = \Sigma_{t=1}^{n} \frac{A_t - F_t - T_t}{(1 + i)^t} + \frac{S_n - B_n - G_n}{(1 + i)^n}$$

Where:

n = projection period.
A_t = net operating income in period t.
F_t = debt service in period t.
T_t = income taxes in period t.
S_n = resale price at the end of the projection period, less expenses of sale.
B_n = unpaid mortgage balance at the end of the projection period.
G_n = taxes upon sale of the property.
E = investment outflow.

For the benchmark property, the after-tax internal rate of return for a ten-year holding period is approximately 17.5% as shown on Table 19–5.

Modified Internal Rate

The modified internal rate (MIR) method avoids the reinvestment assumption of the IRR. Instead, the analyst specifies a reinvestment rate. Cash inflows are assumed to be reinvested at that rate to a terminal amount and are added to the proceeds from a sale to derive a total terminal value. Then the compounded rate of growth (MIR) that equates the inflows with the terminal value is sought.

TABLE 19-5

Internal Rate of Return

Year		After-Tax Cash Flow		17.5% Discount Factor		Amount @ Present Value
0	Investment	($100,000)	×	1.00	=	($100,000)
1		14,787	×	.851	=	12,585
2		14,650	×	.724	=	10,611
3		14,496	×	.616	=	8,936
4		14,322	×	.525	=	7,514
5		14,126	×	.446	=	6,307
6		13,905	×	.380	=	5,284
7		13,656	×	.323	=	4,416
8		13,376	×	.275	=	3,681
9		13,060	×	.234	=	3,059
10		12,704	×	.199	=	2,532
Resale price		178,000	×	.199	=	35,485
Net present value at 17.5% discount rate					=	$ +410

Note: The difference for the present value of inflows versus outflows is only $410 at a 17.5% rate. The present value of outflows at a 17.5% rate is almost equal to the present value of inflows. The rate at which inflows and outflows are exactly equal is the internal rate of return. In this example, it is slightly higher than 17.5%.

To illustrate:

$$E = \Sigma_{t=1}^{n} \frac{(A_t - F_t - T_t) \times (1 + r)^{(n-1)} + (S_n - B_n - G_n)}{(1 + mi)^n}$$

Where:

r = reinvestment rate
mi = modified internal rate

and other variables are as previously defined.

Financial Management Rate of Return

M. Chapman Findlay III and Stephen D. Messner developed the financial management rate of return (FMRR) to remedy some of the deficiencies of the IRR technique.[1] The FMRR consists of a modification of the IRR technique that is especially important when more than one outflow is forecast from an investment. Two rates are considered by the FMRR:

1. A safe, liquid after-tax rate *(i_L)*.
2. A "run-of-the-mill" reinvestment rate *(i_R)*.

There are four steps in applying this technique:

1. Future outflows are "removed" by utilizing prior inflows where possible. Removal is accomplished by deducting from prior inflows the value of future outflows discounted at i_L to the period of prior inflows.
2. Remaining outflows (those that cannot be offset by prior inflows) are discounted to their present value at i_R, then summed.
3. The inflows that were not offset by outflows are compounded forward at i_R and summed.
4. The compounded rate of growth that would equate step 2 with step 3 is found. The result is the FMRR.

Applying the FMRR to the benchmark property would produce the same results as the modified IRR. Investment inflows are compounded forward to a terminal value considering that income is to be reinvested at a specified i_R rate. The initial equity investment is compared to the terminal value; then the compounded growth rate from start to terminal value is derived.

The FMRR has an important place in evaluating new projects. Developers often sell income-producing property with equity to be contributed in the following intallments:

1. One-third of the total equity to be contributed is due upon signing the agreement.
2. Another third is due upon completion of construction.

[1]M. Chapman Findlay, III, and Stephen D. Messner, "Real Estate Investment Analysis: IRR versus FMRR," *The Real Estate Appraiser,* V. 41 July/August 1975, 5–20.

3. The remaining one-third is due upon attainment of a specified occupancy rate, often at the expected cash flow break-even point.

Since the second and third installments must be met with certainty and on short notice, investors must remain adequately liquid or else forfeit the property. Therefore, discounting the certain outflows at a safe, liquid rate is appropriate unless the investor plans to (a) borrow the funds when they are due or (b) earn them from nonproject sources during the construction or rent-up period.

Another situation where an outflow may be forecast is where a property is financed with a rather lengthy (40-year) mortgage, as in certain subsidized housing programs. Projections for these programs are likely to be prepared with the assumption that the property will be worth no more than the outstanding mortgage balance at some future date. Although the investor may then sell the equity for only $1, there may be a substantial tax because of earlier depreciation write-offs, especially when accelerated depreciation is used. It is appropriate to discount such taxes at a low rate (i_L) and subtract them from prior inflows.

Often real property is financed at least partly with balloon payment mortgage loans. If an investor plans to meet the future payment with cash rather than a substitute loan, subtracting the discounted present value of the necessary payments at a low rate is in order because of the certainty that these must be paid.

INVESTMENT CRITERIA

Table 19–6 offers a summary of factors considered by various investment criteria. Those criteria that consider the time value of money are more sophisticated. It is suggested that others be used only as a preliminary screening device.

Analyst's Considerations

When selecting the criteria to be used, an analyst should consider:

1. The motivations and objectives of an investor.
2. The adequacy of information on the subject property and comparables.
3. Confidence in financial pro forma projections.
4. Time, money, and equipment availability.

TABLE 19-6

Factors Considered by Selected Investment Criteria

Factor	Payback Period	Gross Rent Multiplier	Overall Rate of Return	Equity Dividend Rate	Net Spendable Income	Total Annual Equity Returns	Average Annual Method	Net Present Value	Ellwood Technique	Internal Rate of Return	Modified Internal Rate	Financial Management Rate of Return
Vacancy allowance	*	*	Yes	Yes	Yes	Yes	Yes	Yes	Yes	Yes	Yes	Yes
Operating expenses	Yes	No	Yes	Yes	Yes	Yes	Yes	Yes	Yes	Yes	Yes	Yes
Return on total capital	*	No	Yes	No	No	No	No	*	Yes	*	No*	No*
Return on equity	No	No	No	Yes	Yes	Yes	Yes	Yes	Yes	Yes	Yes	Yes
Interest expense	No	No	No	Yes	Yes	Yes	Yes	Yes	Yes	Yes	Yes	Yes
Mortgage principal retirement	No	No	No	No	No	Yes	Yes	Yes	Yes	Yes	Yes	Yes
Depreciation (tax)	No	No	No	No	Yes	Yes*	Yes*	Yes*	No	Yes*	Yes*	Yes*
Property value changes	No	No	No	No	No	Yes	Yes	Yes	Yes	Yes	Yes	Yes
Holding period length	No	No	No	No	No	Yes	Yes	Yes	Yes	Yes	Yes	Yes
Income taxes	No	No	No	No	Yes	Yes	Yes	Yes*	No	Yes*	Yes*	Yes*
Capital gains tax	No	No	No	No	No	Yes	Yes	Yes*	No	Yes*	Yes*	Yes*
Time value of money	No	No	No	No	No	No	No	Yes	Yes	Yes	Yes	Yes
Specified reinvestment rate	No	No	No	No	No	No	No	Yes	Yes	No	Yes	Yes

*Depends on use.

REVIEW OF CAPITALIZATION RATES

A *capitalization rate* is defined in real estate literature as a rate used to convert an income stream into one capital (present) value, using the formula $V = I/R$; that is, the present value of an income stream is equal to the annual income divided by a capitalization rate.

The capitalization rate in real estate terminology is composed of two main elements:

1. The rate of return *on* investment.
2. The rate of return *of* investment.

The first element, the return *on* investment, is applicable to all income streams and is composed of four subelements:

1. A safe, liquid rate.
2. A rate for illiquidity.
3. A rate for the burdens of investment management (not property management).
4. A rate for the risk or uncertainty of the income stream and resale proceeds.

The second main element of a capitalization rate, the rate of return *of* investment (capital recovery rate), is applied to the *wasting* (depreciating) portion of assets. When the income is expected forever, as when there is no capital recovery, or when the same amount of capital paid for an investment is expected to remain intact and be realized upon a resale, a provision for capital recovery is unnecessary. Then the rate of return *on* investment is the capitalization rate. But when the asset is wasting—and all man-made assets have a limited useful life—a capital recovery rate is added to the rate of return on investment to derive a capitalization rate. If a real estate asset has a limited economic useful life of, say, 30 years, an investor would want a return *on* investment each year, plus recovery of the wasting, economically depreciating portion of the investment over its useful life.

Capital recovery rates can be derived by any of three methods:

1. Straight-line
2. Sinking fund
3. Annuity

Table 19-7 shows the three capital recovery methods considering a 12% discount rate.

TABLE 19-7
Capitalization Rate Derivation

Return on investment:		
Subelement 1.	Safe, liquid rate	9%
Subelement 2.	Illiquidity provision	1
Subelement 3.	Investment management	1
Subelement 4.	Risk provision	1
Subtotal:	Return on investment	12%
Plus return of investment, sinking fund factors:		
Ring, 0% straight-line for 30 years	= .0333 =	3.33%
Hoskold, 5% for 30 years	= .0150 =	1.50%
Inwood, 12% for 30 years	= .0041 =	.41%
Total capitalization rates are:		
Straight-line:	12% + 3.33% =	15.33%
Sinking fund:	12% + 1.50% =	13.50%
Annuity:	12% + .41% =	12.41%

The Straight-Line Method

The straight-line method is called the *Ring method.* It is defensible only when the income stream is expected to decline systematically. For example, an asset with a 30-year remaining life would have a 3⅓% per year straight-line capital recovery rate. This is because 100% of the asset must be recovered over 30 years, which is 3⅓% per year. The capitalization rate is therefore 15⅓%, comprised of a 12% return on investment plus 3⅓% capital recovery rate.

Sinking Fund Method

The sinking fund method is also called the *Hoskold method.* In this method, a conservative reinvestment rate is applied to the portion of income that is considered to be a return *of* investment. For example, consider again the asset with a 30-year useful life. If one were to attempt to put aside each year in a savings account a portion of the cost of the asset, an annual deposit of less than 3⅓% of its cost would be more than adequate to fully recover the asset cost over 30 years. A deposit of 3⅓% per year would recover the entire cost in 30 years even without interest. If the earnings assumption is conservative, say, a savings fund that pays a 5% rate of compound interest, then the capital recovery rate would be .01505, which is the sinking fund factor at 5% for 30 years. If 1½% (.015) of the asset cost is deposited each year in a fund that earns at a 5% rate of interest, that fund would grow to 100% of the asset cost after 30 years. The capitalization rate is then 12% plus 1½%, or 13.5%.

The Annuity Method

The annuity method is also called the *Inwood method.* It is used when income is expected to remain constant over the income projection period as with a secure net-net lease. If the portion of periodic income considered to be capital recovery is assumed to be reinvested at the same rate as the return *on* investment, then the annuity method is to be used. For example, when the desired return on the subject investment is 12%, the sinking fund factor at that rate for 30 years is .0041. The sum of these would be a capitalization rate of .1241. This figure is the same as the installment to amortize one. The annuity capitalization rate is equivalent to treating level annual income as a series of individual reversions and applying the present worth of one factor to each annual amount of income.

Effect of Capitalization Rates on Value

Higher capitalization rates result in lower values on a given income stream; conversely, lower capitalization rates place higher values on the same income stream. Low capitalization rates are justified when (a) the safe, liquid rate of return—such as that offered on passbook savings accounts—is low, and (b) there is little investment management, (c) the asset is highly liquid with little risk, and (d) little or no economic depreciation is expected. Higher capitalization rates (and hence lower property values) are justified when at least one of the above conditions does not exist. Capitalization rates used should reflect current local market conditions.

When considering the net operating income of a real estate investment, an overall capital rate can be used to convert all of the net operating income into the property value. Therefore, if forecast net operating income is $65,000, and the overall rate is 15⅓%, the value of the income is $65,000 divided by .1533, or $424,005. If the overall rate drops to 13.5%, the value increases to $481,481. An overall rate of 12.41% gives a value of $523,771. Note that a small change in the capitalization rate results in a significant change in the property value estimate.

Use of Capital Recovery Rates

The *Ring straight-line capital recovery rate* should be used when income is expected to decline, as in older property that is continually sustaining higher operating expenses for repairs and maintenance and/or lower rentals. In such a case, divide the straight-line capitalization rate into the current year's net operating income to derive the property value estimate.

The amount of income decline assumed by the straight-line technique is the amount of capital recaptured each year multiplied by the rate of interest. For example, suppose the first year's income is \$65,000. The property value is \$65,000 divided by .15333 or about \$424,000. This figure divided by 30 years gives an annual capital recovery of \$14,133 per year. Twelve percent interest applied to \$14,133 is \$1,696; this amount is the annual income decline, using the straight-line presumption. The second year, presumed net operating income is \$63,304 (\$65,000 minus \$1,696).

The *Hoskold method* should be used when the rate of return generated by the subject property is especially high and is not expected to be matched in a reinvestment situation. For example, suppose that an investor struck an oil well that generates substantial profits but has a limited supply of oil. Some of the returns are a recovery *of* the costs (as the well is depleted), and some are a return *on* investment. However, it is doubtful that the investor will be so lucky on his next try for oil. Therefore, the investor should save, so that when the well runs dry, the same amount as his initial capital will have been saved. If he assumes that the interest rate on his savings account will be 5%, instead of a higher rate that is available only on risky ventures, the Hoskold method is being applied.

The *Inwood method* (annuity capital recovery) implicitly assumes that return of capital can be reinvested at the same rate as the yield to maturity of the subject investment. It would be properly applied to level periodic income as in a net lease, or where rental increases will offset operating expense increases, or to the income stream generated by mortgage receipts.

Capital recovery is not necessary when the principal remains intact or when the income stream is perpetual. Then, the capitalization rate is the same as the interest or discount rate.

Composite Rates

The *overall capitalization rate* (OAR) applied to a real estate asset may be considered as a composite rate of return. An appraiser can approach the asset from two points of view: (1) physical, and (2) financial. From a physical standpoint, the overall capitalization rate represents a return *on* the nonwasting land, and a return *on* and *of* the improvements because they have a limited useful life. From a financial standpoint, an overall rate represents a composite of interest and principal repayment to a lender, with return *on* and *of* investment to the equity investor.

Residual capitalization techniques include *land, buildings,* and *property.* The land residual technique can be used best when the building represents the highest and best use of the site and the cost of construction approximates its value. The building residual technique can be used *only* when the site value estimate and income claims are known. The property residual technique values all of the income that is forecast to be received over a projection period; then adds the present value of the resale amount, which is called the *reversion.*

Selection of Capitalization Rates

When selecting a capitalization rate, remember that:

1. The higher the rate, the lower the value.
2. Conversely, the lower the rate, the higher the value.
3. Always consider return *on* and *of* investment.
4. Capitalization rates are applied to a stream of income, not to a lump-sum payment.

Capitalization rates should be applied to the appropriate segment of income. When dealing with net operating income, use an overall capitalization rate that accounts for both land and improvements, or for mortgage and equity, with proportions and rates properly weighted.

Capitalization rates are convenient for valuing income streams. The selection of a rate must be carefully studied from the market and reflect both return *on* and *of* investment.

SUMMARY

There are various decision tools used to value real estate and as criteria to rank investment offerings. They range in sophistication from simple relationships of purchase price to gross income, to complex geometric (compounded) types applied to after-tax cash flow. The analyst or appraiser, in order to arrive at a conclusion, should evaluate the subject property using the most meaningful criteria. Generally, the less sophisticated techniques can be used as rough measures or as checks by appraisers and as screening devices by investment counselors. More sophisticated techniques can be applied to derive value estimates or rank investment opportunities.

Capitalization of income is defined as estimating the lump-sum present value of a stream of income. Capitalization rates are composed of two elements: one is return on investment; the other is a recovery of investment. Overall capitalization rates consider property value estimates based on net operating income. They should include a *return on* and a *recovery of* investment, and should be an appropriate composite of building and land value estimates, and/or mortgage and equity value estimates.

Only with an understanding of the various tools for income property analysis does one become prepared to meet the variety of challenges that are encountered in appraisal and analysis of real estate.

Questions

1. A small office building is for sale for $1,000,000, subject to a $600,000 first mortgage at 10% interest, self-amortizing over 20 years with monthly payments. The present tenant has a 50-year lease at a rental of $120,000 per year and must pay all operating expenses in excess of $40,000 per year. (Operating expenses are presently $50,000 and are expected to increase each year.) The property value depreciates by $10,000 per year and will be resold in 15 years. Disregard income taxes.
   a. How much is the net operating income?
   b. How much is the before-tax cash flow?
   c. How much is the forecast reversion upon resale, after the mortgage balance at resale is subtracted?
   d. How long is the payback period?
   e. What is the overall rate of return?
   f. What is the equity dividend rate?
   g. What is the net present value of equity returns, discounted at a 15% rate?
   h. Estimate the internal rate of return to equity.

Essay Questions

1. Define:
   a. Payback period.
   b. Gross rent multiplier.
   c. Overall rate of return.
   d. Equity divided rate.
   e. Internal rate of return.
2. How does the overall rate of return (OAR) improve on the gross rent multiplier? What factors does the OAR fail to consider?
3. Why is it important to consider the timing of investment inflows and outflows?
4. How does the net present value technique differ from the internal rate of return?
5. What is the main element that is common to both the modified internal rate and financial management rate of return? How does that element cause those techniques to differ from the internal rate of return? What capitalization method is similar to the modified internal rate of return?
6. What main elements must real estate capitalization rate consider? What are the various methods of deriving an overall capitalization rate?

Chapter 20

Partial Interest in Real Estate

The concept of rights to real estate is often expressed by the *bundle of sticks* method. Visualize a person holding a bundle of sticks in his/her hand. Each stick represents a right to the property. Some sticks (rights) may be sold or donated by the owner, or some may be taken away by law. The result is that at least some ownership rights (and perhaps obligations) are transferred to another party. Thus, each party is left with only a partial interest in the property. This chapter addresses many of the various partial interests, the value of them, and the value of the fee interest.

Partial interests include financial claims against the property, restrictions that limit the time duration of one's possession, restrictions that limit the use of property, and restrictions that physically divide the property. Each of the various restrictions and the manner in which they are used will have an effect on the property value.

In lieu of using a bundle of sticks to illustrate various ownership interests, circles are used as illustrations in this chapter. Fee simple absolute, which is complete ownership with full disposition rights, is represented by an entire circle in Figure 20-1. Portions of circles are interests that are not held by the fee owner or that limit the owner's use.

FINANCIAL CLAIMS

There are various types of financial claims against real property. Some of the claims are so strong that they must be satisfied before the fee owner can sell any interest.

The most commonly encountered financial claim is the mortgage. There are also fractional interests in real estate whereby vari-

FIGURE 20-1. Illustration of Fee Simple Absolute Ownership.

ous parties own different portions of the real estate. These portions can include joint ventures, options, sales contracts, contracts for deed, and liens. A brief discussion on the financial analysis of these partial interests follows.

Mortgage

A mortgage is a pledge of property as collateral for a debt. (In some states, title to the property is transferred to the lender, but the transferor retains the rights to use of the property and to ownership, providing there is no default on the debt.) Mortgages have various provisions that financially affect the property value such as for *equity participation.* See Figure 20-2.

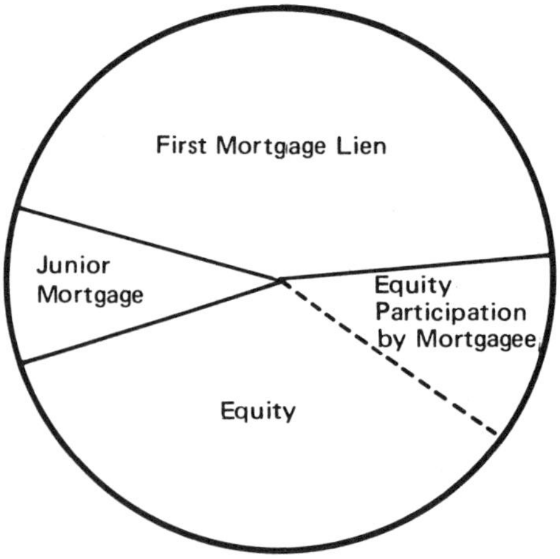

FIGURE 20-2. Mortgage Claims: Effect on Equity.

The mortgage loan that is first to be borrowed against previously free and clear property is called the *first mortgage.* The equity owner may borrow additional amounts on mortgaged property by arranging *junior mortgages* against the property, such as for second and third claims. The priority of each subsequent mortgage is lower. Upon default and a foreclosure sale, the first mortgage lender is repaid in full before junior lenders receive anything. In the absence of an agreement to the contrary, junior mortgages move to a higher priority when those that had higher priority are paid off or subordinated. *Subordination* is moving a lien to a lower priority.

Valuation of the income from mortgage loans was described in Chapter 9. Generally, the value of a mortgage loan is based on the present worth of expected income. The lower in priority a mortgage loan, the higher the interest rate should be to reflect additional risk.

The influence of financing instruments on the price of real estate was discussed in Chapter 10. Generally, financing, either good or poor, is likely to be reflected in the price of the real estate.

Most mortgages include special provisions that require equity owners to do (or not to do) specified things. Among such provisions are those dealing with financial matters, such as requiring more to be paid than minimal interest and principal. On income-producing property, *participation* is frequently encountered.

Equity participation (also called *mortgage participation)* entitles a lender to receive a share of income and/or appreciation from the property in addition to payments for interest and principal retirement. Each participation agreement is unique. Some agreements require the payment of a stated percentage of effective gross income, net operating income, or cash flow. Other agreements require a share of income in excess of a base amount, such as 5% of effective gross income above $500,000. Still other agreements allow the lender to share in the appreciation or resale proceeds. Definitions of annual income or of resale proceeds for the purposes of determining the participation amount will not necessarily agree with those definitions that are typically used in general real estate literature. Consequently, appraisers and analysts must understand the details of such agreements and the manner in which terms are defined.

After understanding the agreements and considering relevant market data, forecasts can be prepared of amounts expected to be paid under participation agreements. These amounts can be discounted to a present value estimate. It is suggested that the interest or discount rate applied should exceed the mortgage rate of interest to reflect the uncertainty of the excess earnings that will be paid pursuant to the participation agreement.

Fractional Interests

Ownership of land and improvements are sometimes separated in order to accomplish tax and/or financial objectives. By splitting property ownership, the various parties can receive the particular ownership interest and collateral that they desire. The sum of the prices paid for each component should exceed the price that would be realized from the sale of the property as a whole, or else fractionating is not worthwhile.

It is possible to sell the land that is beneath a shopping center or office building, and simultaneously lease it back for a long term (over 25 years). The lease allows the seller to retain control of the property, and the simultaneous sale generates substantial cash for the seller. The landowner receives periodic lease payments and rights to the resale of the property. An improvement may be sold to another party who may gain the right to depreciate it for tax purposes. One mortgage may encumber land and improvements; alternatively, the building and land may be encumbered by separate mortgages. Management rights, including the privilege of sharing in property income, may be sold separately. See Figure 20-3. With careful tax and legal planning, ownership of the total property is separated so that benefits to different parties fit the objectives of each. This type of property fractionating is sometimes called William Zeckendorf's "Hawaiian technique."[1]

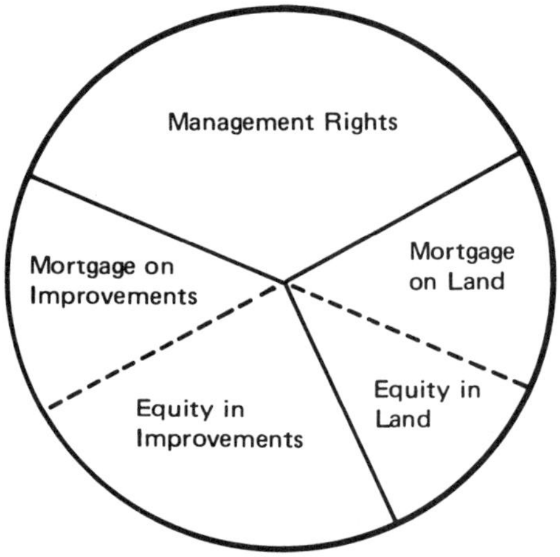

FIGURE 20-3. Fractional Interests: Share of Property Value.

[1]William Zeckendorf, *Autobiography of Zeckendorf* (New York: Holt, Rinehart, and Winston, 1970).

When attempting to value a partial interest such as a land lease, or the right to income from improvements, the appraiser must understand the entire agreement in order to estimate the risks and potential returns from the particular interest being considered. It is preferable to estimate annual income for the entire property, then subtract requirements for prior claims, to derive the income or cash flow available to the interest being considered. The income to the interest and the forecast residual can be capitalized to estimate the value of the interest.

Joint Ventures

A property or an interest in real property can be sold to investors who pool their resources for a specific investment. The pooling of investment funds for a specific project is called a *joint venture.*

Joint ventures can take on a myriad of forms (see Figure 20-4). They can be a *tenancy in common,* whereby each participant's share is alike; a *general partnership,* whereby each participant is a partner; a *limited partnership,* in which at least one partner is liable beyond the amount invested and at least one partner's liability is limited; or an agreement that gives one participant preferred returns. *Preferred returns* allow an investor to claim a certain amount of income or cash flow before other participants receive any income.

The distinction between a partnership and a joint venture is that the joint venture is formed for just one investment purpose; whereas in a partnership, the general partners may bind other partners to another venture provided the new business is within the scope of the partnership. However, many partnerships are formed for the purpose of owning just one parcel of real estate; so they, as a practical matter, are a form of a joint venture.

Partnerships, tenancy in common arrangements, corporations, trusts, and other ownership vehicles are subject to certain uniform and/or individual state laws concerning transferability, continuity, control, and taxation. It is necessary to understand the distinctions when structuring a transaction.

An appraiser attempting to estimate the value of an interest should understand the entire agreement. Risks and returns are balanced using different discount rates depending on whether the interest is subordinated, the degree of risk, and personal liability.

Options and Conditional Sales Contracts

An *option* is the right but not the obligation to buy certain property at a stated price within a time period. A *conditional sales contract* imposes the obligation to buy unless the stipulated conditions are

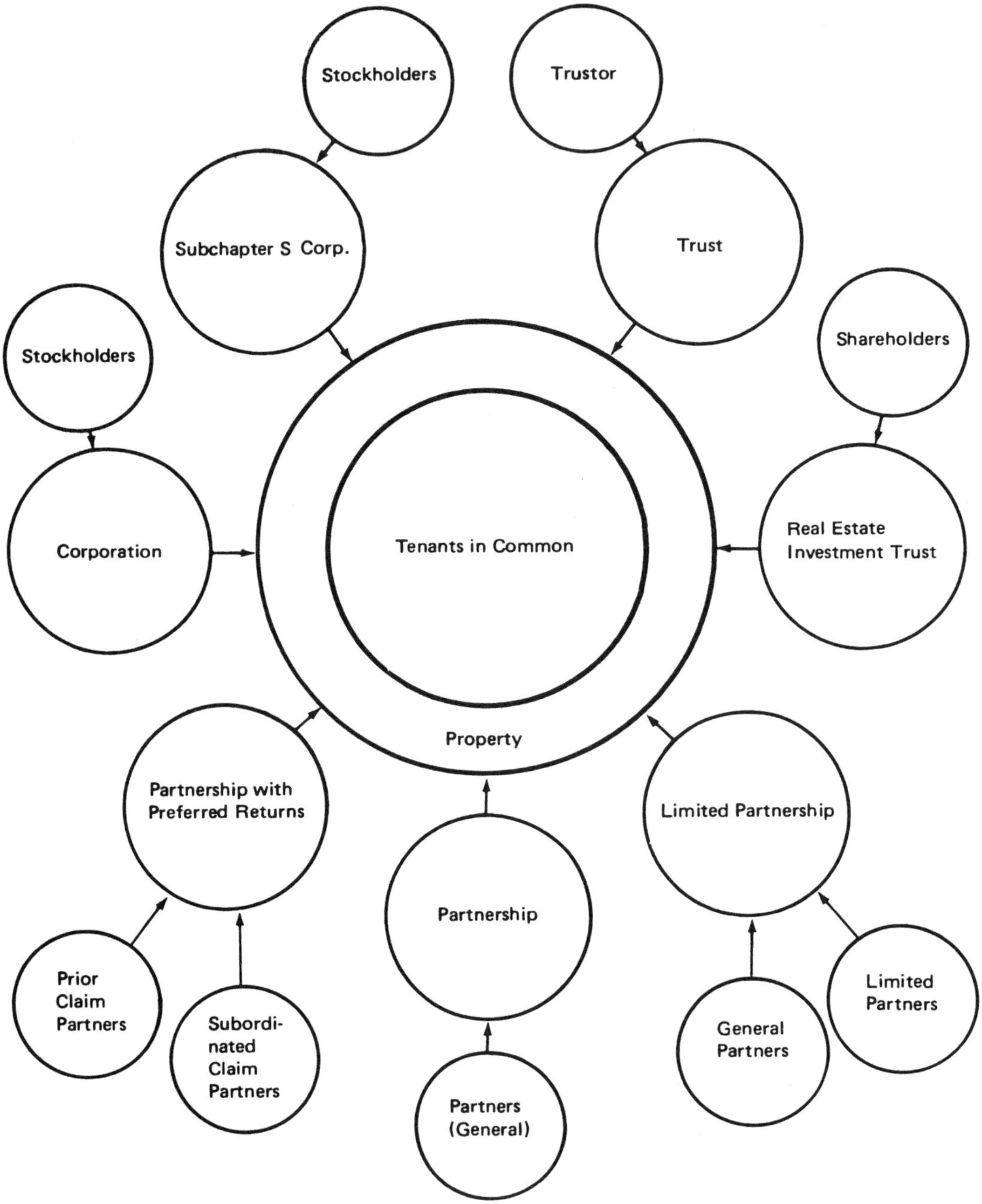

FIGURE 20-4. Forms of a Joint Venture.

not met. Commonly used conditions include financing, rezoning, approval by partners, soil-boring test results, transfer of marketable title, and others. See Figure 20-5.

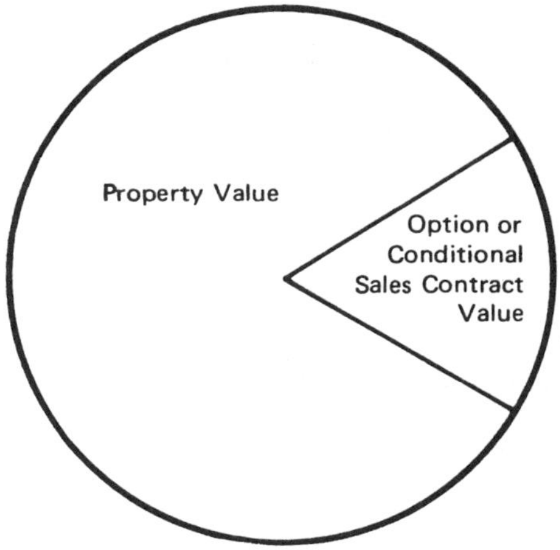

FIGURE 20-5. Potential Value of an Option or Conditional Sales Contract.

When an option or conditional sales contract encumbers property, it must be recognized. Generally, the highest price that the fee owner can realize at that time is the amount specified in the option or contract, although the price ultimately realized may be less. Opportunities for further value appreciation for the fee owner are limited to those situations when the contract is not exercised. However, an option or contract holder will seldom default knowing that the property has appreciated above the contractual amount; therefore property value gains above the contractual price seldom accrue to the fee owner.

The option or contract can be quite valuable. With appreciation, the agreed contractual price for the property may be or soon becomes less than the property's market value. The excess of property value over the agreed price accrues to the option or contract holder, who can sell or assign rights without acquiring title to the property. The estimated market value of an option or contract is generally the difference between the market value of the property and the contractual price. During an option's exercise period, some speculators would pay a premium for the extreme leverage if the market is active and rising. In calm markets, an option or contract may have little value because of the approaching expiration or closing date.

Contract for Deed

A contract for deed, also called an *installment sales contract* or a *land contract,* does not normally transfer a deed until the purchaser has completed all of the payments on the property. This type of contract is frequently used for recreational lot sales and for sales in which the purchaser's credit is uncertain. Since title does not pass until the final payment, it is easy for the owner to regain possession upon default. It should be noted that each state may pass laws modifying the rules as to when title passes under a contract for deed.

The borrower, under a contract for deed, is frequently not considered to be a serious buyer until many payments have been met and therefore substantial equity has been built up. To estimate the amount of equity, an appraiser should estimate the property value, then subtract the present value of remaining payments. See Figure 20-6.

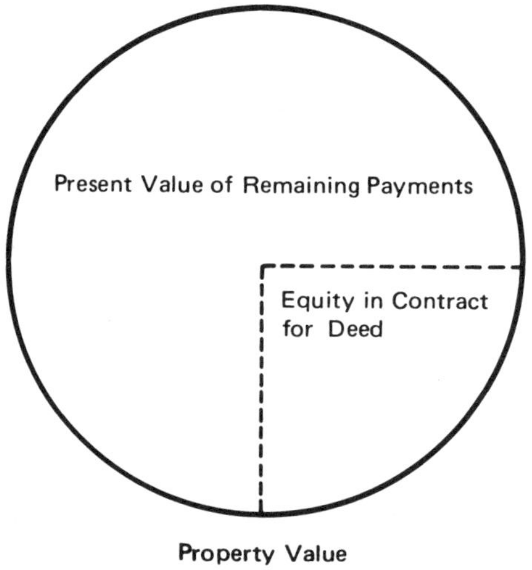

FIGURE 20-6. Property Subject to Contract for Deed.

Other Liens

Judgments against property, as well as mechanics' and tax liens, must be satisfied currently; if not, then through a foreclosure sale. The amount of a lien plus interest and penalties should be subtracted from the estimated property value to derive the owner's estimated equity. It should also be noted that the threat of imminent foreclosure is likely to cause a further reduction of property value. See Figure 20-7.

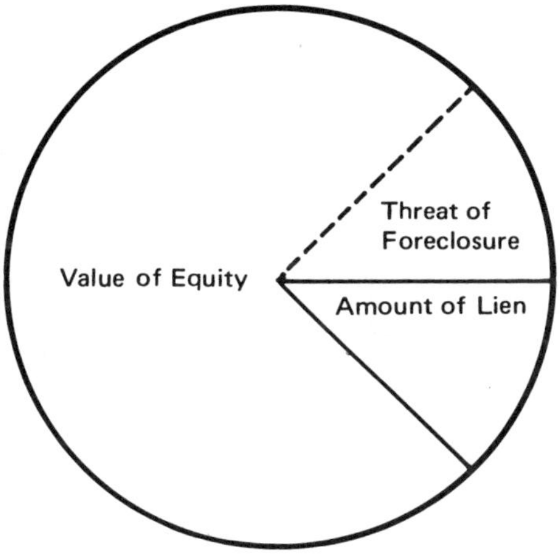

FIGURE 20–7. Liens and Judgments Affect Value of Equity.

TIME DURATION OF POSSESSION

The time duration of possession of real estate can be divided among different interests, with a value approximated for each interest. Two common time-splitting devices are leases and life estates.

Leases

A lease transfers possession with rights to use property, but not fee ownership. The tenant (lessee) has a leasehold estate. The landlord owns the leased fee.

The value of a leasehold can be substantial. Long-term leases at rents that are fixed and below market have a market value; the value can be estimated from the remaining term and below-market rent. For example, if the lease requires $1,000 as the annual net rent for the next 50 years, and the market rental rate is $5,000 per year, the $4,000 per year difference may be capitalized to estimate the leasehold value. The leased fee is worth the present value of the $1,000 annual payment (discounted at a riskless rate because the tenant is unlikely to default) plus the discounted present value of the property upon the lease expiration date. Taken together, the two interests should approximate the total market value of the property. The leasehold, if it is sublet, creates another ownership interest that may have value depending on its terms. See Figure 20–8.

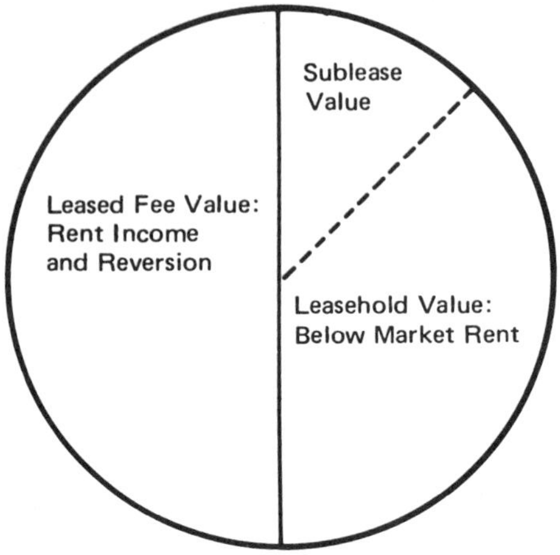

FIGURE 20-8. Leasehold and Leased Fee Valuation.

Life Estate

A life estate allows one to use property for a person's lifetime or for the life of another (*pur autre vie*). Upon death, the remainderman becomes the sole owner. Thus, the market value of the property is divided among two persons: one with the right of use for life; the other's use commences upon the life tenant's death.

Either the life tenant or the remainderman is permitted to sell the interest owned. One who buys the life tenant's interest loses it upon the life tenant's death; a purchaser of the remainderman's interest cannot use the property until the life tenant dies. Therefore, the prices paid (and hence market value of the interests) will vary depending on the life expectancy of the life tenant, and a purchaser's willingness to accept the life tenant's life span as either the termination or beginning period for use. See Figure 20-9.

For estate and inheritance tax purposes, annuity and mortality tables are typically allowed (or required) to estimate the value of a life estate and remainder. For example, if the mortality tables indicate that the life tenant has 20 years of life remaining, and the appropriate interest rate is 8%, the life tenant's share of the value is \$78.55 per \$100 of the property's current value (annuity of \$8 per year for 20 years at 8%); whereas the remainderman's interest is worth \$21.45 (reversion of \$100 in 20 years at 8%) per \$100 of the property's present value.

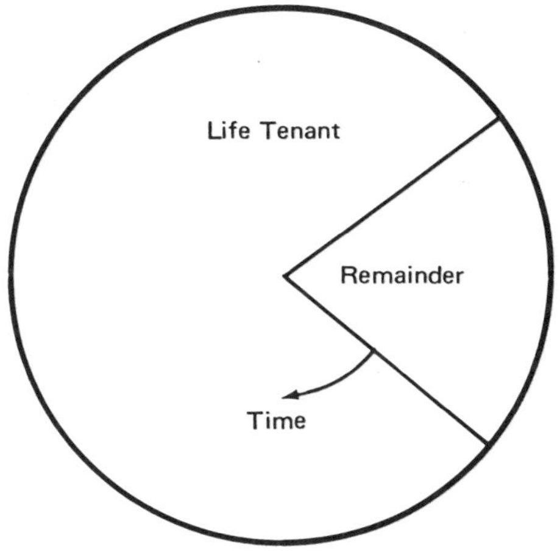

FIGURE 20-9. Life Tenant and Remainder Interests Share in Property Value.

USE OF PROPERTY

Rights in real estate may be limited by agreements that allow or prevent certain uses. Parties with the privilege of using (or not using) property may receive financial benefits. Commonly encountered situations that limit the use of real estate include easements, deed or subdivision restrictions, restrictions set by grant, exercise of police powers, condominium controls, and the creation of rights in separate physical layers of property. See Figure 20-10.

FIGURE 20-10. Influence on Value of Restrictions on Use.

Easements

Easements are the right to use property owned by another for a special purpose. For example, billboards may be erected on easements; or power company transmission line paths and other land needs of utilities are often satisfied by the use of easements. Easements may enhance the value of real estate when they generate adequate revenue (billboard rent), attract desired services (utilities to the property), or provide access to other properties. They may detract from value when they represent nuisances (unsightly utility wires), indicate flood plains, or prevent alternative profitable property uses. See Figure 20-11. Unless specifically excluded by the appraisal report, appraisers should ascertain the effect of easements on the property being considered and easements on other's properties that the subject property owner can enjoy.

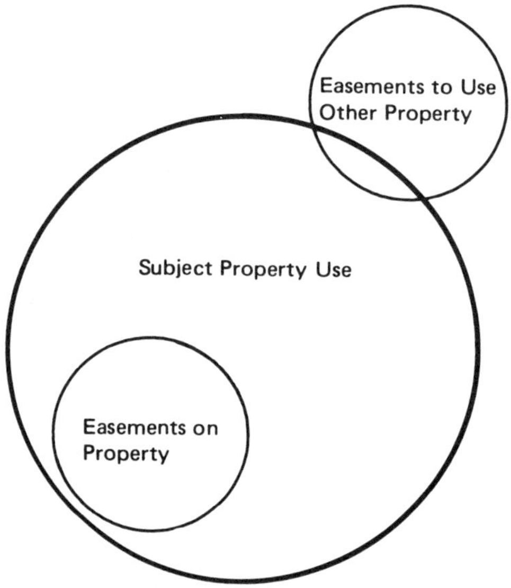

FIGURE 20-11. Easements That Affect Value.

Deed and Subdivision Restrictions

Restrictions may be created in several ways and for several purposes. They include deed restrictions, subdivision restrictions, and restrictions set by grant or will.

Deed restrictions may limit or prohibit certain property uses. Examples are restrictions that prohibit businesses on the subject property from being open on Sundays, or prohibit the sale of alcoholic beverages on the property; or there may be covenants that specify the property may not compete with certain enterprises. If a restriction is upheld in court, the value of the property may be affected. The restriction may result in preventing property from being developed in a manner consistent with its highest and best use. Although the restriction may have only psychic value to one party, it could significantly affect the property value.

Subdivision restrictions are typically imposed prior to the development of improvements. These are usually intended to require harmonious use of the lots within a subdivision. Examples include prohibition of business establishments within the subdivision, a requirement for a minimum size of home, or specification of architectural styles, etc. Although intended to insulate all homes against unwanted uses within the subdivision and thus maintain the subdivision's integrity, the restriction may also prevent alternative profitable uses of certain lots. Lots on busy intersections would be more valuable as commercial property if not for the deed restriction. Consequently, the value of some lots within a subdivision will be enhanced due to the restriction, and the value of others will be decreased.

Restrictions may be set by *grant* or by *will.* The use of property for a park, school, or other purpose will limit its value in the open market; it may also positively affect the value of surrounding property. See Figure 20-12.

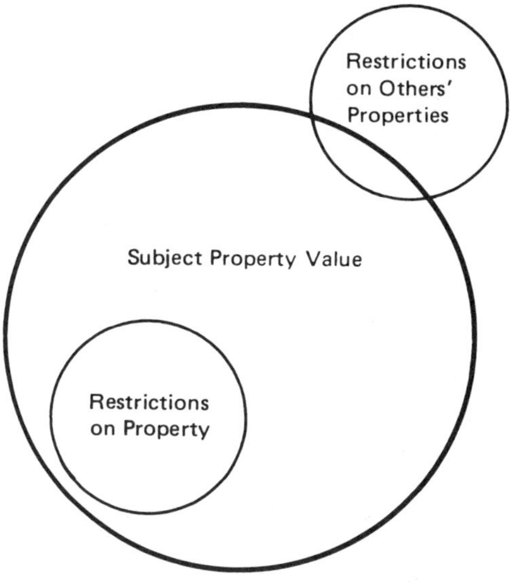

FIGURE 20-12. Effect of Restrictions on Property Value.

Governmental Regulations

Governments will exercise their rights of police power to protect the health, safety, and welfare of their citizens by promulgating and enforcing zoning laws, building codes, and environmental requirements. They also have the right of *eminent domain,* which allows taking private property for public use.

Zoning limits the use of property, thus preventing certain improvements from being built. The effect on property values can be substantial. Unless the appraisal report specifically notes that present zoning requirements are not considered, value estimates derived should be based on the existing legal framework.

Building codes are intended to require safe and sanitary structures. However, unless there is substantial variation among communities, or unless there have been significant changes in building code requirements, adjustments for differences among comparable properties described in appraisal reports should be minor. When variations are significant, both site and improvement values may be affected. For example, if building codes have recently been made more rigorous, development may be more expensive. This will, at least temporarily, enhance the value of existing structures. Simultaneously, it may reduce the value of suitable land because added construction costs, without a corresponding increase in market rental rates, will cause a project to be less feasible considering the land residual capitalization process.

Environmental protection requirements may have the same effect; the compliance time and effort itself will cause added costs. See Figure 20–12.

Condemnation or its threat will also cause changes in the subject property's value. Or a man-made lake constructed to meet local water needs will create lakefront lots as well as underwater property from the same tract.

Condominium Controls

Common areas of condominiums, whether apartment-style or office, may create the need for use restrictions. Common areas include corridors of a building, access roads, parking areas, elevators, swimming pool, tennis courts, and others that are owned by an association. See Figure 20–13. Rules must be established for the use of such areas and for the sharing of maintenance expenses. When estimating the value of an office condominium, for example, an appraiser must consider not only the unit or floor owned but also the amenities of the common areas and their maintenance expenses.

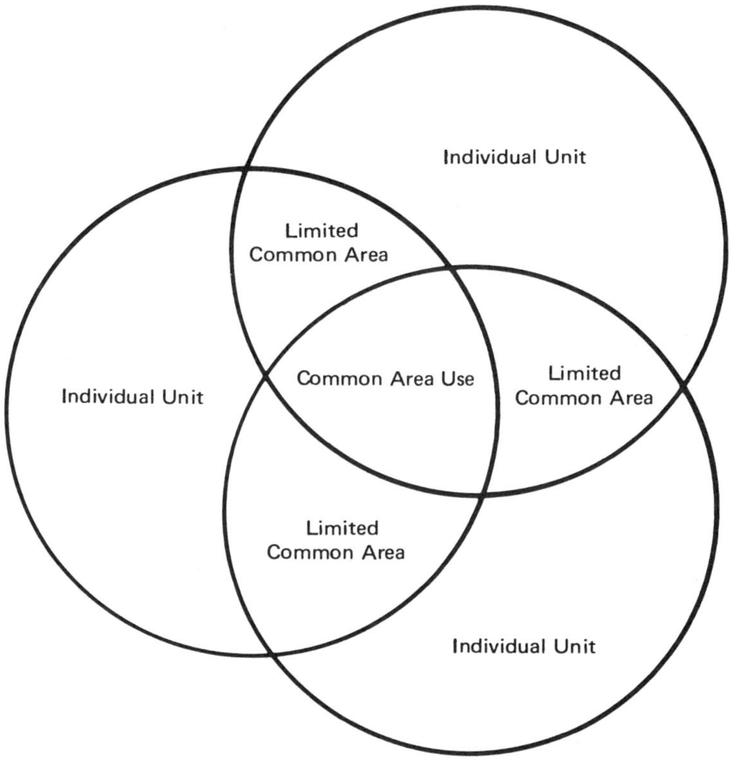

FIGURE 20-13. Condominium Ownership: Common Area Uses.

Physical Layers of Property

Property may be divided physically by the distinction between surface, mineral, and air rights. For example, the surface of a tract can be used for a railroad yard; and simultaneously it is possible to construct an office building over the tracks and to lease rights to minerals that are beneath the surface. In some situations it is desirable to carve the layers such that the value of the entire tract is enhanced. As for other partial interests, it is important to understand all agreements and how potential conflicts will be resolved. The value of each activity can then be estimated, as well as the property value as a whole.

SUMMARY

Rights to real estate may be partitioned in a number of ways: financially, by duration, and by use. In order to estimate the value of the fractional or partial interest, and of the remaining fee, an appraiser must first develop an understanding of the entire transaction. An estimate of the forecast income or loss for each interest should be determined, followed by an attempt to value the interest(s).

Complex financial, legal, and physical divisions of property are commonplace in real estate. Efforts to value property or interests must consider all relevant matters, including financial claims, duration of possession, and rights to use property.

Essay Questions

1. List and explain the influence of the following on the value of real estate:
   a. Mortgage debt.
   b. Equity participation.
   c. Options and contract.
   d. Liens.
   e. Leaseholds.
   f. Life estates.
   g. Easements.
   h. Deed restrictions.
   i. Government regulations.
   j. Air rights.
   k. Mineral rights.
2. Explain how the appraisal process is applied to estimate the value of partial interests.

Appendix A

Solutions to Practice Problems in Chapters 12 and 13

Chapter 12

PRACTICE PROBLEM 1

Solve for value, given estimate of resale price or dollar changes.

The mechanics are simplified when an estimate of the expected resale price is known instead of a percentage value change. For example, suppose it is estimated that the property would resell for $500,000 in ten years. The present value estimate is then:

V = PWAF(CF) + PWF(PS) + MP
V = 5.01877 ($14,445) + .2472 ($500,000 − $351,000) + $400,000
V = $72,496 + .2472 ($149,000) + $400,000
V = $72,496 + $36,833 + $400,000
V = $509,328
Rounded to $509,000

If it were estimated that the property would resell for a certain dollar change from the present value, the resale portion of the equation would change. Suppose the property is expected to decline by $50,000. The equation will be:

V = PWCF + PWF(V − $50,000 − OS) + MP
V = $72,496 + .2472 ($V$ − $50,000 − $351,000) + $400,000
V = $72,496 + .2472 V − $12,360 − $86,767 + $400,000

Collecting terms:

$$.7528\ V = \$373{,}369$$
$$V = \$373{,}369/.7528$$
$$V = \$495{,}974$$
Rounded to \$496,000

PRACTICE PROBLEM 2

Solve for value, given NOI, mortgage principal and terms, and percentage property value changes.

Given:

\$65,000 annual NOI
\$400,000 mortgage at 12% interest, 25 years
Therefore, debt service = \$50,555 per year
10% property value increase
10-year projection period
15% equity yield rate

V = PWAF(NOI − DS) + PWF (RP − OS) + MP

Insert known values:

PWAF @ 15%, for 10 years	= 5.01877
NOI	= \$65,000
DS	= \$50,555
PWF	= .2472
RP = 10% above V	= 1.1V
OS	= \$351,000
MP	= \$400,000

Then:

$$V = 5.01877\ (\$65{,}000 - \$50{,}555) + .2472\ (1.1V - \$351{,}000) + \$400{,}000$$
$$V = \$72{,}496 + .2719V - \$86{,}767 + \$400{,}000$$

Collecting terms:

$$.7281V = \$385{,}729$$
$$V = \$385{,}729/.7281$$
$$V = \$529{,}775$$

As a check, assume that the value is $529,775 as indicated. The resale price in ten years will be 10% higher than that amount, which is $582,752 ($529,775 + $52,977 = $582,752).

Treating the cash flow and reversion separately, the property value is checked as follows:

Stage I.	Estimate present worth of cash flow		
	Net operating income	$ 65,000	
	Less: Debt service	− 50,555	
	Annual cash flow	$ 14,445	
	Multiply by present worth annuity factor	× 5.01877	
	Present value of cash flow		$ 72,496
Stage II.	Estimate proceeds from resale		
	Resale price	$582,752	
	Less: Mortgage debt in 10 years	−351,000	
	Proceeds from resale	$231,752	
	Multiply by present worth factor	× .2472	$ 57,289
Stage III.	Present value of mortgage		$400,000
	Present property value		$529,785
	Rounded to		$530,000

Modification of Practice Problem 2 That Considers Forecast Value Decline

Had a 10% property value decline been forecast, the present property value would be estimated at $496,000 as shown below:

$$V = 5.01877\ (\$14{,}445) + .2472\ (.9V - \$351{,}000) + \$400{,}000$$
$$V = \$72{,}496 + .22248V - \$86{,}767 \times \$400{,}000$$

Collecting terms:

$$.77752V = \$385{,}729$$
$$V = \$385{,}729/.77752$$
$$V = \$496{,}102$$
Rounded to $496,000

Note: It is not inconsistent that the present price varies with the resale value estimate. Investors will pay more for property when they expect appreciation. Therefore, the values of $530,000 anticipating

10% appreciation and of $496,000 anticipating a 10% value decline are both technically correct. The higher the rate of forecast appreciation, the greater the present value.

PRACTICE PROBLEM 3

Solve for value, given a loan-to-value estimate.

Often, a market-derived loan-to-value ratio and mortgage terms are known, but not the mortgage principal. The mortgage principal has an effect on the annual debt service and on the proceeds from resale. In this case, algebraic computations by the conventional technique are cumbersome when the loan-to-value ratio is given in lieu of a principal balance. Therefore, the Ellwood formulation, described in Chapter 13 is mechanically easier to apply.

With the conventional technique, given only the loan-to-value ratio and mortgage terms (interest rate, amortization term), the debt service constant is applied to the loan-to-value ratio. This result offers the fraction of present value that must be paid annually as debt service. Assuming an 80% loan-to-value ratio and no property value change over the holding period e.g. ($V = \text{RP}$), the conventional technique becomes:

$$V = \text{PWAF}\ [\text{NOI} - .8V(f)] + \text{PWR}\ [\text{RP} - .8V(b)] + .8V$$

In the example consistently used throughout, the numbers are:

$$V = 5.01877\ [\$65{,}000 - .8V\,(.126387)] + .2472\ [V - .8V\,(.8775)] + .8V$$

Multiplying inner terms:

$$V = 5.01877\ (\$65{,}000 - .1011096V) + .2472\ (V - .702V) + .8V$$

Multiplication by outer terms:

$$V = \$326{,}220 - .50744584V + .2472V - .1735344V + .8V$$

Collecting terms:

$$V = \$326{,}220 + .3662178V$$
$$.6337822\ V = \$326{,}220$$
$$V = \$514{,}719$$

Thus, the result of the manipulation offers a value estimate of \$514,719. An 80% loan of that amount is \$411,776 (80% of \$514,719 = \$411,776). In 10 years, the remaining mortgage balance will be 87.75% of its present balance.

As a check, presume a loan of that principal amount, 25-year term, 12% interest rate, as shown below:

Stage I

NOI		\$ 65,000	
Less: DS .126387 × \$411,776	=	−52,043	
CF		\$ 12,957	
Multiply by annuity factor @ 15%		× 5.01877	
PWCF			\$ 65,028

Stage II

Resale price (no value change)		\$514,719	
Less: O S Mortgage: .8775 × \$411,776	=	−361,333	
Reversion		\$153,386	
Multiply by PWR PWF		× .2472	
			\$ 37,917

Stage III

Mortgage balance	\$411,776
Total property value	\$514,721

Note: A slight difference in the results of the two techniques occurs because of rounding.

PRACTICE PROBLEM 4

Solve for value, given loan-to-value ratio and value change.

The preceding example can be modified to reflect an anticipated value change over the projection period, whether in dollars or percentages. The only modification needed is in the resale proceeds (RP) term. An anticipated value decline of 30% over the projection period can be accomplished by changing RP to $.7V$. Anticipated appreciation of 30% requires RP to be $1.3V$.

$$V = 5.01877\ (\$65{,}000 - .1011096V) + .32136V - .173534V + .8V$$
$$V = \$326{,}220 - .507446V + .32136V - .173534V + .8V$$
$$V = \$326{,}220 - .44038V$$

Collecting terms:

$$.55962V = \$326,220$$
$$V = \$582,931$$

Dollar estimates of RP can also be substituted, as can dollars of gain. As an example, RP of $600,000 can be substituted to represent a $600,000 resale price. Or in lieu of $100,000 appreciation, $V+$ $100,000 can be substituted for RP.

PRACTICE PROBLEM 5

Solve for equity yield rate, given the present property value.

In previous practice problems, a 15% equity yield rate was assumed. The price of the real estate was unknown. Should the equity yield rate be unknown at a given property price, a trial-and-error process is needed to estimate the rate. At various equity yield rates, substitute in the equation the appropriate factors for PWAF and PWF, until an equality is found.

For example, assume a $500,000 price with no forecast change in value over the projection period, and a $400,000 mortgage at 12% interest, 25-year term. The equation is:

$$V = \text{PWAF (NOI} - \text{DS)} + \text{PWF (RP} - \text{OS)} + \text{MP}$$

Try 16%:

$$V = 4.833\ (\$65,000 - \$50,555) + .2267\ (\$500,000 - \$351,000) + \$400,000$$
$$V = 4.833\ (\$14,445) + .2267\ (\$149,000) + \$400,000$$
$$V = \$69,813 + \$33,778 + \$400,000$$
$$V = \$503,591$$

Since the result of $503,591 exceeds the $500,000 price, the equity yield rate is too low. Therefore, try 17%:

$$V = 4.6586\ (\$14,445) + .208\ (\$149,000) + \$400,000$$
$$V = \$67,293 + \$30,992 + \$400,000$$
$$V = \$498,285$$

At a 17% equity yield rate, the present worth of the property is under $500,000. Therefore, since a 16% equity yield rate is too low and a 17% rate is too high, the equity yield offered at the $500,000 price will be between 16% and 17%.

Chapter 13

PRACTICE PROBLEM 1

Solve for value, given mortgage principal and a dollar estimate of the resale price.

$$\frac{65{,}000}{V} = .15 - \frac{\$400{,}000}{V}(.02964) + \frac{V - \$500{,}000}{V}(.049252)$$

Multiply by V:

$$\$65{,}000 = .15V - [(\$400{,}000)(.02964)] + [(V - \$500{,}000)(.049252)]$$

Multiply inner terms:

$$\$65{,}000 = .15V - 11856 + .049252V - 24626$$

Collecting terms:

$$\$65{,}000 = .199252V - 36482$$
$$101{,}482 = .199252V$$
$$101{,}482/.199252 = V$$
$$\$509{,}314 = V$$

PRACTICE PROBLEM 2

Solve for value, given mortgage principal and percentage of property value change.

$$\frac{\$65{,}000}{V} = .15 - \frac{\$400{,}000}{V}(.02964) - .1(.049252)$$

Multiply by V:

$$\$65{,}000 = .15V - \$400{,}000\,(.02964) - .1V\,(.049252)$$

Multiply inner terms:

$$\$65{,}000 = .15V - 11856 - .0049252V$$

Collecting terms:

$$76{,}856 = .1450748V$$
$$76{,}856/.1450748 = V$$
$$\$529{,}768 = V$$

PRACTICE PROBLEM 3

Solve for value, given a loan-to-value ratio and dollar estimate of resale price.

$$\frac{\$65{,}000}{V} = .15 - .8(.02964) + \frac{\text{V} - \text{RP}}{V}(.049252)$$

Note: Since no value change is forecast, $V = \text{RP}$, so $V - \text{RP} = 0$. Then multiply by V:

$$\$65{,}000 = .15V - .8V(.02964)$$

Multiply inner terms:

$$\$65{,}000 = .15V - .023712V$$

Collecting terms:

$$\$65{,}000 = .126288V$$

Solve for V:

$$\$65{,}000/.126288 = V$$
$$\$514{,}696 = V$$

PRACTICE PROBLEM 4

Solve for value, given a loan-to-value ratio and value change fraction.

$$\frac{\$65{,}000}{V} = .15 - .8(.02964) - .30(.049252)$$

Multiply inner terms:

$$\frac{\$65{,}000}{V} = .15 - .023712 - .0147756$$

Collect terms:

$$\frac{\$65{,}000}{V} = .1115124$$

Solve for V:

$$V = \$65{,}000/.1115124$$
$$V = \$582{,}895$$

PRACTICE PROBLEM 5

Solve for equity yield rate, given present price and other variables.

$$r = \frac{\$65{,}000}{\$500{,}000}$$

$$r = .13$$
$$r = Y - mC$$

Substitute .13 for r and $\frac{\text{Loan principal}}{\text{Price/Value}}$ for m.

$$.13 = Y - \frac{\$400{,}000}{\$500{,}000}\ (C)$$

Try $Y = 16\%$:

$$.13 = .16 - \frac{\$400{,}000}{\$500{,}000}\ (C)$$

$$.13 = .16 - .8\ (C)$$
$$.13 = .16 - .8\ (.039346)$$
$$.13 = .16 - .0314768$$
$$.13 = .1285232 \text{ (too low)}$$

Try $Y = 17\%$:

$$.13 = .17 - .8\ (.049067)$$
$$.13 = .17 - .0392536$$
$$.13 = .1307464 \text{ (too high)}$$

Conclusion: Y is between 16% and 17%.

Note: If the analyst requires a more refined result, further iterations would be required. Alternatively, interpolation will allow the derivation of an *approximate* answer. In this problem, Y is approximately 16.7%.

*Six-Function Compound Interest Tables**

* Annual tables from 5 to 30 percent
* Monthly tables from 8 to 16 percent

5 % = ANNUAL RATE   **COMPOUND INTEREST TABLES**   ANNUAL RATE = 5 %

NOMINAL ANNUAL INTEREST RATE = 5 %   COMPOUNDING FREQUENCY (PER YEAR) = 1

YEAR	AMOUNT OF 1 AT COMPOUND INTEREST (COL 1)	ACCUM OF 1 PER PERIOD (COL 2)	SINKING FUND FACTOR (COL 3)	PRESENT VALUE REVERSN OF 1 (COL 4)	PRESENT VALUE ORD ANN 1 PER PERIOD (COL 5)	INSTALL TO AMORT 1 (COL 6)	PERIOD
1	1.0500	1.0000	1.000000	0.9524	0.9524	1.0500000	1
2	1.1025	2.0500	0.487805	0.9070	1.8594	0.5378049	2
3	1.1576	3.1525	0.317209	0.8638	2.7232	0.3672086	3
4	1.2155	4.3101	0.232012	0.8227	3.5460	0.2820118	4
5	1.2763	5.5256	0.180975	0.7835	4.3295	0.2309748	5
6	1.3401	6.8019	0.147017	0.7462	5.0757	0.1970175	6
7	1.4071	8.1420	0.122820	0.7107	5.7864	0.1728198	7
8	1.4775	9.5491	0.104722	0.6768	6.4632	0.1547218	8
9	1.5513	11.0266	0.090690	0.6446	7.1078	0.1406901	9
10	1.6289	12.5779	0.079505	0.6139	7.7217	0.1295046	10
11	1.7103	14.2068	0.070389	0.5847	8.3064	0.1203889	11
12	1.7959	15.9171	0.062825	0.5568	8.8633	0.1128254	12
13	1.8856	17.7130	0.056456	0.5303	9.3936	0.1064558	13
14	1.9799	19.5986	0.051024	0.5051	9.8986	0.1010240	14
15	2.0789	21.5786	0.046342	0.4810	10.3797	0.0963423	15
16	2.1829	23.6575	0.042270	0.4581	10.8378	0.0922699	16
17	2.2920	25.8404	0.038699	0.4363	11.2741	0.0886991	17
18	2.4066	28.1324	0.035546	0.4155	11.6896	0.0855462	18
19	2.5270	30.5390	0.032745	0.3957	12.0853	0.0827450	19
20	2.6533	33.0660	0.030243	0.3769	12.4622	0.0802426	20
21	2.7860	35.7193	0.027996	0.3589	12.8212	0.0779961	21
22	2.9253	38.5052	0.025971	0.3418	13.1630	0.0759705	22
23	3.0715	41.4305	0.024137	0.3256	13.4886	0.0741368	23
24	3.2251	44.5020	0.022471	0.3101	13.7986	0.0724709	24
25	3.3864	47.7271	0.020952	0.2953	14.0939	0.0709525	25
26	3.5557	51.1135	0.019564	0.2812	14.3752	0.0695643	26
27	3.7335	54.6691	0.018292	0.2678	14.6430	0.0682919	27
28	3.9201	58.4026	0.017123	0.2551	14.8981	0.0671225	28
29	4.1161	62.3227	0.016046	0.2429	15.1411	0.0660455	29
30	4.3219	66.4388	0.015051	0.2314	15.3725	0.0650514	30
31	4.5380	70.7608	0.014132	0.2204	15.5928	0.0641321	31
32	4.7649	75.2988	0.013280	0.2099	15.8027	0.0632804	32
33	5.0032	80.0638	0.012490	0.1999	16.0025	0.0624900	33
34	5.2533	85.0670	0.011755	0.1904	16.1929	0.0617554	34
35	5.5160	90.3203	0.011072	0.1813	16.3742	0.0610717	35
36	5.7918	95.8363	0.010434	0.1727	16.5469	0.0604345	36
37	6.0814	101.6281	0.009840	0.1644	16.7113	0.0598398	37
38	6.3855	107.7095	0.009284	0.1566	16.8679	0.0592842	38
39	6.7048	114.0950	0.008765	0.1491	17.0170	0.0587646	39
40	7.0400	120.7998	0.008278	0.1420	17.1591	0.0582782	40
41	7.3920	127.8398	0.007822	0.1353	17.2944	0.0578223	41
42	7.7616	135.2318	0.007395	0.1288	17.4232	0.0573947	42
43	8.1497	142.9933	0.006993	0.1227	17.5459	0.0569933	43
44	8.5572	151.1430	0.006616	0.1169	17.6628	0.0566163	44
45	8.9850	159.7002	0.006262	0.1113	17.7741	0.0562617	45
46	9.4343	168.6852	0.005928	0.1060	17.8801	0.0559282	46
47	9.9060	178.1194	0.005614	0.1009	17.9810	0.0556142	47
48	10.4013	188.0254	0.005318	0.0961	18.0772	0.0553184	48
49	10.9213	198.4267	0.005040	0.0916	18.1687	0.0550396	49
50	11.4674	209.3480	0.004777	0.0872	18.2559	0.0547767	50

6 % = ANNUAL RATE COMPOUND INTEREST TABLES ANNUAL RATE = 6 %

NOMINAL ANNUAL INTEREST RATE = 6 % COMPOUNDING FREQUENCY (PER YEAR) = 1

YEAR	AMOUNT OF 1 AT COMPOUND INTEREST (COL 1)	ACCUM OF 1 PER PERIOD (COL 2)	SINKING FUND FACTOR (COL 3)	PRESENT VALUE REVERSN OF 1 (COL 4)	PRESENT VALUE ORD ANN 1 PER PERIOD (COL 5)	INSTALL TO AMORT 1 (COL 6)	PERIOD
1	1.0600	1.0000	1.000000	0.9434	0.9434	1.0600000	1
2	1.1236	2.0600	0.485437	0.8900	1.8334	0.5454369	2
3	1.1910	3.1836	0.314110	0.8396	2.6730	0.3741098	3
4	1.2625	4.3746	0.228591	0.7921	3.4651	0.2885915	4
5	1.3382	5.6371	0.177396	0.7473	4.2124	0.2373964	5
6	1.4185	6.9753	0.143363	0.7050	4.9173	0.2033626	6
7	1.5036	8.3938	0.119135	0.6651	5.5824	0.1791350	7
8	1.5938	9.8975	0.101036	0.6274	6.2098	0.1610359	8
9	1.6895	11.4913	0.087022	0.5919	6.8017	0.1470222	9
10	1.7908	13.1808	0.075868	0.5584	7.3601	0.1358680	10
11	1.8983	14.9716	0.066793	0.5268	7.8869	0.1267929	11
12	2.0122	16.8699	0.059277	0.4970	8.3838	0.1192770	12
13	2.1329	18.8821	0.052960	0.4688	8.8527	0.1129601	13
14	2.2609	21.0151	0.047585	0.4423	9.2950	0.1075849	14
15	2.3966	23.2760	0.042963	0.4173	9.7122	0.1029628	15
16	2.5404	25.6725	0.038952	0.3936	10.1059	0.0989521	16
17	2.6928	28.2129	0.035445	0.3714	10.4773	0.0954448	17
18	2.8543	30.9057	0.032357	0.3503	10.8276	0.0923565	18
19	3.0256	33.7600	0.029621	0.3305	11.1581	0.0896209	19
20	3.2071	36.7856	0.027185	0.3118	11.4699	0.0871846	20
21	3.3996	39.9927	0.025005	0.2942	11.7641	0.0850045	21
22	3.6035	43.3923	0.023046	0.2775	12.0416	0.0830456	22
23	3.8197	46.9958	0.021278	0.2618	12.3034	0.0812785	23
24	4.0489	50.8156	0.019679	0.2470	12.5504	0.0796790	24
25	4.2919	54.8645	0.018227	0.2330	12.7834	0.0782267	25
26	4.5494	59.1564	0.016904	0.2198	13.0032	0.0769043	26
27	4.8223	63.7058	0.015697	0.2074	13.2105	0.0756972	27
28	5.1117	68.5281	0.014593	0.1956	13.4062	0.0745926	28
29	5.4184	73.6398	0.013580	0.1846	13.5907	0.0735796	29
30	5.7435	79.0582	0.012649	0.1741	13.7648	0.0726489	30
31	6.0881	84.8017	0.011792	0.1643	13.9291	0.0717922	31
32	6.4534	90.8898	0.011002	0.1550	14.0840	0.0710023	32
33	6.8406	97.3432	0.010273	0.1462	14.2302	0.0702729	33
34	7.2510	104.1838	0.009598	0.1379	14.3681	0.0695984	34
35	7.6861	111.4348	0.008974	0.1301	14.4982	0.0689739	35
36	8.1473	119.1209	0.008395	0.1227	14.6210	0.0683948	36
37	8.6361	127.2681	0.007857	0.1158	14.7368	0.0678574	37
38	9.1543	135.9042	0.007358	0.1092	14.8460	0.0673581	38
39	9.7035	145.0585	0.006894	0.1031	14.9491	0.0668938	39
40	10.2857	154.7620	0.006462	0.0972	15.0463	0.0664615	40
41	10.9029	165.0477	0.006059	0.0917	15.1380	0.0660589	41
42	11.5570	175.9505	0.005683	0.0865	15.2245	0.0656834	42
43	12.2505	187.5076	0.005333	0.0816	15.3062	0.0653331	43
44	12.9855	199.7580	0.005006	0.0770	15.3832	0.0650061	44
45	13.7646	212.7435	0.004700	0.0727	15.4558	0.0647005	45
46	14.5905	226.5081	0.004415	0.0685	15.5244	0.0644149	46
47	15.4659	241.0986	0.004148	0.0647	15.5890	0.0641477	47
48	16.3939	256.5645	0.003898	0.0610	15.6500	0.0638977	48
49	17.3775	272.9584	0.003664	0.0575	15.7076	0.0636636	49
50	18.4202	290.3359	0.003444	0.0543	15.7619	0.0634443	50

NOMINAL ANNUAL INTEREST RATE = 7 %   COMPOUNDING FREQUENCY (PER YEAR) = 1

YEAR	AMOUNT OF 1 AT COMPOUND INTEREST (COL 1)	ACCUM OF 1 PER PERIOD (COL 2)	SINKING FUND FACTOR (COL 3)	PRESENT VALUE REVERSN OF 1 (COL 4)	PRESENT VALUE ORD ANN 1 PER PERIOD (COL 5)	INSTALL TO AMORT 1 (COL 6)	PERIOD
1	1.0700	1.0000	1.000000	0.9346	0.9346	1.0700000	1
2	1.1449	2.0700	0.483092	0.8734	1.8080	0.5530918	2
3	1.2250	3.2149	0.311052	0.8163	2.6243	0.3810517	3
4	1.3108	4.4399	0.225228	0.7629	3.3872	0.2952281	4
5	1.4026	5.7507	0.173891	0.7130	4.1002	0.2438907	5
6	1.5007	7.1533	0.139796	0.6663	4.7665	0.2097958	6
7	1.6058	8.6540	0.115553	0.6227	5.3893	0.1855532	7
8	1.7182	10.2598	0.097468	0.5820	5.9713	0.1674678	8
9	1.8385	11.9780	0.083486	0.5439	6.5152	0.1534865	9
10	1.9672	13.8164	0.072378	0.5083	7.0236	0.1423775	10
11	2.1049	15.7836	0.063357	0.4751	7.4987	0.1333569	11
12	2.2522	17.8885	0.055902	0.4440	7.9427	0.1259020	12
13	2.4098	20.1406	0.049651	0.4150	8.3577	0.1196508	13
14	2.5785	22.5505	0.044345	0.3878	8.7455	0.1143449	14
15	2.7590	25.1290	0.039795	0.3624	9.1079	0.1097946	15
16	2.9522	27.8881	0.035858	0.3387	9.4466	0.1058576	16
17	3.1588	30.8402	0.032425	0.3166	9.7632	0.1024252	17
18	3.3799	33.9990	0.029413	0.2959	10.0591	0.0994126	18
19	3.6165	37.3790	0.026753	0.2765	10.3356	0.0967530	19
20	3.8697	40.9955	0.024393	0.2584	10.5940	0.0943929	20
21	4.1406	44.8652	0.022289	0.2415	10.8355	0.0922890	21
22	4.4304	49.0057	0.020406	0.2257	11.0612	0.0904058	22
23	4.7405	53.4361	0.018714	0.2109	11.2722	0.0887139	23
24	5.0724	58.1767	0.017189	0.1971	11.4693	0.0871890	24
25	5.4274	63.2490	0.015811	0.1842	11.6536	0.0858105	25
26	5.8074	68.6765	0.014561	0.1722	11.8258	0.0845610	26
27	6.2139	74.4838	0.013426	0.1609	11.9867	0.0834257	27
28	6.6488	80.6977	0.012392	0.1504	12.1371	0.0823919	28
29	7.1143	87.3465	0.011449	0.1406	12.2777	0.0814487	29
30	7.6123	94.4608	0.010586	0.1314	12.4090	0.0805864	30
31	8.1451	102.0730	0.009797	0.1228	12.5318	0.0797969	31
32	8.7153	110.2182	0.009073	0.1147	12.6466	0.0790729	32
33	9.3253	118.9334	0.008408	0.1072	12.7538	0.0784081	33
34	9.9781	128.2588	0.007797	0.1002	12.8540	0.0777967	34
35	10.6766	138.2369	0.007234	0.0937	12.9477	0.0772340	35
36	11.4239	148.9135	0.006715	0.0875	13.0352	0.0767153	36
37	12.2236	160.3374	0.006237	0.0818	13.1170	0.0762368	37
38	13.0793	172.5610	0.005795	0.0765	13.1935	0.0757951	38
39	13.9948	185.6403	0.005387	0.0715	13.2649	0.0753868	39
40	14.9745	199.6351	0.005009	0.0668	13.3317	0.0750091	40
41	16.0227	214.6096	0.004660	0.0624	13.3941	0.0746596	41
42	17.1443	230.6322	0.004336	0.0583	13.4524	0.0743359	42
43	18.3444	247.7765	0.004036	0.0545	13.5070	0.0740359	43
44	19.6285	266.1209	0.003758	0.0509	13.5579	0.0737577	44
45	21.0025	285.7493	0.003500	0.0476	13.6055	0.0734996	45
46	22.4726	306.7518	0.003260	0.0445	13.6500	0.0732600	46
47	24.0457	329.2244	0.003037	0.0416	13.6916	0.0730374	47
48	25.7289	353.2701	0.002831	0.0389	13.7305	0.0728307	48
49	27.5299	378.9990	0.002639	0.0363	13.7668	0.0726385	49
50	29.4570	406.5289	0.002460	0.0339	13.8007	0.0724598	50

8 % = ANNUAL RATE　　COMPOUND INTEREST TABLES　　ANNUAL RATE = 8 %

NOMINAL ANNUAL INTEREST RATE = 8 %　　COMPOUNDING FREQUENCY (PER YEAR) = 1

YEAR	AMOUNT OF 1 AT COMPOUND INTEREST (COL 1)	ACCUM OF 1 PER PERIOD (COL 2)	SINKING FUND FACTOR (COL 3)	PRESENT VALUE REVERSN OF 1 (COL 4)	PRESENT VALUE ORD ANN 1 PER PERIOD (COL 5)	INSTALL TO AMORT 1 (COL 6)	PERIOD
1	1.0800	1.0000	1.000000	0.9259	0.9259	1.0800000	1
2	1.1664	2.0800	0.480769	0.8573	1.7833	0.5607692	2
3	1.2597	3.2464	0.308034	0.7938	2.5771	0.3880335	3
4	1.3605	4.5061	0.221921	0.7350	3.3121	0.3019208	4
5	1.4693	5.8666	0.170456	0.6806	3.9927	0.2504565	5
6	1.5869	7.3359	0.136315	0.6302	4.6229	0.2163154	6
7	1.7138	8.9228	0.112072	0.5835	5.2064	0.1920724	7
8	1.8509	10.6366	0.094015	0.5403	5.7466	0.1740148	8
9	1.9990	12.4876	0.080080	0.5002	6.2469	0.1600797	9
10	2.1589	14.4866	0.069029	0.4632	6.7101	0.1490295	10
11	2.3316	16.6455	0.060076	0.4289	7.1390	0.1400763	11
12	2.5182	18.9771	0.052695	0.3971	7.5361	0.1326950	12
13	2.7196	21.4953	0.046522	0.3677	7.9038	0.1265218	13
14	2.9372	24.2149	0.041297	0.3405	8.2442	0.1212969	14
15	3.1722	27.1521	0.036830	0.3152	8.5595	0.1168295	15
16	3.4259	30.3243	0.032977	0.2919	8.8514	0.1129769	16
17	3.7000	33.7502	0.029629	0.2703	9.1216	0.1096294	17
18	3.9960	37.4502	0.026702	0.2502	9.3719	0.1067021	18
19	4.3157	41.4463	0.024128	0.2317	9.6036	0.1041276	19
20	4.6610	45.7620	0.021852	0.2145	9.8181	0.1018522	20
21	5.0338	50.4229	0.019832	0.1987	10.0168	0.0998322	21
22	5.4365	55.4568	0.018032	0.1839	10.2007	0.0980321	22
23	5.8715	60.8933	0.016422	0.1703	10.3711	0.0964222	23
24	6.3412	66.7648	0.014978	0.1577	10.5288	0.0949780	24
25	6.8485	73.1059	0.013679	0.1460	10.6748	0.0936788	25
26	7.3964	79.9544	0.012507	0.1352	10.8100	0.0925071	26
27	7.9881	87.3508	0.011448	0.1252	10.9352	0.0914481	27
28	8.6271	95.3388	0.010489	0.1159	11.0511	0.0904889	28
29	9.3173	103.9659	0.009619	0.1073	11.1584	0.0896185	29
30	10.0627	113.2832	0.008827	0.0994	11.2578	0.0888274	30
31	10.8677	123.3459	0.008107	0.0920	11.3498	0.0881073	31
32	11.7371	134.2135	0.007451	0.0852	11.4350	0.0874508	32
33	12.6760	145.9506	0.006852	0.0789	11.5139	0.0868516	33
34	13.6901	158.6267	0.006304	0.0730	11.5869	0.0863041	34
35	14.7853	172.3168	0.005803	0.0676	11.6546	0.0858033	35
36	15.9682	187.1021	0.005345	0.0626	11.7172	0.0853447	36
37	17.2456	203.0703	0.004924	0.0580	11.7752	0.0849244	37
38	18.6253	220.3159	0.004539	0.0537	11.8289	0.0845389	38
39	20.1153	238.9412	0.004185	0.0497	11.8786	0.0841851	39
40	21.7245	259.0565	0.003860	0.0460	11.9246	0.0838602	40
41	23.4625	280.7810	0.003561	0.0426	11.9672	0.0835615	41
42	25.3395	304.2435	0.003287	0.0395	12.0067	0.0832868	42
43	27.3666	329.5830	0.003034	0.0365	12.0432	0.0830341	43
44	29.5560	356.9496	0.002802	0.0338	12.0771	0.0828015	44
45	31.9204	386.5056	0.002587	0.0313	12.1084	0.0825873	45
46	34.4741	418.4260	0.002390	0.0290	12.1374	0.0823899	46
47	37.2320	452.9001	0.002208	0.0269	12.1643	0.0822080	47
48	40.2106	490.1321	0.002040	0.0249	12.1891	0.0820403	48
49	43.4274	530.3427	0.001886	0.0230	12.2122	0.0818856	49
50	46.9016	573.7701	0.001743	0.0213	12.2335	0.0817429	50

NOMINAL ANNUAL INTEREST RATE = 9 % COMPOUNDING FREQUENCY (PER YEAR) = 1

YEAR	AMOUNT OF 1 AT COMPOUND INTEREST (COL 1)	ACCUM OF 1 PER PERIOD (COL 2)	SINKING FUND FACTOR (COL 3)	PRESENT VALUE REVERSN OF 1 (COL 4)	PRESENT VALUE ORD ANN 1 PER PERIOD (COL 5)	INSTALL TO AMORT 1 (COL 6)	PERIOD
1	1.0900	1.0000	1.000000	0.9174	0.9174	1.0900000	1
2	1.1881	2.0900	0.478469	0.8417	1.7591	0.5684689	2
3	1.2950	3.2781	0.305055	0.7722	2.5313	0.3950548	3
4	1.4116	4.5731	0.218669	0.7084	3.2397	0.3086687	4
5	1.5386	5.9847	0.167092	0.6499	3.8897	0.2570925	5
6	1.6771	7.5233	0.132920	0.5963	4.4859	0.2229198	6
7	1.8280	9.2004	0.108691	0.5470	5.0330	0.1986905	7
8	1.9926	11.0285	0.090674	0.5019	5.5348	0.1806744	8
9	2.1719	13.0210	0.076799	0.4604	5.9952	0.1667988	9
10	2.3674	15.1929	0.065820	0.4224	6.4177	0.1558201	10
11	2.5804	17.5603	0.056947	0.3875	6.8052	0.1469467	11
12	2.8127	20.1407	0.049651	0.3555	7.1607	0.1396507	12
13	3.0658	22.9534	0.043567	0.3262	7.4869	0.1335666	13
14	3.3417	26.0192	0.038433	0.2992	7.7862	0.1284332	14
15	3.6425	29.3609	0.034059	0.2745	8.0607	0.1240589	15
16	3.9703	33.0034	0.030300	0.2519	8.3126	0.1202999	16
17	4.3276	36.9737	0.027046	0.2311	8.5436	0.1170463	17
18	4.7171	41.3013	0.024212	0.2120	8.7556	0.1142123	18
19	5.1417	46.0185	0.021730	0.1945	8.9501	0.1117304	19
20	5.6044	51.1601	0.019546	0.1784	9.1285	0.1095465	20
21	6.1088	56.7645	0.017617	0.1637	9.2922	0.1076166	21
22	6.6586	62.8733	0.015905	0.1502	9.4424	0.1059050	22
23	7.2579	69.5319	0.014382	0.1378	9.5802	0.1043819	23
24	7.9111	76.7898	0.013023	0.1264	9.7066	0.1030226	24
25	8.6231	84.7009	0.011806	0.1160	9.8226	0.1018063	25
26	9.3992	93.3240	0.010715	0.1064	9.9290	0.1007154	26
27	10.2451	102.7231	0.009735	0.0976	10.0266	0.0997349	27
28	11.1671	112.9682	0.008852	0.0895	10.1161	0.0988521	28
29	12.1722	124.1354	0.008056	0.0822	10.1983	0.0980557	29
30	13.2677	136.3075	0.007336	0.0754	10.2737	0.0973364	30
31	14.4618	149.5752	0.006686	0.0691	10.3428	0.0966856	31
32	15.7633	164.0370	0.006096	0.0634	10.4062	0.0960962	32
33	17.1820	179.8003	0.005562	0.0582	10.4644	0.0955617	33
34	18.7284	196.9824	0.005077	0.0534	10.5178	0.0950766	34
35	20.4140	215.7108	0.004636	0.0490	10.5668	0.0946358	35
36	22.2512	236.1247	0.004235	0.0449	10.6118	0.0942351	36
37	24.2538	258.3760	0.003870	0.0412	10.6530	0.0938703	37
38	26.4367	282.6298	0.003538	0.0378	10.6908	0.0935382	38
39	28.8160	309.0665	0.003236	0.0347	10.7255	0.0932356	39
40	31.4094	337.8825	0.002960	0.0318	10.7574	0.0929596	40
41	34.2363	369.2919	0.002708	0.0292	10.7866	0.0927079	41
42	37.3175	403.5282	0.002478	0.0268	10.8134	0.0924781	42
43	40.6761	440.8457	0.002268	0.0246	10.8380	0.0922684	43
44	44.3370	481.5218	0.002077	0.0226	10.8605	0.0920768	44
45	48.3273	525.8588	0.001902	0.0207	10.8812	0.0919017	45
46	52.6767	574.1861	0.001742	0.0190	10.9002	0.0917416	46
47	57.4177	626.8628	0.001595	0.0174	10.9176	0.0915952	47
48	62.5852	684.2805	0.001461	0.0160	10.9336	0.0914614	48
49	68.2179	746.8657	0.001339	0.0147	10.9482	0.0913389	49
50	74.3575	815.0837	0.001227	0.0134	10.9617	0.0912269	50

10 % = ANNUAL RATE COMPOUND INTEREST TABLES ANNUAL RATE = 10 %

NOMINAL ANNUAL INTEREST RATE = 10 % COMPOUNDING FREQUENCY (PER YEAR) = 1

YEAR	AMOUNT OF 1 AT COMPOUND INTEREST (COL 1)	ACCUM OF 1 PER PERIOD (COL 2)	SINKING FUND FACTOR (COL 3)	PRESENT VALUE REVERSN OF 1 (COL 4)	PRESENT VALUE ORD ANN 1 PER PERIOD (COL 5)	INSTALL TO AMORT 1 (COL 6)	PERIOD
1	1.1000	1.0000	1.000000	0.9091	0.9091	1.1000000	1
2	1.2100	2.1000	0.476190	0.8264	1.7355	0.5761905	2
3	1.3310	3.3100	0.302115	0.7513	2.4869	0.4021148	3
4	1.4641	4.6410	0.215471	0.6830	3.1699	0.3154708	4
5	1.6105	6.1051	0.163797	0.6209	3.7908	0.2637975	5
6	1.7716	7.7156	0.129607	0.5645	4.3553	0.2296074	6
7	1.9487	9.4872	0.105405	0.5132	4.8684	0.2054055	7
8	2.1436	11.4359	0.087444	0.4665	5.3349	0.1874440	8
9	2.3579	13.5795	0.073641	0.4241	5.7590	0.1736405	9
10	2.5937	15.9374	0.062745	0.3855	6.1446	0.1627454	10
11	2.8531	18.5312	0.053963	0.3505	6.4951	0.1539631	11
12	3.1384	21.3843	0.046763	0.3186	6.8137	0.1467633	12
13	3.4523	24.5227	0.040779	0.2897	7.1034	0.1407785	13
14	3.7975	27.9750	0.035746	0.2633	7.3667	0.1357462	14
15	4.1772	31.7725	0.031474	0.2394	7.6061	0.1314738	15
16	4.5950	35.9497	0.027817	0.2176	7.8237	0.1278166	16
17	5.0545	40.5447	0.024664	0.1978	8.0216	0.1246641	17
18	5.5599	45.5992	0.021930	0.1799	8.2014	0.1219302	18
19	6.1159	51.1591	0.019547	0.1635	8.3649	0.1195469	19
20	6.7275	57.2750	0.017460	0.1486	8.5136	0.1174596	20
21	7.4003	64.0025	0.015624	0.1351	8.6487	0.1156244	21
22	8.1403	71.4028	0.014005	0.1228	8.7715	0.1140051	22
23	8.9543	79.5430	0.012572	0.1117	8.8832	0.1125718	23
24	9.8497	88.4973	0.011300	0.1015	8.9847	0.1112998	24
25	10.8347	98.3471	0.010168	0.0923	9.0770	0.1101681	25
26	11.9182	109.1818	0.009159	0.0839	9.1609	0.1091590	26
27	13.1100	121.0999	0.008258	0.0763	9.2372	0.1082576	27
28	14.4210	134.2099	0.007451	0.0693	9.3066	0.1074510	28
29	15.8631	148.6309	0.006728	0.0630	9.3696	0.1067281	29
30	17.4494	164.4940	0.006079	0.0573	9.4269	0.1060792	30
31	19.1943	181.9434	0.005496	0.0521	9.4790	0.1054962	31
32	21.1138	201.1378	0.004972	0.0474	9.5264	0.1049717	32
33	23.2252	222.2516	0.004499	0.0431	9.5694	0.1044994	33
34	25.5477	245.4767	0.004074	0.0391	9.6086	0.1040737	34
35	28.1024	271.0244	0.003690	0.0356	9.6442	0.1036897	35
36	30.9127	299.1268	0.003343	0.0323	9.6765	0.1033431	36
37	34.0040	330.0395	0.003030	0.0294	9.7059	0.1030299	37
38	37.4043	364.0434	0.002747	0.0267	9.7327	0.1027469	38
39	41.1448	401.4478	0.002491	0.0243	9.7570	0.1024910	39
40	45.2593	442.5926	0.002259	0.0221	9.7791	0.1022594	40
41	49.7852	487.8518	0.002050	0.0201	9.7991	0.1020498	41
42	54.7637	537.6370	0.001860	0.0183	9.8174	0.1018600	42
43	60.2401	592.4007	0.001688	0.0166	9.8340	0.1016880	43
44	66.2641	652.6408	0.001532	0.0151	9.8491	0.1015322	44
45	72.8905	718.9049	0.001391	0.0137	9.8628	0.1013910	45
46	80.1795	791.7954	0.001263	0.0125	9.8753	0.1012630	46
47	88.1975	871.9749	0.001147	0.0113	9.8866	0.1011468	47
48	97.0172	960.1724	0.001041	0.0103	9.8969	0.1010415	48
49	106.7190	1057.1896	0.000946	0.0094	9.9063	0.1009459	49
50	117.3909	1163.9086	0.000859	0.0085	9.9148	0.1008592	50

11 % = ANNUAL RATE

COMPOUND INTEREST TABLES

ANNUAL RATE = 11 %

NOMINAL ANNUAL INTEREST RATE = 11 %   COMPOUNDING FREQUENCY (PER YEAR) = 1

YEAR	AMOUNT OF 1 AT COMPOUND INTEREST (COL 1)	ACCUM OF 1 PER PERIOD (COL 2)	SINKING FUND FACTOR (COL 3)	PRESENT VALUE REVERSN OF 1 (COL 4)	PRESENT VALUE ORD ANN 1 PER PERIOD (COL 5)	INSTALL TO AMORT 1 (COL 6)	PERIOD
1	1.1100	1.0000	1.000000	0.9009	0.9009	1.1100000	1
2	1.2321	2.1100	0.473934	0.8116	1.7125	0.5839336	2
3	1.3676	3.3421	0.299213	0.7312	2.4437	0.4092131	3
4	1.5181	4.7097	0.212326	0.6587	3.1024	0.3223264	4
5	1.6851	6.2278	0.160570	0.5935	3.6959	0.2705703	5
6	1.8704	7.9129	0.126377	0.5346	4.2305	0.2363766	6
7	2.0762	9.7833	0.102215	0.4817	4.7122	0.2122153	7
8	2.3045	11.8594	0.084321	0.4339	5.1461	0.1943211	8
9	2.5580	14.1640	0.070602	0.3909	5.5370	0.1806017	9
10	2.8394	16.7220	0.059801	0.3522	5.8892	0.1698014	10
11	3.1518	19.5614	0.051121	0.3173	6.2065	0.1611210	11
12	3.4985	22.7132	0.044027	0.2858	6.4924	0.1540273	12
13	3.8833	26.2116	0.038151	0.2575	6.7499	0.1481510	13
14	4.3104	30.0949	0.033228	0.2320	6.9819	0.1432282	14
15	4.7846	34.4054	0.029065	0.2090	7.1909	0.1390652	15
16	5.3109	39.1899	0.025517	0.1883	7.3792	0.1355167	16
17	5.8951	44.5008	0.022471	0.1696	7.5488	0.1324715	17
18	6.5436	50.3959	0.019843	0.1528	7.7016	0.1298429	18
19	7.2633	56.9395	0.017563	0.1377	7.8393	0.1275625	19
20	8.0623	64.2028	0.015576	0.1240	7.9633	0.1255756	20
21	8.9492	72.2651	0.013838	0.1117	8.0751	0.1238379	21
22	9.9336	81.2143	0.012313	0.1007	8.1757	0.1223131	22
23	11.0263	91.1479	0.010971	0.0907	8.2664	0.1209712	23
24	12.2392	102.1741	0.009787	0.0817	8.3481	0.1197872	24
25	13.5855	114.4133	0.008740	0.0736	8.4217	0.1187402	25
26	15.0799	127.9988	0.007813	0.0663	8.4881	0.1178126	26
27	16.7386	143.0786	0.006989	0.0597	8.5478	0.1169892	27
28	18.5799	159.8173	0.006257	0.0538	8.6016	0.1162571	28
29	20.6237	178.3972	0.005605	0.0485	8.6501	0.1156055	29
30	22.8923	199.0209	0.005025	0.0437	8.6938	0.1150246	30
31	25.4104	221.9132	0.004506	0.0394	8.7331	0.1145063	31
32	28.2056	247.3236	0.004043	0.0355	8.7686	0.1140433	32
33	31.3082	275.5292	0.003629	0.0319	8.8005	0.1136294	33
34	34.7521	306.8374	0.003259	0.0288	8.8293	0.1132591	34
35	38.5749	341.5896	0.002927	0.0259	8.8552	0.1129275	35
36	42.8181	380.1644	0.002630	0.0234	8.8786	0.1126304	36
37	47.5281	422.9825	0.002364	0.0210	8.8996	0.1123642	37
38	52.7562	470.5106	0.002125	0.0190	8.9186	0.1121254	38
39	58.5593	523.2667	0.001911	0.0171	8.9357	0.1119111	39
40	65.0009	581.8261	0.001719	0.0154	8.9511	0.1117187	40
41	72.1510	646.8269	0.001546	0.0139	8.9649	0.1115460	41
42	80.0876	718.9779	0.001391	0.0125	8.9774	0.1113909	42
43	88.8972	799.0655	0.001251	0.0112	8.9886	0.1112515	43
44	98.6759	887.9626	0.001126	0.0101	8.9988	0.1111262	44
45	109.5302	986.6385	0.001014	0.0091	9.0079	0.1110135	45
46	121.5786	1096.1688	0.000912	0.0082	9.0161	0.1109123	46
47	134.9522	1217.7473	0.000821	0.0074	9.0235	0.1108212	47
48	149.7969	1352.6996	0.000739	0.0067	9.0302	0.1107393	48
49	166.2746	1502.4965	0.000666	0.0060	9.0362	0.1106656	49
50	184.5648	1668.7711	0.000599	0.0054	9.0417	0.1105992	50

12 % = ANNUAL RATE   COMPOUND INTEREST TABLES   ANNUAL RATE = 12 %

NOMINAL ANNUAL INTEREST RATE = 12 %   COMPOUNDING FREQUENCY (PER YEAR) = 1

YEAR	AMOUNT OF 1 AT COMPOUND INTEREST (COL 1)	ACCUM OF 1 PER PERIOD (COL 2)	SINKING FUND FACTOR (COL 3)	PRESENT VALUE REVERSN OF 1 (COL 4)	PRESENT VALUE ORD ANN 1 PER PERIOD (COL 5)	INSTALL TO AMORT 1 (COL 6)	PERIOD
1	1.1200	1.0000	1.000000	0.8929	0.8929	1.1200000	1
2	1.2544	2.1200	0.471698	0.7972	1.6901	0.5916981	2
3	1.4049	3.3744	0.296349	0.7118	2.4018	0.4163490	3
4	1.5735	4.7793	0.209234	0.6355	3.0373	0.3292344	4
5	1.7623	6.3528	0.157410	0.5674	3.6048	0.2774097	5
6	1.9738	8.1152	0.123226	0.5066	4.1114	0.2432257	6
7	2.2107	10.0890	0.099118	0.4523	4.5638	0.2191177	7
8	2.4760	12.2997	0.081303	0.4039	4.9676	0.2013028	8
9	2.7731	14.7757	0.067679	0.3606	5.3282	0.1876789	9
10	3.1058	17.5487	0.056984	0.3220	5.6502	0.1769842	10
11	3.4785	20.6546	0.048415	0.2875	5.9377	0.1684154	11
12	3.8960	24.1331	0.041437	0.2567	6.1944	0.1614368	12
13	4.3635	28.0291	0.035677	0.2292	6.4235	0.1556772	13
14	4.8871	32.3926	0.030871	0.2046	6.6282	0.1508712	14
15	5.4736	37.2797	0.026824	0.1827	6.8109	0.1468242	15
16	6.1304	42.7533	0.023390	0.1631	6.9740	0.1433900	16
17	6.8660	48.8837	0.020457	0.1456	7.1196	0.1404567	17
18	7.6900	55.7497	0.017937	0.1300	7.2497	0.1379373	18
19	8.6128	63.4397	0.015763	0.1161	7.3658	0.1357630	19
20	9.6463	72.0524	0.013879	0.1037	7.4694	0.1338788	20
21	10.8038	81.6987	0.012240	0.0926	7.5620	0.1322401	21
22	12.1003	92.5026	0.010811	0.0826	7.6446	0.1308105	22
23	13.5523	104.6029	0.009560	0.0738	7.7184	0.1295600	23
24	15.1786	118.1552	0.008463	0.0659	7.7843	0.1284634	24
25	17.0001	133.3339	0.007500	0.0588	7.8431	0.1275000	25
26	19.0401	150.3339	0.006652	0.0525	7.8957	0.1266519	26
27	21.3249	169.3740	0.005904	0.0469	7.9426	0.1259041	27
28	23.8839	190.6989	0.005244	0.0419	7.9844	0.1252439	28
29	26.7499	214.5827	0.004660	0.0374	8.0218	0.1246602	29
30	29.9599	241.3327	0.004144	0.0334	8.0552	0.1241437	30
31	33.5551	271.2926	0.003686	0.0298	8.0850	0.1236861	31
32	37.5817	304.8477	0.003280	0.0266	8.1116	0.1232803	32
33	42.0915	342.4294	0.002920	0.0238	8.1354	0.1229203	33
34	47.1425	384.5210	0.002601	0.0212	8.1566	0.1226006	34
35	52.7996	431.6635	0.002317	0.0189	8.1755	0.1223166	35
36	59.1356	484.4631	0.002064	0.0169	8.1924	0.1220641	36
37	66.2318	543.5987	0.001840	0.0151	8.2075	0.1218396	37
38	74.1797	609.8305	0.001640	0.0135	8.2210	0.1216398	38
39	83.0812	684.0101	0.001462	0.0120	8.2330	0.1214620	39
40	93.0510	767.0914	0.001304	0.0107	8.2438	0.1213036	40
41	104.2171	860.1423	0.001163	0.0096	8.2534	0.1211626	41
42	116.7231	964.3594	0.001037	0.0086	8.2619	0.1210370	42
43	130.7299	1081.0825	0.000925	0.0076	8.2696	0.1209250	43
44	146.4175	1211.8124	0.000825	0.0068	8.2764	0.1208252	44
45	163.9876	1358.2299	0.000736	0.0061	8.2825	0.1207362	45
46	183.6661	1522.2175	0.000657	0.0054	8.2880	0.1206569	46
47	205.7060	1705.8836	0.000586	0.0049	8.2928	0.1205862	47
48	230.3907	1911.5896	0.000523	0.0043	8.2972	0.1205231	48
49	258.0376	2141.9804	0.000467	0.0039	8.3010	0.1204669	49
50	289.0022	2400.0180	0.000417	0.0035	8.3045	0.1204167	50

NOMINAL ANNUAL INTEREST RATE = 13 %   COMPOUNDING FREQUENCY (PER YEAR) = 1

YEAR	AMOUNT OF 1 AT COMPOUND INTEREST (COL 1)	ACCUM OF 1 PER PERIOD (COL 2)	SINKING FUND FACTOR (COL 3)	PRESENT VALUE REVERSN OF 1 (COL 4)	PRESENT VALUE ORD ANN 1 PER PERIOD (COL 5)	INSTALL TO AMORT 1 (COL 6)	PERIOD
1	1.1300	1.0000	1.000000	0.8850	0.8850	1.1300000	1
2	1.2769	2.1300	0.469484	0.7831	1.6681	0.5994836	2
3	1.4429	3.4069	0.293522	0.6931	2.3612	0.4235220	3
4	1.6305	4.8498	0.206194	0.6133	2.9745	0.3361942	4
5	1.8424	6.4803	0.154315	0.5428	3.5172	0.2843145	5
6	2.0820	8.3227	0.120153	0.4803	3.9975	0.2501532	6
7	2.3526	10.4047	0.096111	0.4251	4.4226	0.2261108	7
8	2.6584	12.7573	0.078387	0.3762	4.7988	0.2083867	8
9	3.0040	15.4157	0.064869	0.3329	5.1317	0.1948689	9
10	3.3946	18.4197	0.054290	0.2946	5.4262	0.1842896	10
11	3.8359	21.8143	0.045841	0.2607	5.6869	0.1758415	11
12	4.3345	25.6502	0.038986	0.2307	5.9176	0.1689861	12
13	4.8980	29.9847	0.033350	0.2042	6.1218	0.1633503	13
14	5.5348	34.8827	0.028667	0.1807	6.3025	0.1586675	14
15	6.2543	40.4175	0.024742	0.1599	6.4624	0.1547418	15
16	7.0673	46.6717	0.021426	0.1415	6.6039	0.1514262	16
17	7.9861	53.7391	0.018608	0.1252	6.7291	0.1486084	17
18	9.0243	61.7251	0.016201	0.1108	6.8399	0.1462009	18
19	10.1974	70.7494	0.014134	0.0981	6.9380	0.1441344	19
20	11.5231	80.9468	0.012354	0.0868	7.0248	0.1423538	20
21	13.0211	92.4699	0.010814	0.0768	7.1016	0.1408143	21
22	14.7138	105.4910	0.009479	0.0680	7.1695	0.1394795	22
23	16.6266	120.2048	0.008319	0.0601	7.2297	0.1383191	23
24	18.7881	136.8315	0.007308	0.0532	7.2829	0.1373083	24
25	21.2305	155.6195	0.006426	0.0471	7.3300	0.1364259	25
26	23.9905	176.8501	0.005655	0.0417	7.3717	0.1356545	26
27	27.1093	200.8406	0.004979	0.0369	7.4086	0.1349791	27
28	30.6335	227.9499	0.004387	0.0326	7.4412	0.1343869	28
29	34.6158	258.5834	0.003867	0.0289	7.4701	0.1338672	29
30	39.1159	293.1992	0.003411	0.0256	7.4957	0.1334106	30
31	44.2010	332.3151	0.003009	0.0226	7.5183	0.1330092	31
32	49.9471	376.5160	0.002656	0.0200	7.5383	0.1326559	32
33	56.4402	426.4631	0.002345	0.0177	7.5560	0.1323449	33
34	63.7774	482.9033	0.002071	0.0157	7.5717	0.1320708	34
35	72.0685	546.6808	0.001829	0.0139	7.5856	0.1318292	35
36	81.4374	618.7493	0.001616	0.0123	7.5979	0.1316162	36
37	92.0243	700.1867	0.001428	0.0109	7.6087	0.1314282	37
38	103.9874	792.2109	0.001262	0.0096	7.6183	0.1312623	38
39	117.5058	896.1983	0.001116	0.0085	7.6268	0.1311158	39
40	132.7815	1013.7041	0.000986	0.0075	7.6344	0.1309865	40
41	150.0431	1146.4856	0.000872	0.0067	7.6410	0.1308722	41
42	169.5487	1296.5288	0.000771	0.0059	7.6469	0.1307713	42
43	191.5901	1466.0775	0.000682	0.0052	7.6522	0.1306821	43
44	216.4968	1657.6676	0.000603	0.0046	7.6568	0.1306033	44
45	244.6414	1874.1643	0.000534	0.0041	7.6609	0.1305336	45
46	276.4447	2118.8057	0.000472	0.0036	7.6645	0.1304720	46
47	312.3825	2395.2504	0.000417	0.0032	7.6677	0.1304175	47
48	352.9923	2707.6330	0.000369	0.0028	7.6705	0.1303693	48
49	398.8813	3060.6252	0.000327	0.0025	7.6730	0.1303267	49
50	450.7358	3459.5065	0.000289	0.0022	7.6752	0.1302891	50

NOMINAL ANNUAL INTEREST RATE = 14 % COMPOUNDING FREQUENCY (PER YEAR) = 1

YEAR	AMOUNT OF 1 AT COMPOUND INTEREST (COL 1)	ACCUM OF 1 PER PERIOD (COL 2)	SINKING FUND FACTOR (COL 3)	PRESENT VALUE REVERSN OF 1 (COL 4)	PRESENT VALUE ORD ANN 1 PER PERIOD (COL 5)	INSTALL TO AMORT 1 (COL 6)	PERIOD
1	1.1400	1.0000	1.000000	0.8772	0.8772	1.1400000	1
2	1.2996	2.1400	0.467290	0.7695	1.6467	0.6072897	2
3	1.4815	3.4396	0.290731	0.6750	2.3216	0.4307315	3
4	1.6890	4.9211	0.203205	0.5921	2.9137	0.3432048	4
5	1.9254	6.6101	0.151284	0.5194	3.4331	0.2912835	5
6	2.1950	8.5355	0.117157	0.4556	3.8887	0.2571575	6
7	2.5023	10.7305	0.093192	0.3996	4.2883	0.2331924	7
8	2.8526	13.2328	0.075570	0.3506	4.6389	0.2155700	8
9	3.2519	16.0853	0.062168	0.3075	4.9464	0.2021684	9
10	3.7072	19.3373	0.051714	0.2697	5.2161	0.1917135	10
11	4.2262	23.0445	0.043394	0.2366	5.4527	0.1833943	11
12	4.8179	27.2707	0.036669	0.2076	5.6603	0.1766693	12
13	5.4924	32.0887	0.031164	0.1821	5.8424	0.1711637	13
14	6.2613	37.5811	0.026609	0.1597	6.0021	0.1666091	14
15	7.1379	43.8424	0.022809	0.1401	6.1422	0.1628090	15
16	8.1372	50.9804	0.019615	0.1229	6.2651	0.1596154	16
17	9.2765	59.1176	0.016915	0.1078	6.3729	0.1569154	17
18	10.5752	68.3941	0.014621	0.0946	6.4674	0.1546212	18
19	12.0557	78.9692	0.012663	0.0829	6.5504	0.1526632	19
20	13.7435	91.0249	0.010986	0.0728	6.6231	0.1509860	20
21	15.6676	104.7684	0.009545	0.0638	6.6870	0.1495449	21
22	17.8610	120.4360	0.008303	0.0560	6.7429	0.1483032	22
23	20.3616	138.2970	0.007231	0.0491	6.7921	0.1472308	23
24	23.2122	158.6586	0.006303	0.0431	6.8351	0.1463028	24
25	26.4619	181.8708	0.005498	0.0378	6.8729	0.1454984	25
26	30.1666	208.3327	0.004800	0.0331	6.9061	0.1448000	26
27	34.3899	238.4993	0.004193	0.0291	6.9352	0.1441929	27
28	39.2045	272.8892	0.003664	0.0255	6.9607	0.1436645	28
29	44.6931	312.0937	0.003204	0.0224	6.9830	0.1432042	29
30	50.9502	356.7869	0.002803	0.0196	7.0027	0.1428028	30
31	58.0832	407.7370	0.002453	0.0172	7.0199	0.1424526	31
32	66.2148	465.8202	0.002147	0.0151	7.0350	0.1421468	32
33	75.4849	532.0350	0.001880	0.0132	7.0482	0.1418796	33
34	86.0528	607.5199	0.001646	0.0116	7.0599	0.1416460	34
35	98.1002	693.5727	0.001442	0.0102	7.0700	0.1414418	35
36	111.8342	791.6729	0.001263	0.0089	7.0790	0.1412631	36
37	127.4910	903.5071	0.001107	0.0078	7.0868	0.1411068	37
38	145.3397	1030.9981	0.000970	0.0069	7.0937	0.1409699	38
39	165.6873	1176.3378	0.000850	0.0060	7.0997	0.1408501	39
40	188.8835	1342.0251	0.000745	0.0053	7.1050	0.1407451	40
41	215.3272	1530.9086	0.000653	0.0046	7.1097	0.1406532	41
42	245.4730	1746.2358	0.000573	0.0041	7.1138	0.1405727	42
43	279.8392	1991.7089	0.000502	0.0036	7.1173	0.1405021	43
44	319.0167	2271.5481	0.000440	0.0031	7.1205	0.1404402	44
45	363.6791	2590.5648	0.000386	0.0027	7.1232	0.1403860	45
46	414.5942	2954.2439	0.000338	0.0024	7.1256	0.1403385	46
47	472.6373	3368.8381	0.000297	0.0021	7.1277	0.1402968	47
48	538.8066	3841.4754	0.000260	0.0019	7.1296	0.1402603	48
49	614.2395	4380.2820	0.000228	0.0016	7.1312	0.1402283	49
50	700.2330	4994.5215	0.000200	0.0014	7.1327	0.1402002	50

15 % = ANNUAL RATE   COMPOUND INTEREST TABLES   ANNUAL RATE = 15 %

NOMINAL ANNUAL INTEREST RATE = 15 %   COMPOUNDING FREQUENCY (PER YEAR) = 1

YEAR	AMOUNT OF 1 AT COMPOUND INTEREST (COL 1)	ACCUM OF 1 PER PERIOD (COL 2)	SINKING FUND FACTOR (COL 3)	PRESENT VALUE REVERSN OF 1 (COL 4)	PRESENT VALUE ORD ANN 1 PER PERIOD (COL 5)	INSTALL TO AMORT 1 (COL 6)	PERIOD
1	1.1500	1.0000	1.000000	0.8696	0.8696	1.1500000	1
2	1.3225	2.1500	0.465116	0.7561	1.6257	0.6151163	2
3	1.5209	3.4725	0.287977	0.6575	2.2832	0.4379770	3
4	1.7490	4.9934	0.200265	0.5718	2.8550	0.3502654	4
5	2.0114	6.7424	0.148316	0.4972	3.3522	0.2983156	5
6	2.3131	8.7537	0.114237	0.4323	3.7845	0.2642369	6
7	2.6600	11.0668	0.090360	0.3759	4.1604	0.2403604	7
8	3.0590	13.7268	0.072850	0.3269	4.4873	0.2228501	8
9	3.5179	16.7858	0.059574	0.2843	4.7716	0.2095740	9
10	4.0456	20.3037	0.049252	0.2472	5.0188	0.1992521	10
11	4.6524	24.3493	0.041069	0.2149	5.2337	0.1910690	11
12	5.3503	29.0017	0.034481	0.1869	5.4206	0.1844808	12
13	6.1528	34.3519	0.029110	0.1625	5.5831	0.1791105	13
14	7.0757	40.5047	0.024688	0.1413	5.7245	0.1746885	14
15	8.1371	47.5804	0.021017	0.1229	5.8474	0.1710171	15
16	9.3576	55.7175	0.017948	0.1069	5.9542	0.1679477	16
17	10.7613	65.0751	0.015367	0.0929	6.0472	0.1653669	17
18	12.3755	75.8364	0.013186	0.0808	6.1280	0.1631863	18
19	14.2318	88.2118	0.011336	0.0703	6.1982	0.1613364	19
20	16.3665	102.4436	0.009761	0.0611	6.2593	0.1597615	20
21	18.8215	118.8101	0.008417	0.0531	6.3125	0.1584168	21
22	21.6447	137.6316	0.007266	0.0462	6.3587	0.1572658	22
23	24.8915	159.2764	0.006278	0.0402	6.3988	0.1562784	23
24	28.6252	184.1679	0.005430	0.0349	6.4338	0.1554298	24
25	32.9190	212.7930	0.004699	0.0304	6.4641	0.1546994	25
26	37.8568	245.7120	0.004070	0.0264	6.4906	0.1540698	26
27	43.5353	283.5688	0.003526	0.0230	6.5135	0.1535265	27
28	50.0656	327.1041	0.003057	0.0200	6.5335	0.1530571	28
29	57.5755	377.1697	0.002651	0.0174	6.5509	0.1526513	29
30	66.2118	434.7452	0.002300	0.0151	6.5660	0.1523002	30
31	76.1435	500.9570	0.001996	0.0131	6.5791	0.1519962	31
32	87.5651	577.1005	0.001733	0.0114	6.5905	0.1517328	32
33	100.6998	664.6656	0.001505	0.0099	6.6005	0.1515045	33
34	115.8048	765.3655	0.001307	0.0086	6.6091	0.1513066	34
35	133.1755	881.1703	0.001135	0.0075	6.6166	0.1511349	35
36	153.1519	1014.3458	0.000986	0.0065	6.6231	0.1509859	36
37	176.1247	1167.4977	0.000857	0.0057	6.6288	0.1508565	37
38	202.5434	1343.6224	0.000744	0.0049	6.6338	0.1507443	38
39	232.9249	1546.1657	0.000647	0.0043	6.6380	0.1506468	39
40	267.8636	1779.0906	0.000562	0.0037	6.6418	0.1505621	40

NOMINAL ANNUAL INTEREST RATE = 16 % COMPOUNDING FREQUENCY (PER YEAR) = 1

YEAR	AMOUNT OF 1 AT COMPOUND INTEREST (COL 1)	ACCUM OF 1 PER PERIOD (COL 2)	SINKING FUND FACTOR (COL 3)	PRESENT VALUE REVERSN OF 1 (COL 4)	PRESENT VALUE ORD ANN 1 PER PERIOD (COL 5)	INSTALL TO AMORT 1 (COL 6)	PERIOD
1	1.1600	1.0000	1.000000	0.8621	0.8621	1.1600000	1
2	1.3456	2.1600	0.462963	0.7432	1.6052	0.6229630	2
3	1.5609	3.5056	0.285258	0.6407	2.2459	0.4452579	3
4	1.8106	5.0665	0.197375	0.5523	2.7982	0.3573751	4
5	2.1003	6.8771	0.145409	0.4761	3.2743	0.3054094	5
6	2.4364	8.9775	0.111390	0.4104	3.6847	0.2713899	6
7	2.8262	11.4139	0.087613	0.3538	4.0386	0.2476127	7
8	3.2784	14.2401	0.070224	0.3050	4.3436	0.2302243	8
9	3.8030	17.5185	0.057082	0.2630	4.6065	0.2170825	9
10	4.4114	21.3215	0.046901	0.2267	4.8332	0.2069011	10
11	5.1173	25.7329	0.038861	0.1954	5.0286	0.1988607	11
12	5.9360	30.8502	0.032415	0.1685	5.1971	0.1924147	12
13	6.8858	36.7862	0.027184	0.1452	5.3423	0.1871841	13
14	7.9875	43.6720	0.022898	0.1252	5.4675	0.1828980	14
15	9.2655	51.6595	0.019358	0.1079	5.5755	0.1793575	15
16	10.7480	60.9250	0.016414	0.0930	5.6685	0.1764136	16
17	12.4677	71.6730	0.013952	0.0802	5.7487	0.1739522	17
18	14.4625	84.1407	0.011885	0.0691	5.8178	0.1718848	18
19	16.7765	98.6032	0.010142	0.0596	5.8775	0.1701417	19
20	19.4608	115.3797	0.008667	0.0514	5.9288	0.1686670	20
21	22.5745	134.8405	0.007416	0.0443	5.9731	0.1674162	21
22	26.1864	157.4150	0.006353	0.0382	6.0113	0.1663526	22
23	30.3762	183.6014	0.005447	0.0329	6.0442	0.1654466	23
24	35.2364	213.9776	0.004673	0.0284	6.0726	0.1646734	24
25	40.8742	249.2140	0.004013	0.0245	6.0971	0.1640126	25
26	47.4141	290.0883	0.003447	0.0211	6.1182	0.1634472	26
27	55.0004	337.5024	0.002963	0.0182	6.1364	0.1629629	27
28	63.8004	392.5027	0.002548	0.0157	6.1520	0.1625477	28
29	74.0085	456.3032	0.002192	0.0135	6.1656	0.1621915	29
30	85.8499	530.3117	0.001886	0.0116	6.1772	0.1618857	30
31	99.5858	616.1616	0.001623	0.0100	6.1872	0.1616229	31
32	115.5196	715.7474	0.001397	0.0087	6.1959	0.1613971	32
33	134.0027	831.2670	0.001203	0.0075	6.2034	0.1612030	33
34	155.4431	965.2697	0.001036	0.0064	6.2098	0.1610360	34
35	180.3141	1120.7129	0.000892	0.0055	6.2153	0.1608923	35
36	209.1643	1301.0269	0.000769	0.0048	6.2201	0.1607686	36
37	242.6306	1510.1912	0.000662	0.0041	6.2242	0.1606622	37
38	281.4515	1752.8218	0.000571	0.0036	6.2278	0.1605705	38
39	326.4837	2034.2733	0.000492	0.0031	6.2309	0.1604916	39
40	378.7211	2360.7570	0.000424	0.0026	6.2335	0.1604236	40

17 % = ANNUAL RATE   COMPOUND INTEREST TABLES   ANNUAL RATE = 17 %

NOMINAL ANNUAL INTEREST RATE = 17 %   COMPOUNDING FREQUENCY (PER YEAR) = 1

YEAR	AMOUNT OF 1 AT COMPOUND INTEREST (COL 1)	ACCUM OF 1 PER PERIOD (COL 2)	SINKING FUND FACTOR (COL 3)	PRESENT VALUE REVERSN OF 1 (COL 4)	PRESENT VALUE ORD ANN 1 PER PERIOD (COL 5)	INSTALL TO AMORT 1 (COL 6)	PERIOD
1	1.1700	1.0000	1.000000	0.8547	0.8547	1.1700000	1
2	1.3689	2.1700	0.460829	0.7305	1.5852	0.6308295	2
3	1.6016	3.5389	0.282574	0.6244	2.2096	0.4525737	3
4	1.8739	5.1405	0.194533	0.5337	2.7432	0.3645331	4
5	2.1924	7.0144	0.142564	0.4561	3.1993	0.3125639	5
6	2.5652	9.2068	0.108615	0.3898	3.5892	0.2786148	6
7	3.0012	11.7720	0.084947	0.3332	3.9224	0.2549472	7
8	3.5115	14.7733	0.067690	0.2848	4.2072	0.2376899	8
9	4.1084	18.2847	0.054691	0.2434	4.4506	0.2246905	9
10	4.8068	22.3931	0.044657	0.2080	4.6586	0.2146566	10
11	5.6240	27.1999	0.036765	0.1778	4.8364	0.2067648	11
12	6.5801	32.8239	0.030466	0.1520	4.9884	0.2004656	12
13	7.6987	39.4040	0.025378	0.1299	5.1183	0.1953781	13
14	9.0075	47.1027	0.021230	0.1110	5.2293	0.1912302	14
15	10.5387	56.1101	0.017822	0.0949	5.3242	0.1878221	15
16	12.3303	66.6488	0.015004	0.0811	5.4053	0.1850040	16
17	14.4265	78.9792	0.012662	0.0693	5.4746	0.1826616	17
18	16.8790	93.4056	0.010706	0.0592	5.5339	0.1807060	18
19	19.7484	110.2846	0.009067	0.0506	5.5845	0.1790675	19
20	23.1056	130.0329	0.007690	0.0433	5.6278	0.1776904	20
21	27.0336	153.1385	0.006530	0.0370	5.6648	0.1765300	21
22	31.6293	180.1721	0.005550	0.0316	5.6964	0.1755503	22
23	37.0062	211.8013	0.004721	0.0270	5.7234	0.1747214	23
24	43.2973	248.8076	0.004019	0.0231	5.7465	0.1740192	24
25	50.6578	292.1049	0.003423	0.0197	5.7662	0.1734234	25
26	59.2697	342.7627	0.002917	0.0169	5.7831	0.1729175	26
27	69.3455	402.0323	0.002487	0.0144	5.7975	0.1724874	27
28	81.1342	471.3779	0.002121	0.0123	5.8099	0.1721214	28
29	94.9271	552.5121	0.001810	0.0105	5.8204	0.1718099	29
30	111.0647	647.4391	0.001545	0.0090	5.8294	0.1715445	30
31	129.9456	758.5038	0.001318	0.0077	5.8371	0.1713184	31
32	152.0364	888.4494	0.001126	0.0066	5.8437	0.1711256	32
33	177.8826	1040.4858	0.000961	0.0056	5.8493	0.1709611	33
34	208.1226	1218.3684	0.000821	0.0048	5.8541	0.1708208	34
35	243.5035	1426.4911	0.000701	0.0041	5.8582	0.1707010	35
36	284.8991	1669.9946	0.000599	0.0035	5.8617	0.1705988	36
37	333.3319	1954.8937	0.000512	0.0030	5.8647	0.1705115	37
38	389.9984	2288.2256	0.000437	0.0026	5.8673	0.1704370	38
39	456.2981	2678.2239	0.000373	0.0022	5.8695	0.1703734	39
40	533.8687	3134.5220	0.000319	0.0019	5.8713	0.1703190	40

18 % = ANNUAL RATE   COMPOUND INTEREST TABLES   ANNUAL RATE = 18 %

NOMINAL ANNUAL INTEREST RATE = 18 %   COMPOUNDING FREQUENCY (PER YEAR) = 1

YEAR	AMOUNT OF 1 AT COMPOUND INTEREST (COL 1)	ACCUM OF 1 PER PERIOD (COL 2)	SINKING FUND FACTOR (COL 3)	PRESENT VALUE REVERSN OF 1 (COL 4)	PRESENT VALUE ORD ANN 1 PER PERIOD (COL 5)	INSTALL TO AMORT 1 (COL 6)	PERIOD
1	1.1800	1.0000	1.000000	0.8475	0.8475	1.1800000	1
2	1.3924	2.1800	0.458716	0.7182	1.5656	0.6387156	2
3	1.6430	3.5724	0.279924	0.6086	2.1743	0.4599239	3
4	1.9388	5.2154	0.191739	0.5158	2.6901	0.3717387	4
5	2.2878	7.1542	0.139778	0.4371	3.1272	0.3197778	5
6	2.6996	9.4420	0.105910	0.3704	3.4976	0.2859101	6
7	3.1855	12.1415	0.082362	0.3139	3.8115	0.2623620	7
8	3.7589	15.3270	0.065244	0.2660	4.0776	0.2452444	8
9	4.4355	19.0859	0.052395	0.2255	4.3030	0.2323948	9
10	5.2338	23.5213	0.042515	0.1911	4.4941	0.2225146	10
11	6.1759	28.7551	0.034776	0.1619	4.6560	0.2147764	11
12	7.2876	34.9311	0.028628	0.1372	4.7932	0.2086278	12
13	8.5994	42.2187	0.023686	0.1163	4.9095	0.2036862	13
14	10.1472	50.8180	0.019678	0.0985	5.0081	0.1996781	14
15	11.9737	60.9653	0.016403	0.0835	5.0916	0.1964028	15
16	14.1290	72.9390	0.013710	0.0708	5.1624	0.1937101	16
17	16.6722	87.0680	0.011485	0.0600	5.2223	0.1914853	17
18	19.6733	103.7403	0.009639	0.0508	5.2732	0.1896395	18
19	23.2144	123.4135	0.008103	0.0431	5.3162	0.1881028	19
20	27.3930	146.6280	0.006820	0.0365	5.3527	0.1868200	20
21	32.3238	174.0210	0.005746	0.0309	5.3837	0.1857464	21
22	38.1421	206.3448	0.004846	0.0262	5.4099	0.1848463	22
23	45.0076	244.4869	0.004090	0.0222	5.4321	0.1840902	23
24	53.1090	289.4945	0.003454	0.0188	5.4509	0.1834543	24
25	62.6686	342.6035	0.002919	0.0160	5.4669	0.1829188	25
26	73.9490	405.2722	0.002467	0.0135	5.4804	0.1824675	26
27	87.2598	479.2212	0.002087	0.0115	5.4919	0.1820867	27
28	102.9666	566.4810	0.001765	0.0097	5.5016	0.1817653	28
29	121.5006	669.4475	0.001494	0.0082	5.5098	0.1814938	29
30	143.3707	790.9481	0.001264	0.0070	5.5168	0.1812643	30
31	169.1774	934.3188	0.001070	0.0059	5.5227	0.1810703	31
32	199.6293	1103.4962	0.000906	0.0050	5.5277	0.1809062	32
33	235.5626	1303.1255	0.000767	0.0042	5.5320	0.1807674	33
34	277.9639	1538.6881	0.000650	0.0036	5.5356	0.1806499	34
35	327.9974	1816.6519	0.000550	0.0030	5.5386	0.1805505	35
36	387.0369	2144.6493	0.000466	0.0026	5.5412	0.1804663	36
37	456.7035	2531.6862	0.000395	0.0022	5.5434	0.1803950	37
38	538.9102	2988.3897	0.000335	0.0019	5.5452	0.1803346	38
39	635.9140	3527.2999	0.000284	0.0016	5.5468	0.1802835	39
40	750.3785	4163.2139	0.000240	0.0013	5.5482	0.1802402	40

19 % = ANNUAL RATE   COMPOUND INTEREST TABLES   ANNUAL RATE = 19 %

NOMINAL ANNUAL INTEREST RATE = 19 %   COMPOUNDING FREQUENCY (PER YEAR) = 1

YEAR	AMOUNT OF 1 AT COMPOUND INTEREST (COL 1)	ACCUM OF 1 PER PERIOD (COL 2)	SINKING FUND FACTOR (COL 3)	PRESENT VALUE REVERSN OF 1 (COL 4)	PRESENT VALUE ORD ANN 1 PER PERIOD (COL 5)	INSTALL TO AMORT 1 (COL 6)	PERIOD
1	1.1900	1.0000	1.000000	0.8403	0.8403	1.1900000	1
2	1.4161	2.1900	0.456621	0.7062	1.5465	0.6466210	2
3	1.6852	3.6061	0.277308	0.5934	2.1399	0.4673079	3
4	2.0053	5.2913	0.188991	0.4987	2.6386	0.3789909	4
5	2.3864	7.2966	0.137050	0.4190	3.0576	0.3270502	5
6	2.8398	9.6830	0.103274	0.3521	3.4098	0.2932743	6
7	3.3793	12.5227	0.079855	0.2959	3.7057	0.2698549	7
8	4.0214	15.9020	0.062885	0.2487	3.9544	0.2528851	8
9	4.7854	19.9234	0.050192	0.2090	4.1633	0.2401922	9
10	5.6947	24.7089	0.040471	0.1756	4.3389	0.2304713	10
11	6.7767	30.4035	0.032891	0.1476	4.4865	0.2228909	11
12	8.0642	37.1802	0.026896	0.1240	4.6105	0.2168960	12
13	9.5964	45.2445	0.022102	0.1042	4.7147	0.2121022	13
14	11.4198	54.8409	0.018235	0.0876	4.8023	0.2082346	14
15	13.5895	66.2607	0.015092	0.0736	4.8759	0.2050919	15
16	16.1715	79.8502	0.012523	0.0618	4.9377	0.2025234	16
17	19.2441	96.0217	0.010414	0.0520	4.9897	0.2004143	17
18	22.9005	115.2659	0.008676	0.0437	5.0333	0.1986756	18
19	27.2516	138.1664	0.007238	0.0367	5.0700	0.1972376	19
20	32.4294	165.4180	0.006045	0.0308	5.1009	0.1960453	20
21	38.5910	197.8474	0.005054	0.0259	5.1268	0.1950544	21
22	45.9233	236.4384	0.004229	0.0218	5.1486	0.1942294	22
23	54.6487	282.3618	0.003542	0.0183	5.1668	0.1935416	23
24	65.0320	337.0105	0.002967	0.0154	5.1822	0.1929673	24
25	77.3881	402.0425	0.002487	0.0129	5.1951	0.1924873	25
26	92.0918	479.4305	0.002086	0.0109	5.2060	0.1920858	26
27	109.5892	571.5223	0.001750	0.0091	5.2151	0.1917497	27
28	130.4112	681.1116	0.001468	0.0077	5.2228	0.1914682	28
29	155.1893	811.5228	0.001232	0.0064	5.2292	0.1912322	29
30	184.6753	966.7121	0.001034	0.0054	5.2347	0.1910344	30
31	219.7636	1151.3874	0.000869	0.0046	5.2392	0.1908685	31
32	261.5187	1371.1510	0.000729	0.0038	5.2430	0.1907293	32
33	311.2072	1632.6697	0.000612	0.0032	5.2462	0.1906125	33
34	370.3366	1943.8770	0.000514	0.0027	5.2489	0.1905144	34
35	440.7006	2314.2136	0.000432	0.0023	5.2512	0.1904321	35
36	524.4337	2754.9142	0.000363	0.0019	5.2531	0.1903630	36
37	624.0761	3279.3478	0.000305	0.0016	5.2547	0.1903049	37
38	742.6505	3903.4239	0.000256	0.0013	5.2561	0.1902562	38
39	883.7541	4646.0745	0.000215	0.0011	5.2572	0.1902152	39
40	1051.6674	5529.8286	0.000181	0.0010	5.2582	0.1901808	40

20 % = ANNUAL RATE — COMPOUND INTEREST TABLES — ANNUAL RATE = 20 %

NOMINAL ANNUAL INTEREST RATE = 20 %   COMPOUNDING FREQUENCY (PER YEAR) = 1

YEAR	AMOUNT OF 1 AT COMPOUND INTEREST (COL 1)	ACCUM OF 1 PER PERIOD (COL 2)	SINKING FUND FACTOR (COL 3)	PRESENT VALUE REVERSN OF 1 (COL 4)	PRESENT VALUE ORD ANN 1 PER PERIOD (COL 5)	INSTALL TO AMORT 1 (COL 6)	PERIOD
1	1.2000	1.0000	1.000000	0.8333	0.8333	1.2000000	1
2	1.4400	2.2000	0.454545	0.6944	1.5278	0.6545455	2
3	1.7280	3.6400	0.274725	0.5787	2.1065	0.4747253	3
4	2.0736	5.3680	0.186289	0.4823	2.5887	0.3862891	4
5	2.4883	7.4416	0.134380	0.4019	2.9906	0.3343797	5
6	2.9860	9.9299	0.100706	0.3349	3.3255	0.3007057	6
7	3.5832	12.9159	0.077424	0.2791	3.6046	0.2774239	7
8	4.2998	16.4991	0.060609	0.2326	3.8372	0.2606094	8
9	5.1598	20.7989	0.048079	0.1938	4.0310	0.2480795	9
10	6.1917	25.9587	0.038523	0.1615	4.1925	0.2385228	10
11	7.4301	32.1504	0.031104	0.1346	4.3271	0.2311038	11
12	8.9161	39.5805	0.025265	0.1122	4.4392	0.2252650	12
13	10.6993	48.4966	0.020620	0.0935	4.5327	0.2206200	13
14	12.8392	59.1959	0.016893	0.0779	4.6106	0.2168931	14
15	15.4070	72.0351	0.013882	0.0649	4.6755	0.2138821	15
16	18.4884	87.4421	0.011436	0.0541	4.7296	0.2114361	16
17	22.1861	105.9306	0.009440	0.0451	4.7746	0.2094401	17
18	26.6233	128.1167	0.007805	0.0376	4.8122	0.2078054	18
19	31.9480	154.7400	0.006462	0.0313	4.8435	0.2064625	19
20	38.3376	186.6880	0.005357	0.0261	4.8696	0.2053565	20
21	46.0051	225.0256	0.004444	0.0217	4.8913	0.2044439	21
22	55.2061	271.0307	0.003690	0.0181	4.9094	0.2036896	22
23	66.2474	326.2369	0.003065	0.0151	4.9245	0.2030653	23
24	79.4969	392.4843	0.002548	0.0126	4.9371	0.2025479	24
25	95.3962	471.9811	0.002119	0.0105	4.9476	0.2021187	25
26	114.4755	567.3773	0.001762	0.0087	4.9563	0.2017625	26
27	137.3706	681.8528	0.001467	0.0073	4.9636	0.2014666	27
28	164.8447	819.2234	0.001221	0.0061	4.9697	0.2012207	28
29	197.8136	984.0680	0.001016	0.0051	4.9747	0.2010162	29
30	237.3763	1181.8816	0.000846	0.0042	4.9789	0.2008461	30
31	284.8516	1419.2580	0.000705	0.0035	4.9824	0.2007046	31
32	341.8219	1704.1096	0.000587	0.0029	4.9854	0.2005868	32
33	410.1863	2045.9315	0.000489	0.0024	4.9878	0.2004888	33
34	492.2236	2456.1178	0.000407	0.0020	4.9898	0.2004071	34
35	590.6683	2948.3414	0.000339	0.0017	4.9915	0.2003392	35
36	708.8019	3539.0096	0.000283	0.0014	4.9929	0.2002826	36
37	850.5623	4247.8116	0.000235	0.0012	4.9941	0.2002354	37
38	1020.6748	5098.3739	0.000196	0.0010	4.9951	0.2001961	38
39	1224.8098	6119.0487	0.000163	0.0008	4.9959	0.2001634	39
40	1469.7717	7343.8585	0.000136	0.0007	4.9966	0.2001362	40

21 % = ANNUAL RATE COMPOUND INTEREST TABLES ANNUAL RATE = 21 %

NOMINAL ANNUAL INTEREST RATE = 21 % COMPOUNDING FREQUENCY (PER YEAR) = 1

YEAR	AMOUNT OF 1 AT COMPOUND INTEREST (COL 1)	ACCUM OF 1 PER PERIOD (COL 2)	SINKING FUND FACTOR (COL 3)	PRESENT VALUE REVERSN OF 1 (COL 4)	PRESENT VALUE ORD ANN 1 PER PERIOD (COL 5)	INSTALL TO AMORT 1 (COL 6)	PERIOD
1	1.2100	1.0000	1.000000	0.8264	0.8264	1.2100000	1
2	1.4641	2.2100	0.452489	0.6830	1.5095	0.6624887	2
3	1.7716	3.6741	0.272176	0.5645	2.0739	0.4821755	3
4	2.1436	5.4457	0.183632	0.4665	2.5404	0.3936324	4
5	2.5937	7.5892	0.131765	0.3855	2.9260	0.3417653	5
6	3.1384	10.1830	0.098203	0.3186	3.2446	0.3082030	6
7	3.7975	13.3214	0.075067	0.2633	3.5079	0.2850671	7
8	4.5950	17.1189	0.058415	0.2176	3.7256	0.2684149	8
9	5.5599	21.7139	0.046053	0.1799	3.9054	0.2560535	9
10	6.7275	27.2738	0.036665	0.1486	4.0541	0.2466652	10
11	8.1403	34.0013	0.029411	0.1228	4.1769	0.2394106	11
12	9.8497	42.1416	0.023730	0.1015	4.2784	0.2337295	12
13	11.9182	51.9913	0.019234	0.0839	4.3624	0.2292340	13
14	14.4210	63.9095	0.015647	0.0693	4.4317	0.2256471	14
15	17.4494	78.3305	0.012766	0.0573	4.4890	0.2227664	15
16	21.1138	95.7799	0.010441	0.0474	4.5364	0.2204406	16
17	25.5477	116.8937	0.008555	0.0391	4.5755	0.2185548	17
18	30.9127	142.4413	0.007020	0.0323	4.6079	0.2170204	18
19	37.4043	173.3540	0.005769	0.0267	4.6346	0.2157685	19
20	45.2593	210.7583	0.004745	0.0221	4.6567	0.2147448	20
21	54.7637	256.0176	0.003906	0.0183	4.6750	0.2139060	21
22	66.2641	310.7813	0.003218	0.0151	4.6900	0.2132177	22
23	80.1795	377.0454	0.002652	0.0125	4.7025	0.2126522	23
24	97.0172	457.2249	0.002187	0.0103	4.7128	0.2121871	24
25	117.3908	554.2421	0.001804	0.0085	4.7213	0.2118043	25
26	142.0429	671.6329	0.001489	0.0070	4.7284	0.2114889	26
27	171.8719	813.6758	0.001229	0.0058	4.7342	0.2112290	27
28	207.9650	985.5478	0.001015	0.0048	4.7390	0.2110147	28
29	251.6377	1193.5128	0.000838	0.0040	4.7430	0.2108379	29
30	304.4816	1445.1505	0.000692	0.0033	4.7463	0.2106920	30

NOMINAL ANNUAL INTEREST RATE = 22 % COMPOUNDING FREQUENCY (PER YEAR) = 1

YEAR	AMOUNT OF 1 AT COMPOUND INTEREST (COL 1)	ACCUM OF 1 PER PERIOD (COL 2)	SINKING FUND FACTOR (COL 3)	PRESENT VALUE REVERSN OF 1 (COL 4)	PRESENT VALUE ORD ANN 1 PER PERIOD (COL 5)	INSTALL TO AMORT 1 (COL 6)	PERIOD
1	1.2200	1.0000	1.000000	0.8197	0.8197	1.2200000	1
2	1.4884	2.2200	0.450450	0.6719	1.4915	0.6704504	2
3	1.8158	3.7084	0.269658	0.5507	2.0422	0.4896581	3
4	2.2153	5.5242	0.181020	0.4514	2.4936	0.4010201	4
5	2.7027	7.7396	0.129206	0.3700	2.8636	0.3492059	5
6	3.2973	10.4423	0.095764	0.3033	3.1669	0.3157644	6
7	4.0227	13.7396	0.072782	0.2486	3.4155	0.2927823	7
8	4.9077	17.7623	0.056299	0.2038	3.6193	0.2762990	8
9	5.9874	22.6700	0.044111	0.1670	3.7863	0.2641111	9
10	7.3046	28.6574	0.034895	0.1369	3.9232	0.2548950	10
11	8.9117	35.9620	0.027807	0.1122	4.0354	0.2478071	11
12	10.8722	44.8737	0.022285	0.0920	4.1274	0.2422848	12
13	13.2641	55.7459	0.017939	0.0754	4.2028	0.2379385	13
14	16.1822	69.0100	0.014491	0.0618	4.2646	0.2344907	14
15	19.7423	85.1922	0.011738	0.0507	4.3152	0.2317382	15
16	24.0856	104.9345	0.009530	0.0415	4.3567	0.2295298	16
17	29.3844	129.0201	0.007751	0.0340	4.3908	0.2277507	17
18	35.8490	158.4045	0.006313	0.0279	4.4187	0.2263130	18
19	43.7358	194.2535	0.005148	0.0229	4.4415	0.2251479	19
20	53.3576	237.9893	0.004202	0.0187	4.4603	0.2242019	20
21	65.0963	291.3469	0.003432	0.0154	4.4756	0.2234323	21
22	79.4175	356.4432	0.002805	0.0126	4.4882	0.2228055	22
23	96.8894	435.8607	0.002294	0.0103	4.4985	0.2222943	23
24	118.2050	532.7501	0.001877	0.0085	4.5070	0.2218771	24
25	144.2101	650.9551	0.001536	0.0069	4.5139	0.2215362	25
26	175.9364	795.1652	0.001258	0.0057	4.5196	0.2212576	26
27	214.6424	971.1016	0.001030	0.0047	4.5243	0.2210298	27
28	261.8637	1185.7440	0.000843	0.0038	4.5281	0.2208434	28
29	319.4737	1447.6076	0.000691	0.0031	4.5312	0.2206908	29
30	389.7579	1767.0813	0.000566	0.0026	4.5338	0.2205659	30

23 % = ANNUAL RATE   COMPOUND INTEREST TABLES   ANNUAL RATE = 23 %

NOMINAL ANNUAL INTEREST RATE = 23 %   COMPOUNDING FREQUENCY (PER YEAR) = 1

YEAR	AMOUNT OF 1 AT COMPOUND INTEREST (COL 1)	ACCUM OF 1 PER PERIOD (COL 2)	SINKING FUND FACTOR (COL 3)	PRESENT VALUE REVERSN OF 1 (COL 4)	PRESENT VALUE ORD ANN 1 PER PERIOD (COL 5)	INSTALL TO AMORT 1 (COL 6)	PERIOD
1	1.2300	1.0000	1.000000	0.8130	0.8130	1.2300000	1
2	1.5129	2.2300	0.448430	0.6610	1.4740	0.6784305	2
3	1.8609	3.7429	0.267173	0.5374	2.0114	0.4971725	3
4	2.2889	5.6038	0.178451	0.4369	2.4483	0.4084514	4
5	2.8153	7.8926	0.126700	0.3552	2.8035	0.3567004	5
6	3.4628	10.7079	0.093389	0.2888	3.0923	0.3233887	6
7	4.2593	14.1708	0.070568	0.2348	3.3270	0.3005678	7
8	5.2389	18.4300	0.054259	0.1909	3.5179	0.2842592	8
9	6.4439	23.6690	0.042249	0.1552	3.6731	0.2722494	9
10	7.9259	30.1128	0.033208	0.1262	3.7993	0.2632085	10
11	9.7489	38.0388	0.026289	0.1026	3.9018	0.2562890	11
12	11.9912	47.7877	0.020926	0.0834	3.9852	0.2509259	12
13	14.7491	59.7788	0.016728	0.0678	4.0530	0.2467283	13
14	18.1414	74.5280	0.013418	0.0551	4.1082	0.2434178	14
15	22.3140	92.6694	0.010791	0.0448	4.1530	0.2407911	15
16	27.4462	114.9834	0.008697	0.0364	4.1894	0.2386969	16
17	33.7588	142.4295	0.007021	0.0296	4.2190	0.2370210	17
18	41.5233	176.1883	0.005676	0.0241	4.2431	0.2356757	18
19	51.0737	217.7116	0.004593	0.0196	4.2627	0.2345932	19
20	62.8206	268.7853	0.003720	0.0159	4.2786	0.2337204	20
21	77.2694	331.6060	0.003016	0.0129	4.2916	0.2330156	21
22	95.0413	408.8753	0.002446	0.0105	4.3021	0.2324457	22
23	116.9008	503.9166	0.001984	0.0086	4.3106	0.2319845	23
24	143.7880	620.8175	0.001611	0.0070	4.3176	0.2316108	24
25	176.8593	764.6055	0.001308	0.0057	4.3232	0.2313079	25
26	217.5369	941.4648	0.001062	0.0046	4.3278	0.2310622	26
27	267.5704	1159.0017	0.000863	0.0037	4.3316	0.2308628	27
28	329.1116	1426.5721	0.000701	0.0030	4.3346	0.2307010	28
29	404.8072	1755.6836	0.000570	0.0025	4.3371	0.2305696	29
30	497.9129	2160.4909	0.000463	0.0020	4.3391	0.2304629	30

24 % = ANNUAL RATE COMPOUND INTEREST TABLES ANNUAL RATE = 24 %

NOMINAL ANNUAL INTEREST RATE = 24 % COMPOUNDING FREQUENCY (PER YEAR) = 1

YEAR	AMOUNT OF 1 AT COMPOUND INTEREST (COL 1)	ACCUM OF 1 PER PERIOD (COL 2)	SINKING FUND FACTOR (COL 3)	PRESENT VALUE REVERSN OF 1 (COL 4)	PRESENT VALUE ORD ANN 1 PER PERIOD (COL 5)	INSTALL TO AMORT 1 (COL 6)	PERIOD
1	1.2400	1.0000	1.000000	0.8065	0.8065	1.2400000	1
2	1.5376	2.2400	0.446429	0.6504	1.4568	0.6864286	2
3	1.9066	3.7776	0.264718	0.5245	1.9813	0.5047183	3
4	2.3642	5.6842	0.175926	0.4230	2.4043	0.4159255	4
5	2.9316	8.0484	0.124248	0.3411	2.7454	0.3642477	5
6	3.6352	10.9801	0.091074	0.2751	3.0205	0.3310742	6
7	4.5077	14.6153	0.068422	0.2218	3.2423	0.3084215	7
8	5.5895	19.1229	0.052293	0.1789	3.4212	0.2922932	8
9	6.9310	24.7125	0.040465	0.1443	3.5655	0.2804654	9
10	8.5944	31.6434	0.031602	0.1164	3.6819	0.2716021	10
11	10.6571	40.2379	0.024852	0.0938	3.7757	0.2648522	11
12	13.2148	50.8950	0.019648	0.0757	3.8514	0.2596483	12
13	16.3863	64.1097	0.015598	0.0610	3.9124	0.2555982	13
14	20.3191	80.4961	0.012423	0.0492	3.9616	0.2524230	14
15	25.1956	100.8151	0.009919	0.0397	4.0013	0.2499191	15
16	31.2426	126.0108	0.007936	0.0320	4.0333	0.2479358	16
17	38.7408	157.2533	0.006359	0.0258	4.0591	0.2463592	17
18	48.0386	195.9942	0.005102	0.0208	4.0799	0.2451022	18
19	59.5679	244.0327	0.004098	0.0168	4.0967	0.2440978	19
20	73.8641	303.6006	0.003294	0.0135	4.1103	0.2432938	20
21	91.5915	377.4647	0.002649	0.0109	4.1212	0.2426492	21
22	113.5735	469.0563	0.002132	0.0088	4.1300	0.2421319	22
23	140.8311	582.6298	0.001716	0.0071	4.1371	0.2417164	23
24	174.6306	723.4609	0.001382	0.0057	4.1428	0.2413822	24
25	216.5420	898.0916	0.001113	0.0046	4.1474	0.2411135	25
26	268.5120	1114.6335	0.000897	0.0037	4.1511	0.2408972	26
27	332.9549	1383.1456	0.000723	0.0030	4.1542	0.2407230	27
28	412.8641	1716.1005	0.000583	0.0024	4.1566	0.2405827	28
29	511.9515	2128.9646	0.000470	0.0020	4.1585	0.2404697	29
30	634.8199	2640.9161	0.000379	0.0016	4.1601	0.2403787	30

NOMINAL ANNUAL INTEREST RATE = 25 % COMPOUNDING FREQUENCY (PER YEAR) = 1

YEAR	AMOUNT OF 1 AT COMPOUND INTEREST (COL 1)	ACCUM OF 1 PER PERIOD (COL 2)	SINKING FUND FACTOR (COL 3)	PRESENT VALUE REVERSN OF 1 (COL 4)	PRESENT VALUE ORD ANN 1 PER PERIOD (COL 5)	INSTALL TO AMORT 1 (COL 6)	PERIOD
1	1.2500	1.0000	1.000000	0.8000	0.8000	1.2500000	1
2	1.5625	2.2500	0.444444	0.6400	1.4400	0.6944444	2
3	1.9531	3.8125	0.262295	0.5120	1.9520	0.5122951	3
4	2.4414	5.7656	0.173442	0.4096	2.3616	0.4234417	4
5	3.0518	8.2070	0.121847	0.3277	2.6893	0.3718467	5
6	3.8147	11.2588	0.088819	0.2621	2.9514	0.3388195	6
7	4.7684	15.0735	0.066342	0.2097	3.1611	0.3163417	7
8	5.9605	19.8419	0.050399	0.1678	3.3289	0.3003985	8
9	7.4506	25.8023	0.038756	0.1342	3.4631	0.2887562	9
10	9.3132	33.2529	0.030073	0.1074	3.5705	0.2800726	10
11	11.6415	42.5661	0.023493	0.0859	3.6564	0.2734929	11
12	14.5519	54.2077	0.018448	0.0687	3.7251	0.2684476	12
13	18.1899	68.7596	0.014543	0.0550	3.7801	0.2645434	13
14	22.7374	86.9495	0.011501	0.0440	3.8241	0.2615009	14
15	28.4217	109.6868	0.009117	0.0352	3.8593	0.2591169	15
16	35.5271	138.1085	0.007241	0.0281	3.8874	0.2572407	16
17	44.4089	173.6357	0.005759	0.0225	3.9099	0.2557592	17
18	55.5112	218.0446	0.004586	0.0180	3.9279	0.2545862	18
19	69.3889	273.5558	0.003656	0.0144	3.9424	0.2536556	19
20	86.7362	342.9447	0.002916	0.0115	3.9539	0.2529159	20
21	108.4202	429.6809	0.002327	0.0092	3.9631	0.2523273	21
22	135.5253	538.1011	0.001858	0.0074	3.9705	0.2518584	22
23	169.4066	673.6264	0.001485	0.0059	3.9764	0.2514845	23
24	211.7582	843.0329	0.001186	0.0047	3.9811	0.2511862	24
25	264.6978	1054.7912	0.000948	0.0038	3.9849	0.2509481	25
26	330.8722	1319.4890	0.000758	0.0030	3.9879	0.2507579	26
27	413.5903	1650.3612	0.000606	0.0024	3.9903	0.2506059	27
28	516.9879	2063.9515	0.000485	0.0019	3.9923	0.2504845	28
29	646.2349	2580.9394	0.000387	0.0015	3.9938	0.2503875	29
30	807.7936	3227.1743	0.000310	0.0012	3.9950	0.2503099	30

NOMINAL ANNUAL INTEREST RATE = 26 % COMPOUNDING FREQUENCY (PER YEAR) = 1

YEAR	AMOUNT OF 1 AT COMPOUND INTEREST (COL 1)	ACCUM OF 1 PER PERIOD (COL 2)	SINKING FUND FACTOR (COL 3)	PRESENT VALUE REVERSN OF 1 (COL 4)	PRESENT VALUE ORD ANN 1 PER PERIOD (COL 5)	INSTALL TO AMORT 1 (COL 6)	PERIOD
1	1.2600	1.0000	1.000000	0.7937	0.7937	1.2600000	1
2	1.5876	2.2600	0.442478	0.6299	1.4235	0.7024779	2
3	2.0004	3.8476	0.259902	0.4999	1.9234	0.5199023	3
4	2.5205	5.8480	0.170999	0.3968	2.3202	0.4309993	4
5	3.1758	8.3684	0.119496	0.3149	2.6351	0.3794964	5
6	4.0015	11.5442	0.086623	0.2499	2.8850	0.3466232	6
7	5.0419	15.5458	0.064326	0.1983	3.0833	0.3243263	7
8	6.3528	20.5876	0.048573	0.1574	3.2407	0.3085728	8
9	8.0045	26.9404	0.037119	0.1249	3.3657	0.2971189	9
10	10.0857	34.9449	0.028616	0.0992	3.4648	0.2886164	10
11	12.7080	45.0306	0.022207	0.0787	3.5435	0.2822071	11
12	16.0120	57.7386	0.017319	0.0625	3.6060	0.2773194	12
13	20.1752	73.7506	0.013559	0.0496	3.6555	0.2735592	13
14	25.4207	93.9258	0.010647	0.0393	3.6949	0.2706467	14
15	32.0301	119.3465	0.008379	0.0312	3.7261	0.2683790	15
16	40.3579	151.3766	0.006606	0.0248	3.7509	0.2666060	16
17	50.8510	191.7345	0.005216	0.0197	3.7705	0.2652155	17
18	64.0722	242.5855	0.004122	0.0156	3.7861	0.2641222	18
19	80.7310	306.6577	0.003261	0.0124	3.7985	0.2632610	19
20	101.7211	387.3887	0.002581	0.0098	3.8083	0.2625814	20
21	128.1685	489.1097	0.002045	0.0078	3.8161	0.2620445	21
22	161.4923	617.2782	0.001620	0.0062	3.8223	0.2616200	22
23	203.4803	778.7706	0.001284	0.0049	3.8273	0.2612841	23
24	256.3852	982.2509	0.001018	0.0039	3.8312	0.2610181	24
25	323.0454	1238.6362	0.000807	0.0031	3.8342	0.2608073	25
26	407.0372	1561.6815	0.000640	0.0025	3.8367	0.2606403	26
27	512.8669	1968.7187	0.000508	0.0019	3.8387	0.2605079	27
28	646.2122	2481.5856	0.000403	0.0015	3.8402	0.2604030	28
29	814.2274	3127.7978	0.000320	0.0012	3.8414	0.2603197	29
30	1025.9265	3942.0252	0.000254	0.0010	3.8424	0.2602537	30

27 % = ANNUAL RATE COMPOUND INTEREST TABLES ANNUAL RATE = 27 %

NOMINAL ANNUAL INTEREST RATE = 27 % COMPOUNDING FREQUENCY (PER YEAR) = 1

YEAR	AMOUNT OF 1 AT COMPOUND INTEREST (COL 1)	ACCUM OF 1 PER PERIOD (COL 2)	SINKING FUND FACTOR (COL 3)	PRESENT VALUE REVERSN OF 1 (COL 4)	PRESENT VALUE ORD ANN 1 PER PERIOD (COL 5)	INSTALL TO AMORT 1 (COL 6)	PERIOD
1	1.2700	1.0000	1.000000	0.7874	0.7874	1.2700000	1
2	1.6129	2.2700	0.440529	0.6200	1.4074	0.7105286	2
3	2.0484	3.8829	0.257539	0.4882	1.8956	0.5275395	3
4	2.6014	5.9313	0.168598	0.3844	2.2800	0.4385976	4
5	3.3038	8.5327	0.117196	0.3027	2.5827	0.3871958	5
6	4.1959	11.8366	0.084484	0.2383	2.8210	0.3544840	6
7	5.3288	16.0324	0.062374	0.1877	3.0087	0.3323735	7
8	6.7675	21.3612	0.046814	0.1478	3.1564	0.3168139	8
9	8.5948	28.1287	0.035551	0.1164	3.2728	0.3055509	9
10	10.9153	36.7235	0.027231	0.0916	3.3644	0.2972305	10
11	13.8625	47.6388	0.020991	0.0721	3.4365	0.2909913	11
12	17.6054	61.5013	0.016260	0.0568	3.4933	0.2862598	12
13	22.3588	79.1066	0.012641	0.0447	3.5381	0.2826412	13
14	28.3957	101.4654	0.009856	0.0352	3.5733	0.2798556	14
15	36.0625	129.8611	0.007701	0.0277	3.6010	0.2777005	15
16	45.7994	165.9236	0.006027	0.0218	3.6228	0.2760269	16
17	58.1652	211.7230	0.004723	0.0172	3.6400	0.2747232	17
18	73.8698	269.8882	0.003705	0.0135	3.6536	0.2737052	18
19	93.8147	343.7580	0.002909	0.0107	3.6642	0.2729090	19
20	119.1446	437.5727	0.002285	0.0084	3.6726	0.2722853	20
21	151.3137	556.7173	0.001796	0.0066	3.6792	0.2717963	21
22	192.1684	708.0310	0.001412	0.0052	3.6844	0.2714124	22
23	244.0539	900.1994	0.001111	0.0041	3.6885	0.2711109	23
24	309.9484	1144.2533	0.000874	0.0032	3.6918	0.2708739	24
25	393.6345	1454.2017	0.000688	0.0025	3.6943	0.2706877	25
26	499.9158	1847.8361	0.000541	0.0020	3.6963	0.2705412	26
27	634.8930	2347.7519	0.000426	0.0016	3.6979	0.2704260	27
28	806.3142	2982.6449	0.000335	0.0012	3.6991	0.2703353	28
29	1024.0190	3788.9591	0.000264	0.0010	3.7001	0.2702639	29
30	1300.5041	4812.9781	0.000208	0.0008	3.7009	0.2702078	30

28 % = ANNUAL RATE　　COMPOUND INTEREST TABLES　　ANNUAL RATE = 28 %

NOMINAL ANNUAL INTEREST RATE = 28 %　　COMPOUNDING FREQUENCY (PER YEAR) = 1

YEAR	AMOUNT OF 1 AT COMPOUND INTEREST (COL 1)	ACCUM OF 1 PER PERIOD (COL 2)	SINKING FUND FACTOR (COL 3)	PRESENT VALUE REVERSN OF 1 (COL 4)	PRESENT VALUE ORD ANN 1 PER PERIOD (COL 5)	INSTALL TO AMORT 1 (COL 6)	PERIOD
1	1.2800	1.0000	1.000000	0.7812	0.7812	1.2800000	1
2	1.6384	2.2800	0.438596	0.6104	1.3916	0.7185965	2
3	2.0972	3.9184	0.255206	0.4768	1.8684	0.5352062	3
4	2.6844	6.0156	0.166236	0.3725	2.2410	0.4462358	4
5	3.4360	8.6999	0.114944	0.2910	2.5320	0.3949438	5
6	4.3980	12.1359	0.082400	0.2274	2.7594	0.3624003	6
7	5.6295	16.5339	0.060482	0.1776	2.9370	0.3404817	7
8	7.2058	22.1634	0.045119	0.1388	3.0758	0.3251194	8
9	9.2234	29.3692	0.034049	0.1084	3.1842	0.3140493	9
10	11.8059	38.5926	0.025912	0.0847	3.2689	0.3059117	10
11	15.1116	50.3985	0.019842	0.0662	3.3351	0.2998419	11
12	19.3428	65.5100	0.015265	0.0517	3.3868	0.2952648	12
13	24.7588	84.8529	0.011785	0.0404	3.4272	0.2917851	13
14	31.6913	109.6117	0.009123	0.0316	3.4587	0.2891231	14
15	40.5648	141.3029	0.007077	0.0247	3.4834	0.2870770	15
16	51.9230	181.8677	0.005499	0.0193	3.5026	0.2854985	16
17	66.4614	233.7907	0.004277	0.0150	3.5177	0.2842773	17
18	85.0706	300.2521	0.003331	0.0118	3.5294	0.2833305	18
19	108.8904	385.3227	0.002595	0.0092	3.5386	0.2825952	19
20	139.3797	494.2131	0.002023	0.0072	3.5458	0.2820234	20
21	178.4060	633.5927	0.001578	0.0056	3.5514	0.2815783	21
22	228.3596	811.9987	0.001232	0.0044	3.5558	0.2812315	22
23	292.3003	1040.3583	0.000961	0.0034	3.5592	0.2809612	23
24	374.1444	1332.6587	0.000750	0.0027	3.5619	0.2807504	24
25	478.9049	1706.8031	0.000586	0.0021	3.5640	0.2805859	25
26	612.9982	2185.7080	0.000458	0.0016	3.5656	0.2804575	26
27	784.6377	2798.7062	0.000357	0.0013	3.5669	0.2803573	27
28	1004.3363	3583.3439	0.000279	0.0010	3.5679	0.2802791	28
29	1285.5505	4587.6802	0.000218	0.0008	3.5687	0.2802180	29
30	1645.5046	5873.2307	0.000170	0.0006	3.5693	0.2801703	30

29 % = ANNUAL RATE   COMPOUND INTEREST TABLES   ANNUAL RATE = 29 %

NOMINAL ANNUAL INTEREST RATE = 29 %   COMPOUNDING FREQUENCY (PER YEAR) = 1

YEAR	AMOUNT OF 1 AT COMPOUND INTEREST (COL 1)	ACCUM OF 1 PER PERIOD (COL 2)	SINKING FUND FACTOR (COL 3)	PRESENT VALUE REVERSN OF 1 (COL 4)	PRESENT VALUE ORD ANN 1 PER PERIOD (COL 5)	INSTALL TO AMORT 1 (COL 6)	PERIOD
1	1.2900	1.0000	1.000000	0.7752	0.7752	1.2900000	1
2	1.6641	2.2900	0.436681	0.6009	1.3761	0.7266812	2
3	2.1467	3.9541	0.252902	0.4658	1.8420	0.5429020	3
4	2.7692	6.1008	0.163913	0.3611	2.2031	0.4539132	4
5	3.5723	8.8700	0.112739	0.2799	2.4830	0.4027393	5
6	4.6083	12.4423	0.080371	0.2170	2.7000	0.3703708	6
7	5.9447	17.0506	0.058649	0.1682	2.8682	0.3486490	7
8	7.6686	22.9953	0.043487	0.1304	2.9986	0.3334872	8
9	9.8925	30.6639	0.032612	0.1011	3.0997	0.3226116	9
10	12.7614	40.5564	0.024657	0.0784	3.1781	0.3146570	10
11	16.4622	53.3178	0.018755	0.0607	3.2388	0.3087555	11
12	21.2362	69.7799	0.014331	0.0471	3.2859	0.3043308	12
13	27.3947	91.0161	0.010987	0.0365	3.3224	0.3009871	13
14	35.3391	118.4108	0.008445	0.0283	3.3507	0.2984452	14
15	45.5875	153.7499	0.006504	0.0219	3.3726	0.2965041	15
16	58.8079	199.3374	0.005017	0.0170	3.3896	0.2950166	16
17	75.8621	258.1453	0.003874	0.0132	3.4028	0.2938738	17
18	97.8621	334.0074	0.002994	0.0102	3.4130	0.2929939	18
19	126.2422	431.8696	0.002316	0.0079	3.4210	0.2923155	19
20	162.8524	558.1117	0.001792	0.0061	3.4271	0.2917917	20
21	210.0796	720.9641	0.001387	0.0048	3.4319	0.2913870	21
22	271.0027	931.0437	0.001074	0.0037	3.4356	0.2910741	22
23	349.5934	1202.0464	0.000832	0.0029	3.4384	0.2908319	23
24	450.9755	1551.6398	0.000644	0.0022	3.4406	0.2906445	24
25	581.7584	2002.6153	0.000499	0.0017	3.4423	0.2904993	25
26	750.4684	2584.3738	0.000387	0.0013	3.4437	0.2903869	26
27	968.1042	3334.8421	0.000300	0.0010	3.4447	0.2902999	27
28	1248.8544	4302.9463	0.000232	0.0008	3.4455	0.2902324	28
29	1611.0222	5551.8007	0.000180	0.0006	3.4461	0.2901801	29
30	2078.2186	7162.8229	0.000140	0.0005	3.4466	0.2901396	30

NOMINAL ANNUAL INTEREST RATE = 30 % COMPOUNDING FREQUENCY (PER YEAR) = 1

YEAR	AMOUNT OF 1 AT COMPOUND INTEREST (COL 1)	ACCUM OF 1 PER PERIOD (COL 2)	SINKING FUND FACTOR (COL 3)	PRESENT VALUE REVERSN OF 1 (COL 4)	PRESENT VALUE ORD ANN 1 PER PERIOD (COL 5)	INSTALL TO AMORT 1 (COL 6)	PERIOD
1	1.3000	1.0000	1.000000	0.7692	0.7692	1.3000000	1
2	1.6900	2.3000	0.434783	0.5917	1.3609	0.7347826	2
3	2.1970	3.9900	0.250627	0.4552	1.8161	0.5506266	3
4	2.8561	6.1870	0.161629	0.3501	2.1662	0.4616292	4
5	3.7129	9.0431	0.110582	0.2693	2.4356	0.4105816	5
6	4.8268	12.7560	0.078394	0.2072	2.6427	0.3783943	6
7	6.2749	17.5828	0.056874	0.1594	2.8021	0.3568736	7
8	8.1573	23.8577	0.041915	0.1226	2.9247	0.3419152	8
9	10.6045	32.0150	0.031235	0.0943	3.0190	0.3312354	9
10	13.7859	42.6195	0.023463	0.0725	3.0915	0.3234635	10
11	17.9216	56.4054	0.017729	0.0558	3.1473	0.3177288	11
12	23.2981	74.3270	0.013454	0.0429	3.1903	0.3134541	12
13	30.2875	97.6250	0.010243	0.0330	3.2233	0.3102433	13
14	39.3738	127.9126	0.007818	0.0254	3.2487	0.3078179	14
15	51.1859	167.2863	0.005978	0.0195	3.2682	0.3059778	15
16	66.5417	218.4722	0.004577	0.0150	3.2832	0.3045773	16
17	86.5042	285.0139	0.003509	0.0116	3.2948	0.3035086	17
18	112.4554	371.5181	0.002692	0.0089	3.3037	0.3026917	18
19	146.1921	483.9735	0.002066	0.0068	3.3105	0.3020662	19
20	190.0497	630.1656	0.001587	0.0053	3.3158	0.3015869	20
21	247.0646	820.2152	0.001219	0.0040	3.3198	0.3012192	21
22	321.1840	1067.2798	0.000937	0.0031	3.3230	0.3009370	22
23	417.5391	1388.4638	0.000720	0.0024	3.3253	0.3007202	23
24	542.8009	1806.0029	0.000554	0.0018	3.3272	0.3005537	24
25	705.6412	2348.8038	0.000426	0.0014	3.3286	0.3004258	25
26	917.3335	3054.4449	0.000327	0.0011	3.3297	0.3003274	26
27	1192.5336	3971.7785	0.000252	0.0008	3.3305	0.3002518	27
28	1550.2937	5164.3121	0.000194	0.0006	3.3312	0.3001936	28
29	2015.3818	6714.6057	0.000149	0.0005	3.3317	0.3001489	29
30	2619.9964	8729.9875	0.000115	0.0004	3.3321	0.3001146	30

COMPOUND INTEREST TABLES

8 % MONTHLY COMPOUNDING MONTHLY COMPOUNDING 8 %

NOMINAL ANNUAL INTEREST RATE = 8 % COMPOUNDING PERIODS PER YEAR = 12

YEAR	AMOUNT OF 1 AT COMPOUND INTEREST (COL 1)	ACCUM OF 1 PER PERIOD (COL 2)	SINKING FUND FACTOR (COL 3)	PRESENT VALUE REVERSN OF 1 (COL 4)	PRESENT VALUE ORD ANN 1 PER PERIOD (COL 5)	INSTALL TO AMORT 1 (COL 6)	PERIOD
1	1.0830	12.4499	0.080322	0.9234	11.4958	0.08698843	12
2	1.1729	25.9332	0.038561	0.8526	22.1105	0.04522729	24
3	1.2702	40.5356	0.024670	0.7873	31.9118	0.03133637	36
4	1.3757	56.3499	0.017746	0.7269	40.9619	0.02441292	48
5	1.4898	73.4769	0.013610	0.6712	49.3184	0.02027639	60
6	1.6135	92.0253	0.010867	0.6198	57.0345	0.01753324	72
7	1.7474	112.1133	0.008920	0.5723	64.1593	0.01558621	84
8	1.8925	133.8686	0.007470	0.5284	70.7380	0.01413668	96
9	2.0495	157.4295	0.006352	0.4879	76.8125	0.01301871	108
10	2.2196	182.9460	0.005466	0.4505	82.4215	0.01213276	120
11	2.4039	210.5804	0.004749	0.4160	87.6006	0.01141545	132
12	2.6034	240.5084	0.004158	0.3841	92.3828	0.01082453	144
13	2.8195	272.9204	0.003664	0.3547	96.7985	0.01033074	156
14	3.0535	308.0226	0.003247	0.3275	100.8758	0.00991318	168
15	3.3069	346.0382	0.002890	0.3024	104.6406	0.00955652	180
16	3.5814	387.2092	0.002583	0.2792	108.1169	0.00924925	192
17	3.8786	431.7973	0.002316	0.2578	111.3267	0.00898257	204
18	4.2006	480.0861	0.002083	0.2381	114.2906	0.00874963	216
19	4.5492	532.3830	0.001878	0.2198	117.0273	0.00854501	228
20	4.9268	589.0204	0.001698	0.2030	119.5543	0.00836440	240
21	5.3357	650.3588	0.001538	0.1874	121.8876	0.00820428	252
22	5.7786	716.7881	0.001395	0.1731	124.0421	0.00806178	264
23	6.2582	788.7311	0.001268	0.1598	126.0315	0.00793453	276
24	6.7776	866.6454	0.001154	0.1475	127.8684	0.00782054	288
25	7.3402	951.0264	0.001051	0.1362	129.5645	0.00771816	300
26	7.9494	1042.4111	0.000959	0.1258	131.1307	0.00762598	312
27	8.6092	1141.3806	0.000876	0.1162	132.5768	0.00754280	324
28	9.3238	1248.5646	0.000801	0.1073	133.9121	0.00746759	336
29	10.0976	1364.6447	0.000733	0.0990	135.1450	0.00739946	348
30	10.9357	1490.3595	0.000671	0.0914	136.2835	0.00733765	360
31	11.8434	1626.5085	0.000615	0.0844	137.3347	0.00728148	372
32	12.8264	1773.9579	0.000564	0.0780	138.3054	0.00723038	384
33	13.8910	1933.6454	0.000517	0.0720	139.2016	0.00718382	396
34	15.0439	2106.5870	0.000475	0.0665	140.0292	0.00714137	408
35	16.2926	2293.8826	0.000436	0.0614	140.7933	0.00710261	420
36	17.6448	2496.7236	0.000401	0.0567	141.4989	0.00706719	432
37	19.1093	2716.4004	0.000368	0.0523	142.1504	0.00703480	444
38	20.6954	2954.3102	0.000338	0.0483	142.7520	0 00700516	456
39	22.4131	3211.9665	0.000311	0.0446	143.3075	0.00697800	468
40	24.2734	3491.0080	0.000286	0.0412	143.8204	0.00695312	480

COMPOUND INTEREST TABLES

9 % MONTHLY COMPOUNDING MONTHLY COMPOUNDING 9 %

NOMINAL ANNUAL INTEREST RATE = 9 % COMPOUNDING PERIODS PER YEAR = 12

YEAR	AMOUNT OF 1 AT COMPOUND INTEREST (COL 1)	ACCUM OF 1 PER PERIOD (COL 2)	SINKING FUND FACTOR (COL 3)	PRESENT VALUE REVERSN OF 1 (COL 4)	PRESENT VALUE ORD ANN 1 PER PERIOD (COL 5)	INSTALL TO AMORT 1 (COL 6)	PERIOD
1	1.0938	12.5076	0.079951	0.9142	11.4349	0.08745148	12
2	1.1964	26.1885	0.038185	0.8358	21.8891	0.04568474	24
3	1.3086	41.1527	0.024300	0.7641	31.4468	0.03179973	36
4	1.4314	57.5207	0.017385	0.6986	40.1848	0.02488504	48
5	1.5657	75.4241	0.013258	0.6387	48.1734	0.02075836	60
6	1.7126	95.0070	0.010526	0.5839	55.4768	0.01802554	72
7	1.8732	116.4269	0.008589	0.5338	62.1540	0.01608908	84
8	2.0489	139.8562	0.007150	0.4881	68.2584	0.01465020	96
9	2.2411	165.4832	0.006043	0.4462	73.8394	0.01354291	108
10	2.4514	193.5143	0.005168	0.4079	78.9417	0.01266758	120
11	2.6813	224.1748	0.004461	0.3730	83.6064	0.01196080	132
12	2.9328	257.7116	0.003880	0.3410	87.8711	0.01138031	144
13	3.2080	294.3943	0.003397	0.3117	91.7700	0.01089681	156
14	3.5089	334.5181	0.002989	0.2850	95.3346	0.01048937	168
15	3.8380	378.4058	0.002643	0.2605	98.5934	0.01014267	180
16	4.1981	426.4104	0.002345	0.2382	101.5728	0.00984516	192
17	4.5919	478.9182	0.002088	0.2178	104.2966	0.00958804	204
18	5.0226	536.3517	0.001864	0.1991	106.7869	0.00936445	216
19	5.4938	599.1727	0.001669	0.1820	109.0635	0.00916897	228
20	6.0092	667.8869	0.001497	0.1664	111.1450	0.00899726	240
21	6.5729	743.0468	0.001346	0.1521	113.0479	0.00884581	252
22	7.1894	825.2573	0.001212	0.1391	114.7876	0.00871174	264
23	7.8638	915.1797	0.001093	0.1272	116.3781	0.00859268	276
24	8.6015	1013.5375	0.000987	0.1163	117.8322	0.00848664	288
25	9.4084	1121.1219	0.000892	0.1063	119.1616	0.00839196	300
26	10.2910	1238.7985	0.000807	0.0972	120.3770	0.00830723	312
27	11.2564	1367.5139	0.000731	0.0888	121.4882	0.00823125	324
28	12.3123	1508.3037	0.000663	0.0812	122.5040	0.00816300	336
29	13.4673	1662.3006	0.000602	0.0743	123.4328	0.00810158	348
30	14.7306	1830.7434	0.000546	0.0679	124.2819	0.00804623	360
31	16.1124	2014.9873	0.000496	0.0621	125.0581	0.00799628	372
32	17.6239	2216.5146	0.000451	0.0567	125.7678	0.00795116	384
33	19.2771	2436.9466	0.000410	0.0519	126.4167	0.00791035	396
34	21.0854	2678.0566	0.000373	0.0474	127.0099	0.00787340	408
35	23.0634	2941.7843	0.000340	0.0434	127.5522	0.00783993	420
36	25.2269	3230.2516	0.000310	0.0396	128.0480	0.00780957	432
37	27.5933	3545.7790	0.000282	0.0362	128.5013	0.00778203	444
38	30.1818	3890.9051	0.000257	0.0331	128.9157	0.00775701	456
39	33.0130	4268.4064	0.000234	0.0303	129.2945	0.00773428	468
40	36.1099	4681.3200	0.000214	0.0277	129.6409	0.00771361	480

COMPOUND INTEREST TABLES

10 % MONTHLY COMPOUNDING MONTHLY COMPOUNDING 10 %

NOMINAL ANNUAL INTEREST RATE = 10 % COMPOUNDING PERIODS PER YEAR = 12

YEAR	AMOUNT OF 1 AT COMPOUND INTEREST (COL 1)	ACCUM OF 1 PER PERIOD (COL 2)	SINKING FUND FACTOR (COL 3)	PRESENT VALUE REVERSN OF 1 (COL 4)	PRESENT VALUE ORD ANN 1 PER PERIOD (COL 5)	INSTALL TO AMORT 1 (COL 6)	PERIOD
1	1.1047	12.5656	0.079583	0.9052	11.3745	0.08791589	12
2	1.2204	26.4469	0.037812	0.8194	21.6709	0.04614493	24
3	1.3482	41.7818	0.023934	0.7417	30.9912	0.03226719	36
4	1.4894	58.7225	0.017029	0.6714	39.4282	0.02536258	48
5	1.6453	77.4371	0.012914	0.6078	47.0654	0.02124704	60
6	1.8176	98.1113	0.010193	0.5502	53.9787	0.01852584	72
7	2.0079	120.9504	0.008268	0.4980	60.2367	0.01660118	84
8	2.2182	146.1811	0.006841	0.4508	65.9015	0.01517416	96
9	2.4504	174.0537	0.005745	0.4081	71.0294	0.01407869	108
10	2.7070	204.8450	0.004882	0.3694	75.6712	0.01321507	120
11	2.9905	238.8605	0.004187	0.3344	79.8730	0.01251988	132
12	3.3036	276.4379	0.003617	0.3027	83.6765	0.01195078	144
13	3.6496	317.9501	0.003145	0.2740	87.1195	0.01147848	156
14	4.0317	363.8092	0.002749	0.2480	90.2362	0.01108203	168
15	4.4539	414.4703	0.002413	0.2245	93.0574	0.01074605	180
16	4.9203	470.4363	0.002126	0.2032	95.6113	0.01045902	192
17	5.4355	532.2627	0.001879	0.1840	97.9230	0.01021210	204
18	6.0047	600.5632	0.001665	0.1665	100.0156	0.00999844	216
19	6.6335	676.0156	0.001479	0.1508	101.9099	0.00981259	228
20	7.3281	759.3688	0.001317	0.1365	103.6246	0.00965022	240
21	8.0954	851.4502	0.001174	0.1235	105.1768	0.00950780	252
22	8.9431	953.1737	0.001049	0.1118	106.5819	0.00938246	264
23	9.8796	1065.5490	0.000938	0.1012	107.8537	0.00927182	276
24	10.9141	1189.6915	0.000841	0.0916	109.0050	0.00917389	288
25	12.0569	1326.8333	0.000754	0.0829	110.0472	0.00908701	300
26	13.3195	1478.3356	0.000676	0.0751	110.9906	0.00900977	312
27	14.7142	1645.7022	0.000608	0.0680	111.8446	0.00894098	324
28	16.2550	1830.5943	0.000546	0.0615	112.6176	0.00887960	336
29	17.9571	2034.8470	0.000491	0.0557	113.3174	0.00882477	348
30	19.8374	2260.4876	0.000442	0.0504	113.9508	0.00877572	360
31	21.9146	2509.7558	0.000398	0.0456	114.5242	0.00873178	372
32	24.2094	2785.1256	0.000359	0.0413	115.0433	0.00869238	384
33	26.7444	3089.3302	0.000324	0.0374	115.5131	0.00865703	396
34	29.5449	3425.3889	0.000292	0.0338	115.9384	0.00862527	408
35	32.6386	3796.6375	0.000263	0.0306	116.3234	0.00859672	420
36	36.0563	4206.7606	0.000238	0.0277	116.6719	0.00857105	432
37	39.8319	4659.8289	0.000215	0.0251	116.9873	0.00854793	444
38	44.0028	5160.3394	0.000194	0.0227	117.2729	0.00852712	456
39	48.6105	5713.2599	0.000175	0.0206	117.5314	0.00850836	468
40	53.7007	6324.0784	0.000158	0.0186	117.7654	0.00849146	480

COMPOUND INTEREST TABLES

11 % MONTHLY COMPOUNDING MONTHLY COMPOUNDING 11 %

NOMINAL ANNUAL INTEREST RATE = 11 % COMPOUNDING PERIODS PER YEAR = 12

YEAR	AMOUNT OF 1 AT COMPOUND INTEREST (COL 1)	ACCUM OF 1 PER PERIOD (COL 2)	SINKING FUND FACTOR (COL 3)	PRESENT VALUE REVERSN OF 1 (COL 4)	PRESENT VALUE ORD ANN 1 PER PERIOD (COL 5)	INSTALL TO AMORT 1 (COL 6)	PERIOD
1	1.1157	12.6239	0.079215	0.8963	11.3146	0.08838166	12
2	1.2448	26.7086	0.037441	0.8033	21.4556	0.04660784	24
3	1.3889	42.4231	0.023572	0.7200	30.5449	0.03273872	36
4	1.5496	59.9562	0.016679	0.6453	38.6914	0.02584552	48
5	1.7289	79.5181	0.012576	0.5784	45.9930	0.02174242	60
6	1.9290	101.3437	0.009867	0.5184	52.5373	0.01903408	72
7	2.1522	125.6949	0.007956	0.4646	58.4029	0.01712244	84
8	2.4013	152.8641	0.006542	0.4164	63.6601	0.01570843	96
9	2.6791	183.1772	0.005459	0.3733	68.3720	0.01462586	108
10	2.9891	216.9981	0.004608	0.3345	72.5953	0.01377500	120
11	3.3351	254.7328	0.003926	0.2998	76.3805	0.01309235	132
12	3.7210	296.8341	0.003369	0.2687	79.7731	0.01253555	144
13	4.1516	343.8072	0.002909	0.2409	82.8139	0.01207527	156
14	4.6320	396.2161	0.002524	0.2159	85.5392	0.01169054	168
15	5.1680	454.6896	0.002199	0.1935	87.9819	0.01136597	180
16	5.7660	519.9296	0.001923	0.1734	90.1713	0.01109000	192
17	6.4333	592.7192	0.001687	0.1554	92.1336	0.01085381	204
18	7.1777	673.9318	0.001484	0.1393	93.8923	0.01065050	216
19	8.0083	764.5423	0.001308	0.1249	95.4687	0.01047464	228
20	8.9350	865.6381	0.001155	0.1119	96.8815	0.01032188	240
21	9.9690	978.4326	0.001022	0.1003	98.1479	0.01018871	252
22	11.1226	1104.2796	0.000906	0.0899	99.2828	0.01007223	264
23	12.4097	1244.6894	0.000803	0.0806	100.3001	0.00997008	276
24	13.8457	1401.3473	0.000714	0.0722	101.2118	0.00988027	288
25	15.4479	1576.1335	0.000634	0.0647	102.0290	0.00980113	300
26	17.2355	1771.1457	0.000565	0.0580	102.7615	0.00973127	312
27	19.2300	1988.7245	0.000503	0.0520	103.4179	0.00966950	324
28	21.4552	2231.4813	0.000448	0.0466	104.0063	0.00961480	336
29	23.9380	2502.3296	0.000400	0.0418	104.5337	0.00956629	348
30	26.7081	2804.5202	0.000357	0.0374	105.0063	0.00952323	360
31	29.7987	3141.6799	0.000318	0.0336	105.4300	0.00948497	372
32	33.2470	3517.8553	0.000284	0.0301	105.8097	0.00945093	384
33	37.0943	3937.5613	0.000254	0.0270	106.1500	0.00942063	396
34	41.3868	4405.8352	0.000227	0.0242	106.4550	0.00939364	408
35	46.1761	4928.2973	0.000203	0.0217	106.7284	0.00936958	420
36	51.5195	5511.2180	0.000181	0.0194	106.9734	0.00934812	432
37	57.4813	6161.5936	0.000162	0.0174	107.1931	0.00932896	444
38	64.1329	6887.2300	0.000145	0.0156	107.3899	0.00931186	456
39	71.5543	7696.8362	0.000130	0.0140	107.5663	0.00929659	468
40	79.8345	8600.1290	0.000116	0.0125	107.7244	0.00928294	480

COMPOUND INTEREST TABLES

12 % MONTHLY COMPOUNDING MONTHLY COMPOUNDING 12 %

NOMINAL ANNUAL INTEREST RATE = 12 % COMPOUNDING PERIODS PER YEAR = 12

YEAR	AMOUNT OF 1 AT COMPOUND INTEREST (COL 1)	ACCUM OF 1 PER PERIOD (COL 2)	SINKING FUND FACTOR (COL 3)	PRESENT VALUE REVERSN OF 1 (COL 4)	PRESENT VALUE ORD ANN 1 PER PERIOD (COL 5)	INSTALL TO AMORT 1 (COL 6)	PERIOD
1	1.1268	12.6825	0.078849	0.8874	11.2551	0.08884879	12
2	1.2697	26.9735	0.037073	0.7876	21.2434	0.04707347	24
3	1.4308	43.0769	0.023214	0.6989	30.1075	0.03321431	36
4	1.6122	61.2226	0.016334	0.6203	37.9740	0.02633384	48
5	1.8167	81.6697	0.012244	0.5504	44.9550	0.02224445	60
6	2.0471	104.7099	0.009550	0.4885	51.1504	0.01955019	72
7	2.3067	130.6723	0.007653	0.4335	56.6485	0.01765273	84
8	2.5993	159.9273	0.006253	0.3847	61.5277	0.01625284	96
9	2.9289	192.8926	0.005184	0.3414	65.8578	0.01518423	108
10	3.3004	230.0387	0.004347	0.3030	69.7005	0.01434709	120
11	3.7190	271.8959	0.003678	0.2689	73.1108	0.01367788	132
12	4.1906	319.0616	0.003134	0.2386	76.1372	0.01313419	144
13	4.7221	372.2090	0.002687	0.2118	78.8229	0.01268666	156
14	5.3210	432.0970	0.002314	0.1879	81.2064	0.01231430	168
15	5.9958	499.5802	0.002002	0.1668	83.3217	0.01200168	180
16	6.7562	575.6220	0.001737	0.1480	85.1988	0.01173725	192
17	7.6131	661.3077	0.001512	0.1314	86.8647	0.01151216	204
18	8.5786	757.8606	0.001320	0.1166	88.3431	0.01131950	216
19	9.6666	866.6588	0.001154	0.1034	89.6551	0.01115386	228
20	10.8926	989.2553	0.001011	0.0918	90.8194	0.01101086	240
21	12.2740	1127.4002	0.000887	0.0815	91.8527	0.01088700	252
22	13.8307	1283.0652	0.000779	0.0723	92.7697	0.01077938	264
23	15.5847	1458.4725	0.000686	0.0642	93.5835	0.01068565	276
24	17.5613	1656.1258	0.000604	0.0569	94.3056	0.01060382	288
25	19.7885	1878.8465	0.000532	0.0505	94.9466	0.01053224	300
26	22.2981	2129.8138	0.000470	0.0448	95.5153	0.01046952	312
27	25.1261	2412.6100	0.000414	0.0398	96.0201	0.01041449	324
28	28.3127	2731.2718	0.000366	0.0353	96.4680	0.01036613	336
29	31.9035	3090.3480	0.000324	0.0313	96.8655	0.01032359	348
30	35.9496	3494.9639	0.000286	0.0278	97.2183	0.01028613	360
31	40.5090	3950.8953	0.000253	0.0247	97.5314	0.01025311	372
32	45.6465	4464.6502	0.000224	0.0219	97.8093	0.01022398	384
33	51.4356	5043.5621	0.000198	0.0194	98.0558	0.01019827	396
34	57.9589	5695.8945	0.000176	0.0173	98.2746	0.01017556	408
35	65.3096	6430.9590	0.000155	0.0153	98.4688	0.01015550	420
36	73.5925	7259.2481	0.000138	0.0136	98.6412	0.01013776	432
37	82.9258	8192.5849	0.000122	0.0121	98.7941	0.01012206	444
38	93.4429	9244.2922	0.000108	0.0107	98.9298	0.01010817	456
39	105.2938	10429.3823	0.000096	0.0095	99.0503	0.01009588	468
40	118.6477	11764.7715	0.000085	0.0084	99.1572	0.01008500	480

COMPOUND INTEREST TABLES

13 % MONTHLY COMPOUNDING MONTHLY COMPOUNDING 13 %

NOMINAL ANNUAL INTEREST RATE = 13 % COMPOUNDING PERIODS PER YEAR = 12

YEAR	AMOUNT OF 1 AT COMPOUND INTEREST (COL 1)	ACCUM OF 1 PER PERIOD (COL 2)	SINKING FUND FACTOR (COL 3)	PRESENT VALUE REVERSN OF 1 (COL 4)	PRESENT VALUE ORD ANN 1 PER PERIOD (COL 5)	INSTALL TO AMORT 1 (COL 6)	PERIOD
1	1.1380	12.7415	0.078484	0.8787	11.1960	0.08931728	12
2	1.2951	27.2417	0.036708	0.7721	21.0341	0.04754182	24
3	1.4739	43.7433	0.022861	0.6785	29.6789	0.03369395	36
4	1.6773	62.5228	0.015994	0.5962	37.2752	0.02682750	48
5	1.9089	83.8945	0.011920	0.5239	43.9501	0.02275307	60
6	2.1723	108.2161	0.009241	0.4603	49.8154	0.02007411	72
7	2.4722	135.8949	0.007359	0.4045	54.9693	0.01819196	84
8	2.8134	167.3942	0.005974	0.3554	59.4981	0.01680726	96
9	3.2018	203.2415	0.004920	0.3123	63.4776	0.01575359	108
10	3.6437	244.0369	0.004098	0.2744	66.9744	0.01493107	120
11	4.1467	290.4634	0.003443	0.2412	70.0471	0.01427611	132
12	4.7191	343.2983	0.002913	0.2119	72.7471	0.01374625	144
13	5.3704	403.4260	0.002479	0.1862	75.1196	0.01331210	156
14	6.1117	471.8534	0.002119	0.1636	77.2044	0.01295264	168
15	6.9554	549.7260	0.001819	0.1438	79.0362	0.01265242	180
16	7.9154	638.3475	0.001567	0.1263	80.6459	0.01239988	192
17	9.0080	739.2016	0.001353	0.1110	82.0604	0.01218615	204
18	10.2514	853.9769	0.001171	0.0975	83.3033	0.01200433	216
19	11.6664	984.5950	0.001016	0.0857	84.3954	0.01184898	228
20	13.2768	1133.2425	0.000882	0.0753	85.3551	0.01171576	240
21	15.1094	1302.4083	0.000768	0.0662	86.1984	0.01160114	252
22	17.1950	1494.9244	0.000669	0.0582	86.9394	0.01150226	264
23	19.5685	1714.0140	0.000583	0.0511	87.5905	0.01141676	276
24	22.2696	1963.3451	0.000509	0.0449	88.1627	0.01134267	288
25	25.3435	2247.0919	0.000445	0.0395	88.6654	0.01127835	300
26	28.8417	2570.0051	0.000389	0.0347	89.1072	0.01122244	312
27	32.8228	2937.4908	0.000340	0.0305	89.4954	0.01117376	324
28	37.3534	3355.7014	0.000298	0.0268	89.8365	0.01113133	336
29	42.5094	3831.6387	0.000261	0.0235	90.1362	0.01109432	348
30	48.3771	4373.2708	0.000229	0.0207	90.3996	0.01106200	360
31	55.0547	4989.6657	0.000200	0.0182	90.6310	0.01103375	372
32	62.6541	5691.1432	0.000176	0.0160	90.8344	0.01100905	384
33	71.3024	6489.4473	0.000154	0.0140	91.0131	0.01098743	396
34	81.1444	7397.9434	0.000135	0.0123	91.1701	0.01096851	408
35	92.3450	8431.8414	0.000119	0.0108	91.3081	0.01095193	420
36	105.0916	9608.4509	0.000104	0.0095	91.4293	0.01093741	432
37	119.5976	10947.4708	0.000091	0.0084	91.5359	0.01092468	444
38	136.1060	12471.3190	0.000080	0.0073	91.6295	0.01091352	456
39	154.8930	14205.5077	0.000070	0.0065	91.7117	0.01090373	468
40	176.2733	16179.0708	0.000062	0.0057	91.7840	0.01089514	480

COMPOUND INTEREST TABLES

14 % MONTHLY COMPOUNDING MONTHLY COMPOUNDING 14 %

NOMINAL ANNUAL INTEREST RATE = 14 % COMPOUNDING PERIODS PER YEAR = 12

YEAR	AMOUNT OF 1 AT COMPOUND INTEREST (COL 1)	ACCUM OF 1 PER PERIOD (COL 2)	SINKING FUND FACTOR (COL 3)	PRESENT VALUE REVERSN OF 1 (COL 4)	PRESENT VALUE ORD ANN 1 PER PERIOD (COL 5)	INSTALL TO AMORT 1 (COL 6)	PERIOD
1	1.1493	12.8007	0.078120	0.8701	11.1375	0.08978712	12
2	1.3210	27.5132	0.036346	0.7570	20.8277	0.04801288	24
3	1.5183	44.4228	0.022511	0.6586	29.2589	0.03417763	36
4	1.7450	63.8577	0.015660	0.5731	36.5945	0.02732648	48
5	2.0056	86.1951	0.011602	0.4986	42.9770	0.02326825	60
6	2.3051	111.8684	0.008939	0.4338	48.5302	0.02060574	72
7	2.6494	141.3758	0.007073	0.3774	53.3618	0.01874001	84
8	3.0450	175.2899	0.005705	0.3284	57.5655	0.01737150	96
9	3.4998	214.2688	0.004667	0.2857	61.2231	0.01633370	108
10	4.0225	259.0689	0.003860	0.2486	64.4054	0.01552664	120
11	4.6232	310.5595	0.003220	0.2163	67.1742	0.01488666	132
12	5.3136	369.7399	0.002705	0.1882	69.5833	0.01437127	144
13	6.1072	437.7583	0.002284	0.1637	71.6793	0.01395103	156
14	7.0192	515.9348	0.001938	0.1425	73.5029	0.01360490	168
15	8.0675	605.7863	0.001651	0.1240	75.0897	0.01331741	180
16	9.2723	709.0564	0.001410	0.1078	76.4702	0.01307699	192
17	10.6571	827.7490	0.001208	0.0938	77.6713	0.01287476	204
18	12.2486	964.1675	0.001037	0.0816	78.7164	0.01270383	216
19	14.0779	1120.9590	0.000892	0.0710	79.6257	0.01255876	228
20	16.1803	1301.1660	0.000769	0.0618	80.4168	0.01243521	240
21	18.5967	1508.2855	0.000663	0.0538	81.1052	0.01232967	252
22	21.3739	1746.3367	0.000573	0.0468	81.7041	0.01223929	264
23	24.5660	2019.9389	0.000495	0.0407	82.2251	0.01216173	276
24	28.2347	2334.4014	0.000428	0.0354	82.6785	0.01209504	288
25	32.4513	2695.8264	0.000371	0.0308	83.0730	0.01203761	300
26	37.2977	3111.2274	0.000321	0.0268	83.4162	0.01198808	312
27	42.8678	3588.6651	0.000279	0.0233	83.7148	0.01194532	324
28	49.2697	4137.4044	0.000242	0.0203	83.9746	0.01190836	336
29	56.6278	4768.0935	0.000210	0.0177	84.2006	0.01187639	348
30	65.0847	5492.9710	0.000182	0.0154	84.3973	0.01184872	360
31	74.8045	6326.1032	0.000158	0.0134	84.5684	0.01182474	372
32	85.9760	7283.6571	0.000137	0.0116	84.7173	0.01180396	384
33	98.8158	8384.2140	0.000119	0.0101	84.8469	0.01178594	396
34	113.5732	9649.1302	0.000104	0.0088	84.9596	0.01177030	408
35	130.5344	11102.9517	0.000090	0.0077	85.0576	0.01175673	420
36	150.0287	12773.8898	0.000078	0.0067	85.1430	0.01174495	432
37	172.4343	14694.3691	0.000068	0.0058	85.2172	0.01173472	444
38	198.1860	16901.6568	0.000059	0.0050	85.2818	0.01172583	456
39	227.7835	19438.5853	0.000051	0.0044	85.3380	0.01171811	468
40	261.8011	22354.3838	0.000045	0.0038	85.3869	0.01171140	480

COMPOUND INTEREST TABLES

15 % MONTHLY COMPOUNDING | MONTHLY COMPOUNDING 15 %

NOMINAL ANNUAL INTEREST RATE = 15 % COMPOUNDING PERIODS PER YEAR = 12

YEAR	AMOUNT OF 1 AT COMPOUND INTEREST (COL 1)	ACCUM OF 1 PER PERIOD (COL 2)	SINKING FUND FACTOR (COL 3)	PRESENT VALUE REVERSN OF 1 (COL 4)	PRESENT VALUE ORD ANN 1 PER PERIOD (COL 5)	INSTALL TO AMORT 1 (COL 6)	PERIOD
1	1.1608	12.8604	0.077758	0.8615	11.0793	0.09025831	12
2	1.3474	27.7881	0.035987	0.7422	20.6242	0.04848665	24
3	1.5639	45.1155	0.022165	0.6394	28.8473	0.03466533	36
4	1.8154	65.2284	0.015331	0.5509	35.9315	0.02783075	48
5	2.1072	88.5745	0.011290	0.4746	42.0346	0.02378993	60
6	2.4459	115.6736	0.008645	0.4088	47.2925	0.02114501	72
7	2.8391	147.1290	0.006797	0.3522	51.8222	0.01929675	84
8	3.2955	183.6411	0.005445	0.3034	55.7246	0.01794541	96
9	3.8253	226.0226	0.004424	0.2614	59.0865	0.01692434	108
10	4.4402	275.2171	0.003633	0.2252	61.9828	0.01613350	120
11	5.1540	332.3198	0.003009	0.1940	64.4781	0.01550915	132
12	5.9825	398.6021	0.002509	0.1672	66.6277	0.01500877	144
13	6.9442	475.5395	0.002103	0.1440	68.4797	0.01460287	156
14	8.0606	564.8450	0.001770	0.1241	70.0751	0.01427040	168
15	9.3563	668.5068	0.001496	0.1069	71.4496	0.01399587	180
16	10.8604	788.8326	0.001268	0.0921	72.6338	0.01376770	192
17	12.6063	928.5014	0.001077	0.0793	73.6539	0.01357700	204
18	14.6328	1090.6225	0.000917	0.0683	74.5328	0.01341691	216
19	16.9851	1278.8054	0.000782	0.0589	75.2900	0.01328198	228
20	19.7155	1497.2395	0.000668	0.0507	75.9423	0.01316790	240
21	22.8848	1750.7879	0.000571	0.0437	76.5042	0.01307117	252
22	26.5637	2045.0953	0.000489	0.0376	76.9884	0.01298897	264
23	30.8339	2386.7140	0.000419	0.0324	77.4055	0.01291899	276
24	35.7906	2783.2495	0.000359	0.0279	77.7648	0.01285929	288
25	41.5441	3243.5298	0.000308	0.0241	78.0743	0.01280831	300
26	48.2225	3777.8022	0.000265	0.0207	78.3410	0.01276470	312
27	55.9745	4397.9613	0.000227	0.0179	78.5708	0.01272738	324
28	64.9727	5117.8138	0.000195	0.0154	78.7687	0.01269540	336
29	75.4173	5953.3859	0.000168	0.0133	78.9392	0.01266797	348
30	87.5410	6923.2800	0.000144	0.0114	79.0861	0.01264444	360
31	101.6136	8049.0889	0.000124	0.0098	79.2127	0.01262424	372
32	117.9485	9355.8767	0.000107	0.0085	79.3217	0.01260688	384
33	136.9092	10872.7365	0.000092	0.0073	79.4157	0.01259197	396
34	158.9180	12633.4384	0.000079	0.0063	79.4966	0.01257916	408
35	184.4648	14677.1811	0.000068	0.0054	79.5663	0.01256813	420
36	214.1183	17049.4647	0.000059	0.0047	79.6264	0.01255865	432
37	248.5388	19803.1035	0.000050	0.0040	79.6781	0.01255050	444
38	288.4925	22999.4023	0.000043	0.0035	79.7227	0.01254348	456
39	334.8690	26709.5205	0.000037	0.0030	79.7611	0.01253744	468
40	388.7007	31016.0571	0.000032	0.0026	79.7942	0.01253224	480

The National Society of Real Estate Appraisers, Inc. Constitution

ARTICLE I

NAME

The name of this Society shall be:

"THE NATIONAL SOCIETY OF REAL ESTATE APPRAISERS, INCORPORATED"

MOTTO

"Professionalism with Integrity"

ARTICLE II

PURPOSE

The purpose of this Society shall be:

A. To formulate rules of ethics and professional conduct and enforce these rules for the benefit of its members and those desirious of joining the Society.

B. To examine carefully all applications for membership, conduct examinations in all major subjects directly related to real estate appraising and its allied fields, through its chapters and through the National Office of the Society.

C. To award professional designations to successful applicants after completion of a prescribed course of study and final examination of "MASTER REAL ESTATE APPRAISER," the abbreviation of which shall be letters in capital (M.R.E.A.); "CERTIFIED REAL ESTATE APPRAISER," the abbreviation of which shall be the letters in capital (C.R.A.); and "RESIDENTIAL APPRAISER," the abbreviation of which shall be the letters in capital (R.A.).

D. To provide an equal opportunity and give direction to all interested men and women.

E. To exchange ideas and to advance the profession of real property valuation through education and experience.

F. To encourage each member to preserve and increase their competency as an appraiser.

ARTICLE III

MEMBERSHIP

All persons who are members of this Society shall be members in good standing in the NATIONAL ASSOCIATION OF REAL ESTATE BROKERS, INCORPORATED. Membership in a chapter that is affiliated with a local Real Estate Board of NATIONAL ASSOCIATION OF REAL ESTATE BROKERS shall be deemed members in good standing with the NATIONAL ASSOCIATION OF REAL ESTATE BROKERS.

The membership in this Society shall be divided into five (5) classes:

A. CANDIDATE MEMBER

Applicant must be engaged in or interested in Real Estate Appraising. Applicant shall agree in writing by signing the Society's application form, to be governed by and uphold the Constitution and By-Laws of the Society, its Code of Ethics, Uniform Standards of Professional Appraisal Practice, and the legal actions of its Officers and Directors. A Candidate Member shall have no voting rights nor should he or she hold office in any capacity within the Society or its chapters. Application and all necessary fees must be submitted through a chapter except if no chapter exists in the applicant's city. Applicant shall then submit application to National office of the Society.

The maximum period of time for Candidate Membership is 5 years. After this time his or her name will be dropped from our list.

B. JUNIOR MEMBER (R.A.)

Applicant must be a Candidate Member and have at least two (2) years in Residential Appraising. Said applicant will have passed the National Society of Real Estate Appraisers Course No. 1001 — "An Introduction to the Professional Process of Appraising Real Estate" or a similar course conducted by other appraisal organizations or colleges, which has been approved by the National Society's Education Committee. Applicant must submit a Narrative Residential Appraisal report which must be approved by the National Society's Education Committee. Applicant must submit a Narrative Residential Appraisal report which must be approved by Education Committee and Board of Directors. All persons who have successfully passed all qualifying procedures shall be entitled to use the designation, Residential Appraiser (R.A.) and be entitled to all rights and privileges of the Society.

C. SENIOR MEMBER (C.R.A.)

Applicant must have at least three (3) additional years experience in appraising in addition to the two (2) years requirement for R.A. Designation. Said applicant will be required to successfully pass National Society of Real Estate Appraisers Course No. 1001 and Course No. 2001 — "Advanced Course in Principles Income Property Appraising," or similar courses given by other appraisal organizations or colleges which have been approved by the National Society's Education Committee. The applicant must submit a complete Narrative Appraisal report covering the approaches to value, using an income producing property, (Apartment, Commercial or Industrial Property) which must be approved by the Education Committee and Board of Directors. All persons who have successfully passed all qualifying procedures shall be entitled to use the designation "CERTIFIED REAL ESTATE APPRAISERS" (C.R.A.) and be entitled to all rights and privileges of the Society.

D. MASTER MEMBER (M.R.E.A.)

Applicant member must submit an application with fee for admission into the Master Designation Program.

Applicant Member must qualify in the following manner:

1. Must be a member in good standing of the National Society.
2. Must be the holder of a CRA Designation in the National Society of Real Estate Appraisers, Inc., or a designation of similar quality in a recognized appraisal organization.
3. Must have a minimum of two years college or its equivalent in college credit.
4. Application Fee for admission into the Master Designation Program must be paid as well as any subsequent fee set by the Board of Directors.
5. Three Appraisal Reports of any of the items 1 thru 7 plus item 8, listed below must be submitted within a period of three years from date of application:

ITEM 1. A Shopping Center.

ITEM 2. Assessment review on a Commercial or Industrial Building.

ITEM 3. Measuring damages resulting from a partial taking.

ITEM 4. Industrial Property (Fair Market Value, Fair Market Rental and Leasehold value).

ITEM 5. Air Rights Evaluation.

ITEM 6. Office Building Complex.
ITEM 7. Multi-Story parking structure.
ITEM 8. Prepare a feasibility analysis study of any commercial or industrial property.

The three narrative appraisal reports and feasibility analysis, as listed above must be submitted and if approved by the review panel, will count as 75 points toward the 145 points required to receive the MREA designation. Points for education, basic knowledge and experience, plus satisfactory completion of an oral examination would make up the other 70 required points.

The Master Designation Program is designed to attract the best qualified men and women in the Real Estate Profession to do any type of appraisal work as well as do feasibility analysis, cash flow estimation and income projection.

E. HONORARY MEMBER
Honorary Members shall be individuals not necessarily engaged in the appraisal business who have performed outstanding notable service for the appraisal profession and/or for this Society. This person could have attained distinction and renown in rendering services to the general public. This designation shall be awarded by a ⅔ vote of the Board of Directors at a regular meeting. Inactive members of this Society may also be designated Honorary Members. Honorary Members shall not be eligible to vote or hold any elective or appointed position within the Society unless he also holds a R.A., C.R.A. or M.R.E.A.

F. A member may be expelled, suspended or disciplined if:

1. He or she violated any of the Rules of Ethics or Professional conduct or Regulations of the Society.
2. He or she has been found guilty by the Board of Directors of any act discrediting to the appraisal profession.
3. He or she is declared by any court of competent jurisdiction to have committed any fraud; to be mentally incompetent, or otherwise not a fit person to continue to practice his profession.
4. He or she fails to pay his or her dues for one (1) year, at the end of the first year, such failuire continuing, shall constitute automatic suspension of membership.
5. Any designated member of the Society who fails to comply with the four (4) year re-certification requirements shall automatically be suspended and restricted from further use of his or her designation, until such member has successfully completed a minimum of forty (40) hours of appraisal credits as follows:
   1. A minumum of twenty (20) credit hours shall be taken at any annual recertification conference.
   2. A minimum of twenty (20) credit hours shall be taken from any recognized or acceptable appraisal course.

ARTICLE IV

STRUCTURE OF SOCIETY

BOARD OF DIRECTORS

The government of the Society shall be vested in a BOARD OF DIRECTORS composed of all elected officers, all Standing Committee Chairpersons and six (6) other persons elected from the membership. A majority of the members of the Board of Directors shall constitute a quorum. The Board of Directors shall meet at such time and place as determined by the Board or at the call of the President. The President of this Society shall be the chairman of the Board of Directors until otherwise provided for:

CHAPTERS

FORMATION OF A CHAPTER

Any group having five (5) or more Master Members, Senior Members, or Junior Members may petition the Board of Directors for a Chapter Charter if there is no Chapter in the immediate vicinity. Upon approval of this Chapter by the Board of Directors the respective Chapter shall appoint convening officer to set up a date for election of officers.

The Board of Directors should immediately outline the area of operations and any member falling within this jurisdiction will automatically be a member of that Chapter and shall be duly notified thereof, by the Board of Directors.

Nothing in the Constitution and By-Laws of a Chapter shall infringe upon or conflict with any provision of the NSREA's Constitution or By-Laws.

OFFICERS

The elective officers of the Society shall be a President, a Vice-President, a Secretary, and Assistant Secretary, a Treasurer, Executive Vice President and a Chaplain.

All vacancies in elective offices shall be filled by the President for the unexpired term subject to ratification of the Board of Directors at the regular meeting.

There shall be a Legal Advisor and Assistant, who shall be appointed by the President and approved by the Board of Directors, and must be members in good standing of the National Association of Real Estate Brokers, Incorporated. Only "MASTER MEMBERS," "SENIOR MEMBERS," or "JUNIOR MEMBERS" may be elective officers or chairman of standing committees.

ELECTION OF OFFICERS

The officers of the Society, except the Executive Vice President, shall be elected at the annual meeting and shall serve for a period of one (1) year or until their successor or successors are duly elected and qualified. They shall assume office immediately after the election.

The Executive Vice President shall be elected for a term of two years.

NOMINATING COMMITTEE

The President shall appoint a Nominating Committee of two (2) members within thirty (30) days of the annual meeting. Board of Directors to elect three (3) members at Mid-Winter Meeting, and the said committee shall publish its report not less than ten (10) days prior to the election. A member shall have the right to nominate any Master, Senior or Junior Member for an office from the floor on the day of election.

STANDING COMMITTEES

There shall be Standing Committees known as:

A. Membership Committee
B. Education Committee
C. Grievance Committee
D. Public Affairs Committee
E. Appraisal Standards Committee

The chairman and the membership of these committees shall be appointed by the President to serve for one (1) year, but shall be eligible for reappointment. All committees shall make annual reports to the President and at such other times as requested.

EXECUTIVE COUNCIL

There shall be an Executive Council composed of the duly elected officers and one appointed by the President and approved by the Board of Directors.

ARTICLE V

MEETINGS

A. There shall be an annual meeting to be held concurrent with the annual meeting of the National Association of Real Estate Brokers, Incorporated, if feasible.

B. Special meetings may be called by the President or by a majority of members of the Board of Directors. The call for the special meeting must state the business to be transacted and no business shall be transacted except that business specified in the call. The call when made by the Board of Directors must be made by petition to the Secretary and signed by at least nine (9) members of the Board of Directors, and shall specify the purpose of the meeting, the time, and place of such meeting, allowing reasonable time for travel to such place of meeting. Upon receipt of the petition for the call of the special meeting, the Secretary must issue the call.

ARTICLE VI

PROPERTY

All emblems, seals and other paraphernalia showing identification with the Society shall be the property of the Society and when leased or entrusted to the care of a member or members, shall be returned forthwith to the Society upon request of the proper officials of the Society.

Any member who has become inactive (non-paying) within one year shall be restricted from use of emblems, logos, seals and other paraphernalia showing identification with the Society and any person found in violation shall be called before an arbitration or the grievance committee for necessary action.

ARTICLE VII

GENERAL PROVISIONS

A. A Master Member may use the title "Master Member, National Society of Real Estate Appraisers" on individual letterheads, business cards, appraisal reports, and on professional forms. This designation may not be used at any time by or in connection with any firm, corporation or partnership.

A Master Member may identify himself or herself by the designation "M.R.E.A." which shall be the abbreviation for the words "Master Real Estate Appraiser." A Master Member may use the designation "M.R.E.A." following his signature in signing professional letters, in articles and books for publication and on appraisal reports.

B. A "Senior Member" may use the title "Senior Member, National Society of Real Estate Appraisers" on individual letterheads, business cards, appraisal reports and on professional forms. This designation may not be used at any time by or in connection with any firm, corporation or partnership.

C. A "Senior Member" may identify himself or herself by the designation "C.R.A." which shall be the abbreviation for the words "Certified Real Estate Appraiser." A "Senior Member" may use the designation "C.R.A." following his signature in signing professional letters, in articles and books for publication and on appraisal reports.

D. A "Junior Member" may use the title "Junior Member, National Society of Real Estate Appraisers" on individual letterheads, business cards, appraisal reports, and on professional forms. This designation may not be used at any time by or in connection with any firm, corporation or partnership. A "Junior Member" may identify himself or herself by the designation "R.A." which shall be the abbreviation for the words "Residential Appraisers."

E. The rights and privileges of the "Candidate Member" shall be determined by the Board of Directors upon the recommendation of the Education Committee.

In lieu of the above, an applicant of 50 years of age could obtain designated membership by qualifying in all three (3) listed categories. (1) 10 years appraisal experience; (2) passing an oral test given by the Appraisal Committee; (3) presents a portfolio of appraisals which have been completed.

RULES OF ORDER

All meetings of this Society and Committees shall be conducted under Robert's Rules of Order, latest edition.

THE SEAL

The Seal of this Society shall be used only by the Society in the manner prescribed by the Board of Directors.

VOTING

Voting shall be by secret ballot if deemed necessary by the Board of Directors.

QUORUM

Fifteen percent (15%) of the voting members in good standing shall constitute a quorum at any meeting.

LIMITATION OF LIABILITY

The National Society of Real Estate Appraisers, Incorporated shall not assume nor be responsible for any liability or commitment for expenditures made by any committee or officer or members unless it shall have been first approved by the Board of Directors.

AMENDMENTS

This Constitution may be amended at any annual meeting of the Society by a two-thirds (⅔) vote of the members present and in good standing.

This Constitution may also be amended at a special meeting of the membership by a two-thirds (⅔) vote of the members present and in good standing. The proposed amendment must be submitted in writing to the membership at least thirty (30) days prior to such special meeting.

ARTICLE VIII

Uniform Standards of Professional Appraisal Practice were approved and adopted at the annual meeting on August 9, 1986, in Dallas, Texas.

BY-LAWS

ARTICLE I

DUES AND ASSESSMENTS

1. First Year Dues. The first year dues for active membership in the National Society of Real Estate Appraisers, Inc. shall be Sixty Dollars ($60.00).
2. The annual dues for active membership in the Society shall be Sixty Dollars ($60.00) which shall be due and payable on January 1st each succeeding year. (Effective January 1, 1982.)
3. Each application for membership shall be accompanied by an application fee of Twenty-Five Dollars ($25.00).

   If the application is not approved by the Board of Directors, Ten Dollars ($10.00) shall be refunded to the applicant forthwith and Fifteen Dollars ($15.00) retained by the Society as cost of investigation of the applicant's credits and technical data submitted
4. The cost of courses of instruction and examination shall be determined by the Board of Directors and shall be in addition to the annual dues.

ARTICLE II

DUTIES OF BOARD OF DIRECTORS

1. It shall be the duty of the Board of Directors to act on all matters of policy subject to the constitutional

limitations and to determine, upon recommendation of the Executive Council, the course of study, number of credit hours and other formal training necessary to complete a thorough course of real estate appraising upon which the award to the various classes of membership shall be based.

2. It shall be the further duty of the Board of Directors to determine the rights, privileges and duties of all officers, Standing Committees, Executive Council, Special Committees, members and employees subject to the Constitution and By-Laws of the National Society of Real Estate Appraisers, Incorporated.

3. It shall be the further duty of the Board of Directors to protect the Society's interest and safeguard its welfare at all times and to report its findings and actions to the meetings of the Society.

ELECTION TO THE BOARD OF DIRECTORS

4. In the first election of the members of the Board of Directors, the two (2) persons receiving the two (2) highest number of votes cast for membership on the Baord of Directors, shall be declared to serve a three (3) year term. The next two (2) persons receiving the next two (2) highest number of votes shall be declared elected to serve a two (2) year term, and the next two persons receiving the third group of high number of votes shall be declared to serve a one (1) year term. At all subsequent elections, the election for members of the Board of Directors shall be for a three (3) year term.

ARTICLE III

DUTIES OF OFFICERS

1. It shall be the duty of all officers to conduct the activities of the Society in an efficient and businesslike manner and to safeguard the interest and welfare of the Society at all times.

2. The President shall president at all the meetings of the Society and perform all other duties as properly pertain to his office.

3. The Vice-President shall preside at the meetings of the Society and act as President in the absence of the President. In the event of the absence of both President and Vice-President at any regular or special meeting, a chairman shall be chosen by the members present at such meeting.

4. The Executive Vice President, who shall be elected by the body for a term of two years beginning in 1984, shall perform such duties as may be prescribed by the Executive Council and shall assist the President in the day to day administration and operation of the National Society of Real Estate Appraisers, Inc. The duties shall include but not be limited to the following:

   (a) Shall carry out the necessary and advisable business activity of the National Office in a professional and effective manner.

   (b) Have regular distributes to membership made of all necessary or pertinent information and communication related to N.S.R.E.A.'s policies, objectives and activities, such as: all official Board and committee meeting announcements, workshops and educational material.

   (c) Act in no way to bind the N.S.R.E.A. by statement or communication, except as authorized by the President together with the Board of Directors.

   (d) Hire and supervise administrative employees, when necessary, with the approval of the Executive Council and Board of Directors and maintain accurate records for all taxes or fees due and payable or paid for such employees to any private, municipal, state or federal agency.

   (e) Handle and disburse finances strictly in accordance with the direction and manner prescribed by the Executive Council and Board of Directors.

   (f) Exert continual affirmative efforts through the office of Executive Vice President to foster and advance the policies and ideals of N.S.R.E.A. and the National Association of Real Estate Brokers.

5. The Secretary shall have charge of the records and property and shall keep an accurate classified list of the membership of the Society with the address of each member; receive all money due the Society and pay the same to the Treasurer, giving or taking a receipt for each sum transferred; notify delinquent members of their deliquency and on the first day of each fiscal year shall make a separate list of all delinquents. The Secretary shall also mail membership cards and keep a record of members to whom cards were sent.

6. The Assistant Secretary shall take minutes, keep an accurate record of proceedings and shall notify applicants of their election or rejection; also notify all officers of their election and committees of their appointments, and in general conduct the cor-

respondence of the Society; and shall perform such other duties as delegated by the Secretary or Board of Directors.

7. The Treasurer shall pay bills only upon warrants signed by the President and Secretary; keep an itemized account of all receipts and disbursements, and present a written report at each meeting of the Board of Directors, and to the membership at each regular meeting. The funds of the Society shall be deposited in a bank subject to withdrawal by check only. The book in which the record of receipts and disbursements for the years has been kept, together with the warrants vouchers, also the annual report of the Treasurer shall be submitted to the Auditor at the close of the calendar year. The Treasurer shall be bounded in an amount to be determined by the Board of Directors. The cost of such bond shall be paid by the Society.

MECHANICS OF FUND CONTROL

1. Secretary perpares a voucher in triplicate and check.
2. Forward two (2) vouchers and check to President for signature.
3. President forwards one (1) voucher and check to Treasurer for other signature.
4. Treasurer signs check and forwards it to payee; retains voucher.

EXECUTIVE COUNCIL

1. The Exective Council shall consult with the President on matters of policy and advise him on programs for the good and welfare of the Society. All proposed programs shall be approved by the Board of Directors.
2. The rights and privileges of the "Candidate Member" shall be determined by "Board of Directors" upon recommendation of the Executive Council.
3. The Executive Council shall report its recommendations to the Board of Directors for approval before admissions may be had or awards granted.

ARTICLE IV

STANDING COMMITTEES

MEMBERSHIP COMMITTEE

The Membership Committee shall have the duty to receive all applications for membership and shall secure as nearly as possible all information oral or written relating to applicant's fitness with respect to his or her reputation, moral character, formal training and quality of experience and submit a written report to the Board of Directors.

Upon approval of candidate by the Board of Directors of this Society, the Membership Committee shall issue to the new member a copy of the Constitution and By-Laws and a roster of all members, their designation and their chapter.

It shall report its recommendations to the Board of Directors for approval before admissions may be had or awards granted.

EDUCATION COMMITTEE

The Education Committee shall have the duty to study the standard procedure and latest editions of books, treatises, studies and articles relating to the methods of appraising real property and its allied fields; to prepare the courses of study for Junior Members, Senior Members and Master Members for approval by the Board of Directors and shall report promptly all data to the Board of Directors for use in the conduct of classes and examination of applicants for the various awards of the Society.

It shall have the duty to approve the courses of study and determine the number of points required for the award for the certificate of "Master Member," "Senior Member" and "Junior Member" of the National Society of Real Estate Appraisers, Incorporated.

GRIEVANCE COMMITTEE

The Grievance Committee shall have the duty to investigate all charges made by or against any of the members of the Society. They shall investigate fully such charges and report their findings and recommendations to the Board of Directors for final determination of action.

PUBLIC AFFAIRS COMMITTEE

The Public Affairs Committee shall have the duty to see that all local, County, State and Federal agencies concerned with Real Estate and its allied fields are made aware of the Society and its members. It shall place in their possession the names of all members and the scope of their experience.

They shall monitor and investigate all charges of bias and/or discrimination in the selection of Appraisers for governmental panels and report their findings and recommendations to the Board of Directors.

It shall further keep aware of legislation dealing with Real Estate and report to the membership the possible effect of such legislation on the Appraising Profession.

Furthermore, this Committee shall feel free to consult and coordinate with the Executive Vice President of NAREB on any matter or subject the Committee feels is pertinent to this Society.

ARTICLE V
GENERAL PROVISIONS

1. Admission to National Society of Real Estate Appraisers. Junior Membership may be attained in the following manner:
   A. By securing 50 points or more as follows:

      Class 1 — Education

      (1) A passing grade in Residential appraising under the auspices of approved appraisal organization or a passing grade in NSREA Course No. 1001 — 20 points.

      (2) Appraisal course given in accredited colleges — 7 points.

      (3) Courses in real estate and related subjects in accredited colleges — 3 points.

      Class 2 — Experience

      (1) Two years — 10 points each year.

      (2) Over two years — 10 points each year.

      (3) Non-concurrent collateral real estate experience — 5 points each year.

      Class 3 — Appraisal Reports — 10 points each accepted report.

      At least twenty (20) Class 1 points must be obtained.

      At least twenty (20) Class 2 points must be obtained in appraisal experience.

      At least ten (10) points must be obtained in Class 3.
2. Admission to National Society of Real Estate Appraisers. Senior Membership may be attained in the following manner:
   A. By securing 100 points or more as follows:

      Class 1 — Education

      (1) A passing grade in an Introductory Appraisal course and an Advance Appraisal course under the auspices f an approved appraisal organization or a pasing grade in NSREA courses No. 1001 and No. 2001 — 20 points.

      (2) Appraisal courses given in accredited colleges — 15 points.

      (3) Courses in real estate and related subjects in accredited colleges — 5 points.

      Class 2 — Experience

      (1) Five years — 10 points each year.

      (2) Over five years — 10 points each year.

      (3) Non-concurrent collateral real estate experience — 5 points each year.

      (4) Demonstration of a Commercial or Industrial Appraisal Project.

      Class 3 — Appraisal Reports — 10 points each accepted report.

      Appraisal Reports — 10 points each accepted report of a commercial or industrial.

      At least forty (40) Class 1 points must be obtained.

      At least fifty (50) Class 2 points must be obtained in appraisal experience.

      At least ten (10) points must be obtained in Class 3.
3. Admission to National Society of Real Estate Appraisers Master Membership may be attained in the following manner:
   A. By securing 145 or more credit points as follows:

      Class 1 — Education

      1. Two years or more college or its equivalent in college credits — 20 points.
      2. An examination to test basic knowledge of market, feasibility, and investment analysis, and cash flow estimation. This is a self-graded examination taken at home to determine need to up-date knowledge in these listed areas — 20 points.
      3. Advanced courses in Appraising problem solving and statistics — 10 points.

      Class II — Experience

      Over five years — 5 points each year.

      Class III — Appraisal Reports — 75 points total

      (1) Item 1. A shopping center.

      Item 2. Assessment review on a Commercial or Industrial Building.

      Item 3. Measuring damages resulting from a partial taking.

Item 4. Industrial Property (Fair Market Value, Fair Market Rental and Leasehold value.)

Item 5. Air Rights Evaluation.

Item 6. Office Building Complex.

Item 7. Multi-Story parking structure.

(2) 21 points for an accepted feasibility analysis study of any commercial or industrial property.

Class IV — Oral interview by Masters Appraisal review panel — 25 points.

At least forty (40) Class I points must be obtained.

At least five (5) Class II points must be obtained.

At least Seventy-Five (75) Class III points must be obtained including 21 points for (2)

At least twenty-five (25) Class IV points must be obtained.

ORDER OF BUSINESS

The order of business for the annual meeting shall be:

1. Call to order
2. Reading of minutes
3. Annual reports of officers
   a. Secretary
   b. Treasurer
   c. Auditor
   d. Standing committees
4. Address of President
5. New business
6. Election of officers
7. Installation of officers
8. Adjournment

AMENDMENTS

There has been a change in our By-Laws as to the use of Insignia by our membership:

A Master member can use the Master Insignia;
A Senior member can use the Senior Insignia;
A Junior member can use the Junior Insignia.

The use is on individual's letterheads, business cards, appraisal reports and on professional forms.

The NSREA INSIGNIA is to be used only by the National Organization and its Chapters, never by individual members.

NSREA will publish a newsletter called "National Report," will be published quarterly and the cost of the report ($12.00) will be included in the annual dues of each member.

These By-Laws may be amended at any annual, regular or special meeting of the Association by a two-thirds (2/3) vote of the active members present. The proposed amendment must be in writing and must have been read to the Society at a prior meeting.

These By-Laws may also be amended at any annual meeting without prior notice by the unanimous vote of the members present.

UNIFORM STANDARDS

OF

PROFESSIONAL APPRAISAL PRACTICE

PREAMBLE

It is essential that a professional appraiser arrive at and communicate his or her analyses, opinions, and advice in a manner that will be meaningful to the client and will not be misleading in the marketplace. These Uniform Standards of Professional Appraisal Practice reflect the current standards of the appraisal profession.

These standards include a Competency Provision which places an immediate responsibility on the appraiser prior to acceptance of an assignment. The standards contain binding requirements, as well as specific guidelines to which a Departure Provision applies under certain conditions. Definitions applicable to these standards are also included.

These standards deal with the procedures to be followed in developing an appraisal, analysis, or opinion and the manner in which an appraisal, analysis, or opinion is communicated. Standards 1 and 2 relate to the development and communication of a real estate appraisal. Standard 3 establishes guidelines for reviewing an appraisal and reporting on that review. Standards 4 and 5 address the development and communication of various real estate analysis functions. Standard 6 sets forth criteria for the development and reporting of mass appraisals for ad valorem tax purposes. Standards 7 and 8 establish guidelines for developing and communicating personal property appraisals.

These standards are developed for appraisers and the users of appraisal services. To maintain the highest level of professional practice, appraisers will observe these standards. The users of appraisal services should demand work performed in conformance with these standards.

COMPETENCY PROVISION

Prior to entering into an agreement to perform any assignment, an appraiser must carefully consider the knowledge and experience that will be required to complete the assignment competently and either:

1. have the knowledge and experience necessary to complete the assignment competently; or
2. with regard to appraisal, review, and analysis as defined herein, immediately disclose the lack of knowledge or experience to the client, and take all steps necessary or appropriate to complete the assignment competently; or
3. with regard to mass appraisal as defined herein, immediately take all necessary or appropriate steps to ensure the mass appraisal is developed under the supervision of an appraiser who has the qualifications referred to in Standard 6.

DEPARTURE PROVISION

An appraiser may enter into an agreement to perform an assignment that calls for something less than, or different from, the work that would otherwise be required by the specific guidelines, provided that prior to entering into such agreement:

1. the appraiser has determined that the assignment to be performed is not so limited in scope that the resulting appraisal, review, or analysis would tend to mislead or confuse the client, the users of the report, or the public; and
2. the appraiser has advised the client that the assignment calls for something less than, or different from, the work required by the specific guidelines, and therefore the report will include a qualification that reflects the limited or differing scope of the appraisal, review, or analysis.

In the context of this departure provision, exceptions to the following binding requirements are not permitted: S.R. 1-1, S.R. 1-5, S.R. 2-1, S.R. 2-3, S.R. 2-5, S.R. 3-3, S.R. 4-1, S.R. 5-1, S.R. 5-3, S.R. 6-1, S.R. 6-5, S.R. 6-6, S.R. 7-1, S.R. 8-1 and S.R. 8-3.

JURISDICTIONAL EXCEPTION

If any part of these standards is contrary to the law or public policy of any jurisdiction, only that part shall be void and of no force or effect in that jurisdiction.

DEFINITIONS

For the purpose of these standards, the following definitions apply:

ANALYSIS: the act or process of providing information, recommendations and/or conclusions on diversified problems in real estate other than estimating value.

APPRAISAL: the act or process of estimating value.

CASH FLOW ANALYSIS: a study of the anticipated movement of cash in or out of real estate.

CLIENT: any party for whom an appraiser performs a service.

FEASIBILITY ANALYSIS: a study of the cost-benefit relationship of an economic endeavor.

INVESTMENT ANALYSIS: a study that reflects the relationship between acquisition price and anticipated future benefits of a real estate investment.

MARKET ANALYSIS: a study of real estate market conditions for a specific type of property.

MASS APPRAISAL: the process of valuing a universe of properties as of a given date utilizing standard methodology, employing common data, and allowing for statistical testing.

MASS APPRAISAL MODEL: a mathematical expression of how supply and demand factors interact in a market.

PERSONAL PROPERTY: identifiable portable and tangible objects which are considered by the general public as being "personal," e.g., furnishings, artwork, antiques, gems and jewelry, collectibles, machinery and equipment.

REAL ESTATE: an identified parcel or tract of land, including improvements, if any.

REAL PROPERTY: the interests, benefits, and rights inherent in the ownership of real estate.

REPORT: any communication, written or oral, of an appraisal, review, or analysis; the document that is transmitted to the client upon completion of an assignment.

REVIEW: the act or process of critically studying a report prepared by another.

STANDARD 1

In developing a real estate appraisal, an appraiser must be aware of, understand, and correctly employ those recognized methods and techniques that are necessary to produce a credible appraisal.

STANDARDS RULES RELATING TO STANDARD 1

S.R. 1-1

In developing a real estate appraisal, an appraiser must:

(a) be aware of, understand, and correctly employ those recognized methods and techniques that are necessary to produce a credible appraisal;

(b) not commit a substantial error of omission or commission that significantly affects an appraisal;

(c) not render appraisal services in a careless or negligent manner, such as a series of errors that, considered individually, may not significantly affect the results of an appraisal, but which, when considered in the aggregate, would be misleading.

S.R. 1-2

In developing a real estate appraisal, an appraiser must observe the following apecific appraisal guidelines:

(a) adequately identify the real estate, identify the real property interest under consideration, define the purpose and intended use of the appraisal, consider the scope of the appraisal, describe any special limiting conditions, and identify the effective date of the appraisal;

(b) define the value being considered; if the value to be estimated is market value, the appraiser must clearly indicate whether the estimate is the most probable price:

(i) in terms of cash; or

(ii) in terms of financial arrangements equivalent to cash; or

(iii)in such other terms as may be precisely defined;

if an estimate of value is based on submarket financing or financing with unusual conditions or incentives, the terms of such financing must be clearly set forth, their contributions to or negative influence on value must be described and estimated, and the market data supporting the valuation estimate must be described and explained;

(c) consider easements, restrictions, encumbrances, leases, reservations, covenants, contracts, declarations, special assignments, ordinances, or other items of a similar nature;

(d) consider whether an appraised fractional interest, physical segment, or partial holding contributes pro rata to the value of the whole;

(e) identify and consider any personal property, fixtures or tangible items that are not real property but are included in the appraisal.

S.R. 1-3

In developing a real estate appraisal, an appraiser must observe the following specific appraisal guidelines:

(a) consider the effect on use and value of the following factors: existing land use regulations, reasonably probable modifications of such land use regulations, economic demand, the physic adaptability of the property, neighborhood trends, and the highest and best use of the property;

(b) recognize that land is appraised as though vacant and available for development to its highest and best use and that the appraisal of improvements is based on their actual contribution to the site.

S.R. 1-4

In developing a real estate appraisal, an appraiser must observe the following specific appraisal guidelines when applicable:

(a) value the site by an appropriate appraisal method or technique;

(b) collect, verify, analyze, and reconcile:

(i) such comparable cost data as are available to estimate the cost new of the improvements (if any);

(ii) such comparable data as are available to estimate the difference between cost new and the present worth of the improvements (accrued depreciation);

(iii) such comparable sales data, adequately identified and described, as are available to indicate a value conclusion;

(iv) such comparable rental data as are available to estimate the market rental of the property being appraised;

(v) such comparable operating expense data as are available to estimate the operating expenses of the property being appraised;

(vi) such comparable data as are available to estimate rates of captalization and/or rates of discount.

No pertinent information shall be withheld.

(c) base projections of future rent and expenses on reasonably clear and appropriate evidence.

(d) when estimating the value of a leased fee estate or a leasehold estate, consider and analyze the effect on value, if any, of the terms and conditions of the lease(s);

(e) consider and analyze the effect on value, if any, of the assemblage of the various estates or component parts of a property and refrain from estimating the value of the whole solely by adding together the individual values of the various estates or component parts;

(f) consider and analyze the effect on value, if any, of anticipated public or private improvements, located on or off the site, to the extent that market actions reflect such anticipated improvements as of the effective appraisal date;

(g) identify and consider the appropriate procedures and market information required to perform the appraisal, including all physical, functional, and external market factors as they may affect the appraisal;

(h) appraise proposed improvements only after examining and having available for future examination:

(i) plans, specifications, or other documentation sufficient to identify the scope and character of the proposed improvements;

(ii) evidence indicating the probable time of completion of the proposed improvements;

(iii) reasonably clear and appropriate evidence supporting development costs, anticipated earnings, occupancy projections, and the anticipated competition at the time of completion.

S.R. 1-5

In developing a real estate appraisal, an appraiser must:

(a) consider and analyze any current Agreement of Sale, option, or listing of the property being appraised, if such information is available to the appraiser in the normal course of business;

(b) consider and analyze any prior sales of property being appraised that occurred within the following time periods:

(i) one year for one-to-four family residential property; and

(ii) three years for all other property types;

(c) consider the quality and quantity of data available and analyzed within the approaches used, and the applicability or suitability of the approaches used in the final reconciliation.

STANDARD 2

In reporting the results of a real estate appraisal, an appraiser must communicate each analysis, opinion, and conclusion in a manner that is not misleading.

STANDARDS RULES RELATING TO STANDARD 2

S.R. 2-1

Each written or oral real estate appraisal report must:

(a) clearly and accurately set forth the appraisal in a manner that will not be misleading;

(b) contain sufficient information to enable the person(s) who receive or rely on the report to understand it properly;

(c) clearly and accurately disclose any extraordinary assumption or limiting condition that directly affects the appraisal and indicate its impact on value.

S.R. 2-2

Each written real estate appraisal report must comply with the following specific reporting guidelines:

(a) identify and describe the real estate being appraised;

(b) identify the real property interest being appraised;

(c) define the purpose of the appraisal;

(d) define the value to be estimated;

(e) set forth the effective date of the appraisal and the date of the report;

(f) describe the scope of the appraisal;

(g) set forth all assumptions and limiting conditions that affect the analyses, opinions, and conclusions;

(h) set forth the information considered, the appraisal procedures followed, and the reasoning that supports the analyses, opinions, and conclusions;

(i) set forth the appraiser's opinion of the highest and best use of the real estate being appraised when such an opinion is necessary and appropriate;

(j) explain and support the exclusion of any of the usual valuation approaches;

(k) set forth any additional information that may be appropriate to show compliance with, or clearly identify and explain permitted departures from, the requirements of Standard 1;

(l) include a signed certification in accordance with Standards Rule 2-3.

S.R. 2-3

Each written real estate appraisal report must contain a certification that is similar in content to the following form:

(a) I certify that, to the best of my knowledge and belief:

the statements of fact contained in this report are true and correct.

the reported analyses, opinions, and conclusions are limited only by the reported assumptions and limiting conditions, and are my personal, unbiased professional analyses, opinions, and conclusions.

- I have no (or the specified) present or prospective interest in the property that is the subject of this report, and I have no (or the specified) personal interest or bias with respect to the parties involved.
- my compensation is not contingent on an action or event resulting from the analyses, opinions, or conclusions in, or the use of, this report.
- my analyses, opinions, and conclusions were developed, and this report has been prepared, in conformity with the Uniform Standards of Professional Appraisal Practice.
- I have (or have not) made a personal inspection of the property that is the subject of this report. (If more than one person signs the report, this certification must clearly specify which individuals did and which individuals did not make a personal inspection of the appraised property.)
- no one provided significant professional assistance to the person signing this report. (If there are exceptions, the name of each individual providing significant professional assistance must be stated.)

S.R. 2-4

To the extent that it is both possible and appropriate, each oral real estate appraisal report (including expert testimony) must address the substantive matters set forth in Standards Rule 2-2.

S.R. 2-5

An appraiser who signs a real estate appraisal report prepared by another, even under the label of "review appraiser," must accept full responsibility for the contents of the report.

STANDARD 3

In reviewing an appraisal and reporting the results of that review, an appraiser must form an opinion as to the adequacy and appropriateness of the report being reviewed and must clearly disclose the nature of the review process undertaken.

STANDARDS RULES RELATING TO STANDARD 3

S.R. 3-1

In reviewing an appraisal, an appraiser must observe the following specific guidelines:

(a) identify the report being reviewed, the real estate and real property interest being appraised, the effective date of the opinion in the report being reviewed, and the date of the review;

(b) identify the scope of the review process to be conducted;

(c) form an opinion as to the adequacy and relevance of the data and the propriety of any adjustments to the data;

(d) form an opinion as to the appropriateness of the appraisal methods and techniques used and develop the reasons for any disagreement;

(e) form an opinion as to the correctness and appropriateness of the analyses, opinions, and/or conclusions in the report being reviewed and develop the reasons for any disagreement.

S.R. 3-2

In reporting the results of an appraisal review, an appraiser must:

(a) disclose the nature, extent, and detail of the review process undertaken;

(b) disclose the information that must be considered in S.R. 3-1 (a) and (b);

(c) set forth the opinions, reasons, and conclusions required in S.R. 3-1 (c), (d) and (e).

No pertinent information shall be withheld.

S.R. 3-3

In reviewing an appraisal and reporting the results of that review, an appraiser must separate the review function from any other functions.

STANDARD 4

In developing a real estate analysis, an analyst must be aware of, understand, and correctly employ those recognized methods and techniques that are necessary to produce a credible analysis.

STANDARDS RULES RELATING TO STANDARD 4

S.R. 4-1

In developing a real estate analysis, an analyst must:

(a) be aware of, understand, and correctly employ those recognized methods and techniques that are necessary to produce a credible analysis;

(b) not commit a substantial error of omission or commission that significantly affects an analysis;

(c) not render analyst services in a careless or negligent manner, such as a series of errors that, considered individually, may not significantly affect the results of an analysis, but which, when considered in the aggregate, would be misleading.

S.R. 4-2

In developing a real estate analysis, an analyst must observe the following specific analysis guidelines:

(a) clearly identify the client's objective;

(b) define the problem to be considered, define the purpose and intended use of the analysis, consider the scope of the assignment, adequately identify the real estate under consideration (if any), describe any special limiting conditions, and identify the effective date of the analysis;

(c) collect, verify, and reconcile such data as may be required to complete the assignment;

(i) if the market value of a specific property is pertinent to the analysis assignment, an appraisal in conformance with Standard 1 should be included in the data collection.

No pertinent information shall be withheld.

(d) apply the appropriate tools and techniques of analysis to the data collected;

(e) base all projections on reasonably clear and appropriate evidence.

S.R. 4-3

In developing a real estate analysis, an analyst must observe the following specific analysis guidelines when a conclusion or recommendation is required by the nature of the assignment:

(a) identify alternative courses of action to achieve the client's objective, and analyze their implications;

(b) identify both known and anticipated constraints to each alternative and measure their probable impact;

(c) identify the resources actually or expected to be available to each alternative and measure their probable impact;

(d) identify the optimum course of action to achieve the client's objective.

S.R. 4-4

In developing a real estate market analysis, an analyst must observe the following specific analysis guidelines when applicable:

(a) define and delineate the market area;

(b) identify and analyze the current supply and demand conditions that make up the specific real estate market;

(c) identify, measure, and forecast the effect of anticipated development or other changes and future supply;

(d) identify, measure, and forecast the effect of anticipated economic or other changes and future demand.

S.R. 4-5

In developing a real estate cash flow and/or investment analysis, an analyst must observe the following specific analysis guidelines when applicable:

(a) consider and analyze the quantity and quality of the income stream;

(b) consider and analyze the history of expenses and reserves;

(c) consider and analyze financing availability and terms;

(d) select and support the appropriate method of processing the income stream;

(e) consider and analyze the cash flow return(s) and reversion(s) to the specified investment position over a projected time period(s).

S.R. 4-6

In developing a real estate feasibility analysis, an analyst must observe the following specific analysis guidelines when applicable:

(a) prepare a complete market analysis;

(b) apply the results of the market analysis to alternative courses of action to achieve the client's objective;

(i) consider and analyze the probable costs of each alternative;

(ii) consider and analyze the probability of altering any constraints to each alternative;

(iii) consider and analyze the probable outcome of each alternative.

STANDARD 5

In reporting the results of a real estate analysis, an analyst must communicate each analysis, opinion, and conclusion in a manner that is not misleading.

STANDARDS RULES RELATING TO STANDARD 5

S.R. 5-1

Each written or oral analysis report must:

(a) clearly and accurately set forth the analysis in a manner that will not be misleading;

(b) contain sufficient information to enable the person(s) who receive or rely on the report to understand it properly;

(c) clearly and accurately disclose any extraordinary assumption or limiting condition that directly affects the analysis and indicate its impact on the final conclusion or recommendation (if any).

S.R. 5-2

Each written analysis report must comply with the following specific reporting guidelines:

(a) define the problem to be considered;

(b) define the purpose of the analysis;

(c) identify and describe the real estate under consideration (if any);

(d) set forth the effective date of the analysis and the date of the report;

(e) describe the scope of the assignment;

(f) set forth all assumptions and limiting conditions that affect the analyses, opinions, and conclusions;

(g) set forth the information considered, the analysis procedures followed, and the reasoning that supports the analyses, opinions, and conclusions;

(h) set forth the analyst's final conclusions or recommendations (if any);

(i) set forth any additional information that may be appropriate to show compliance with, or clearly identify and explain permitted departures from, the requirements of Standard 4;

(j) include a signed certification in accordance with Standards Rule 5-3.

S.R. 5-3

Each written analysis report must contain a certification that is similar in content to the following form:

(a) I certify that, to the best of my knowledge and belief:

- the statements of fact contained in this report are true and correct.
- the reported analyses, opinions, and conclusions are limited only by the reported assumptions and limiting conditions, and are my personal, unbiased professional analyses, opinions and conclusions.
- I have no (or the specified) present or prospective interest in the property (if any) that is the

subject of this report, and I have no (or the specified) personal interest or bias with respect to the parties involved.

- my compensation is not (or is) contingent on an action or event resulting from the analyses, opinions, or conclusions in, or the use of, this report. (If the compensation is contingent, the basis of such contingency must be explained)
- my analyses, opinions, and conclusions were developed, and this report has been prepared, in conformity with the Uniform Standards of Professional Appraisal Practice.
- I have (or have not) made a personal inspection of the property (if any) that is the subject of this report. (If more than one person signs the report, this certification must clearly specify which individuals did and which individuals did not make a personal inspection of the property.)
- no one provided significant professional assistance to the person signing this report. (If there are exceptions, the name of each individual providing significant professional assistance must be stated.)

S.R. 5-4

To the extent that it is both possible and appropriate, each oral analysis report (including expert testimony) must address the substantive matters set forth in Standards Rule 5-2.

STANDARD 6

In developing and reporting a mass appraisal for ad valorem tax purposes, an appraiser must be aware of, undestand, and correctly employ those recognized methods and techniques that are necessary to produce and communicate credible appraisals within the context of the property tax laws.

STANDARDS RULES RELATING TO STANDARD 6

S.R. 6-1

In developing a mass appraisal for ad valorem tax purposes, an appraiser must:

(a) be aware of, understand, and correctly employ those recognized methods and techniques that are necessary to produce a credible appraisal;

(b) not commit a substantial error of omission or commission that significantly affects an appraisal;

(c) not render an appraisal in a careless or negligent manner;

(d) employ those recognized mass appraisal procedures and techniques that are necessary to minimize errors in the data and analyses;

(e) employ those recognized techniques for formulating and calibrating mass appraisal models; and

(f) employ those recognized mass appraisal testing procedures and techniques that are necessary to ensure that standards of accuracy are maintained.

S.R. 6-2

In developing a mass appraisal for ad valorem tax purposes, an appraiser must:

(a) adequately identify the real estate, identify the real property interest under consideration, define the purpose and intended use of the appraisal, consider the scope of the appraisal, describe any special limiting conditions, and identify the effective date of the appraisal;

(b) define the value being considered;

if the value to be estimated is market value, the appraiser must clearly indicate whether the estimate is the most probable price:

(i) in terms of cash; or
(ii) in terms of financial arrangements equivalent to cash; or
(iii) in such other terms as may be precisely defined;

(c) when applicable and when the information is available to the appraiser in the normal course of business, consider easements, restrictions, encumbrances, leases, reservations, covenants, contracts, declarations, special assessments, ordinances, or other items of a similar nature;

(d) consider whether an appraised fractional interest, physical segment, or partial holding contributes pro rata to the value of the whole, if applicable;

(e) identify and consider any personal property, fixtures or intangible items that are not real property but are included in the appraisal.

S.R. 6-3

In developing a mass appraisal for ad valorem tax purposes, an appraiser must:

(a) consider the effect on use and value of the following factors: existing land use regulations, reasonably probable modifications of such land use regulations, economic demand, the physical adaptability of the property, neighborhood trends, and the highest and best use of the property;

(b) recognize that land is appraised as though vacant and available for development to its highest and best use and that the appraisal of improvements is based on their actual contribution to the site.

S.R. 6-4

In developing a mass appraisal for ad valorem tax purposes, an appraiser must:

(a) value the site by an appropriate method or technique;

(b) collect, verify, analyze, and reconcile:

(i) such comparable cost data as are available to estimate the cost new of the improvement (if any);

(ii) such comparable data as are available to estimate the difference between cost new and the present worth of the improvements (accrued depreciation);

(iii) such comparable sales data, adequately identified and described, as are available to indicate a value conclusion;

(iv) such comparable rental data as are available to estimate the market rental of the property being appraised;

(v) such comparable operating expense data as are available to estimate the operating expenses of the property being appraised;

(vi) such comparable data as are available to estimate rates of capitalization and/or rates of discount.

No pertinent information shall be withheld.

(c) base projections of future rent and expenses on reasonably clear and appropriate evidence;

(d) when estimating the value of a leased fee estate or a leasehold estate, consider and analyze the effect on value, if any, of the terms and conditions of the lease;

(e) consider and analyze the effect on value, if any, of the assemblage of the various estates or component parts of a property and refrain from estimating the value of the whole solely by adding together the individual values of the various estates or component parts;

(f) consider and analyze the effect on value, if any, of anticipated public or private improvements, located on or off the site, to the extent that market actions reflect such anticipated improvements as of the effective appraisal date;

(g) identify and consider the appropriate procedures and market information to perform the appraisal, including all physical, functional, and external market factors as they may affect the appraisal;

(h) appraise proposed improvements only after examining and having available for future examination:

(i) plans, specifications, or other documentation sufficient to identify the scope and character of the proposed improvements;

(ii) evidence indicating the probable time of completion of the proposed improvements; and

(iii) reasonably clear and appropriate evidence supporting development costs, anticipated earnings, occupancy projections, and the anticipated competition at the time of completion.

S.R. 6-5

In developing a mass appraisal for ad valorem tax purposes, an appraiser must:

(a) consider and analyze any current agreement of sale, option, or listing of the property being appraised, if such information is available to the appraiser in the normal course of business;

(b) consider and analyze any prior sales of the property being appraised;

(c) consider the quality and quantity of data available and analyzed within the approaches used, and the adaptability or suitability of the approaches used in the final reconciliation.

S.R. 6-6

Mass appraisals for ad valorem tax purposes must be supported by documentation that is reasonably accessible to the public and communicated in ways that are not misleading. Documentation may be in the form of (1) records and files in electromagnetic, micrographic, paper, or other storage media, (2) reports, (3) manuals, (4) regulations, (5) statutes, or other acceptable forms. The documentation should substantially conform to the factual requirements of Standards Rule 2-2. Appraisals for ad valorem tax purposes should be certified in a manner consistent with law and with generally accepted practices.

STANDARD 7

In developing a personal property appraisal, an appraiser must be aware of, understand, and correctly employ those recognized methods and techniques that are necessary to produce a credible appraisal.

STANDARDS RULES RELATING TO STANDARD 7

S.R. 7-1

In developing a personal property appraisal, an appraiser must:

(a) be aware of, understand, and correctly employ those recognized methods and techniques that are necessary to produce a credible appraisal;

(b) not commit a substantial error of omission or commission that significantly affects an appraisal;

(c) not render appraisal services in a careless or negligent manner, such as series of errors that, considered individually, may not significantly affect the results of an appraisal, but which, when considered in the aggregate, would be misleading.

S.R. 7-2

In developing a personal property appraisal, an appraiser must observe the following specific appraisal guidelines:

(a) adequately identify the object(s) to be valued, including the method of identification;

(b) define the purpose and intended use of the appraisal, including any special limiting conditions;

(c) identify the effective date of the appraisal, clearly distinguishing the appraisal date from the report date when appropriate;

(d) define the value to be considered consistent with the purpose of the appraisal;

(e) value the object(s) by an appropriate appraisal method or technique;

(f) collect, verify, analyze and reconcile such data as are available, adequately identified and described, to indicate a value conclusion.

No pertinent information shall be withheld.

S.R. 7-3

In developing an appraisal of certain types of fine art, when applicable, consider and analyze the effect on value of:

(a) any relevant damage or imperfections;

(b) the importance of the object(s) as compared to other items of the same type and classification, or as relating to an artist's total work, or as enhancing other parts of a specific collection;

(c) any historical factors (provenance) which would affect value;

(d) the market acceptability of the style and scale of the object(s);

(e) the utility, if any, in today's society as it relates to the originally intended use of the object(s);

(f) any prior sales of the object(s) being appraised.

STANDARD 8

In reporting the results of a personal property appraisal, an appraiser must communicate each analysis, opinion, and conclusion in a manner that is not misleading.

STANDARDS RULES RELATING TO STANDARD 8

S.R. 8-1

Each written or oral personal property appraisal report must:

(a) clearly and accurately set forth the appraisal in a manner that will not be misleading;

(b) contain sufficient information to enable the person(s) who receive or rely on the report to understand it properly;

(c) clearly and accurately disclose any extraordinary assumption or limiting condition that directly affects the appraisal and indicate its impact on value.

S.R. 8-2

Each written personal property appraisal report must comply with the following specific reporting guidelines:

(a) identify and describe the personal property being appraised;

(b) define the purpose and scope of the appraisal;

(c) define the value to be estimated;

(d) set forth the effective date of the appraisal and the date of the report;

(e) set forth all assumptions and limiting conditions that affect the analyses, opinions, conclusions and valuations;

(f) where appropriate, set forth the information considered, the appraisal procedures followed, and the reasoning that supports the analyses, opinions, conclusions and valuations;

(g) when analysis of comparable sales is one of the methods used in the appraisal of personal property for sale purposes, carefully document the sales and analysis;

(h) set forth any additional information that may be appropriate to show compliance with, or clearly identify and explain permitted departures from, the requirements of Standard 7;

(i) include a signed certification in accordance with Standards Rule 8-3.

S.R. 8-3

Each written personal property appraisal report must contain a certification that is similar in content to the following form:

(a) I certify that, to the best of my knowledge and belief:

- the statements of fact contained in this report are true and correct.
- the reported analyses, opinions, and conclusions are limited only by the reported assumptions and limiting conditions, and are my personal , unbiased professional analyses, opinions, and conclusions.
- I have no (or the specified) present or prospective interest in the property that is the subject of this report, and I have no (or the specified) personal interest or bias with respect to the parties involved.
- my compensation is not contingent on an action or event resulting from the analyses, opinions, or conclusions in, or the use of, this report.
- my analyses, opinions, and conclusions were developed, and this report has been prepared, in conformity with the Uniform Standards of Professional Appraisal Practice.
- I have (or have not) made a personal inspection of the personal property that is the subject of this report. (If more than one person signs the report, this certification must clearly specify which individuals did and which individuals did not make a personal inspection of the appraised property.)
- no one provided significant professional assistance to the person signing this report. (If there are exceptions, the name of each individual providing significant professional assistance must be stated.)

S.R. 8-4

To the extent that it is both possible and appropriate, each oral personal property appraisal report (including expert testimony) must address the substantive matters set forth in Standards rule 8-2.

There are to be added additional Standards as they are promigated by the Ad Hoc Committee and/or a Standards Board.

Glossary of Appraisal and Investment Terms

AAA tenant: A tenant who is given the highest credit rating and is considered the least risky.

Accelerated depreciation: The methods of depreciation for income tax purposes that permit a faster write-off than is permitted by straight-line depreciation.

Acceleration of debt: Occurs whenever the future principal installments on a mortgage note become due immediately. This may be due to default, a "due on sale clause," or some other contractual provision specified in the mortgage instrument or the note.

Accrued depreciation: In appraisal, any loss of utility that causes the actual value of a property to be less than the reproduction cost new. *Same as* Diminished utility.

Accrued interest: Unpaid interest that has already been earned.

Accumulation of one per period: *Same as* Compound amount of one per period and Amount of one per period.

Acre: Area measurement that is 43,560 square feet, 1,840 square yards, or 160 square rods.

Actual age: *See* Chronological age.

Add-on interest: Interest calculated by taking the simple interest that would be charged if the loan principal amount is not amortized over the term of the loan. Periodic installments are calculated by dividing the sum of the add-on interest and original principal by the number of periods in the term. Add-on interest is often used in consumer loans and in some second mortgages.

Adjusted tax basis: The tax basis of an asset reflecting adjustments for depreciation accounting and other pertinent factors.

Adjustments: Used in the sales comparison approach to value. These are the additions and subtractions that are made to account for differences between comparable properties and the subject property.

After-tax cash flow: Before-tax cash flow adjusted for income taxes that result from ownership of property or from income tax savings realized by property ownership. *Same as* Net spendable income or spendable income.

After-tax equity yield rate: The internal rate of return on the equity investment after considering federal income taxes.

After-tax income: *Same as* After-tax cash flow and Net spendable income.

After-tax proceeds from resale: The amount a property seller would receive from a property sale after subtracting transaction costs, capital gains taxes, and other expenses. Generally, the selling price less the sum of the existing debt, the income or capital gains taxes, and the expenses of sale.

Age-life method: A method of estimating accrued depreciation by applying to the reproduction cost new the ratio of effective age to economic useful life.

Air rights: The right to use, control, and occupy the space or a portion of the space above a particular surface of land.

Amenity: A feature in real property creating psychological benefits or other attractions. Examples of amenities include a scenic view, a swimming pool, a fireplace in the living room, etc.

Amortization: Reduction of the principal balance of a loan.

Amortization rate: The percentage of a periodic payment that is applied to the reduction of the principal; in a level-payment mortgage this corresponds to the sinking fund factor.

Amortization term: The time period over which the principal amount would be retired on the basis of the periodic installments paid.

Amortized mortgage: A financial debt that is paid off over a term by a series of periodic payments. A loan can be fully amortized, in which case the entire principal is paid back over the term, or it can be partially amortized, in which case a balloon payment is due to satisfy the debt at the end of the term.

Amount of one: *See* Compound amount of one.

Amount of one per period: *See* Compound amount of one per period.

Analyst: An individual who performs studies and calculations to help make decisions or solve problems concerning real estate investments.

Anchor tenant: Major tenant in a shopping center that serves as a magnet to attract customers to the center.

Annual debt service: Total payments required in one year by a loan.

Annual percentage rate (APR): The effective annual cost of credit calculated on the basis of procedures specified by Regulation Z (Truth-in-Lending).

Annuity: A series of equal payments either made or received at even intervals over a period of time. An example is the series of payments made to satisfy a level-payment mortgage debt. *Same as* annuity due.

Annuity in advance: An annuity in which payments are made at the beginning of each period as contrasted with an ordinary annuity, in which payments are made at the end of each period.

Annuity method: A means of capitalizing future income streams from an investment. The procedure uses compound interest formulas that treat the income stream as an annuity providing for both a return on investment and a return of investment.

Anticipation, principle of: The value principle that holds that value is determined by the present worth of income or of other benefits one expects to receive in the future from the ownership of property.

Appraisal: An opinion or estimate of value.

Appraisal approaches: Conventional approaches to value used by the appraisal profession. *See* separate entries for:

- Direct sales comparison approach—*same as* Market data approach. Also known as *market approach, market sales approach,* and *sales comparison approach.*
- Cost approach—*same as* Summation approach.
- Income approach—*same as* Capitalization approach. Also known as *income capitalization approach.*

Appraisal date: *See* Date of appraisal.

Appraisal process: A systematic problem-solving procedure for collecting and analyzing data to reach an opinion of value.

Appraisal report: A document submitted by an appraiser to support an opinion of value. The report may consist of a single-page standard form report or a lengthy narrative report. Ordinarily the report will consist of: (a) a letter of transmittal; (b) identification of property and interests being appraised; (c) value estimate; (d) date of appraisal; (e) assumptions and limiting conditions; (f) body of report, indicating data collected and appraisal methods used to reach an opinion of value; (g) reconciliation; and (h) exhibits, photographs, and other material.

Appraised value: An estimate of value based on the appraiser's analysis of data within the context of the appraisal problem that the appraiser was hired to solve.

Appraiser: An individual who has the experience, training, and legal qualifications to appraise real or personal property.

Appreciation: Increase in value.

ARA: An appraisal designation for Accredited Rural Appraiser, which is given by the American Society of Farm Managers and Rural Appraisers.

Arm's-length transaction: A contractual transaction negotiated between two or more unrelated parties who are knowledgeable, under no undue pressure, and capable in the context of the local market.

Assemblage: The process of bringing two or more parcels of land together under one ownership.

Assessed value: The valuation of a property for the purpose of imposing an ad valorem (property) tax.

Asset: Something of value possessed by an individual or entity. This includes both real and personal property.

Assumed mortgage: A mortgage obligation transferred to a purchaser, who becomes liable for any deficiencies that could arise in the event of a foreclosure sale; the original borrower remains secondarily liable.

Average rate of return: A technique used to estimate a rate of return. To compute this rate, investment outflows are subtracted from total investment inflows. The result is divided by the number of years the investment was held, and that result is divided by the total investment to arrive at the average annual rate of return.

Balance, principle of: The value principle that holds that for any type of land use there are optimal amounts of different agents in production that can be combined to create maximum land values. Also known as the *principle of proportionality*.

Balance sheet: A statement that measures from an accounting viewpoint the financial position of a business enterprise as of a given date.

Balloon mortgage: A partially amortized mortgage with a portion of the original principal due at the end of the term; also a straight term mortgage having interest-only payments during the term with the entire principal due at the end of the term.

Balloon payment: The remaining balance owed at maturity of a loan that has not been completely repaid through periodic installments.

Band of investment: A technique for deriving a capitalization rate related to the capital structure of a project and the necessary compensation required by each provider of funds.

Base (base interest rate): In compound interest, one plus the interest rate per period. Mathematically this is expressed as:

$$S = (1 + i)$$

where S represents the base, and i is the interest rate for the compounding period.

Base period: A period that serves as a reference point for establishing an index for price changes. The index for the base period is normally set at 100. If, for example, a price change of 8% occurred, the new index would be 108.

Base rent: In percentage leases and leases that provide operating expense escalation, the minimum rent due to the landlord.

Basis, original tax: Except for special situations such as property acquired by gift or inheritance, the basis is the cost of acquisition. The adjusted basis is the original basis plus all capital improvements, minus depreciation.

Basis point: There are one hundred basis points in 1% of an interest rate.

Before-tax cash flow: Net operating income minus debt service. The amount available to the equity owner of the income-producing real estate after cash operating expenses and debt service are subtracted from the effective gross income. *Same as* Cash flow and Cash throw-off.

Before-tax resale proceeds: The amount left over from the sales price after subtracting selling expenses, the remaining principal balance on existing mortgages, and any prepayment penalties. *Same as* Reversion.

Benchmark: A reference point.

Bond: (1) In finance, a long-term promissory note; also an interest-bearing certificate of indebtedness. (2) In law, the amount put up to secure the performance of some obligation.

Book depreciation: An accounting concept; an allowance taken to provide for recovery of capital invested in wasting assets.

Book value: The worth of property as reflected in an accounting balance sheet.

Boot: In federal taxation, this is anything that is not considered "like kind" property in a tax-free exchange; included to equalize the value of properties exchanged.

Break-even point: In finance, the point at which total income is equal to total expenses. *Same as* Default ratio.

Broker: A person acting as an intermediary for another, who, for a fee, offers to perform certain functions such as those done by real estate brokers or mortgage brokers. Generally, this intermediary is responsible for bringing buyers and sellers together. A license in real estate is generally required.

Building capitalization rate: A rate used in the residual techniques to capitalize the income attributable to the improvements; it includes both a return on and a return of capital invested in the improvements.

Building code: Ordinances passed by local governments that specify minimum standards of construction for new buildings or major additions to old buildings.

Building residual technique: A method of estimating the value of improvements by which the income attributable to the improvements is the remainder of net operating income after subtracting income attributable to land. The rate used to capitalize the income attributable to the improvement includes a return on and a return of capital. The income attributable to the land is capitalized at a rate that provides for a return on investment. Together these two values are added to estimate the total value.

Build-up method: A technique for deriving a capitalization rate that begins with a risk-free or safe rate, to which are added allowances for risk, illiquidity, and investment management.

Bundle of rights: A legal theory used to define the nature of property. It states that property is composed of a number of rights that can be separately sold, namely the rights to possess, use, control, enjoy the benefits of, and dispose of property.

Buyer's market: A market in which buyers are able to achieve very favorable terms and prices. It is usually due to general economic conditions or an oversupply of a particular land use in a community.

Canadian rollover mortgage: A renegotiated loan where the maturity is fixed (for example, 25 or 30 years), but the interest rates and, hence, the monthly mortgage payment are renegotiated periodically (for example, every 3 or 5 years). *See also* Renegotiated rate mortgage.

Capital: The accumulated wealth of a person or a business.

Capital asset: In taxation, property other than inventory, receivables, or depreciable property used in a trade or business, and certain other assets. In general, assets of a more or less permanent nature.

Capital expenditure: In accounting, an amount paid to acquire something of lasting value in contrast to something that will be consumed in the current year.

Capital gain: In taxation, gain from the sale of a capital asset that is sold for more than its adjusted tax basis. In general, a gain when a long-term asset is sold for more than its book value.

Capital recovery: A return of capital. This refers to a recapture of the portion of an investment that is expected to reflect a loss of value over the investment holding period.

Capital recovery period: The period over which a property is expected to produce income to the particular investor and over which any loss in the capital must be recaptured through the operating income stream.

Capital recovery rate: The percentage of the capital that is recaptured in each year. *Same as* Rate of return of investment. *See also* Recapture rate.

Capitalization approach: *See* Income approach.

Capitalization in perpetuity: Capitalization of income that is expected not to change and will last indefinitely, or capitalization of an asset that is expected to be sold for exactly the same price as it was purchased for and thus requires no capital recovery.

Capitalization rate (cap rate): A rate used to convert an income stream into a lump-sum capital value. The periodic income is divided by the capitalization rate to estimate the capital value of the income stream. In real estate, the capitalization rate must include a provision for interest and, in many cases, a provision for a return of capital.

Capitalize: To convert a future income stream to a present lump-sum value.

Capitalized value: The present worth of future benefits expected from the income stream and resale proceeds.

Carrying charges: The cost of owning nonincome-producing land or land under development or construction.

Cash: Money in U.S. legal tender, or its equivalent payable on demand. Cash is a purely liquid asset. The liquidity of other assets depends on how easily these can be converted into cash. *Same as* Money.

Cash equivalent: The price of a property reduced to a present value cash sum that takes into account the value of financial terms and any noncash items or services included as part of the consideration.

Cash flow: *See* Before-tax cash flow. *Same as* Cash throw-off.

Cash-on-cash: The before-tax cash flow divided by the equity invested. *Same as* Equity dividend rate.

Cash throw-off: *See* Before-tax cash flow. *Same as* Cash flow.

Certified real estate appraiser: A senior designation offered by the National Society of Real Estate Appraisers. Abbreviated CRA, the designation is a registered trademark.

Chronological age: The actual age of an item as measured by a standard calendar. *Same as* Actual age.

Coefficient: A factor that precedes another. For example, in the expression "5x," the coefficient is 5.

Commercial property: Income property used for offices, stores, or services, not including residential, public, or industrial uses.

Comparative unit method: A method of estimating construction costs by finding the completed cost per square foot or other measure of an entire benchmark structure. *See also* Cost estimating.

Comparison method: *See* Direct sales comparison approach.

Competition, principle of: A value principle that holds that where profits exist beyond the income necessary to pay for the agents (factors) in production, competition will tend to enter the market, causing average net incomes to fall.

Component depreciation: Depreciation estimated by breaking a depreciable capital asset down into separate parts such as the roof, carpeting, foundation, shell, and mechanical equipment and depreciating each part individually.

Composite rate: A blended rate that is a weighted average of different rates applicable to the property. In the Ellwood approach, R is a composite rate.

Compound amount of one: A factor used to calculate how much a present sum will be worth in the future if it is held for a certain period of time and earns an interest rate that is compounded periodically. The factor is calculated using the formula:

$$S^n = (1 + i)^n$$

Same as Amount of one and Future worth of one.

Compound amount of one per period: A factor used to calculate how much a series of equal sums deposited at the end of periodic compounding time intervals will be worth at the end of the total term. The factor is calculated using the formula:

$$S_n = \frac{(1 + i)^n - 1}{i}$$

Same as Amount of one per period, and Future worth of one per period, and Accumulation of one per period.

Compound interest: Interest earned on both principal and on any accrued interest earned in a previous compounding period.

Condemnation: The process of acquiring private land by the exercise of the power of eminent domain. On the basis of constitutional law the property may be taken for public use with the payment of just compensation.

Condominium: A legal form of ownership involving a separation of property into individual ownership elements and common ownership elements.

Conformity, principle of: The value principle that holds that value is influenced by how well the architectural style and level of amenities and services offered by a real estate development measure up to surrounding market needs and expectations. Also known as the *principle of consistency.*

Consideration: Anything of value offered to induce someone to enter into a contract.

Constant: A number that does not vary in size or amount (for example, a debt service constant).

Construction loan: An interim loan that provides the funds necessary for the construction of improvements. It is usually characterized by progress payments tied to different phases of the construction and by a floating interest rate tied to some index such as the prime rate.

Contract for deed: A type of financing agreement between a seller of property and a purchaser. The seller passes possession but retains title to the property until the total or a substantial portion of the purchase price is paid. If the purchaser defaults, the seller can normally cancel the contract and keep all payments as rent. *Same as* Installment contract and Land contract. Also known as *land sales contract* and *installment land contract.*

Contract rent: The amount of rent specified in the lease agreement.

Contribution, principle of: Value principle that is a measurement of the amount by which the value or net income of an economic good is increased or decreased by the presence or absence of some additional factor of production. *Same as* Marginal productivity.

Conventional mortgage: A mortgage other than one guaranteed by the Veteran's Administration or insured by the Federal Housing Administration.

Cost approach: An approach in appraisal analysis based on the premise that an informed purchaser would generally pay no more for a property than the cost of producing a substitute property having the same usefulness. Requires an estimate of current reproduction cost new (replacement cost new in some situations) and accrued depreciation. *Same as* Summation approach.

Cost estimating: The process of calculating the approximate construction cost of an improvement through one of several alternative methods. *See also* Quantity survey method, Unit-in-place method, Trade breakdown method, and Comparative unit method.

Curable depreciation: Depreciation that can be corrected at a cost that would be worthwhile from a prudent, profit-motivated standpoint.

Current assets: Assets that are liquid, including cash and items such as merchandise inventory or accounts receivable that generally will be converted into cash within a year.

Current liabilities: Short-term obligations, generally due within one year.

Current yield: A measurement of the present productivity of the current cash returns from an investment compared to investment cost. The current yield does not measure changes in the value of the capital invested. The following formula can be used to calculate this yield:

$$\text{Current yield} = \frac{\text{Annual income}}{\text{Investment outlay}}$$

See also Yield and Yield to maturity.

Date of appraisal: The date as of which the opinion of value is effective. *Same as* Appraisal date.

Debt financing: The use of borrowed funds to make a real estate purchase.

Debt service: Interest and principal payments for a loan. *Same as* Mortgage requirement.

Debt service constant (percentage): The relationship, stated as a percentage, of the principal and interest payments to the initial amount borrowed. *See also* Annual debt service.

Debt service coverage ratio: Percentage relationship found by dividing the annual debt service (principal amortization and interest) into the net operating income.

Declining-balance depreciation: Accelerated depreciation method in which the remaining undepreciated balance is the base for calculating the next year's depreciation.

Decreasing annuity: A series of periodic payments or receipts that progressively decline over time.

Deed of trust: A deed in real property financing transactions that serves the same purpose as a mortgage but involves three parties instead of two. The third party (trustee) holds title for the benefit of the lender (beneficiary). *Same as* Trust deed.

Deed restriction: A covenant in a deed that restricts the use of property. *Same as* Restrictive covenant.

Default: In mortgage financing, any failure to perform contractual obligations that would justify steps by the lender to institute foreclosure proceedings.

Default ratio: *See* Break-even point.

Deferred annuity: A series of periodic payments or receipts that begin at some point in the future.

Deferred charges: In accounting, expenditures for intangible assets, such as mortgage placement fees or property leasing commissions, that are to be written off over the life of the service provided.

Deferred liability: A debt that need not be paid currently. Accelerated depreciation frequently causes a deferred income tax liability.

Deferred maintenance: Needed repairs that have not been made. Sometimes repairs are postponed to understate the expenses in a particular year.

Deficiency: The lack of an item or its inadequate capacity.

Deficiency judgment: A personal claim based on a judicial order against a debtor. This occurs when the price paid for a property at a foreclosure sale fails to cover the unpaid mortgage amount.

Deflation: A decline in the general level of prices.

Demand: A basic economic concept that refers to the quantity of a good or service that will be purchased at a particular price level.

Depreciated cost: In taxation, the cost new minus any depreciation taken. *See also* Adjusted tax basis.

Depreciation: In appraisal, the loss in market value of an asset; also a forecast value change. *See also* Depreciation accounting.

Depreciation accounting: A systematic method of allocating the cost of an asset over time. *See also* Depreciation.

Depreciation allowance: The amount reported in accounting statements to reflect how much has been set aside to replace the assets of a firm; or the amount of an asset used in a previous period.

Depreciation method: In taxation, the method used to determine the depreciation deduction for qualified assets. In general, depreciation methods can be classified as straight-line or accelerated.

Depreciation recapture: Treatment as ordinary income of that portion of gain that is a result of excess accelerated depreciation over straight line as described in Sections 1245 and 1250 of the Internal Revenue Code.

Depreciation reserve: The account where accruals for depreciation are tabulated. *See also* Depreciation allowance.

Depth table: A table showing the percentage relationship between the depth of a lot being appraised and the value as compared to values indicated by a standard lot in the market.

Diminished utility; *See* Accrued depreciation.

Diminishing returns, point of: The point where returns fail to increase in proportion to additional investments of labor, capital, management, or land.

Direct overall capitalization: A method of capitalizing income based on a procedure of dividing net operating income by a rate derived by analyzing similar properties and comparing their income to their selling price.

Direct costs: Costs directly associated with the physical construction of a project, such as steel, bricks, lumber, and labor.

Direct sales comparison approach: A means of estimating value by comparing recent sales of comparable properties to the subject property after making appropriate adjustments for any differences. This method is effective in an active market in which sales comparables can be identified and information collected. *Same as* Market data approach. Also known as *market approach* and the *market sales approach.*

Discount: The amount of money paid at the front end to acquire a loan. This amount is deducted from the principal at the time the loan is made.

Discounted cash flow: Present worth of a future income stream.

Discounted mortgage: A mortgage sold below the amount of the remaining principal balance in order to provide a satisfactory yield to the purchasing mortgage investor.

Discounting: The process of converting investment inflows to a present value.

Discount point: One percent (1%) of the loan amount. Discount points are a fee charged by a lender at the time a loan is made; they have the result of increasing the lender's effective yield above the contract interest rate. *See also* Point.

Discount rate: *See* Interest rate.

Double-declining balance depreciation: In accounting, an accelerated depreciation method restricted to certain qualified properties. It calculates depreciation at twice the rate of the straight-line method on a balance that is reduced each year as the depreciation is taken. Also known as *200% declining balance depreciation* and *DDB depreciation.*

Down payment: The amount of cash paid by a purchaser which, added to the mortgage amount, equals the total sales price. At the time of closing this is referred to as *equity. See also* Original equity.

Due-on-sale clause: A clause in a mortgage that permits the lender to accelerate the loan if an attempt is made to sell or transfer mortgaged property without obtaining prior approval by the lender. Also known as *due-on-transfer clause.*

Easement: A right to limited use or enjoyment by one or more persons of the land of another.

Economic obsolescence: A loss in value due to factors outside the subject property, such as changes in competition or surrounding land uses. *Same as* Locational obsolescence and Environmental obsolescence. *See also* Obsolescence.

Economic rent: The amount of rental revenues a building would receive if the amount was set by the market, as opposed to contract rent, which is specified in the lease. *See also* Market rent. In economics, surplus receipts over the amount necessary to employ a factor in production.

Effective age: The age of an item as indicated by its physical condition and utility compared to its useful life, in contrast to its chronological age.

Effective capital recovery rate: The difference between the overall rate and the discount rate. An annual capital recovery rate weighted by the fraction of property considered to be wasting.

Effective gross income: Gross actual cash receipts (net of vacancy and collection losses) from income-producing property. Includes rental receipts, parking income, and other miscellaneous income. *See also* Income.

Effective interest rate: The percentage rate of interest actually being paid by a borrower.

Effective tax rate: In property taxation, the percentage relationship between the ad valorem taxes imposed and the market value.

Efficiency ratio: The ratio of leasable space to total space.

Ellwood technique: A mortgage-equity technique for estimating the value of property on the basis of the present value of cash flows and resale proceeds, before income taxes; named after L. W. Ellwood.

Encumbrance: Any interest in or claim on the land of another that in some manner burdens or diminishes the value of that property.

Environmental obsolescence: *See* Economic obsolescence.

Equity: The excess of a property's fair market value over the outstanding indebtedness.

Equity build-up: The increase of the owner's share of the property as a percentage of the total as the property appreciates and the mortgage principal is amortized over time.

Equity dividend: *See* Before-tax cash flow.

Equity dividend rate: *See* Cash-on-cash.

Equity kicker: *See* Kicker.

Equity participation: A lender's share in the equity in addition to the interest earned on the mortgage note.

Equity purchaser: One who purchases another's equity in a project without necessarily assuming personal liability for the loan.

Equity ratio: The percentage relationship between the down payment and the total purchase price; or equity value at any point in time to total property value.

Equity yield rate: The internal rate of return on an equity investment without regard to income taxes.

Escalation: Raising the interest rate or rent upon the occurrence of certain stipulated events or conditions, or passing expense increases to tenants.

Excess accelerated depreciation: The amount by which annual or accumulated depreciation, under a rapid method of depreciation, exceeds straight-line depreciation, considering the same asset useful life. *See also* Depreciation recapture.

Exculpation: A contractual agreement by which one party is held to be immune from personal liability in certain specified situations. *Same as* Hold-harmless clause.

Expense ratio: The fraction found by dividing stabilized operating expenses by the effective gross income.

Factor: Any number or symbol that when multiplied by another forms a product; the reciprocal of a rate.

Fair market value: A legal concept defined as the price, in terms of money, at which a willing seller and willing buyer will agree when both parties are acting prudently, knowledgeably, and under no compulsion.

Feasibility: The reasonable likelihood of satisfying certain investment objectives within the context of the market, finances, and other resources or constraints.

Fee simple: The highest quantum of ownership rights in real property recognized by law.

Final value estimate: Estimate of value reached after the appraiser has analyzed the data, reconciled the value indications provided by the application of the three approaches to value, and made a final judgment.

Financial leverage: Use of borrowed funds to complete the acquisition of an investment. *See also* Leverage and Operating leverage.

Financial management rate of return (FMRR): A modified internal rate of return model developed by M. Chapman Findlay and Stephen D. Messner.

Financial statement: Statement containing a report of assets and liabilities, or income and expenses.

Financial structure: The mix of equity and debt dollars from various sources used in the purchase price of a project; alternatively, the mix of equity and debt dollars used to establish a corporation or other entity.

Financing costs: Fees and other charges that must be paid in order to acquire a loan.

First mortgage: A first lien on property securing the payment of a loan. It is superior to the rights of subsequent lenders.

Fixed expenses: Expenses such as property taxes or insurance that do not vary with changes in the occupancy level.

Flexible-payment mortgage: A variation of the graduated payment mortgage. It frequently requires a savings account deposit in addition to the cash down payment for the property. The instrument may have other names.

Floating rate: A variable interest rate tied to some mutually agreeable index.

Floor area ratio (FAR): Indicates the relationship between the building area and land. For example, a 2:1 FAR means that two square feet of floor space may be constructed on one square foot of land. If only one-half of the land is to be covered, a four-story building could be constructed.

Floor loan: Minimum loan amount that will be distributed by the lender when the improvements are completed.

Forecasting: An estimate of future events based on present knowledge, facts, theory, and judgment.

Fractional appraisal: An appraisal of one component or legal interest of the whole property. For example, an appraisal of the air rights separated from the surface and subsurface rights.

Fractional interest: A partial interest in real estate, for example, an easement.

Front foot: A property measurement for purposes of valuation that is measured by the front footage on the street line.

Front money: Money that must be raised before obtaining financing in order to start a project.

Functional obsolescence: Impairment of capacity or efficiency due to changes in tastes, preferences, technical innovations, or market standards.

Functional utility: A measurement of how compatible a project is with respect to market standards.

Future worth of one: *See* Compound amount of one.

Future worth of one per period: *See* Compound amount of one per period.

Gap loan: (1) A loan covering the period between the time when the construction loan is due and the time when the conditions set by the permanent lender will be met. (2) Any loan filling the deficiency created when the permanent financing and the equity are unable to cover the total cost of a project.

General partner: In a partnership, one who manages the firm and is subject to personal liability for the firm's obligations.

Graduated lease: A lease whose provisions provide for periodic increases in the rental payments.

Graduated-payment mortgage (GPM): A financing arrangement by which monthly payments early in the term are lower than what monthly payments for a level-payment mortgage would be. These payments increase periodically in graduated steps until the monthly payment is sufficient to fully amortize the loan.

Gross leasable area (GLA): Total floor area designed for exclusive tenant use and occupancy, expressed in square feet. Generally measured from the center line of joint partitions and from outside walls.

Gross lease: A lease in which the landlord pays for most of the operating expenses, including property taxes, maintenance, repairs. Specific details vary according to the lease agreement provisions and local market custom.

Gross rent (income) multiplier: The result of dividing the sales price of property by the potential or effective gross income. *See also* Multiplier.

Ground lease: Lease of land, usually for a long term.

Ground rent: A payment made by a tenant under a ground lease.

Guideline life: The asset depreciable life suggested by Revenue Procedure 62–21 of the Internal Revenue Service's *Cumulative Bulletin* (1962).

Guidelines: A list of suggested useful asset lives, for income tax depreciation deductions, published in Revenue Procedure 62–21 of the Internal Revenue Service's *Cumulative Bulletin* (1962).

Highest and best use, principle of: The legal, physically possible, financially feasible, and probable use of a parcel of land creating an income stream that when capitalized will result in the highest present value attributable to the land.

Historical cost: Actual cost of a project when it was first constructed.

Hold-harmless clause: *See* Exculpation.

Holding period: The period of property ownership, from the date of purchase to the date of sale.

Hoskold factor: A factor used to value an annuity and based on reinvesting capital recapture at a safe rate of interest, named after H. E. Hoskold.

Hundred percent location: The location that generates the highest revenues per square foot for a particular type of use in a geographic area.

Illiquidity: Inability (of an asset) to be readily converted into cash.

Improvement ratio: A ratio or fraction that compares the value of improvements to the value of all property.

Improvements: All real estate except land. Includes buildings, fixtures, fences, curbs, sewers, etc.

Income: Financial and other benefits. Income should be qualified as to the degree of "netness." *See also* Potential gross income, Effective gross income, Net operating income, Net income, Before-tax cash flow, After-tax cash flow, and Netness.

Income approach: One of the traditional means of appraising property, based on the assumption that the value is equal to the present worth of the rights to future income. *Same as* Capitalization approach.

Income multiplier: A factor that expresses the value of property as a multiple of the periodic income that the property generates. *See also* Gross rent (income) multiplier.

Income participation: The right of a party to share in part or all of the income generated by an investment. *See also* Equity participation and Kicker.

Income-producing property: Property that generates periodic income for its owner, for example, an office building or apartment complex.

Income tax liability: The tax a property owner must pay, based on the taxpayer's taxable income multiplied by the tax rate in each marginal tax bracket.

Increasing and decreasing returns, principle of: The principle stating that as resources are added to fixed factors of production, net returns will tend to increase at an increasing rate up to a point. Once that point is reached total returns will increase at a declining rate until additions to value are less than the cost of additional resources. *See also* Marginal utility.

Increasing annuity: An income stream that promises or requires systematic increases in the periodic payment.

Incurable depreciation: Depreciation that would cost more to correct than the value added by correction.

Independent appraisal: An estimate of the value of property, performed by a qualified, disinterested party.

Index lease: A lease whereby the rental is tied to some commonly agreed-upon price index such as the Consumer Price Index or the Wholesale Price Index.

Indirect costs: Costs associated with construction that cannot be actually identified in the structure, including insurance, interest, and taxes during construction, architects' fees, management costs, and the like.

Industrial property: Real property that is used as a manufacturing facility; also a zoning classification that restricts land to certain uses.

Inflation: Decrease in the purchasing power of currency, typically measured by the Consumer Price Index published by the Bureau of Labor Statistics.

Initial equity: The amount of cash and/or other valuable contribution used as a down payment by a real estate owner.

Installment contract: *See* Contract for deed.

Installment payment: One payment of principal and interest, required as a periodic payment on a mortgage loan.

Installment sale: A seller-financed sale whereby, for income tax purposes, the receipts are spread over a number of years, and the transaction meets certain requirements.

Installment to amortize one: The periodic payment necessary to retire a one dollar loan with interest computed on the declining loan balance.

Insurable value: The highest reasonable value that can be placed on property for hazard insurance purposes.

Interest: The sum paid for the use of money; the degree of rights in the ownership of land.

Interest-only mortgage: A balloon mortgage that requires installment payments of interest only.

Interest rate: Rate of return on a principal amount. The rate used to compound principal amounts to a future value, or to discount anticipated future amounts to a present value. The interest rate does not include a capital recovery provision. Should be further classified as to effective rate or nominal face rate.

Internal rate of return (IRR): The rate at which discounted returns from an investment equal the cost of the investment.

Interest rate risk: The probability that market interest rates will change, affecting the value of an investment that bears a stated fixed rate.

Interpolation: The process of deriving a value that is known to lie between two given amounts.

Investment: The outlay of money for income or profit; property acquired for income or profit.

Investment analysis: An examination of investment property that considers its suitability for the unique situation of a particular investor.

Investment appetite: Characteristics of an investment that are desired by a particular investor.

Investment property: An asset acquired for income or profit.

Investment value: The worth of investment property to a specific investor.

Investment yield: The internal rate of return on an investment.

Investor: One who acquires investment property.

Inwood factor: A multiplier to value an ordinary annuity, named after William Inwood; the present worth of one per period.

J factor: A factor used to derive the change in net operating income that is required to realize a certain equity yield rate.

Joint venture: An agreement by two or more individuals or entities to engage in a single project or undertaking.

Junior lien: An encumbrance second in priority to a previously recorded lien or to a lien to which the encumbrance has been subordinated.

Junior member: **Appraisal designation offered by the National Society of Real Estate Appraisers. Members use abbreviation RA.**

Kicker: The right of a mortgage lender or other investor to share in income, in addition to principal and interest receipts. *Same as* Equity kicker and Lender participation.

Land contract: A contract whereby the seller accepts a down payment on a parcel of land but generally does not give title to the property until the last principal payment has been received. *Same as* Contract for deed.

Land residual technique: A method of estimating the value of land when the value of a building is given.

Lease: An agreement by which a landlord gives a tenant the right to use and to have exclusive possession but not ownership of realty for a specified period in consideration for the payment of rent.

Leased fee: The landlord's interest in leased property.

Leasehold: The interest that the tenant has, created by a lease.

Leasehold improvements: Fixtures and other improvements to leased property, made by or for a specific tenant.

Lease-purchase agreement: An arrangement whereby part of the rent payment is applied to the purchase price, and when the prearranged total amount has been paid, title is transferred.

Lender participation: *See* Kicker.

Lessee: Tenant.

Lessor: Landlord.

Level annuity: A series of periodic receipts or payments that are each equal in amount.

Level-payment mortgage: A method of loan repayment in which the dollar amount of each payment is the same.

Leverage: Use of borrowed capital to finance the purchase of real estate or other assets. *See also* Financial leverage and Operating leverage.

Lien: A legally recognized right to enforce a claim or charge on the property of another for payment of some debt, duty, or obligation.

Life annuity: The right of an individual to receive periodic payments until death.

Life estate: An interest that lasts only for the term of the life or lives of one or more persons.

Limited partnership: An entity with one or more general partners and one or more passive investors, called *limited partners.*

Limiting condition: A statement in an appraisal report that describes an impediment or circumstance that caused the appraiser to qualify the value estimate.

Linkage: Refers to the time and distance cost necessary to reach a supporting facility or land use from the subject property.

Liquidity: The ease with which an asset may be converted into cash.

Loan constant: *See* Mortgage constant.

Loan-to-value ratio: The relationship between the amount borrowed and the appraised value of the property.

Local adjustment factor: A factor used to recognize construction cost variations found in different cities in the United States. The average city is 100%; high-cost areas exceed 100%; low-cost areas are below 100%.

Locational obsolescence: *See* Economic obsolescence.

Long-lived assets: Components of a building that have a relatively long useful life, such as the foundation and framework.

Long-term capital gain: The gain realized from the sale or exchange of a capital asset held for more than one year.

MAI: Member of the American Institute of Real Estate Appraisers.

Management fee: An operating expense paid for overseeing the operations of real estate.

Marginal tax bracket: The rate of federal income tax that will apply to the next increment of taxable income.

Marginal productivity: *See* Contribution, principle of.

Marginal utility: The addition to total utility of the last unit of a resource. *See also* Increasing and decreasing returns, principle of.

Market: The economic function of bringing buyers and sellers together through the price mechanism.

Market data approach: *See* Direct sales comparison approach.

Market price: The amount paid in a transaction; a historical fact.

Market rent: The rental income that a property is likely to command in the current market. *See also* Economic rent.

Market rental risk: The probability that market rental rates will change, affecting the value of a property that is subject to fixed rent.

Market value: The price in terms of cash or its equivalent at which a willing buyer and a willing seller will agree upon, where neither is under any undue pressure and both are typically motivated, have adequate knowledge, and are acting in their own best interest. *See also* Fair market value.

Master member (MREA): Designation awarded by the National Society of Real Estate Appraisers for extensive appraisal expertise.

Mechanic's lien: A statutory lien levied on property by a person who is wrongfully not compensated after providing labor (mechanic) or material (materialman) for the improvement to land.

Mineral rights: The right to share in the sale of minerals that may be extracted from land.

Money: *See* Cash.

Mortgage: The financing obligation by which the borrower or mortgagor pledges property to secure the debt represented by a promissory note or bond.

Mortgage coefficient: An amount multiplied by a financial mortgage feature, particularly the Ellwood *C* factor.

Mortgage commitment: An agreement whereby a mortgage lender agrees to fund a certain mortgage loan and a borrower agrees to comply with its requirements.

Mortgage constant: The relationship between annual mortgage loan requirements and the initial mortgage loan principal, expressed as a decimal or percentage, for level-payment mortgage loans. *Same as* Loan constant.

Mortgagee: A lender who receives a pledge of property to secure a debt.

Mortgage-equity technique: A technique for estimating the value of income-producing property, based on the sum of the mortgage principal added to the discounted present value of forecast cash flow and reversion to equity.

Mortgage requirement: *See* Debt service.

Mortgage value: The value of an asset for purposes of securing a mortgage loan; also the market value of a mortgage loan.

Mortgagor: A borrower who pledges property through a mortgage to secure a debt.

Most probable selling price: The likely price a property will bring, given current market conditions, buyer and seller motivations, and the financing terms that are likely to be employed.

Multiple regression: A mathematical technique for estimating the amount of value for a subject property based on known variables and prices for comparable properties.

Multiplier: A rate to be multiplied by an amount. *See also* Gross rent (income) multiplier.

National Society of Real Estate Appraisers: An organization of professional appraisers headquartered in Cleveland, affiliated with the National Association of Real Estate Brokers, most of whom are minorities. Offers RA, CRA, and MREA designations.

Neighborhood life cycle: The growth, maturity, decline, and potential for renewal phases of the life of a neighborhood.

Net: After subtracting expenses.

Net income: In accounting and taxation, income after all expenses or deductions; in real estate, see Net operating income.

Net lease: A lease that imposes on the lessee an obligation to pay such costs as property taxes, special assessments, and insurance premiums, as agreed upon by the parties. *See also* Triple-net lease.

Netness: A colloquial term use to indicate the degree to which expenses have been subtracted from income.

Net operating income (NOI): Property operating expenses subtracted from effective gross income. *Same as* Operating income. *See also* Income and NIBD.

Net present value: The value of an income stream and reversion at a given discount rate, less the original investment cost.

Net spendable income: *See* After-tax cash flow. *Same as* Spendable income.

Net worth: Equity; total assets minus total liabilities.

New property: Property improvements, the original use of which commences with the taxpayer.

NIBD: Net income before depreciation. *See also* Net operating income.

NOI: *See* Net operating income.

Nominal interest rate: The face rate of interest as stated in the contract.

Obsolescence: A loss in value due to a decrease in the usefulness of property caused by decay, changes in technology, people's behavior patterns and tastes, or environmental changes. *See also* Economic obsolescence, Functional obsolescence, Locational obsolescence, and Depreciation.

Occupancy rate: The ratio of the space rented to the total amount of space available for rent.

Operating expense ratio: The relationship of operating expenses to potential gross income or effective gross income.

Operating expenses: Expenses of operating income-producing property other than debt service and income taxes.

Operating income: *See* Net operating income.

Operating leverage: The effect of increasing gross income while maintaining expenses at a fixed or semivariable rate. *See also* Leverage and Financial leverage.

Opportunity cost: The principle that a prudent investor would pay no more for a particular piece of property than for equally attractive substitutes, whether those substitutes are real estate or other investments that promise to offer equal financial benefits and the same risk.

Option: A right, given for consideration to a party (optionee) by property owner (optionor), to purchase or lease property within a specified time at a specified price and terms.

Original equity: The cash down payment applied to purchase property. *See also* Down payment.

Ordinary annuity: A series of equal periodic receipts or payments, receivable or payable at the end of each period.

Ordinary income: Income that is subject to regular rates of taxation, as contrasted with capital gains or tax-free cash flow.

Overage income: Percentage rent based on retail sales, in addition to a base rent. *See also* percentage rent.

Overall rate of return: The mathematical rate obtained by dividing net operating income by the selling price or value of income-producing real estate. Also called *overall capitalization rate.*

Overimprovement: Occurs when the owner combines more factors of production with the land than can be profitably employed.

Partial interest: A less than fee-simple interest in real property.

Partially amortized mortgage: A method of loan repayment in which the balance of the outstanding loan is not zero at maturity, so that a balloon payment is required.

Participation: Sharing in income and/or ownership.

Participation mortgage: An agreement between a mortgagee and a mortgagor that provides the lender with a certain percentage of ownership in the project, and/or income.

Payback period: The time necessary for the cash flow generated from a project to equal the initial amount invested.

Percentage lease: A lease whereby the lessor receives a percentage of the gross sales or net profits as the rental payment for the lease on the property.

Percentage rent: Rent based on a percentage of a retail tenant's sales, usually in addition to a base rent. *Same as* Overage income.

Permanent mortgage: A long-term loan secured by real estate.

Perpetuity, in: Forever; something perpetual as an income stream expected to continue without an end. *See also* Capitalization in perpetuity.

Physical depreciation: A reduction in the usefulness or attractiveness of property due to impairment of its physical condition.

Plottage: Occurs when two or more sites are combined with the result that the value of the assembled site is worth more than the sum of the values of the individual sites.

Point: One percent (1%). *See also* Discount point and Basis point.

Point of diminishing returns: *See* Diminishing returns, point of.

Potential gross income: Gross receipts that would be collected if all available rental units were leased and all rents were paid by tenants. *See also* Income and Net income.

Prepayment penalty: The charge levied by the lender for paying off a mortgage before its maturity date.

Present value: The value of an income stream and/or reversion at a given discount rate.

Present worth (value) of an annuity: The value, at a specified discount rate, of a stream of level cash flow or payments.

Present worth of an annuity factor (PWAF): The value, at a specified discount rate, of a stream of cash flow having $1.00 payable or receivable at the end of each period.

Present worth of one factor: The present value, at a specified discount rate, of $1.00 to be received at the end of a specified period.

Price: An amount paid for property. Any amount, usually expressed in terms of money.

Prime rate: The interest rate charged to a bank's highest credit rated customers for short-term loans.

Principal: A lump sum of money or capital. Also, a buyer or seller.

Principal risk: The possibility that the resale price of an investment will be less than was originally forecast.

Principle: A fundamental idea upon which other ideas are based.

Productivity: Effective use of an agent (factor) of production.

Pro forma statement: A financial statement that shows forecast or projected amounts.

Projection period: The forecast holding period for an investment under consideration.

Property: Anything in which there may be ownership.

Property residual technique: A form of income approach that estimates the present value of property by combining the present value of forecast income with the present value of the forecast resale proceeds.

Pro rata: In proportion.

Purchase capital: Amounts used to acquire property.

Purchase-money mortgage: A loan given by the seller to the buyer to cover all or part of the sales price.

Purchasing power risk: The possibility that cash flow to be received from an investment and the resale price will have less purchasing power due to inflation.

Quantity survey method: A method of estimating reproduction cost by totaling the cost of each individual part to be used in construction and the cost of labor per part, plus additions for indirect costs. *See also* Cost estimating.

Rate of interest: The rate at which borrowed money earns money.

Rate of return of investment: *See also* Recapture rate and Capital recovery rate.

Real estate: Land and everything permanently affixed to it.

Real estate investment trust (REIT): An association whereby investors pool their funds. If certain tax requirements are met, it allows a pass-through of income without double taxation.

REALTIST®: A registered trademark of the National Association of Real Estate Brokers (NAREB) whose members are concerned with all real estate matters including those pertaining to fair housing policies.

REALTOR®: A registered trademark of the NATIONAL ASSO-

CIATION OF REALTORS®. It is used by brokers and salespersons who hold active membership in the association.

Realty: A term used to refer to land and the improvements on and to the land.

Reappraisal lease: A lease that includes a provision for periodic reevaluation of property, the rent to be set as a percentage of the appraised value. *Same as* Reevaluation lease.

Reassessment: A change in the assessed value of property for ad valorem tax purposes.

Recapture of depreciation: *See* Depreciation recapture.

Recapture rate: The annual rate at which capital invested in a declining-value asset is recovered through the income provided by the asset. *Same as* Rate of return of investment. *See also* Capital recovery rate.

Reciprocal: Inverse; the result obtained after dividing 1 by the given number.

Reconciliation: In appraisal, the adjustment process whereby comparables are adjusted to the subject property. Formerly called *correlation.*

Reevaluation lease: *See* Reappraisal lease.

Refinance: To repay one or more existing mortgage loans by simultaneously borrowing funds through another mortgage loan.

Reinvestment rate: The interest rate at which cash flows from income-producing property, particularly the portion of cash flows that represent a recovery of capital, are presumed to be reinvested.

Remainder: A future interest that is created simultaneously with the granting of an estate of limited or potentially limited duration.

Remaining economic life: The estimated number of remaining years of usefulness of a structure or component.

Renegotiated rate mortgage: A type of rollover mortgage whereby the interest rate is adjusted to prevailing rates at fixed time intervals. *See also* Canadian rollover mortgage.

Rent: The payment made for the use of real estate.

Rent multiplier: *See* Gross rent (income) multiplier.

Rent-up period: The period that begins with completion of construction and ends upon attainment of a normal occupancy rate.

Replacement cost new: The current cost of constructing a new building having utility equivalent to that of the subject being appraised, but built with modern materials and techniques and designed in accordance with current tastes and standards.

Replacement reserve: A fund established to replace assets when they wear out. Also, contributions to such a fund.

Reproduction cost new: The current cost of constructing an exact duplicate of the property being appraised.

Resale price: The gross selling amount of an asset at the end of the investment holding period. *See also* Terminal value.

Resale proceeds: Resale price minus selling expenses, closing costs, and unpaid debts on the property at resale.

Reserve for depreciation: In accounting, the accumulation of book depreciation for assets.

Residential rental property: Property from which 80% or more of the gross rental income is rental income from dwelling units.

Residual: Left over. Real estate is said to be *residual* in that its value is dependent on how much compensation is left after the other factors of production have been compensated.

Residual techniques: Techniques used to estimate the value of improvements or land, given net operating income and a known value and income requirement for the improvements or land. Net operating income not required by the known value is capitalized into the value for the unknown.

Restrictive covenant: *See* Deed restriction.

Return on equity: The internal rate of return on initial equity based on cash flows and resale proceeds. Status should be qualified as to before- or after-tax.

Reverse annuity mortgage: A financing arrangement whereby the lender advances periodic payments to the borrower; the principal balance of the loan increases by the periodic payments and all accrued interest.

Reverse leverage: *See* Negative leverage.

Reversion: *See* Before-tax resale proceeds.

Reversion factor: The present worth of one factor applied to resale proceeds.

Risk: Variability; the possibility that a real estate investor will not receive expected returns; also, the possibility of a loss.

Risk-free rate: The interest rate available on investments having the least risk, such as short-term U.S. Treasury obligations and liquid deposits insured by an agency of the U.S. government.

Risk rate: The rate of return on an investment that is necessary to attract capital; the rate of earnings that is perceived to be commensurate with the risk.

RM: Residential Member of the American Institute of Real Estate Appraisers.

Rollover mortgage: At specified intervals the mortgage is due; the lender agrees to renew, but at a new interest rate.

Safe rate: A rate of return on investment that can be earned through relatively risk-free investments.

Sale-leaseback: A technique used by owners of property as a means of raising capital. The process involves the simultaneous selling and leasing back of the property, usually through a net lease.

Salvage value: The expected worth of a piece of property at the end of its economic life.

Sandwich lease: A lease created when a sublessee sublets property.

Secondary mortgage market: The means by which existing first mortgages are bought and sold. It provides a lender with an opportunity to sell a loan before its maturity date.

Second mortgage: A mortgage that is second in priority because of time of recording or subordination. *See also* Junior mortgage.

Section 1231: Section 1231 of the *Internal Revenue Code,* which refers to real and personal property used in a trade or business. Net gains on Section 1231 assets are taxed at long-term capital gains rates; net losses are ordinary.

Section 1250: Section 1250 of the *Internal Revenue Code.* Real property used in trade or business on which accelerated depreciation is claimed is subject to the recapture of excess accelerated depreciation as ordinary income upon a sale.

Self-amortizing mortgage loan: A mortgage loan that requires level annual payments adequate to meet interest requirements and fully amortize the principal over its term.

Shared appreciation mortgage: A mortgage in which the lender shares in the appreciation of the real estate.

Simple interest: Interest earned only on the initial principal, not on accrued interest.

Sinking fund: Periodic deposits of money into an account that, with its interest earnings, will be used to replace assets or to retire loans.

Sinking fund factor: A computed figure that indicates the periodic deposit that is necessary for a fund to reach $1.00 after a certain number of periods at a given interest rate.

Site: A lot ready for development.

Site analysis: A study of the economic or physical characteristics of a parcel of land.

Site development costs: The costs of changing property from raw land to a site; included are surveying, grading, bringing utilities to the property, and other costs.

Situs: Refers to the economic location of real estate.

Six functions of one: See separate entries for each of these six functions:

- Compound interest.
- Accumulation of one per period.
- Sinking fund.
- Present worth of one.
- Present worth (value) of an annuity.
- Installment to amortize one.

Software: Programs that logically instruct computers; as contrasted with *hardware,* which is the computer and peripheral equipment.

Special-purpose property: A building that is intended for only one use, such as a church, nursery, school, automobile service station, or theater. Conversion to alternate uses would require substantial expenditures.

Speculative value: The value that property is expected to realize, provided certain goals or forecasts are achieved.

Speculator: A type of investor who accepts much greater risk in exchange for the possibility of much higher returns.

Spendable income: *See* After-tax cash flow. *Same as* net spendable income.

Split rate capitalization: Capitalization where two different interest or discount rates are applied to cash inflows and/or outflows forecast from the same property.

Springfield mortgage: A mortgage that requires equal periodic payments of principal, with interest in addition so that the total payment declines each period.

SRA: Senior Residential Appraiser of the Society of Real Estate Appraisers.

SREA: Senior Real Estate Analyst of the Society of Real Estate Appraisers.

SRPA: Senior Real Property Appraiser of the Society of Real Estate Appraisers.

Stabilized expenses: The level annual equivalent, preferably on a present value basis, of operating expenses that are expected to vary from one year to another.

Stabilized income: The level annual equivalent, preferably on a present value basis, usually for net operating income, of income that is expected to vary from one year to another.

Standby commitment: An agreement between a lender and a developer whereby, for a fee, the lender stands ready to make a certain loan amount for a specific period of time.

Straight-line capitalization: A method of deriving a capitalization rate for real estate by adding the straight-line capital recapture rate to the interest rate.

Straight-line capital recovery (recapture) rate: A component of a capitalization rate in real estate whereby the periodic loss of asset value is deemed to occur equally over the life of the asset, such as at the rate of 2% per year for 50 years.

Straight-line depreciation: A method of computing depreciation for income tax purposes in which the difference between the original cost and the salvage value is deducted in equal installments over the depreciable life of the asset.

Subject property: The property under appraisal or analysis.

Subject to mortgage: An obligation created when a person purchases property and takes over the mortgage payments but assumes no personal liability. The original borrower remains liable.

Sublease: A lease from one tenant to another who rents from the tenant.

Substitution, principle of: The principle that holds that the maximum value of a property is set by the lowest price or cost of acquiring another property of equivalent utility.

Subsurface rights: Rights to use the subsurface area of a piece of property, as for mineral extraction.

Summation approach: *See* Cost approach.

Sum-of-the-years'-digits (SYD): An accelerated method for calculating depreciation for income tax purposes.

Superadequacy: Presence of unnecessary or unwanted land improvements.

Supply and demand, principle of: The principle that together supply and demand interact to establish prices. Supply is the quantity of goods available at a given price schedule; demand is the quantity of goods desired at a price schedule.

Surplus productivity, principle of: The net income attributed to land after the costs of material, labor, and entrepreneurship have been paid.

Syndicate: A group of investors who pool capital for a business venture.

Taxable income: Income that is subject to taxation.

Tax-free cash throw-off: Money produced by an investment that is not subject to income tax. Frequently caused by depreciation deductions.

Tax rate: A rate defining the proportion of income or value to be paid as a tax.

Tax shelter: A reduction of taxable income allowed by an investment.

Terminal value: *See* Resale price and Resale proceeds.

Term mortgage (straight term): A method of financing in which interest only is paid during the time of the loan. At maturity the entire principal is due.

Time value of money: A concept based on the idea that money is assumed to earn interest; the concept that money today is more valuable than the same amount to be received in the future.

Trade breakdown method: A method of cost estimation that categorizes costs by the various trades such as carpentry, masonry, and plumbing. *See also* Cost estimating.

Trading on the equity: Increasing the rate of return on the owner's equity by borrowing part or all of the purchase price at a rate of interest less than the expected rate of return generated by the net income of the property.

Triple-net lease: Emphasizes the "netness" of a lease.

Trust deed: *See* Deed of trust.

Underimproved land: Land that has been improved to a lesser extent than can be profitable.

Unearned increment: An increase in the value of property caused by forces outside of the property; a windfall gain.

Unencumbered property: Property that is free and clear of any liens.

Unit-in-place method: A method of estimating construction costs by estimating the total per-unit cost of each component of the property, then multiplying by the total number of units (square feet of roof, etc.) in the property. *See also* Cost estimating.

Units of comparison: A measuring unit that is common to the subject property and the comparables.

Unit value: The value of property expressed in terms of a measuring unit, such as land per square foot, or a motel per room.

Upset price: The minimum price set for property when offered at auction or public sale.

Useful life: The period over which property is expected to have utility in the function the property was designed for.

Usury: Charging more than legal rate of interest for the use of money.

Vacancy allowance (vacancy rate): the percentage of a building's space that is not rented due to oversupply, tenant turnover, etc.

Valuation: Appraisal.

Valuation principles: The logic, rules, and economic roots that explain the forces affecting value.

Value: The worth of a good or service in terms of money.

Value in exchange: The ability of a good or service to command other goods or services; the present worth of rights to future income.

Value in use: The worth of property in a particular use, such as the contribution to income provided by a particular building. The value in use may vary from the market value.

Variable: A factor that may change.

Variable annuity: A nonlevel stream of income.

Variable expenses: Expenses that change generally in proportion to production or use, contrasted with those that remain fixed regardless of the level of use.

Variable proportions: This principle holds that land can be developed in different ways which changes the productivity of the land itself.

Variable-rate mortgage (VRM): A mortgage loan that allows the interest rate to change periodically, such as every year.

Wasting asset: Something of value that depreciates over time.

Weighted rate: An overall capitalization rate that considers the portions of purchase capital contributed by various investors and their respective risk rates.

Wraparound mortgage: A junior mortgage that includes one or more mortgages in its balance.

Yield: The interest earned by an investor on the investment. *See also* Current yield and Yield to maturity.

Yield to maturity: The effective annual rate of return on an investment, including periodic income and resale proceeds. The internal rate of return on investment. *See also* Yield and Current yield.

Zoning: The police power device that allows for legislative division of space into districts and imposition of regulations prescribing the use and intensity of use to which land within each designated district may be put. Districts may be zoned for residential use, for example, or for commercial use.

Bibliography of Books on Appraisal, Finance, and Investment Analysis.

Appraisal

Babcock, Frederick M. *Valuation of Real Estate.* New York: McGraw-Hill Book Company, 1932.

Babcock, Henry. *Appraisal Principles and Procedures.* Homewood, Ill.: Richard D. Irwin, 1968.

Bartless, Charles R. *Assessing and the Appraisal Process.* 4th ed. Chicago: International Association of Assessing Officers, 1971.

Boyce, Byrl N. *Real Estate Appraisal Terminology.* Cambridge, Mass.: Ballinger Publishing Company, 1975.

Friedman, Edith J., ed. *Encyclopedia of Real Estate Appraising.* 3rd. ed. Englewood Cliffs, N.J.: Prentice-Hall, Inc., 1978.

Johnson, Irwin E. *The Instant Mortgage Equity Technique.* Lexington, Mass.: D.C. Heath and Co., 1971.

Kahn, Sanders A., and Case, Frederick E. *Real Estate Appraisal and Investment.* 2d ed. New York: The Ronald Press Company, 1977.

Kinnard, William N. *Income Property Valuation.* Lexington, Mass.: Heath Lexington Books, 1971.

McMichael, Stanley L. *McMichael's Appraising Manual.* Englewood Cliffs, N.J.: Prentice-Hall, Inc., 1951.

North, Lincoln W. *Real Estate Investment Analysis and Valuation.* Winnipeg, Canada: Saults & Pollard Limited, 1973.

Rams, Edwin M. *Rams' Real Estate Appraising Handbook.* Englewood Cliffs, N.J.: Prentice-Hall, Inc., 1975.

Rams, Edwin M. *Valuation for Eminent Domain.* Englewood Cliffs, N.J.: Prentice-Hall, Inc., 1973.

Ring, Alfred A. *The Valuation of Real Estate.* 2d ed. Englewood Cliffs, N.J.: Prentice-Hall, Inc., 1970.

Schmutz, George L. *The Appraisal Process.* North Hollywood, Calif.: George L. Schmutz, 1953.

Shenkel, William M. *Modern Real Estate Appraisal.* New York: McGraw-Hill Book Company, 1978.

Smith, Halbert C. *Real Estate Appraisal.* Columbus, Ohio: Grid, Inc., 1976.

Wendt, Paul F. *Real Estate Appraisal.* Athens: University of Georgia Press, 1974.

Finance

Atteberry, William. *Modern Real Estate Finance.* 2d ed. Columbus, Ohio: Grid, Inc., 1976.

Bagby, Joseph R. *Real Estate Financing Desk Book.* 2d ed. Englewood Cliffs, N.J.: Institute for Business Planning, Inc., 1977.

Beaton, William R. *Real Estate Finance.* Englewood Cliffs, N.J.: Prentice-Hall, Inc., 1975.

Boykin, James H. *Financing Real Estate.* Lexington, Mass.: Heath Lexington Books, 1979.

Britton, James A. Jr., and Kerwood, Lewis O. *Financing Income-Producing Real Estate.* New York: McGraw-Hill Book Company, 1977.

Case, Frederick E., and Clapp, John M. *Real Estate Financing.* New York: John Wiley & Sons, 1978.

Dennis, Marshall. *Fundamentals of Mortgage Lending.* Reston, Va.: Reston Publishing Company, Inc., 1978.

Freshman, Samuel K. *Principles of Real Estate Syndication.* 2d ed. Los Angeles: Parker & Son, Inc., 1973.

Goleman, Harry A., ed. *Financing Real Estate Development.* Englewood, N.J.: Aloray Publisher, 1974.

Hines, Mary Alice. *Real Estate Finance.* Englewood Cliffs, N.J.: Prentice-Hall, Inc., 1978.

Hoagland, Henry E., Stone, Leo D., and Brueggman, William B. *Real Estate Finance.* 6th ed. Homewood, Ill.: Richard D. Irwin, Inc., 1977.

Unger, Maurice A., and Melicher, Ronald. *Real Estate Finance.* Cincinnati: South-Western Publishing Co., 1978.

Wiedemer, John P. *Real Estate Finance.* 3rd ed. Reston, Va.: Reston Publishing Company, Inc., 1980.

Investment Analysis

Beaton, William R., and Robertson, Terry. *Real Estate Investment.* 2d ed. Englewood Cliffs, N.J.: Prentice-Hall, Inc., 1977.

Benke, William. *All About Land Investment.* New York: McGraw-Hill Book Company, 1976.

Creedy, Judith, and Wall, Norbert F. *Real Estate Investment by Objective.* New York: McGraw-Hill Book Company, 1979.

Epley, Donald R., and Millar, James A. *Basic Real Estate Finance and Investments.* New York: John Wiley & Sons, 1980.

Gettel, Ronald E. *Real Estate Guidelines & Rules of Thumb.* New York: McGraw-Hill Book Company, 1976.

Hines, Mary Alice. *Real Estate Investment.* New York: Macmillan Publishing Co., Inc., 1980.

Maisel, Sherman J., and Roulac, Stephen E. *Real Estate Investment and Finance.* New York: McGraw-Hill Book Company, 1976.

Messner, Stephen D., Schreiber, Irving, and Lyon, Victor L. *Marketing Investment Real Estate.* Chicago: Realtors National Marketing Institute, 1975.

Roulac, Stephen E. *Modern Real Estate Investment.* San Francisco, Calif.: Property Press, 1976.

Seldin, Maury. *Land Investment.* Homewood, Ill.: Dow Jones-Irwin, 1975.

Swesnik, Richard H. *Acquiring and Developing Income-Producing Real Estate.* Reston, Va.: Reston Publishing Company, Inc., 1979.

Wendt, Paul F., and Cerf, Alan R. *Real Estate Investment Analysis and Taxation.* 2d ed. New York: McGraw-Hill Book Company, 1979.

Wiley, Robert J. *Real Estate Investment.* New York: John Wiley & Sons, 1977.

Index

A

B

C

D

E

F

L

M

N

O

P

W

Y

Z